Mac OS® X
Snow Leopard™ Bible

Mac OS® X
Snow Leopard™ Bible

Galen Gruman

Mark Hattersley

with Timothy R. Butler

WILEY

Wiley Publishing, Inc.

Mac OS® X Snow Leopard™ Bible

Published by
Wiley Publishing, Inc.
10475 Crosspoint Boulevard
Indianapolis, IN 46256
www.wiley.com

Copyright © 2009 by Wiley Publishing, Inc., Indianapolis, Indiana

Published by Wiley Publishing, Inc., Indianapolis, Indiana

Published simultaneously in Canada

ISBN: 978-0-470-45363-6

Manufactured in the United States of America

10 9 8 7 6 5 4 3 2 1

For general information on our other products and services or to obtain technical support, please contact our Customer Care Department within the U.S. at (877) 762-2974, outside the U.S. at (317) 572-3993 or fax (317) 572-4002.

Library of Congress Control Number: 2009932707

To all the Mac users who've endured Apple's troubled 1990s and are now enjoying the Mac's renaissance.
— Galen Gruman

For my darling wife, Rosemary, with all my heart. And to my parents for buying me my first computer and filling my childhood with happiness, but inspiring me to work hard. Thank you. This book is also for the forum posters on Macworld UK, for their priceless advice, suggestions, thoughts, and opinions. It's good to be a Mac!
— Mark Hattersley

To Mom and Dad. Thank you for all of your support for my writing and everything else. And most of all, your love.
— Tim Butler

About the Authors

Galen Gruman is the principal at The Zango Group, an editorial development and book production firm. As such, he has produced several books for Wiley Publishing and is a regular contributor to *Macworld* and *CIO*. He is also author or co-author of 24 books on desktop publishing. Gruman has covered Macintosh technology since then for several publications, including the trade weekly *InfoWorld*, for which he began writing in 1986 and of which he is now executive editor, and *Macworld*, whose staff he was a member of from 1991 to 1998.

Mark Hattersley is the editor in chief of *Macworld UK*. He is a writer and editor of various technology publications including *Macworld, iPod User, Digital Arts*, and *MacVideo*. Mark has spent much of his working life covering Apple products and is an unabashed enthusiast of what Macs enable people to create, rather than merely consume.

Mark is a key name on the UK Mac scene, and he has tremendously enjoyed covering Apple's Pheonix-like rise; emerging from the ashes when he first began writing about technology, to making some of the UK's most popular tech products.

Mark lives in London with his wife, Rosemary, who is the deputy editor of *PC Advisor* (the UK edition of *PC World* magazine). This causes much mirth to their friends, although the home networking issues have finally been sorted.

Timothy R. Butler is the editor in chief of *Open for Business* (www.ofb.biz). At *OFB* he started by covering the GNU/Linux beat, particularly focusing on Linux as a desktop system in business environments. In recent years his coverage has broadened to cover Macs, along with non-tech subjects such as politics and religion. He is a happy desktop-Linux-to-Mac "switcher" and now enjoys doing his little part for Mac world domination. Tim is also the founder of Universal Networks, where he has worked as a system administrator for Mac, Unix, Linux and Windows systems since 1998.

Credits

Acquisitions Editor
Aaron Black

Project Editor
Martin V. Minner

Technical Editor
Paul Sihvonen-Binder

Copy Editor
Lauren Kennedy

Editorial Director
Robyn Siesky

Editorial Manager
Cricket Krengel

Business Manager
Amy Knies

Senior Marketing Manager
Sandy Smith

Vice President and Executive Group Publisher
Richard Swadley

Vice President and Executive Publisher
Barry Pruett

Project Coordinator
Patrick Redmond

Graphics and Production Specialists
Andrea Hornberger
Jennifer Mayberry
Christin Swinford
Ronald Terry

Quality Control Technician
Melissa Cossell

Proofreading
Bonnie Mikkelson

Indexing
Broccoli Information Management

Contents

Contents

Contents

Contents

Contents

Contents

Contents

Contents

Contents

Contents

Contents

Contents

Contents

Contents

Contents

Contents

Contents

Contents

Introduction

For those who've used the Mac since the mid-1980s, it's hard to believe that it's been eight years since the first version of Mac OS X (10.0 Cheetah) was released, in March 2001, at a period when Apple's very survival seemed uncertain after years of chaotic management. Returned CEO Steve Jobs changed that chaos into focus and innovation, and a steady stream of improved Mac OS "big cats" have followed ever since: Mac OS X 10.1 Puma in September 2001, followed by Mac OS X 10.2 Jaguar in August 2002, Mac OS X 10.3 Panther in October 2003, Mac OS X 10.4 Tiger in April 2005, and Mac OS X 10.5 Leopard in October 2007. Now the newest big cat is here: Mac OS X 10.6 Snow Leopard.

Of the Mac OS X lineage, Snow Leopard in many ways is the oddest. Apple publicly proclaimed that this seventh version would not introduce significant new functionalities, the kinds of "Wow!" features like Time Machine or the Dock Apple is famous for. Instead, it would be retooled to be lighter and faster — less fat, more muscle — by taking advantage of multiple cores now standard on computer processors. That means a boost to application performance, speedier QuickTime streaming media, and faster JavaScripts on Web pages. Oh yeah, and take less disk space. Many of us believe these under-the-hood changes are not only to make the Mac faster, but to prepare for the use of Mac OS in new kinds of devices that the iPhone (also based on some of the Mac OS) can only suggest.

But of course, Apple can't just do things under the hood. Mac OS X 10.6 Snow Leopard is certainly very familiar, with few interface changes or obvious visual cues that it's different. You'll notice the speed, of course — sort of like getting a new Mac without buying one — but we expect you'll also discover the more subtle differences throughout.

For example, Safari 4.0 adds tabbed pane support that was sorely lacking in previous versions, while adding the zing of Cover Flow navigation. The Finder gets a slider for icon size, plus a more customizable Sidebar, while the Dock now allows for folder navigation and includes Exposé-based window switching for running applications. Older Mac laptops with a Multi-Touch trackpad now have all the same gesture capabilities as the newest models. Preview now makes it easier to select text in multicolumn PDFs, Spotlight now lets you both change the default search locations and sort your results, and better handling of Web page content is available in the VoiceOver Utility for the visually impaired.

Other changes are more pronounced, such as support for multiple Braille readers; the ability to create your own text auto-replacement rules for Mail, TextEdit, and other programs; a reworked set of controls for the built-in security firewall; the inclusion of many QuickTIme Pro features into the built-in QuickTime Player (that'll save you $35); the ability to have multiple active Unix sessions in Terminal; and a revamped, editable Services capability.

And there are in fact some "Wow!" additions that Apple could not resist, such as the ability to enter Chinese characters on Multi-Touch trackpad and the automatic time zone detection that means your Mac laptop will always have the correct time when you travel.

There is one big change that many users won't appreciate, but that is a potential game-changer for Mac users in business settings: support for Microsoft's ActiveSync technology. Mac OS X 10.6 Snow Leopard is now natively able to work with Microsoft Exchange 2007, the server that powers a lot of business's e-mails, shared calendars, shared to-dos, and shared contacts. This tears down a huge barrier at many businesses that held back Mac adoption. Sure, home and graphics users won't notice the ActiveSync support, but the rest of the world will. And the elimination of Apple's proprietary AppleTalk protocol underscores the fact that the Mac simply fits right into the corporate world, all without giving up one inch of its personality, innovation, or distinctive advantages.

Just as Mac OS X 10.6 Snow Leopard at first glance may seem like it doesn't have many new features, though it is really different under the hood and has dozens of enhancements that make your day-to-day work easier, this book has undergone a similar transformation. The cover and many of the chapter titles will look familiar if you've read previous editions, but the text and presentation are all new. As a new author team, we have focused much more on providing tips and how-to context so you can get more out of your Mac than ever before. We believe you'll learn a lot about making things happen on the Mac that you probably didn't know it could do.

What This Book Offers

So, given the Mac OS's reputation for being intuitive, why do you need this book? For one, because Mac OS X packs a lot of capabilities that you may never realize exist unless you go looking for them. This book does the looking for you, so you can take the most advantage of the Mac OS's many capabilities.

We also identify any weaknesses in the Mac OS's interface and tools and explain how to overcome them — these situations are rare, but they do exist.

Macintosh users fall into several classes:

- Users new to the Mac but familiar with other computer operating systems (namely, Windows)
- Users new to computers, period
- Experienced Mac users looking to see what's new and different in the latest version of Mac OS X

No matter which class you're in, this book addresses your needs. Regardless of your level of experience with Macs, this book can help you use Mac OS X efficiently and guide you to discovering more of the operating system's potential.

How to Read This Book

Mac OS X Snow Leopard Bible is made up of 26 chapters divided into five parts, plus a glossary. The parts cover different aspects of the Mac OS X, so you're likely to read parts in the order of interest to you. Still, we suggest that everyone read Part I first to get the basic lay of the land in how Mac OS X operates, so you have the fundamentals in place for the rest of the book.

Following is a brief description of the parts in *Mac OS X Snow Leopard Bible*.

Part I: Getting Started with Mac OS X 10.6 Snow Leopard

This part walks you through the basic user interface and tools in the Mac OS, beginning with how to install it and then explaining main user interface components such as the menu bar, Dock, desktop, and Finder. It also has a chapter that explains how to set up Mac OS X for people with disabilities. This part also explains key operations such as backing up your Mac's data, using its help system, using application software, both the software that comes with Mac OS X 10.6 Snow Leopard and software you may acquire on your own. There's a chapter dedicated to the suite of Mac OS X applications used to play music and movies, a key Mac strength.

Part II: Networking and the Internet

This part explains how to use the Mac to connect with the rest of the world, both through a local network and over the Internet. It explains how to use Mac OS X's Safari Web browser, Mail e-mail program, and iChat instant-messaging application, as well as how to share your Address Book contacts and iCal calendars. Three chapters explains the ins and outs of setting up and working with networks, such as to reach the Internet, share files with other users in a workgroup, host your own Web site, and make files available via the File Transfer Protocol service. You'll also learn about the different kinds of networking technologies — Ethernet, Wi-Fi, and Bluetooth — available to you. Another chapter explains how to use Apple's MobileMe service, which enables you to synchronize multiple computers' contents, as well as make files, contacts, and calendar entries available publicly via the Web.

Part III: At Work with Mac OS X

This part explains how to use Mac OS X's more specialized but widely useful capabilities. For example, one chapter covers the helper services that Mac OS X makes available to applications, while another explains how to print and fax from your Mac. The third chapter covers how to work with Windows users, and even run Windows on your Mac, while the fourth chapter in this part explains how to set up your Mac to work with Microsoft's Exchange e-mail, contacts, and calendar server — something that Mac OS X 10.6 Snow Leopard greatly enhances.

Part IV: Maintaining Your Mac with Mac OS X

This part shows you how to manage and fine-tune the Mac OS X itself, from setting up user accounts so more than one person can work on the Mac without interfering with other users' preferences to understanding all the system preferences you can set, such as screen display and sound defaults. You'll also learn how to use and manage fonts and secure your Mac from viruses and other dangers.

Part V: Beyond the Basics

This part covers the features of Mac OS X 10.6 Snow Leopard that are highly specialized and, therefore, typically of interest to advanced users. You'll learn about utilities to enhance Mac OS X, how to use the AppleScript and Automator tools to create your own automated actions, and how to use the Unix operating system that is included with Mac OS X.

Conventions Used in This Book

Before we begin showing you the ins and outs of Mac OS X 10.6 Snow Leopard, we need to spend a few minutes reviewing the terms and conventions used in this book.

Menu commands

The Mac OS X commands that you select by using the program menus appear in this book in normal typeface. When you choose some menu commands, a related popup menu appears. If this book describes a situation in which you need to select one menu, and then choose a command from a secondary menu or list box, it uses an arrow symbol. For example, Choose File ➪ Open means that you should choose the Open command from the File menu.

Literal text

This book uses a special font to indicate literal text; that is, text that you should type exactly as is. We use the font to indicate text that we instruct you to type for URLs (Web addresses), AppleScript and other code, and pathnames for Mac OS X folders. For example: "Type **localhost** and press Return to see local services."

Windows, dialog boxes, and panes

Mac OS X also a mechanism called a *window* that opens in an application for its contents, such as text or movies. Some applications have an *application window* that contains all its controls and contents; most applications have *document windows* that contain the contents of whatever you're working on within the application. The Finder — the application that you use to work with disks, folders, and files — has its own type of window called the Finder window. And there are other windows that you may see that, such as informational and status windows that show the progress of a disk copy or the details on a disk's contents and settings.

Within applications, Mac OS X uses dialog boxes to offer up a bunch of related features in one place. Dialog boxes may have options that open a subsidiary group of options, called a *settings sheet*. Dialog boxes are the most common way to access options in programs; when a dialog box is open, you can't use other features in that application.

In many dialog boxes and in some windows, you may see a feature that has proved to be quite popular called *tabbed panes*. This is a method of stuffing several dialog boxes into one dialog box or window. You see tabs, somewhat like those in file folders, and when you click a tab, the pane of options for that tab comes to the front of the dialog box or window. This book will tell you to go to the pane, which you do by clicking the tab where the name of the pane is to display the pane. For example, "Go to the General pane" means click the General tab in the current dialog box or window. There are also panes that don't have tabs but instead are accessed via a button. Then there are panes that are essentially subdivisions of a dialog box or window, a defined space in the existing dialog box or window, rather than something you switch to via a button or tab.

Mouse conventions

Here's what we mean when we talk about using the mouse:

- **Click.** Most Mac mice have only one button, but some have two or more; the Mighty Mouse that Apple has included with Macs for the last several years appears to have one button but can detect which side of the mouse you are pressing, so it in effect has two buttons. If you have a multibutton mouse, quickly press and release the leftmost mouse button once when we say to click the mouse. (If your mouse has only one button — you guessed it — just press and release the button you have.)

- **Double-click.** When we say to double-click, quickly press and release the leftmost mouse button twice. (If your mouse has only one button, just press and release the button you have two times.) On some multibutton mice, one of the buttons can function as a double-click (you click it once, the mouse clicks twice); if your mouse has this feature, use it — it saves strain on your hand.

- **Right-click.** If your mouse has at least two buttons, right-clicking means clicking the right-hand mouse button. (On multibutton Mac mice, Mac OS X automatically assigns the right-hand button to Control+click.) On a one-button mouse, hold the Control key when clicking the mouse button to achieve the right-click effect.

- **Drag.** Dragging is used for moving and sizing items in a document. To drag an item, position the mouse pointer on it. Press and hold down the mouse button, and then slide the mouse across a flat surface to drag the item. Release the mouse button to drop the dragged item in its new location.

Touchpad conventions

In 2008, Apple began shipping Macs that have a touchpad (adapted from its iPhone and iPod Touch) that supports *gestures*, so you can use finger actions on the touchpad instead of using a mouse. The actions include:

- **Tap.** This is the equivalent of mouse-clicking on a touch screen, using your finger or stylus rather than a mouse.

- **Swipe.** This means to move your finger across the touchpad in one direction, such as for scrolling.

- **Pinch.** This means to put two fingers apart on the touchpad and then move them together, to zoom out the view (include more of the content on the screen).

- **Expand.** This means to put two fingers together on the touchpad and then move them apart to zoom in the view (magnify part of the content on the screen).

Keyboard conventions

Keyboard shortcuts are widely used in Mac OS X to provide quick access to various controls and options. These shortcuts usually include pressing and holding one or more modifier keys — a special key such as ⌘, Option, Shift, and Control — then pressing a "regular" key such as number, punctuation symbol, or letter, and finally letting go of the keys.

- The Mac's Command key (⌘) is the most-used shortcut key. This key is sometimes known as the Apple key because the key has both the ⌘ symbol and an open Apple logo printed on it. But because there is also the Apple menu, indicated by a solid Apple logo (), in the Mac OS, it's best *not* to call this key the Apple key and then get confused with the Apple menu.

- Shift is used both to capitalize text and in keyboard shortcuts. In Mac OS X and in many Mac program menus, Shift is displayed by the symbol ⇧.

- The Option key is used in keyboard shortcuts. In Mac OS X and in many Mac program menus, you see the symbol ⌥ used. Note that Mac keyboards often add the label Alt to the Option key; this is for the convenience of Windows users because the Option key functions as the Windows Alt key when you are running Windows on a Mac.

- The Control key is used infrequently for shortcuts; its main use is to Control+click an object to display a contextual menu. In Mac OS X and in many Mac programs, you see the symbol ⌃ used.

- The Tab key is used both to move within fields in panes and dialog boxes and to insert the tab character in text. Mac OS X and many Mac programs indicate it in menus with the symbol .

- The Esc key is typically used to close a dialog box or pane and cancel any settings you entered in it. It's also used in a few keyboard shortcuts.

- The Return key is used to apply a dialog box's settings and close the dialog box (equivalent to clicking OK or Done), as well as to insert a hard paragraph return in text. In Mac OS X and Mac programs, it is indicated in menus by the symbol . Note that there is another key labeled Enter on most keyboards, in the numeric keypad. This sometimes works like the regular Return, but not always. (We refer to it as *keypad Enter* in this book.) In Mac OS X and many Mac programs, it is indicated in menus by the symbol .

- The Delete key deletes text, one character at a time, to the *left* of the text-insertion point (what a typewriter or a Windows PC would call Backspace). In Mac OS X and many Mac programs, the Delete key is indicated in menus by the symbol ⌫.

- The Eject key lets you quickly eject an optical disc, such as a DVD or CD, in the Mac's SuperDrive. But it is also occasionally used in shortcuts, such as for putting the Mac to sleep. In Mac OS X and many Mac programs, the Eject key is indicated in menus by the symbol ⏏.

- Macs with an extended keyboard — one with a numeric keypad — have a second Delete key (below Help or Fn and next to End) that deletes text to the right of the text-insertion pointer. Called Forward Delete, newer Mac keys label it Delete ⌦. In Mac OS X and many Mac programs, the Forward Delete key is indicated in menus by the symbol ⌦.

If you're supposed to press several keys at the same time, we indicate that by placing plus signs (+) between them. Thus, Shift+⌘+A means press and hold the Shift and ⌘ keys, then press A. After you've pressed A, let go of all three keys. (You don't need to hold down the last character in the sequence.)

We also use the plus sign (+) to join keys to mouse movements. For example, Option+drag means to press and hold the Option key while dragging the mouse on the Mac.

Icons

We've used special graphic symbols, or *icons,* throughout this book. These icons call your attention to points that are particularly important or worth noting:

New Feature
The New Feature icon indicates a technique or action that is new to or revised in Mac OS X 10.6 Snow Leopard.

Tip
The Tip icon indicates a technique or action in Mac OS X 10.6 Snow Leopard that will save you time or effort.

Note
The Note icon indicates information that you should remember for future use — something that may seem minor or inconsequential but will, in reality, resurface.

Caution
The Caution icon is used to warn you of potential hang-ups or pitfalls you may encounter while using Mac OS X 10.6 Snow Leopard (and how to avoid them).

Cross-Ref
The Cross-Ref icon points you to different parts of the book that contain related or expanded information on a particular topic.

Part I

Getting Started with Mac OS X 10.6 Snow Leopard

Starting with Mac OS X 10.6 Snow Leopard

Apple's operating system for its Mac computers (named Mac OS X) is now in its seventh incarnation (10.6) and has been given the moniker Snow Leopard. This follows Apple's tradition of naming the Mac OS X operating system after big cats, which started when the code name for Mac OS X 10.0 Cheetah was leaked and Apple decided to stick with it.

Users familiar with Mac OS X will find themselves right at home with Mac OS X 10.6 Snow Leopard, while users migrating from a Windows PC will discover a big wow factor when they run Mac OS X for the first time. Whereas the Windows operating system acts a base to launch other applications, Mac OS X technologies and information in applications permeate throughout the system.

The result is a very different experience because users can seamlessly perform tasks. But Windows users need not fear working in a different operating system; OS X is surprisingly simple and effective, and it follows many computing conventions: Technologies such as the desktop, folders, and windows work in the same way on an Apple system as a Microsoft-based one.

In this chapter, we first look at some of the key technologies that make up Mac OS X, and at some of the new technologies that have been introduced in Mac OS X 10.6 Snow Leopard. Then we take you through the system requirements and installation methods for getting Mac OS X 10.6 Snow Leopard on your Mac.

IN THIS CHAPTER

Getting to know Mac OS X 10.6 Snow Leopard

Preparing for the installation

Running the Mac OS X installer

Getting to Know Mac OS X 10.6 Snow Leopard

Apple CEO Steve Jobs first announced Mac OS X 10.6 Snow Leopard at Apple's Worldwide Developers Conference in June 2008, and the new operating system went on sale about a year later.

On the surface, Mac OS X 10.6 Snow Leopard has hardly any new features (notable exceptions include support for Microsoft Exchange 2007 and QuickTime X); instead, most of the changes have taken place under the hood. Mac OS X 10.6 Snow Leopard is a complete reworking of the operating system designed specifically to run faster on the latest generation of multicore processors, such as the Core 2 Duo and quad-core Intel Xeon processors, and is scaled down to work on Arm processors such as those used by the iPhone and iPod touch.

Mac OS X 10.6 Snow Leopard also sports other features that promise to use your graphics card for additional computing oomph when it's not being used for visual prowess. Owners of Intel-based Mac computers should see huge performance gains when upgrading from Mac OS X 10.5 Leopard to Mac OS X 10.6 Snow Leopard.

Note
Apple never refers to its operating system as Mac OS "ex." Instead it is always referred to as Mac OS "ten."

Understanding the technologies in Mac OS X 10.6 Snow Leopard

Mac OS X has an extremely slick interface, but underneath it is a world-class operating system based on open standards. Below the shiny exterior of the Mac OS X interface sits a rock-solid Unix-based operating system core called Darwin. (The "X" in Mac OS X refers to Unix.)

Mac OS X was designed from the ground up to replace the older, or "classic," Mac operating system that Apple had been using since the original Mac launched in 1984. Because it is based on Unix, it provides an extremely stable environment for applications to run in. And because Unix is so Internet-centric, Mac OS X can be integrated to virtually any computing environment (although it is designed to only work on an Apple-branded computer).

The Unix operating system is widely used in servers and workstations managed by technical experts; this has given Unix a reputation for being a complex OS sitting in the domain of the technical elite. Mac users need not fear Mac OS X's Unix core because Apple has created a world-class GUI (graphical user interface); users need not be concerned with Unix's command-line interface.

Mac OS X merged Unix's reliability with Apple's famous ease of use, creating an operating system like no other. But Unix is still at the heart of the Mac OS X operating system and those users who want to explore the underside of the Mac OS X operating system can do so by using a program called Terminal. As Apple says: The command line is there for those who would like to use it, but it isn't required for day-to-day operations. You can make as much or as little use of it as you want. We take a closer look at Terminal in Chapter 26.

In the meantime, let's take a closer look at all the different parts that make up Mac OS X.

What's New in Mac OS X 10.6 Snow Leopard

Despite its similar appearance (and name) to its predecessor, Mac OS X 10.5 Leopard, and the lack of stand-out application functionality to rival, for example, the introduction of the Time Machine backup utility in the previous version, Mac OS X 10.6 Snow Leopard has a lot of new capabilities under the hood:

- ActiveSync: This is the Microsoft technology that lets Mac OS X itself and its applications communicate instantly with Microsoft Exchange 2007 Server, so your e-mail, contacts, to-do items, and appointments are automatically kept up-to-date in a business environment.

- Grand Central Dispatch: This technology lets applications take advantage of multicore processors, so tasks can run in a parallel instead of running one at a time. This should make many Mac applications run much faster on the same systems.

- Open CL: This technology lets applications tap into newer Macs' graphics processors, giving them extra computing power when needed.

- 64-bit OS: "64-bit" refers to the size of the data and instructions that can be processed at any time by the processor and the OS. 64-bit applications run faster than the 32-bit applications of yesteryear, so by rewriting the Mac OS X to be 64-bit, the whole OS speeds up. Plus much more RAM can be used by the Mac and its applications: 32TB rather than the previous Mac OS's general 4GB limit.

- QuickTime X: The core of the Mac's media playback capabilities, Mac OS X Snow Leopard's revised version of this technology is optimized for greater speed and visual smoothness.

- Java processing: Here too, Apple has upped the ante on an existing technology. In this case, the revised Java processing lets Web pages that contain Java or Ajax programs run much faster.

In addition, Mac OS X 10.6 Snow Leopard removes the AppleTalk networking protocol, from which Apple has been slowly shifting to the Internet Protocol (IP) standard for some time. And Mac OS X 10.6 Snow Leopard no longer installs the Rosetta technology by default; Rosetta let applications designed for Macs that used the PowerPC chip to run on Macs with the Intel chip. (You can still install Rosetta as an option.)

Mac OS X 10.6 Snow Leopard also tweaks the user interface of several system preferences, such as renaming the International system preference to Language & Text. It also tweaks some of the icons and visuals in the Finder, and makes small adjustments to applications such as Address Book. But the vast majority of these tweaks are so subtle that most people won't notice them.

Grand Central Dispatch

In recent years, the race for faster processors has switched from clock speeds to multiple cores — the now-standard multicore processor essentially places multiple processors onto one chip, theoretically letting the processor do two, four, or eight times as much processing. But not all programmers know how to take full advantage of multicore computing. Grand Central Dispatch is designed to take advantage for these multicore processors by making the entire Mac OS X operating system "multicore aware" and optimizing it to allocate tasks across multiple cores and multiple processors. It aims to make it easier for programmers to get the full performance from modern computer systems.

New Feature

New to Mac OS X 10.6 Snow Leopard, Grand Central Dispatch is comprised of a set of technologies designed to take advantage of the latest generation of multicore processors (such as Intel's Core 2 Duo, quad-core, and i7 processors).

OpenCL

OpenCL (Open Computing Language) joins OpenGL (Open Graphics Library) in enabling Mac OS X 10.6 Snow Leopard to take full advantage of the incredibly fast graphics cards shipping with modern computers. Whereas OpenGL is designed to harness the power of graphics cards to draw visual effects, OpenCL is designed to extend this power beyond graphics and provide parallel processing with your main CPU.

New Feature

The introduction of OpenCL in Mac OS X Snow Leopard lets complex programs that don't require powerful graphical effects tap into the power of your graphics card to provide additional horsepower.

64-bit kernel

The journey from older 32-bit processors and applications to the 64-bit ones has been a long, but worthwhile, process. 32-bit processors are limited to 4GB of RAM, with 2GB application support — a figure that is looking increasingly tame as computer technology marches onwards.

The real advantage in offering 64-bit support is that it enables the operating system and applications to address more than 4GB of RAM, and Mac OS X Snow Leopard can support up to a theoretical 32TB (terabytes) of RAM. Although this amount sounds ridiculous today, it places Mac OS X in good stead for the future.

The underlying 64-bit support was first introduced in Mac OS X 10.3 Panther, which expanded a virtual address space in the kernel to 64 bits — this enabled a single non-GUI (graphical user interface) process to access the 8GB of memory that the Mac Pro offered, but doing so required specialized programming.

Mac OS X 10.4 Tiger took the process further by enabling any non-GUI process that was coded for 64-bit to see a 64-bit address space (the idea being that a program could spin off a worker thread to do the 64-bit number crunching and report back to the 32-bit GUI); Mac OS X 10.5 Leopard introduced full 64-bit support for any GUI application to access 4TB of RAM.

New Feature

Mac OS X 10.6 Snow Leopard takes 64-bit support all the way down into the kernel itself, so everything in Mac OS X 10.6 Snow Leopard (including all the applications) has been recompiled for 64-bit.

Note

Mac OS X 10.6 Snow Leopard installs as a complete 32-bit or 64-bit system depending on your processor. Intel Core Duo processors, used on early MacBooks, iMacs, and Mac Minis are 32-bit whereas all Intel Core 2 Duo-based and Intel Xeon-based Macs are 64-bit.

QuickTime X

QuickTime is the technology used throughout Mac OS X (and other operating systems) to handle media playback. Most people's experience of QuickTime is with the QuickTime Player, but iTunes, iPhoto, and the Finder also use it extensively.

New Feature

QuickTime X optimizes the familiar QuickTime to support modern audio and video formats, which enables it to play back media more efficiently.

Core Location

Core Location is a technology that uses known WiFi hotspots to triangulate your current position. In Mac OS X 10.6 Snow Leopard it is used to automatically determine your present time zone and adjusts the clock accordingly.

New Feature

Core Location triangulates your position from a list of known WiFi hotspots. It uses this information to set the Time Zone.

Darwin

Underneath Mac OS X 10.6 Snow Leopard sits Darwin 10.0, which is a result of a joint operation between the open source community and Apple. Darwin is a complete open source Posix (Portable Operating System Interface) operating system released by Apple in 2000 and continuously developed alongside Mac OS X.

Darwin forms the base of Mac OS X, and also the base of the iPhone and Apple TV operating systems. It is composed of code created by Apple, as well as code from NextStep, Free BSD (Berkeley Software Distribution), and other open source software projects.

Darwin is released under the Apple Public Source License, which the Free Software Foundation approved as a free software license from Darwin 2.0. Thus, there are many independent projects modifying or enhancing Darwin.

XNU kernel

At the heart of Darwin lies a XNU (X Is Not Unix) kernel developed by NeXT, and later Apple. The kernel is the central component of most computer operating systems and sits between the hardware and software components. It is responsible for managing system resources, especially memory, the CPU, and I/O (input/output) devices.

XNU combines the Mach microkernel developed by Carnegie Mellon University with BSD and a device driver framework called I/O Kit.

The XNU kernel is a complicated beast, but at its heart, the Mach kernel handles threads and processing; BSD sits between the GUI and the kernel and handles users' IDs, permissions, and the network file system; the I/O Kit enables drivers to run from the user space instead of the kernel space — this ensures that if these drivers crash, the kernel does not crash. If a kernel space driver crashes, then it may cause a "kernel panic" that requires your Mac to be restarted.

Kernel panics are extremely rare in Mac OS X. When one occurs, the screen fades to a dark gray with white text. This message appears in several languages: "You need to restart your computer. Press the power button for several seconds or press the Restart button." Figure 1.1 shows Mac OS X suffering from a kernel panic.

FIGURE 1.1

Mac OS X rarely suffers from a kernel panic crash. When it does, you need to restart your computer.

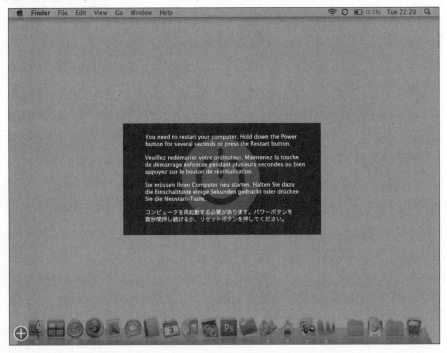

Protected memory

Protected memory ensures that applications run inside their own memory spaces and prevents applications from going beyond memory that is allocated to them. Protected memory also ensures that if an application crashes, it can be terminated without having a negative effect on other applications.

Advance memory management

The physical RAM in your Mac is managed automatically by Mac OS X, and is augmented with virtual memory dynamically as it is needed. (Virtual memory uses space on your hard drive in lieu of physical RAM.) This means that users no longer have to set allocated memory amounts manually to applications, as they did in the "classic" Mac OS. Advance memory management also alleviates the out-of-memory conditions that used to affect Mac users.

Preemptive multitasking

Since Mac OS 7 (then called System 7), every Mac operating system has allowed more than one application to be open at the same time. This capability is known as *multitasking*. Before the introduction of Mac OS X, Mac computers used a technology known as *cooperative multitasking*, in which they would negotiate which applications got the Mac's resources and for how long before switching to the next application. (This switching among applications happened so quickly that, to a person, it appeared as if they were running simultaneously.) But for cooperative multitasking to work, tasks had to be programmed to yield when they did not require system resources, and not everyone played nicely by the rules.

The first version of Mac OS X replaced this cooperative approach with *preemptive multitasking*, which enables privileged tasks or parts of the system to interrupt, and then later resume, other tasks. Thus, no task could hog all the resources. Preemptive multitasking is a more efficient method of task management and it enables Mac OS X to remain responsive even during processor-intensive tasks.

Symmetric multiprocessing

Symmetric multiprocessing (SMP) is the computing term for a multiprocessor computer architecture where two or more processors can connect to a single shared main memory. In the case of multicore processors, such as those used in Intel-based Macs, the SMP architecture treats individual cores as separate processors.

SMP technology takes advantage of multiple processors by assigning applications to specific processors, or by splitting up parts of applications (known as *threads*) between multiple processors simultaneously. Mac OS X is also optimized to take advantage of a technique known as *optimized kernel resource locking*, which provides superior SMP performance by enabling multiple CPUs to access different portions of the kernel simultaneously.

Mac OS X 10.5 Leopard introduced multiprocessor competency, with support for up to eight simultaneous cores (found in the dual quad-core Mac Pro computer).

New Feature

Mac OS X 10.6 Snow Leopard takes great strides with SMP, thanks to its Grand Central Dispatch technology. This technology implements FreeBSD's ULE scheduler into Mac OS X (ULE is short for SCHED_ULE). ULE was designed from the ground up for symmetric multiprocessing and can set CPU affinity per processor, per thread, producing a great speed boost to multi-threaded applications.

Graphics technologies in Mac OS X

The visual muscle of Mac OS X is the stuff of legend. Apple's operating system is one of the most graphically powerful on earth. Mac OS X harnesses several of the best technologies around to achieve this visual prowess: Quartz, OpenGL, and QuickTime form the three pillars that Apple's graphical competence stands on.

Over the last decade some of the greatest strides in hardware performance have come from increasingly powerful graphics cards. Apple has taken advantage of this with two software technologies: Core image and Core Animation. These technologies improve performance by reducing floating-point unit (FPU) utilization by offloading it to the graphics processing unit (GPU).

New Feature

Mac OS X 10.6 Snow Leopard introduces a new technology called OpenCL. This takes the power of these graphics cards a step farther, outside of the realm of creating visual effects, and uses them to create additional parallel computing alongside the GPU.

Quartz

Quartz is a two-dimensional graphics-rendering system known as Quartz 2D and a composition engine that sends instructions to the graphics card called Quartz Compositor. Together they are generally referred to as either Quartz or Core Graphics. Key features of Quartz include built-in support for the Portable Document Format (PDF); plus on-the-fly rendering, compositing, and anti aliasing. It supports multiple font formats, including TrueType, PostScript Type 1, and OpenType (see Chapter 22). Apple's ColorSync technology is also supported by Quartz to enable accurate color calibration in the print/graphics environment (see Chapter 21).

OpenGL

Open Graphics Library began its life with Silicon Graphics in 1992 and is a cross-platform API (application programming interface) for applications that produce 2-D and 3-D graphics. It consists of more than 250 different functions that are used to create three-dimensional scenes. It is widely used by any application that requires intensive three-dimensional graphics (CAD/CAM [computer-aided design and computer-aided manufacturing], medical imaging, computer simulation, video games, and so on) and it is a direct competitor to Microsoft's DirectX technology. The capabilities of OpenGL have extended with each incarnation of Mac OS X and increasingly powerful graphics cards included in Mac computers. You can find a table of capabilities plus general information on OpenGL at `http://developer.apple.com/graphicsimaging/opengl/`.

QuickTime

QuickTime is a cross-platform (Mac and Windows PC) media-authoring and distribution engine. It is used by a variety of different applications to play and edit media files. It supports more than 50 video, audio, and still-image formats. Some examples include MOV, ACC, MP3, MPEG-1, JPEG, and TIFF. QuickTime has a plug-in architecture that enables third-party developers to create additional components; these widen the range of media format types. QuickTime also supports video streaming, enabling viewers to watch video or listen to audio as it is streamed over the Internet.

Apple ships an application called QuickTime Player with Mac OS X, which is used to play or stream media (see Chapter 8).

Aqua

Aqua is the name of Mac OS X's GUI; it also refers to the primary visual theme of the Mac OS X operating system. As the name implies, it is based around water, with translucent and reflection effects, some areas of Mac OS X — such as Dashboard — take the effect to extremes with water-rippling visual animations. The Aqua interface also pays many visual nods to the Mac hardware, the original two-tone style of menu bars complemented the Bondi Blue iMacs, whereas the metal look used today ties closely to the aluminum used on many Mac computers.

Visually Aqua has moved a considerable distance from the look of the "classic" OS, and each successive implementation of Mac OS X has refined the visual theme of the Aqua interfaceMac OS X application environments.

The Mac OS X 10.6 Snow Leopard operating system has a distinguished history and, as such, Apple has had to build several application environments over time and include them with Mac OS X so it can run both modern software and older, legacy applications.

An application environment consists of various system resources, components, and services that enable an application to function. Mac OS X has numerous application environments, including Cocoa, Carbon, Java, AppleScript, and WebObjects, plus BSD and X11.

Cocoa

Cocoa is Mac OS X's native object-orientated application environment. Applications developed in Cocoa are designed exclusively for Mac OS X and will not run on any other operating system, including Mac OS 9.

The Cocoa programming environment automates many aspects of the application to comply with Apple's human interface standards; as such, Cocoa applications usually have a distinctive look in keeping with Mac OS X's Aqua interface. Common Cocoa applications include Mail, Safari, and Preview.

Cocoa applications take full advantage of some of the key Mac OS X features covered earlier in this chapter, including advanced memory management, preemptive multitasking, and symmetric multi-processing. Apple promotes Cocoa over Carbon among developers, citing the modern object-orientated programming techniques and rapid application development tools as distinct advantages.

New Feature

Before Mac OS X 10.6 Snow Leopard, many of Apple's programs, including the Finder itself, were written in Carbon; however, Apple has completely rewritten the Finder in Cocoa for Mac OS X 10.6 Snow Leopard.

Carbon

Carbon is Mac OS X's second application environment. The great advantage that Carbon offers is that developers can create applications that run in "classic" versions of Mac OS (versions 8.1 and 9) and in Mac OS X. But as Mac OS X is now more than a decade old, there are very few applications in use that require Carbon to operate.

When running in Mac OS X, Carbon applications take advantage of Mac OS X's modern feature set, including the Aqua interface. This can make it difficult to tell if an application is written in Carbon or Cocoa. One disadvantage to Carbon applications is that they cannot use 64-bit processes in the GUI and it is not possible to compile 64-bit Carbon applications.

Tip

To tell if an application is created with Cocoa or Carbon in Mac OS X, click on the desktop to put an application window in the background, then press ⌘ and try to resize the window. If it is a Cocoa application, it stays in the background, whereas a Carbon application pops to the foreground.

Java

Java is a programming language originally developed by Sun Microsystems. Mac OS X comes with the latest version of Java installed as an application environment (updates to Java are frequently installed for you via Software Update). The advantage to developing in Java is that applications can run on any platform that contains a compatible Java virtual machine. Java development is increasingly rare, though, because it is generally considered to be more time consuming to develop for than rival cross-platform environments; still, Java is commonly used in Web-based applications. Sun released most of Java to the open source community in 2006.

BSD and X11

BSD (Berkley Software Distribution) is a Unix application environment that usually deals with command-line executable shell scripts, command-line tools, and daemons (programs that run in the background). X11 extends the BSD environment by adding a set of interfaces for graphical applications, in effect enabling a GUI environment for BSD Unix applications.

Packages and bundles

Cocoa and Carbon applications in Mac OS X are often contained in *packages* (also known as *bundles*). These appear in the Finder (usually in the Applications folder) as a single icon, but they actually contain all the files and folders used by the application. So, instead of having to open an application's folder (as you must in Windows) to find the program itself, you just double-click the package and the Mac OS X finds and loads the program for you.

Note

You can see the contents of a package by Control+clicking or right-clicking the package and choosing Show Package Contents from the contextual menu (see Figure 1.2).

FIGURE 1.2

Control+click or right-click an application icon and choose Show Package Contents from the contextual menu to see the files and folders that make up the application package.

Frameworks

Mac OS X frameworks contain code that is dynamically loaded and shared by multiple applications. The presence of frameworks reduces the need for applications that share common code to each load an individual version of the code.

Installing Mac OS X 10.6 Snow Leopard

Now that you're familiar with some of the technology underlying Apple's newest operating system, it's time to install a copy onto your Apple Mac computer. If you've recently bought a brand-new Apple Mac, it's likely that Mac OS X 10.6 Snow Leopard is already installed, although you should still check the information regarding Software Update later in this chapter.

However, many people will be required to upgrade from an earlier version of Mac OS X to Mac OS X 10.6 Snow Leopard. Alternatively, you may have no operating system present on a Mac, such as due to a hard disk crash, and require a fresh install.

Upgrading or installing Mac OS X is a relatively easy process, and Apple has created a custom installer that leads you through the process step by step. We'll take a look at these steps shortly, but first you need to ensure that your Mac can run Mac OS X 10.6 Snow Leopard.

Checking the system requirements

Mac OS X 10.6 Snow Leopard is designed to take full advantage of the multicore processors found in the latest generation of Intel computers. Because of this, you need to have a Mac computer with an Intel CPU. This includes all Mac Pro towers, all MacBook and MacBook Pro laptops, every iMac released since January 2006, and every Mac Mini released since March 2006.

New Feature

PowerPC-based Macs cannot run Mac OS X 10.6 Snow Leopard, so stick with Mac OS X 10.5 Leopard on these old systems.

The official system requirements are:

- An Intel processor

- An internal, external, or shared DVD drive

- At least 512MB of RAM (more is recommended for development); 2GB is recommended

- A built-in display or display connected to an Apple-supplied video card supported by your computer

- At least 9GB of disk space available for Mac OS X itself, or 12GB of disk space if you install the developer tools. You should also allow at least an extra 10GB for application installation, file saving, and free space for Mac OS X to move data around.

Preparing for the installation

After you have confirmed that your Mac computer meets the system requirements for Mac OS X 10.6 Snow Leopard, you need to prepare your computer for the update.

The first step is to ensure that your computer's firmware is up-to-date. Firmware is a computer program that resides in the Mac's motherboard and controls it; as with application software, it can be updated with new instructions.

Ever since Mac OS X 10.3 Panther, the easiest way to ensure that both software and firmware is up-to-date has been to use the built-in Software Update program. Choose ➪ Software Update from the menu bar. If any updates are available, they appear in the main window; click the Install button and enter your administrator password. You can also download firmware updates from `www.apple.com/support/downloads`.

Caution

Do not interrupt a firmware upgrade; you could permanently damage your Mac by doing so. If you are installing a firmware update on a Mac laptop, make sure that you connect it to a main power source so there's no chance of the battery dying mid-upgrade.

A Caution on Applications before Upgrading

When you perform a clean installation, you must reinstall all of your applications. Some applications limit the number of times they can be installed, so you run the risk of not being able to install them in the "clean" Mac OS X 10.6 Snow Leopard's Applications folder. So you may need to uninstall such applications first (look for an uninstall utility on the application's install disk), because you may not be able to uninstall them after you upgrade to Mac OS X 10.6 Snow Leopard.

Others — notably QuarkXPress and Adobe Creative Suite — use a technology called activation that tracks the number of installations and prevents further installations when you've exceeded your limit; but it also lets you deactivate the software in any location to free up a new installation in another location. In such cases, be sure to deactivate the original installation (you don't have to actually uninstall the software) before installing the software in a "clean" location, because you may not be able to deactivate them after you upgrade to Mac OS X 10.6 Snow Leopard.

Setting up a drive for installation

It is likely that you will be installing Mac OS X 10.6 Snow Leopard on a hard drive already containing a previous version of the Mac OS X operating system, replacing the existing Mac OS X with Mac OS X 10.6 Snow Leopard.

However, it is possible to perform a clean install on an additional internal or external hard drive (or on a partition within a hard drive). Doing so offers the advantage of leaving your original Mac OS X installation intact. (You can then boot back and forth between the old and new Mac OSes until you're satisfied that everything works in Mac OS X 10.6 Snow Leopard.)

In Mac OS X, hard drives are formatted by using a program called Disk Utility (see Chapter 8). You can find it in the Utilities folder inside the Applications folder; it is also on the Mac OS X 10.6 Snow Leopard installation DVD and can be used during the installation process. To erase your Mac's startup disk, you must start up from another disk, such as the Mac OS X installation DVD.

The Mac OS X Disk Utility offers five formatting options:

- Mac OS X Extended (Journaled)
- Mac OS X Extended
- Mac OS X Extended (Case-sensitive, Journaled)
- Mac OS X Extended (Journaled)
- MS-DOS (FAT)

If you are erasing your drive during the DVD installation process, you can choose to erase your drive by using just these two options: Mac OS X Extended, and Mac OS X Extended (Journaled).

We advise using Mac OS X Extended (Journaled). *Journaling* is a feature that was first introduced in Mac OS X Server 10.2.2 and then brought to non-Server users in Mac OS X 10.3 Panther. This feature protects the integrity of the file system in the event of an unplanned shutdown (such as a power failure) by keeping a log, or journal, of all changes so it can more easily recover the data if a repair is needed.

The Case-sensitive option (versus its counterpart, known as *Case preserving*) enables multiple files with the same name, but different capitalization, to exist in the same space, such as a folder. For example, if you selected Case-sensitive, files with the names "dog," "Dog," and "doG" could all appear on your desktop. If you do not select a case-sensitive formatting option, you are prevented from having these files in the same space, which helps prevent confusion.

Making a note of system settings

Before heading into the installation, we recommend that you make a note of your current networking and Internet preferences. If you are upgrading from a previous version of Mac OS X, these system preferences should be transferring from your old installation to the new Mac OS X Snow Leopard one. However, it is still prudent to make a note of them just in case they are not preserved.

Choose ➪ System Preferences and click the Network iconic button to open the Network system preference. Depending on your method of connecting to the Internet (most likely Ethernet or AirPort), you may need to make a record of the settings in the AirPort, TCP/IP (Transmission Control Protocol/Internet Protocol), DNS (Domain Name Service), and Proxies panes. (To see these panes, click the Advanced button. (See Chapter 12 for more on the Network system preference.)

Note
Users of older Macs connecting via dial-up may also have settings contained within an application called Internet Connect. This application was removed from Mac OS X 10.5 Leopard, and its settings are now found in the Network system preference.

Also make a note of any settings in the Sharing system preference (see Chapter 13), especially if you are using features such as remote login or Xgrid sharing, or have any custom file-sharing settings.

Backing up your data

We strongly advise that you back up your Mac's startup hard drive before beginning the upgrade. You can use this backup to restore your current operating system in the case of a mishap during installation. Even if the installation does not go awry, upgrading an operating system can result in applications compatibility issues. In these circumstances, many users revert to the previous operating system while waiting for the developer of any incompatible application to issue an update.

To back up your hard drive, you need a second hard drive. Those with Mac Pros can install an additional internal SATA (Serial Advanced Technology Attachment) hard drive, although most users will opt for an external USB 2.0, FireWire, or eSATA hard drive. Those with iMacs, Mac Minis, or MacBooks will need to use an external hard drive.

There are several ways to go about backing up your hard drive; the most common is to use Apple's Time Machine backup utility. This is covered in detail in Chapter 4.

A second option is to create a complete clone of your hard drive by using a program such as Bombich Software's Carbon Copy Cloner (www.bombich.com). In the event of an emergency, you can boot from this external clone of your hard drive (by pressing and holding the Option key during startup and selecting the cloned drive as the startup disk). After you have booted from your backup, you can use Carbon Copy Cloner to copy the complete hard drive from the backup disk back to your primary drive.

Tip

If you back up your current Mac OS X startup drive, then reformat it to install Mac OS X 10.6 Snow Leopard on a "clean" drive, you can transfer your accounts, settings, and applications to the Mac OS X 10.6 Snow Leopard drive from the backup by using the Migration Assistant, as explained later in this chapter.

Running the Mac OS X installer

Now that you have prepared the hard drive, backed up your current version of Mac OS X, and made a record of your current system settings, it's finally time to begin installing Mac OS X 10.6 Snow Leopard.

First insert the installation DVD into your Mac.

Note

If you are planning to install Mac OS X Snow Leopard on a MacBook Air laptop, you need to either attach an external dual-layer DVD drive (such as an Apple SuperDrive) to the laptop or use the Remote Install Mac OS utility to "borrow" the optical drive from another Mac. First, insert the Mac OS X 10.6 Snow Leopard installation DVD into a Mac or PC with a DVD drive. (That computer must be available on the network through an AirPort Wi-Fi or Ethernet connection, as must the MacBook Air.) Then run the Remote Install Mac OS utility from the Utilities folder in the Mac's Applications folder, or select the Remote Install Mac OS X iconic button from the Install Assistant on the PC, and follow its instructions.

To install Mac OS X 10.6 Snow Leopard, you must boot your Mac from the Mac OS X Install DVD; this launches the Setup Assistant (see Figure 1.3). You can do this in one of four ways:

- Double-click the Install Mac OS X icon inside the Mac OS X Install DVD window that appears on the desktop. Click the Restart button and enter your administrator password.

- Boot the Macintosh while pressing and holding the C key.

- In the Startup Disk system preference, select Mac OS X Install DVD icon, and click Restart.

- Press and hold the Option key while booting the Mac. You are presented with a blue screen with an icon for each valid startup disk. Use the mouse to select the Mac OS X Install DVD icon and press Return, or use the → or ← key to move to the Mac OS X Install DVD icon and press Return.

FIGURE 1.3

Begin the Mac OS X 10.6 Snow Leopard install process by inserting the installation DVD and restarting the Mac.

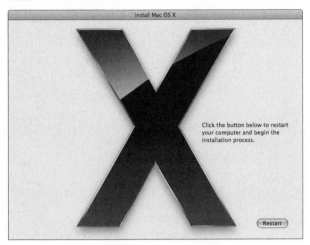

Running the installer

As your Mac boots up, it launches the installer program, which takes you through the process of installing Mac OS X 10.6 Snow Leopard on your Mac. Before the installation begins, you are presented with a series of windows for different installation options, which are covered in the sections that follow.

Select Language window

Mac OS X 10.6 Snow Leopard provides support for multiple languages, and the installer itself is available in 18 languages. Select the appropriate language and click the → button on the bottom right of the window to continue.

Welcome window

The Welcome window introduces you to the installation process. You can click the More Information button to get hints from Apple about installation. Click Continue to carry on with the installation.

Note that at this point you can access the menu bar at the top of the screen, such as to access the utilities on the Mac OS X Install DVD. You can also turn on wireless networking with the AirPort iconic popup menu and change the input language with the Input Sources iconic popup menu.

Note
The utilities available in the Utilities menu as you begin installation are Startup Disk (see Chapter 21), Reset Password (see Chapter 23), Firmware Password Utility (see Chapter 23), Disk Utility (see Chapter 8), Terminal (see Chapter 26), System Profile (see Chapter 8), Network Utility (see Chapter 8), and Restore System from Backup (see Chapter 4).

License window

Before you can install Mac OS X 10.6 Snow Leopard on your Mac, you must agree to the license by clicking the Agree button.

It is tempting to skip the reading of the documentation itself, as it consists of several thousand words, written in fairly complex legalese. However, we advised you to familiarize yourself with the license agreement, particularly if you are preparing to use Mac OS X 10.6 Snow Leopard in a commercial environment. For example, one condition of installation is that you may install Mac OS X 10.6 Snow Leopard only on a single machine, unless you have a Family Pack, in which case you may install it on up to five Macs. While some restrictions may seem remotely implausible (such as the ones relating to using the system as part of terrorist activity), some business restrictions relating to hospital, aircraft control, or nuclear facilities may affect you.

Apple's legal department takes the license agreement very seriously, and it's clear that Apple wants you to read it. You can also click Save to save a copy of the agreement — although if you are preparing to do a clean install, you should save it to an external hard drive.

Select a Destination window

The Select a Destination window enables you to determine where you want to install Mac OS X 10.6 Snow Leopard. Icons for all available drives appear at the center of the window. An exclamation mark in a yellow triangle means that the operating system cannot be installed on the drive (you see this if, for example, you have an iPod attached to your Mac as a drive). Typically, you will see the yellow icon if you have a newer version of the Mac OS X already installed on your Mac or if the drive was not formatted as a startup disk for an Intel Mac (called a GUID partition).

Select the drive you want to install Mac OS X 10.6 Snow Leopard on and click the Options button. Here, you'll find the following choices:

- **Upgrade Mac OS X.** If you are moving from Mac OS X 10.5 Leopard to Mac OS X 10.6 Snow Leopard, you can select this option. This upgrades your operating system while preserving all your system settings, preferences, applications, fonts, and documents. The advantage of selecting this option is that it offers a quick method of migrating from Mac OS X 10.5 Leopard to Mac OS X 10.6 Snow Leopard; the disadvantage is that you lose an opportunity to wipe your Mac computer clean and start with a fresh install.

- **Archive and Install.** This option moves all System files from your current Mac OS X installation to a folder called Previous System. It then installs a fresh copy of Mac OS X 10.6 Snow Leopard onto your Mac. After this option is used, your Mac will boot into the new version of Mac OS X, and the files in Previous System cannot be used as a boot drive. The idea is to produce a clean install of the new operating system that also contains all your old documents, preferences, fonts, and other files that you may need (tucked away in a single folder). You can then copy them from the Previous System folder to your current version of Mac OS X as, and when, you need them. It is wise to choose this option over Erase and Install unless you are absolutely certain you no longer need any files from your computer (or have a cast-iron backup of your current computer).

A suboption is Preserve Users and Network Settings. Selecting this option imports existing user accounts, home folders, and network settings into the new system.

- **Erase and Install.** This is the option for a completely new slate. As the name suggests, it completely wipes your hard drive and installs a fresh copy of Mac OS X 10.6 Snow Leopard. It will be as if you have bought a brand-new Mac. Obviously you should only choose this option if you are happy to lose everything on your hard drive, or have a suitable backup of all your important files and documents.

Note

Both the Archive and Install option and the Erase and Install option, followed by a reinstallation of all your preferred applications, fonts, important documents, and preferences can be a form of extreme housekeeping that results in a clutter-free and faster computing experience. But before installing Mac OS X 10.6 Snow Leopard, be sure to deactivate any software that uses activation licensing and to uninstall any software that may limit you from installing new copies — you may not get the chance after installing Mac OS X 10.6 Snow Leopard and have to buy a new license or activation.

A suboption of the Erase and Install menu is to choose the disk format. Your options are Mac OS Extended (Journaled) and Mac OS Extended (Case-sensitive, Journaled).

As mentioned previously, journaling enables your system to protect itself against sudden power shortages or system freezes. The case-sensitive option relates to filename capitalization; with this option selected, you can have multiple files with the same name, but different capitalization, in the same place.

Select your install option and click OK. The Select a Destination window now lets you know how much space is required to install Mac OS X 10.6 Snow Leopard on your hard drive. Click Continue to move to the next step.

Install Summary window

The Install Summary is the final window you see before you begin the actual installation. Here you have two options: You can either click the Install button (for the default settings) or click Customize.

By default, the Mac OS X 10.6 installer places on your Mac a limited selection of print drivers, additional fonts, and language support files,, as well as X11 (an implementation of the X window system that enables you to run X11-based applications in Mac OS X). It does not install all the printer drivers on the DVD, just those connected to your Mac for which it has drivers, plus the drivers for a few popular printers. Nor does it install the Rosetta technology that lets applications developers for PowerPC-based Macs run on Intel Macs. But it does install the fonts and language support (called Language Translation) files.

The Customize option enables you to choose the installation options, adding drivers, deselecting fonts, deselecting language files, and/or installing Rosetta, for example. (Deselecting any items you consider superfluous will save disk space and may improve performance slightly.)

When you're happy with your selections, click the Install button.

Stopping the Mac OS X 10.6 Snow Leopard Installation

Until you click the Install button and get the install process underway, you can stop the installation at any time by choosing Mac OS X Installer ➪ Quit Mac OS X Installation. If you do this, you are asked to confirm that you really intend to quit the installation; if you quit, the Mac will restart after asking you to select a startup drive. No matter what you select as the startup drive, you can change it by pressing and holding the Option key while your Mac boots up to select a different boot drive. You can also boot up to your original installation by pressing and holding the mouse button during the boot process. (This automatically ejects the DVD.)

You can also quit the installation process while the installation is taking place by choosing Mac OS X Installer ➪ Quit Mac OS X Installer. This isn't really advisable, though, because it leaves you without the operating system fully installed. If you select this option, you get a warning message and the options Restart, Don't Quit, or Select a Startup Disk.

When the process is finished, you get the message "Congratulations! You've installed Mac OS X on your computer." Click the Continue button, then click the Restart button to fire up OS X 10.6 Snow Leopard.

Checking Installation DVD window

The Mac OS X installation begins with the Checking Installation DVD window, which checks for any errors on your installation DVD, to prevent a corrupted version from being installed. You can click the Skip button to bypass this check.

Installing window

The Installing window appears, and the Mac OS X 10.6 Snow Leopard operating system is installed from the DVD to your hard drive. The process is largely automated and takes around an hour (depending on the speed of your system). There is little for you to do other than watch the progress bar, so now might be a good time to read up on some of the underlying technology in Mac OS X 10.6 Snow Leopard.

Starting Mac OS X 10.6 Snow Leopard and setting up your Mac

After the installation process is complete, your Mac boots up. Owners of new Mac systems, and those that have just performed a clean install, get to watch a short and stylish welcome video.

You are then taken to the Welcome window, which guides you through the process of setting up your Mac. Users who have opted to upgrade to Mac OS X 10.6 Snow Leopard, as well as those who chose the Archive and Install with the Preserve Users and Network Settings option, are taken straight to the Mac OS desktop.

Everybody else can get ready to set up his or her new Mac, which Mac OS X helps you do through a series of windows.

Welcome window

The Welcome window begins by asking you to select a country or region; there are six default regions: United States, Canada, United Kingdom, Australia, New Zealand, and Ireland. If you live outside of one of these areas, then select the Show All check box; this brings up a comprehensive list of countries.

If you wait for about 30 seconds, Apple's VoiceOver technology and a large dialog box appear. It informs you that you can enable VoiceOver by pressing the F5 key; if you are unfamiliar with VoiceOver technology, you can access a guide to using VoiceOver by pressing the Escape key. VoiceOver is part of Mac OS X's Universal Access settings, designed for people with different access requirements, such as the hearing impaired and the visually impaired. These technologies are covered in more depth in Chapter 6.

When you're ready, click Continue.

Keyboard window

This window enables you to choose a keyboard layout that matches your region. There is usually an option based on your region selection in the previous window; if this is the wrong area for your keyboard layout or if you want a different layout than the default for your region, click the Show All button and select the appropriate keyboard.

Do You Already Own a Mac? window

This window is useful for users who have upgraded from an older Mac system, or those who have used Time Machine or a program such as Carbon Copy Cloner to back up their data. In this window, you can launch a program called Migration Assistant to transfer system information from one Mac to another. (The original backup source is unaffected by this transfer.) To run Migration Assistant, choose any of the first three options when presented with the question "Would you like to transfer your information?":

- From another Mac
- From another volume on this Mac
- From Time Machine backup
- Do not transfer my information right now

Tip

You can run the Migration Assistant program at any time, not just during initial setup. You can find the Migration Assistant in the Utilities folder inside the Applications folder.

When transferring information from one account to another, you can transfer information from the following areas:

- Users
- Networks and other settings
- The Applications folder
- Files and folders on "*startup drive's name*"

By default, all four areas are checked, and performing this transfer re-creates your original Mac's setup in the new operating system. While you can select to transfer individual users' accounts, you cannot selectively choose what is transferred for each of the areas. (You cannot, for example, choose specific applications to transfer from your old installation to the new one; it's all or none.)

Some applications may not function correctly after they have been migrated from one Mac to another. In particular, some software includes copyright protection that makes a note of what system it is on and refuses to work when moved to a different computer. In these instances, you need to reinstall the software. Thus, it's best to uninstall or deactivate any applications that may have copy or license protection *before* migrating them to the new Mac OS.

Purchases from the iTunes Store will also not work on the transferred computer because you will need to authorize your new computer with your iTunes Store details. For some media, such as music purchases, you can only authorize five machines at any one point, so you may need to deauthorize one Mac before authorizing the new one. Therefore, be sure to deauthorize iTunes in the old Mac OS (see Chapter 9) before migrating your settings to the new Mac OS.

Transferring information from another Mac

Transferring information from another Mac requires you to connect both computers with a FireWire cable. You then need to restart the source Mac (the one you are transferring information from) while pressing and holding the T key. This places the source Mac in Target Disk mode, which in effect turns it into an external hard drive. You can then select the information you want to migrate and click the Transfer button. (When Target Disk mode is enabled, the migration process is the same as for an upgrade.)

Transferring information from another drive on this Mac

This option is for Mac users who have more than one installation of Mac OS X on their Mac. This can be either another hard drive, or a partition on your Mac's sole drive. (Partitioning splits a single hard drive into multiple parts, each of which looks and acts as if it were a separate physical drive.) Select the drive or partition that you want to transfer information from, then highlight the information that you wish to migrate and click the Transfer button. (The migration process is the same as for an upgrade.)

Restoring data from a Time Machine backup

Time Machine is a backup utility first introduced in Mac OS X 10.5 Leopard, and it is useful not just for retrieving lost information but also for transferring system information between computers.

If you plan to transfer information from a complete Time Machine backup of your drive, you should make sure the external hard drive containing the backup is attached to your Mac. If you have used a wireless networking drive (such as Apple's Time Capsule, or a hard drive connected to an Apple AirPort Extreme Base Station or other wireless router), then you will need to join a Wi-Fi network. Click the Join button to open the Network Assistant, click the Show Networks button, and select your network. Enter a password if required.

When the backup drive appears in the main window, click Continue to select the information you want to migrate and then click Transfer to start the migration process. (The migration process is the same as for an upgrade.)

Select a Wireless Service window

As the name suggests, this window enables you to join a Wi-Fi network (provided your Mac possesses AirPort functionality, as most do). A list of wireless networks appears in the main window; select the one you want join and enter the password. Then click Continue.

If your computer isn't connected to a wireless network, you can click the Different Network Setup button. This takes you to a window with a wider range of network options, including Cable Modem, DSL Modem, and Local Network (Ethernet); the My Computer option does not connect to the Internet. If you select this last option, you bypass the Apple ID and Registration Information windows and go straight to the Personalize Your Settings window.

Enter Your Apple ID window

An Apple ID is primarily used to make purchases and download free content from iTunes, iPhoto, and the Apple Store. If you have a MobileMe membership (formerly known as .Mac), simply enter your name and your password. An example Apple ID would be `steve@me.com`; you can also use the `steve@mac.com` variant (they are interchangeable).

If you don't have an Apple ID, leave the boxes blank and click Continue; you can always create an Apple ID later. Advantages of an Apple ID include a 60-day free trial of Apple's MobileMe service, which is explained in depth in Chapter 15.

Registration Information window

The information you fill out in this page is automatically sent to Apple via the Internet. You cannot leave anything in this page blank, and there is no button option to skip registration. However, it is possible to skip registration by pressing ⌘+Q, then selecting the Skip option. If you want to get more information on why Apple is collecting your information, and what it is used for, click the Privacy Policy button.

When you have filled out the registration information, click Continue; this takes you to the A Few More Questions window, which has two pull-down menus requesting information on where you will be primarily using this computer and what best describes what you do. Here you will also find the Stay in Touch check box; selecting this option means Apple sends you e-mails regarding new products, software updates, and newsworthy information.

Create Your Account window

Before you can start using your Mac, you need to create a user account. We take a much more in-depth look at user accounts in Chapter 20, but for now suffice it to say that you need to add information to administer your Mac account.

You need to enter a name and a short name. The name should be your full name, and the short name should be an abbreviation that you will learn to appreciate when authentication is required.

You also need to type in a password, and verify it by typing it in again. It is imperative that you pick a password that is memorable, because there is no way to retrieve a password that you have forgotten, although you can use the Reset Password utility on the installation DVD to set a new password, as Chapter 20 explains. Finally, you can enter a password hint to jog your memory.

When you're done, click Continue.

Select a Picture for This Account window

This part of the setup process attaches a picture to your account. If your Mac has a built-in iSight camera (or you have an older iSight attached to your Mac), you can take a quick snapshot of your-self to attach to your account. Otherwise (or if you are a bit camera-shy), you can choose a picture from the picture library, which brings up a number of pictures provided by Apple. Before taking your photograph, keep in mind that the snapshot will be used throughout Mac OS X and shared by programs such as iSight, although you can easily change it at a later time.

Select Time Zone window

This window enables you to select a time zone for your Mac. You can either use the map to click on a geographic region, or type in the name of a nearby city. After making your selection, click Continue.

Set the Date and Time window

This window enables you to set up the Mac's clock and calendar; enter the correct date and time and click Continue.

Don't Forget to Register window

If you skipped the registration process (by pressing ⌘+Q and selecting Skip on the registration page), you will be prompted once more to register. Click Done to move on.

Automatically Renew MobileMe window

If you are a MobileMe member and entered your Apple ID, you may be presented with an option to automatically renew your membership when it expires. If so, decide whether you want automat-ically renew, or not, and press Continue.

Thank You window

Now you see a window saying your Mac is set up and ready to use. Several icons are displayed, showing all the things you can do based on your chosen settings. Click on the Go button to start using your Mac.

Running Software Update

Apple periodically introduces updates to its Mac OS X operating system and the various applications provided on the Mac OS X Install DVD. It is not uncommon to find that the software provided by Apple has been improved by the time you install it on your Mac.

Note
Most software manufacturers provide software updates via their Web sites and have menu options (typically in the Help menu) that you can use to check for recent updates to their applications.

Apple simplifies the process with the Software Update program (choose ⇨ Software Update). Software Update is covered in depth in Chapter 21, although it is prudent to run Software Update as soon as you have finished installing Mac OS X 10.6 Snow Leopard (see Figure 1.4). The program checks for new software, and clicking the Install button downloads the relevant updates via the Internet and installs them. You may be required to enter your administrator password, and your Mac may have to restart for the update to take place.

FIGURE 1.4

Software Update checks for the latest versions of programs (including upgrades to Mac OS X itself). Be sure to run it right after you have installed Mac OS X 10.6 Snow Leopard.

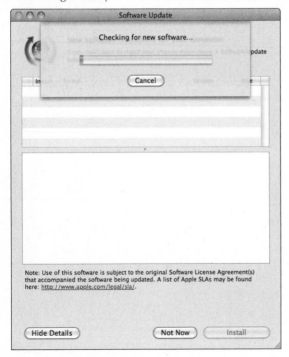

Summary

Mac OS X 10.6 Snow Leopard is Apple's Unix-based operating system designed to take advantage of modern multicore processors and advanced graphics cards. It provides preemptive multitasking, symmetric multiprocessing, protected memory, and advanced memory management, all of which allow the rich applications you'd expect to run on the Mac.

Apple has made many performance-oriented changes to the operating system in Mac OS X 10.6 Snow Leopard, even though on the surface it appears little changed, remaining the most accessible operating system available, with the style and appearance that customers expect from Apple.

New Macs come with Mac OS X preinstalled, but if you own a Mac and want to upgrade to Mac OS X 10.6 Snow Leopard, you have several options for doing so. You can overwrite the old Mac OS (only if it's Mac OS X 10.5 Leopard) and retain all your applications and settings. You can install a "clean" copy of Mac OS X 10.6 Snow Leopard on the same drive as your old Mac OS and have the settings transferred over. You can install Mac OS X onto a separate drive. Or you can reformat your original drive and install a "clean" copy of Mac OS X 10.6 Snow Leopard onto that.

When you begin the installation of Mac OS X 10.6 Snow Leopard, the installer walks you through all the options. After installation, when your Mac is booting into Mac OS X 10.6 Snow Leopard for the first time, a setup utility also walks you through the main setup and registration options, including giving you the option to transfer settings and applications from another Mac, another installation of Mac OS X on the same computer, or from a backup drive.

Exploring Mac OS X 10.6 Snow Leopard

This chapter introduces you to the Mac OS X 10.6 Snow Leopard working environment. Like all modern operating systems, Mac OS X has a graphical user interface (GUI, pronounced "gooey") that consists of windows, menus, icons, buttons, and various types of controls. Apple refers to this graphical interface as Aqua, because its theme takes cues from the transparent and reflective nature of water. Aqua is an extremely elegant interface that is easy to navigate and enables you to perform complex tasks quickly and efficiently. Because of this, Mac OS X is a rich and productive working environment.

In this chapter, you'll discover how to start up and log on to your Mac; you'll learn how to deal with any common startup problems, and the process of logging out, or switching off your Mac.

Next, you'll take a tour of the Mac OS X environment and learn the fundamentals of the menu bar, Dock, and desktop; last, you'll take a look at how you can customize your Mac to give it a personal appearance, as well as set it up so you can work in your own personal style.

After you're familiar with the interface, we'll show you a complete look at working with files and documents, especially with one of Mac OS X's key applications: the Finder. This application is how you navigate through your Mac.

By the end of this chapter, you will be familiar with the Mac OS X working environment, as well as many of the features covered in greater depth throughout the remaining chapters. Before describing the working environment in depth, we begin with how to start up and log in to your computer.

Starting Up and Logging In

Few sounds in life are as satisfying as the chime a Mac makes when it first starts up. This noise signifies that the basic hardware elements inside your Mac (hard disk, CPU [central processing unit], memory, and so on) are all operational. Following this chime, the hardware tests begin as the Mac checks for basic errors; after it confirms that everything is okay, the computer loads the operating system from the hard disk into memory.

Of course, being that it is a sleek operating system, Mac OS X does all this under the hood. Following the power light coming on, you'll hear the chime; then you will see a gray screen with a darker gray Apple logo in the middle; this is followed by a gray, spinning time wheel. After anywhere from 10 to 30 seconds, you see a blue screen with the arrow-shaped mouse pointer. Finally, depending on how your Mac is configured, you see either the login window or the Mac OS X desktop. The entire boot process takes about 30 to 45 seconds, depending on the speed of your Mac. Note that on faster Macs, some of the events may pass too quickly for you to notice.

Starting up your Mac

You start a Mac running Mac OS X 10.6 Snow Leopard in one of the following ways:

- **By pressing the power button on the Mac.**
- **By pressing the power button on some Apple Cinema Display LCD monitors.** Note that on some older models, the power button may simply switch the display off; the Apple LED Cinema Display does not have a power button.

Note
Check if the Mac has already been turned on and is in Sleep mode. In this case, the screen is dark and can easily be confused with the Mac being off. One way to tell if it's in Sleep mode is if the Mac has a pulsating light on. This is a visual cue that the Mac is asleep (the pulsing light is meant to evoke snoring). If this is the case, tapping the mouse or keyboard wakes it up.

Choosing a startup disk

By default, Mac OS X starts up from your primary disk, the hard disk inside your Mac. But it can start from other disks as well, such as DVDs and external hard disks. It can even start up from a drive on the network. You might start from a DVD — such as the Mac OS X installation disc — to upgrade your version of the Mac OS, or to reinstall it. You might start up from an external disk that contains applications or setup configurations you are testing (something developers and IT staff might do, but not regular users).

Dealing with Startup Problems

If your Mac does not start up correctly or at all, try booting up from the installation DVD and make sure that the startup drive still contains its folders and files (in case it was accidentally wiped out or corrupted, such as during a power failure). You can also run utilities such as Disk Utility from the installation DVD to try to repair any disk issues, as Chapter 1 explains. There are also third-party fix-it tools such as TechTool Pro ($98; www.micromat.com) that enables you to create a bootable partition on your hard disk from which you can run its repair utilities.

There are two special startup modes that an advanced user can use to troubleshoot a Mac that is not starting up correctly. One is single-user mode (press and hold ⌘+S during startup), which boots you into the Mac's Unix core, where you can type Unix commands to explore and troubleshoot the system (Chapter 26 has more information on working with Unix). The other is verbose mode (press and hold ⌘+V during startup), which displays a list of all startup activities and any error messages, which may help you identify the problem (such as a login item that is corrupt) and needs to be deleted (you'll have to boot from a different drive to delete or modify any such files if the Mac won't boot from its normal startup drive). Note that neither single-user or verbose mode will work if the Mac has Open Firmware Password Protection enabled (see Chapter 23).

To choose your startup disk, you have several choices.

- Press and hold Option as the Mac's startup chime begins; a screen appears showing icons for each drive available to boot from (you can release Option then). Select the desired disk by using the mouse or by pressing ← or → until the desired disk is highlighted (a ↑ iconic button appears below it). Then press Return or click the ↑ iconic button to boot into the selected drive.

- Press and hold the C key as the Mac's startup chime begins to start up from a CD or DVD. Note that this only works with Apple's SuperDrives.

- Press and hold the D key as the Mac's startup chime begins to start up from the first internal disk in a Mac that has multiple internal disks, such as a Mac Pro.

- Press and hold the N key as the Mac's startup chime begins to start up from the network. (A network startup drive must be properly configured and enabled, and the Mac must be connected to the network.)

- Press and hold the T key as the Mac's startup chime begins to boot the Mac into Target Disk mode, which lets another Mac connected to it via a FireWire cable see it as an external disk.

- Boot your Mac from its default disk, then choose 🍎⇨ System Preferences and click the Startup iconic button. In the Startup system preference, choose a startup disk from the list, then click Restart. Note that this startup-disk choice remains in effect each time you start the Mac until you change the Startup system preference again. (By contrast, pressing and holding one of the keys during startup changes the default startup disk only that one time.)

Logging in to Mac OS X

After the Mac has finished its bootup process, the login procedure begins. The login procedure essentially identifies you to the computer, as a security measure, to ensure that only people authorized to use your Mac can access it; it also serves a second purpose of activating your personal workspace (called a *user account*).

The login process is mandatory, although it is automated by default so the Mac logs into the primary user account created when you first installed Mac OS X. Thus, whenever a user turns on the Mac, he or she is taken directly to the desktop and can begin using the computer.

Login screen options

It is possible to disable the automatic login (Chapter 20 has more information on setting up user accounts and login options). If you disable automatic login, the Mac asks for your username and password before logging in to your user account and taking you to the desktop.

You might disable automatic login for a Mac used at an office or other public space, so no one but you can use your computer after it is shut down. If automatic login is disabled, you might see one of two login screens when you start the Mac:

- **List of users.** One login screen option presents a list of users, where you click your name or the icon representing you from the list of users, then enter your password in the field that appears. (If you accidentally selected the wrong user from the list, you can click the Back button to return to the list of users.)

- **Name and password.** The other login screen option presents a Name text field and a Password text field, and you must type in both to log in.

The login screen displays when you start your Mac with automatic login disabled; it also appears when you restart your Mac, log out of Mac OS X (a process explained later in this chapter), or when you switch users by using Fast User Switching (Chapter 20 has more information regarding Fast User Switching).

Cross-Ref

Chapter 20 covers how to manage your user account, as well as how to create and manage multiple user accounts on the same Mac.

Password entry

If you enter your username or password incorrectly, the login window shakes from left to right, indicating that there has been a problem. The Password text field also clears so you can reenter the password. (Note that the Name text field does not automatically clear; for security reasons, Mac OS X does not inform users if they have entered a wrong username.) If you press the Tab key, it highlights the text in the Name text field, so you can reenter the username.

Note

Passwords are case-sensitive, so capitalization must match that of the password as originally set up.

Logins and Access Permissions

A Mac can be set up with multiple user accounts, giving each user a private space for applications and files, a well as access to shared applications and files. The most common case for having multiple accounts is in home use, where each family member has his or her own "space" on the Mac.

Multiple user accounts are useful in business environments where employees may share the same Mac.

If your Mac is configured with multiple user accounts, be sure to disable automatic login so users have to log in to their accounts each time the Mac is started.

There's more to multiple user accounts than supporting multiple users. User accounts can also be set up with different levels of permissions. At home, that enables parents to have greater rights than children, such as the ability to change the children's user accounts. At a business, IT may have such administrator rights on all Macs, while employees have limited rights

Chapter 20 explains the various permissions levels available for user accounts.

If you enter the password incorrectly three times in a row, a password hint appears at the bottom of the screen. Clicking the Forgot Password button also reveals the password hint. You enter password hints when creating a user account and can use them to jog your memory.

The login screen's iconic buttons

In the login screen, three buttons appear at the bottom of the screen: Sleep, Restart, and Shut Down. You can use these immediately, instead of having to log in to the Mac first. They come in handy when you accidentally turn on the Mac and want to put it back to sleep or shut it down. Restart is handy when you meant to start the Mac from an external drive but didn't press Option in time during the boot process to get the list of alternative startup drives.

You can configure Mac OS X so that the Sleep, Shut Down, and Restart buttons do not appear in the login window. To do so, choose ⇨ System Preferences and go to the Accounts system preference, click the Login Options button, and then deselect the Show Restart, Sleep, and Shut Down Buttons option, as explained in Chapter 20. By coupling this setting with the Open Firmware Password protection utility explained in Chapter 23, you can make it all but impossible for someone to circumvent the requirement to log in.

Turning Off and Logging Out

When you've finished using your Mac, you have several options:

- Put the Mac to sleep.
- Leave the Mac on until the screen saver engages and then, later, the Energy Saver system preference settings put the computer to sleep automatically. (See Chapter 21 for details about the Desktop & Screen Saver and Energy Saver system preferences.)

- Log out of your account so that people cannot access your Mac without first entering your (or their) login password.

- Shut down the Mac, which logs out of your account and closes the operating system, before switching off the power. This option saves energy and provides greater safety in case of power failure.

- Restart the Mac. This isn't really a way to finish working with your Mac, but an option typically used to complete the installation of certain system updates or to allow the computer to run its self-tests on startup.

Caution

If you cut the power to a computer without first switching it off (either by pulling the plug or by removing the battery from an Apple notebook), you risk damaging the files on your Mac. Although this damage may not be immediately noticeable, an accumulation of damage could eventually cause problems, such as applications no longer working correctly or files missing data.

Putting your Mac to sleep (and waking it up)

When you're not going to use your Mac for a while, you can save energy by putting it to sleep. When you want to start using your Mac again, you can quickly wake it up. Waking up the Mac is much quicker than starting it up from being powered off.

You can put your Mac to sleep in any of the following ways:

- If you have a Mac laptop, simply close the screen lid.

- Choose ➪ Sleep.

- If you are using an Apple keyboard with an Eject key, press Control+Eject. Now either click Sleep option from the dialog box that appears, or press the S key.

- Press the power button on your computer (or on your Apple display, if it has a power button). Then click the Sleep button in the dialog box that appears or press the S key.

- If you are using an Apple keyboard with an Eject key, press Control+Shift+Eject to immediately put the Mac to sleep.

- Log out of your Mac and click the Sleep iconic button in the login window that appears.

- Choose ➪ System Preferences and go the Energy Saver system preference, then set the automatic "go to sleep" time by using the Put the Computer to Sleep When It Is Inactive For slider. That makes the Mac go to sleep automatically after it's been inactive for the specified time (meaning you haven't touched the mouse or keyboard and that no applications are running that are reading from or writing to a drive).

You can wake up your Mac in any of the following ways:

- If you have a Mac laptop, simply open the lid.

- Press any key on the keyboard. To prevent the keypress from inserting text into an active document or text field, it's wise to get into the habit of using the Shift key as your wake-up key.

- Click or move the mouse.

Logging out of Mac OS X

You can log out of Mac OS X when you have finished using your computer. This provides an additional level of security over putting the Mac to sleep because it requires people to enter a password before they can begin using the computer. Logging out of Mac OS X is also a way to switch from one user account to another.

You can log out of Mac OS X by choosing ⇨ Log Out username or pressing Shift+⌘+Q. Either way, a dialog box appears that provides two buttons: Log Out and Cancel. Click Log Out or press Return to immediately log out, or wait 60 seconds for the Mac to do it for you. Click Cancel to resume working on the Mac, using your current user account.

When you log out, Mac OS X quits all running applications, then displays the login window. From there, select a user account and enter the corresponding password to log in as that user. You can also click the Sleep, Restart, or Shut Down iconic buttons if you didn't mean to do one of those actions instead of logging out.

Shutting down the Mac

While you can leave your Mac permanently running or let it go to sleep, you may want to completely switch it off at the end of the day. That reduces energy usage and makes it less likely the Mac could be damaged due to heat buildup or an electrical surge.

You can shut down a Mac several ways, including:

- If your keyboard has a power button, press it and then click Shut Down or press Enter when the confirmation dialog box appears.
- If you are using a keyboard with an Eject key, press Control+Eject, then click Shut Down or press Enter when the confirmation dialog box appears.
- Choose ⇨ Shut Down. Then click Shut Down or press Enter when the confirmation dialog box appears — or you can wait 60 seconds and the Mac will shut down automatically.
- Log out and click the Shut Down iconic button in the login window.

When you go through the shut-down process, Mac OS X tells all open applications to quit and proceeds to shut down. If any applications have unsaved data, you will be prompted with a Save dialog window before shutting down.

Tip

When shutting down, it is wise to watch the desktop until the screen goes blank, which lets you know the Mac has actually shut down. When you shut down Mac OS X, it first tries to quit all active applications, but applications may not quit if they have unsaved documents. In this case, the applications present a dialog box asking if you want to save the unsaved documents, and the shutdown is delayed. If you walk away, you'll come back only to find that the shutdown didn't complete, and then you have address the unsaved documents, wait for the Mac to shut down, and start it again to be able to use the Mac — a process that can be quite frustrating.

To Shut Down or to Sleep?

There is much debate within the computer community as to whether you should shut down your computer at the end of a session (or at the end of the day), or whether you should simply put your computer to sleep. Both methods have their merits.

Turning off your computer completely ensures that it isn't using any power when idle, which is the environmentally correct thing to do (not to mention a financially smart move because all those standby hours rack up electricity costs over the years).

If you use Sleep mode, you do use some energy, but less than leaving the Mac fully on — as long as your sleep settings (in the Energy Saver system preference) are set to idle the hard disk (be sure to select the Put the Hard Disk(s) to Sleep When Possible option). Putting the disks to sleep also saves on wear and tear on the hard disks.

Some users claim that the surge of power that enters the Mac when starting up is worse on the system components than having a constant trickle of power. Although this might have mattered on the first computers in the 1980s, there's no evidence that it matters on a Mac today. Like all modern computers, it is designed to be turned on and off.

One reason to put the Mac to sleep rather than shut it down is that Mac OS X is designed to run optimization utilities when the Mac is asleep, so if you turn off the computer every night, you may miss out on these optimizations.

Most people use of a combination of putting the Mac to sleep and shutting it down, choosing between them based on how long they are away from it. That's a good way to approach the issue of sleep versus shutdown.

Note
There is one other method of shutting down the Mac: a forced shutdown. This can be handy in the event of a system crash, when there is no other way to shut down or restart the Mac. To use this method, simply hold down the power button for at least five seconds. However, you should avoid a forced shutdown if at all possible: Any unsaved document data is lost, and it is possible to cause damage to the system.

Restarting the Mac

You need to restart Mac OS X far less than many other operating systems (including previous versions of the Mac OS). That's because Mac OS X is very stable, and doesn't require a restart to clear its memory as Windows does. Plus, many applications can be installed in the Mac OS without requiring a restart to activate their features. Still, there are times that you need to restart the computer after installing some software updates (such as Apple's Mac OS X software updates) or when installing some applications.

You can use the following methods to restart the computer:

- Press the power button on your Mac (or on certain Apple-branded monitors). When the confirmation dialog box appears, click Restart.

- If your keyboard has the Eject key, press Control+Eject. When the confirmation dialog box appears, click Restart.

- If your keyboard has the Eject key, press Control+⌘+Eject; the Mac begins to restart immediately.

- Log out and click the Restart iconic button.

- Choose ⌘ ⇨ Restart. When the confirmation dialog box appears, click Restart or press Enter — or simply wait 60 seconds and let the Mac restart automatically.

During the restart process, Mac OS X tells all open applications running in the system to quit. If an application has an open document with unsaved changes, it asks you if you want to save the changes before quitting. Only when all the applications have quit does the Mac shut down and then start back up again.

Discovering the Mac OS X Environment

When the startup is complete, and you have been through the login processes, you will be taken to the Mac OS X desktop, where you can begin to use your computer.

The desktop is the screen with icons, folders, and windows. By default, it has just one icon on the right-hand side, which represents the Mac's internal startup disk. (If you have a CD or DVD inserted in the Mac, or any external hard disks or thumb drives attached, they appear below the icon for the startup disk.) At the bottom of the desktop, you'll see the Dock. This horizontal bar contains icons that represent quick shortcuts to applications and files. At the top of the screen is a menu bar that changes depending on the application in use, but by default is the Finder's menu bar. (The Finder is the application that you use to manage the Mac itself, letting you work with files and folders.)

Working with menus

Like most operating systems, Mac OS X uses menus to give you multiple lists of commands and functions that can be used by programs and the operating system as a whole. Menus take up considerable space on the screen, so they tend to be hidden except for a single title (usually marked with a word, such as File or Edit); clicking this title brings up a popup menu of commands, such as New Document, Open, and Save.

In Mac OS X, a single menu appears at the top of the screen called the *menu bar*. Some of the titles for the items in the menu bar change, depending upon which application is highlighted at the time. Some, such as ⌘, File, Edit, Window, and Help almost always appear because Apple insists that applications use a consistent interface so users can easily move among them.

Popup menus can appear in a variety of different areas, including windows, side panes, dialog boxes, and control panels. In addition to popup menus. you can also access contextual menus, either by right-clicking on a mouse or by holding down the Control key and clicking the mouse button. Contextual menus are so named because their contents change according to the context (area or item) that you Control+click or right-click on.

The menu bar appears at the top of the screen (see Figure 2.1), and contains commands that are relevant to the application you are working with. If you are working with the desktop, it displays menu options for the Finder application.

FIGURE 2.1

In Mac OS X, the menu bar always appears at the top of the desktop. The menu options change according to which program you are working with.

To access an option in a menu, you typically use the mouse to control the pointer and choose one of the options. You can choose menu options one of two ways:

- **Click and click.** Move the mouse pointer over the menu title and click the mouse button to reveal the list of menu options. Now move the mouse down the list to highlight the menu option you are interested in. Click the menu option to activate it. The highlighted option flashes to indicate that it has been chosen and Mac OS X then executes whatever the menu option is designed to do in the application.

- **Click and release.** Move the mouse pointer over the menu title and click and hold the mouse button. While holding the mouse button down, move down to the menu option you want to select and, with the item highlighted, release the mouse button. The menu option flashes and the application executes whatever it is designed to do.

The method you use is largely a case of personal preference.

Some menu options may also expand to reveal further options. These are called *submenus*; a submenu is indicated by a small black triangle to the right of the menu option (see Figure 2.2). Moving the mouse pointer to one of these menu options makes the submenu expand to the right and present further options. (In some applications, the submenu may expand to the left.) Moving the mouse into the submenu enables you to select these further options. It is rare for a submenu to contain further submenu options, known as *nested submenus*, although some complex programs have nested submenus (Adobe Dreamweaver CS4 is an example).

Note

When you navigate submenus, the mouse pointer must stay within the bounds of submenu; if it leaves its area, the submenu closes.

FIGURE 2.2

Menu options with a small black triangle to the right of them lead to submenu options.

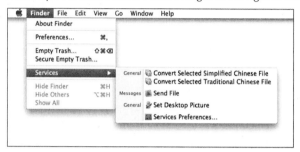

Choosing a menu option generally issues a command to the program, such as the Send a New Message in Mail (found in the File menu) that indicates you want to send a new e-mail to somebody. Alternatively, you can use a menu option to alter the state of something in a document, such as a font size in a word processor. Typically, you select the object (in the case of a word processor by highlighting the text) and then choose a menu option (such as Font ⇨ Bold) to change it.

It is also common for selected menu options to open up dialog boxes. These offer further options relating to the chosen menu option.

Some menu options may appear in a light gray text (this visual effect is often referred to as *grayed out*), which indicates that the menu item is not available at the moment. Common examples are the Save and Print menu options that are grayed out in most applications if no document is open (because there is no document being worked on to save or print).

In Mac OS X, when you click a menu title to display the list of options, the list remains on the screen, regardless of where you move the mouse. This helps prevent accidental mouse movements from irritatingly closing menus. If you have clicked on a menu title and decide that you do not want to select any option, then click anywhere on the screen (other than on a menu option) to close the menu and continue working.

Tip

As you move around menu options, you may notice that certain ones have symbols and letters next to them. These are keyboard shortcuts, and represent key combinations you can use instead the mouse to select menu options.

Understanding Why There's Just One Menu Bar

The menu bar at the top of the screen is a permanent fixture in the Mac OS X desktop, and is a key difference between the Mac OS X environment and the Windows environment. In Mac OS X, that single menu bar's options change, depending on which program is active at the time; in the Windows environment, menus appear at the top of each window open on the desktop, so it's easy to click into the wrong menu when several applications are open because each has its own separate menu bar. The single location for the menu in Mac OS X is one of the reasons the operating system is considered much more user-friendly than Windows.

Becoming familiar with menu bar items

Although the menu bar changes according to which application is currently active, several menu options on the left side of the menu bar are common to all applications: , File, Edit, Window, and Help. On the right-hand side of the menu bar sit several iconic menus that remain the same no matter which application is highlighted. The other menu options vary, based on what application is active.

The (Apple) menu

At the far left-hand side of the menu bar sits the menu (called the *Apple menu*). The options in this menu typically relate to the Mac as a whole, and to system-wide options and commands. You can use the menu options here to get information about your Mac, perform software updates, and change system preferences; you can also log out, put your computer to sleep, or shut it down completely.

Given these menu options remain the same no matter what application is open, let's take a close look at them in depth. The options include:

- **About This Mac.** Choosing this menu option brings up a window displaying information about your Mac. It informs you which version of Mac OS X you are running, what your processor speed is, the amount of memory (random access memory, or RAM) in your Mac, and what your startup disk is. There is also a button in this window labeled More Info; clicking it opens the System Profiler utility that provides detailed information on all aspects of your computer.

- **Software Update.** Choosing this menu option brings up the Software Update application and automatically connects to the Internet to look for updates to Mac OS X and the various Apple programs installed on your Mac.

- **Mac OS X Software.** Choosing this menu option opens your default Web browser and navigates to the Apple Web site's download area (www.apple.com/downloads/).

- **System Preferences.** Choosing this menu option opens up the System Preferences application, where you can adjust various aspects of the Mac OS X environment. The system preferences are explained in depth in Chapter 21.

- **Dock.** Choosing this option opens a submenu that provides controls for the Dock (explained later in this chapter). You can quickly adjust the magnification and position of the Dock from this menu option.

- **Location.** This menu option works with the Network system preference (which enables you to set different networking preferences for different environments). Typically, a laptop owner may connect a Mac to his or her home network, as well as to a work network, and may have different settings depending on the environment. (Networking is explained in depth in Chapter 10.) The Location menu option offers a submenu for selecting different locations, so the appropriate network settings are activated for your current location. This menu option is only present if you have set multiple network locations by using the Network system preferences.

- **Recent Items.** This particularly handy menu option takes you to a submenu with three separate areas: Applications, Documents, and Servers. Each area contains the last ten respective items that you have used on the Mac. So you get a list of the ten recently used applications, documents you have opened, and server locations you have visited.

- **Force Quit.** This menu option brings up the Force Quit dialog box, which shows all running applications on the Mac, and is where you force unruly applications to quit. It is rare that you will need to use the Force Quit menu option, but it can prevent you from having to restart your computer. The Force Quit dialog box is explained in more depth in Chapter 7. (You can also press Option+⌘+Esc to open the Force Quit dialog box.)

- **Sleep, Restart, and Shut Down.** You use these three menu options when you want to break from what you are doing. Sleep turns off your monitor and puts your computer into a low-power mode (tapping the mouse or keyboard wakes it back up). Shut Down switches off your computer. Restart switches off the computer and begins the boot process automatically.

- **Log Out.** The final option is marked Log Out *username*, such as Log Out Mark. This is used to log off your session; you will need to log back in (as described earlier in this chapter) to begin working again on your Mac. This logoff option is often used in a work environment when a computer holds sensitive information and should not be accessible without an authorized user present. (In that case, you would log out when taking a break from your computer.) It's also used to switch among user accounts on the same Mac, as Chapter 20 explains.

The application menu

To the right of the ⌘ menu sits the application menu, the title of which typically signifies the application that is currently running. Because the menu item is limited in space (usually to just one or two words), it doesn't always match exactly the application's name. For example, the application menu for Adobe Photoshop CS4 is listed simply as "Photoshop." This menu serves as a handy indication of what application is currently active, and it also contains a list of items that apply to the application as a whole.

The options in the application menu vary according to the application in question, although some options are common across most applications. They include:

- **About.** This is typically labeled with the name of the program, such as About Safari; selecting this menu option brings up information about the application you are running. Typically, this information is limited to the name of the program, its icon, the version number, and some copyright information.

- **Preferences.** Most applications have a set of preferences that enable you to set up and personalize the program. You access the preferences for all applications through the Preferences menu option. (You can also press ⌘+, [comma] to open the preferences for the current application.)

- **Services.** The Services menu option leads to a submenu of all the services offered by Mac OS X that are available to the current application. Services are explained in depth in Chapter 16.

- **Hide and Show.** These menu options let you hide and show applications. There are two Hide menu options and one Show menu option:

  - Hide *applicationname* (such as Hide Mail). This usually has the shortcut ⌘+H; it hides the application and all its windows.

  - Hide Others. This usually has the shortcut Option+⌘+H; it hides all applications except the active one.

  - Show All. This menu option brings back all windows from all running applications.

Cross-Ref
We explain controlling windows in depth later on in this chapter.

- **Quit.** The Quit menu option (again, usually written as Quit followed by the application name, such as Quit Mail) closes the program. You can also simply press ⌘+Q.

The File menu

The File menu contains options that pertain to documents (or files) used by the active program. It is common across most programs used in the Mac OS X environment, although a few applications and games, such as the Chess game included in Mac OS X, may forgo a File menu because they do not work with documents. The menu options include:

- **New.** Typically the File menu begins with a range of New menu options that often relate to starting a new file or document. Sometimes, such as in the Finder, they are used to create new folders. In Mail, for example, they are used to create new e-mail messages. Typically, the shortcut for choosing File ➪ New is ⌘+N.

- **Open.** The Open menu options are often used to load documents that were previously created and saved by the application. Often there is also an Open Recent command with a submenu that contains a list of documents recently saved by that application. Occasionally there will be other types of Open commands: In Safari, for example, you can find commands to open URLs (Web page addresses). Typically, the shortcut for choosing File ➪ Open is ⌘+O.

- **Save.** Following the Open menu options are typically options to save documents. There are usually both a Save and a Save As menu option. If the document has not been saved, the Save command is grayed out and only the Save As command is available (signifying that you need to select Save As and give the document a name). Typically, the shortcut for choosing File ⇨ Save is ⌘+S, and for choosing File ⇨ Save As, it is Shift+⌘+S.

- **Print.** Typically, near the bottom of the File menu is the Print menu option. It opens the Print dialog box that enables you to export the contents of a document to a sheet of paper. In Mac OS X, it is also possible to print a document as a PDF (Portable Document Format) file, which is an electronic printout that can be retained or shared with other users, or to fax it by using options in the Print dialog box. (Printing is explained in depth in Chapter 17.) Typically, the shortcut for choosing File ⇨ Print is ⌘+P.

The Edit menu

The Edit menu contains menu options used to adjust the contents of a document. As with the File menu, the nature of these options varies greatly, depending on the document in question. Some, such as Undo and Redo, are common across many applications, as are the universal options of Cut, Copy, and Paste. Another commonly found option in the Edit menu is the Find command, which you use to search through documents for specific items (usually words or phrases).

The View menu

Another commonly found menu is View, which is used to control how documents are displayed. The menu options themselves vary by application: In iCal, for example, you use them to view and navigate the calendars by using the By Day, By Week, and By Month menu options.

The Window menu

This menu enables you to control windows. Two common menu options at the top are Minimize (reduce to the Dock) and Zoom (maximize to the full size of your desktop). Another common option is Bring All to Front, which brings all windows relating to the application to the front of other windows in use by Mac OS X. The Window menu also lists other types of windows and panels (which typically are floating windows that hold controls). These vary by application.

The Help menu

This menu gives you access to on-screen help. At the top is the Search field, and typing into it displays menu-option explanations and help topics. The explanations relate to corresponding commands throughout the menu bar, and you can use them to quickly locate items. The help topics open up the Help browser, which offers a range of advice on every area of Mac OS X. More information on using Mac OS X's built-in help system is outlined in Chapter 5. Below the Search field is usually a set of dedicated help options. These correspond to either the application as a whole, or to particular areas of interest relating to the application.

Understanding menu bar icons

On the right-hand side of the menu bar sit a variety of different icons that relate to system-wide functions. These may include:

Time Machine

This iconic menu (a small counterclockwise circular arrow icon) represents the status of the Time Machine backup utility (Time Machine is explained in depth in Chapter 4). It offers options to perform a backup, restore files, and adjust the preferences.

MobileMe and iSync

If you subscribe to Apple's MobileMe service (outlined in Chapter 15), you can use this iconic menu (its icon is a set of curved arrows) to synchronize all your MobileMe data and to open the MobileMe system preference. This iconic menu also displays the status of Mac OS X's iSync utility, which synchronizes applications such as iCal and Microsoft Entourage with each other and with devices such as smartphones, as Chapter 8 explains, and has the Sync menu item to force a synchronization.

Volume

Clicking this iconic menu (the speaker icon) brings up a vertical slider you can to adjust the loudness of noise emanating from your Mac. The icon changes, showing more "sound waves" emanating from the speaker as you increase the volume. You can also adjust sound levels by using the Sound system preference (described in Chapter 21), and moving Volume iconic button's slider adjusts the slider in the Sound system preference accordingly.

AirPort

AirPort is Apple's term for Wi-Fi, and this iconic menu appears if you have a wireless networking card installed in your Mac (all Macs except the Mac Pro line have an AirPort card installed by default). The icon is composed of four arcs, reminiscent of a radar display, and the number of arcs that are lit up corresponds to the strength of the signal from a corresponding wireless router. If the AirPort is switched off, or there is no signal, the symbol is an empty outline (similar in style to the shape of a baseball field). You can use the AirPort iconic menu to join a local wireless network, create a wireless network, or access the Network system preference.

Time

Thu 14:00 The next common iconic menu item on the right-hand side is the time; by default, it displays as an abbreviation of the day and the time in the 24-hour format. Clicking the time shows the full date and options to view the time as analog or digital; you can also access the Date & Time system preference.

New Feature

You can now display both the date and time simultaneously in the menu bar. In previous incarnations of Mac OS X, the menu bar displayed the time, and clicking the time displayed the date. Two new options — Show the Day of the Week and Show Date — in the Date & Time system preference's Clock pane enable you to add this information to the menu bar. Chapter 21 has more information regarding the Date & Time system preference.

User

Mark If you have Fast User Switching enabled, the right of the menu bar displays one of three variations of this menu: the head-and-shoulders icon, your full username, or the Mac OS's short name for your account. (You set the iconic menu's display by using the Fast User Switching option set in the Accounts system preference, as Chapter 20 explains.) Clicking this iconic menu enables you to select a different user account from a popup menu. You can also access the login window from here to switch to another user account while keeping the current user account running. (This differs from the Log Out option found in the menu, which logs out the current user before switching to another one.) Finally, this iconic menu also offers quick access to the Accounts system preferences.

Bluetooth

If you have Bluetooth activated on your Mac, the Bluetooth iconic menu (a stylized B icon) appears in the menu bar. You can use it to set up devices, make your Mac discoverable by other Bluetooth devices, browse devices, and open the Bluetooth system preference.

Spotlight

At the far right of the screen is the Spotlight iconic menu (a magnifying glass icon). Clicking it brings up a search box where you can type a term to be searched throughout your Mac's disks. Spotlight is a powerful technology that permeates the Mac OS X environment, and the terms you enter here search applications, documents, folders, e-mail messages, and even your music and video collections. Spotlight is explained in depth in Chapter 3.

Menu Bar Standards and Options

According to Apple's developer notes, the menu bar itself must be visible (although some games take over the full screen) and the menu bar must contain the menu, the Spotlight iconic menu, the application menu, and the Window menu. All other items are optional, although Apple has comprehensive guidelines that ensure most programs use common menus such a File, Edit, View, and Help in a similar fashion.

While menu items on the left-hand side of the menu bar are fixed by the application in question, you can move and rearrange those on the right (with the exception of the Spotlight iconic menu) that are provided by the Mac OS. Simply ⌘+click an icon and drag it left or right to rearrange it. Note that iconic menus added to the menu bar by individual applications typically cannot be moved this way.

Spaces

 If you have Spaces activated (see Chapter 21), you can switch between different desktop spaces with this iconic menu (the numbered black-square icon). It also offers a quick access area to the Exposé & Spaces system preference.

Input Source

 The Input Sources iconic menu lets you choose different input sources, it also has shortcuts to the Character Viewer and Keyboard Viewer; these enable you to access special characters (see Chapter 22). It also has shortcuts to the Keyboard and Language & Text system preferences. These are used to set up keyboard settings and modify system-wide keyboard shortcuts, as Chapter 21 explains.

If you have enabled the Keyboard & Character Viewer option in the Language & Text system preference's Input Sources pane, the iconic menu appears as an asterisk-in-a-box icon. If you've enabled multiple keyboard layouts for your Mac in the Language & Text system preference's Input Sources pane (see Chapter 21) — such as Canadian English and Canadian French — the Input Source iconic menu's icon changes to the flag of your default keyboard's country, and the popup menu adds two sets of options. First, it adds a menu option for each keyboard layout you've enabled in the Language & Text system preference. Second, it adds the Open Language & Text option to provide quick access to the Language & Text system preference.

New Feature

The Language & Text system preference is the new name in Mac OS X 10.6 Snow Leopard for what had been called the International system preference.

Displays

 The Displays iconic menu (the monitor icon) gives you quick access to several options for the displays used by your Mac. The Detect Displays option enables Mac OS X to determine what type of displays are currently connected to the machine. (This is useful if you frequently change displays.) Below this setting are various recently used screen resolution settings available for your Mac, and a Number of Recent Items submenu. This enables you to determine how many screen resolution settings appear in the menu (0, 3, 5, or 10). The final option enables you to launch the Displays system preference.

Battery status

 Users of Mac notebooks containing batteries also have a Battery Status iconic menu (the battery icon) in the menu bar. If a power connector is attached to your Mac, the battery symbol contains a small graphic of a plug; if the power cable is removed, the battery has a black bar showing approximately how much charge is present in the battery. (The bar turns red when power is running low.) Clicking the icon opens a menu that informs you approximately how much time you have left to use your Mac (or, if the power adaptor is plugged in, approximately how much time it will take to recharge the Mac). Below this is confirmation of which power source (the battery or power adapter) is currently powering your Mac. Although this confirmation information appears as a menu option, you cannot select it. There is also a submenu option labeled Show, which you use to set whether the iconic menu shows just as an icon, or as the icon and battery time remaining, or as an icon with the percentage of battery capacity remaining. The final menu item takes you to the Energy Saver system preference.

Universal Access status

 The Universal Access iconic menu (the icon is a human figure in a circle) offers quick on/off options for all the Mac's accessibility options. These options are available only if they have been enabled in the Universal Access system preference. Chapter 6 has more information on Mac OS X's Universal Access options.

Fax

 If you have a fax set up on your Mac, the Fax iconic menu displays (the phone-on-paper icon). You can answer incoming calls and manage fax status. Chapter 17 has more information on setting up faxing services on your Mac.

Modem

 If you are using a dial-up modem, you can display the Modem iconic menu (the phone icon) to control dial-up services. You can connect and disconnect to the Internet over a phone connection via the options in the iconic menu. More information on accessing the Internet via a dial-up modem is in Chapter 10.

AppleScript

 If you enable display of the AppleScript iconic menu (the styled S icon) in the AppleScript Editor (see Chapter 25), you can use it to edit and run scripts.

Using popup menus

Popup menus are the menus that appear within a dialog box or panel. Popup menus come in several different styles. Common types include horizontal bars with a double-arrow icon on the right-hand side (see Figure 2.3); clicking on these enables you to change the default option. Often, Mac OS X displays buttons marked with a single black arrow pointing down (to emphasize further options); clicking these buttons reveals a submenu of further options; these buttons can be textual or iconic.

FIGURE 2.3

Popup menus are signified by arrow icons. Here, the double-arrow icons next to Printer and Presets signify the presence of alternative choices, as does the small downward-arrow icon next to PDF.

Using contextual menus

As the name suggests, a contextual menu is one that changes based upon its context. This ensures that you only see menu options that are relevant to a particular file, document, or situation. You display a contextual menu by Control+clicking or right-clicking virtually anywhere in the Mac OS X environment, such as an icon, window, or other selection. The options that appear are infinitely varied; Control+clicking or right-clicking on a file on the desktop, for example, brings up options to open the file, move it to the Trash, get information, compress the file, duplicate it, create an alias, take a quick look at its contents, clean it up, change the color of its label, and send it to somebody as an e-mail attachment.

It is also possible to highlight multiple items and Control+click or right-click to bring up a contextual menu that applies to several items; in that case, only options that apply to all the selected items appear in the menu.

Tip
Since 2005, all desktop Macs except Mac Minis have shipped with a multibutton mouse known as a Mighty Mouse. Despite having a single body shell that depresses as the button, it registers as a right or left click depending on where you touch the shell as you depress the mouse. Using a Mighty Mouse to register a primary and secondary click takes some practice; for this reason, the mouse is set by default to act as a single button. You can change that default in the Mouse system preference (see Chapter 21).

Recognizing menu symbols

Several symbols accompany menu items. Here is a guide to the various symbols and their meanings:

✓	A check mark next to a menu option indicates that it is currently selected. These menu options act as toggles: If you select the item from the menu, it usually deselects the item; select it again to select the item.
–	A dash designates an attribute that only applies to some things that are currently selected (and not all of them).
•	The bullet designates a document with unsaved changes. Some applications use it instead of the check mark symbol to refer to an attribute that applies to everything that is currently selected.
◆	A diamond that appears before options in the Window menu signifies that the window is minimized in the Dock.
▸	This indicates that a menu leads to a submenu offering further options.
…	The ellipsis signifies that a menu option will open a dialog box and requires further information before the option can take effect.

Using keyboard shortcuts

Other symbols are used to designate keyboard combinations that you can press instead of highlighting with the mouse and choosing the menu option. Pressing ⌘+P, for example, is commonly used to access the Print option from the File menu.

The modifier keys — those like ⌘ and Option that are used in combination with other keys — are presented in menus as symbols. Some of the symbols, such as ⌘, match the symbol on the keyboard; others, such as ⌃ (for Control), do not appear on the keyboard. Also, Option is also marked as Alt on the keyboard (for the benefit of users running Windows on their Macs), leading to further confusion still.

Note
Apple has been inconsistent in its own keyboard labeling; for example, MacBook keyboards since 2006 and Mac desktop keyboards since 2009 label the Control key as Ctrl, and Mac keyboards since 2009 print Cmd instead of on the keyboard's Command key. MacBook keyboards, since 2006, list Enter and Return instead of using the entr and retr symbols; and have Option instead of the ⌥ option symbol.

Here is a guide to the modifier keys' symbols in menus, and the corresponding keys:

⌘	Command key
⌥	Option key
⇧	Shift key
⌃	Control key
	Return key
	keypad Enter key
⌫	Delete key (backspace)
⌦	Delete ⌦ key (forward delete)
	Tab key
⏏	Eject key (not on all keyboards)
⎋	Escape key

When you press a keyboard shortcut, the item on the menu bar flashes briefly to indicate that a menu option has been selected (although the menu itself does not expand to show the exact option being invoked).

Tip

Keyboard shortcuts can massively increase the speed at which you work and are well worth learning. You can discover many keyboard shortcuts by looking at the Keyboard Shortcuts pane of the Keyboard system preference. Here you will not only learn keyboard shortcuts, but can also create your own, as Chapter 21 explains. Apple also has a comprehensive list of common keyboard shortcuts on its Web site (`http://support.apple.com/kb/HT1343`).

Working with the Dock

Now that you are familiar with the menu bar, it is time to look at Mac OS X's second stalwart interface device, the Dock, shown in Figure 2.4.

Located at the bottom of the screen, the Dock is a container for commonly used applications, files, and Mac OS X functions. The Dock uses many visual effects, including see-through transparency, reflections, and magnification and, as such, demonstrates much of Apple's legendary visual flair. But don't be fooled into thinking of it as a mere visual gimmick. The Dock is a powerful organizational tool that keeps your most important items in front of you for immediate access.

FIGURE 2.4

The Dock is a visual bar used to quickly open and switch between applications, plus access and store files and folders.

The Dock is a surprisingly intuitive device with several different uses. It is, by default, a horizontal bar used for launching applications and accessing commonly used files and folders. The Dock is divided into two halves (an easy-to-overlook gray dividing line of 3-D dashes marks the separation, like a lane divider stripe on a road). The left-hand side is devoted to applications, whereas the right-hand side is used for documents, folders, and minimized windows. It is possible to adjust the position and visual appearance of the Dock, which we look at later in the chapter.

The Dock contains a set of icons that you can rearrange or remove at will. The only two icons that must stay on the Dock are the Finder on the left-hand side and the Trash icon on the right. By default, icons for the following items appear on the Dock:

- **Finder.** The main application used by Mac OS X to manage files and folders present on your computer. The Finder is described in depth later in this chapter, but it remains open at all times and is a permanent fixture on the left-hand side of the Dock.

- **Dashboard.** The control for accessing and managing widgets (small applications used by the Dashboard, covered later in this chapter; widgets are covered in Chapter 8).

- **Mail.** Apple's program used for sending and receiving e-mail.

- **Safari.** Apple's Web browser included with Mac OS X.

- **iChat.** Apple's instant messaging program.

- **Address Book.** An application for storing information on contacts (people and companies). Several applications throughout Mac OS X can use the information stored in Address Book.

- **iCal.** Apple's calendar application for making note of important dates and events, plus a to-do task manager.

- **Preview.** An application for quickly examining the contents of files.

- **iTunes.** An application for storing and playing audio and video files, plus managing and synchronizing other Apple devices such as the iPod and iPhone.

- **Spaces.** A system preference for organizing and moving between multiple desktop environments.

- **Time Machine.** Apple's built-in backup utility. Clicking the icon enables you to recover accidentally deleted documents.

- **System Preferences.** Enables you to adjust various aspects of Mac OS X.

- **Applications.** An alias to the Applications folder.

- **Documents.** An alias to the Documents folder.

- **Downloads.** An alias to the Downloads folder.

- **Trash.** A folder that contains files that you have discarded. Emptying the Trash permanently deletes the files from the Mac. Along with the Finder, the Trash icon is a permanent fixture on the Dock.

Hovering the mouse over the icons in the Dock brings up a text description of the application, window, or document.

Icons are temporarily added to the Dock as you use applications, open documents, and minimize windows. This can be confusing to the newcomer, although it quickly becomes second nature. You can keep icons in the Dock by Control+clicking or right-clicking them, then choosing Keep in Dock from the contextual menu.

New Feature

The Put Back option is new to Mac OS X 10.6 Snow Leopard. Control+click any file you want to recover from the Trash and choose Put Back. Mac OS X remembers where each file existed before it was moved to the Trash, and returns it to its original location.

Tip

To quickly access options for Dock items, Control+click or right-click them to open a contextual menu. Or click and hold the mouse button on a Dock item for a few seconds to open a contextual menu.

Retrieving Items from the Trash

When you throw items in the Trash — whether by dragging them there or deleting them with a menu option or a keyboard shortcut — you're actually putting them in a folder. So you can move items out of the Trash if you deleted them accidentally — as long as you do so before you empty the Trash, of course. There are two ways to get items out of the Trash. Both start with double-clicking the Trash in the Dock to open it as a folder. (You can also select it and choose File ➪ Open, press ⌘+O, or Control+click or right-click it and choose Open from the contextual menu.) With the Trash folder open, you have these options:

- Drag the item to the desktop or other location on your Mac. This lets you put the item anywhere you want.
- Control+click or right-click an item and choose Put Back from the contextual menu. This saves you from having to remember the item's original location; Mac OS X remembers and places the item there.

Looking at the application side of the Dock

Any application that is being used by your Mac has an icon in the Dock. When you open the application, the icon will bounce up and down in the Dock signifying that it is loading. It then sits in the Dock with a small blue-and-white sphere beneath it to signify that the application is running. When you quit the application, the icon disappears from the Dock (unless it has been added to the Dock, in which case the icon will remain although the blue-and-white sphere disappears.) There are three exceptions to this: the Dashboard, Spaces, and Time Machine icons. Clicking any of these will take you straight to the corresponding function. We take a look at Time Machine in Chapter 4, Dashboard in Chapter 8, and Spaces in Chapter 21.

Note
Icons that remain in the Dock are actually aliases, or quick links, to applications; the applications themselves remain in the Applications or Utilities folder.

The application icons can sometimes provide information relating to the program. Mail, for example, checks for new messages periodically and a small red number appears next to the icon in the Dock, signifying the number of unread e-mail messages.

Adding applications to the Dock

As mentioned previously, any application opened in Mac OS X has its icon temporarily added to the Dock. When the application is closed, the icon disappears from the Dock.

If you find that you frequently use an application, it may be helpful to keep the icon in the Dock when the application is closed. This means that you can quickly open the application by clicking its icon. You can add an application item to the Dock two ways:

- **Locate the desired application (usually located in the Applications folder) and drag it to the left-hand side of the Dock.** Note that this does not copy the application from the Applications folder to the Dock; rather it creates an alias in the Dock that links to the application, so when the icon is clicked in the Dock, it opens the application in the Applications folder.

- **Locate the desired application and double-click it to open it.** This temporarily places its icon in the Dock. Now Control+click or right-click the icon in the Dock and select Keep in Dock from the contextual menu. Now when the program is closed, the icon remains in the Dock. (Note: You can use this technique to keep your printer's icon in the Dock.)

Accessing application contextual menus

As with most items in Mac OS X, you can access a contextual menu for each application in the Dock by Control+clicking or right-clicking the icon in the Dock (see Figure 2.5). Note that the contextual menu changes, depending on whether the program is open or not; if just the icon is displayed, the following options appear:

- **Options.** Choosing this submenu reveals two further options:

  - **Remove from Dock.** Choosing this option removes the icon from the Dock; it is effectively the same as dragging the icon out of the Dock.

  - **Open at Login.** Choosing this option ensures that the program starts when you boot up and log in to your Mac. This can be useful if there is a program that you always use as soon as you start your Mac. Login items are set in the Accounts system preference, as explained in Chapter 21.

- **Show in Finder.** Because icons are aliases to items that exist in the Finder, you can quickly open a Finder window and show the original item by choosing this option.

- **Open.** Choosing this option opens the application.

In the Dock, open applications (identified by the blue-and-white glowing sphere underneath) may have additional options depending on the application. Mail, for example, has the following options: Get New Mail, Compose New Message, and Compose New Note; Safari has options for moving between open browser windows; System Preferences has a complete list of all the available system preferences.

As well as their own custom options, open applications always have the following menu options:

- **Hide.** Choosing this option removes the open windows from the desktop. When you choose this option, its name in the contextual menu changes to Show, which you use to bring back the application's windows.

- **Quit.** Choosing this option quits the application.

Using Dock Exposé

Mac OS X 10.6 Snow Leopard has a new Dock feature called Dock Exposé that works with application icons in the Dock. If you click and hold an application icon in the Dock, all of the document windows associated with that application appear on the screen using Apple's Exposé technology. Clicking on an application's icon causes Exposé to display whatever windows are associated with that application. Active windows associated with a Dock item are displayed in the upper half of the screen, whereas minimized windows are displayed with slightly smaller graphics in the lower half of the screen. Chapter 8 has more information on Exposé.

FIGURE 2.5

Control+clicking or right-clicking a Dock item reveals a contextual menu with options relating to the Dock item. These options can vary depending on the Dock item, and whether it has any associated windows.

Tip

Pressing and holding the Option key when accessing an application's contextual menu changes some of the options. The Hide option becomes Hide Others, which is used to hide windows from all other applications other than the one selected; Quit turns into Force Quit, which you can use to close down applications that have frozen (Force Quit is explained in Chapter 7).

Given that the Finder is permanently open, it always displays different options to the other applications. The contextual menu options offered by the Finder include:

- **New Finder Window.** This option opens a new window that can be used to explore files on your Mac. The Finder is explained in depth later in this chapter. You can also simply press ⌘+N.

- **New Smart Folder.** Smart folders are "intelligent" folders that collect files based on predefined criteria. The creation of smart folders is explained in Chapter 3. You can also simply press Option+⌘+N.

- **Find.** The Find option opens a Finder window and takes you directly to the Spotlight search area. You can also simply press ⌘+F.

- **Go to Folder.** The Go to Folder command is used to navigate directly to a folder by using its pathname. The pathname is the name of all the folders surrounded by a slash (/) character; for example, `/Library/Documentation`. You can also simply press Shift+⌘+G.

- **Connect to Server.** This command is used to connect to local and remote servers. You can also simply press ⌘+K.

Tip

If you click the Finder icon in the Dock while holding down both the Control and Option keys (or if you press and hold the Option key and right-click the Finder icon), the contextual menu adds an option: Relaunch This option force-quits the Finder and relaunches it, which you may need to do if the Finder freezes, though this is a very rare occurrence.

Looking at the right-hand side of the Dock

The right-hand side of the Dock is where you place documents, folders, and disks. When you place a document into the Dock, clicking it opens the document using its default application. (It will open the application as well, if necessary.)

Folders that are added to the Dock expand to reveal their contents when selected with the mouse. They expand in one of three ways, depending on the number of items contained within and on your own personal preferences. As with applications and documents, it is important to remember that the folders are not themselves contained in the Dock, but instead the Dock acts as an alias to the folder stored elsewhere on the Mac.

Dragging documents to and from folders on the Dock moves the files to and from the folder that the Dock item points to. As well as folders, you can add aliases for entire drives to the Dock, which can make accessing multiple drives (both those located on your computer and networked attached drives) a quick and easy process.

Adding a document, folder, or disk to the Dock

Adding a document, folder, or disk to the Dock is relatively simple. Click and drag the item from its location (either on the desktop or in the Finder) to the right-hand side of the Dock. Be careful to drag it between other items on the Dock, and not on top of a folder (or it will be moved into that folder). Surrounding items should move out of the way to enable a space for you to drop in the document. Note that the Dock treats a disk as if it were a folder, and uses a folder icon for it.

Removing icons from the Dock

To remove an icon from the Dock, simply click it with the mouse and drag it away from the Dock. The icon appears with a small smoke cloud beneath it; release the mouse button and the icon vanishes into a cloud of smoke (replete with a satisfying whooshing sound effect). Because it is so easy to remove icons from the Dock, you should be careful not to remove items accidentally. If you drag an icon up and the smoke cloud appears, and you don't wish to delete an icon, simply drag it back down to the right-hand side of the Dock before releasing the mouse button.

Tip
You can also Control+click or right-click an icon in the Dock and choose Remove from Dock to remove its icon.

Moving icons around the Dock

You can rearrange items on the Dock by clicking them with the mouse and dragging them left and right. Timing is fairly critical, because if you hold the mouse button down for too long without moving the mouse, a contextual menu appears instead. As you move the icon around, the other icons move to make space for it. Remember that you cannot move applications and documents/folders beyond their respective sides. (If you try to do so, the icon slides back to its original position.) Because icons are not the documents themselves, you cannot move a document icon inside a folder icon.

Caution
Be careful when moving files to keep an eye out for the cloud-of-smoke image appearing on the icon. The appearance of this cloud-of-smoke image means you are about to remove the icon from the Dock, which is easy to do accidentally. If you don't intend to remove the icon from the Dock, keep the mouse button pressed and move the icon back onto the Dock; then you can release the mouse button. (Releasing the mouse button when the cloud-of-smoke graphic appears removes the icon from the Dock.)

Understanding Stacks

Much of the power of the Dock is apparent when you begin to add folders or disks to the Dock, and use it to quickly examine and access their contents. Apple refers to this feature as *Stacks*.

When you add a folder to the Dock it is known as a Stack. This is because the icon is formed from small images from the items in the folder stacked up on top of each other. Clicking the icon in the Dock reveals the stacked contents in one of three ways: as a fan, which shows the contained items in a slightly curved vertical line; as a grid, which shows the items in a popup square grid against a gray translucent background; or as a list, which shows them in a standard linear menu arrangement.

By default, items in a Stack appear in either fan or grid mode automatically, depending on the number of items. If a Stack contains nine items or less, it appears as a fan; if it contains ten items or more, it appears as a grid. (You can override these defaults and choose either the fan or grid mode for individual folders by using options in the contextual menu.)

When a Stack is opened and the contents are on display, you can click an item to open it or drag items to move them out of the Stack (including dragging them to the Trash to delete them).

There are, however, a number of things that you cannot do with items in a Stack. You cannot click and drag to rearrange items in the Stack. (Clicking an item immediately closes the Stack and leaves the item under your mouse.) You cannot drag the mouse to select multiple items — they must be dealt with individually. Finally, you cannot Control+click or right-click to open a contextual menu for items in a Stack.

The Stack is designed to provide quick-and-simple access to items contained within: If you want to do anything more complex with items in the Stack, you need to open the original folder that the Stack refers to. Fortunately each Stack contains a handy Open in Finder icon; clicking it takes you directly to the folder on your Finder containing all the original items.

New Feature

Mac OS X 10.6 Snow Leopard has two new features when using Stacks in Grid mode. First, you can now scroll through the files and folders: If there are more items that can be displayed on the screen, a scrollbar appears that you can use to navigate through the items using the mouse (including the scrollbar or the mouse's scroll ball or wheel). Second, you can navigate through folders: Clicking a folder in a Stack opens up the contents of that folder in a new Stack and, at the top-left of the Stack, you see a Back iconic button containing the name of the previous folder. Clicking this Back iconic button takes you to the contents of the previous folder.

Note

If you hold Shift when opening a Stack, or Shift+click an item in a Stack, the list opens, or closes, very slowly, using a slo-mo effect. This seems to be an Easter egg, one of those useless or humorous gems that developers sometimes insert in applications just for fun.

The folder's contextual menu options

If you Control+click or right-click a folder or Stack on the Dock, you are presented with a contextual menu with several options that affect how the folder and its contents are displayed:

- **Sort by.** Items in the folder are sorted automatically and you cannot manually rearrange them. By default they are sorted alphabetically by name, but here you can change that to Date Added, Date Modified, Date Created, or Kind.

- **Display As.** This option relates to the Dock icon itself, not the Stack that expands. By default, folders dragged to the Dock are displayed as Stacks, which means that the icon is made up of images of the files it contains. If the folder is empty, then a basic folder icon is displayed instead of the Stack; selecting the Folder option ensures that the icon from the Finder is displayed instead of the Stack. This is useful when you are adding disks to the Dock because an icon is displayed on the desktop rather than a Stack of changing contents.

- **View Content As.** This option affects how the Stack's items are presented when expanded. By default, it is set to Automatic, which means that nine or fewer items expand vertically in a fan-shaped arrangement; ten or more items are portrayed in a grid. Control+click or right-click on a folder icon in the Dock and use the View Content As menu option to change the arrangement to Fan, Grid, or List, as you prefer. Displaying items in a list arranges them like any menu's list, plus displays folders as submenus (with the same black triangle used to designate submenu options in a menu), so you can easily navigate through subfolders to locate individual files. However, because the menu items are smaller in list view than in fan or grid view, it can be harder to read the items' labels.

Below these options, you'll find the usual contextual menu items covered earlier: Remove from Dock, Show in Finder, and Open. In the case of folders, Show in Finder and Open options perform the same actionMinimizing windows in the Dock.

The other feature that the Dock is used for is as a placeholder for minimized windows. You can minimize windows into the Dock by clicking the window's yellow Minimize iconic button, choosing Window➪Minimize, or pressing ⌘+M. Minimized windows compress down into a Dock icon with a rather nifty animation called the Genie effect. The Dock icon is itself a miniaturized version of the window and often contains all the elements of the window. If, for example, the window is Apple's QuickTime Player application playing a video, then a small icon of the video continues to play in the Dock. (This is a great way to show off the visual prowess of a Mac to your friends.) Clicking in a minimized window in the Dock restores it to its original size and position on the desktop.

Tip

You can change the minimize effect in the Dock system preferences; you can choose Genie Effect or Scale Effect in the Minimize Using popup menu. The Genie effect is the default, with that genie-in-a-bottle style. The Scale effect is a more straightforward shrinking in a quick series of steps. (It exists because it takes less processing power, but current Macs are fast enough that anyone can use the Genie effect.) Choose ⌘➪System Preferences and then click the Dock icon, or choose ⌘➪Dock➪Dock Preferences, to open the Dock system preference.

Control+clicking or right-clicking in a minimized window in the Dock brings up a contextual menu with the option to open (maximize) the minimized window or close it. If you opt to close the window, you are prompted to save any unsaved data; this prompt also appears if you try to quit a program that has any minimized windows with unsaved data.

Customizing the Dock

By default, the Dock is located at the bottom of the screen and is fairly large. You might want to change its location, change its size, or otherwise customize its appearance.

All the options for adjusting the Dock are located in the Dock system preference, as explained in Chapter 21. You can also adjust many aspects of the Dock via its own contextual menu, which you access by Control+clicking or right-clicking the area on the Dock that has the dividing line.

Tip

A fast way to change several Dock preferences is to choose  ⇒ Dock, and then choose one of the submenu options: Turn Hiding On/Off, Turn Magnification On/Off, Position on Left, Position on Right, Position on Bottom, or Dock Preferences.

Adjusting the Dock's size

As you add and remove items from the Dock, it expands left and right to accommodate the extra items. The Dock system preference's Size slider lets you adjusts the overall size of the icons in the Dock. The overall size of the icons depends largely on how many you have in the Dock, but the slider, in effect, sets the maximize size.

There are two ways to adjust the Dock's size:

- Drag the Size slider in the Dock system preference from left to right to find the desired size (left is smaller; right is larger). If you have numerous icons in the Dock, you will be limited in how large you can resize the Dock. In this case, the slider still moves all the way to the right position, but the Dock itself does not get any larger.

- Hold the mouse over the vertical dividing line until a Dock resizing icon appears. (The icon is a white horizontal line with arrows above and below it.) Click and drag the mouse up or left to make the Dock larger; click and drag the mouse down or right to make the Dock smaller.

Setting the Dock magnification

If you have set the Dock to less than its maximum size, you can use the visual effect called *magnification*. This makes the icons on the Dock that your mouse is hovering over larger than the rest of the Dock, as if you were moving a magnifying glass over it. (Figure 2.6 shows this effect in action.)

To enable magnification quickly, choose  ⇒ Dock ⇒ Turn Magnification On, or Control+click or right-click the white dividing line in the Dock and choose Turn Magnification On from the contextual menu. (If magnification is already on, the menu option is labeled Turn Magnification Off.) Alternatively check the Magnification option in the Dock system preference. You can adjust the size of Dock magnification by using the Magnification slider.

Dock magnification is very much a personal choice, and many users prefer to keep it switched off. Magnification is a great visual effect and can enable you to focus on the icon under the mouse. However, it can also make it more difficult for newcomers to click desired icons as they move slightly when expanding. Experiment with both styles to discover which one works for you.

FIGURE 2.6

The Dock magnification feature makes icons underneath the mouse larger than surrounding icons. The effect shown here has the Size slider's thumb in the middle and the Magnification slider set to the maximum.

Positioning and automatically hiding the Dock

By default, the Dock appears at the bottom of the screen. However, you can position it at either the left or right side of the screen.

The advantage of having the Dock at the bottom of the screen is that you can fit more icons to the Dock (or have a slightly larger Dock) because the bottom of the screen is wider than the sides of the screen.

The flip side to this is that the Dock's positioning at the bottom of the screen limits the maximum vertical size of windows on the screen. Given that widescreen displays have limited the vertical space in favor of horizontal space, positioning the Dock on the side of the screen can reclaim vertical space, which in turn can make scanning long documents or Web sites easier.

One way to deal with this is to move the Dock from its default position to either the left- or right-hand side of the screen. To do so, choose ⇨ Dock ⇨ Position on Left or ⇨ Dock ⇨ Position on Right, or Control+click or right-click the Dock's dividing line and chose Position on Screen ⇨ Left or Position on Screen ⇨ Right from the contextual menu.

A side effect of positioning the Dock on either the left- or right-hand side of the screen is that the Dock has a slightly different visual effect. When the Dock is positioned on the bottom of the screen, it reflects the vertical desktop (and any nearby windows); when it is on either side of the window, it has no reflection effect and thus has slightly more contrast. Many people find the reflective effect of the Dock distracting and prefer the higher contrast effect when it is on the side of the screen.

An alternative to moving the Dock is to have it out of the way when it's not required. You can set it to do this by using one of the following methods:

- Choosing ⇨ Dock ⇨ Turn Hiding On.
- Control+clicking or right-clicking the white divider line in the Dock and choosing Turn Hiding on from the contextual menu.
- Pressing Option+⌘+D.
- Selecting the Automatically Hide and Show the Dock option in the Dock system preference.

When this hiding option is selected, the Dock automatically slides off the screen when not in use. When you slide the mouse to the edge where the dock is hiding, it automatically slides back onto the screen, enabling you to make selections as normal. This automatic Dock hiding is the best way to get the most out of your screen space, although some people prefer the Dock to be on display at all times.

Animating open applications in the Dock

The final visual option in the Dock system preference is Animate Opening Applications. This is selected by default, which means that clicking on an application in the Dock causes it to bounce up and down as it launches. Although we think this is a good visual indicator of an application's status, many users find the bouncing effect distracting. You can switch it off by deselecting the Animate Opening Applications option in the Dock system preference. If this option is deselected, the application icons remain static when you launch them. The only indication that the applications are loading is the blue-and-white sphere underneath the application icon, which flashes as the application loads and remains on as the application is running.

Understanding the Desktop

Now that you are familiar with two stalwarts of Mac OS X, the menu bar and Dock, it is time to turn your attention to another of Apple's innovations, the desktop.

Apple popularized a GUI with a desktop metaphor with its famous Macintosh line, introduced in 1984. As Microsoft followed suit with Windows, it made the desktop metaphor common parlance throughout the world.

However, it is important to distinguish between the desktop metaphor for the GUI and a desktop computer. A desktop computer is one designed to fit on the desk in the office or at home and originally signified a computer designed for the home or office rather than industrial use; these days the *desktop* moniker differentiates computers designed to stay in one place from a laptop, or notebook, which is designed to be portable.

In a GUI, the desktop metaphor is the concept of the screen on the monitor acting as a visual representation of your physical desk. In this sense, the desktop contains folders (which are virtual representations of cardboard folders or drawers), documents (which are virtual pieces of paper), a trash can to dispose of items, and other visual icons designed to imitate real-life objects.

In other words, the desktop metaphor was developed to make computers more user-friendly by imitating the physical workspace that most of us inhabit.

Because the desktop metaphor has been in use for so long, and has achieved such widespread prominence throughout the computing world, most users will be intimately familiar with it already. Younger computer users may never have used a computer without a desktop, and it is hard for many people to imagine a computer that does not use one.

Despite being based on a commonplace metaphor, the desktop used in Mac OS X has many features and functions that may not be immediately apparent.

Getting to know the desktop

In essence, the desktop is the background on the screen — the expanse of space that sits behind the Dock and below the menu bar. By default, every version of Mac OS X has featured a different background signifying which version of Mac OS X is running. But the arrangement of the default disk icons has not changed: The startup disk appears at the upper right of the desktop, and any additional disks' icons appear below the startup disk's icon.

It is important to understand that although the desktop is the space on the screen, it is also a folder inside your Home folder, located in /Users/username/Desktop). Whatever is in that folder appears on the desktop when that user is logged in. And whatever that user puts on the desktop is actually placed in that folder. Because different users have different Home folders, the desktop is individual to each user. (We explain the folder structure of Mac OS X later in this chapter.)

Note

Although the icons of disks appear on the desktop, they do not appear inside the `/Users/username/Desktop` folder, not even as aliases. These icons appear on the desktop purely because it is convenient for Mac OS X to place them there. (They are also accessible via the Finder's Sidebar, as explained later.) The fact that disk icons appear on the desktop, but are not in the `/Users/username/Desktop` folder, is an exception to the Mac OS's rule that all folders display the items they contain.

Changing the desktop background

By default, the desktop comes with a rather spectacular default background called Aurora. This vista (see Figure 2.7) matches the marketing material used to promote Mac OS X 10.6 Snow Leopard. However, you may want to change the background to make for a more personal computing experience.

You can change the desktop background to virtually anything: You can set it to any vibrant color of your choosing, or opt for a functional black, white, or gray shade. Plus, Apple supplies a range of images, abstract artworks, and photographs. You can also use any of your photographs, and the Web is awash with desktop images that you can download and use to personalize your desktop.

FIGURE 2.7

Mac OS X's default desktop features a stunning space vista as its background image. Note the disk icon in the right of the screen.

To change the desktop background, you need to open the Desktop & Screen Saver system preference. You can access this system preference by using any of the following methods:

- **The Dock.** If the System Preferences application icon appears in the Dock, you can click it to open the System Preferences application. Now click the Desktop & Screen Saver icon to access the Desktop & Screen Saver system preference, and go to its Desktop pane.

- **Menu bar.** Choose ⇨ System Preferences. Now click the Desktop & Screen Saver icon to access the Desktop & Screen Saver system preference, and go to its Desktop pane.

- **Contextual menu.** Control+click or right-click the desktop (but not a disk or folder in it) to get the contextual menu, and choose Change Desktop Background. This opens the Desktop & Screen Saver system preference's Desktop pane.

Figure 2.8 shows the Desktop pane. (Chapter 21 explains how to use the Screen Saver pane.)

FIGURE 2.8

The Desktop pane in the Desktop & Screen Saver system preference shows a small picture and the name of the currently selected desktop image, plus options for selecting your own image.

At the top of the Desktop pane is a small preview image of the currently selected desktop background image, and next to it is the image's name. If you have added your own image, you also see a popup menu offering options for adjusting the image.

At the left side of the pane, below the preview of the current desktop image, is a library of different image offerings. By default, it has two sections: Apple and Folders. A third option, iPhoto Library, appears if you have Apple's iPhoto installed.

You can show and hide each section by clicking its disclosure triangle. On the right is a gallery showing the options available for the highlighted selection in the library list. Follow these steps to select a new desktop background image:

1. **Select an option from the library.**
2. **Select one of the images from the preview grid to the right.**

That's it. You don't even have to close the Desktop & Screen Saver system preference for the new desktop background image to take effect. (Though you should close it when done to reduce screen clutter.)

Using the Apple-provided background images

Apple provides several background images with Mac OS X. Here are the options available:

- **Apple Images.** This collection of backgrounds has colored patterns.
- **Nature.** The nature collection includes a series of photographs of natural objects. They range from the extremely close-up image of a drop of water hanging from an earthbound leaf to the default Aurora image (this has changed from the previous Aurora desktop image, which has been renamed Leopard Aurora). Other options include images of the Earth, stones, rock gardens, zebra skins, and tranquil water.
- **Plants.** Similar in theme to Nature, the Plants collection includes photos of a variety of flowers and other vegetation.
- **Black & White.** This collection includes an array of striking landscape photographs rendered without color.
- **Abstract.** Like the Apple images, this is a collection of backgrounds with swirling waves flowing through them. The images here are highly colorful.
- **Solid Colors.** There are ten colors here to choose from. They slightly fade to a lighter color near the bottom of the screen, creating a subtle effect that is not distracting.

Using your own background images

There are several ways to use your own images as the desktop background image.

One way is to choose an image in the library list, using one of these two options:

- **Pictures Folder.** Any pictures you place directly in the Pictures folder in your Home folder appear in this folder. This is one way that you can add your own custom pictures to the desktop.
- **iPhoto Albums.** This is linked to your iPhoto album, which enables you to set personal photos imported to your Mac via Apple's iPhoto image-management application as your desktop background. Under the iPhoto Albums label appears a list of available iPhoto albums in your Home folder. Click an album and the photographs appear on the right-hand side of the screen.

Or, you can add images directly to the Desktop pane of the Desktop & Screen Saver system preference:

1. **Be sure the Desktop pane of the Desktop & Screen Saver pane is open.** If not, open it as described earlier.

2. **Go to the disk or folder that contains your desired image (it may also be on the desktop), and drag it onto the current preview image at the top-left side of the Desktop pane.**

3. **As you move the image over the small preview, a green + icon appears over the file, indicating that it will be added to the library and made the new background image.** Release the mouse button and the image is used as your new background image.

4. **A popup menu appears to the right of the new preview image; use it to select how the background image should appear.** There are five options:

   - **Fit to Screen.** This enlarges or reduces the image so it fits in your screen. But if the image's ratio doesn't match your monitor's ratio, any gap is filled in with a color that you can change by using the color-swatch iconic button to the right of the popup menu. Click it to open the Colors panel and choose a different fill-in color, if desired.

   - **Fill Screen.** This resizes the image so it fills the entire desktop. There is no gap as with Fit to Screen. If the image's proportions don't match the screens, some of the image may fall outside the screen and not be visible.

   - **Stretch to Fill Screen.** This resizes the image and, if necessary, its proportions so it fills the screen. This option can distort the image's perspective.

   - **Center.** This places the image in its original size in the center of the screen. As with Fit to Screen, you can change the fill-in color that appears around it.

   - **Tile.** This places multiple copies of the image in its original size so that the copies end up covering the entire desktop.

A third way to add your own images is to make entire folders accessible in the library list. You can then choose images from those folders as you do the Apple-supplied images, images in the Pictures folder, or images in an iPhoto album.

To add a folder of images to the Desktop pane, click the + iconic button at the bottom of the library list. This opens a Finder window. Navigate through the Finder window to find a folder containing images that you want to add to the list and click the Choose button. A new section called Folders appears below the iPhoto Albums section, containing the name of any folders you've added.

Changing desktop pictures automatically

If variety is the spice of your life, then why not set up the desktop to change background images automatically? To do so in the Desktop pane of the Desktop & Screen Saver system preference, select the Change Picture option at the bottom of the pane, then select an interval from the adjoining popup menu. Options range from every five seconds to once a day; there are also options to change the background image every time you start the Mac or wake it from sleep.

By default, every time the background image changes, it moves to the next one in the selected library list's folder. But, if you select the Random Order option, Mac OS X chooses an image from that library folder randomly.

Caution

Changing the desktop background image can be amusing, but it can also take a lot of system resources, especially if it changes frequently, and thus slow down your Mac. It can also be distracting, and thus slow down your brain.

Choosing a non-translucent menu bar

In keeping with the Aqua theme used throughout Mac OS X, the menu bar at the top of the screen has a translucent background that shows part of the desktop below it. For most desktops, this isn't a problem. However, some of the more complex desktop background images can make the menu bar difficult to read. If this is the case, or if you just prefer the clear visual delineation that a non-transparent menu bar provides, you can turn off the see-through aspect of the menu bar by deselecting the Translucent Menu Bar option in the Desktop pane of the Desktop & Screen Saver system preference.

Working with Windows

Ever since the GUI became prevalent in desktop computing, the window metaphor has been used to describe the square panels of information that appear on-screen. A *window* is a container for information. There are many different kinds of window used by Mac OS X, and each serves a particular function.

Some windows contain complete applications, such as iTunes; these are called *application windows*. Others display documents within applications, such as Microsoft Word; these are called *document windows*. Still others show the contents of hard disks and folders; these are called *Finder windows*. And some windows display images and movies, or play audio files; these are called *playback windows*.

Others alert you with messages you should act on; and some present options to change, modify, and interact with the content in other windows. These alert and options-oriented windows have specific names:

- **Dialog box.** A window that when opened does not let you work elsewhere within an application until the dialog box is closed. (You can work in other applications, however.) It typically contains settings and similar controls, but can also provide alerts that you must acknowledge. You typically close a dialog box by clicking OK to apply or confirm changes or warnings, or by clicking Cancel to ignore the changes or warnings.

- **Sheet.** Also called a *settings sheet*, a window that appears to show a set of additional options related to the active dialog box. Like a dialog box, it prevents you from working in other windows in the active application until you close it.

- **Panel.** A window that when opened lets you work with other windows, such as panels or dialog boxes. It typically contains settings and similar controls. Panels have no OK or Cancel buttons, so changes to their options take effect immediately (though you can often press Esc to undo the last change to an option). Microsoft Office and Adobe Creative Suite heavily use panels.

- **Pane.** A section within a dialog box, panel, or other window. Often, the active pane obscures the other panes in the window, though you can easily switch among them by clicking tabs or buttons. However, a pane can also be a separate, distinct area within a window that groups similar controls.

Windows are, in short, prolific and exceptionally versatile. Figure 2.9 shows a sampling.

Most windows in Mac OS X are rectangular and follow guidelines set by Apple that ensure a unified look and feel. There are common buttons and elements that you can use to resize, maximize, and minimize windows, enabling you to make the most of your desktop real estate.

FIGURE 2.9

Several common windows that can be found in the Mac OS X environment: a window displaying a text document (upper left), a dialog box (upper right), a sheet (lower left), and a panel (lower right)

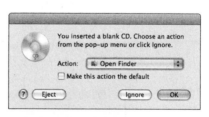

Understanding windows controls

Windows can take many different shapes and forms, as can their controls. As with menus, Apple developers adhere to a set of guidelines as to how windows should appear. These include using a common graphical style with similar visual styling, and commonly used buttons and control surfaces. Some are common to many window types, while others are specific to certain types. You won't find these commonalities on every window; for example, dialog boxes rarely have control surfaces and cannot be resized, and sheets often have no controls at all. However, a unified look and feel is common across Mac OS X, and most document and application windows have the same set of buttons and controls in the same place. Figure 2.10 shows the Safari Web browser window with all the commonly found controls and objects noted:

- **Title bar.** The title bar appears at the top of the window and typically displays the name of the application or document that the window contains. Clicking and dragging the title bar is the common way to move windows around the screen. Double-clicking the title bar minimizes the window to the Dock. A cluster of brightly colored iconic buttons that are common across many windows appears on the left-hand side of the Title bar. They include Close (red), Minimize (yellow), and Zoom (green). Users migrating from the Microsoft Windows environment will find that these buttons offer much the same functionality as the Close, Minimize, and Maximize buttons found in the top right of a window in Windows.

  - **Close.** The Close iconic button is the red button that you'll always find on the far left of the window. When you hover the mouse over it, a red cross appears in center. If you click it, the window disappears (and if there is any data yet to be saved, a dialog box appears, asking if you would like to do so). In some applications, holding down the Option key while clicking the Close iconic button forces all windows attached to that Window to close. Note that a key difference between Mac OS X and Microsoft Windows is that closing all the windows of an application in Mac OS X does not quit the application itself. For this, you need to quit the application by using the menu bar, Dock, or ⌘+Q shortcut as described earlier in this chapter. Note that you can also press ⌘+W to close the active window, and in many programs, pressing Option+⌘+W closes all windows in the active application.

  - **Minimize.** The yellow iconic Minimize iconic button appears next to the red Close iconic button, and when you hover the mouse over it, a minus symbol (–) appears inside the button. Clicking it shrinks the window down into the Dock. (Clicking it in the Dock makes it reappear in the same position on the screen.) In many programs you can also press ⌘+M to minimize the window.

  - **Zoom.** The green button to the right of Minimize is the Zoom iconic button. When you hover the mouse over this button, a small plus sign (+) appears. Clicking the Zoom iconic button adjusts the size of the window according to its contents. A zoomed window will take up as much space as required by the window's contents, up to the size of the entire desktop (leaving space for the Dock if it is visible). Clicking the Zoom iconic button a second time causes it to return to its previous size.

Note

It is incorrect to think of the Zoom iconic button as a Maximize button, and therefore the polar opposite of the Minimize iconic button (as it is in Microsoft Windows). Although it often makes the window full size, it can also make the window smaller because it resizes it to the optimum size for the current contents. Some windows have their size determined by the application and cannot be resized — in this case, the Zoom iconic button is dimmed and no plus sign appears when you hover the mouse over it. There are a few applications that use the Zoom iconic button differently. Clicking the Zoom iconic button in iTunes, for example, causes the application to switch between a full window and a small window that only displays shuttle controls and the currently playing track.

- **Scrollbar.** Scrollbars sit on the right and bottom of a window. They appear only if the contents do not fit in the window. A scrollbar serves as both an indicator that more content is available than can fit inside the window and as a device to navigate through that content. Scrollbars in Mac OS X 10.6 Snow Leopard consist of the scroll track (also known as the *trough*), the slider, and scroll arrows.

  - **Scroll track.** It is easy to confuse the scroll track with the scrollbar itself, although technically the scroll track is the blank area behind the slider. Clicking on an area of the scroll track that does not contain the slider makes the slider move in that direction.

  - **Slider.** The slider serves as an indicator as to what part of a window's content you a currently looking at and how much more content exists off the edges of the window. The slider also lets you navigate that content; you click and drag it to move through the content. The size of the slider is proportional to the amount of extra content that exists. A document, for example, that is twice the size of the window will have a slider half the size of the scroll track. If the document has four times as much information, the slider will be a quarter of the size of the scroll track; the smaller the slider, the more information that exists off the edge of the window.

  - **Scroll arrows.** You can use the scroll arrows to move the slider in the direction of the arrow (up and down, or left and right). Scroll arrows can be used in two ways: In the first way, a single click causes the slider to move in that direction. Unlike clicking the scroll track, which moves a whole window of content, clicking the scroll arrow moves by a single item contained within the window (clicking in Word, for example, moves one document line at a time). In the second way, clicking and holding the scroll arrow lets you scan or page through a window, sort of like a rewind or fast-forward control.

- **Resize control.** The bottom right-hand corner of a window typically lets you resize the window. If a window can be resized, the corner will be marked with three diagonal lines. Click and drag the window by this corner to adjust the size and proportion of the window.

FIGURE 2.10

Mac OS X has a unified look and feel and many windows share a common set of controls. This figure highlights the controls you will find on many windows.

Organizing windows

Most windows used in Mac OS X follow a similar set of rules, and act in a similar manner. In this sense, it is possible to organize and arrange windows to suit your working requirements. Although some programs violate Apple's GUI guidelines and use nonstandard controls and behaviors for windows, most windows follow the rules and act the same way.

Opening items in the Finder

The quickest way to get a window to appear on the desktop is to open an item (such as a folder, document, or application). For example, double-clicking the icon for your main hard disk in the top right of the desktop opens a window displaying its contents. Alternatively, you can click the item and choose File ⇨ Open, press ⌘+O, or Control+click or right-click the item and choose Open from its contextual menu.

Creating a new Finder window

A Finder window is a folder — one that by default shows the contents of the Home folder for the current user account, in fact. When you have lots of disks and folders open on your desktop, opening a new Finder window is a great way to get to the starting point for all your account's folders. To open a Finder, choose Finder ⇨ New Finder Window, press ⌘+N, or click the Finder icon in the Dock.

Recognizing active and inactive windows

Although Mac OS X can have multiple windows operating at once, only one of them is ever considered active at any one time. This is the window you are currently working in. Mac OS X uses a quasi-3-D layered effect with shadows behind windows to help you determine which one is at the front — the active window. Another way of determining which window is active is to check the buttons in the top left of the window. The active window has colored buttons, whereas inactive windows have gray buttons. When a window is inactive, you usually cannot make any changes to its contents; some exceptions include the Close iconic button, which you can click on an inactive window to close it. See Figure 2.11 for an example of active and inactive windows.

FIGURE 2.11

The System Preferences application is currently the active window. You can tell because it is in front of the other windows. Also, the buttons on the left of the window are brightly colored and the window has a slightly stronger hue than the other windows.

Changing the active window

Clicking in any part of an inactive window (other than window items that can be changed when inactive) makes it instantly become the active window. It then moves in front of the other windows and its buttons light up. If the active window has any other panels or dialog boxes open, they also become active. But other windows used by the application may stay where they are, such as document windows.

Tip

If you want all windows associated with an application to move in front of other windows, click the application's icon in the Dock.

Note that if an application has a window with a dialog box open, you may not be able to access other windows being used by the application until you have closed the dialog box (by opening the window relating to the dialog box and closing the dialog box, usually by clicking OK to accept any new settings or Cancel to ignore those changes).

There are four other ways to change the active window.

- Use the Finder's Window menu to select a desired window; all open windows display in this menu.

- Click a minimized window in the Dock to open it.

- Press ⌘+` or choose Window ➪ Cycle Through Windows in the Finder to move from one window to the next.

- Press ⌘+Tab to open the application switcher (see Chapter 7) and cycle through the active applications; hold ⌘ and press Tab repeatedly to move through the applications. When you release ⌘, the selected application's window comes to the fore.

Understanding common controls within windows

The controls we have covered so far relate to the windows. However, you will also encounter a wide range of controls inside the windows themselves. These can take the form of buttons, sliders, check boxes, and a myriad of other forms dreamed up by software designers. While software designers are free to develop whatever control system works for their particular application, many standard controls exist and Apple provides documentation for developers on using a standard set of buttons and controls within applications. And, of course, Apple itself uses these controls within the applications supplied with Mac OS X. Here are some of the common controls you will encounter when using Mac OS X:

- **Button.** As its name suggests, a button is a control that causes an action to take place when you click it with the mouse. (Apple's formal term is *push button*, but everyone calls them simply *buttons*.) Buttons come in a variety of shapes and sizes, and can be marked with either text or a graphic. Buttons with text are generally horizontal with rounded edges; iconic (graphical) buttons can be any shape (sometimes they are accompanied by text descriptions). A sampling of buttons is shown in Figure 2.12.

- **OK and Cancel buttons.** These standard buttons appear in most dialog boxes. Clicking the OK button accepts the settings in the corresponding window, whereas clicking Cancel rejects any changes you made to the settings; both buttons close the dialog box. Occasionally, you may find the buttons marked differently: Deleting a file from a connected server, for example, displays Delete and Cancel buttons instead of OK and Cancel buttons. Some developers use Done instead of OK. Note that if a button is glowing or colored, pressing Return is the same as clicking that button. Also, in most cases, pressing Esc is the same as clicking Cancel.

FIGURE 2.12

Buttons are found throughout the Mac OS X environment. Clicking them performs the action associated with the button.

- **Radio button.** When an action has multiple predefined settings to choose from, you may find radio button options used. They are named after the physical buttons that used to appear on car radios, where pushing one button causes the others to pop out — so only one button can be used at a time. In Mac OS X, radio buttons are small gray circles that turn blue with a black dot in the center when an option is selected. Radio buttons can be displayed either horizontally or vertically. Figure 2.13 shows an example of the radio buttons used to control the position of the Dock.

- **Check boxes.** Another group of settings might be displayed with check box options. A check box is similar to a radio button, except that it is square, and when an option is selected, the check box becomes blue with a small black check mark inside. The key difference between check boxes and radio buttons is that multiple options can be selected at once with check boxes (whereas radio buttons allow for only a single selection). Click in a check box to select it, and click in it again to deselect it. Some check boxes also have a third, intermediate state, marked as a horizontal line. This usually indicates that it has a subselection of check boxes and that some, but not all, of the items are selected. Figure 2.14 shows an example of check boxes.

- **Sliders.** A slider is a track (normally horizontal) that displays a range of values. On the track is a square with a triangular edge known as the *thumb*. You move the thumb along the track to select a value between the two ends of the slider. Sometimes you use sliders to select a numerical range, and the number appears nearby. At other times, you use them to choose from a non-numerical condition (a range between Slow and Fast, for example). An example of sliders is shown in Figure 2.15.

- **Stepper controls.** Also known as *little arrows*, these small arrows are used to raise or lower a value incrementally. Clicking an arrow adjusts the value by one predefined increment. Clicking and holding one of the arrows continuously increases the value until it reaches the end of its range.

- **Disclosure triangles.** One of these devices is a small black triangle that is used to control how much detail is displayed by an item in a window. Typically, a disclosure triangle points to the right, which indicates that its detail is *collapsed* (hidden); clicking it rotates the triangle by 90 degrees to point downward, and the remaining information is *expanded* (revealed). Figure 2.16 shows an example of disclosure triangles.

- **Ordered lists.** This is a less commonly used control, where a list of items is displayed. Typically, you can click and drag the items to arrange them in a different order. In the Language & Text system preference's Language pane, for example, it lets you determine in what order languages are displayed in options. Sometimes an ordered list also uses check boxes that enable you to switch on or off items in the list. See Figure 2.17 for an example of ordered lists.

FIGURE 2.13

Radio buttons enable you to make a single selection from a predefined set of options.

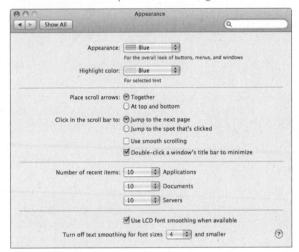

FIGURE 2.14

Check box options enable you to switch settings on or off.

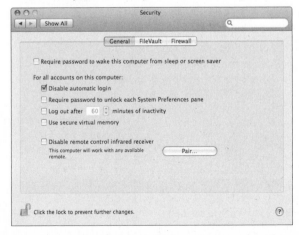

FIGURE 2.15

Sliders enable you adjust settings by moving the thumb across a track.

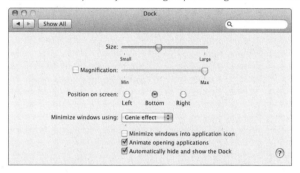

FIGURE 2.16

Clicking a disclosure triangle causes it to reveal the information contained within an item.

- **Tabs.** These controls typically appear at the top of a dialog box or panel. When you click a tab, the window or dialog box displays a different pane of information. (The metaphor is a window divided up into separate panes of glass.) Figure 2.18 shows an example of the tabs used in the MobileMe system preference. (Panes accessed via tabs are often called *tabbed panes*.)

FIGURE 2.17

An example of an ordered list. Items can be dragged and rearranged to adjust the order they appear in.

FIGURE 2.18

The four tabs — Account, Sync, iDisk, and Back to My Mac — take you to different panes that the window displays.

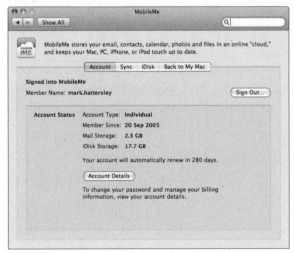

Recognizing Icons

Menus, windows, and buttons are some of the key components that make up a modern computer operating system. But there is one other thing that makes a GUI complete: icons.

Icons are small pictures that represent, well, just about anything. Icons can represent applications, documents (documents that belong to specific applications), files, folders, and fonts. Just about everything on the desktop or in the Finder has an icon associated with it.

Working with objects in Mac OS X largely means finding and manipulating their respective icons. You double-click a document icon to open the document; you drag the icon around to move the document around the various parts of the Finder. Icons for applications appear on the Dock and in the Applications folder; clicking them opens applications.Because Mac OS X is a GUI based upon the desktop metaphor, an icon's basic appearance is designed to visually represent what kind of item it is. A folder, for example, is designed to resemble a cardboard folder; files look like pieces of paper with one corner slightly turned. Other icons have no real-world equivalent; applications are an example, although they share a common visual style that enables you to identify them.

The icons used by various versions of Mac OS X have evolved over time (Figure 2.19 shows an example of icons in the Finder). They have typically become larger and more detailed. Unlike the icons found in previous operating systems, the ones in Mac OS X can be resized up to a substantial size measuring 128 × 128 pixels. In some cases, such as with the desktop, you decide how large you want the Mac OS X icons to be displayed. In some others, such as when you're using the Finder in columns view, the icons are a predetermined size.

FIGURE 2.19

The icons in Mac OS X are large and have a realistic visual style.

Identifying application icons

Application icons are possibly the most varied type of icon used in Mac OS X. Typically, they are a colorful representation of the tool they represent. The iTunes icon, for example, is an image of a CD with a blue musical note. Figure 2.20 shows some examples of application icons.

Examples of application icons

Identifying document icons

In Mac OS X, document icons are designed to look like a sheet of paper with the top right-hand corner curved over. The icon itself often has a visual preview of what the document itself contains. Look at an icon for a word-processing document and you'll notice the document's text has been used to create the icon. Other times, the icon document displays the icon of the application it is associated with: Music files often show the iTunes or QuickTime icon, for example. Icons for images are slightly different in that they don't have the curved-paper design and usually show a small version of the image itself.

Identifying folder icons

Folders are among the most easily identifiable icons in Mac OS X. This is because their appearance rarely changes. Most of the time the folder appears as a blue rectangle with an extended tab on the top left. The design is reminiscent of real-life cardboard folders used to store paper documents. Some folders appear in color or with graphics or logos, and sometimes they have a skewed perspective; these are typically application folders whose developers had some fun.

Some of the folders commonly included with Mac OS X have a small design "etched" onto the blue rectangle. The Applications folder has a stylized A etched in it, the Library folder has an etching of a classical Greek structure, the Pictures folder has an etching of a camera, the System folder has an etching of the letter X, the Users folder has an etching of a person's head and shoulders, and the Utilities folder has an etching of two crossed tools. Other system folders with such etchings are the Desktop, Documents, Movies, Music, Public, and Sites folders for each user account.

Note

The current user account's Home folder has a wholly different look: a color image of a house, not a folder-like icon.

Identifying volume icons

Like folder icons, volume icons are largely easy to identify. (A *volume* is the general name for drives, disks, and partitions — storage containers, essentially.) They are typically designed to appear similar to the real-life object they represent. So the icons for internal disks are gray rectangles styled to look like physical hard disks; the icons for external hard disks have a similar shape but look like external drives and sometimes feature a symbol matching the drive's connection type (USB [Universal Serial Bus] or FireWire). The icons for CD-ROM and DVD drives look like actual CDs and DVDs. Network volumes often appear as a distinctive blue sphere inside a clear square. Figure 2.21 shows examples of volume icons.

Identifying alias icons

An *alias* is a shortcut to a document, or application — or even another alias. Aliases exist to enable quick access to items that may be buried deep within several folder layers within the Mac OS's folder hierarchy. By using aliases, you can drill down to a specific folder or item quickly and with fewer mouse clicks. An alias uses the same icon as the original item but has a small black curved arrow in its bottom-left corner which signifies that it points to another item.

FIGURE 2.21

Examples of different volume icons

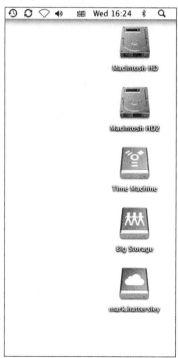

Identifying restricted folders

Some folders on your Mac, or located on a networked server, are restricted to particular users. This is especially true if you have multiple accounts on your computer: You cannot access or edit files and folders in another user's account when you are logged in with your account unless that user has enabled file sharing for those items (see Chapters 13 and 20).

Tip

If you account has administrator privileges, you can access such restricted files, but must enter in your password each time to do so.

Restricted files and folders are pretty easy to spot because they feature a red "no entry" symbol (a red circle with a white horizontal bar across the middle) on the bottom right of the icon. Figure 2.22 shows an example of a restricted file.

FIGURE 2.22

Folders with a red "no entry" symbol are restricted and cannot be accessed or altered unless you enter your administrator password.

Issues with Aliases

Aliases are very handy for providing easy access from the desktop and other locations you frequent to files, folders, and disks buried in your folder hierarchy; or otherwise more mouse clicks away from where you are than you want to traverse.

But sometimes you want to get the original item an alias points to. To do so, select an alias and choose File ⇨ Show Original or press ⌘+R. Or Control+click or right-click an alias and select Show Original from the contextual menu. This opens a Finder window that contains the original item.

Mac OS X tracks aliases as they and the original files are moved around the Finder, so they're kept up-to-date automatically. However, if the original item has been deleted or moved to a disk that has been ejected, the Finder shows an alert dialog box informing you that the original item can't be found when you try to open the alias.

This dialog box offers you three options. You can click OK to accept the warning and continue working without using the alias; you can click the Delete Alias button to move the alias to the Trash; and you can click the Fix Alias button to locate the missing item (or select one you want the alias to point to from now on instead) via the Select New Original dialog box.

Discovering the Finder

The Finder lies at the heart of Mac OS X, and is often mistaken for being the Mac OS. But it is an application almost like any other. Because it is so ubiquitous, many Mac OS X users do not even realize they are using an application.

This is understandable. After all, unlike other applications, you never have to start the Finder; and although you can relaunch the Finder if it gets stuck, without affecting other running programs, it isn't possible to stop running the application. The Finder application starts up when you log in, and keeps running until you log out. Like all applications, the Finder has its own icon, a smiling blue face that permanently appears on the far left of the Dock.

The Finder is responsible for managing the desktop and file structure of Mac OS X. With the Finder, you create, move, copy, and delete folders and files, and you access disks so you can create, move, copy, and delete folders and files to, from, and within them. The Finder also lets you work with these items through four views: list, grid, icon, and Cover Flow. Chapter 3 explains these views and the Finder's folder structure.

Like other applications, it generates its own document windows, only the Finder's document windows — called Finder windows — are primarily used for navigating the file structure. And they have unique elements — the Sidebar at left and the toolbar at top. Chapter 3 explains in detail how these work.

Relaunching the Finder

The Finder is an application, and like other applications, it runs in a protected memory area. This helps to ensure that if there is a problem with the Finder, you don't need to restart the entire computer.

If an application becomes unresponsive in Mac OS X, you can use the Force Quit command to ensure that Mac OS X closes it. (It can then be reopened.). However, because the Finder should be running at all times, the Force Quit command is replaced with one called Relaunch Finder, which forces the Finder to close, then reopens it. This command is specific to the Finder; hence its name, Relaunch Finder.

When the Finder becomes unresponsive (typically both the Finder windows and the desktop will cease to respond to mouse clicks, and the mouse may turn into a spinning wheel), you may need to invoke the Relaunch Finder command. There are several different ways to relaunch the Finder:

- Control+Option+click the Finder icon in the Dock. Choose the Relaunch option from the contextual menu that appears.
- Choose  ⇨ Force Quit from the menu bar. Select the Finder option from the Force Quit menu and click the Relaunch button.
- Press Control+Option+Esc on the keyboard. This opens the Force Quit Applications menu; select the Finder option and click Relaunch.
- In the Terminal, enter the command **killall Finder**. The Terminal application is explained in more depth in Chapter 26.
- Open the Activity Monitor application (located within the Utilities folder, which is inside the Applications folder). Scroll down the list and find the Finder application and click the red Quit Process button. Now click the Quit button (if this fails to quit the Finder, use the Force Quit command). This completely quits the Finder; click the Finder icon in the Dock to relaunch the Finder and continue.

When you invoke the Relaunch Finder command, the Finder's menu bar, plus all the icons on the desktop disappear and then reappear. All the Finder windows close and do not reappear.

Because the Finder is treated as an application, when the Finder is unresponsive, other applications will still be active. You can switch between applications, continue working, and even save files. This is one of the key strengths of Mac OS X. It is extremely rare that you will ever need to restart Mac OS X, and you can continue working and save files even when a key part of the operating system is unresponsive. If the system becomes totally unresponsive, and none of the previously listed solutions work, you can completely restart your Mac by holding down the power button for ten seconds.

Understanding the Finder menus

Like any application, the Finder has its own set of menus, with menu options specific to the Finder's operations. The Finder's menu options all appear on the menu bar — to the right of the  symbol — when the Finder is the active application (click on the desktop, or on the Finder icon in the Dock, to make Finder the active application). Let's look at the Finder-specific menus.

The Finder menu

The application menu for the Finder is, not surprisingly, called the Finder menu.

- **About Finder.** This option opens a dialog box with the Finder icon, the current version of the Finder, and some copyright information.

- **Preferences.** This option brings up a dialog box with many of the preferences that can be adjusted for the Finder. You can also press ⌘+, (comma) to open the Preferences dialog box.

- **Empty Trash.** The Trash can is located on the far right of the Dock and contains files you've deleted from the system. These files stay in the Trash (so they can be recovered) until you choose this menu option. Emptying the Trash permanently removes these items from the Mac.

- **Secure Empty Trash.** The Secure Empty Trash option not only deletes the Trash but also completely overwrites the files with meaningless numbers, preventing anybody from recovering the data with a recovery utility.

- **Services.** This menu option lets you choose services related to the Finder's operations. Chapter 16 covers services in depth.

The File menu

The File menu offers the following menu options:

- **New Finder Window.** Choosing this option opens a new Finder window. The Finder window enables you to browse through volumes, folders, and files, as Chapter 3 describes. (You can also simply press ⌘+N to open a new Finder window.)

- **New Folder.** Choosing this option creates a new folder in the active Finder window or, if no Finder window is open, on the desktop. (You can also simply press Shift+⌘+N.)

- **New Smart Folder.** Choosing this option creates a smart folder. Smart folders are "intelligent" folders that collect files based on predefined criteria. The creation of smart folders is explained in Chapter 3. (You can also simply press Option+⌘+N.)

- **New Burn Folder.** Choosing this option creates a folder that you then place files and folders in that you want to put on a recordable CD or DVD. After you've placed all the files you want recorded, or "burned," to disc, insert a recordable disc into the Mac's SuperDrive and follow the prompts. This is how you can create discs without needing special disc-recording software.

- **Open.** This option opens the selected file or application. If a file is selected, the Finder launches an application that its database says can open the file. (You can also press ⌘+O.)

- **Open With.** This option requires you to select an application from its submenu with which you want to open the selected file. Use it when the regular Open menu option can't find an appropriate application.

- **Print.** This option prints whatever files are selected. (You can also press ⌘+P.)

- **Close Window.** This option closes the active Finder window. (You can also press ⌘+W.)

- **Get Info.** This option gets information on a highlighted item in the Finder, as outlined later in this chapter. (You can also press ⌘+I.)

- **Compress.** The option, also known as the Archive command, creates a Zip-compressed copy of the selected items. These files usually take less space and can be more easily provided to other Mac and Windows users.

- **Duplicate.** This command creates a duplicate of the file, as outlined later in the chapter. (You can also press ⌘+D.)

- **Make Alias.** This command creates a quick-access link, called an *alias* (Windows users will know this as a *shortcut*) to a highlighted item in the Finder. The alias can be used to quickly locate and open files buried deep in the Finder's file structure. (You can also press ⌘+L.)

Tip

Press and hold Option+⌘ while dragging an item to a new location in the Finder. (You can also press and hold the Option+⌘ keys after clicking and dragging the item, but you must be sure to hold them until after you release the mouse button.) This method has the added benefit of enabling you to create the alias in a different location from the original file (which is useful because an alias typically lives in a different location than the item it points to).

- **Quick Look.** The Quick Look option reveals the contents of most files, as described later in this chapter. (You can also press ⌘+Y.)

- **Show Original.** This command is only active when an alias is highlighted in the Finder. It opens a Finder window displaying the item that the alias points to. (You can also press ⌘+R.)

- **Add to Sidebar.** The Sidebar is located on the left-hand side of Finder windows, and provides quick access to disks, folders, and files. This option adds the selected items to the Sidebar for such quick access, as Chapter 3 explains. (You can also press ⌘+T.)

- **Move to Trash.** This option moves any item highlighted in the Finder to the Trash (in effect deleting it). (You can also press ⌘+Delete.)

- **Eject.** Before you can remove CDs, DVDs, external disks, thumb drives, server volumes, and the like from the Mac, you must eject them. Failure to do so can corrupt their data. (You can also press ⌘+E. For a CD or DVD, you can also press the Eject key if your keyboard has this key.) When the icon has disappeared from the desktop, it is safe to disconnect, shut off, or remove the disk.

- **Burn.** This option is used to record selected items to recordable CDs and DVDs. You will be asked to insert a recordable disc if none is present in your Mac's SuperDrive. (If nothing is selected, the option becomes Burn Desktop to Disc.)

- **Find.** The Find option opens a search window and places the cursor in the Search box at the top so you can type in a search term. If a Finder window is active, this menu option changes it to a search window. Chapter 3 explains the Spotlight search technology this menu option invokes. (You can also press ⌘+F.)

- **Label.** You can color any item in the Finder by choosing one of the swatches here. If the item's icon doesn't use a generic icon, only the color behind the item's name gets the label color; otherwise, both the icon and the name are colored. You might color items to visually categorize them, such as by making urgent items orange or personal items purple.

The Edit menu

The Edit menu offers a lot of options you can use to manipulate items in the Finder. The options are as follows:

- **Undo.** This menu option reverses, or undoes, the last task performed in the Finder. (As an aid, the menu option specifies undo action, such as Undo Move of "2009 budget.xls".) When you choose Undo, the menu option changes to Redo, which lets you in effect cancel the undo. (You can also press ⌘+Z.) Note that not all actions can be undone; the menu option becomes Can't Undo and is grayed out in such cases.

- **Cut.** This option cuts the selected items (including text or graphics), putting them in the Pasteboard so they can be pasted elsewhere. Note that if you do not paste the items, they are not deleted. (You can also press ⌘+X.)

- **Copy.** This option copies the selected items into the Pasteboard so they can be pasted elsewhere. (You can also press ⌘+C.)

- **Paste.** This option pastes the last-copied or last-cut items into the current Finder window (or into the desktop if no Finder window is open). (You can also press ⌘+V.)

Note

The Pasteboard is the name for Mac OS X's temporary holding bin. The last item or set of items that you cut or copied are stored in the Pasteboard so they can be pasted elsewhere. They are automatically removed from the Pasteboard the next time you cut or copy items (including text or graphics).

- **Select All.** This option selects all the items in the active Finder window or, if no window is active, in the desktop. (You can also press ⌘+A.)

- **Show Clipboard.** When you use the Cut or Copy commands, the item you are cutting or copying is sent to the Clipboard. Choosing the Show Clipboard option opens a window in the Finder to reveal what is currently held in the Clipboard. If the last item copied or cut was text or a graphic, the window shows the text or graphic. If the last item copied or cut was a file, folder, or disk, the item's name is displayed in the Clipboard window.

- **Special Characters.** This option opens the Character Palette, from which you can choose special characters, as Chapter 22 explains.

The View menu

The View menu provides a number of commands you can use to control how the information inside windows is displayed. Some of the commands offered include:

- **As Icons, As List, As Columns,** and **As Cover Flow.** These menu options change how information is displayed in the Finder window, as Chapter 3 explains.

- **Clean Up.** This option tidies up the icons inside a Finder window, arranging them into a neat grid as specified by the Finder's View Options settings (see Chapter 3). If no window is active, it tidies up the icons on the desktop.

- **Arrange By.** The Arrange By option enables you to sort the items in a window (or on the desktop) according to their name, date, size, kind, or label.

- **Show/Hide Path Bar.** The path bar appears at the bottom of the Finder window and shows where the current location is in relation to the rest of the Finder. This option shows or hides it, depending on whether it is already visible.

- **Show/Hide Status Bar.** The status bar gives information about the files inside a Finder window. It is only available if the toolbar (Chapter 3) is not visible. This option shows or hides the status bar, depending on whether it is already visible.

- **Show/Hide Sidebar.** The Sidebar appears on the left side of a Finder window, and provides shortcuts to a variety of volumes, places, and commonly used folders. Chapter 3 has more information on the Sidebar.

- **Show/Hide Toolbar.** The toolbar appears at the top of a Finder window and provides buttons for forward and backward navigation, different view options, and a text box for searching through text, as Chapter 3 explains. (You can also press Option+⌘+T.)

- **Show View Options.** This option opens the View Options dialog box that lets you fine-tune the appearance of individual Finder windows and the items inside them. The view options are covered in Chapter 3. (You can also press ⌘+J.)

The Go menu

The Go menu gives you a range of options for navigating through the Finder. Options include:

- **Back** and **Forward.** As you navigate through windows, you may find it useful to go back to previous locations, and then later forward to the locations you were at — similar to how you navigate in a Web browser. You can also press ⌘+[to go back and ⌘+] to go forward, or use the iconic buttons in the Finder window's toolbar.

- **Enclosing folder.** When you are in icon view, you can quickly move into folders by double-clicking them. This command does the reverse, taking you out of the current folder and into the folder above it in the file structure. (You can also press ⌘+↑.)

- **Locations.** The Go menu has seven menu options that let you quickly move to standard Finder locations (they're also usually in the Finder window's Sidebar). One is Computer (Shift+⌘+C), which shows you all disks connected to the Mac. Another is Network (Shift+⌘+CN), which shows you all network-accessible computers and volumes. Two are system folders for the current user account: Home (Shift+⌘+H) and Desktop (Shift+⌘+D). Two are folders common to all user accounts: Applications (Shift+⌘+A) and Utilities (Shift+⌘+U). The seventh one is iDisk, which has submenus for My iDisk (Shift+⌘+I), Other User's iDisk, and Other User's Public Folder; Chapter 15 explains iDisk and the MobileMe service it is part of.

- **Recent Folders.** The Recent Folders submenu shows the ten most recently visited folders. This is useful for quickly going back to a folder you were looking at. The Clear Menu option, which removes all the items in the list, appears at the bottom of the submenu.

- **Go to Folder.** The Go to Folder option opens a dialog box in which you type in the exact path of the folder you want to navigate to. For example, the Documents folder is found in /Users/username/Documents. (Note that you don't have to match the destination folder's capitalization.) Press Return after entering the pathname and a Finder window opens for it. (You can also use the keyboard shortcut Shift+⌘+G to open the Go to Folder dialog box.) Users familiar with Unix and MS-DOS environments will have experience with this form of folder navigation, but most people will prefer to stick with the Finder windows for navigation.

- **Connect to Server.** This option opens the Connect to Server dialog box, which enables you to connect to another computer or server by entering the server address. You can also click Browse to search for available servers, click the + iconic button to add a server to the Favorites list for easy access later, or click the clock-shaped iconic menu to get a list of recently visited servers. (You can also use the shortcut ⌘+K to open the Connect to Server dialog box.)

Tip

An easy way to see and access available servers is to select the All item in the Finder window's Sidebar, in its Shared section.

The Window menu

The Window menu has these options:

- **Minimize.** This option shrinks the active Finder window into the right-hand side of the Dock, as explained earlier in this chapter. (You can also press ⌘+M.)

- **Zoom.** This option toggles a Finder window's size between Full Size and its previous size. (You can resize a window by using the resize control, as explained earlier in this chapter, so that the previous size can vary from window to window.)

- **Cycle through Windows.** This option opens the next open Finder window. Each time you choose it, the menu option advances down the list of open widows, then goes back through the list from the top if you keep choosing it. (You can also press ⌘+`.)

- **Bring All to Front.** This option brigs all Finder windows to the fore, on top of any application and document windows that may be obscuring them.

Plus, a list of all open Finder windows appears at the bottom of the menu.

The Help menu

As with all other applications, the Help menu includes a search box you can use to look for information about the Finder, and to quickly locate items in the Finder's menu structure. The Mac Help option opens a window with help topics you can browse or search.

Interacting with items

Whether item's icons are displayed on the desktop or in the Finder, and regardless of whether you look at them in list view or icon view, they can be interacted with in a similar fashion (with the exception of icons in the Dock, which act slightly differently, as outlined earlier in the chapter).

Knowing how to interact with items in the Finder and desktop forms the basis of your interaction with the Mac OS X environment. (Note that in other chapters we expand on some of the areas covered here.)

Selecting items

The beauty of the Mac OS X GUI is its simplicity, which enables most people to intuitively use the system. To select an item, you simply click the icon with the mouse. In Mac OS X, an item that you have selected is highlighted. The item's icon is surrounded with an opaque box that often looks gray against a white background. The text that accompanies the icon is highlighted. (The default color is blue, although you can change this in the Appearance system preference, as Chapter 21 explains).

Selecting items with the keyboard

Selecting items may seem instinctively trivial, but seasoned Mac users know that there are multiple ways of selecting items that can prove useful.

One such way is to use the arrow keys to move from one icon to another. Alternatively you can start typing the name of an item in a folder and the highlight will jump to the appropriate item as you type. You do not need to type in the whole name of the desired item; the highlight jumps from item to item alphabetically and according to the letters you type. This method is particularly useful if you have a folder with lots of items in it and know a specific item you are looking for.

You can also move through items alphabetically by pressing the Tab key (and reverse-alphabetically by pressing Shift+Tab). Typically, the items are sorted alphabetically so this takes you forward and backward through the items in order. However, if you have arranged the items by a different sort (by date, size, kind, or label, for example) you still can move through the items alphabetically. Note that pressing Tab does not work when you are in column view.

Table 2.1 provides a handy reference for different ways to select items via keyboard commands:

TABLE 2.1

Selecting Items with Keyboard Commands

Keyboard Letters	Resulting Name of Item According to Keys Pressed
↑ or ↓	The item above, or below, the currently highlighted item.
← or →	The item to the left or right of the current item on the desktop, or in icon view. Note that in list view, the left and right arrows expand and contract folders.
Tab	The next alphabetical item in the list.
Shift+Tab	The previous alphabetical item in the list.

Selecting multiple items

Clicking an item selects it, while deselecting the item that was previously highlighted. Thus, only one item is highlighted at a time. However, there are many occasions in Mac OS X when selecting multiple items is desirable (typically for moving or deleting a range of items). There are several methods of selecting different items, and the methods available often depend upon which view mode you have selected in a Finder window. Here are some of the methods available:

- **Command+click.** Using the ⌘ key enables you to select multiple items. Hold down the ⌘ key and click multiple items to select them (selected items have the highlight around them). With the ⌘ key held down you can also deselect items. This method works in every Finder mode and on the desktop.

- **Click+drag.** You can also select multiple items by holding down the mouse and dragging the pointer across several items. This method works differently depending on where you are.

  On the desktop, or in a Finder window displaying in icon view, you click an area that does not contain an item and drag the mouse diagonally while holding down the mouse button. This creates an opaque rectangle (known as a *marquee*), and any items within the rectangle when you release the mouse button are selected.

  When you are in column view or Cover Flow view, the selection dragging works slightly differently. You click the white space around an icon or its accompanying text and then drag the mouse over the items you view by dragging.

- **Shift+clicking.** Another method of highlighting a range of files is to hold down the Shift key and click the first and last item in a range. This highlights all the items between the two points. This method is useful for highlighting a lot of items in a list without having to individually select them all, or having to Click+drag across a large area to select all the desired items.

  Shift+clicking works only when you are in list, column, or Cover Flow view. (These views are explained in more depth later in this chapter.) When you are in icon view, or working on the desktop, Shift+clicking selects individual items in the same way as ⌘+clicking.

Note

Selecting multiple items in list view can be confusing because you can highlight individual items and the folders that they are contained within. If you have selected two items and the containing folder above them in the list, then copying the items copies the entire folder and all the items inside.

Using Quick Look to view file contents

As we mention earlier, an icon is sometimes a snapshot of the actual documents contents, such as a photo or movie clip. This is possible because Mac OS X uses powerful graphical rendering technology and has substantial previewing technology that can look inside a file without opening the file itself. That technology enables a feature called Quick Look.

If you highlight a file and press the spacebar, an opaque window opens and shows you the file contents. (You can also Control+click or right-click an item and choose Quick Look from the contextual menu,) This works for just about every type of file imaginable — Word documents, PDF files, images, even music and movie files — without having to open the corresponding application. If you select another item, you get its Quick Look preview; to stop seeing previews, click the Close button in the preview window or press Esc. When you start working with Quick Look, you'll wonder how you ever lived without it.

Tip

At the bottom of the Quick Look preview window is the Full Screen iconic button; click it to expand the preview to the full desktop dimensions. When the preview is at full size, two iconic buttons are available: Exit Full Screen, which returns to the original preview size, and Close, which closes the preview.

Moving and copying items

After you've selected a few items, you are likely to want to move them around (or move them to the Trash to delete them). To move the files you simply select them by using any of the methods outlined previously, and then click and drag them to their new location. This can be to the desktop (or another part of the desktop) or another location inside a Finder window. You can drag items into empty parts of the Finder or desktop, or drag them to the top of a folder, in which case they will be placed within the folder.

Tip

If you are working in list or icon view, hover a selected item over a folder for a few seconds and that folder opens to expose its contents. (Apple calls this capability spring-loaded folders.) This lets you drill down through folders while an item is selected so you can move that item several levels deep in the folder hierarchy. Drag the item outside the folder window if you've drilled down too far or to the wrong location, so you can start over again.

You can drag an item by clicking either its icon or the title underneath the icon. In list view, you can click and drag on any part of the file information on the horizontal line, and in Cover Flow view, you can either drag the item or any part of the horizontal bar or drag the large preview of the item in the Cover Flow area.

When you drag an item to a folder, it is surrounded by a dark opaque area (like a more pronounced version of the highlight around the item itself); this indicates that the folder is the destination area if you release the mouse. When you drag an item over a blank area in a Finder window, the border of the window is highlighted with a blue line — this indicates that the folder is the destination if you release the mouse.

Tip

To copy an item to a folder, rather than move it, hold Option while dragging the item to its new destination.

After releasing the mouse button, the item is moved from its original location to the new one. The exception to this is if you are moving a file from one volume to another. In this case, the file is not moved, but copied to the destination. When you try to move a file from one volume to another, the mouse pointer's icon changes to an image of a green circle with a plus sign (+) in the middle of it. This indicates that the file will be copied, not moved.

Tip

To move an item to another volume, rather than copy it, hold Option while dragging the item to its new destination.

Replacing items

If you move or copy an item (a file or folder) into a folder that contains an item with the same name, you receive a warning dialog box, asking you if you want to replace the file in the destination folder (see Figure 2.23). This is because Mac OS X cannot have two items with the same name in the same location. Typically, the presence of two items with the same name suggests that the same item has been duplicated. In this case, the warning dialog box gives you an indication as to which item is newer. If you click the Replace button, the file you are dragging replaces the file in the selected destination.

You should be careful before replacing an item because it is very difficult to recover the item you overwrite — in fact, it's usually not possible. Instead of being sent to the Trash, the item you are replacing is removed completely. If you are unsure which item you want to keep (or if you want to keep both files), you can click the Stop button to prevent the item in the destination file from being overwritten. Then you can either look at the items to see which one is no longer needed, or you can rename one of the items to ensure that both can sit happily in the same location.

FIGURE 2.23

Moving or copying an item to a location that has an item with the same name produces this warning.

If you are moving or copying multiple items, you may also have the option of replacing all duplicate items or just selected duplicate items. In that case, the warning dialog box now has three buttons, Don't Replace, Stop, and Replace, and an Apply to All option (see Figure 2.24). To replace all items in the destinations whose names match the ones you are moving or copying, select Apply to All and click Replace; to keep all the originals at the destination, select Apply to All and click Don't Replace. Otherwise, the warning dialog box takes you through each of the individual items you are trying to move or copy that have duplicates at the destination, and you click Don't Replace or Replace, as appropriate for each item in turn.

Tip

Clicking the Stop button stops any items from being moved or copied, including those that don't have duplicated versions in the destination folder.

FIGURE 2.24

Moving or copying a selection of items to a location with duplicate items produces this warning. You can choose whether or not to replace individual items, or select the Apply to All option and then click either Replace or Don't Replace to handle all duplicate items the same way.

Using Undo to Move an Item Back

Sometimes, when moving or replacing a folder or a file, you decide that it would be better off the way it was. In this case, you can restore the item to its original location by choosing Edit⇨Undo in the Finder or pressing ⌘+Z. But if you replaced an item, the Undo command does not recover the item that was replaced; it is gone for good. (The Undo command just moves the other item back to its original location. After using the Undo command, the Undo option in the Edit menu is replaced with a Redo option, which if chosen reverses the undo operation.

The Undo command works only on the last action in the Finder, and you cannot perform multiple Undo commands in the Finder (as you can in some applications).

Replicating items

There are times when you need to create an identical copy of an item. Perhaps you want to make changes to a copy of a file while preserving the original, or to copy the file from one place to another. During this process, you typically use the Copy and Duplicate commands; in this case, the two commands are, for all intents and purposes, interchangeable.

To duplicate an item, select it and choose File⇨Duplicate in the Finder or press ⌘+D. Or Control+click or right-click an item and choose Duplicate from its contextual menu. A duplicate of the item is placed in the same location in the Finder as the original; the duplicate has the text "copy" added to the end of the filename. If the highlighted item is a folder, the folder and everything in it is duplicated. Additional duplicates will have numbers added to the end of the filename: "copy 2," "copy 3," and so on.

Another way to replicate a file or folder is to use the Copy command with the Paste command. The notion of copying and pasting is familiar to people who have used word processors.

The key difference between using Copy and Paste versus Duplicate is that Duplicate replicates the item in the same location in the Finder, but amends its name; Copy and Paste, on the other hand, replicates the item with the same name but in a different location in the Finder.

To copy an item, select the desired item, then choose Edit⇨Copy in the Finder and press ⌘+C, or Control+click or right-click it and choose Copy from its contextual menu. Now navigate in the Finder to the location that you desire the copy to be placed and choose Edit⇨Paste, press ⌘+V, or Control+click or right-click an empty area in the destination and choose Paste in the contextual menu. If you paste the item in the same location as the original, Mac OS X adds a number to the end of the item's name, starting with 2 and increasing the number for each subsequent paste.

Tip

A fast way to copy an item from one location to another is to press and hold the Option key and then drag the file to a new location. As you drag the file, the pointer turns into a green plus sign (+), indicating that you are copying the file. Release the mouse at the destination to make the copy, then release the Option key.

Note that it is not possible to copy and paste a folder within itself, or within one of its subfolders. Any attempt to do so brings up an error message.

Renaming items

You can rename items in the Finder so they better serve your organizational needs. For example, you may want to add "version 2" to the end of a filename to identify that it is an updated version of something, or you may simply want to rename a file so it is more readily identifiable; for example, change Picture 2 to Zoe's Birthday Cake.

Changing filenames (and folder names) is something you will do on a regular basis in Mac OS X. However, some filenames are best left unchanged. Documents and folders containing documents can be changed with impunity; however, application files and system folders should be left alone. Some important files and folders cannot be changed (for example, most folders sitting in the root level of your main hard disk resist any attempts to change them). However, applications and system folders inside your Home folder can be changed, — although we advise you not to do so in case you need to locate files during troubleshooting.

You can rename entire volumes, such as your hard disks, with complete freedom, and indeed it is often wise to rename your hard disks to something memorable. Be warned, though, that renaming hard disks may interfere with aliases.

Tip

In Mac OS X, you can rename only one file at a time. If you find you regularly have to rename a lot of files (or example, those created by a digital camera), use the Automator utility that comes with Mac OS to create a rename workflow so you can batch-rename files easily. Chapter 25 covers the Automator. If you're not afraid to use Unix, you can use command lines in the Terminal to batch-rename items as well, as Chapter 26 explains.

Users migrating from Microsoft Windows will undoubtedly look for a contextual menu option called Rename. However, Mac OS X has no equivalent contextual menu option. To rename an item, you must highlight its current name by using one of the following methods, in order from least preferred to most preferred:

- **Click the name twice.** This method requires a pause between clicks — do *not* double-click the item, as that opens it. You first click an item's name, pause for a fraction of a second, and then click again on the name.

- **Select the item and press the Return key.** In this method, you first highlight an item and press the Return key. This highlights the text in the item and you will be able to rename it. But be careful: A slip of the finger and whatever else you type replaces the current name.

- **Select the item and click the item name.** After selecting the item, click its name once.

If the filename has an extension, such as .txt, only the file part of the filename is highlighted, not the extension. That's so you don't change the file type accidentally. You should avoid changing the filename extension because doing so can cause the file to open in a different application, or not at all.

After you've highlighted the filename, either type new text (which replaces the existing text), or edit the existing filename. To edit the existing text, click in the text where you want to begin editing, or navigate to that location by using the ↑ and ← keys. When the text cursor is at the desired location, delete unwanted characters with the Delete and Delete ⌦ keys and type in new text — just as you would in a word processor.

Tip

You can even paste in text, as well as copy and cut text by using the standard shortcuts: ⌘+V, ⌘+C, and ⌘+X, respectively. Or you can use the standard menu options: Edit ⇨ Paste, Edit ⇨ Copy, and Edit ⇨ Cut. You can also delete selected text by using the Delete and Delete ⊗ keys; such deleted text is not saved on the Clipboard and so cannot be pasted elsewhere.

When done replacing or editing the text, either press Return or simply click elsewhere in the Finder to complete the renaming.

If you decide that you do not want to rename the item after you have selected the text, press Esc to restore the original name. If you have changed the name and want to return to the original name, use the Undo command (choose Edit ⇨ Undo or press ⌘+Z). See Table 2.2 for a list of keyboard commands you can use when renaming files.

TABLE 2.2

Keyboard Commands for Selecting Text	
↑	Moves the insertion point to the beginning of the name when it is first selected, and up one line thereafter.
↓	Moves the insertion point to the end of the name when it is first selected, and down one line thereafter.
←	Moves the insertion point to the beginning of the name when it is first selected, and to the left one character thereafter.
→	Moves the insertion point to the end of the name when it is first selected, and to the right one character thereafter.
Option+←, Option+→	Moves the insertion point one word to the right or left.
Shift+←, Option+→	Selects more (or less) of the name to the right or left.

Understanding naming conventions

Mac OS X is very versatile when it comes to renaming files. A filename can be up to 255 characters long and contain most characters and symbols imaginable. Having said that, the same isn't true of Windows computers, which are not so forgiving of imaginative filenames. If you ever plan to share, or access, your files on a Windows-based computer, you should stick to a few conventions:

- **Avoid special characters.** Avoid using bullet points (•) and currency symbols, such as the euro (€). Also avoid any odd characters such as the infinity symbol (∞). This is because other operating systems may not be able to render these symbols correctly, and consequently the file may not open.

- **Don't use colons.** Do not use colons (:) in character names. This is because Mac OS X uses the colon character internally to specify the path through the folder structure. For example, the Documents folder is located in `Macintosh HD:Users:username:Documents`. (In an actual path, *username* is replaced by the name of your user account.) Using colons in your filenames interferes with this file structure, so Mac OS X will not allow you to use colons in your filenames.

- **Don't use slashes.** Although Mac OS X forbids you from using colons in filenames, it permits you to use the forward slash (/) and backslash (\) characters. However, we strongly encourage you to never use slash characters in your filenames. That's because Windows uses the slash characters to indicate the file structure, in the same way that the colon character is used by Mac OS X, so Mac files whose names include slashes will not work on a Windows PC.

- **Do use common characters.** Except for :, /, and \, it's fine to use the characters on a keyboard that you access by pressing the keys or by holding and pressing Shift with the keys. All alphabetical characters, whether uppercase or lowercase, are acceptable, as are numerical (0 through 9) characters and any symbols in the numbers row. Also acceptable are blank spaces, hyphens (–), underscores (_) and commas (,).

Note
Periods (.) are acceptable in filenames, but they can cause some mischief: Because the filename extension follows a period, some programs can't tell what part of the filename has the extension if there are multiple periods in the filename, and they end up cutting off part of the name (often the actual filename extension). This is usually an issue only when trading files between Macs and Windows PCs.

Getting info on files

As well as the filename itself, Mac OS X keeps a great deal of information about files, folders, and disks. All this information goes far beyond what appears on the desktop. This information could be the size of the file on the hard disk, the location within the file structure, and the date it was created or modified, and any Spotlight information.

At some point you will want to take a closer look at some of the information about an item, and you may need to change some of the information associated with an item. For this, you need to use the Info window (also known as the Get Info window, or just Get Info). The Info window displays a variety of information about the files, folders, and other items displayed in the Finder and is well worth getting to know in depth.

To access the Info window, simply highlight an item in the Finder and choose File ⇨ Get Info or press ⌘+I. You can also Control+click or right-click the item and choose Get Info from the contextual menu. Figure 2.25 shows the Info window.

FIGURE 2.25

The Info window has several sections of information about an item. Use the disclosure triangles to collapse and expand those sections. There are also some controls over what application is set to open the file type by default and over sharing of the file with other users.

The anatomy of the Info window's sections is as follows.

Icon and summary

At the top of the Info window is a preview of the item's icon, as well as the item's filename, its size, and the date it was last modified. You can copy and paste icon previews from one Info window to another, as well as copy icons from pretty much any graphic into an Info window. You might do so to give favorite files and folders custom icons.

Spotlight comments

Spotlight is Mac OS X's technology for searching throughout files, folders, and application data in Mac OS X. You can populate this field in the Info window with any information that you want, and Spotlight associates this information to the file. For example, you can add the names of people to images of them by using this field; then when you search for them by name, using Spotlight, it returns these images in its results. Spotlight is covered in depth in Chapter 3.

General

The General section contains the bulk of the information pertaining to an item. The information presented changes, depending on the nature of the item highlighted in the Finder. But files, folders, and disks all have the following information: kind, creation date, last-modified date, and label. Files and folders also have location (Where) information, while disks also have total capacity, available capacity, and used capacity information.

Note

A label is a color you can associate to an item as a way to distinguish different kinds of items from each other based on your own criteria; you can select a label color in the Info window, or select an item and choose File and then a color swatch in the Label area of the menu.

The General section also has one or two options, depending on the item type that you can select or deselect to change the item's status:

- **Shared Folder.** This option appears when the Info window relates to a volume or folders. If the Shared Folder option is selected, the folder will be available to whomever has appropriate file-sharing privileges as indicated in the Sharing & Permissions section of the Info window. (Chapter 13 explains how to share files.)

- **Stationery Pad.** Available only for files, the Stationery Pad option, if selected, means the file is a template, so if you open it and save it, a copy is saved instead, leaving the original file untouched.

- **Locked.** Available for disks and folders only; if this option is selected, items cannot be added, renamed, or deleted unless you either enter an administrator password or deselect Locked in the Info window. (A lock icon appears on the folder or disk if Locked is selected.) Note that the Locked status is not that strong: You can open items in the folder or disk, edit them, and save them. And you can add, rename, or delete items in the folder's or disk's subfolders.

More Info

The More Info section of the Info window presents detailed information about the item. As with the General window, this varies depending upon the item in question. Image files, for example, have information relating to the dimensions of the image, its color space, profile name, alpha channel, and when it was last opened. Word documents may have information on when they were created and modified. HTML documents may have the `<title>` tag information displayed. Music files may have artist, genre, and track information displayed.

Name & Extension

The name of the current file appears in the Name & Extensions section, and you can select the name and change it. You can also hide or show the filename extension by selecting or deselecting the Hide Extension option.

Open With

Available for files only, this section has a popup menu from which you choose which application opens the file automatically when you double-click it. This change affects only the current file, unless you click the Change All button as well, in which case all files of this type are opened with the new application specified in the popup menu. Note that Mac OS X tries to limit the options in the popup menu to those that are comparable with the file type, but it may include incompatible options as well. If you select an incompatible option, you will get an error message when you open the file by double-clicking it, letting you know the file is not compatible with the application.

Preview

The Preview area of the Info window shows a small graphic displaying the contents of the item, if available. For folders and disks, the preview is simply a larger version of the icon at the top of the Info window. For graphics, you usually see the actual graphic. For movies and audio files, you see the movie poster or album cover if available and a generic icon if not. If you move the mouse pointer over the preview image, a play button appears. Click it to play the file; the button then turns into a stop button you can click to stop playing the file.

Sharing & Permissions

Sharing and the permissions is a complex business that is explained in Chapter 13. After you've set up who has permissions to share files on your Mac, you can change those permissions on individual items in this section of the Info window. Below the Sharing & Permissions label, Mac OS X displays your permissions for the item, such as "You can only read" or "You can read and write."

As a general rule, the creator of an item is its owner. That person can choose to share the file with others. But a Mac's administrator also has rights to change sharing permissions no matter which user account is active. To change permissions, first click the bronze lock iconic button at the bottom right of the Info window and enter the administrator's or owner's password. This makes the Sharing & Permissions settings available to be changed.

First, choose a name or group whose permissions you want to change from the Name list. Then choose a permissions level from the adjoining popup menu in the Privilege list. There are two or three choices, depending on the item type: Read & Write, Read Only, and Write Only (Drop Box). The Write Only (Drop Box) permission is available only for disks and folders.

You can add and delete users by clicking the + and – iconic buttons, and choose to apply your changes to all folders within the selected disk or folder by choosing Apply to Enclosed Items from the gear iconic popup menu. (This can take several minutes to complete, so be warned.) And you can undo your changes by choosing Revert Changes from the same gear iconic popup menu.

Finally, for nonstartup disks only, you can select the Ignore Ownership on This Volume option. If selected, any user account is considered to be the disk's owner and thus has all the privileges assigned to an owner. In the Name list, look for the user account that has "(Me)" following its name; that's the current owner, and those are the permissions everyone gets when this option is selected — handy for a shared drive of, say, family photos you pass around. If the Ignore Ownership on This Volume option is deselected, then people who access the drive from their user accounts will have the access permissions set for their specific user account in the Info window.

Using Gestures

One of the more recent additions to Mac OS X is a technology called Multi-Touch. This technology applies to finger-operating interface devices, specifically the trackpads on Mac laptops and Apple devices that use touch screens (the iPod touch and iPhone, for example).

As its name suggests, Multi-Touch lets you use multiple fingers to interact with the device. This technology is relatively new and is being popularized by Apple.

Understanding which Macs support gestures

Whether you can use Multi-Touch to interact with Mac OS X, and the kinds of Multi-Touch commands that are available to you, depends on which Mac you own. Desktop Macs, such as the iMac, Mac Pro, and Mac mini do not come with trackpads and, because there are no options to buy a plug-in trackpad (at least as of when this book went to press), the Multi-Touch technology doesn't apply to them. But Apple's MacBook and MacBook Pro laptops come with Multi-Touch trackpads, though with different levels of capability depending on when they were produced. The oldest supported models support two-finger input; all models from 2008 support four-finger input.

New Feature

Previously, some models of the MacBook Pro and MacBook Air only supported three-finger gestures, and the four-finger gestures were only available to owners of MacBook and MacBook Pro laptops with the new glass trackpad. In Mac OS X 10.6 Snow Leopard, these older MacBook Pro and MacBook Air laptops can now take advantage of four-finger gestures.

Note

Apple began referring to the technology as Multi-Touch only in 2006, when it became possible to use more than two fingers and to perform complex movements (such as Pinch Open & Close). However, before then, MacBook and MacBook Pro laptops' trackpads did support the use of a simple two-finger gesture to perform the equivalent of right-clicking with a mouse.

One way to determine the level of Multi-Touch input you have is to choose ⇨ System Preferences and go to the Trackpad system preference. On the left-hand side of the system preference is a list of options divided into categories labeled One Finger, Two Fingers, and so on (see Figure 2.26). By looking at these options, you can determine which Multi-Touch commands are available to you. Apple has also provides some short video clips accessible from the system preference that demonstrate how the Multi-Touch gestures work. For more information on the Trackpad system preference, see Chapter 21.

New Feature

Mac OS X 10.6 Snow Leopard has expanded Multi-Touch gesture interface to developers, enabling them to quickly add support for Multi-Touch in their own applications. Some applications, such as Adobe Create Suite 4 and Firefox 3.1 already supported Multi-Touch (because the developers had created the control interface), but in Mac OS X 10.6 Snow Leopard, many other applications should be able to support the feature.

FIGURE 2.26

The Trackpad system preference is a great way to become familiar with the Multi-Touch options available on your Mac.

Controlling Mac OS X with more than one finger

Apple has created several stock Multi-Touch gestures that can be used throughout the operating system and in various programs:

- **Two-finger click.** Place two fingers on the trackpad and press the button with your thumb. This gesture acts like a Control+click or a right-click.

- **Two-finger scroll.** Place two fingers on the trackpad and move both fingers up and down (or left and right). This gesture scrolls the active window, and is the equivalent of moving the scrollbars to the right or bottom of the window.

- **Two-finger rotate.** Place two fingers (or your index finger and thumb) on the trackpad and rotate clockwise or counterclockwise. This gesture typically applies to images opened in graphics applications, such as Preview and iPhoto, to rotate images.

- **Pinch Open and Close.** This gesture is used to zoom in and out, as well as to enlarge and shrink items. Place two fingers (typically the thumb and index finger) on the trackpad and move them apart to expand an item, and pinch them together to shrink it. The same gestures increase and decrease the size of icons on the desktop.

- **Screen zoom.** This is another two-finger gesture. Press and hold Control+Option+⌘, then place two fingers on the trackpad and scroll up to zoom in or down to zoom out. If you move the mouse around the screen at the same time, the zoom's center follows the mouse.

- **Three-finger swipe.** This gesture involves placing three fingers on the trackpad and moving them quickly to the left or right. You typically do it to invoke the Back and Forward commands, such as in the Safari Web browser. You can also use it to move back and forward through folders in a Finder window.

- **Four-finger swipe (up and down).** This gesture provides access to Exposé's All Windows and Show Desktop capabilities (see Chapter 21). You place all four fingers on the trackpad and swipe them quickly up or down. Swiping four fingers up shows all the windows open in Mac OS X; swiping the four fingers down moves all the windows off the side of the screen to reveal the desktop.

- **Four-finger swipe (left and right).** This gesture enables you to quickly switch between open applications. Place all four fingers on the trackpad and quickly swipe them left or right to open the Application Switcher (which shows icons for all active applications in an opaque horizontal bar across the center of the window). Use the mouse to select the application you want to switch to. (This gesture is the same as pressing ⌘+Tab.)

Learning to use Multi-Touch effectively can enable you to work on a Mac laptop much faster, and the process is often more intuitive than using a mouse.

Summary

Starting up the Mac is as easy as pressing the power button, but more sophisticated capabilities exist when you need them, such as the ability to start up from different disks and to require login so only authorized users can access the Mac. This combination of simplicity and rich capabilities extends to the Mac's option to go to sleep, restart, and shut down, as well as to switch among authorized users.

A key distinguishing feature of Mac OS X is its GUI, which sets the standard for ease of use. Mac OS X has four main GUI components that users interact with: the menu bar, Dock, desktop, and Finder. They let you not only personalize the Mac, but get extraordinary control over the manipulation and use of applications, files, folders, and disks. The menu bar provides access to both applications' and Mac OS X's commands via the mouse; the Dock provides quick access to applications, document windows, and files and folders; the desktop provides a simple starting point you can also use to hold items of your choice; and the Finder lets you navigate and work with files, folders, and disks.

The extensive use of keyboard shortcuts and contextual menus makes it easy to initiate actions at times when navigating the menu bar can be inefficient. Furthermore, the Mac's consistent use of controls such as buttons and dialog boxes — plus its conventions for using windows as containers for applications and documents — makes using the Mac and your Mac OS applications much easier after you learn the basics. Yet Mac OS X also supports extensive customization of the environment, so you can fine-tune it to your work style.

Mac OS X also provides lots of helpful functions, such as Quick Look and Get Info, that provide extra context about the items you're working with. And its innovative use of finger-based gestures on recent laptops' trackpads extends its sophisticated ease of use into a new interface realm.

Using the Finder and Searching with Spotlight

Mac OS X contains two very powerful tools that enable you to manage and locate files stored on your Mac's hard disk. The first, an application called the Finder, is used to locate, adjust, and move files around the Mac OS X. Because the Finder application is the most commonly used tool in Mac OS X, we outlined it in Chapter 2 as an example of how menus, buttons, and windows work in a Mac OS X application. In this chapter, we examine the Finder in action and how it can be put to practical use.

The second Mac OS X feature we look at is called Spotlight. This technology was first introduced in Mac OS X 10.4 Tiger and has revolutionized the way people interact with their Macs. Spotlight helps you discover files, folders, and information contained throughout the Mac OS X at blistering speed.

Searching with Spotlight can be either extremely simple or very sophisticated. Spotlight can search for files and folders by name, in much the same way that traditional search tools have operated on computers for countless years. It can also search for combinations of other attributes, such as a file's size, creator, modification date, and label color.

Where Spotlight starts to get clever is when it's searching through files themselves. Spotlight can look through the contents of Word documents, PDF (Portable Document Format) files, and even the metadata attached to music and image files. Spotlight even searches through the information in Mac OS X's built-in applications, such as your e-mail messages, contacts, and calendar events. You'll quickly find yourself turning to Spotlight not just to find information that you've lost, but also to quickly access e-mails, people, and documents without diving through the Finder. You can even open applications by just typing in the first part of an application name and pressing Enter.

Indeed, so successful is Spotlight at finding files and information, many Mac users are no longer as careful at managing files with the Finder as they used to be, knowing that Spotlight will help them find whatever they are looking for no matter how disorganized their hard drive structure has become.

While highly organized Mac OS X users may look on in dismay at the virtual flotsam and jetsam crammed on some user's computers, it's comforting to note that Macs can be used efficiently by all users, regardless of how organized they are.

Whatever your level of personal efficiency is, the two tools offered by Mac OS X for managing and finding data on your Mac are a powerful combination. In this chapter, we'll take a close look at what both tools can do.

Opening and Using Finder Windows

You typically navigate the myriad of files and folders in Mac OS X via a Finder window. It is a visual representation of the files and folders contained within the various disks on your computer. It presents the information in a variety of different ways, some straightforward, others more abstract. A standard Finder window (see Figure 3.1) is a good place to start.

You can open a new Finder Window quite a few ways if the Finder is active: Choose File ⇨ New Finder Window, press ⌘+N, or Control+click or right-click the Finder icon in the Dock and choose New Finder Window from the contextual menu. (To make the Finder the active application, click the desktop or click the Finder icon in the Dock.) The new Finder window opens to your Home folder, unless you change the default location in the Finder's Preferences dialog box, as explained later in this chapter.

If you double-click a disk's or folder's icon on the desktop, or click an item in the Sidebar, its Finder window opens. (And if you have several disks and/or folders selected, double-clicking any of them opens them all.) If you ⌘+double-click a folder in an open Finder window, that internal folder is opened in its own Finder window. Likewise, ⌘+clicking a drive or folder in the Sidebar also opens the item in its own Finder window.

You can also see open Finder windows simply by clicking them on the desktop or, if they are minimized to the Dock, by clicking their icon on the Dock.

Tip
Pressing and holding the Option key while clicking a disk or folder in the Sidebar or double-clicking a disk or folder on the desktop closes the current Finder window and opens a new one with the new item's contents.

When you open a Finder window, you are presented with several areas you can use to navigate the files, folders, and volumes on your Mac. The Finder window is designed by Apple to be as intuitive as possible, and you'll use most elements of instinctively. Figure 3.1 shows a Finder window.

FIGURE 3.1

The Finder window is used to view and manage the files and folders on your Mac.

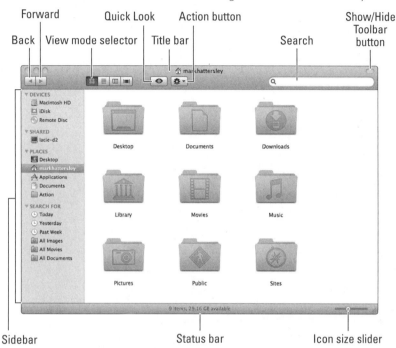

Outside of these buttons, the Finder window is composed of the standard buttons that apply to most windows used by Mac OS X (notably, Close, Minimize, and Zoom); it also sports the sliders and draggable areas outlined in Chapter 2. However, there are also several unique items in a Finder window not available in other windows.

Working with the Sidebar

On the left-hand side of the window is the Sidebar. It contains aliases to common areas on the Mac. The aliases are divided into four sections, each with a disclosure triangle you can use to expand or collapse the area's options: Devices, Shared, Places, and Search For. (The Shared section appears only if your Mac is connected to other computers on the network.)

To use an item in the Sidebar, simply click its icon. For example, in the Places section, icons for the Music and Movies folders appear; clicking these icons takes you immediately to those specific areas in the Finder window.

You can add aliases to your own items from a Finder window or from the desktop to the Sidebar. To do so, simply drag the items to the Sidebar, or select them and then choose File ⇨ Add to Sidebar or press ⌘+T; to remove aliases from the Sidebar, simply drag them out of the Sidebar, or Control+click or right-click them and choose Remove from Sidebar from the contextual menu.

New Feature

If you remove all items under the Devices, Places, or Search For header in the Sidebar, the header disappears, too. If you drag an item into the Sidebar that belongs to one of those headers, the header automatically reappears.

You cannot add new sections to the Sidebar, but you can specify what disks, shared items, places, and searches appear in the Sidebar's sections via the Finder's Preferences dialog box, as explained later in this chapter. First, let's take a look at the areas that make up the Sidebar:

- **Devices.** This section lists hard disks (both internal and external), inserted CDs and DVDs, and iDisk (an Internet volume provided as part of Apple's MobileMe service). If you own a Mac without a built-in DVD drive (such as a MacBook Air), you will also see a Remote Disc option, which enables you to "borrow" an optical drive over a network connection from another computer so you can read data and install programs from an optical disc. (The other Mac must have enabled CD or DVD sharing in the Sharing system preference, as Chapter 13 explains.)

- **Shared.** Computers and shared volumes on the same local area network are listed here. If you have multiple Macs connected to the network, you can remotely search through hard disks and even control the screen on one Mac while working on another. (Creating networks and sharing files and screens are covered in detail in Chapter 13.)

- **Places.** This section organizes the shortcuts to popular destinations on your hard disk. The default areas include the desktop, Documents, Applications, and your Home folder.

- **Search For.** This section includes smart folders (detailed later in the chapter). *Smart folders* are Finder windows that show files based on Spotlight search information you specify, such as all the Word documents on your computer, or all the files containing the term "work." The default items in the Search For section are Today, Yesterday, Past Week, All Images, All Movies, and All Documents.

Looking at the title bar

At the very top of the Finder window is the title bar. It displays a folder, disk, or other icon (depending on what is open) and the name of the folder whose contents are displaying in the Finder window. You can move the window on the desktop by dragging its title bar.

If you ⌘+click, Control+click, or right-click the icon or the folder or disk name in the title bar, a popup menu displays the folder hierarchy, as Figure 3.2 shows. (The folder hierarchy is the list of "parent" folders that traces the path from the current folder to the folder that contains it, and all the way to the topmost level, the root of the volume.) Click one of the folders in the hierarchy to have its contents displayed in the Finder window (it will replace the currently displayed Finder window contents).

Tip

If you Shift+click or Option+click the folder or disk icon, it should be selected; you can then drag the icon elsewhere to copy the folder's, or disk's, contents to wherever you drag the icon to. Note that sometimes the Shift+click or Option+click doesn't select the icon; if that occurs, release the key and the mouse and try again.

FIGURE 3.2

You can discover the path from the current folder or item to the root of the volume — the folder hierarchy — by ⌘+clicking, Control+clicking, or right-clicking the icon or name at the top of a Finder window.

In addition to the standard Close, Minimize, and Zoom iconic buttons at the left side of the title bar (see Chapter 2), the title bar also has the Show/Hide Toolbar iconic button at the far right side. This pill-shaped iconic button controls the display of the toolbar and Sidebar. Clicking it radically changes the look of the Finder window. When the Sidebar and Toolbar are hidden, the Finder window has a much simpler style that some users prefer. However, the compromise is that you will have to access many options offered by the toolbar through the Finder's menus or by learning keyboard shortcuts.

Tip

You can hide just the toolbar for the current window by choosing View ➪ Hide Toolbar or pressing Option+⌘+T. And you can hide just the Sidebar for the current window by choosing View ➪ Hide Sidebar or pressing Option+⌘+S.

Investigating the toolbar

The toolbar is located on the top of the window just below the title bar. It contains several useful iconic buttons that enable you to navigate the Finder and access Finder options without having to go through the Finder's menu. You can change some of the iconic buttons on the toolbar to suit your own purposes, although other iconic buttons are a permanent fixture.

The standard iconic buttons are Back, Forward, View as Icons, View as List, View as Columns, View as Cover Flow, and Quick Look. There's also the Action iconic popup menu and the Spotlight-powered Search field. Here's what these iconic controls do:

- **Back.** Pressing the Back iconic button (the left-facing triangle icon) takes the Finder window to the previous folder or other item that was open, or to the previous viewing mode for that item.

- **Forward.** If you have pressed the Back iconic button, pressing the Forward iconic button (the right-facing arrow icon) returns you to the item or viewing mode that you were originally looking at.

- **View mode selectors.** These four iconic buttons change how the Finder presents its contents, in what are called *view modes* or *list views*: Icons, List, Columns, and Cover Flow. Each icon has a small graphic that depicts how the contents will display in the Finder window. Working in these different view modes is outlined later in this chapter.

- **Quick Look.** Clicking the Quick Look iconic button (the eye icon) enables you to quickly examine the contents of many files and folders. Its function is identical to highlighting an item in the Finder and pressing the spacebar or Control+clicking or right-clicking an item and choosing Quick Look from the contextual menu. (Chapter 7 covers Quick Look.).

- **Action.** The Action iconic popup menu (the gear icon) provides a set of options extremely similar to the contextual menu, and its options change depending on what is highlighted in the Finder.

- **Search field.** Typing into the search field marked with the magnifying glass icon enables you to search for files by using Mac OS X's Spotlight technology. Searching via Spotlight is outlined later in this chapter.

You can change the contents and arrangement of the toolbar by choosing View ➪ Customize Toolbar or by Control+clicking or right-clicking the toolbar and choosing Customize Toolbar from the contextual menu. The Customize Toolbar settings sheet, shown in Figure 3.3, appears.

FIGURE 3.3

You can add, remove, and rearrange buttons in the Finder window by using the Customize Toolbar settings sheet.

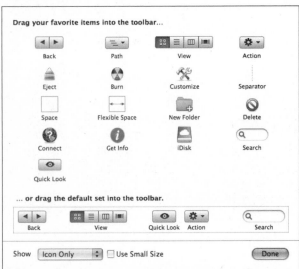

You can perform the following options with the Customize Toolbar settings sheet:

- **Drag your favorite items into the toolbar.** Click and drag any of the iconic buttons from the Customize Toolbar dialog box to the toolbar of the active window to add it as a favorite. The following items are available: Back, Path, View, Action, Eject, Burn, Customize, Separator, Space, Flexible Space, New Folder, Delete, Connect, Get Info, iDisk, Search, and Quick Look. You can add new items to any point on the toolbar, and the other items will spread apart to make room for the new button. If you drag more iconic buttons to the toolbar than can physically fit, then an iconic button displaying two arrows pointing right appears on the right side of the toolbar. Clicking this iconic button displays a popup menu with the hidden iconic buttons. Click Done when you are happy with the selection.

- **Drag the default set into the toolbar.** The default set of iconic buttons offers a good selection of tools without cluttering up the toolbar. If you decide that you want to restore the default icon set, you can drag the complete set from the bottom of the Customize Toolbar window to the toolbar. All the icons currently in the toolbar are replaced with the default set.

- **Arrange the iconic buttons.** You can drag the iconic buttons to the left and right to rearrange their positions in the toolbar. As you move an iconic button, the other iconic buttons move to accommodate it.

- **Removing iconic buttons.** To remove iconic buttons from the toolbar, click and drag them away from the Finder window. As you drag them away, the button's icons will have small dust clouds added to them, indicating that they are about to be trashed. Release the mouse, and the iconic buttons disappear into a cloud of dust.

- **Change the buttons' display.** At the bottom of the Customize Toolbar window is a popup menu that you can use to adjust the appearance of the buttons. The options are Icon & Text, Icon Only, and Text Only, as Figure 3.1 shows. Next to the popup menu is the Use Small Size option; selecting it slightly reduces the size of the icons and text descriptions.

When done, click Done to apply your changes to all Finder windows.

Tip

You can add, remove, and arrange items on the toolbar without opening the Customize Toolbar settings sheet. To do this, press and hold the ⌘ key, then drag iconic buttons to remove and rearrange them in any active Finder window. Likewise, ⌘+drag items such as folders, files, and even volumes into the toolbar. When dragging items to the toolbar, a green circle with a + icon appears to indicate that it will be an addition. You may have to hold the ⌘ key for a second or two before dragging the item.) When you've dragged the item to the desired location in the toolbar, release the mouse button.

Here are the controls you can add to the toolbar from the Customize Toolbar settings sheet:

- **Path.** This iconic popup menu shows the file hierarchy. Choosing any of the folders in the popup menu opens that folder's contents in the current Finder window. (This function is identical to ⌘+clicking the item's icon or name in the title bar.)

- **Eject.** This iconic button disconnects any selected attached servers, network-connected computers, optical discs, or external disks. It also physically ejects any CD or DVDs inserted into the computer.

- **Burn.** This iconic button opens the Burn Disc dialog box, which walks you through the steps of copying ("burning") the selected items to a recordable CD or DVD. If no CD or DVD is inserted, you are asked to insert an optical disc.

- **Customize.** This iconic button opens the Customize Toolbar settings sheet.

- **Separator.** This control places a vertical line in the toolbar, for use as a visual divider between items on the toolbar.

- **Space** and **Flexible Space.** Using the Space and Flexible Space controls, you can move iconic buttons apart. The Space control creates a square block of space that is about the same size as most toolbar icons. The Flexible Space control expands and contracts depending on the width of the Finder window.

- **New Folder.** This iconic button opens a new Finder window.

- **Delete.** This iconic button moves any highlighted items in the Finder to the Trash.

- **Connect.** This iconic button opens the Connect to Server dialog box. Connecting to servers is outlined in Chapter 13.

- **Get Info.** This iconic button opens the Info window, as outlined in Chapter 2.

- **iDisk.** This iconic button displays the contents of your iDisk folder in the Finder window. iDisk is part of Apple's MobileMe service and is outlined in Chapter 15.

Looking at the bottom of the Finder window

At the bottom of the Finder window is a gray horizontal bar that provides a space for further information, and some limited controls. Although the bottom part of the Finder window is much less complex than the toolbar, it still has areas worth looking at.

- **File path.** The file path appears at the bottom of the Finder window when you have typed something into the Search field. From left to right it displays the path from the root of the hard drive to the file that is currently highlighted in the Finder search window (in other words, the folder hierarchy). Double-clicking any of the folders in the file path causes it to open in a new Finder window. (Note that you cannot use the Columns view mode in a Finder search window; it is grayed out.)

  You can also display the file path at the bottom of the Finder window in any view mode by choosing View ➪ Show Path Bar. Choose View ➪ Hide Path Bar to hide it.

- **Status bar.** At the very bottom of a Finder window sits the status bar, which presents information about the window's contents. It typically shows how many items are available in the Finder window and how much free space is available. If you have items selected in the Finder, it lists how many items of the total number are selected. If you do not have write privileges for a folder or item, a small icon that looks like a crossed-out pencil appears on the left-hand side of the status bar.

- **Icon size slider.** Available only in the Icons view mode, a slider at the right-hand side of the status bar lets you increase or decrease the icon's size for the current Finder window. (You can also use the View Options controls as explained in later in this chapter.)

New Feature
The Icon size slider is new to Mac OS X 10.6 Snow Leopard.

Working with Finder view modes

You can view the Finder window in one of four view modes. Each offers a different approach to interacting with the files on your Mac, and each has its own advantages in different circumstances. Whichever method you use is largely a case of personal preference. The four view modes are Icon, List, Column, and Cover Flow.

Choosing a different view mode

You can choose a different Finder view mode several different ways:

- **Via the Finder menu.** Choose View from the menu bar and then choose from the following menu options: As Icons, As List, As Columns, and As Cover Flow.

- **Using keyboard shortcuts.** Press ⌘+1, ⌘+2, ⌘+3, or ⌘+4 to access the Icons, List, Columns, and Cover Flow view modes, respectively.

- **Using the toolbar icons.** You can use the four iconic buttons on the toolbar to change the view mode, as Figure 3.4 shows. From left to right, the iconic buttons enable the icon, list, column, and Cover Flow views. Each icon has a small graphic showing what the view mode will look like in the Finder.

FIGURE 3.4

You use the four iconic buttons on the Finder toolbar to change the view mode. From left to right, they enable the Icons, List, Columns, and Cover Flow view modes.

Working in icon view

Icon view is the oldest view mode used by Mac operating systems, dating all the way back to the original Macintosh computer that shipped in 1984. Over the years, the icon view has been updated and improved, and in Mac OS X 10.6 Snow Leopard, the icons provide a lot of visual detail about the item they represent, as Chapter 2 explains. But they provide very little additional information beyond the item's name and — if you enable it via the Finder view options explained later in this chapter — basic item information such as file size and number of items in a folder.

Tip

The big advantage of the icon view is the size of the preview, which enables you to get an idea of the contents of icons without opening them. You can increase or decrease their size by using the slider that appears at the right-hand side of the status bar at the bottom of the Finder window when in icon view.

If you use icon view, it is easy to end up with various icons in disarray. It is also a simple task to get the Finder to tidy up icons by choosing View ➪ Clean Up. Alternatively you can press and hold the ⌘ key while dragging icons around; this automatically lines them up to the grid you set with the View Options controls explained later in this chapter.

Note

Icon view is the only view mode available to the desktop.

Working in list view

List view emphasizes textual information about the items in the Finder window, relegating the icon to a small element no taller than the text. The background has alternate blue and white rows, which makes it easier to visually distinguish between different items.

As Figure 3.5 shows, folders are presented with disclosure triangles that enable you to display or hide the files or folders they contain. A right-facing disclosure triangle to the left of a folder's name means it has contents not being shown; a down-facing disclosure triangle means its contents are being displayed (notice how they are also indented to give you an outline-like, *nested* organization.)

Note

When you expand a folder by clicking the disclosure triangle, the next time you open that Finder window, the Finder remembers whether the folders contained within were previously expanded or collapsed.

Tip

If you press and hold the Option key while clicking a folder's disclosure triangle to reveal its items, the Finder automatically also expands the first level of subfolders within that folder.

Tip

You can expand folders in list view (and in Cover Flow view) by pressing ⌘+→; press ⌘+← to collapse expanded folders.

One key advantage of working in list view is that you can drill down through folder structures and select multiple items from different folders within the same Finder window (by using the disclosure triangles to show the contents of all subfolders so everything is visible in the Finder window).

The other key advantage of working in list view is the ability to sort information quickly. As Figure 3.5 shows, list view has by default four columns of information: Name, Date Modified, Size, and Kind (file type). You can click these column headers to sort the contents; by default they sort alphabetically (A to Z) for Names and Kind, newest to oldest for Date, largest to smallest for Size. If you click the active column again, it reverses the sort; note how the triangle to the right of the active column header's name flips between up-facing and down-facing as you click the column header. (The column header highlighted in blue is the one currently sorting the window's contents.)

FIGURE 3.5

The Finder window in list view with both expanded and collapsed folders

As well as sorting by columns in list view, you can adjust the columns themselves. One adjustment is the ability to change the width of columns, which is useful because many items' labels are too long to fit within the Name or Kind column, as indicated by text truncated with an ellipsis (...).

Tip

You can add columns to list view by using the view options described later in this chapter. For example, you might add the Label column to a Finder window so you can sort files based on the color labels you assigned them (see Chapter 2).

Follow these steps to change a column's size:

1. **Highlight the column edge.** Position the mouse over the line that divides one column from another. You can tell when the position is correct because the mouse pointer changes from a pointer to a vertical line with two arrows protruding to the left and right.

2. **Click and hold the mouse button on that vertical line.**

3. **Drag the mouse left and right.**

Tip

You don't need to adjust column widths if you just want to view just a particular item that doesn't fit inside a column view. If you hover the mouse over an item in list view whose label is truncated, a light yellow box appears showing the full name. Pressing the Option key speeds up how quickly the description box appears.

You can also change the order in which the Date Modified, Size, and Kind columns appear. To do this, click the column title and drag the column left or right. As you drag the column header, the pointer transforms into a hand tool and a grayed-out preview of the column appears where it will move. Release the mouse button and the column moves to its new position, rearranging the other columns as it slides into place (see Figure 3.6). Unfortunately, you cannot move the Name column.

FIGURE 3.6

List view has four columns of information you can use to sort the order that items are displayed. The columns, apart from the Name column, can be rearranged.

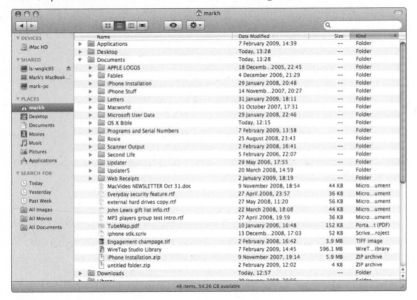

Column view was first formally introduced in Mac OS X 10.4 Tiger, although it has its roots in the NeXT operating system and had been available on the Mac in the form of a shareware utility called Greg's Browser.

Understanding and using the column view in Mac OS X is important, not just because it is one of the fastest ways to navigate through the Finder, but also because it is the default view presented in dialog boxes when you are asked to open or save an item by an application. (Chapter 7 has more information on opening and saving items from within documents.)

The real advantage of column view is the ease with which you can review your path through the folder structure on a volume; it also presents a comprehensive preview and substantial file information in the final column when you have selected an item other than a folder. Consequently, it is many Mac OS X users' preferred view mode. The disadvantage is that it lacks the sorted options offered by list view, and it does not offer the capability to view and manage the contents of multiple folders that are not nested within each other that list view provides.

When you select a folder in column view, the column to the right immediately displays the contents of that folder (including any folders). Column view shows the contents of that folder in the first column, and then displays the contents of a selected subfolder in the next column, then the contents of a selected subfolder in the next column, until there are no more subfolders to select. In this manner you can delve down through the contents of a volume to find the file or folder you are looking for, as Figure 3.7 shows. This makes it possible to drill down through a menu structure and at any point to return to a previous file or folder found in earlier columns.

If the number of columns exceeds the width of the Finder window, new columns will continue to appear on the right-hand side of the Finder window, with the columns to the left scrolling out of sight. A scrollbar appears at the bottom of the Finder window so you can navigate back and forth through the menu structure.

If you select an alias of a folder, the Finder displays the contents of the folder that the alias points to, while keeping the folder structure leading to the alias intact. When you select a file, the column to the right displays basic information for that file, as well as a large preview of the item (see Figure 3.7). As in icon view, whether you see a preview of the file's contents or an icon of the application associated with that file depends on the nature of the file itself. And although the preview icon is fairly large, you may want to get a larger look by using the Quick Look feature described in Chapter 7.

For an application, you always see a large picture of the icon used by the application, plus the name, kind (in this case, "application"), size, date the application was created (or installed), and date the application was modified and last opened; you also see the version number of the application. You can show and hide the preview by using the disclosure triangle next to the text labeled Preview.

Note

Opening and closing the preview in column view applies to all items you select in the Finder, not just the currently selected item.

For some text or graphic items, the preview shows the contents of the file rather than the application associated with it. For most documents, you will also see all the information that you see for an application (with the exception of the version number). If you have selected an image, the final column also displays information on the dimensions of the picture, which is measured in pixels horizontally, then vertically. So if the dimensions are listed as 400 × 200, the image is 400 pixels high and 200 pixels wide. If you have selected an audio or video file, you also get duration information. When you have a movie or sound file selected, hovering the mouse over the preview in the final column reveals a small white circle with a play triangle inside. Clicking this iconic button plays the movie or sound file.

FIGURE 3.7

A Finder window in column view. Each column shows the contents of a folder, and the final column displays information about a selected file and a preview of the item's contents.

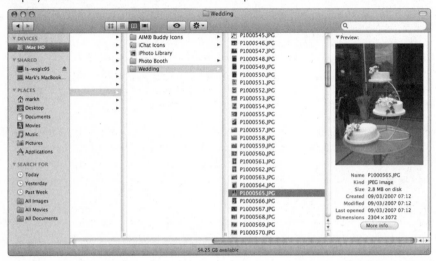

The width of the columns in column view is adjustable. You can adjust the width of individual columns, or all columns uniformly. To adjust the column width, perform one of the following actions:

- To resize a single column, click the handle at the bottom of the column divider (the handle is a small square icon with two vertical lines) and drag it to the left or right.

- To resize all of the columns to a uniform size, hold down the Option key while dragging a handle left and right. All the columns snap to the size of the one you are adjusting. As you drag the handle left and right, all the columns will snap to the same size.

Working in Cover Flow view

Cover Flow is an Apple technology that first appeared in iTunes, and it has slowly permeated into many of Apple's applications. Cover Flow is by far the most visually stimulating of all the view modes, offering a highly graphical way of interacting with the Finder. Cover Flow splits the Finder window in half, with the bottom half using the list view to present files and folders, and the top half providing a horizontal presentation of the items as large icons that you can "thumb through." The currently selected item faces straight out in the middle of the other items, which are arranged in a fan- or carousel-like view, as Figure 3.8 shows.

Tip

You can adjust the size of the Cover Flow part of the window to get a larger (or smaller) visual display. Below the Cover Flow scrollbar is a handle marked by three small horizontal white lines. If you hover the mouse over this handle, the pointer turns into a hand. Click and drag the white lines up for a smaller Cover Flow display or down for a larger Cover Flow display.

You can navigate the bottom half of the window in the same manner as using list view (as outlined earlier). The key difference is that when you highlight an item, the top half flips to a large preview of it.

However, you can also use the top half of the Cover Flow window to flip through the files. You can interact with the Cover Flow window in five ways:

- **Using the scrollbar.** Click and drag the scrollbar directly beneath the images to scroll through the current windows.

- **Using the scroll arrows.** Two arrows appear to the left and right of the scrollbar. Clicking these moves one item at a time.

- **Clicking images.** You can directly click any visual image in the Cover Flow to go directly to that image. By repeatedly clicking an image to the left or right of the current one, you can scroll through all the images in Cover Flow view.

- **Using the arrow keys.** If you press the ← and → keys, you move the Cover Flow images left and right, respectively. You can also use the ↑ and ↓ keys to move up and down the list of items in the bottom half of the Finder window; this has the same effect as using ← and →, respectively.

- **Using the scroll wheel.** If you have a Mighty Mouse or other scroll-wheel mouse attached to your Mac, you can move the scroll wheel on the top of the mouse to move through the items represented in the Cover Flow window. If the scroll wheel moves just up and down, it works like the ↑ and ↓ keys. If the scroll wheel is actually a ball, as in the Mighty Mouse, that can move in several directions, scrolling down or to the right moves through the Cover Flow images to the right, while moving the ball up or to the left moves through the Cover Flow images to the left.

FIGURE 3.8

The Finder window in Cover Flow view splits the window in half, with the bottom showing a list of items and the top half providing a scrollable 3-D fanlike or carousel-like view that you can "thumb through."

Cover Flow view is not without detractors. Many OS X users complain that it provides visual aplomb at the expense of usability. While it offers little navigational functionality that can't be found in other view modes, the ability to visually scan through files is great for looking through collections of images. And if you don't like it, don't use it.

Tip

Cover Flow works exceptionally well in tandem with Apple's Quick Look technology (see Chapter 7). As you scan the items in the Cover Flow window, pressing the spacebar makes the highlighted item zoom out to show a larger preview. Using Cover Flow and Quick Look together is a great way to scan through your files.

Adjusting Finder preferences settings

Most of the Finder preferences reside in the Finder Preferences dialog box, which you access by choosing Finder➪Preferences or pressing ⌘+; (semicolon). This dialog box has four panes, as Figure 3.9 shows.

You use the Sidebar pane to configure which standard disks and folders appear in the sidebar of all Finder windows (such as when you open a disk or folder). Select the ones you want to appear, and deselect those you don't want to appear. Note that when a Finder window is open, you can drag any disk or folder into it so that disk or folder is permanently available in the Sidebar. To delete them, just drag them out of a Finder window one at a time, or Control+click or right-click them one at a time and choose Remove from Sidebar in the contextual menu.

New Feature

Mac OS X 10.6 Snow Leopard now lets you choose File➪Add to Sidebar or just press ⌘+T to add a selected disk or folder.

The General pane provides several controls:

- **Show These Items on the Desktop.** Select and deselect the options in this area to control what always displays on the desktop when available: Hard Disks; External Disks; CDs, DVDs, and iPods; and Connected Servers.

- **New Finder Windows Open.** Use this popup menu to choose which folder should open when you open a new Finder Window. (Choose File➪Open New Finder Window or press ⌘+N when in the Finder to open a new Finder window.) By default, this option is set to the active user account's Home folder.

- **Always Open Folders in a New Window.** Select this option or deselect it to have folders open in place of the current window (the default behavior).

- **Spring-Loaded Folders and Windows.** When you drag files or folders to put them in other ones, you often aren't sure where the destination folder actually is. If the Spring-Loaded Folders and Windows option is selected, when you drag a file or a folder over another folder or disk drive and then hover, the folder or drive opens automatically so you can drop the file or folder into it — or hover over a subfolder to open it. (Move the hovering file or folder out of the window to close it.) You can thus explore multiple folders and drives before deciding where to drop the selected folder or file into. Adjust the hovering time by using the Delay slider.

FIGURE 3.9

The Finder Preferences dialog box and its four panes, General, Labels, Sidebar, and Advanced

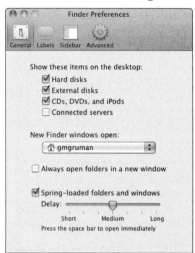

The Labels pane is very simple: It shows the seven colors you can apply to folders and enables you to change the labels for each. (You can apply a color to a folder by selecting the folder and then choosing File and the desired color square at the bottom of the File menu.)

The Advanced pane controls the behavior for filename extensions and the Trash Can:

- **Show All Filename Extensions.** A filename extension is the typically three- or four-character code that follows a period at the end of the filename to identify what kind of file it is. For example, a `.tiff` file is a TIFF image file, while a `.doc` or `.docx` file is a Microsoft Word document file. The Mac OS uses icons to tell you what type a file is, so by default it hides the filename extensions as unneeded. But if you prefer to see them, select the Show All File Extensions option.

- **Show Warning Before Changing an Extension.** This is related to filename extensions. If you edit a filename in a way that changes its extension, Mac OS X will ask if you are sure. (Typically, you should not change the filename extension, as that could confuse the Mac OS and applications as to what the file is, perhaps making applications "believe" that they can no longer open the file.)

- **Show Warning Before Emptying the Trash.** When you delete files and folders from the Trash Can (choose Finder⇨Empty Trash, press Shift+⌘+Delete, or Control+click or right-click the Trash icon in the Dock and choose Empty Trash from the contextual menu), the Mac OS displays an alert asking if you are sure because after they are deleted, the files cannot be recovered. To turn off this alert, deselect the Show Warning Before Emptying the Trash option.

- **Empty Trash Securely.** Although it's not easy to recover deleted Trash items, there is software that can do so in some circumstances. If you deal with sensitive data, you may not want anyone to recover your deleted files. To empty the Trash items in a way they can't be recovered, select the Empty Trash Securely option.

- **When Performing a Search.** This popup menu lets you control what is searched by default in the Finder, using Mac OS X's Spotlight capability. There are three options: Search This Macintosh (the default option), Search the Enclosing Folder, and Use the Previous Search Scope (which uses whatever search criteria you last set in a Finder search window, as we explain later in this chapter).

New Feature

The When Performing a Search popup menu is new to Mac OS X 10.6 Snow Leopard.

Using Finder view menu settings

Another place to configure the Finder window's display is in the Finder's View menu.

Choose View⇨Show View Options or press ⌘+J to control how Finder windows display their contents. If no disk or folder is selected, you get a limited set of options that apply to the desktop compared to the options that display when a disk or folder is selected. Note that these settings apply only to the desktop (if no disk or file is selected) or just to the selected disk or folder.

Desktop view settings

For the desktop, you can set the icon size by using the Icon Size slider, as well as the space between icons by using the Grid Spacing slider. (Figure 3.10 shows the settings available.) You can also choose the text label's size for the items that display within the desktop, folder, or disk by using the Text Size popup menu, as well as determine where that label appears by selecting either the Bottom or Right radio button.

Select the Show Item Info option to have details about the disk or folder — such as its size and number of items — display under the item's name. Deselect the Show Icon Preview option so the Mac no longer creates a thumbnail of the image or document as its icon; instead, the Mac uses the icon for the application that created it.

Finally, you can control how items are arranged in the window by using the Arrange By popup menu. Your options are None (leave the items where they were placed), Snap to Grid (shift them to the settings specified in the Grid Spacing slider; this setting only affects items you move or add, leaving items in their original location otherwise), Name, Date Modified, Date Created, Size, Kind and Label. These last six options sort the items automatically.

FIGURE 3.10

The view options for the desktop

Folder and disk view settings

When you open a folder or disk and open the view options, the options vary based on what view you have set for the folder or disk window — icon view, list view, column view, and Cover Flow view — using the View iconic buttons at the top of the window or by choosing an option in the Finder's View menu. Figure 3.11 shows the four sets of options.

FIGURE 3.11

The view options for the folder and disk windows vary based on what type of display is active. From left to right: the options for icon view, list view, column view, and Cover Flow view.

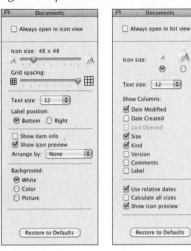  

Note

If you click Use as Defaults, the settings you apply to the current Finder window become the default background for all Finder windows, except those previously customized.

In icon view, you get many of the same options as for the desktop: Icon Size, Grid Spacing, Text Size, Label Position, Show Item Info, Show Icon Preview, and Arrange By. But you also get the Always Open in Icon View option, as well as the capability to set a background color or image for the window.

In list view, you also get the Text Size popup menu and Show Icon Preview option, but that's all it has in common with the desktop view options. In the list view, you get a choice of two icon sizes, as well as the capability to select which columns you want to display in the list: Date Modified, Date Created, Last Opened, Size, Kind, Version, Comments, and Label. Select those columns you want to display, and deselect those you don't. The Use Relative Dates option, if selected, replaces today's date with Today and yesterday's date with Yesterday in the date-oriented columns. The calculate All Sizes option, if selected, shows the size for folders, not just for files. (Note that this option can slow down the display of window information.) Plus you get the Always Open in List View option.

In column view, there are just a few options, several of which are familiar: Always Open in Column View, Text Size, Show Icon Preview, and Arrange By. The two unique options are Show Icons (if deselected, only the text label appears for each item) and Show Preview Column (if deselected, no quick-look preview of the selected file appears in the rightmost column).

In Cover Flow view, the options are identical to those in list view, except of course that the Always Open in Cover Flow View option replaces the Always Open in List View one.

Tip

If you want all Finder windows to open in one of the view modes with the view options you've set for the current Finder, be sure to select the Always Open in mode View option. This option makes that view mode and its view options the default view mode (until you change it again). But do note that any Finder windows to which you applied custom view settings will not use these new defaults; you must change them by choosing View ➪ View Options for each such window.

Customizing Finder windows in icon view

So far we have looked at how to customize Finder windows globally on your Mac. But you can also customize individual Finder windows in icon view.

Arranging icons

In icon view, all icons inside a folder are manually arranged. That is to say, you can drag them to wherever you want and they remain where you place them, even when you close the Finder window and reopen it later; the Finder remembers where you last left them.

But a manually arranged Finder window can soon be a mess. That's why the Finder has the Arrange By menu (available in the Finder's View menu and in its contextual menu). It offers several options that can help you maintain a tidier Finder window.

The Snap to Grid menu option still enables you to manually move around icons, but it ensures they always remain lined up with each other (horizontally and vertically). You set the grid by using the view options explained earlier in this chapter.

The other options automatically sort the icons as their names indicate: Name, Date Modified, Date Created, Size, Kind, or Label. When you choose one of these options, it "cleans up" the Finder window, rearranging the icons so they are aligned to the grid.

You can also arrange the icons so they snap in place within the grid without having to sort them, using an Arrange By option. To do so, make sure no item is selected in the Finder window, then choose View ➪ Clean Up. If the menu option is Clean Up Selection, that means one or more items is selected, and only they will be snapped to the grid.

Changing the background of a window

By default, the background of every Finder window is white. However, you change that background in icon view by using the view options controls covered earlier in this chapter. There are three options:

- **White.** This is the default option. Use it to reset the Finder window's background back to white.

- **Color.** This option enables you to change the background of a Finder window to a solid color of your own choosing. When you select this option, a color swatch appears to its right; click it to open the Mac OS X Color Picker, which lets you create any color the monitor can display. As you select colors in the Color Picker, the background of the Finder window changes to show you how it will appear. Click OK to apply the color to the Finder window's background.

- **Picture.** This option enables you to use any supported image available to your Mac as a background for the Finder window. Figure 3.12 shows a Finder window with an image used as the background. When you select this option, a square appears to the right. Drag an image from your Mac or any disk or computer connected to it onto that square to make it the Finder window's background.

Note

If you click Use as Defaults, the custom background for the current Finder window becomes the default background for all Finder windows, except those previously customized.

FIGURE 3.12

A Finder window using an image in the background

Using the Color Picker

Some of the Finder appearance settings outlined in this chapter use the Color Picker, a tool used through Mac OS X as a standard tool that can be used in a variety of situations, from picking the desktop background to selecting text colors in applications.

In the top left of the Color Picker is a small magnifying glass icon. Clicking it brings up the Loupe tool (a magnifying glass icon with a cross hair in the middle). Move the Loupe tool around the screen and click an object whose color you want to add to the Color Picker.

At the bottom of each color pane is a set of white boxes known as the *color shelf* (there is one row by default, but you can drag the shelf down to add rows). If you find a color that you like in any of the five subpanes, drag it to one of the squares on the color shelf, which makes the color available in the future simply by clicking it in the color shelf.

The Color Picker has five panes, each offering its own method for choosing a color, as the figure shows.

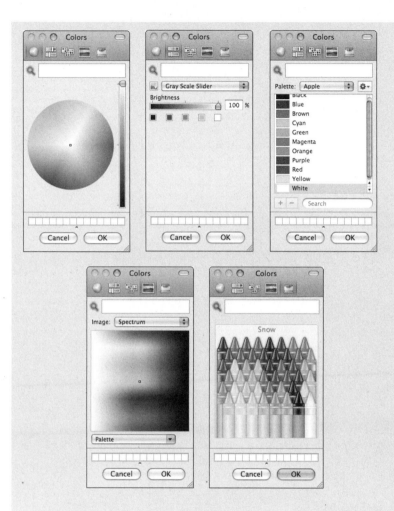

- **Color Wheel.** The pane's color wheel is a circle based upon the RGB (red, green, blue) color space. At the center is white; the three colors get more saturated as you move to the edge of the circle. In the middle of the circle is a small square dot; click and drag this through the color wheel to pick a color. To the right of the color wheel is the brightness slider; moving the slider down darkens the colors, while moving it up lightens them. The rectangular area at the top shows the current color selection.

- **Sliders.** This pane offers four different slider options: Gray Scale, RGB, CMYK (cyan, magenta, yellow, black), and HSB (hue, saturation, brightness). Moving the various sliders left and right enables you to choose from the spectrum of colors according to the color spaces they represent. You can also choose the colors by entering numbers into the boxes to the right of the sliders. These are also useful if you want to exactly reproduce a color based upon its numerical code, such as a color from a Web site or sampled in a tool such as Adobe Photoshop.

continued

continued

- **List.** This pane enables you to choose a color from a list of swatches. There are four palettes (or lists) to choose from: Apple (the default), Web Safe Colors, Crayons, and Developer. The Action iconic popup menu (the gear icon) to the right enables you to create, rename, and remove palettes; you drag colors from the color shelf into the new palette.

- **Image.** This pane enables you to pick a color from an image. By default, the image is of the color spectrum available to Mac OS X, although the Palette popup menu at the bottom enables you to add any image of your own choosing as the image. This is useful if you have an image you frequently refer to for color selection, although for one-off purposes it is quicker to use the Loupe tool.

- **Crayons.** This pane offers a range of crayons to choose from. Like the List pane, it offers a quick way to choose from a set of predetermined colors.

Working with Folder Actions

Mac OS X comes with a collection of AppleScripts known as *folder actions* that enable folders to not just store items, but also to act on any items placed within them. Some folder actions change the way information is displayed inside the folders, while others perform basic editing actions (such as rotating all images by 90 degrees). The actions can do whatever the accompanying AppleScript demands (AppleScript is outlined in more detail in Chapter 25).

New Feature

Mac OS X 10.6 Snow Leopard slightly changes the process for managing folder actions. The Folder Actions Setup menu option is now available in the contextual menu for any folder; you no longer need to access it as a submenu option in the More menu option. To disable folder actions, there is also no longer the Disable Folder Action contextual menu option for folders that have folder actions attached; instead, you use the Folder Actions Setup dialog box to both enable and disable folder actions for any folder.

Attaching actions to folders

You can create your own AppleScripts to attach to folders, although creating them is an advanced area of Mac OS X usage. Fortunately, Apple provides several scripts that perform useful functions. To attach an action to a folder, do the following:

1. **Control+click or right-click a disk or a folder to open the contextual menu, and choose Folder Actions Setup.**

2. **Choose a script to attach to the folder from the list that appears, and click the Attach button.** Alternatively, press the Cancel button and use the + iconic button in Step 4 to select scripts.

3. **Select the Enable Folder Actions option in the upper-left side of the Folder Actions Setup dialog box.**

4. **Click the + iconic button in the bottom left of the Folder Actions Setup dialog box to attach further scripts.** See Figure 3.13 for an example of the Folder Actions Setup dialog box.

5. **Click Open to launch the Open dialog box, from which you navigate to the folder you want to attach an Action Script to.**

6. **In the sheet that appears, select the AppleScripts you want to attach, and click Attach.** (⌘+click items to select multiple actions.)

7. **The Folder Actions Setup dialog box reappears, listing the folder in its left pane and the associated actions in its right pane.** You can turn folder actions on and off by selecting and deselecting the check boxes to the left of the folder and script names.

8. **Click the red Close iconic button to complete the folder action assignment.** The selected actions are now active for the folder.

FIGURE 3.13

The Folder Actions Setup dialog box enables you to attach action script actions to folders.

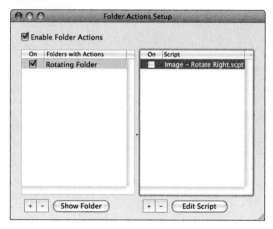

Using actions

When an action script is attached to a folder, the standard method of using a folder action is to drag an item (or items) to the folder. As the item is placed into the folder, the action's AppleScripts are run and perform their action on the items selected. (If a script doesn't apply to the items, nothing happens.) An action creates a subfolder for the results inside the folder with a name determined by the script; for example, if you use the Image – Rotate Right script, the new subfolder is named Rotated Images.

Editing actions

To edit an action, open the Folder Actions Setup dialog box, then select the folder whose actions you want to edit. Deselect the On check boxes to the left of a script name to stop it from running. Select a script and click the – iconic button under the Script list to completely remove the script from the folder action. Click the + iconic button under the Script list to add a script to the folder action.

Click the Edit Script button under the Script list to launch the AppleScript Editor and open the script in it so you can edit it. This is also a great way to simply take a look at the code that underlies the script to understand what it does. (Chapter 25 has more information on AppleScript.)

Click the + iconic button under the Folders with Actions list to add additional folders to which you can apply scripts. Select a folder and click the – iconic button to remove folder actions from that folder. Click the Show Folder button to open the selected folder in a new Finder window.

Understanding Mac OS X's Special Folders

Now that you are familiar with the Finder, and the various things you can use it to do, it is time to become acquainted with the main folder structure of the Mac OS X environment. As mentioned previously, Mac OS X has many folders that are created along with the installation of the operating system. Some are contained within your Home folder and some are contained in the root of your main volume and are used by Mac OS X.

The system folders

On your desktop is an icon in the top right for your startup disk, usually named Macintosh HD. (You can rename it as you would any folder or disk: by selecting it, then clicking its name, and changing the text that becomes selected.) Double-clicking the disk's icon opens the first level (called the *root level*) of folders on the startup disk. Figure 3.14 shows the folders in the startup disk; by default, it contains just four folders:

- **Applications.** As the name suggest, this folder contains programs used for a variety of different purposes.
- **System.** This folder contains the actual files that represent the heart of Mac OS X. Most of the items stored here are used to make your Mac work, so interfering with this folder is usually a bad idea. To prevent unintentional changes, this folder isn't easily editable, and you are asked to provide an administrator password before moving, deleting, or editing any files in it.
- **Library.** The Library folder contains a set of system-wide settings, as well as some additional files that are used to help the Mac operate. The settings inside this Library folder apply to all users of the Mac, although each user also has his or her own Library folder within his or her Home folder.
- **Users.** Each user account set up in Mac OS X has its own Home folder inside the Users folder. Each Home folder acts as a central storage area for all the files and Mac OS X settings for each user, including a Desktop, Documents, Downloads, Library, Movies, Music, Pictures, Public, and Sites folder, as Table 3.1 details.

FIGURE 3.14

The root level of the startup disk contains just four folders by default: Applications, System, Library, and Users.

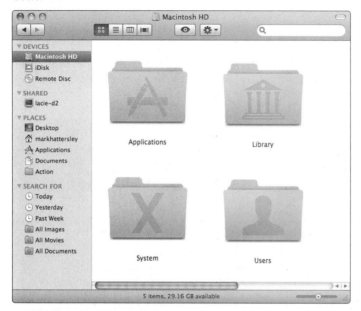

Working with the Home folder

Mac OS X is designed to be a multiuser operating system that different people can use, with their own personal files, preferences, and even applications. Mac OS X segregates each user account's files in what is called the Home folder, one of which exists for each user in the Users folder. This area is appropriately named *home*. Each user's Home folder is protected from the prying eyes of other users, unless the user gives others permission to access their files, as Chapters 13 and 20 explain. When you customize any aspect of Mac OS X, those settings are saved in your Home folder's Library folder — and they don't apply to other user accounts.

When you create or save documents, the documents are stored by default within your Home folder's Documents folder; of course, you can choose a different location in the Save As dialog box of the applications you are saving from.

The Home folder is not named Home. Instead, it uses the short name you set up for your user account when first installing the Mac OS (see Chapter 1) or when creating a user account (see Chapter 20). But the Home folder for the active user account has a house icon (thus the name Home), while those of inactive users use standard folder icons.

You can access the Home folder in several ways:

- Click the Home folder in the Finder's Sidebar, in the Places section. (The Home folder's name will be your short name, not "Home.")

- Choose Go➪Home in the Finder or press Shift+⌘+H in the Finder.
- Choose New➪Finder Window or press ⌘+N to open a new Finder window that opens to the Home folder (unless you changed that default folder, as explained earlier in this chapter.)
- Open the startup disk, open the Users folder, then open the Home folder.

Note

Only the currently logged in user can access his or her Home folder. This security measure ensures that user's system settings and personal documents remain private. But people with administrator passwords can access anyone's Home folder, as Chapter 20 explains.

TABLE 3.1

Folders Contained in the Home Folder

Name	Contents
Applications	Contains any applications that are unique to that user.
Desktop	Contains all the files and folders shown on the desktop. Note that volume icons are not displayed here.
Documents	Stores miscellaneous documents created by the user.
Downloads	Temporarily stores files downloaded from the Web by Safari and other applications.
Library	Contains applications preferences and other system settings that are unique to the user.
Movies	Is the default location for any files created by Apple's movie-making software. It is also a good place to store any movie files.
Music	Is the default location for the iTunes library, and is a good place to keep any audio files.
Pictures	Is the default location for the iPhoto picture library, and is a good place to store any pictures.
Public	Is used to share files with other users across the network. The Public folder is outlined in more depth in Chapter 13.
Sites	Is the default location for Web sites that you want to make available over the network or Internet from your Mac. Chapter 14 explains such personal Web hosting.

Working with Disks and Other Volumes

A *volume* is a set amount of storage on your computer. Typically, a volume means an internal or external hard disk, a recordable optical disc (such as a CD-R or a DVD-R), or an attached USB (Universal Serial Bus) flash drive. The terms *volume*, *drive*, and *disk* are often used interchangeably, but there are some differences:

- Volumes can be any storage container that a Mac sees as a distinct container, including disks, partitions, and network file shares.
- Drives are the physical mechanisms that contain one or more disks.

- Disks are the media (magnetic, such as used in hard disks and floppy disks; optical, such as used in CDs and DVDs; or solid-state, such as used in flash "thumb" drives) that actually stores data.

- Partitions are sections of a disk that are presented to Mac OS X as if they were separate disks. (You create such partitions when formatting the disk by using Mac OS X's Disk Utility, as Chapter 8 explains.)

Note

Optical media, such as CD and DVD drives are always referred to as discs (written with the letter c); the magnetic-based drive such as internal and external hard disks are referred to as disks, written with the letter k. Solid-state devices are often referred to as disks (with a k), though the USB devices variously called flash drives, thumb drives, and USB keys aren't usually called disks or discs.

Examining drives and partitions and recognizing volumes

If you open a Finder window and select the Computer option (look for the Mac icon) in the Sidebar's Devices section, you will see all the volumes available to your Mac. Typically you have only the single volume available, which will be your hard disk. However, if you have an optical disc inserted, an external hard disk attached, an iDisk set up via Apple's MobileMe service, or a network connection to other devices, these items also appear in the Devices section.

Volumes also appear on the desktop, as outlined earlier in this chapter in the section on setting Finder preferences.

Note

The name of your Mac may not be "Computer." Mac OS X may have named it something along the lines of "your name's Macintosh model," or you may have renamed it. To rename your Mac, go to the Sharing system preference and change the text in the Computer Name field. (Choose ⇨ System Preferences, or press ⌘+, [comma], and click the Sharing icon to go to the Sharing system preference.)

There are also files known as *disk images* (which have the filename extension .dmg) that can be mounted as virtual volumes. Double-clicking a .dmg file or using the Disk Utility to mount these files turns them into volumes that operate identically to other volumes.

Cross-Ref

Chapter 8 has more information on using the Disk Utility to format and manage disks. Chapter 4 explains how to back up disks. Chapter 13 has more information on file servers, while Chapter 15 has more information on using iDisk.

Each type of volume is displayed in Mac OS X with a distinctive icon that represents the type of drive it is:

- Volumes on internal hard drives are displayed with a gray icon that looks similar to an actual internal hard disk.

- External hard disks' icons are yellow and have a symbol on them that represents the connection type (FireWire or USB).

- Floppy disks, flash drives, and other removable disks have a white icon that is shaped like a flat box.

- iDisk is indicated by a magenta-colored flat box with the MobileMe logo.

- Network volumes use a globe icon.

Ejecting volumes

Volumes attached to the Mac should be ejected before the physical device is removed from the computer. (Mac OS X sometimes refers to this action as *putting away* the volume.) Thus, before disconnecting server volumes, external hard disks, and USB flash drives, you should first eject the volume from the Mac. For optical discs and old-fashioned floppy disks, ejecting them sends a signal to the drive to physically pop out the disc (or disk).

To eject a volume, use one of these techniques:

- For optical discs only, press the Eject button on your keyboard, if it has one, or F12 if it does not. If your Mac has two optical drives attached, you can eject the second drive by pressing Option+Eject (this method only works with an optical drive designed to work with Mac OS X).

- Select the volume and drag it to the Trash. The Trash icon changes to the Eject icon, so you know you're not deleting the volume's contents.

- Select the volume and choose File ➪ Eject "*volumename*" or press ⌘+E.

- Control+click or right-click the volume and choose Eject "*volumename*" from the contextual menu.

If you do not eject a volume before removing the physical device from your Mac, a warning appears (see Figure 3.15). It warns you that the device was not properly put away (ejected), and that data might have been lost or damaged. It's not likely that you'll cause physical damage to the device, but you may lose data because of a technique called *write-behind caching*. Mac OS X uses this technique to store changes to the hard disk in a temporary file called a cache. This is then later transferred to the disk. (This process speeds up the operation of Mac OS X.) When you eject a volume, the data in the cache is transferred to it first. So if you physically remove the disk before that cache has been transferred, that cached data is lost.

Recording to optical discs

Most modern Macs can write data to optical media. This process is commonly known as *burning* (or recording) to disc. There are lots of different recordable media available, including CD-R, CD-RW, DVD-R, DVD+R, DVD-RW, DVD-RAM, and DVD+-R. Mac OS X supports all these formats, so you don't have to worry about them. (One exception is the Blu-ray DVD format, which Mac OS X can't write to, but third-party programs such as Roxio's Toast can — if you have a recordable Blu-ray drive, of course.)

FIGURE 3.15

This warning appears if you do not eject a volume before physically removing it from your Mac.

Device Removal

The device you removed was not properly put away. Data might have been lost or damaged. Before you unplug your device, you must first select its icon in the Finder and choose Eject from the File menu.

OK

Creating a burn folder

Burn folders are an easy way of organizing content that you want to take from your Finder to an optical disc. The great thing about burn folders is that after you've recorded the contents to the optical disc, you still have the burn folder so you make new copies easily later, as well as update it and make copies of the changed version, without starting from scratch. This is handy if you want to back up a changing set of documents, such as project files or family photo albums.

To create a burn folder, choose File ➪ New Burn Folder. The burn folder is created in the active Finder window or on the desktop (if no Finder window is open), as Figure 3.16 shows. By default, the name of the folder is Burn Folder, instead of a regular folder's default name of Untitled; but like other newly created folders, the name is highlighted so you can change it.

Now you can drag items from the Finder into the burn folder. As you drag items into the burn folder, aliases from the original items are placed inside it. (Unlike normal folders, items dragged to burn folders remain in their original position.) You can open the burn folder to examine its contents, and you can remove or reorganize these files at will — just as with any folder.

Tip

If you think you'll work with a burn folder repeatedly, you might drag it in the Sidebar for one-click access at any time, as explained earlier in this chapter.

When you are happy with the contents, you can burn the disc by selecting the burn folder, then choosing File ➪ Burn "*foldername*@dp to Disc, or by Control+clicking or right-clicking the folder and choosing Burn "*foldername*@dp to Disc from the contextual menu. If you don't have a blank disc inserted into the computer, Mac OS X requests that you insert one before continuing.

Tip

If you burn lots of discs, you might want to modify the toolbar, as explained earlier in this chapter, to add the Burn iconic button. Then you just need to select a burn folder and click the Burn iconic button in the toolbar to burn the contents to disc.

FIGURE 3.16

A burn folder used by Mac OS X to store files before they are recorded to an optical disc

Using Finder burn

There is an alternative to using burn folders called *Finder burn*. This is where you drag items from the Finder directly to an optical disc mounted in the Finder.

First, insert a blank optical disc into the drive. A dialog box appears asking what action you want to perform: Open Finder, Open iTunes, or Open Disk Utility. In the Action popup menu, choose Open Finder to inform the Finder that it is responsible for recording the disc. Then click OK. This creates a folder on the desktop called Untitled CD or Untitled DVD, which for all intents and purposes is a burn folder.

Note

The dialog box has an Eject button so you can eject the disc immediately; this is handy if you inserted a blank disc by mistake. There's also the Ignore button, which tells the Finder to do nothing wit the disc. That can be dangerous, as no icon appears in the Finder, so you may forget you have a disc in your SuperDrive, which might lead someone to jam in a new disc later, not knowing there's already a disc in it, and damage the SuperDrive.

If you double-click the burn folder, it opens to reveal its contents (empty to begin with). Drag files to this folder and when you are ready to commit the files to the optical disc, click the Burn iconic button in the Sidebar (the icon appears to the right of the disc's name) or use one of the burn commands described in the section on using burn folders.

Finishing the burn

Whether you created your own burn folder or use a Finder burn, when you tell Mac OS X to burn the disc, an alert dialog box appears requesting confirmation that you are ready to burn. Some discs can only be recorded on once, so this request helps you from ruining discs by burning to them before you are ready. This dialog box also contains the Burn Speed popup menu, which is set to Maximum by default. You can choose a slower speed, which is useful if you find the discs aren't burning correctly; using a slower speed can help with lower quality discs that can't accept data as fast as the Mac can provide it.

After clicking Burn in the confirmation dialog box, the burn process begins and a progress bar tells you how it is going. The Finder follows this process: It first prepares the data, then writes the data, and finally verifies the condition of the optical disc. When the burn is complete, the disc is ejected.

At any time you can halt the burn process by clicking the Stop button. However, doing so usually makes the optical disc useless.

Using Get Info to change disk and folder permissions

As noted previously, you can share folders and disks with other users, both those with user accounts on your Mac (see Chapter 20) and those who have been given file-sharing access to your Mac (see Chapter 13).

You can quickly enable and change sharing privileges for individual folders and disks by using the Info window. To do so, choose File ⇨ Get Info, press ⌘+I, or Control+click or right-click the item and choose Get Info from the contextual menu. You'll get an Info window such as the one shown in Figure 3.17. Most of what displays is information on the disk or folder, but there are a few sharing settings you can change a the bottom of the window:

- **Shared Folder.** You can share a folder or disk by selecting the Shared Folder option, or stop sharing by deselecting it.

- **Sharing & Permissions.** You can change who has access permissions in the Sharing & Permissions section. Select Name and then choose a Privilege for that name; your options are Read & Write, Read Only, and Write Only (Drop Box). You can add and delete users by using the + and − iconic buttons, and choose to apply your changes to all folders within the selected disk or folder by choosing Apply to Enclosed Items from the Action iconic popup menu (the gear icon). (This can take several minutes to complete, so be warned.) And you can undo your changes by choosing Action ⇨ Revert Changes.

Note

If the Sharing & Permissions settings are grayed out, click the Lock button (the bronze-colored lock icon) and enter your user account password (if your account has permissions to change sharing options) or an administrator's password.

Cross-Ref

Chapter 2 covers the other capabilities in the Info window.

FIGURE 3.17

The Info window lets you get a lot of detail on a file, folder, or disk, as well as enable or disable sharing for the selected disk or folder.

Using Spotlight to Find Items

Spotlight is a powerful search engine tool that enables you to search through information on your Mac. Searching with Spotlight can be extremely simple or exceptionally complicated, depending on what you want to do.

How Spotlight works

Spotlight can search for a file by its name, or it can search for information inside the file, such as text embedded in PDF documents or inside text documents; it can even search through what is called *metadata* attached to images, so you can search for the exposure setting of a picture imported from a digital camera. Because Spotlight is also integrated throughout the applications in Mac OS X, it can also search through mail messages for contacts, and even through your calendar. More important, Spotlight can search for Mac OS X items, including applications and system preferences. More recent additions to the Spotlight search scope include definitions from Mac OS X's built-in dictionary and recent Web locations visited in Safari. You can even perform basic math equations by typing them into Spotlight. And, if you're logically inclined, you can search with Boolean logic, so you can search with terms such as AND, NOT, and OR. All these capabilities can be used to create smarter searches.

Spotlight is incredibly powerful, and so easy to use; you'll quickly find yourself turning to Spotlight much of the time when you want to do anything on your Mac. You do this through the Spotlight iconic button at the far right of the menu bar.

Spotlight natively supports the following file types, meaning it can read their metadata and contents:

- plain text
- RTF (Rich Text Format)
- PDF
- Mail
- Address Book contacts
- Microsoft Office Word and Excel documents
- Apple Keynote presentations
- Adobe Photoshop images
- applications
- folders
- Web pages (HTML and associated formats)
- video and audio files: MP3, MP4, AAC, and MOV (QuickTime movie)
- image files: JPEG, GIF, TIFF, PNG, and EXIF

This list doesn't mean that other files types are left out of the loop: Apple has made Spotlight extensible so that non-Apple applications can take advantage of the technology. Microsoft, for example, has created a Spotlight extension for its Entourage e-mail program so its users can search their mail messages in Spotlight.

Despite the huge wealth of information on your hard drive, using Spotlight is a fast process. This is because it doesn't actually search through the data and metadata of every single file on your Mac each time you search; instead, it takes all the data and metadata and keeps an index to it in a database called the Spotlight Store — this is very much like the index in a book, but much more detailed. Every time a file is created, copied, moved, saved, or deleted, the Spotlight Store is updated with new information about the file. The Spotlight Store keeps information on all the metadata associated with a file in a file known as the Metadata Store. And it keeps an index to the contents of your files in its Content Store.

Just What Is Metadata?

All files contain data of some type, such as the text inside Word, PDF, InDesign, and other text-containing documents. Image files include the series of bits that make up their pictures.

But all files also contain metadata. Metadata literally means *data about data*. One type of metadata that all files have is their filename. That's not part of the actual file, but is part of the file's attributes stored by the Finder. File size is another such universal type of metadata, as are the file's location in the Mac's folder hierarchy and its file type.

Some files have metadata specific to their type. For example, an image file's metadata may include information from the camera that took the image, such as the bit depth, color mode (RGB or CMYK), dimensions in pixels, and even the location data of where the photo was taken (such as if you use an iPhone).

The Info window offers a lot of information about a file's metadata, though files may contain even more metadata than the Info window displays. (To open an Info window for an item, select it and press ⌘+I or choose File ➪ Get Info, or Control+click or right-click the item and choose Get Info from the contextual menu.

There's one area of the Info window where you can add your own metadata for Spotlight to search: the Spotlight Comments box. Any comments you type in it are attached to the file, and Spotlight searches them automatically.

Note

Be aware that Spotlight maintains a single Spotlight Store per file system. This store is a folder called `.Spotlight-V100` that is hidden in the root folder of the disk. If you attach another storage device, say an external USB disk, Mac OS X creates a Spotlight Store in its root folder to store information related to that disk. Spotlight data always stays with the volumes; this is crucial when working with networked volumes, as Spotlight has no access to their indexes unless they are visible to your Mac.

Note

Because Spotlight must index your disk's contents to find them, when you first attach a disk to your Mac, Spotlight is at a disadvantage. Give it some time — several hours for a large hard disk — to index the disk the first time you attach it. A good idea when you first set up your Mac is to connect all your common disks and network volumes to the Mac and let Spotlight index them all overnight or during the day while you're working.

Using Spotlight

Now that you're aware of what Spotlight is and have a rough understanding of how it works, it's time to put it into action. Searching in Spotlight couldn't be easier (at least not when you do a simple text search). In its most basic form, a Spotlight search is a single word, such as the name of an application, a contact, or a file you know the name of but not its immediate location.

You can perform a Spotlight search in one of three ways:

- By clicking the Spotlight iconic menu in the menu bar. This opens the Spotlight search window at the upper right of your screen, in which you can type a search term, as Figure 3.18 shows.

- By pressing ⌘+spacebar in most applications, including the Finder. This also opens the Spotlight search window at the upper right of your screen, in which you can type a search term.

- From the Search field in a Finder window. This option gives you more options for your search, as we explain shortly.

Spotlight searches from the menu bar

Running Spotlight from the menu bar is the easiest, and typically the most common method of searching — especially if you are looking to perform a straightforward, no-nonsense search. Typically, more complex searches take place from a Finder window.

Tip
Of all the shortcuts offered by Mac OS X, ⌘+spacebar is probably the most important to learn. This quick keyboard command enables you to quickly get to the Spotlight and search for something without even taking your hands off the keyboard.

FIGURE 3.18

Enter search terms into the Spotlight text box to find items on your Mac.

As soon as you start typing letters into the search field, results appear in a drop-down sheet (see Figure 3.19). The results are divided into categories of information. Top Hit is at the top; this is the file Mac OS X thinks you are most likely looking for. The remaining information is divided into the following categories (categories that don't apply to the results don't appear):

- **Top Hit.** The item that Spotlight thinks you are most likely looking for

- **Definition.** Articles from Mac OS X's built-in dictionary and thesaurus

- **Applications.** Programs that you can run

- **System Preferences.** Items from the System Preferences application

- **Documents.** Files on the Mac and attached volumes

- **Folders.** Folders on the Mac and attached volumes

- **Messages.** E-mail messages contained in Mail

- **Contacts.** People and companies stored in Address Book

- **Events & To-Dos.** Any events or tasks you have stored in iCal

- **Images.** Graphic files stored on your Mac and its attached volumes, as well as within iPhoto
- **PDF Documents.** PDF files stored on the Mac and attached volumes
- **Webpages.** Any recent Web pages you have visited
- **Music.** Audio tracks on the Mac and attached volumes, plus those found in iTunes
- **Movies.** Video tracks on the Mac and attached volumes, plus those found in iTunes
- **Fonts.** Any fonts you have installed on your Mac
- **Presentations.** Any Apple Keynote presentations you have created

There may be other categories in the results sheet; these are created by applications that have Spotlight extensions.

Tip

Notice that Spotlight starts searching as soon as you begin typing, and if you make a mistake, or decide to search for something else, simply press the Backspace key to delete any or all of the search text. You can also clear the text inside the Spotlight search field by pressing the Close iconic button (the X-in-a-gray-circle icon).

FIGURE 3.19

As soon as you begin to type letters, Spotlight offers suggestions based upon what you have entered.

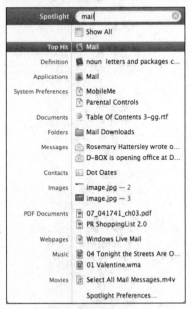

Selecting an item couldn't be easier. Simply use the mouse and click the item you want. Alternatively you can use the arrow keys to move up and down the items and press Return to select the one you want. By default, the Top Hit is highlighted, and pressing Return takes you straight to it.

When you select an item, Spotlight opens a folder with it, if it's a file or folder, or opens the item in the application needed to view it.

Tip

Spotlight is a fantastic alternative to the Dock or Applications folder for launching applications. If you know the name of the application you want to launch, Spotlight invariably places it as the Top Hit. By accessing Spotlight via the ⌘+spacebar shortcut, any application is just a few keystrokes away.

The Spotlight results sheet has two options beyond the results: Show All (at the top of the sheet) and Spotlight Preferences (at the bottom of the sheet):

- Choosing Show All opens a Finder window and runs the search, showing you the complete results, rather than the selective results shown in the sheet. You can then narrow down those complete results by using the tools in the Finder window, which we explain in the next section.
- Choosing Spotlight Preferences opens the Spotlight system preference so you can control where Spotlight searches, as Chapter 21 explains.

Spotlight searches from a Finder window

Each Finder window also contains its own Spotlight search field on the right-hand side of the toolbar. As soon as you begin to enter text into this field, the Finder window's contents of the displayed folder are replaced with those relating to the Spotlight search. The window also changes to a Finder search window, displayed in icon view by default, with extra search options appearing below the toolbar, as Figure 3.20 shows.

When you use Spotlight in a Finder window, Spotlight searches just for files and folders, so it won't display recent Web pages or e-mails, for example, like the menu bar Spotlight search does. As with the menu bar Spotlight search, the Finder search windows' results are aliases to the files and folders, which remain in their existing locations.

Note

Spotlight results in the Finder window can be displayed only in Icons, List, or Cover Flow view modes, and not in Columns view mode. If the Finder window is in column view when you begin a Spotlight search, it is automatically switched to icon view.

Notice that the list of items automatically appears according to when an item was most recently opened; if you are in list or Cover Flow view, you see the Last Opened column automatically highlighted. As with other Finder windows, you can change the sort order by clicking the Name or Kind columns. (The other columns normally shown in a Finder window in list view do not appear in a Finder search window.)

The number of results provided by Spotlight in the Finder window can be huge, so Spotlight caps the results at 10,000 items and places a blue More link at the bottom of the list (see Figure 3.21). Clicking this opens up the remaining results.

FIGURE 3.20

A Finder window that has text entered into the Spotlight field

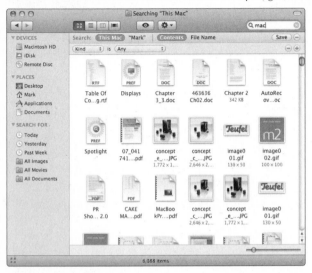

FIGURE 3.21

If more than 10,000 results are returned in a Spotlight search, the More link appears. Clicking it loads the remaining results.

Using Spotlight in the Finder search window also provides several options you can use to narrow down the search results. Two menu bars inside the Finder search window, above the results: the location menu bar and the customization menu bar.

Identified by the term Search, the location menu bar contains several buttons that enable you to decide where to search:

- **This Mac.** This is the default option, and with this option selected Spotlight returns results based upon files located on your boot volume.

- **Current folder.** This option is marked with the name of the current folder that the Finder window was displaying when you entered text in Spotlight. Selecting it narrows the Spotlight search to that specfic folder.

- **Contents and File Name.** There are also two buttons that determine what is searched: either the contents within a file, or just the filename.

- **Save.** The Save button enables you to save your search for reuse later. By default, saved searches are stored in the Saved Searched folder in your Home folder's Library folder, but you can choose a different location; you can also select the Add to Sidebar option to place the saved search in the Search For section of the Sidebar.

- **Customization menu bar.** To see the customization menu bar, you must click the + iconic button on the far-right side of the location menu bar. The customization menu bar lets you choose additional search conditions by using the popup menu at its left side. Based on which option you choose in that popup menu, other popup menus and text fields appear that let you choose further options to refine the search. The standard options are:

  - **Kind.** This is the type of item you are looking for, as defined in the Kind column in the Finder. Its companion popup options are Any, Applications, Documents, Folders, Images, Movies, Music, PDF, Presentations, Text, and Other (selecting Other brings up a text field enabling you to enter any item that matches a Kind field).

  - **Last Opened Date.** This enables you to select the date, or range of dates, that the file was last opened by an application. Its companion popup menus are Within Last, Exactly, Before, After, Today, Yesterday, This Week, This Month, and This Year. Some of these open additional fields and popup menus to refine their settings; for example, Within Last provides a text field to enter a numeric value and a popup menu to choose Days, Weeks, Months, or Years.

  - **Last Modified Date.** This offers the same options as the Last Opened Date filter, but it checks when an item was last changed rather than merely opened.

  - **Created Date.** This checks for items that were created in the date range you specify. Its options are the same as for Last Opened Date.

  - **Name.** This looks for items by name. Its companion popup menu lets you choose the criteria for filtering items — Matches, Contains, Begins With, Ends With, and Is — based on the text you enter in the adjacent text field.

  - **Contents.** This searches through the contents of a file for the text entered in the adjacent text field.

- **Other.** This opens a sheet with a list of more than 100 other metadata options. Select the In Menu option for each that you want to appear in the customization menu bar's popup menu from now on, then click OK.

At the far right of the customization menu bar are the + and – iconic buttons; + lets you add another condition, while – deletes the conditions in that row.

Working with Spotlight results

You can work with items that appear in the Finder search window much like any other items in the Finder. You can drag them from the Spotlight window to a new location, double-click them to open them in their default application, and drag them to the Dock to create aliases.

If you Control+click or right-click items, you get a contextual menu that lets you open them, copy them, label them with a color, open their enclosing folder, perform a Quick Look on them, open an Info Window, move them to the Trash, send them to a Bluetooth device, and rename the files (although if you rename them, they may disappear from the results list if the new name doesn't fit the search criteria).

At the bottom of the Finder search window is the path bar, which shows the folder hierarchy for the selected item in relation to your Home folder. If the Finder search window is too narrow to display the title of each folder, the bar is truncated and just the folder icons appear; hovering the mouse over these icons causes their titles to appear. Double-clicking any of the folder icons in the path bar opens a separate Finder window revealing that folder's contents.

Another way to open the folder that an item is contained within is to select it and choose File ⇨ Open Containing Folder or press ⌘+R, or Control+click or right-click the item and choose Open Containing Folder from the contextual menu.

Boolean Spotlight searching

Boolean searching (named after an English mathematician named George Boole) is a method of searching for items via an algebraic logic system. Boolean logic is familiar to anybody who has created computer code, and its terms are familiar to many users and can be used within Spotlight. Note that the Boolean operators must be entered in all-uppercase. The common Boolean operators that Spotlight uses are as follows:

- **AND.** This looks for items containing both terms. Normally you don't have to type this because entering two or more terms looks for items that contain both the terms by default. For example, if you search for *apple mac*, Spotlight looks for items that contain both the term *apple* and *mac*. You can also search for *apple AND mac* to get the same results. Where AND is useful is when you are using other Boolean operators as well.

- **OR.** If you want to look for items that contain either search term, you can place an OR between the two terms. For example, the Spotlight search *apple OR mac* looks for items containing either term on its own (or items with both Apple and Mac included).

- **NOT.** What if you want to look for things that have *apple* and *mac* but not *fruit* (if you have any files containing references to the edible kind of apple). Typing *apple AND mac NOT fruit* gives you the desired result.

Discovering smart folders

If you find yourself using the same search tool on a regular basis, you can turn the Finder window into an item known as *smart folder*. This is like a regular folder, except when you open the folder, it automatically runs the Spotlight search associated with it. There are two ways of creating a smart folder:

- **Choose File ➪ New Smart Folder in the Finder or press ⌘+Option+N.** This opens a new Finder search window that you can use to enter the search terms. This can then be saved.
- **Enter a search term into a Finder window and click the Save button.** This opens a dialog box that enables you to select a location for the smart folder, and a check box setting that gives you the option of adding the folder to the Search area of the Sidebar.

Smart folders are easily identified by their purple color and a gear icon embedded into the folder icon.

Note

A smart folder is simply a saved Spotlight search; refer to the previous sections for details on using Spotlight.

Double-clicking a smart folder (or selecting it in the Sidebar) reveals its contents. Because smart folders are dynamic, their contents change over time, making them a great way to keep tabs on changing content, such as files from the current week or files with specific image dimensions.

There are several smart folders that come with Mac OS X. You can find them in the Sidebar of any Finder window. There are two basic kinds: content-based (All Documents, All Movies, and All Images) and time-based (Yesterday, Today, and Past Week). The time-based ones are identified in the Sidebar with a clock icon.

Using Spotlight with applications

As we mentioned previously, Spotlight is a system-wide service that is integrated throughout the Mac OS X. As such, Spotlight services are available in a wide variety of Mac OS X applications. Some of these offer unique functions that enable you to search through the data contained in that particular application; others enable you to take the data in the application and perform Spotlight searches on it.

Using the Spotlight contextual menu

Many Apple applications have a Spotlight area in a contextual menu. If you use Apple's Safari Web browser, for example, you can highlight text and Control+click or right-click it to get a contextual menu that includes the Search in Spotlight option. Choosing that option opens a Finder search window with the search term entered into the search field. Other applications such as Mail and TextEdit also sport this function.

Note

These applications also have a Search in Google contextual menu option. It enables you to enter the term into the Google search engine and look for it online.

Using Spotlight with supported applications

Several applications built by Apple have their own Spotlight search fields in the upper right of their windows. These search fields enable you to search through the data contained within the application without having to go through the Finder. It also ensures that you search only through the data applying to that application instead of having to sift through other results. Typical examples of applications that include Spotlight search fields are Mail, Address Book, iCal, and Automator.

Tip

A great use of Spotlight is found in the System Preferences application. Typing in the name of a function in the search field in the System Preferences application window darkens the whole window and highlights the system preference that offers that function. See Figure 3.22 to see this in action.

FIGURE 3.22

The Spotlight search field available in the System Preferences application window enables you to search for items by entering their names in the search field.

Summary

In this chapter, you've seen how to use the Finder to manage and navigate the files on your Mac in its Finder windows, as well as understanding its key areas for providing controls: the title bar, toolbar, and Sidebar. You can switch among four view modes — Icons, List, Columns, and Cover Flow — to navigate the file structure used by Mac OS X.

There are separate options to customize the appearance of the Finder window and its contents: using the Finder's Preferences dialog box, using the view options controls, and using the Customize Toolbar dialog box. The view options controls, by default, apply only to the open Finder window (though you can make them apply to all Finder windows); the options in the Preferences dialog box and Customize Toolbar dialog box always apply to all Finder windows.

The Mac OS has four key folders in which all files on the startup disk are kept: Applications, System, Library, and Users. The Users folder contains Home folders for each user account set up on the Mac, and those Home Folders contain all the files, applications, and settings specific to each user.

There are several special actions that the Finder enables. One is the ability to have AppleScripts run automatically any time a folder's contents change (a feature called *folder actions*). Another is the capability to enable and disable sharing for disks and folders by using the Info window.

Disks and other volumes are essentially just a type of folder as far as the Finder is concerned. But there are some differences. For example, you must eject volumes from the Mac in the Finder before physically removing or disconnecting them; otherwise, data may be lost. The Finder also lets you create burn folders containing files and folders that you can then easily write to a recordable CD or DVD by using Finder commands.

A key technology in Mac OS X is Spotlight, which indexes all the information on your Mac to make it quickly accessible in searches. You can use Spotlight to quickly search for various types of information, from applications to the content within documents, as well as attributes of files, such as image size and last modification date. You can create complex Spotlight search queries and save Spotlight searches as smart folders. Some applications support Spotlight internally, bringing its capabilities to the application's files and functions.

Backing Up Files

I n this chapter, we take a look at effectively backing up and restoring files. Backing up files, as well as restoring them, is fundamentally important, and we highly advise that you become familiar with the process, set up your own backup system, and routinely maintain it.

Backing up data on a computer has always been a laborious process that many people overlook. In Mac OS X 10.5 Leopard, Apple introduced a new backup tool called Time Machine. It makes the backup process quick and simple to set up, virtually unnoticeable in operation, and reliable for restoring files. It even comes with an attractive 3-D interface that adds a touch of life to the otherwise insipidly dull process of file restoration.

Because Time Machine is such a highly integrated Mac OS X tool, we spend the bulk of this chapter looking at using it as your backup solution. However, Time Machine isn't the only backup solution available to Mac OS X users; we also look at some alternatives, including Apple's Backup program (included as part of its MobileMe service).

Finally, we investigate how you can use RAID (redundant array of independent disks) to protect your data against hard-disk failure. We look at how to install, or attach, multiple disks to your Mac, and how to use Disk Utility to turn these drives into a single RAID system that keeps your data safe, even if one of the hard disks malfunctions.

Practicing Good Housekeeping

Any disk-based operating system requires a certain amount of maintenance, both to ensure that it operates efficiently and to prevent mishaps from occurring. As with any storage area used in the real world, debris will accumulate over time and the organizational structure becomes disorganized as data is moved around (on a hard disk, this is known as *fragmentation*). Performing a few standard operations on a regular basis can help provide performance and stability.

Of all the maintenance actions, by far the most important is backing up your data. We cannot stress how critical it is to set up a good backup system. A computer user who doesn't back up files will one day be very sorry for his or her indiscretion. Most of the time, you will be lucky, but sooner or later you will accidentally delete a file or suffer a technical failure and will rue the day you didn't back up your data.

Creating backups

A backup is — as the name suggests — a reserve force that comes into play when something has gone wrong, typically when something has been lost from your Mac. Usually you use a backup in two different circumstances. The first is when a file is lost, either because it was accidentally deleted or it became corrupted and is no longer useable. The second — a more serious use — is for disaster recovery. In this case, your Mac is essentially unusable. It may be because of a physical failure of the hard disk or because something critical has happened to the file structure of Mac OS X. Either way, you'll be glad to have a backup on hand.

A backup enables to you to roll back part of your Mac's data to an earlier point — a point where you still had a file that has now been deleted or where the data on your hard disk wasn't corrupted. Fittingly then, Apple offers a comprehensive backup solution called Time Machine. Time Machine is a seamless backup tool that records changes made to your hard disk and uses a 3-D interface to enable you to move back in time to recover files and data on your Mac. The advantage to using Time Machine — aside from its aforementioned ease of use — is that it's highly integrated with Mac OS X, and has functionality implemented directly within many of Apple's key applications. Because of this we focus on setting up and using Time Machine for most of this chapter. Time Machine is designed to work with an external hard drive, but this is by no means the only backup solution.

Choosing a backup medium

Because the data on your Mac is stored on its hard disk, it makes a lot of sense to ensure that your backup is stored elsewhere. And the most obvious place is on removable media. At one time, personal computer users stored pretty much everything on floppy disks (first the 5.25-inch variety, then the smaller 3.5-inch versions).

Fast-forward to the present day and floppy disks are no longer a practical option. Not only did Apple remove the floppy disk from its computer range with the introduction of the iMac, but also the limited capacity of the disks themselves is dwarfed by the data held on modern computers. Even the Zip disks that provided data storage of up to 750MB are no longer practical (although the Zip's maker, Iomega, has a similar product called the Rev that provides up to 120GB of storage on a single removable disk; however, the disks are expensive).

Businesses working in the enterprise environment often use tape drives to back up large amounts of data. Tape drives work on the same principle as video recording (or early audio recording) equipment, and modern tapes can contain up to a terabyte (1,024GB) of data. These solutions tend to be overkill for the home environment, and with the cost of setting up and maintaining them (not to mention the time involved with retrieving data), tape-based backups are even losing popularity in the enterprise environment.

For many years using CD and DVD drives was the backup solution of choice for many people, and even these days it is an option worth considering. However, the relative size of DVDs (4.7GB for a single layer [SL] disc; 8.5GB for a dual-layer [DL] disc) is quite small, especially compared to modern hard disks. Having said that, the ease with which optical discs can be recorded, the prevalence of optical drives on Macs, and the relative price and availability of optical media make this backup method one that many people still choose — especially when they want a permanent store of a specific kind of data (such as photographs from a wedding).

However, it is the external hard disk that has become the de facto backup system of choice. These hard disks are cheap and readily available. They are essentially based on the same hard-disk technology used in your Mac's startup disk, except they are encased in a separate plastic shell and are connected to the Mac typically via FireWire or USB (Universal Serial Bus), but it can also be via a third, emerging option called eSATA (external Serial Advanced Technology Attachment).

Tip

If you use a USB disk for backup, be sure that it is the USB 2.0 standard rather than the USB 1.0 variant. USB 1.0's slower transfer speeds can make backups interminably slow.

Of course, if you own a Mac Pro, you can install up to four separate hard disks internally, and use one for backup storage.

Caution

It is also possible to partition a single hard disk, such as your startup disk, and use the second partition to store a backup. But this is not particularly wise. A second partition may provide a backup for retrieving files that have been accidentally deleted or corrupted, but it provides no disaster recovery protection from a total hard-disk failure. That's why, if you try to use Time Machine on a partition existing on the same disk you are backing up, Time Machine will repeatedly warn you against doing so.

Finally, it is becoming more common to back up your data to an online storage space. Apple enables you to do this via its MobileMe service, which provides 20GB of online space for backing up or storing files (Chapter 15 has more information on MobileMe). Other dedicated services include Mozy (`http://mozy.com`), iDrive (`www.idrive.com`), and Carbonite (`www.carbonite.com`). Many of these services come with dedicated backup software. For example, MobileMe includes an extra Mac OS X program called Backup.

Selecting backup software

If you decide to create backups to an external hard disk, several applications are available:

- **Time Machine.** Ever since Apple introduced Time Machine, Mac OS X users interested in quickly setting up a backup solution have opted for this straightforward application, which comes with Mac OS X at no additional charge. Most of this chapter discusses setting up and using Time Machine.

- **Backup.** Subscribers to Apple's MobileMe service might want to investigate Backup (outlined later in this chapter). This application predates Time Machine and is, in many ways, a more rudimentary backup application.

- **EMC Retrospect.** If you are looking for a more high-end solution than Time Machine, or are looking for a solution for a small- or medium-sized business with multiple computers, then EMC's Retrospect (http://retrospect.com) is a popular choice. This program offers a wide array of customization options, and supports a wide range of backup media. It is also cross-platform, which makes it useful for network environments with both Mac OS X and Windows computers.

- **SuperDuper.** Before Apple released Time Machine, SuperDuper (www.shirt-pocket. com) had been a popular choice among Mac OS X users. Although it lacks the highly integrated restore functions of Time Machine, SuperDuper is a simple backup tool, and its capability to back up to networked drives and optical discs make it an option still worth considering.

- **Carbon Copy Cloner.** Another popular solution among Mac OS X users is a program called Carbon Copy Cloner (www.bombich.com). Rather than creating incremental backups (those that save just the changes to your disk since the last backup), this program clones your entire hard disk onto an external source (usually another hard disk). The target hard disk has to be larger than your original hard disk, and the cloning process can be time consuming; however, it is a good way to create a complete backup of your hard disk. In the event of a disaster, you can even boot your Mac from the cloned hard disk and use Carbon Copy Cloner to restore your regular boot disk from the backup.

Of course, you do not have to use software to create a backup. You can manually copy files that you want to back up. You can copy important files to an external hard disk, and you can burn files you want to back up to an optical disc. (The process of recording files to a recordable CD or DVD is outlined in Chapter 3.) You can also use Mac OS X's Automator feature to create actions that add a layer of intelligence to the process of backing up files in the Finder. Using Automator, you can schedule the process of copying files, and only copy files that have changed. Automator is described in more depth in Chapter 25.

Tip

You can find a useful Automator function for backing up files at www.apple.com/downloads/macosx/automator/backupfolder.html.

The problems inherent with any backup solution are largely related to setting up and maintaining a regular backup process. You need to determine which files to back up, and then regularly transfer these files to another storage location for the backup to be effective. Performing regular backups is a time-consuming and largely unrewarding process (until, of course, a disaster strikes and you need to restore vital data).

Using Time Machine to Back Up Files

By now we've hopefully ingrained in you both the importance of putting a backup procedure in place, and our recommendation to use Time Machine.

Time Machine has revolutionized the way that the backup process works. Time Machine was designed to be incredibly easy to set up; virtually invisible in operation; and, thanks to some flashy eye candy (its space-themed background), it even makes the normally tedious process of restoring files fun.

Time Machine boasts some great features that cement its status as the number-one backup app for Mac OS X users. The most important of these is automatic stop and resume functionality. If you remove an external disk or unplug your Mac (or disconnect from a network volume), Time Machine just stops where it is, with no fuss, not even a notification; when you reconnect, Time Machine quietly resumes the backup as if nothing had ever happened. This is great: It means you don't have to wait for backups to complete, and, therefore don't have to schedule backups.

Time Machine is a permanent, always-on solution. You don't have to take time out to perform backups.

Because Time Machine is constantly tracking changes on your Mac, you can use it to recover files and data that have been accidentally deleted. It also is a superb disaster recovery tool; if your Mac is so badly damaged that you can't even use it, simply plug the Time Machine drive into another Mac and you can restore your entire computer.

You can even restore your version of Mac OS X to a completely different Mac and carry on working. This is because Time Machine works in tandem with a Mac OS X technology called Migration Assistant (outlined in Chapter 8). So if you set up a new Mac, you can plug in your Time Machine drive and use Migration Assistant to copy all of your files, programs, and settings, and set up the new computer just like your original machine.

Using external disks for backup

The main requirement of Time Machine is that you have a second hard disk to store the backup on. Typically this is an external hard disk, although those of you with Mac Pros can use a second internal hard disk. The advantage to using an external hard disk is that you can take the disk with you and connect it to another Mac with relative ease. This enables you to use it to migrate data from one Mac to another.

Tip

When installing a second hard disk for Time Machine, it's wise to make sure that the disk is larger than the disk that you are backing up. Time Machine uses compression technology to save space, but each incremental backup increases the size of the file stored on the backup disk, so the backups keep growing. A smart move is to buy the largest external hard disk you can afford, and 1TB external disks are readily available at reasonable prices. Time Machine saves backups until it runs out of room and then starts deleting the older versions of files, so the larger your backup disk, the farther in the past you can retrieve files from.

Backing Up Wirelessly

Those of you with a MacBook or other Mac who want back up wirelessly have two options (both of which involve additional Apple hardware).

The first option is to buy an Apple-branded AirPort Extreme router and connect an external USB 2.0 hard disk to the router. Time Machine can use this hard disk to store the backup files. Note that Mac OS X supports this feature only on its AirPort Extreme router; those of you with other Wi-Fi routers that let you connect a hard disk to them cannot use this feature.

The second option for wireless backups is to buy an Apple device called Time Capsule. It is essentially an AirPort Extreme router with a built-in hard disk. Time Capsule acts as a dedicated hub for creating a wireless network and backing up files. While investing in a Time Capsule device isn't as cost-effective as using a USB 2.0 hard disk tethered to your Mac, it is an incredibly simple way to create backups for one or more Macs without worrying about cables. Best of all, setting up a Time Capsule is as simple as setting up Time Machine. Together they make a great backup combination.

Do note that wireless connections are much slower than USB or FireWire connections, so your backups take longer. You trade the advantage of sharing a backup disk and worrying about cabling each Mac to a disk for the disadvantages of lower speed and higher cost.

With today's high-capacity hard disks, you can use a single disk to back up multiple Macs. Just partition the disk so each Mac has its own dedicated volume to keep the backups separate. Of course, this technique means that you have to remember to plug the disk into each Mac long enough for Time Machine to back each one up, and you don't get automatic backup on the Macs not currently connected to the disk, so there is danger of data loss in between backup rotations.

When Apple first released Time Machine, it stated that you would have to use a disk that wasn't bootable and that you wouldn't be able to copy files to a hard disk being used by Time Machine. In fact, you can back up to a bootable disk and you can write files to a Time Machine backup disk. But we don't advise that you do either. In both cases, you're putting files and data that are not being backed up onto the Time Machine disk and you risk accidentally corrupting the Time Machine backup files. So use a disk that has no other function other than to hold backup data as your Time Machine disk.

Setting up Time Machine

Setting up Time Machine really couldn't be simpler. You set it up in the Time Machine system preference, which you can access in any of the following ways.

- **Plug in a new drive.** If Time Machine is not already configured on your Mac, then connecting an external hard disk prompts Mac OS X to open a dialog box that asks if you want to use that disk to back up with Time Machine (see Figure 4.1). Click Use as Backup Disk to open the Time Machine system preference.

- **Via System Preferences.** Open System Preferences by choosing ⌘ ⇨ System Preferences and click the Time Machine icon.

- **Via the menu bar.** If the Time Machine iconic popup menu is available in the menu bar, choose Open Time Machine Preferences from it.

FIGURE 4.1

Setting up Time Machine really couldn't be easier. Simply attaching an external hard disk automatically brings up this dialog box.

Configuring Time Machine for backups

The Time Machine system preference has a large Off/On iconic toggle, the Select Disk and the Options buttons, and the Show Time Machine Status in the Menu Bar option (see Figure 4.2).

If you clicked Use as Backup Disk when you plugged in a new disk, the Off/On switch is set to On and the attached disk is automatically selected as the Time Machine backup disk. In this case, you really are good to go: Time Machine automatically begins backing up the contents of your main hard disk to the backup disk. Kick back, relax, you're done.

When you first create a backup with Time Machine, a status window opens to show you the progress of the backup. The initial backup may take a couple of hours (or longer if you are backing up over a network). Subsequent backups are incremental, so they copy only over files that have changed since the last backup; consequently, all backups after the first are much quicker.

Like all Time Machine activity, the initial backup is designed not to interfere with the operation of Mac OS X, so you can minimize the Time Machine status window (by clicking the yellow Minimize iconic button) and close the Time Machine system preference (by clicking the red Close iconic button); now just continue with your work.

Tip

Time Machine is designed to work seamlessly, regardless of interruptions. However, we advise that you let the initial backup take place uninterrupted. You can carry on using your Mac, but it's best not to remove the hard disk, disconnect from a network volume, or turn off your Mac until the first Time Machine backup is complete.

Choosing a backup disk

If you have more than two disks attached to your Mac, you need to tell Mac OS X which disk to use. Click Select Disk in the Time Machine system preference to open a settings sheet listing all the disks accessible to Mac OS X (see Figure 4.3). Select the disk you want to use and click Use for Backup.

FIGURE 4.2

The Time Machine system preference enables you to switch the backup on and off, and offers basic options for adjusting the nature of the backup.

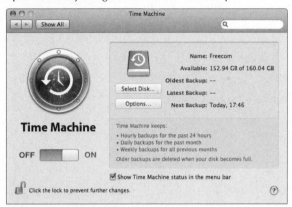

FIGURE 4.3

Time Machine can perform a backup to most of the disks accessible by Mac OS X.

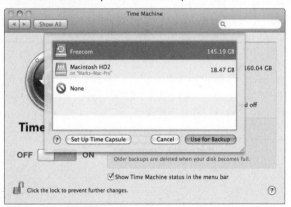

If the hard disk you have selected does not contain enough free space to store the backup, the Time Machine Error dialog box appears (see Figure 4.4). This dialog box informs you of the size that the current backup requires and the amount of space free on the hard drive you have selected. This dialog box has two options: You can click OK, which cancels the backup and turns off Time Machine, or you can click Preferences; from here you can click Select Disk and either choose another disk with more free space or use the Time Machine options to reduce the amount of data backed up on your hard drive.

FIGURE 4.4

Time Machine requires a certain amount of free space on the external hard disk for the initial backup. If there isn't enough space, you receive this warning dialog box.

Time Machine Error

This backup is too large for the backup volume. The backup requires 234.3 GB but only 74.1 GB are available.

To select a larger volume, or make the backup smaller by excluding files, open System Preferences and choose Time Machine.

[Preferences]   [OK]

Setting Time Machine options

When you click the Options button in the Time Machine system preference, a settings sheet appears with options to control the backup.

The main area of the Time Machine options sheet enables you to set areas from the Finder that you do *not* want Time Machine to back up. Not all parts of your Mac OS X volume are vital, and cutting back the backup offers two advantages: It reduces the size of the backup and it reduces the amount of time required to make a backup. There are many types of files that you may consider less important than others; many users consider movies and music to be less important than photographs and documents, although your own priorities may differ.

If you decide there are disks or folders that you don't want to include in the Time Machine backup, you add them to the main area labeled Do Not Back Up. By default, this contains the Time Machine backup volume, but you can add items to this window from other volumes in one of two ways:

- **Drag and drop.** Open a new Finder window and locate a file or folder that you do not want Time Machine to include in the backup. Drag it to the Do Not Back Up window. As you hover over the window, a horizontal blue line appears; let go of the mouse to add the item to the window.

- **Click the plus (+) iconic button below the list of disks.** A dialog box appears from which you navigate to the disk, folder, or file you want; select it and click Exclude. Note the Show Invisible Items option; selecting it reveals the files and folders that are usually hidden on your hard disk, such as internal Mac OS system files.

Note
Folders and files displayed in the Do Not Back Up list include the path structure to the item, so when you come back to this sheet, you can see exactly where these excluded files and folders reside. Next to the + and – iconic buttons is a display showing the amount of space that the current backup will require.

To remove items from the Do Not Back Up list, select them and press the Backspace key or click the – iconic button.

Two Time Machine options appear below the Do Not Back Up list:

- **Back Up while on Battery Power.** This option appears for owners of Mac laptops, and is selected by default. Deselecting the option prevents Time Machine from backing up a Mac laptop unless it is powered via its cord.

- **Notify after Old Backups Are Deleted.** Time Machine backs up data daily, weekly, and monthly. When the hard disk begins to fill up, the program consolidates older backups (days into weeks, and weeks into months). By default, Time Machine warns you when it is going to delete older backups; deselecting this option prevents Time Machine from warning you when it is going to delete older backups.

Setting up Time Machine with a Time Capsule

If you have an Apple Time Capsule device, you can set it up to work with Time Machine. The process of setting up a Time Capsule is identical to that of setting up an Apple Airport Extreme Wi-Fi router. When you first attach a Time Capsule to your home network, the AirPort Utility automatically opens, enabling you to set up the Time Capsule (see Figure 4.5). You can also access the AirPort Utility by opening the Time Machine system preference, clicking Select Disk, and clicking Set Up Time Capsule.

FIGURE 4.5

The AirPort Utility opens up automatically when you attach a Time Capsule to your home network.

You set up a Time Capsule as follows:

1. **Turn on AirPort.** If AirPort is not already switched on, you will need to activate it. You can do this by clicking the AirPort iconic popup menu and choosing Turn AirPort On, or by choosing ⇨ System Preferences, clicking the Network icon, selecting AirPort from the list on the left of the Network system preference, and clicking Turn AirPort On.

2. **Connect to the network.** By default, the Time Capsule is called Apple Network followed by a six-digit alphanumeric identifier (for example, *Apple Network a8a4d8*). Choose this name from the AirPort iconic popup menu, or in the Network system preference choose the name in the Network Name popup menu.

3. **Open AirPort Utility.** AirPort Utility should open automatically if a new Time Capsule is attached to your network. If not, you can locate the AirPort Utility inside the Utilities folder (inside the Applications folder in the Finder).

4. **Highlight Time Machine.** An icon for Time Machine appears in the list on the left-hand side of the AirPort Utility (see Figure 4.5). Select it and click Continue.

5. **Enter a name and password.** You can personalize your Time Capsule by giving it a name (by default, it uses your username). You must also enter a password (and then reenter the same password in the Verify Password text field) to protect the settings of your Time Capsule. By default, the password is saved to your Keychain so you do not need to enter it every time you make changes to the Time Capsule (the Keychain is explained in Chapter 23). If you deselect the Remember This Password in My Keychain option, you are prompted to enter the password whenever you want to make changes to the Time Capsule. By default, the same password also gives you access to the Time Capsule disk through the Finder. If you select the Use a Different Password to Secure Disks option, you can set a different password for disk access. When you've entered your name and password, click Continue.

6. **Select what you want to do with Time Capsule.** Your Time Capsule may be attached to your current router or to your DSL or cable modem. In that case, you need to tell it how to interact with the network. You have three options to choose from:

   - I Want to Create a New Network.
   - I Want to Replace an Existing Base Station or Wireless Router with Time Capsule.
   - I Want Time Capsule to Join My Current Network.

   Select the appropriate option and click Continue.

7. **Update the Time Capsule.** When you have selected the appropriate settings for attaching the Time Capsule to your network, click the Update button. A dialog box appears warning you that the Time Capsule will be unavailable during the update. The update shouldn't take longer than a couple of minutes, after which the AirPort Utility shows a congratulations message (see Figure 4.6). Click Quit to finish setting up your Time Capsule.

When the Time Capsule is set up, Time Machine can back up to it. Open the Time Machine system preference, click Select Disk, select the Time Capsule volume and click Use for Backup. You are prompted to enter the password you entered during the Time Capsule setup; enter it and click Connect. Time Machine begins backing up your volume wirelessly.

FIGURE 4.6

After you have set up a Time Capsule, you will see this message, informing you that everything is set up correctly.

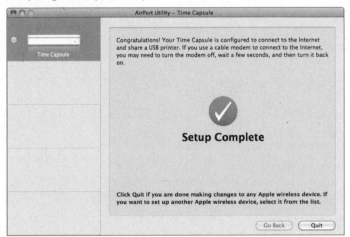

Moving Your Backup to a Bigger Disk

As your Time Machine backup disk gets full — whether from you backing up additional external disks onto it or from backing up the ever-increasing number of files on your Mac — you may decide you want a bigger disk to back up to. The process is not quite as straightforward as you might expect.

First, if you simply connect a new backup drive and set it up in Time Machine, that new backup drive will not have all the previous backups; instead, it starts from scratch by copying all your currently files and then doing the incremental backup after that.

You might think that all you have to do is connect your new disk and copy or move the old files to the new disk, then set it up as the new Time Machine backup disk. But if you do so, Time Machine ignores those previous backup files and starts the backup process from scratch, so again your old backups aren't available via Time Machine.

What you have to do is clone the old disk's contents to the new disk, so Time Machine sees it as the same disk. To do so, first turn off Time Machine, then connect the old and new backup disks. Now open Mac OS X's Disk Utility and go to the Restore pane. At the left of the Disk Utility window is a list of connected disks. Drag the old disk's icon into the Source field, and drag the new disk's icon into the Destination field. Then click Restore.

After Disk Utility has cloned the old disk to the new disk, close Disk Utility and rename the old disk something else so Time Machine doesn't get confused. (We suggest you not delete the old disk's contents or reformat it until you are sure that the new backup disk is working correctly.) Turn Time Machine back on, and you should be set.

Using Time Machine to Restore Files

The point of having a backup is to be able to restore files — a process that Time Machine makes so visually spectacular that you'll find yourself looking forward to it. When you restore files, the Time Machine browser replaces your desktop with a starry background and a row of Finder windows zooming off into infinity, each window representing the Mac's files at a different point in time, as Figure 4.7 shows.

There are typically three reasons for wanting to retrieve a file from an earlier point in time:

- **Accidental deletion.** You may have moved a file to the Trash, and then emptied the Trash. If you decide at a later point that you need the file, Time Machine can help you retrieve it.

- **File corruption.** Even though Mac OS X is a stable operating system, it is possible for a file to become corrupted and unworkable. In this case, you can use Time Machine to retrieve an earlier instance of the file when it was in fully working order.

- **Version rollback.** Say you have made substantial changes to a file and then saved it, but decide at a later point that you want to revert to the earlier version of the file. Although it's usually wiser to track changes in documents and undo the ones you don't want, not all applications have this capability, so Time Machine can come in very handy in those cases.

You can access the Time Machine browser by using any of the following methods:

- **Use the Dock icon.** By default a Time Machine icon is present in the Mac OS X Dock. Click it to open Time Machine.

- **Use the menu bar's icon popup menu.** In the Time Machine iconic popup menu in the menu bar (if one is present), choose Enter Time Machine.

- **Open the application.** Time Machine is an application and, as such, is located in the Applications folder. Double-click the Time Machine icon to access the program.

Using the Time Machine browser

By default, accessing Time Machine replaces the desktop with a starfield window and a Finder window. Behind the Finder window is a cascade of other Finder windows, each one representing an earlier instance in time. The initial Finder window represents the current state of all the files on the Mac. You can navigate the Finder window in the same manner as a Finder window opened in Mac OS X (as explained in Chapter 3). You can also use Spotlight search to locate files in the Finder window displayed in the Time Machine browser. (Spotlight search is also covered in Chapter 3.)

Where the Time Machine browser differs from the regular desktop is the vertical time bar and arrows on the right-hand side. Move the mouse over the time bar and it expands, with a visual effect similar to the dock in magnification mode. Each horizontal line on the time bar represents a different instance in time. Use the mouse to select a time instance.

FIGURE 4.7

The Time Machine interface depicts a star field with windows stretching out back in time. You use controls to the right to move back through different instances.

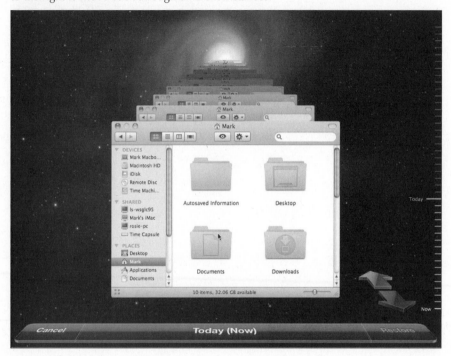

Time Machine backs up files according to the following schedule:

- Hourly backups for the last 24 hours
- Daily backups for the last month
- Weekly backups for all previous months

The lowest line on the vertical time bar represents the present; each horizontal line moving upward represents the next instance back in time (moving through hourly, weekly, and monthly backups). To the left of each bar is the time and date that the line represents. Clicking any of these lines takes the Finder window to that point in time (complete with a swooshing display as the windows in the Time Machine browser flip through to the appropriate one). The Finder window then displays all the files that were present on the Mac and its attached disks at that point in time.

Restoring files with Time Machine

If you see a file that you want to restore, highlight the file in the Finder window in the Time Machine browser and click Restore. The Finder windows flips forward to the foremost instance (the one that represents the present) and the file is deposited into it, in its original location.

If the restored file exists in the present Finder window, a dialog box opens with three options (see Figure 4.8):

- **Keep Original.** Choosing this option cancels the retrieval and keeps the file that is in the present Finder window.

- **Keep Both.** Choosing this option retains the original file into the past Finder window and copies it into the present Finder window. (A number is added to the copied, past filename to differentiate the two files.)

- **Replace.** Choosing this option deletes the file in the present Finder window and replaces it with the past version being retrieved from Time Machine.

FIGURE 4.8

Select a file from a past Finder window in the Time Machine browser and click the Restore button to retrieve it. If the same file still exists in the present Finder window, you see this dialog box.

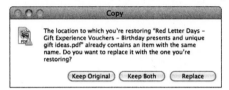

Searching for changes

Just as you can use the vertical timeline to search through folders, you can also skim through Finder windows and look for changes. Clicking the ↑ iconic button in the Time Machine browser flips back in time, moving through the various save points, until one of the files in the Finder's location changes. This is useful for when you know the location of a file, but not the point at which it was changed or deleted. Clicking the ↓ iconic button moves forward through time, again stopping at the point at which the location displayed in the Finder window changes.

Exiting the Time Machine browser

When you have decided to finish restoring files from the Time Machine browser, you can return to the main Mac OS X in three ways:

- By clicking the Cancel button.
- By pressing the Escape key.
- By clicking the Close iconic button in the foremost window in the Time Machine browser.

Using the Time Machine with Applications

Because Time Machine works to back up and restore files on your Mac, you can use it within the Finder to restore anything used by Mac OS X. However, you can also use it to restore some Mac OS X applications to a previous state, such as to restore Address Book contacts if they get corrupted in a file sync or to roll back to old e-mail lists in Mail. The applications supported by the Time Machine browser include:

- Mail
- Address Book
- iPhoto 08 and later
- GarageBand 08 and later

To use Time Machine with these applications, first open the application, then open the Time Machine browser. You see the same series of windows stretching into the past as you do for files, and you move through the browser and restore past application states the same way as you do for files.

Using MobileMe Backup to Save Important Files

Backup is an application that predates Time Machine, but Apple still offers it as an option for backing up files on your Mac for subscribers to its MobileMe service. (Chapter 15 has more information on MobileMe.)

Unlike Time Machine, which is a complete solution for backing up your Mac's disks, Backup enables you to make backups of specific files (or types of files) and then schedules different backup methods. For example, you can back up your files to an external hard disk on a daily basis, and to a CD or DVD once per month. Backup also enables you to save files to iDisk, Apple's online storage space that Apple offers as part of its MobileMe service. (Chapter 15 has more information on iDisk.)

You can set your own plan for backing up files and determine exactly which files or folders you want to back up; you can also use the Backup utility with Spotlight to save certain types of files rather than specific file locations. However, the key difference between Backup and Time Machine is that Backup requires you to determine the files you want to preserve and the backup method you want to use. In this sense, it is a more complex option than Time Machine, which is why Apple promoted Time Machine as the more appropriate option for most users.

Backup is only available to subscribers to Apple's MobileMe service, and is not installed by default within Mac OS X. Subscribers to MobileMe can find the installation files for Backup inside the Software folder contained on the root location of their iDisk volume.

Note

The default amount of data storage on an iDisk was 20GB as this book went to press (although Apple adds more periodically). Using iDisk as a location for backing up files quickly eats up the amount of allocated iDisk space. You can buy more space on iDisk through the account settings in MobileMe (see Chapter 15).

Creating a backup plan

When you first launch Backup, a dialog box opens, prompting you to Choose a Plan Template (Figure 4.9). On subsequent launches of Backup, you can create a new backup plan by clicking on the + iconic button in the Backup window, choosing Plan⇨New Plan, or pressing ⌘+N. You have five options when creating a new backup plan:

- **Home Folder.** This option backs up your Home folder to your hard disk daily and to a CD or DVD monthly.

- **Personal Data & Settings.** This option backs up your Address Book, Stickies notes, iCal calendars, Safari settings, and Keychain settings to your iDisk once per day.

- **iLife.** This option backs up the data relating to iLife (photos, music, and movies) to CD or DVD weekly.

- **iTunes Library.** This option backs up the music used by iTunes to CD or DVD once per month.

- **Custom.** Choosing this option enables you to select your own backup plan.

To begin using Backup, select one of the options and click Choose Plan.

Customizing your backup plan

After you have selected a template option (or custom option) for the new plan, you are presented with a dialog box (see Figure 4.10) named after the option you selected in the Backup dialog box. It opens to the Back Up pane, which has two subpanes:

- **Backup Items.** This subpane shows the data located in Mac OS X (either in the Finder or within specific applications) that will be backed up. The total size of the data that is set to be backed up is displayed below the pane. You can add items by clicking the + iconic button; selecting an item and clicking the – iconic button removes an item from the backup list.

- **Destination and Schedule.** This subpane displays the intended destination of the backup. Typically this is your hard disk or iDisk. The green bar to the right of this area shows the amount of available free space available on the destination. You can add a destination and schedule by clicking the + iconic button; selecting a destination and its schedule, and clicking the – iconic button removes it from the schedule list.

FIGURE 4.9

MobileMe's Backup offers several preset backup templates that you can use to automate the process of making backups.

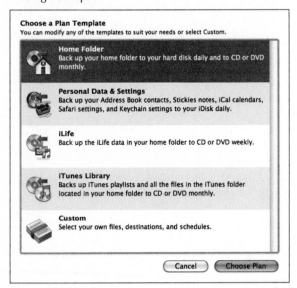

FIGURE 4.10

The Backup dialog box shows the items that you have decided to back up and the destination that they will be added to.

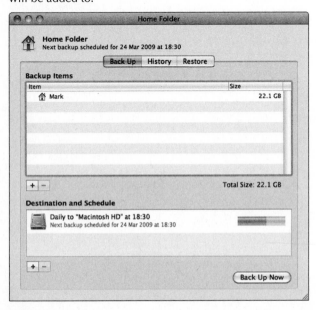

Adding items to the backup

The + and – iconic buttons that appear below the Backup Items subpane enable you to add and remove items to the backup plan. If you click the + iconic button, a settings sheet called Choose Items to Back Up opens with three panes of its own:

- **QuickPicks.** These are links to common items found on Mac OS X, such as Address Book, iTunes Library, and Microsoft Word documents. They tend to be file types, or files associated with certain applications, rather than file collections. Use the check boxes to select items that you want to add to the backup plan and click Done.

- **Files & Folders.** This pane enables you to pick files and folders from the Finder. Below the pane are two options: Include This File/Folder and Do Not Include This File/Folder. Select the desired option and click Done.

- **Spotlight.** This pane enables you to use Spotlight technology and search for items to include or exclude from the backup. Enter a search term in the text field and use the main pane to locate items. (Note that the Spotlight technology used in Backup is more primitive than that used in the Finder.) Click Done when you have finished.

Adjusting the schedule and destination

In the Backup dialog box's Back Up pane, click the + iconic button below the Destination and Schedule subpane to open a settings sheet with a set of options for determining the backup location and frequency of the backup. First click Destination Folder to select an alternative volume, a folder in your Home folder, or your iDisk as the backup location. Use the Folder popup menu to choose the folder in the chosen destination in which you want to store the backup. By default, this is a folder called Backups.

The Automatically Back Up at the Following Times option is selected by default. Its settings enable you to set a frequency (day, week, month, three months, or six months) for the backup, the day of the week or month, and the exact time that you want Mac OS X to perform the backup. Click OK when you have selected the required settings.

Viewing the history

To open a record of when backups have taken place, go to the History pane in the backup dialog box. This pane shows the date, event, and destination of the backup. Select a backup and click the View Details button for more detailed information. Click the Clear History button to remove the backups from the History (note that this does not delete the backups themselves, just the recorded history of them in this pane).

Starting the backup

When you have finished creating a backup plan, click Back Up Now to begin the first backup. This opens the Backup dialog box and starts copying the files (see Figure 4.11).

Note

Files saved by the Backup utility are compressed into a single bundle in the folder. In that folder, look for files with the orange umbrella icon and the Kind description Full Backup Package.

FIGURE 4.11

The Backup dialog box shows you the progress of the backup as it takes place.

Restoring files from Backup

To restore these files, again use the Backup program. Select the backup plan whose files you want to restore, then click Restore.

Managing items in Backup

When you open the Backup application, note its Action iconic popup menu (the gear icon). It provides the following options:

- **New.** Like the + iconic button, this option lets you add a new backup plan to the Backup program.

- **Rename.** This option enables you to rename the selected backup plan.

- **Edit.** Select a plan in the Backup dialog box and choose this option to adjust its settings.

- **Remove.** Select a plan in the Backup dialog box and choose this option to remove the selected plan from Backup.

- **Back Up.** When you choose this menu option, the selected backup plan immediately backs up the items it refers to, regardless of its schedule. It will still back up when the next scheduled point is reached.

- **Restore.** Choose this option to restore the items saved in the last backup of the highlighted option.

Using RAID Redundancy

RAID (redundant array of inexpensive disks) is a technology with two distinct uses.

First, it can use multiple disks to create a single volume. For example, you can install four 512GB hard disks to create a single volume providing 2TB of space. This is particularly useful for server space and for users who use large files. (For example, high-definition video editing takes up a significant amount of space.)

You have two ways to use RAID to create shared disks. One is called a *concatenated disk set*, which stores the files on whatever disk is available but presents the array of disks to the Finder as if it were one disk so the Mac can put the file on the most accessible disk at the moment. The other is called *striping*, which saves files in pieces across multiple disks so data can be pulled simultaneously from multiple locations to get it to the Mac faster (very useful for video). But the risk is if one disk in the array fails, any file with a piece of itself on that failed disk is now corrupted because it is incomplete.

The second use of RAID is to keep an ongoing copy of all data in a mirrored set in case one disk fails — a key issue for Macs used as servers or for other heavy production uses. A failed disk can be replaced without the loss of any data (because a complete set of data still exists on the other drive). When a replacement drive is installed, the data is copied from the remaining hard disk to the new hard disk, and you will be able to continue working as before.

Understanding RAID

RAID is a high-end technology that can be quite complex for the computer novice to understand and set up, although Mac OS X goes a long way to making the technology as accessible as possible for the beginner.

The first thing to understand is that you need to have a set of identical disks to create a RAID array. Typically you need between two to four identical hard disks to create an array and two identical disks to create a mirrored set.

At the time of writing, the only Macs currently available that have internal storage for multiple disks are the Mac Pro, which has bays to contain up to four hard drives, and Apple's Xserve server, which has space for three internal hard drives.

The next thing to understand is that RAID can be controlled via hardware or software configurations. By default, a Mac Pro controls RAID via software contained within Mac OS X. However, a RAID card can be installed to control the RAID via hardware instead. A hardware approach offers numerous benefits: It opens up a wider range of RAID configurations, it contains a 512MB cache of memory for increased performance and stability, and it enables faster hard disks (up to 15,000 rpm) to be installed.

There is a wide range of different types of RAID configurations, each with different requirements and offering different benefits. Table 4.1 explains the different types of RAID configurations available and what each configuration offers.

TABLE 4.1

Different Types of RAID Configurations

RAID Level	Drive Requirements	Description and Benefits
RAID 0 (striping)	One to four identical hard disks	Up to four identical hard disks can be used to create a single volume. The size of the volume is the sum of all the hard disks' space. When data is written to the striped array, it is sent in pieces to all drives in parallel; therefore, a striped array offers faster performance. It also provides a volume larger than the physical size of a single hard disk. However, if any of the hard disks fail, the whole volume is lost, because the files on the surviving disks are incomplete. Therefore, a separate backup system is critical.
RAID 1 (mirroring)	Two identical hard disks	Two identical hard disks are used to create a single volume. The volume size is identical to one of the hard disks. The data on each disk is kept identical at all times, so if one of the hard disks suffers a mechanical problem, the other can replace it immediately without any data loss.
Concatenated RAID (also called JBOD, or "just a bunch of disks")	One to four hard disks	This is a RAID array similar to RAID 0 (striping). However, it does not split (stripe) data across multiple drives, instead keeping files intact on whatever disk they are stored. Thus, there is no performance advantage as with striped drives, but there's also less risk of data loss, because only the files on a failed disk are lost.
Enhanced JBOD	One to four hard drives	This format stands for Just a Bunch of Disks. It isn't technically an array; however, it is a format whereby individual disks can be turned into a RAID without requiring them to be reformatted. If you order a Mac Pro with multiple drives, they will be supplied as individual drives using the JBOD format. This means that you have multiple individual drives, with Mac OS X installed on the first drive, but the JBOD format enables you to turn the drives into a single RAID array without reinstalling Mac OS X.
RAID 0+1	Four identical hard disks	As the name suggests, this format uses four hard disks and combines both features of RAID 0 and RAID 1. The first two disks are striped to create a single volume the sum of both disks. The second two disks are striped and used to mirror the first set.
RAID 5	Three or four hard drives	RAID 5 is a new format that uses block-level striping and redundancy to create a hard disk that has some of the advantages of RAID 0, while implementing redundancy features of RAID 1. In this sense it is similar to RAID 0+1 but its technology creates a larger disk space. For example, if you have four 1TB drives, you can create a 4TB array in RAID 0 or a 2TB redundant array with RAID 0+1. In RAID 5, you can create a 3TB drive with redundancy features. If any of the disks fail, you can replace them.

Tip

Hot swapping is a term often associated with RAID. It is a process where you are able to remove a mirrored hard drive while a computer is still running and insert a replacement drive without having to turn off the computer (or without even interrupting your work). Obviously a hard-disk failure is a rare occurrence, so the hot-swappable feature is only really required in time-critical work environments. The hard disks in Apple's Xserve servers are hot-swappable, whereas the disks in its Mac Pros are not.

Installing internal hard disks

If you own a Mac Pro with a single hard disk, you need to install additional hard disks to create a RAID volume. Installing additional hard disks into the Mac Pro is a relatively easy process (at least, when compared to many other computers). The Mac Pro contains SATA (Serial Advanced Technology Attachment) 3 Gbps, 3.5-inch, single-height (1U) hard disks — that is, the commonly sold as 3.5-inch desktop SATA drives.

The only tool you need is a Phillips #1 screwdriver. (It's the one with a cross head.) Follow these steps to install the hard drive into your Mac Pro:

1. **Shut down your Mac Pro.**

2. **Wait five to ten minutes.** Apple recommends this to allow the internal systems to cool.

3. **Unplug all external cables except for the power cord.**

4. **Discharge any static electricity from your body.** You can do this by touching the metal PCI (Peripheral Component Interconnect) slots' access covers. Another common technique is to touch a heat radiator. Professionals also invest in wearing antistatic wristbands.

5. **Unplug the power cord.**

6. **Lift the latch on the rear of the Mac Pro.**

7. **Remove the side panel from the Mac Pro.**

8. **Locate the hard disk bays.** These are four metal rectangular openings, arranged in a horizontal row, located near the top half of the computer.

9. **Remove the metal carrier.** The first hard disk bay (the one to the left) typically contains the boot disk. This disk can be replaced, but if you are adding an additional disk, you should install it in the adjacent disk bay to the right. Installation is easy: Pull the metal carrier out from the bay. Note: The latch on the rear of the computer (used in Step 6) must be still open, or the disk is locked in place.

10. **Insert the hard disk.** The disk is attached to the carrier via four metal screws. Each carrier has four screws on the bottom. You can remove these by hand, or you can use the Phillips screwdriver. All hard disks have four matching screw sockets. Place the hard disk into the carrier and use the screws to attach the hard disk to the carrier.

11. **Slide the carrier back into the hard disk bay.** Push it firmly in so the connections in the Mac Pro insert into the hard disk. The carrier should slide smoothly back in to the Mac Pro. Do not force it in.

12. **Replace the metal access panel to the side of the Mac Pro.**

13. Close the latch on the rear of the Mac Pro to lock the access panel and disks in place.

14. Reattach all the cables and power up your Mac Pro.

Installing external hard disks

Of course, not everybody owns a Mac Pro. Fortunately, these users are not left completely out in the cold. There are many external RAID drives containing multiple disks available that connect via FireWire and USB 2.0.

Some external RAID drives come with hardware RAID cards, and are designed for the Mac Pro. These typically connect via an eSATA connection. (Refer to their documentation for their specific setup and operations.)

Tip

Data Robotics has created an interesting device called the Drobo, which offers similar functionality to an external RAID drive, but with an interesting twist. Rather than requiring you to install identical disks, the Drobo accepts up to four disks that can be any size. The built-in hardware controller then uses the disks to create a single volume that is approximately three-quarters of the total space of all the disks installed. The advantage is that any single disk can be removed without any loss of data. And you can pull out a single disk and insert a larger one, and the device will automatically increase the total amount of storage available on a volume. The technology has attracted a lot of attention, and it could point to a future of RAID-style storage that is more user friendly and accessible to the general public, while offering both striped and mirrored functionality. You can find more information at www.drobo.com.

Using Disk Utility to format a RAID drive

When you have multiple identical disks installed on your Mac, you need to convert them into a RAID set. You do this by using the Disk Utility application. Disk Utility has a wide range of functionality, much of which is covered in Chapter 8. This chapter covers its RAID features.

Note

Disk Utility cannot create a RAID array by using a volume that is currently running Mac OS X. If you want to create a RAID array with Disk Utility, you must boot Mac OS X from the installation DVD and select Disk Utility during the installation process (see Chapter 1 for more information). Creating a RAID from the installation volume erases all information on the disk, so you need to install Mac OS X from scratch. Combining Time Machine with the Migration Assistant (as outlined earlier in this chapter) enables you to copy all your information back to the disk.

Identifying the disks

The disks available to your Mac appear on the list to the left-hand side of Disk Utility, and any volumes (such as partitions) on the disk appear indented below the disk. When you select a disk or volume, information on it appears at the bottom of the Disk Utility window. This includes the Disk Description, Connection Bus and Type, Connection ID, Capacity, Write Status, S.M.A.R.T. (Self Monitoring Analysis and Reporting Technology) status, and Partition Map Scheme.

Tip

Disk Utility can also access S.M.A.R.T. information supplied by SATA or ATA drives installed in your Mac. S.M.A.R.T. was developed to provide information on predicted drive failures and diagnose the media and mechanics of a hard disk. The S.M.A.R.T. status of a disk is displayed at the bottom of the Disk Utility when a disk is selected in the list. When a disk is functioning correctly, Disk Utility reports a status of "Verified." If the words "About to Fail" appear in red text, you should immediately make a backup of your disk and replace the defective disk.

Formatting new disks

If you have recently inserted a new hard disk, you may need to format it before you can continue:

1. **Select the disk.**

2. **Go to the Erase pane.** This shows all the options in Disk Utility relating to formatting a disk.

3. **Select a volume format.** Use the Format popup menu to select the appropriate volume format, as Chapter 8 explains. Typically, you should choose Mac OS X Extended (Journaled).

4. **Give it a name.** Give the volume a name in the Name text field.

5. **Click Erase.** Click the Erase button; then click Erase again on the confirmation dialog box that appears.

Creating the RAID array

Now that you have your disks ready, it's time to convert them into a single RAID array. In Disk Utility, follow these steps to create a RAID array (see Figure 4.12):

1. **Select a disk.** Select one of the disks in the list that you want to use in the set and go to the RAID pane.

2. **Name the RAID.** Enter a name for the RAID set in the Raid Set Name text field.

3. **Choose a format.** Select a volume format from the Format popup menu. Typically you should choose Mac OS X (Journaled).

4. **Choose a RAID type.** Three options are available to you in the RAID Type popup menu: Mirrored RAID Set, Striped RAID Set, and Concatenated RAID Set.

5. **Add the first disk.** Locate the first disk in the list at left that you want to include in your RAID array. Click and drag the disk from the list to the main window in the center of Disk Utility. It appears as New Member: "*diskname*" (a number appears after *diskname*, identifying which disk it is in your Mac. (To remove a disk, just drag it out of the window.)

6. **Add the remaining disks.** Now drag the remaining disks that will be used in the RAID below the first disk. Each one will be listed as New Member: "*diskname*" and have an identifying number.

Tip

You can create additional RAID sets by clicking the + iconic button. You can also drag the disks around the main window to reconfigure the RAID sets.

7. **Choose RAID Spare or RAID Slice.** Select any of the disks (not the RAID sets) in the window; the RAID Type popup menu becomes the Disk Type popup menu. Choose area, and the pull-down menu marked RAID type turns into Disk Type, which offers two options for each drive: RAID Slice and RAID Spare. By default, the option is set to RAID Slice, which ensures that the disk is used as part of the RAID array. Choosing RAID Spare designates that the disk is not to be used as part of the main RAID volume but is to be automatically used in event of a failure of one of the other disks. When you are creating a Mirrored RAID Set, you can use this option with a third drive. Set it as a RAID Spare to have it automatically substitute one of the other drives in the event of a drive failure.

8. **Select your options.** Click the Options button to open a settings sheet in which you choose the block size by using the RAID Block Size popup menu. (A block is a contiguous area on the hard disk in which data is stored. You can think of them as the equivalent bricks that make up your files. Larger blocks are accessed faster but store data less efficiently.) By default the block size is 32K, although your options are 16K, 32K, 64K, 128K, and 256K. You are advised by Mac OS X to select a block size that matches the kind of data you will be accessing. For example, video may access large blocks of data, but a database will access smaller blocks.

9. **Decide whether to enable automatic rebuilding.** If you are creating a RAID mirrored set, select the Automatically Rebuild RAID Mirrored Sets option. Click OK to close the sheet.

10. **Create the RAID.** Now that you are ready to set up your disks, click Create to begin building the RAID array. Mac OS X gives you a dialog box warning that you will destroy all the information contained on the disks (which it lists for you) used in the RAID array. Click Create to confirm that you are happy to wipe the disks and create the RAID array.

FIGURE 4.12

You use Disk Utility to turn a collection of disks into a RAID array.

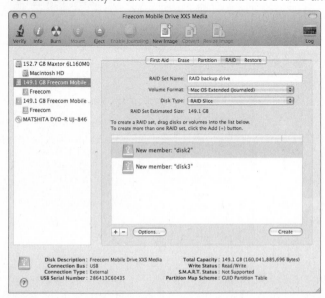

Investigating RAID Utility

If you are managing an Xserve server, you must use a program called RAID Admin to manage RAID systems. However, Mac users who have purchased a hardware RAID card have an additional tool called RAID Utility, which is located in the Utilities folder. This utility provides more options than Disk Utility, including the capability to create RAID 5 volumes.

Summary

It is critical to have a backup plan in place in case files are accidentally deleted or corrupted. Mac OS X's Time Machine utility is an easy-to-use, powerful backup-and-restore tool that everyone should use.

Time Machine backs up data automatically to external hard disks, and it provides options as to what disks on your Mac to back up, as well as what disks, folders, and files to not back up. Apple's Time Capsule combines a wireless router and a hard disk to allow wireless backup for one or more Macs.

If you need to restore old files and folders, the Time Machine browser enables you to navigate through Finder windows that contain those old items; you can then tell Time Machine to restore those old files into the current Finder window, thus bringing back a missing file or replacing a damaged one. Time Machine can restore past settings in some applications, such as Mail and Address Book. Time Machine also enables you to restore an entire volume, such as in the case of disk failure, to another disk. It can also restore one Mac's contents to another Mac when used with the Migration Assistant.

Apple's MobileMe service comes with a utility named Backup that enables you to schedule backup of user-specified files and folders to your choice of external disks, optical discs, and the online iDisk service.

The RAID technology provided by Mac OS X lets you combine multiple disks, either to do instant backup of files so you have a backup disk always ready to go, or to create large arrays — or groups — of disks that the Mac sees as a single disk. One form of combined disk, called striping, can significantly increase disk performance for video processing and other high-performance needs. Only the Mac Pro and Xserve computers can have multiple disks installed internally. For other Macs, you can use external disks to create a RAID array or buy RAID drives that have multiple disks already included. Use Disk Utility to set up the RAID arrays on most Macs, the RAID Utility on Mac Pros and Xserves to gain extra RAID features, or the software that comes with a third-party RAID drive or RAID card.

Getting Help Inside Mac OS X

A s you explore Mac OS X, you will increasingly come across new and exciting areas of the operating system. Mac OS X is a huge, and complex, operating system and sooner or later everybody needs help. When you come across unfamiliar territory, Mac OS X offers a number of methods of built-in assistance.

The main method of reading help files is through a built-in application called the Help Viewer. The Help Viewer provides explanations for most basic tasks, as well as documentation relating to Mac OS X 10.6 Snow Leopard. You can use it to learn basic features about Mac OS X and discover how to use basic hardware, and it acts as a showcase for new features found in Mac OS X 10.6 Snow Leopard.

Another type of assistance offered by Mac OS X is help tags. These are yellow labels that appear when the mouse is positioned over various GUI (graphical user interface) elements and offer further explanation as to what function the element provides.

A further help service is available via man pages in Terminal. These pages outline command-line tasks used in the Terminal application.

In addition to the Mac OS X help, many applications provide their own comprehensive help sections. Furthermore, you can use the Internet as a resource. Apple provides comprehensive help through its Web site, and many product manufacturers provide comprehensive online support. One thing is certain: You'll rarely be short of help if you know where to look. In this chapter, we take a close look at the various options that are available to you when you're learning how to use the features found in Mac OS X.

The Help Viewer Application

The Help Viewer is your main source of information on Mac OS X, as well as for features found within various Apple applications and Apple technologies (such as QuickTime X). In addition to the standard help included with Mac OS X, many applications include sections of specialized help, which in combination with the Help Viewer provides a more complete system that accurately represents the contents of your operating system.

The Help Viewer is reminiscent of a Web browser (see Figure 5.1) and has a table of contents that can take you through common items. Links taking you to more detailed information on the item specified are highlighted in blue, and hovering the mouse over them makes an underline appear. As in a Web browser, clicking the links navigates you to an area that expands on the information outlined in the link.

Other links in the Help Viewer can take you to specific areas within the Mac OS X environment, such as system preference panes, while giving you information on the changes you need to make. Links in the Help Viewer can also take you to associated Web sites, such as the Apple Support pages.

You can access the Help Viewer in different ways, but typically you will do so via the Help option in the menu bar or by clicking an iconic help button — often shown as a circle with a question mark (?) inside. The application that is currently active, or part of the application that appears when you click a help button, determines what initially is displayed in the Help Viewer. You may see a list of help articles or the contents of an individual article relating to the application, or area, of Mac OS X you are working on when seeking help.

FIGURE 5.1

Here, the Help Viewer in Mac OS X shows the default Mac Help area.

Accessing Mac Help

When you're using the Finder, you can use the Help Viewer to display a list of generic help topics to get you started. This is a great starting point for browsing all the help topics available inside the Help Viewer. It also lets you see what's new inside Mac OS X 10.6 Snow Leopard, as well as understand options for various points. To access the Mac Help section in the Help Viewer, follow these steps:

1. **Switch to the Finder.** Click in any Finder window, click the Finder icon in the Dock, or click on the desktop. This brings up the Finder options in the menu bar.

2. **Choose Help⇨Mac Help or press Shift+⌘+/.** The Help menu option in the Finder contains a search box and the solitary option Mac Help (as shown in Figure 5.2). Click this option to open the Help Viewer containing the Mac Help section.

FIGURE 5.2

The Help menu provides a search box and an option to access the Help Viewer. The description inside the Help Menu tells you what content will be displayed in the Help Viewer; in this case, it is Mac Help.

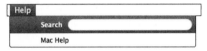

Tip

It's easier to remember the shortcut Shift+⌘+/ as ⌘+?, because Shift+/ gives you the ? character.

Browsing the Mac Help Viewer

The options available in the default Mac Help Viewer are as follows:

- **Learn the Basics.** This link takes you to information on getting started with Mac OS X.

- **Learn about Your Computer's Devices.** This link takes you to information regarding the hardware that makes up your computer. You'll learn all about the display, keyboard, mouse, and other devices.

- **Get to Work.** This link shows you how to set up various parts of Mac OS X's default applications, including Mail, Address Book, iCal, and TextEdit.

- **Have Fun.** This link takes you to information regarding music, photos, movies, and videos.

- **Network, Share, and Go Online.** This link takes you to information on setting up a network, sharing, and Web browsing.

The Mac Help Viewer application window also contains a section labeled *Solving Problems,* which provides links to advice on common problems. These include connecting to the Internet, recovering forgotten passwords, and a link to more help topics. It also provides a link to other help resources (including the Apple Support Web site and Apple community discussion Web site). A final link takes you to a complete index of all help items available in the Mac Help section. Mac Help is a great way to find out a lot of information right on your desktop.

Looking at active application help

As we mention earlier, most applications running in Mac OS X provide their own help. You usually access it the same way as Mac Help, but it provides specific information relating to that particular application. For example, when Address Book is the active application, choosing Help ⇨ Address Book Help or pressing Shift+⌘+/ opens the Help Viewer and displays a range of topics relating to Address Book (as shown in Figure 5.3).

FIGURE 5.3

The Help Viewer displaying a list of help topics relating to a specific application; in this case, Address Book

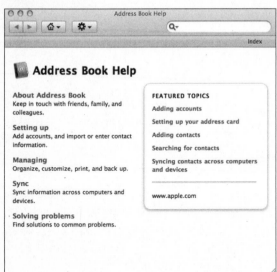

Navigating the Help Viewer

The Help Viewer works in much the same way as a Web browser, and you navigate it via a system of links. (These are specific areas of text that you can click to navigate to another section of text.) You can identify the links in the Help Viewer by their color, which is blue (as opposed to the black text of a regular font). Hover the cursor over a link with the mouse and an underline appears, indicating that the link is ready to be clicked. Clicking it with the mouse navigates away from the current window and toward whatever article is associated with the link. Clicking the Learn the Basics link (as shown in Figure 5.1) takes you to a list of topics titled Learn the Basics About your Mac (as shown in Figure 5.4). This, in turn, provides another list of links that you can use to find more specific information on all the different types of devices (keyboards, monitors, printers, and so on) that make up your Mac.

FIGURE 5.4

Links inside Mac Help are used to move between the various help articles.

Navigating with the Help Viewer toolbar

As with most applications, the Help Viewer contains its own toolbar (as shown in Figure 5.5). However it is wrong to think of it as an application in its own right, because it does not have its own menu at the top of the screen; instead it displays the menu of the active application.

FIGURE 5.5

The Help Viewer menu bar has a series of navigation buttons and a search box.

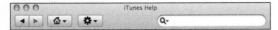

Navigation buttons

You can use the Back and Forward iconic buttons (the left-facing and right-facing triangle icons, respectively) to navigate through windows you have previously browsed. Clicking the Back iconic button takes you to the previous page you looked at; clicking the Forward iconic button takes you forward through your history. Because navigation through linked files is central to the Mac Help Viewer, the navigation iconic buttons are extremely helpful.

The Home button/popup menu

The next iconic control on the Help Viewer toolbar is the Home iconic button/popup menu, which is represented as a small house. Clicking the Home iconic button/popup menu makes it work as a button, taking you back to the main Mac Help Viewer contents. If you click and hold the Home iconic button/popup menu, you are presented with a menu of help options available to Mac OS X. Typically, it includes help topics for all the standard Mac OS X applications (Address Book, AirPort Utility, and so on). It also contains quick links to help for other commonly used Apple hardware, such as the iPod, iPhone, and Apple TV. Finally, the list grows as you install applications, and help links for these applications are included in this popup menu.

The Action button

The next item in the menu bar is the Action iconic popup menu (the gear icon). Its options are commands for the text size (Make Text Smaller and Make Text Bigger), a Find command (whose shortcut is ⌘+F), and a Print command.

Note

Because the Help Viewer acts to support other applications, many shortcuts — such as ⌘+P to print — do not work inside the Help Viewer. Instead, pressing ⌘+P instructs the active application to print. Therefore to print an article from the Help Viewer you must use its Action iconic popup menu's Print command.

Choosing the Find option brings up a search box beneath the menu bar. Entering a term in this box starts a search throughout the current help page. Any items in the Help Viewer that match the term you entered in the text field are highlighted (see Figure 5.6). Next to it are two smaller navigation arrows — Forward and Back iconic buttons that apply just to the search — that move to the next and previous occurrence of the search term. Click the small Close iconic button (the X icon) to remove the search box.

FIGURE 5.6

You can use the Find command (located in the Action iconic popup menu) to search for specific text terms within the currently displayed page.

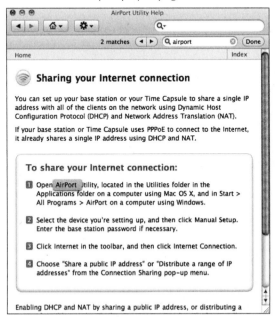

Looking through the index

Most of the help categories have an Index link on their main pages. This index contains an alphabetical list of all the pages associated with that particular category (see Figure 5.7). You can find the link to the index on many pages relating to a particular topic. It appears on the right-hand side of the window, in a gray horizontal strip just below the menu bar. A Home link often appears on the left-hand side of the window; it takes you back to the main page for that subject. Clicking the index brings up the alphabetical list of subjects.

Searching for help

More often than not, you begin not by looking for help by browsing from a menu subject's home page or index, but by searching for help on a particular topic. There are two ways to search for help in Mac OS X:

- **From the menu.** If you choose Help from the menu, you will notice that the first item is a blue box called Search with a text field.

- **From the Help Viewer.** A text field appears on the top right of the Help Viewer window. You enter search terms here to look for help on a particular topic.

FIGURE 5.7

The index contains a list of all the pages associated with a particular help subject.

Getting help from the menu

To search for a help item via the menu, choose Help from the menu and start typing into the search box. As with Spotlight (see Chapter 3), the results appear as soon as you begin typing and change as you enter more letters (see Figure 5.8). The results listed in the help menu are divided into two categories:

- **Menu Items.** Items in the current menu that match the search term are listed here. Highlighting items in the Menu Item category opens that item in the menu and highlights it in blue (and just to drive the message home, a large blue arrow hovers to the right of the menu item). Figure 5.9 shows this menu item highlighting system in action. This help search enables you to quickly find any item in even the most complex application menu structure.

- **Help Topics.** This is a list of all the pages in the Help Viewer that relate to the term entered. Choose an item from the menu to open the Help Viewer and go directly to the information.

Tip

A good trick to learn with the Help menu is to combine the shortcut Shift+⌘+/ with the arrow keys to search for menu items. For example, press Shift+⌘+/ to choose the Help option in the menu, and type in the name of a menu item (open, for example). Now you can use the arrow keys to move through the menu options and press Return to choose the desired option.

FIGURE 5.8

When you enter a term into the Help section of the menu, you will find it displays menu items relating to the term as well as help topics that you can view in the Help Viewer.

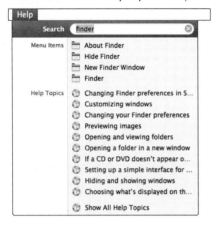

FIGURE 5.9

Searching for menu item terms in the Help search box

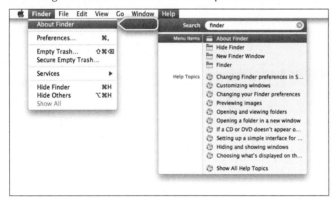

Searching in the Help Viewer

The other way to search for information is to open a Help Viewer, typically by choosing Help and the default help menu option (Mac Help, for example) in the Finder menu. To the top right of the Help Viewer is a text field (see Figure 5.10). Type in a search term and press Return to access a list of help topics relating to the term. Each term has the title of the page of help and a brief description of what the help topic will enable you to achieve. If the description is truncated (indicated by ending with an ellipsis […]), then hovering the mouse over the description brings up a longer description in a yellow box.

FIGURE 5.10

You can search for help topics in the Help Viewer by entering terms into the search box in the top right of the window.

Retrieving Help from the Internet

At times, the Help Viewer will access the Internet to retrieve help articles. An application may only have the most commonly accessed help topics stored on your Mac, but offer a search index that links to the Internet for more details. If you click on a help article that is located on the Internet, the Help Viewer automatically caches the information inside Mac OS X for later use. If you want to read the same article at a later point, the Help Viewer automatically displays the document from the cache. However, Help Viewer also checks the Internet to see if the article has been updated; if a newer version is available, it is displayed instead.

The Help Viewer also adds articles to your Mac's help topics from the Internet as they become available, so your help system continually is expanded and updated. Of course, the Help Viewer can only access online articles if your computer is connected to the Internet.

Using Help Viewer quick clicks

Quick clicks are links within the Help Viewer that take you to places, both inside the Help Viewer and throughout Mac OS X. You should have a clear idea of where the link is going to take you, but some of the options include:

- **A link to another article inside the Help Viewer.**

- **An Open link to a part of an application.** This is typically at the part of the application that the Help Viewer article is describing.

- **A More link.** This brings up a larger list of links.

- **A Support Articles link.** This opens the default Web browser and takes you to the Apple Service and Support pages.

- **A Go to Website link.** This opens the default Web browser and takes you to a site related to the help article in question. Note that the Help Viewer often displays non-linkable Web URL addresses (`www.apple.com`, for example). If a Web URL is listed in the Help Viewer but isn't in blue text, clicking it does not open the Web browser and visit the address.

Creating complex search terms

As we mention earlier, entering search terms into the Help Viewer is a great way to access specific material without having to search through various links to find the article you need. You can enter basic search terms into the field at the top right of the Help Viewer. However, you may find it more productive to use special characters when searching; these enable you to create more complex search terms that are more likely to deliver the exact article you are looking for. Table 5.1 describes these special characters.

TABLE 5.1

Special Characters for Help Searching

Character	Meaning	Search Example	Search Results
+	And	desktop + Finder	This example finds articles that include both "desktop" and "Finder."
|	Or	desktop | Finder	This example finds articles that include either "desktop" or "Finder."
!	Not	desktop ! Finder	This example finds articles that include "desktop" but exclude "Finder."
()	Grouping	picture + (Finder | desktop)	This example finds articles that include "picture" and either "Finder" or "Desktop."

Understanding Help Tags

Help tags are a quick form of help that can offer expanded information on items found throughout the Mac OS X environment. Many applications enable you to get immediate information about GUI items (buttons and icons, for example) via expanded information contained within help tags. If an object in the Mac OS X environment has a help tag description, when you hover the mouse over it for a few seconds, a yellow box appears. Inside the box is a description of what action the item performs (see Figure 5.11). If no such box appears, then the object has no help tag associated with it.

Note
Some applications call these help tags Tool Tips.

FIGURE 5.11

Help tags are enabled throughout Mac OS X, and provide quick information regarding items used in the GUI.

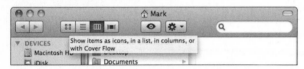

Not all objects have help tags. Common menu items — such as scroll arrows and menus — do not have help tags because they are considered self-explanatory. And not all applications offer the same level of help tag functionality as those created by Apple. Help tags are primarily used by custom buttons and icons to describe what the image used by the icon represents.

Note
Mac OS X users familiar with Balloon Help offered by Apple in Mac OS 9 and earlier will probably draw close comparisons between help tags and the Balloon Help feature. Balloon Help was an optional feature in Mac OS 9 and earlier, whereas help tags are a permanent feature of Mac OS X. Despite their permanence, help tags are not as intrusive as Balloon Help.

Working with Command-Line Help

Most of the help offered by Mac OS X is displayed in the GUI. However, Mac OS X has a comprehensive command-line interface that you can access through the Terminal application. Mac OS X's command-line interface has an integrated help system referred to as the *man pages* (*man* is short for *manual*). The man pages provide an online user manual that contains information on just about every command used in Terminal (see Figure 5.12). Chapter 26 covers Terminal in detail and provides more detailed information regarding the man command.

FIGURE 5.12

The man command, used in Terminal, provides user-manual entries relating to various command-line functions.

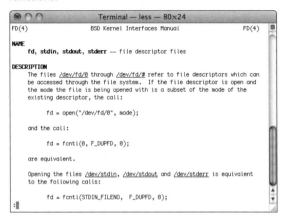

Exploring Other Avenues of Help

Many applications add help items to the Mac OS X help system and provide reference material (both on-screen and physical printed material). In addition to this, you'll find that many applications include documentation in PDF format, typically supplied with the program. Alternatively, a program may include links to the manufacturer's Web site, which will have information relating to the program. As a general rule, if you pull up a company's Web site and search for Support, you will find information relating to its program (see Figure 5.13). Most companies offer a mixture of some reference resources or all of the above.

The Internet is a fantastic resource for discovering additional help, as well as articles on all aspects of Mac OS X, popular applications, and additional hardware. Bookmark the following Web sites:

- **AppleCare Service and Support:** www.apple.com/support
- **AppleCare Knowledge Base:** http://kbase.info.apple.com
- **Apple Manuals:** www.apple.com/support/manuals
- **Apple Mac OS X Support:** www.apple.com/macosx/snowleopard/
- **MacFixIt:** www.macfixit.com

FIGURE 5.13

A typical company online product support page with additional information on their product

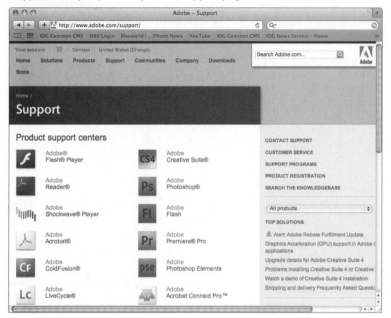

Summary

In this chapter, you learned how to access help articles contained within Mac OS X, using the Help menu in the Finder and most applications or through the shortcut Shift+⌘+/.

In the Help Viewer, you can search for help articles relating to Mac OS X or active applications, and narrow down your choices by using special search characters. The Help browser also enables you to navigate through the Help Viewer, using its Web browser-like interface.

Popup labels called help tags provide a quick reminder of some GUI elements' functions, while the man commands in the Terminal lets you access help articles in the Mac's Unix environment.

Many manufacturers offer a range of support through additional materials, both supplied with installed software and hardware and through online support pages. And several key Web sites are a great place to start for help for Mac computers, hardware, software, and the Mac OS X environment.

Accessing Mac OS X with Universal Access

Mac OS X is designed from the ground up to work effectively for everybody, including people with special needs. People with limited hearing, sight, or ability to control a keyboard or mouse will find Mac OS X is an extremely effective operating system. Apple has always facilitated access to its system for people of all abilities.

These features are mostly located in Mac OS X inside the Universal Access system preference, but Mac OS X's sound input and speech capabilities (found in the Sound and Speech system preferences, respectively) are also extremely useful.

A key support application for the visually impaired, VoiceOver Utility enables Mac OS X to read aloud information displayed on the screen. In many ways, VoiceOver Utility is an extension of Universal Access. The application can be configured to provide the voice a user understands best when the app speaks the text on-screen. A nice touch is that VoiceOver Utility can be used to speak chat combinations such as smiling face :-) or lol (which stands for "laughing out loud"), and so on. You can customize VoiceOver Utility so it reads out an appropriate command for your personalized text chats.

In this chapter, we take an in-depth look at the Universal Access system preference, and the speech and sound controls found in Mac OS X; we also look at how you can set up VoiceOver Utility to personalize your experience.

You'll find Mac OS X is a great operating system for everybody, regardless of what abilities they possess.

Setting Up Mac OS X with Universal Access

If you have a special requirement for Mac OS X, you should start by investigating the Universal Access system preference. Open the System Preferences application (choose ⇨ System Preferences) and click the Universal Access icon.

The Universal Access system preference has four tabs: Seeing, Hearing, Keyboard, and Mouse & Trackpad (see Figure 6.1). Each one enables you to set up a different array of assistive options for a variety of different access needs. The options are as follows:

- **Seeing.** In this section, you can turn on VoiceOver technology and set custom zoom and display contrast levels.

- **Hearing.** In this section, you can adjust the volume and set up screen flash alerts to complement the usual audio alerts.

- **Keyboard.** In this section, you can use the keyboard options to activate sticky keys, which enable you to type key combinations (such as ⌘+O) one letter at a time; there are also options to assist with key repeat options.

- **Mouse & Trackpad.** In this section, the options enable you to activate *mouse keys*. These enable you to use the keyboard as a replacement for the mouse. There are also options to control the speed, delay, and size of the cursor.

FIGURE 6.1

The Universal Access system preference enables you to select a variety of assistance options.

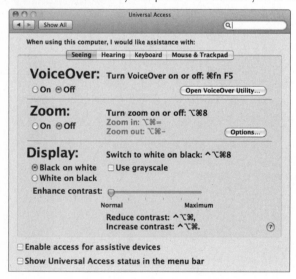

Setting Up Access for Assistive Devices

Note that the bottom of each pane in the Universal Access system preference has the Enable Access for Assistive Devices option. Selecting it enables third-party devices to harness the capabilities of Universal Access. And it must be selected for GUI AppleScripts to run. (These are scripts that can interact with the Mac OS X graphical interface.) Many applications designed to assist people require that this option be selected.

It is a mistake to think that the Enable Access for Assistive Devices option relates only to applications that improve access for people with disabilities. Many regular applications make ingenious use of the GUI AppleScripts to control parts of the screen for all users.

Enabling Visual Assistance

The first pane in the Universal Access system preference is Seeing, and all the options here relate to improving the visual performance of Mac OS, or to substituting visual information with audio equivalents. The technologies available are designed to enable people with limited visual abilities to realize the full potential of Mac OS X.

Hearing your Mac with VoiceOver

The first section in the Seeing pane in the Universal Access preference is VoiceOver. You can turn on VoiceOver two ways:

- **Select the On option in the Seeing pane's VoiceOver section.** Select On to switch on VoiceOver; Off to disable it.
- **Press ⌘+F5.** Use this keyboard shortcut to toggle VoiceOver on and off. Note that on most keyboards, you need to hold the Fn key as well, thus pressing ⌘+Fn+F5. (If you selected the Use all F1, F2, etc. Keys as Standard Function Keys in the Keyboard pane of the Keyboard & Shortcuts system preference, you do *not* need to also hold Fn.)

As soon as you turn on VoiceOver, a dialog box appears with a welcome message (see Figure 6.2). VoiceOver immediately begins speaking the welcome message. This dialog box also asks if you want to learn how to use VoiceOver. To view the VoiceOver tutorial, press the spacebar or click Quick Start Tutorial. If you are already familiar with VoiceOver technology, you can begin using the system immediately by pressing V or clicking Quit.

Automatically turning on Voice Over

Keen readers may have noticed a flaw in the standard method of turning on VoiceOver. It requires you to visually navigate through Mac OS X to activate, something of a flaw in a system designed to replace visual information verbally.

FIGURE 6.2

Turning on VoiceOver in the system preferences displays this dialog box. Mac OS X reads the text and you can access a Quick Start tutorial that takes you through many aspects of using VoiceOver.

However, a technique is available that enables Mac OS X users who rely on audio information to interact with the Mac right from the start. During the welcome video (outlined in Chapter 1), if you wait for 30 seconds without interacting with the visual menu, a dialog box appears informing users that they can enable VoiceOver by pressing the F5 key.

The VoiceOver Quick Start

If you click the Quick Start Tutorial button in the VoiceOver welcome message, a brief tutorial shows you the basics of interacting with your Mac via VoiceOver (see Figure 6.3). You navigate through the tutorial with the arrow keys (press → to move to the next page of the tutorial; press ← to move back to the previous page of the tutorial). You can also navigate the Quick Start tutorial by clicking Continue and Go Back.

VoiceOver verbally announces the information displayed on each page of the Quick Start. You can press Escape or click Quit at any point to leave the tutorial.

Understanding the VoiceOver keys

The VoiceOver keys (also known as the *VO keys*) are used to enter VoiceOver commands. By default, the VO keys are Control+Option. Typically, you hold down both keys while pressing another key to issue a VoiceOver command — just like any other keyboard shortcut.

A wide range of VO key commands are available, and they do everything from reading a currently selected item to interacting with Mac OS X interface elements. You can also use them to navigate around the screen.

General VoiceOver keyboard commands

VoiceOver is an incredibly in-depth program, and it features a wide range of keyboard commands. Many are outlined in the Quick Start tutorial, and you can find even more in the Help Viewer. To find a list of these commands, open VoiceOver Utility (outlined later in this chapter) and choose Help⇨VoiceOver Commands. The commands are split up into six sections: General, Orientation, Navigation, Text, Interaction, and Search.

FIGURE 6.3

The VoiceOver Quick Start tutorial takes you through the process of setting up and using VoiceOver with Mac OS X.

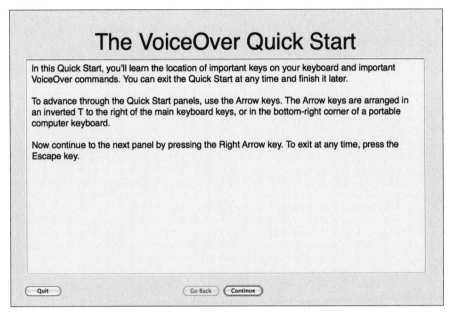

The VoiceOver Quick Start

In this Quick Start, you'll learn the location of important keys on your keyboard and important VoiceOver commands. You can exit the Quick Start at any time and finish it later.

To advance through the Quick Start panels, use the Arrow keys. The Arrow keys are arranged in an inverted T to the right of the main keyboard keys, or in the bottom-right corner of a portable computer keyboard.

Now continue to the next panel by pressing the Right Arrow key. To exit at any time, press the Escape key.

Quit   Go Back   Continue

Using keyboard help

Pressing Control+Option+K brings up the keyboard help function. In keyboard help mode, you hear the name of each key as it is pressed. Someone who cannot clearly see the keys to find his or her way around can use this function to learn the keyboard. When you press the VoiceOver keys (Control+Option) and press a key, the function speaks the associated command along with a brief description of what the command does.

Tip

A standard feature on most keyboards (including all Apple keyboards) is a slight protruding line on the F and J keys. These are designed for touch typists, enabling users to quickly locate their positions on the keyboard without having to look at the keys. The F and J keys also serve as a great navigation tool for the visually impaired. The two keys are located where you place your index fingers, and your other fingers are on the adjacent keys. (The keys your left hand rests on are A, S, D, and F; the keys your right hand rests on are J, K, L, and the semicolon [;] key.) From this position, your fingers can move up and down to reach any key on the keyboard, and you naturally return back to the position. Consequently, you can navigate the entire keyboard without needing to look at it.

Hearing what's on the screen

VoiceOver works by speaking aloud the things that normally appear on the screen. The part of the screen that is being spoken is surrounded by a small black rectangle. Figure 6.4 shows a screen displaying the VoiceOver rectangle. VoiceOver also verbalizes the currently active application, part of application (or part of the Finder), and the currently outlined item.

For example, clicking on the main hard disk on the desktop causes VoiceOver to say the following: "Finder, Desktop, Macintosh HD currently selected volume image."

VoiceOver provides other information as well. It informs you when the screen saver has been activated, for example. It also gives you guidance on what navigation options you have. When you are in a dialog box, window, or panel with multiple options, it informs you to click down to select options. As you move through the options, VoiceOver reads them out to you.

FIGURE 6.4

VoiceOver highlights an item on the screen with a black rectangle, and speaks aloud a description of that item. You can interact with menu options by using VoiceOver commands.

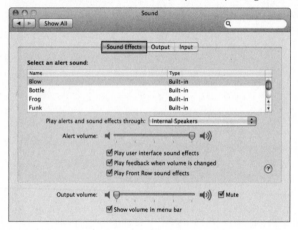

Navigating with VoiceOver

To move the VoiceOver cursor (the black rectangle that surrounds items), press Control+Option and the arrow keys. The VoiceOver cursor moves in that direction to the next item on the horizontal, or vertical, line. You hear a description of each item as the cursor surrounds it. You select items by pressing Control+Option+spacebar, which is the equivalent of pressing the mouse button.

New Feature

In Mac OS X 10.6 Snow Leopard, you can navigate the Mac using the Multi-Touch trackpad of recent laptops, and VoiceOver guides you using voice prompts. When using the Multi-Touch trackpad this way, the trackpad's surface represents the active window (such as the desktop, Finder window, or application window), so your finger works as if it were a mouse moving in that window.

Note

You move around items within a list by pressing the arrow keys as normal, but holding down the VoiceOver keys (Control+Option) while pressing the arrow keys takes you to the next section.

Using the Dock

To move to the Dock, press Control+Option+D. By default, the VoiceOver cursor is placed around the Finder item in the Dock. To move to the next item in the Dock, press Control+Option+→; to move to the previous item, press Control+Option+←. You select an item in the Dock by pressing Control+Option+spacebar.

Using the menu bar

Another quick command to help you get started is Control+Option+M. This takes you to the menu bar, and you can use the arrow keys to move through menu items and press Control+⌘+spacebar (or press Return) to choose a menu item.

Selecting buttons, check boxes, and sliders

To click a button, you typically press Control+Option+spacebar (although you can also press the Return key, as you could when VoiceOver is switched off). This works for selection buttons, check boxes, and radio buttons.

To open a popup menu, you navigate to it with VoiceOver and press Control+Option+spacebar, then use the arrow keys (↑ and ↓) to move through the options; press Control+Option+spacebar to select the appropriate option.

To move a slider, you highlight it with the VoiceOver cursor, then press Control+Option+Shift+↓ to begin interacting with it. Then you use the arrow keys (↑ and ↓ for vertical slider; ← and → for a horizontal slider) to move the slider. As you move the slider, you hear audio feedback regarding the amount (such as a percentage, or number, relating to the slider).

Entering text into text fields

When you move the VoiceOver cursor to a text field, any text that is currently inside the field is spoken. As you type letters into the field, VoiceOver will speak out each letter as you type. The exception is when you are typing text into a secure field (such as a password entry point); at this point, no text will be spoken out loud.

Navigating rows and columns

When you are navigating a table, some additional commands enable you to move between rows and columns. They include:

- **Control+Option+R.** Read a row.
- **Control+Option+C.** Read the column header.
- **Control+Option+C then C.** Read a table column. Upon the first press of the C key, it reads the column header (as above), and on the second press of C it reads the content of the table column.

Using smart groups in Web pages

One more unique feature in VoiceOver is worth mentioning: smart groups. They are a unique way to browse Web pages based upon their visual layout. Web pages are designed to group information together in boxes, which may not be visible on the screen but internally hold related content together. The smart groups capability uses this information to determine what related information should be handled by VoiceOver. The following commands work with smart groups:

- **Control+Option+⌘+N.** Move to the next smart group.
- **Control+Option+Shift+⌘+N.** Move to the previous smart group.
- **Control+Option+→.** Move to the next item in a smart group.
- **Control+Option+←.** Move to the previous item in a smart group.

VoiceOver help

To get help with VoiceOver, press Control+Option+H. This brings up a VoiceOver help menu with the following options:

- Online Help
- Commands Help
- Keyboard Help
- Sounds Help
- Quick Start Tutorial
- Getting Started Guide

Tip

Accidental activation of VoiceOver is a commonly reported error among Mac OS X novices. When using your Mac, it is easy to unintentionally activate VoiceOver by pressing ⌘+F5. This causes the black rectangle to appear around screen items, which to the untrained user can look like a system fault. If you know of a Mac OS X user who is complaining of random squares appearing on the screen, tell him or her to press ⌘+F5 to turn off VoiceOver.

Zooming in on the screen

Another way to provide access to the Mac OS X environment for visually impaired individuals is to enable the zoom option. As the name suggests, zoom homes in on a part of the screen (around the cursor) and magnifies everything, making it clear and easy to see. As you move the cursor to the edge of the screen, the zoomed area scrolls over to that part of the screen.

To activate the zoom in Mac OS X, select the On option underneath the Zoom section in the Universal Access system preference's Seeing pane.

The zoom level can be increased, or decreased, as you move around the Mac OS X in one of two ways:

- **Using keyboard commands.** Press Control+⌘+= to zoom in and Control+⌘+− to zoom out.

- **Using the mouse scroll ball.** Press ⌘ and move the scroll ball or wheel on the mouse up to zoom in and back down to zoom out. Laptop users can press ⌘ and push two fingers up on the trackpad to zoom in and down to zoom out.

Adjusting zoom options

You can personalize the zoom settings in several ways. Click Options to open a range of settings (see Figure 6.5).

FIGURE 6.5

The Zoom options are used to customize the zoom, and can completely change the way it works.

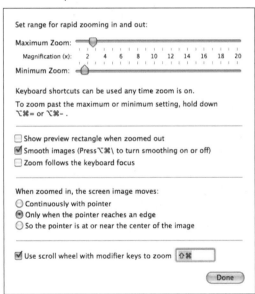

Maximum Zoom and Minimum Zoom sliders

By default, the Maximum Zoom and Minimum Zoom sliders are both set to 0, and you zoom in one incremental step at a time. However, each slider can be moved up to a maximum of 20×. What these sliders do is set a point at which zooming in (maximum) and out (minimum) automatically moves to. So, if you set the maximum slider at 20×, and the minimum at 10× magnification, clicking Control+⌘+= to zoom in automatically takes you straight to a 20× level of magnification; zooming out then takes you to a 10× level of magnification.

Show Preview Rectangle When Zoomed Out option

Selecting the Show Preview Rectangle When Zoomed Out option places a rectangular square around the pointer. This square displays the area of the screen that will be zoomed in to when you press Control+⌘+= (see Figure 6.6). Note that by default the zoom area is set to 0× magnification, and therefore no box appears. The preview rectangle appears on-screen only when you adjust the maximum zoom settings.

Tip

Zoom isn't just for people who need visual assistance. It is a very handy tool for anybody who wants to focus on a specific area of a display. The zoom tool is often used by people wanting to demonstrate a feature or function of an item in Mac OS X (such as an application). By zooming in on a specific part of the screen, you can focus on the feature close up, without any of the distractions of other GUI elements.

Smooth Images option

The images on the screen are made up of pixels, which are small squares. By default, these are so small that the items that make up the Mac OS X interface are smooth and rounded. However, when you zoom in, you quickly see the jagged edges that make up most interface items. When the Smooth Images option is selected (the default), it helps to keep items on the screen smoother when highly magnified. The trade-off is that items can appear slightly blurry when you zoom.

FIGURE 6.6

The preview rectangle displays exactly which part of the GUI will fill the screen when you zoom in.

Zoom Follows the Keyboard Focus option

When you zoom in, the zoom level automatically follows the pointer. If you zoom in on a text area (a large text box or word-processing document, for example), the text you type may go off the edge of the screen. Selecting the Zoom Follows the Keyboard Focus option ensures that the zoom follows the cursor as you type.

When Zoomed In, the Screen Image Moves options

Because a zoomed screen no longer displays the desktop in its entirety, you must scroll around a zoomed-in screen view to see different parts of the interface. There are three ways that this screen movement can occur:

- **Continuously with Pointer.** When this option is selected, the zoomed screen moves in time with the cursor. As you move the cursor, it moves independently, and then the screen starts to move with it. This is one of the most natural zoom modes you can use.

- **Only When the Pointer Reaches an Edge.** When this option is selected, the screen zooms in around the cursor, and you can move the cursor around the zoomed portion of the screen without changing the view at all. If you move the cursor to the edge of the screen, the zoomed area moves in that direction.

- **So the Pointer Is At or Near the Center of the Image.** When this option is selected, the screen zooms in with the cursor in the center. As you move the cursor, it stays in the center of the screen and the zoomed background moves around it. The exception is when you move to the edge of the interface, at which point the cursor moves instead of the background.

Use Scroll Wheel with Modifier Keys to Zoom option

The Use Scroll Wheel with Modifier Keys to Zoom option at the bottom of the screen enables you to zoom in and out by using the scroll ball or wheel on a mouse (or by using two fingers on a Multi-Touch trackpad on a Mac laptop). If you want to zoom in and out with the scroll ball or wheel, select this option. (Note that it is selected by default.)

Beside the option is a text field that enables you to determine which modifier key has to be pressed along with the movement of the scroll ball or wheel (or Multi-Touch trackpad gesture) for the zoom to occur. By default, this is the Control key; however, you can change this to any combination of the modifier keys (⌘, Shift, Control, or Option). To change the option, click in the text field or press Tab until it is highlighted; then press the modifier key or keys you want to assign.

Adjusting display options

The next set of commands in the Seeing pane of the Universal Access system preference appears in the Display section. They enable you to adjust how the Mac OS X GUI is displayed and to determine a higher level of contrast. Adjusting these settings can make the display easier to read for some visually impaired individuals. The options available include:

- **Black on White.** This is the default setting, and it means a standard display, where black is black, white is white, and all other colors are unchanged.

- **White on black.** This is the polar opposite of the Black on white settings, and clicking this option reverses the whole color spectrum. Areas that were black now become white, and white areas become black. It this sense it is like viewing an old-fashioned negative photograph. However, it also applies to all colors; the purple of the Aurora desktop, for example, is shown in green. Figure 6.7 shows a desktop with the White on black setting enabled.

- **Use Grayscale.** Selecting this option removes all the color from the screen; instead, everything displays in monochrome.

- **Enhance Contrast.** As the name suggests, the Enhance Contrast slider makes the contrast of the Mac OS X GUI more pronounced. The gentle fades between colors are replaced with light whites and dark blacks, and the medium grays are gone.

It is important to note that these controls are not all independent of each other; they can be used together to great effect. You can, for example, create a white-on-black background with a grayscale setting and high level of contrast to produce a highly readable display (see Figure 6.8).

FIGURE 6.7

The White on Black setting in the Display area of Universal Access system preference reverses all the displayed colors. This can make the display easier to read for some people.

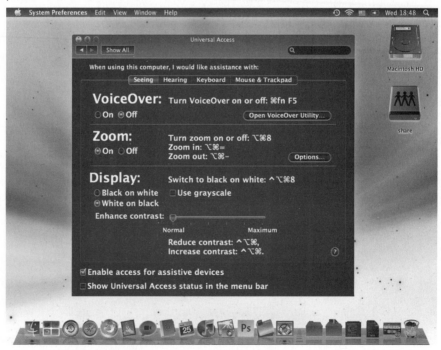

FIGURE 6.8

The Display settings can be combined to create a vastly different look to the Mac OS X interface, one that can be much easier for some people to read.

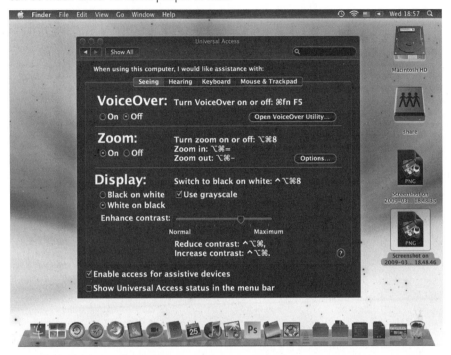

Tip

As with VoiceAssist, the Display settings are another part of the Mac OS X interface that can be accidentally changed through unintentional key presses (typically a user presses Control+Option+⌘+8, which is the shortcut for White on Black). This reverses the screen color. To a person unfamiliar with Universal Access options, it can appear to be a GUI error. If a person complains that his or her Mac OS X display appears wrong, chances are that he or she has accidentally activated the White on Black display mode. Clicking Control+Option+⌘+8 reverts the screen back to the more typical Black on White display mode.

Enabling Hearing Assistance

The second pane on the Universal Access system preference is Hearing. Click it to see some options designed to assist people with limited hearing abilities. There are fewer options here than those for people who need visual assistance.

The first option is to flash the screen in place of an alert sound (see Figure 6.9). If you select the Flash the Screen When an Alert Sound Occurs option, any sound alerts (specified in the Sound system preference) are accompanied with a flash of the screen. The screen quickly flashes white, and then returns to normal, drawing your attention to whatever the alert may be. (You can test the flashing alert by clicking Flash Screen.)

The second option is the Play Stereo as Mono option. If selected, this option combines the left and right speakers' audio into one signal sent to all connected speakers and headsets. This helps people who may hear poorly in one ear and thus miss sounds that come out of, say, just the right-hand speaker.

The final setting in the Hearing pane is the Adjust Volume button, which if clicked opens the Sound system preference. There, you can adjust both the Alert volume and the Output volume. (This affects all sounds outputted by your Mac.)

FIGURE 6.9

Screen flash alerts are useful for people with limited hearing. Whenever an alert takes place, the usual audio noise is accompanied by a flash of the screen. (It quickly turns white, and then back to normal.)

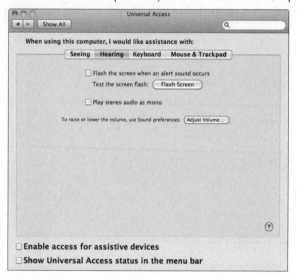

Enabling Keyboard Assistance

The third pane in the Universal Access system preference is Keyboard. Click it to discover a range of options designed for people who need assistance using a keyboard attached to the Mac. These options include help for people who have difficulty pressing more than one key at the same time, people who have difficulty with initial key presses, or people who have difficulty with repeated keystrokes.

Pressing more than one key at a time

Mac OS X offers several options designed to help people overcome difficulties with pressing multiple keys simultaneously.

The first option in the Keyboard pane controls sticky keys. If On is selected, this setting enables you to press modifier keys (Shift, Control, Option, and ⌘) individually (one at a time) and use them to create keyboard combinations. With sticky keys activated, you can press ⌘ and then N, for example, to open a new Finder window, rather than use the standard method of holding ⌘ then pressing N.

You can build modifier key combinations for different commands; for example, you can press ⌘, then Shift, and then N to create a new folder.

Tip

When sticky keys are enabled and you press a modifier key a second time, you lock it. This means that you can use it repeatedly for multiple keyboard commands. Modifier keys pressed accidentally can be cancelled by pressing the key a third time. Alternatively, pressing the Escape key cancels the whole modifier key sequence, unless you have locked down the key (in which case, you must press the same key again to unlock it).

Three options appear beneath the Sticky Keys option:

- **Press the Shift Key Five times to Turn Sticky Keys On or Off.** As the name suggests, this enables you to activate or deactivate the sticky keys functions through multiple presses of the Shift key.

- **Beep When a Modifier Key Is Set.** By default, Mac OS X makes a small clicking sound when a modifier key is set, and a slightly firmer sound when you press it a second time to lock it. (No sound is made for canceling a modifier key.) By default, this sound is active. Deselecting this option cancels the audio feedback.

- **Display Pressed Keys On Screen.** When you press a modifier key, a small symbol of the key appears on-screen (see Figure 6.10). The symbol fades slightly for a single press, but remains bold when locked with a second key press. This option is selected by default.

FIGURE 6.10

When Sticky Keys is activated, pressing modifier keys causes their icons to appear on the desktop, displaying which key is currently active.

Pressing keys accidentally

Some people may find accidental key presses make it difficult for them to accurately enter text. Mac OS X's solution for this is *slow keys*. With this feature activated, a key must be pressed and held for a short period before it is registered by Mac OS X. If the key is released before the required period, the keystroke is ignored.

This feature can be extremely useful for people who find themselves accidentally brushing the wrong key.

Select the On option next to Slow Keys to turn on the feature. Now, when you press a key, you must wait until a noise (reminiscent of a camera clicking) before the keystroke is registered. The delay is less than a second, but it does prevent you from typing quickly.

Below the Slow Keys option are three control configurations:

- **Use Click Key Sounds.** This option is selected by default, and when slow keys is activated, a sound notifies you that the key press has been registered. Deselecting this option silences the associated noise.

- **Acceptance Delay.** This slider determines how long you must wait when using slow keys before a key press is registered. Moving the slider to the left (marked Long) increases the delay between pressing the key and the input; moving the slider to the right (marked Short) decreases the delay between the key press and the input.

- **Set Key Repeat.** By default, a key that is held down for a short period is repeated. This is another area that can cause problems for users who have difficulty pressing and releasing keys quickly. Clicking the Set Key Repeat button takes you to the Keyboard & Shortcuts system preference's Keyboard pane, where you can use the Delay Until Repeat slider to increase the delay (by moving the slider to the left). You can also move the slider all they way to the Off position to cancel the repeat-key function entirely. In the Keyboard & Shortcuts system preference, you can also use the Key Repeat Rate to control how many key presses occur as you hold down a key.

Enabling Mouse Assistance

The pane on the far right of the Universal Access system preference is Mouse & Trackpad and, as the name suggests, it offers several functions that enable assistance for people who have difficulty using either a mouse or a trackpad.

Getting help with using the mouse

Users who have difficulty using the mouse can use the keyboard to control the mouse pointer instead. This feature is known as *mouse keys* (see Figure 6.11).

To enable mouse keys, select the On option in the Mouse Keys section (see Figure 6.11). Mouse keys use the numeric keypad to control the mouse pointer. The 8 key moves the mouse up, 4 moves it left, 6 moves it right, and 2 moves it down; the 5 key (in the middle) indicates a mouse press. Note that the 1, 3, 7, and 9 keys move the mouse pointer diagonally.

Users of a Mac laptop, or those who have a keyboard without the separate numeric keypad, can use the 8, K, U, and O keys for up, down, left, and right, respectively, the I key as a mouse click, and the 7, 9, J, and L keys for diagonal movement. On some older laptops, you can also use the keys surrounding K as a numeric keypad (these keys have smaller numbers located alongside the letters). On such keyboards, press F6 to activate the number lock so you can use these keys as a replacement for the numeric keypad.

Note

Apple currently ships a keyboard without a numeric pad with its popular iMac line, although a larger keyboard with a numeric keypad is available as an option. If you are likely to use mouse keys, you may want to get the larger keyboard for your Mac.

The Mouse Keys section has the following options:

- **Press the Option Key Five Times to Turn Mouse Keys On or Off.** This option enables you to activate and deactivate mouse keys without entering the Universal Access system preference. This is especially useful for laptop owners who need to share the mouse keys with regular keyboard input.

- **Initial Delay.** This slider controls how long you must hold the appropriate mouse key down before the cursor begins to move. Move the slider to the left for a short delay, and to the right for a long delay.

- **Maximum Speed.** As you hold down the mouse key, the pointer speeds up from an initial slow speed to a fairly rapid movement. This technique enables you to perform small mouse movements and also move around the interface reasonably quickly. The slider enables you to set the speed that the cursor moves at when you hold down the mouse key. Move the slider to the left (the Slow setting) to limit the pointer speed, move it farther to the right (the Fast setting) to enable the pointer to move rapidly around the screen.

- **Ignore Trackpad when Mouse Keys Is On.** Users of Mac laptops may want to enable this setting. Selecting it ensures that accidental touches of the trackpad do not interfere with movement of the mouse.

Tip

Although the mouse is ubiquitous in the computer world, don't be fooled into thinking it is the only physical means to interact with the Mac OS X GUI. There are a range of alternatives to using a mouse. People with limited hand movement but accurate control may find trackpads a more suitable alternative. If you have difficulty holding a mouse, a trackball may be more suitable; there are also special joysticks available (not to be confused with gaming joysticks, incidentally) that can be used as effective mouse replacements. Disabled Online (www. disabledonline.com) has lots of alternative input devices that are worth looking at.

Getting help with seeing the pointer

The third slider in the Mouse Keys section is Cursor Size. You can use it to increase the size of the mouse pointer, making it easier to see. By default, the slider is set all the way to the left; dragging it to the right increases the size (see Figure 6.12). Note that this option affects the size of both the text cursor and the mouse pointer.

FIGURE 6.11

Activating mouse keys enables you to use the buttons on the numeric keypad in place of the mouse.

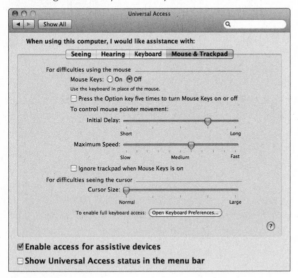

FIGURE 6.12

Making the pointer larger in the Universal Access system preference's Mouse & Trackpad pane can make the mouse pointer (as well as text cursor) easier to view.

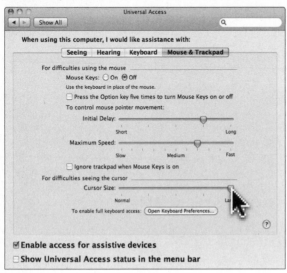

Activating full keyboard access

A final option in the Mouse & Keyboard pane in the Universal Access system preference relates to full keyboard access. Click Open Keyboard Preferences to be taken to the Keyboard & Shortcuts system preference, which has keyboard access controls (see Figure 6.13).

In the Full Keyboard Access section at the bottom of the Keyboard & Shortcuts system preference's Keyboard Shortcuts pane, you have two options:

- **Text Boxes and Lists Only.** This is the default option. When it is selected, pressing the Tab key moves the keyboard focus between text fields (text boxes) and lists, but ignores other options, such as check boxes.

- **All Controls.** When this option is selected, pressing the Tab key moves the focus between all elements in a list, including check boxes, radio buttons, and push buttons.

FIGURE 6.13

Full keyboard access widens the range of objects in lists that the Tab key moves between.

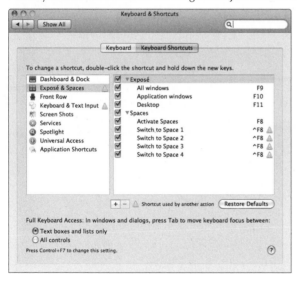

Setting Up Speech Recognition

The idea of being able to verbally communicate with a computer has been a staple of science fiction for decades, but recently the idea has started to make serious movement from science fiction to science fact.

At the introduction of the Macintosh in 1984, the computer introduced itself by speaking aloud to an audience. Over time, Macs have become increasingly verbose.

Listening is, of course, a slightly more complex matter than speaking. The wide range of human languages, regional dialects, semantic variations, and, of course, personal pronunciation differences all pose a real challenge for any speech recognition system.

But Apple has, over time, chipped away at the concept of speech recognition, and every version of Mac OS X has increased the capability of the Mac to understand what people are saying.

Mac OS X has a built-in English speech recognition program that can be activated in the Speech system preference. Speech recognition in Mac OS X is designed to recognize hundreds of commonly spoken commands. You can use it to control the interface, switch between applications, and even start iChat conversations.

Tip

What you can't use Mac OS X's speech recognition for is general dictation. If you want to take full control of your Mac verbally, you need to invest in a separate program. A good one to look at is MacSpeech Dictate ($199; www.macspeech.com).

Tip

It's not just people with limited movement that need to consider speech-based input. Voice recognition technology is especially useful to people suffering, or worried about developing, RSI (repetitive strain injury). Repeated small movements caused by typing on keyboards, or moving a mouse, can lead to RSI-related problems. Voice recognition technology can be a great boon to preventing or adjusting to RSIs.

Using a microphone

Speech recognition requires a microphone. Fortunately, most Mac users are in luck because most Macs have a built-in microphone. (It accompanies the built-in iSight camera, usually located just above the screen.)

The built-in microphones in MacBooks, MacBook Pros, iMacs, and Mac Minis, as well as in some of the latest LED (light-emitting diode) flat-panel monitors made by Apple, are all high-quality affairs, and most of them work just fine for speech recognition.

Using a built-in microphone is fine for Mac OS X's speech recognition, but if you find you have difficulty with the built-in microphone, you might want to consider upgrading to a dedicated external microphone. Some speech recognition systems, such as MacSpeech Dictate, often come supplied with high-quality microphones. If you use speech recognition permanently, you might want to consider a dedicated noise-canceling microphone and earphone headset. Many makes and models are available.

Configuring speech recognition

Open the System Preferences application (choose ⇨ System Preferences) and click the Speech icon to access the Speech system preference (see Figure 6.14), then go to the Speech Recognition pane. To activate speech recognition, you need to select the On option next to Speakable Items. When you do this, a circular window, known as the Speech Feedback window, appears, indicating that speech recognition is up and running. You can now turn speech recognition on and off, and the feedback window lets you know when Mac OS X is listening.

FIGURE 6.14

You can set Mac OS X to listen to you via its Speech system preference. (But it doesn't always do exactly what you ask it to.)

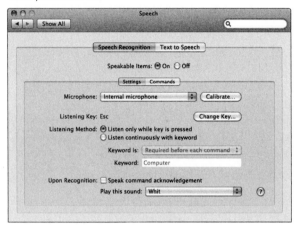

Turning on speech recognition is very simple. Getting it to work, however, takes a little more practice. We start by showing you some of the options.

Adjusting speech recognition settings

The Speech Recognition pane has two subpanes: Settings and Commands. The Settings subpane enables you to adjust various options related to activating the speech input. They are described next.

Microphone popup menu

There is a popup menu which will, by default, have Internal Microphone listed. If you have multiple microphones attached to your Mac, you can choose which one to use with this menu.

Calibrate button

To the right of the Microphone popup menu is the Calibrate button; click it to open the Microphone Calibration dialog box (see Figure 6.15).

To calibrate the microphone, you need to speak naturally (as you will when speaking to your Mac) and watch the meter. The meter lights up as you speak, through the blue, green, and into the red area. As you speak, move the slider between Low and High until the meter stays in the green area as you speak. You may find it easier to read something out loud while calibrating the meter.

When you have the meter calibrated (so it's in the green area), start saying the various items listed on the left-hand side of the window. As each command is recognized, its text blinks. If Mac OS X is having difficulty recognizing any of the commands, you may need to adjust the slider again until all the spoken commands are recognized.

FIGURE 6.15

The Microphone Calibration dialog box is where you set up the microphone for speech recognition. Calibrating the microphone enables speech recognition to more accurately understand what you're saying.

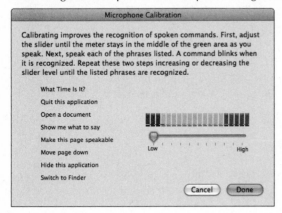

Change Key button

By default, speech recognition on Mac OS X works by listening when you are holding down a key. (The Esc key is used by default.) Click Change Key to change this key to another of your own choosing.

Listening Method options

If you do not want to hold down a key to activate speech recognition, you can opt to use a keyword instead. The way this works is that the speech recognition function continuously listens for you to say a specific word. When it hears that word, it treats whatever you say next as a command. By default, the keyword is "computer" — saying the word "computer" out loud activates the speech recognition. So to open iTunes, you would say, "Computer, open iTunes."

Select the Listen Continuously with Keyword option to switch to this mode.

Underneath the Listen Continuously with Keyword option is the Keyword Is popup menu with the following options: Optional before Commands, Required before Each Command, Required 15 Seconds after Last Command, and Required 30 Seconds after Last Command. Changing these settings adjusts when the keyword needs to be said in relation to the command.

Underneath the Keyword Is popup menu is a text field containing the keyword. You can change the keyword to something else by typing it in this field.

Upon Recognition options

By default, when a command has been recognized, Mac OS X plays a sound called Whit. (It sounds like an extremely short whistle.) The Speak Command Acknowledgment option enables you to set up Mac OS X to speak out loud the command you have just spoken, so if you say, "Open iTunes," your Mac responds with "opening iTunes." This is a cool way to interact with your computer, although it can become tiresome eventually.

The Play This Sound popup menu enables you choose from a range of sound effects to replace Whit. Aside from Whit and Single Click, all are the same as the system alerts found in the Sound system preference. Be careful not to choose the same sound effect as your system alert, because this can lead to confusion.

Using the Speech Feedback window

When you turn on speech recognition, a small round window appears. This is the Speech Feedback window. This in an unusual window in many respects. It has no associated menu bar, for one thing; it has no Minimize, Close, or Zoom iconic buttons; and it floats above all other windows. Figure 6.16 shows the feedback window in several states.

FIGURE 6.16

The Speech Feedback window indicates when speech recognition is idle (left) and displays the key press required to activate it; in this case, Esc. The microphone icon lights up when it is waiting for a command (middle), and two small arrows point to the microphone icon (right) when it is hearing a command.

Getting to know the Speech Feedback window

The Speech Feedback window provides several visual clues regarding speech recognition:

- **Attention mode.** The top half of the feedback window contains an icon of an old-fashioned microphone. This icon indicates whether the Mac is standing by, actively listening to, or recognizing commands. The microphone icon has the following states: not listening, listening, and hearing.

  - **Not listening.** If the small microphone icon is grayed out, speech recognition is not currently listening for commands.

  - **Listening (but not hearing).** If the small microphone icon turns solid black, it is actively listening, but not currently hearing a command.

  - **Hearing a command.** If you see small arrowheads moving toward the microphone icon, speech recognition is currently hearing a command (usually because you are talking).

- **Listening method.** The middle section of the Speech Feedback window indicates how you can make the computer switch from not listening to listening mode. By default it shows Esc, which indicates that you must press Esc before speaking. You may also see the name of the word you must speak to activate listening mode.

- **Loudness.** There are four colored bars at the bottom of the Speech Feedback window. These measure the loudness of your voice. In use, there seems to be little relationship between loudness and successful speech recognition (assuming, of course, that your voice is loud enough to be heard at all). One bar indicates that you're speaking quietly; a blue bar and one or two green bars means you're speaking at a moderate volume; these three bars plus a red bar indicate that you're speaking very loudly (probably shouting). Apple recommends that you speak loudly enough to have green bars appear, but not so loud that the red bar appears.

- **Recognition.** When speech recognizes a command that you speak, it displays the corresponding command in a yellow tag above the Speech Feedback window. The displayed command may not completely match the command you uttered, because speech recognition offers a degree of flexibility when understanding what you speak. For example, if you say, "Close window," the feedback window displays "Close This Window." If speech recognition has a response to your command, it displays it in a help tag below the feedback window.

Using Speech Feedback window controls

At the bottom of the Speech Feedback window is an iconic popup menu, indicated by a small downward-facing triangle (see Figure 6.17). Clicking this iconic popup menu reveals two menu options:

- **Open Speech Commands Window.** Choosing this option opens a window displaying all the available speech commands (see Figure 6.18).

- **Speech Preferences.** Choosing this option takes you to the Speech system preference.

FIGURE 6.17

Clicking the triangle iconic popup menu at the bottom of the Speech Feedback window reveals these two menu options.

Minimizing the Speech Feedback window

As noted earlier, the Speech Feedback window is slightly odd in that it does not have a Minimize iconic button. However, you can minimize it to the Dock by double-clicking the window or by speaking the command "Minimize Speech Feedback window." Figure 6.19 shows a feedback window that has been minimized to the Dock.

While sitting in the Dock, the Speech Feedback window continues to offer much the same functionality as before. You continue to press Esc (or the appropriate key or verbal command) to activate speech recognition, and the feedback window displays the same symbols for speech recognition. Two notable differences are that it no longer displays yellow boxes displaying recognized commands and, because it is minimized, you can no longer access the popup menu. It's also worth noting that because it is smaller when minimized, you may no longer be able to clearly identify the different feedback states.

FIGURE 6.18

The Speech Commands window displays a list of available commands.

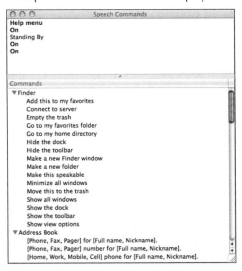

Opening the feedback window from the Dock and returning it to the main part of the interface is easy: Simply click on it in the Dock, or you Control+click or right-click it and choose Open Speech Feedback from the contextual menu. Alternatively you can speak the command "Open Speech Feedback window."

FIGURE 6.19

When minimized in the Dock, the Speech Feedback window (second from the right) continues to provide information regarding speech recognition.

Investigating the Speech Commands window

The Speech Commands window provides a list of all your recently spoken commands and the responses to them; it also displays a list of the commands you can speak in the current context. You access this window by clicking on the iconic popup menu (the arrow icon) at the bottom of the Speech Feedback window and choosing Open Speech Commands Window. Fittingly, you can also open the Speech Commands window by saying the command "Open Speech Commands window."

The tools offered by the Speech Commands window make it a great tool for learning what you can do with the speech function of your Mac.

The commands you have recently spoken appear in bold at the top of the Speech Commands window, and any responses appear below in plain text. The bottom part of the window displays the commands available in the current context. The list is organized into these categories:

- **Current application.** This category only appears if the active application has its own speakable commands. For example, if Mail is the currently active application, the first menu option in Commands is Mail.

- **Address Book.** In this category, you find commands relating to your contacts. As well as with Address Book, these commands interact with Mail and iChat.

- **Speakable Items.** The items in this category are available no matter which application is currently active.

- **Application Switching.** The commands in this category enable you to move between applications. There are also commands here for opening and quitting applications used by Mac OS X.

Each category has a disclosure triangle that can be used to hide or show the various commands contained within each category. You can resize the two parts of the Speech Commands window by dragging the handle located between the two windows (identified as a horizontal gray bar with a small gray thumb [a drag handle] in the middle.) You can also add extra speakable commands to this window, as we explain shortly.

Specifying active commands

The Speech Commands window organizes commands into groups (known as *command sets*). You can choose which groups of commands Mac OS X listens for by going to the Commands subpane in the Speech system preference's Speech Recognition pane (see Figure 6.20).

FIGURE 6.20

The command sets can be identified, and activated or deactivated, in the Commands subpane in the Speech system preference's Speech Recognition pane.

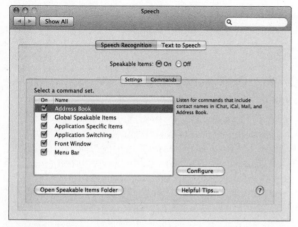

To choose commands by group, follow these steps:

1. **Go to the Speech Recognition pane in the Speech system preference.**

2. **Go to the Commands subpane.**

3. **Use the options in the Select a Command Set list to select or deselect command sets.** Selecting an option activates a particular command set. Note that if you want to activate the Front Window and Menu Bar command sets, you must select the Enable Access for Assistive Devices option in the Universal Access system preference (as outlined earlier in this chapter).

4. **Configure global speakable items.** Highlight the Global Speakable Items command set in the list and click Configure. This brings up a dialog box with the Speak Command Names Exactly as Written option (see Figure 6.21). If selected, this option requires the speaker to use the exact name of the command. This option is selected by default, which improves accuracy and system speed. Deselecting this option has Mac OS X try to understand a more relaxed speech pattern.

5. **Click OK to continue.**

FIGURE 6.21

When the Speak Command Names Exactly as Written option is selected, you must speak command names exactly as they are written. Although this speeds up system time, deselecting this option enables Mac OS X to recognize a more variable speech pattern.

Setting up the Text to Speech option

Text to Speech is the other half of the conversation, where the Mac talks to you. Computer speech has come along in leaps and bounds in recent years, and if your last memory of computer speech is a monotone robotic voice droning on, you're in for a pleasant surprise.

You can investigate the different vocal options for Mac OS X by going to the Text to Speech pane in the Speech preference pane (see Figure 6.22). Here, you can specify what voice to use, the speed at which Mac OS X speaks, and define what, when, and how things are spoken. You can determine alert options, choose from a built-in list of alerts, and even add your own phrases. There's plenty of room for customization: You can set different voices for alerts than normal speech and specify a time delay. There are even options for speaking text, as well as the date and time.

FIGURE 6.22

The Text to Speech pane in the Speech system preference offers a wide range of options for adjusting how Mac OS X talks to you.

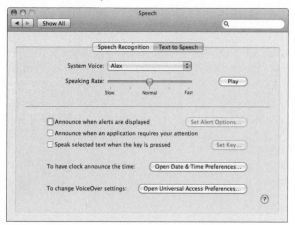

There are several voices included with Mac OS X 10.6 Snow Leopard. But you should note that some are more advanced than others. Each one is given a name, and Alex is the most advanced so far. This is the default voice and by far the clearest and most adept at speaking. Still, there are several voices to choose from, both male and female, plus a range of comic effect voices you can investigate. You can also adjust the rate at which each voice speaks, changing how it sounds.

Follow these steps to change the voice and adjust the rate at which Mac OS X talks to you:

1. **Open the System Preferences application (choose ⇨ System Preferences), click the Speech icon, and go to the Text to Speech pane.**

2. **Select a voice from the System Voice popup menu.** There are several male and female voices. Choosing the Show More Voices option increases the number of voices, including older "human" voices and several novelty voice options such as the spacey Trinoids and the aquatic Bubbles. Figure 6.23 shows all the voices available to you.

3. **Click Play to hear what the voice sounds like.** Mac OS X speaks a single sentence randomly picked from a selection. If you choose another voice before the sentence has finished, Mac OS X starts another random sentence in the desired voice. Click Stop or wait for the sentence to end.

4. **Adjust the speaking rate.** You can speed up the rate that a voice talks by moving the Speaking Rate slider to the right; moving it to the left slows the rate a voice talks.

Selecting text-to-speech options

Below the System Voice popup menu are several options you can use to customize how speech is used by Mac OS X.

FIGURE 6.23

Here are all the voices in Mac OS X. Alex is by far the most natural sounding, and most of the others have mainly novelty value these days.

Announce When Alerts Are Displayed option

Selecting the Announce When Alerts Are Displayed option has Mac OS X read aloud system alerts. Click Set Alert Options to bring up an additional dialog box (see Figure 6.24), which enables you to set a separate voice from the system voice to speak alerts. The Delay slider enables you set a delay between 0 and 60 seconds between when the alert appears on-screen and when Mac OS X speaks it.

FIGURE 6.24

The Set Alert Options window enables you to choose a specific voice, and phrase, associated with system alerts.

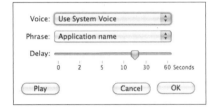

The Phrase popup menu enables you to choose how that the alert is phrased. Choices include:

- **Application Name.** This option has Mac OS X inform you which application has an alert.
- **Next in the Phrase List.** This option moves through a set of phrases.
- **Random in the Phrase List:** This option picks random phrases from the phrase list.
- **Phrase List.** This option enables you to set a particular phrase from the phrase list. The options are Alert!, Attention!, Excuse Me!, and Pardon Me!.
- **Edit Phrase List.** This option brings up the Alert Phrases dialog box (see Figure 6.25). Click Add and type in a phrase that you want Mac OS X to speak during an alert. You can remove alerts from the list by selecting them and clicking Remove.

FIGURE 6.25

The Set Alert Phrases dialog box enables you to create your own alert phrases for Mac OS X to speak.

Announce When an Application Requires Your Attention option

Selecting the Announce When an Application Requires Your Attention option causes Mac OS X to speak when an application requires your attention. This coincides with the usual alert, whereby an application icon in the Dock bounces up and down (see Chapter 2).

Speak Selected Text When a Key Is Pressed option

Select the Speak Selected Text When a Key Is Pressed option to enable a key combination that will, when pressed, cause Mac OS X to speak whatever text is currently highlighted. Click the Set Key button and a dialog box appears (see Figure 6.26) asking you to enter a key combination. Hold down one or more modifier keys (Control, Option, Shift, and ⌘) and then press the desired key to set the command. For example, you might choose Control+Option+S. Now, when you highlight a piece of text in Mac OS X, pressing this key combination causes Mac OS X to read the text aloud.

FIGURE 6.26

The Speak Selected Text When a Key Is Pressed option enables you to set a key combination that can be used to instantly speak whatever text is highlighted in Mac OS X.

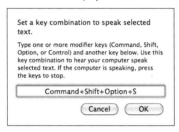

Note

It is also possible to have Mac OS X read text by using Mac OS X services that some applications support. In TextEdit, for example, you can Control+click or right-click a highlighted piece of text and choose Speech ⇨ Start Speaking from the contextual menu to have Mac OS X read out the highlighted text.

Open Date & Time Preferences button

You can click the Open Date & Time Preferences button next to the To Have Clock Announce the Time label to make Mac OS X speak the date and time. Clicking it takes you to the Date & Time system preference. Go to the Clock pane and select the Announce the Time option. A popup menu enables you to choose between On the Hour, On the Half Hour, and On the Quarter Hour. Click Customize Voice to choose the audio style you would like the time announced with. (The options are the same as for system alerts, mentioned earlier.)

Open Universal Access Preferences button

The final option in the Text to Speech pane in the Speech system preference — the Open Universal Access Preferences button — takes you to the Universal Access system preference. From here you can enable VoiceOver (as outlined earlier in the chapter) or — from the Seeing pane — click the Open VoiceOver Utility button to further customize voice settings of Mac OS X. In the remainder of this chapter, we look closely at VoiceOver Utility.

Setting Up the VoiceOver Utility

The VoiceOver Utility is (see Figure 6.27) something of an oddity in Mac OS X. In many ways, it is an extension of the Universal Access system preference (as described at the start of this chapter), although in other ways it is clearly an application in its own right.

VoiceOver, as outlined earlier, is a technology that enables Mac OS X to read aloud whatever is on the screen, underneath the mouse pointer, or underneath the VoiceOver cursor (a square rectangle that appears over items in the GUI).

The VoiceOver Utility enables you to fine-tune almost every aspect of VoiceOver, including the amount of punctuation it interacts with, how it navigates applications and Web pages, the visual effects that accompany it, and even how it interacts with a Braille display (if one is attached to your Mac).

FIGURE 6.27

VoiceOver Utility offers a wide range of settings you can use to fine-tune the way VoiceOver interacts with Mac OS X.

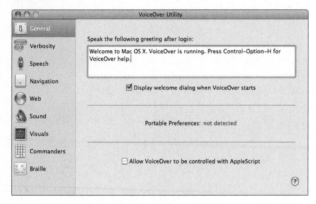

Adjusting the General settings

Click General in the list to the left to access the General pane. Here you can change the VoiceOver message that greets you when you log in (see Figure 6.28). By default, this welcomes you to Mac OS X and informs you that VoiceOver is running; it also tells you that you can access help by pressing Control+Option+H. You can change this message to anything you want.

Setting up VoiceOver

The portable preferences capability is a means of taking your VoiceOver settings with you via an external disk. This could be an external hard disk or, more commonly, a USB (Universal Serial Bus) flash drive. To set up portable preferences, attach an external storage device and choose File➪Set Up Portable Preferences or press Shift+⌘+V. Select the storage device in the settings sheet (see Figure 6.29) and click OK.

New Feature

Portable preferences was called VO-to-Go in previous incarnations of Mac OS X.

FIGURE 6.28

The General settings enable you to enter a personalized message that greets you when you first log in with VoiceOver running.

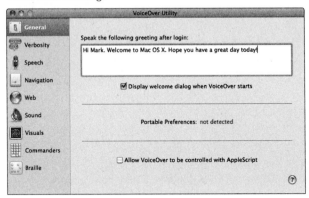

Now the settings you make in the VoiceOver Utility are also saved to the external storage device. When you plug this device into another Mac, that Mac automatically asks if you would like to use portable preferences. Click Yes so you can use all your settings on that computer, without having to set everything up from scratch. Note that those preferences are available to the other Mac as long as that storage device is attached to it.

FIGURE 6.29

The portable preferences capability uses an external storage device (such as a USB flash drive) to save VoiceOver settings for use on other Macs. These preferences are activated when the device is attached to any other Mac.

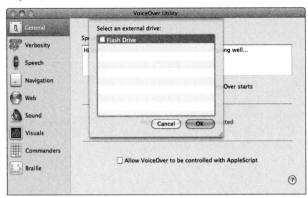

Allow VoiceOver to Be Controlled with AppleScript option

Selecting the Allow VoiceOver to Be Controlled with AppleScript option enables AppleScript to control VoiceOver. Chapter 25 has more information on how you can use AppleScript to interact with Mac OS X.

Adjusting the Verbosity settings

VoiceOver is, by nature, quite verbose. Put simply, it likes to talk a lot. The VoiceOver Utility enables you to fine-tune, almost to a granular level, how much VoiceOver talks and the kind of things it likes to talk about. Clicking the Verbosity option in the list brings up four subpanes: General, Text, Announcements, and Hints.

New Feature

The Verbosity pane offers greater control over VoiceOver's speaking settings than in previous versions of Mac OS X. The General and Hints subpanes are new to Mac OS X 10.6 Snow Leopard, as are their controls.

General subpane

In the General subpane of the Verbosity pane is the Default Verbosity popup menu. It is set to High by default, but there are also Medium and Low settings. Clicking the disclosure triangle labeled Details reveals exactly what each of the settings has for every part of Mac OS X. You can also set different levels of verbosity for different Mac OS X controls by choosing an option for a specific control in its Verbosity popup menu; the options are Low, Medium, High, and Custom. Choosing Custom brings up a settings sheet with options for each individual item spoken by that control (see Figure 6.30).

FIGURE 6.30

You can fine-tune the verbal prowess of Mac OS X. You can do this across the board, or to an extremely granular level.

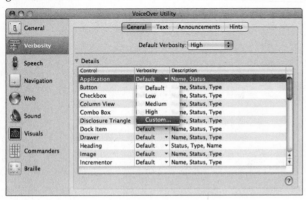

Text subpane

In the Text subpane of the Verbosity pane is a series of popup menus (see Figure 6.31) that enable you to adjust various aspects of VoiceOver when you are working with text. You can change the way that text-to-speech handles punctuation, typing, text cursor location, text attributes, misspelled words, links, numbers, capital letters, deleting text, and word separation. Each popup menu has several options to choose from.

Announcements subpane

VoiceOver announces various aspects of Mac OS X. The Announcements subpane in the Verbosity pane contains a set of options that can increase the number of announcements. The options are:

- Announce When Mouse Cursor Enters a Window.
- Announce When a Modifier Key Is Pressed.
- Announce When the Caps Lock Key Is Pressed.
- Speak Header When Navigating Across a Table Row.
- Automatically Speak Text in Dialog Boxes.

There are several other controls in this subpane:

- **When Status Text Changes Under VoiceOver Cursor popup menu.** The options are Play Tone, Speak Text, and Do Nothing.
- **When Progress Indicator Changes Under VoiceOver Cursor popup menu.** The options are Play Tone, Speak Text, and Do Nothing.
- **Speak Size and Position In popup menu.** The options are Inches, Millimeters, and Pixels.
- **Speak Text under Mouse After Delay slider.** Use the slider to set how long VoiceOver waits to speak the text under the mouse pointer's current location.

Hints pane

VoiceOver gives several hints relating to items under the VoiceOver cursor. The Speak Instructions for Using the Item in the VoiceOver Cursor option (selected by default) activates these instructions. The When an Item Has a Help Tag popup menu enables you to choose from the following options: Do Nothing, Speak Notification, and Speak Help Tag. The final option is a slider marked Speak Hints After Delay, with options from Short to Long.

Adjusting the Speech settings

The Speech pane in the VoiceOver Utility dialog box enables you to fine-tune the voices used by Mac OS X. Click the Speech item in the list on the left to access the settings; there are two subpanes: Voices and Pronunciation (see Figure 6.31).

Voices subpane

There are several options available in the Voices subpane:

- **Mute Speech.** This option enables you to silence the speech.
- **Default.** Here, you set the default options for how Mac OS X speaks. The Voice popup menu lets you choose the default voice, and the fields in the same row enable you to choose the rate, pitch, volume, and intonation values. If you click the disclosure triangle next to Default, you get the same options for several other categories of speaking: Content, Status, Type, Attributes, and VoiceOver Menu.

FIGURE 6.31

The Speech pane in VoiceOver Utility enables you to fine-tune the sound of different voices used in Mac OS X.

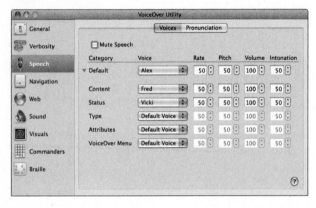

Pronunciation subpane

The Pronunciation subpane in the Speech pane in the VoiceOver Utility dialog box enables you to substitute spoken terms for specific text (see Figure 6.32). This is useful for many of the acronyms that make up computer terminology (for example, GUI is pronounced "gooey," and emoticons such as :-) are pronounced "smiley").

You can change the pronunciation of any of the items in the list by clicking on the text in the Substitution column. New substitutions can be added by clicking the + iconic button and entering the details in the appropriate columns. Clicking the – iconic button enables you to remove substitutions from the list.

FIGURE 6.32

Substitutions are used by VoiceOver to pronounce terms and symbols differently from their visual appearance. You can customize them to correctly pronounce any text in any manner you choose.

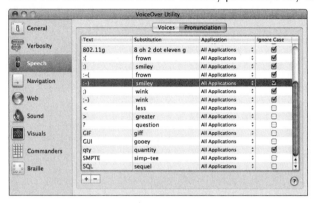

Adjusting Navigation settings

The Navigation pane of the VoiceOver Utility enables you to adjust how the VoiceOver cursor moves around the screen. The following controls are available:

- **Initial Position of VoiceOver Cursor popup menu.** Two options are available in this popup menu. The default is Keyboard Focused Item, or you can choose First Item in Window.

- **Keyboard Focus Follows VoiceOver Cursor option.**

- **Mouse Cursor Follows VoiceOver Cursor option.**

- **VoiceOver Cursor Follows Mouse Cursor option.**

- **Insertion Point Follows VoiceOver Cursor option.**

- **VoiceOver Cursor Follows Insertion Point option.**

- **Mouse Cursor popup menu.** This popup menu lets you specify how the mouse pointer interacts with the VoiceOver cursor: Ignores VoiceOver Cursor, Follows VoiceOver Cursor, or Moves VoiceOver Cursor.

- **Allow Cursor Wrapping option.** If selected, this option specifies that the mouse pointer should be able to move off the side of the screen and appear on the other side. The mouse pointer can wrap horizontally, and vertically, in a continuous loop.

- **Skip Redundant Labels option.**

- **Automatically Interact When Using Tab Key option.**

Adjusting Web settings

You can adjust how VoiceOver interacts with Web pages (misspelled by Apple as "Webpages" in the VoiceOver Utility) several ways, using the Web pane:

- **Navigate Webpages By option.** You have two options: You can either navigate by DOM Order (DOM means Document Object Model, a technical standard for Web pages' internal organization), which uses the layout of a Web page to determine what objects are grouped together; or you can use Grouping Items, which moves the VoiceOver cursor from one group of information to the next, such as from paragraph to paragraph.

- **When Loading a New Webpage option.** Three options are available here: Speak Webpage Summary, Move the VoiceOver Cursor to It, and Automatically Speak the Webpage. The third option is available only if Move the VoiceOver Cursor to It option is selected.

- **When Navigating Tables option.** You have two options: The first is to group items within the table; the second is to speak column and row numbers.

- **Navigate Images popup menu.** This popup menu offers the choices of Never, With Descriptions (the default option), and Always.

- **Web Item Rotor Includes popup menu.** The Web Item Rotor Includes popup menu enables you to select several items in the Web chooser. By default, all options are selected. The options are Headers, Links, Visited Links, Non-Visited Links, Auto Web Spots, Form Controls, Web Spots, Tables, Images, and Frames. These options indicate what types of Web content VoiceOver pays attention to when helping you navigate Web pages. (Web spots use an Apple technology that lets Universal Access find and navigate to content blocks, such as stories, on Web pages through visual indicators and VoiceOver.)

New Feature

The ability to begin reading a Web page when it loads is new to Mac OS X 10.6 Snow Leopard. So is the ability to navigate HTML tables on Web sites using the standard VoiceOver commands used for other elements. Support for Web spots and control over what specific Web page attributes VocieOver works with are also new to Mac OS X 10.6 Snow Leopard.

Adjusting Sound settings

You can choose from two options in the Sound Settings pane of VoiceOver Utility:

- **Mute Sound Effects option.** Selecting this option turns off all sound effects other than VoiceOver.

- **Enable Positional Audio option.** This option (selected by default) enables you to use dual speakers, or headphones, to hear audio positioned in different locations.

Adjusting the Visuals settings

The Visuals pane has four subpanes, each offering different ways that VoiceOver displays information on the screen. Customizing these sections can be extremely useful for those with limited sight abilities.

VoiceOver Cursor subpane

The controls here enable you to adjust how the VoiceOver cursor appears on the screen.

- **Show VoiceOver Cursor option.** This option enables you turn on or off the VoiceOver cursor (the square rectangle that surrounds items being read out on-screen).

- **VoiceOver Cursor Magnification slider.** This slider enables you to magnify the VoiceOver cursor and the contents displayed within it. Moving the slider to the right sets it to the Large setting (see Figure 6.33), which can make the VoiceOver cursor extremely useful for people who see partially.

- **When Reading Text, Move VoiceOver Cursor By popup menu.** This popup menu has two options: Sentence and Word. By default, the VoiceOver cursor moves by each sentence that is read, but here you can tell VoiceOver to move by each individual word.

FIGURE 6.33

The VoiceOver cursor can be magnified to give a larger visual view of the contents currently being verbally communicated.

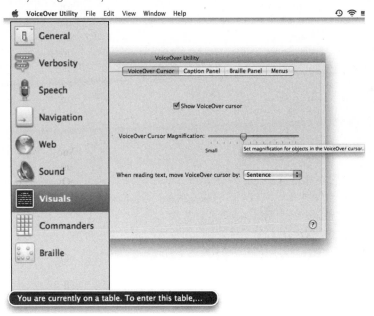

Caption Panel subpane

The caption panel is a gray translucent bubble (normally positioned on the bottom left of the screen) that provides information regarding the VoiceOver caption. Figure 6.34 shows an example of the caption panel. Several settings here control the caption panel:

- **Show Caption Panel option.** This option shows or hides the caption panel. It is selected by default.

- **Caption Panel Font Size slider.** Moving this slider to the right increases the size of the text in the caption panel.

- **Rows in Caption Panel.** By default, the caption panel has only a single row of text, with overflow text indicated with ellipses (...). Moving this slider to the right enables you to expand the caption panel to accommodate up to ten rows of text.

- **Caption Panel Transparency slider.** Moving this slider farther to the right makes the caption panel more opaque, and thus less obtrusive.

FIGURE 6.34

The caption panel displays information relating to the VoiceOver Cursor. These settings enable you to increase the size, or reduce the obtrusiveness, of the caption panel.

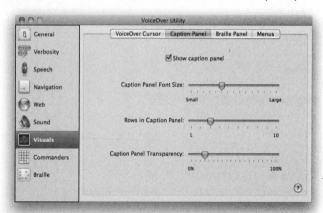

Braille Panel subpane

A refreshable Braille display can be attached to a Mac, and VoiceOver automatically sends information from the screen to that display. The Braille panel also displays this information on the screen (see Figure 6.35). There are several options here that relate to the Braille panel:

- **Show Braille Panel popup menu.** The options here are Automatic, On, and Off.

- **Braille Font Color popup menu.** The color is yellow by default, but this popup menu enables you to select from five colors.

- **Braille Panel Font Size slider.** This slider enables you to adjust the size of the Braille panel's font. Move the slider to the right to make it larger, and to the left to make it smaller.

- **Braille Panel Transparency slider.** Moving this slide to the right decreases the opacity of the Braille panel, making it more transparent.

FIGURE 6.35

The Braille panel displays on-screen the information sent to a Braille display device.

Menus subpane

The options in this subpane adjust the display of VoiceOver Help menu (accessed by clicking Control+Option+H when VoiceOver is running):

- **VoiceOver Menus Font Size slider.** Moving this slider to the right makes the VoiceOver menu larger.
- **VoiceOver Menus Transparency slider.** Moving this slider to the right increases the transparency of the VoiceOver Menu, making it less obtrusive.

Adjusting the Commanders settings

The Commanders pane lets you map commands to both the numeric keypad and the keyboard. Use it to attach commonly used commands (such as Go To Desktop, Open Item Chooser, and open specific applications) to specific keys. This is a useful feature that simplifies complex commands by assigning them to single keys or key combinations.

There are two subpanes: NumPad and Keyboard.

NumPad subpane

The NumPad subpane contains a list of commands that are mapped to the numeric keypad (the numeric keys found to the right of Apple extended keyboards; these keys are not present on Apple laptops and some iMac keyboards).

You must select the Enable NumPad Commander option to enable the mapping capability.

The list of commands in the subpane shows what command VoiceOver performs when you press the appropriate key. VoiceOver commands are available for more than just the regular keyboard keys. You can see the assignments for specific modifier combinations by using the No Modifier popup menu to choose a modifier option: Command (the ⌘ key), Option, Control, Shift, and NumPad Zero (the numeric keypad's 0 key). When you choose an option, the list of VoiceOver command assignments changes to those using that particular modifier key.

You can also replace any of the default commands used by NumPad Commander with your own. Each command listed is actually a popup menu (indicated by the small down-pointing arrow to the right of each command). Then navigate through the popup menu to find the desired replacement command (see Figure 6.36).

Note

You cannot use mouse keys (a feature outlined earlier in the chapter) while using NumPad Commander.

FIGURE 6.36

You can adjust the commands used by NumPad Commander to any one of several different VoiceOver commands available.

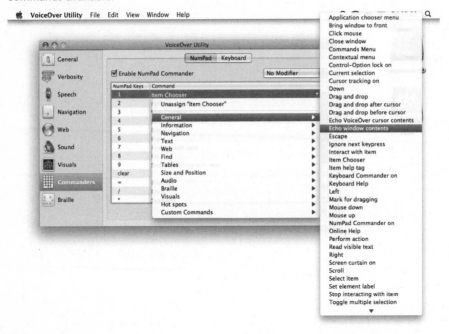

Keyboard subpane

Keyboard Commander works in much the same way as NumPad Commander. Selecting the Enable Keyboard Command option at the top of the subpane enables Keyboard Commander (see Figure 6.37).

One key difference is that the keyboard commands must be used with a modifier key. This is because you are likely to need the keyboard for general tasks. Because you are also likely to require regular keyboard commands, complete with modifier keys, Keyboard Commander uses only one of the Mac keyboard's two Option keys. (Normally, Mac OS doesn't care which Option key you press; it treats them as if they were the same key.) You select which Option key the Keyboard Commander uses by selecting one of the options from Use options: Left Option Key and Right Option Key. If you select Right Option key, pressing the right Option key invokes a VoiceOver keyboard shortcut, while pressing a left-hand Option key invokes the Mac OS's or application's normal keyboard shortcut using Option.

The number of keyboard commands in Keyboard Commander is much more limited than in NumPad Commander. However, you can add new keyboard commands by using the + iconic button in the bottom left of the subpane.

The Keyboard section enables you to map commands to individual keys on the keyboard. You then access them with either the left or right Option key.

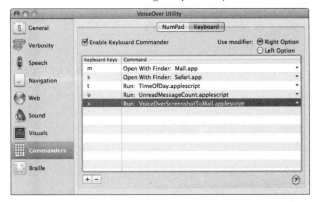

Setting up Braille

Braille converts text shown in VoiceOver into a form readable by touch. There are many Braille readers available for Mac OS X. If you attach a compatible Braille display to the Mac, it is detected automatically, and you can adjust its settings in the VoiceOver Utility's Braille pane. The Braille pane has two subpanes: Layout and Displays.

Layout subpane

The settings available in the Layout subpane of the Braille pane are:

- **Braille Display indicator.** The model of your connected display appears here.
- **Braille Translation section.** This section has three options on how certain items are converted to Braille:
    - **Braille Translation popup menu.** The default option is Apple American English. This popup menu shows any further options installed in Mac OS X.
    - **Show Contracted Braille option.** Contracted Braille is a set of about two dozen words represented by a single symbol each, for faster communication.
    - **Use Dots 7 and 8 to Indicate Cursor option.**

- **Status Cells section.** This section has three options that control how status cells are used: Show General Display Status, Show Text Style, and Show Extended Text Style.
- **Show Status On The option.** Two options are available: Left and Right.

Displays subpane

Any Braille displays attached to your Mac are listed here. If a display is connected via USB, it is automatically connected and listed. However, if your Braille display operates via Bluetooth, you can connect it by using the following method:

1. **Make sure the Braille display is discoverable.** Consult the instructions with the display to discover how to put it in discoverable mode.

2. **Click the + iconic button.**

3. **Find the device.** A dialog box appears that searches for all available Bluetooth devices. When the Braille display appears in the list, click it.

4. **Select the Remember This Device option.** If you want Mac OS X to remember the device so it automatically reconnects in the future, make sure you select this option.

5. **Click Select.**

New Feature

Mac OS X 10.6 Snow Leopard now allows multiple USB Braille readers to be used simultaneously, such as in a classroom setting, so the same screen is displayed on the multiple readers. Also, Snow Leopard now supports Bluetooth Braille readers (only one can be active at a time, however).

Cross-Ref

Chapter 21 explains Bluetooth device setup in more detail; the process is the same for Braille displays as for other devices.

Summary

Universal Access lets you interact with Mac OS X in a variety of ways. Although primarily designed to help those with impaired sight, hearing, or hand usage, some of these interaction controls can benefit anyone.

For example, for those with visual impairment, the VoiceOver technology that enables users to hear what is displayed on the screen, as well as to control output to Braille devices. But it can also give everyone more awareness of alerts. Similarly, options for the hearing impaired provide extra visual feedback for anyone. And controls over keyboard and mouse interactions help not only those with difficulty using keyboards and mice, but also poor typists.

Apple's speech technology lets the Mac both listen to and execute your spoken commands, plus speak aloud alerts and user interface elements. The VoiceOver Utility enables you to fine-tune the VoiceOver text-to-speech technology to your exact needs.

Working with Applications and Documents

N ow that you've set up your Mac and become familiar with the Finder, it's time to get down to the business of working with applications and the day-to-day activity of creating, saving, and working with documents.

Most of the time you spend working on your Mac is in the traditional manner: opening applications, creating documents, printing and sharing them, and saving them for future posterity. In this sense, applications are the tools; documents are the things you create and share.

Having said that, a number of rapid changes are taking place in the computing world, not least of which is the rise of so called "cloud computing." This is where documents and applications are stored on online servers, and accessed via the Internet. Google Docs (www.docs.google.com) and Apple's MobileMe Web applications (www.me.com) are typical examples of this sort of service. (More information on using MobileMe can be found in Chapter 15.)

In this chapter, we look at the different types of applications that are available in Mac OS X. We explore how to locate applications, open them, and start using them. The Mac OS includes a huge range of applications, as Chapter 8 covers, but of course, the beauty of computers is that you can install and run programs built by other people. We cover the process of installing applications — and removing them when they are no longer wanted.

Mac OS X is a multitasking environment, which means you can run several applications at once (both in the foreground and background). We look at the process of managing multiple applications, and the multiple windows that each application may provide.

Applications and documents go hand in hand, so in this chapter, we also explain some basic elements of editing documents by using methods such as copy and paste, and drag and drop. We also address different methods of creating documents, saving documents, and quitting applications when you're done using them.

This chapter covers the general methods of working with applications, plus includes specific techniques that apply to most (but not all) applications. Every application is different, and ones that you install may have different methods of doing things. Chapter 8 includes a lot of information about working with each application that comes with Mac OS X; other applications you install will have their own documentation.

Note

Several terms are used interchangeably by those who produce applications and use them: software, application (and its nickname app), program, utility, tool, and solution. Software is the general term for code that runs on a computer to perform a task, whether in the form of its own application, a plug-in to another application, or a component of the operating system. Application, app, and program all refer to the same thing: software that you think of as collection of related functions, such as iTunes or Photoshop. Utility usually means a specialized program with a small set of functions, often designed to help you prepare for other tasks; examples are Disk Utility and the QuickTime Player. Tool is more of a marketing term to describe software, though sometimes people use it to mean software that people use to produce a result (such as making a movie or indexing a book). Solution is purely marketing-speak for software, hardware, and combinations of the two. Note that none of these terms is exact, so don't worry about trying to differentiate them.

Working with Mac OS X Applications

As we explain in Chapter 1, Mac OS X 10.6 Snow Leopard has many application environments, including Cocoa, Carbon, Java, and BSD (Berkeley Software Distribution) Unix. This diversity represents the history and lineage of the Macintosh, and — in the case of BSD — Mac OS X's Unix roots.

Of all these environments, Cocoa is by far the one most users will experience, with Carbon increasingly becoming a distant second. Apple has decided to push the one environment, and Cocoa is it. In this chapter, we primarily look at these two application environments:

- **Cocoa applications.** These are programs designed exclusively for Mac OS X. Mac OS X 10.6 Snow Leopard consolidates Cocoa and the Finder, which has now been completely rewritten in Cocoa. Cocoa applications have full access to the 64-bit capabilities of the Mac, as well as the latest Snow Leopard APIs (application programming interfaces).

- **Carbon applications.** Typically, these are older programs that were designed to run on PowerPC processors. Carbon applications run on Mac OS X 10.6 Snow Leopard just fine, although they are limited to 32-bit functionality.

Cross-Ref

Chapter 1 has more information on the differences between 64-bit and 32-bit applications.

The great thing is that to the user, Cocoa and Carbon are virtually indistinguishable. In terms of interaction with the Mac OS X graphical user interface (GUI), most users are unlikely to ever know that there are different application environments.

Note

You may have also heard of an older environment called Classic Mode. This Mac OS X environment was used to run earlier programs designed for Mac OS 9. Classic was a great tool that enabled users to migrate from Mac OS 9 to Mac OS X and still use the library of available software. Over time, Classic support has become less important, and Mac OS X 10.5 Leopard removed support for Classic. If you have any legacy applications that require Classic, you have three options. One is to see if a Mac OS X update to the program is available. The second option is to set up an older PowerPC-based (not Intel-based) Mac running Mac OS 9 or Mac OS X 10.4 or earlier (with Classic installed). The third option is to use an open source application called SheepShaver (`http://gwenole.beauchesne.info/en/projects/sheepshaver`) that emulates the Classic environment on an Intel Mac, enabling some (but not all) programs to run.

Discovering the preinstalled applications

Mac OS X comes with a large number of preinstalled applications. Most reside within the Applications folder, or within another folder inside Applications called Utilities. These applications cover virtually every aspect of computing, from surfing the Web; sending and receiving e-mail; and managing your music, video, and digital photographs to writing letters. Indeed, you can have a rich computing experience on Mac OS X without ever having to install a single application other than those supplied with the operating system.

Cross-Ref

Chapter 8 covers all the applications, utilities, and widgets that come bundled with Mac OS X 10.6 Snow Leopard. Chapter 16 covers the add-on capabilities called services that come with Mac OS X.

Table 7.1 lists all the applications within the Applications folder, and Table 7.2 lists all the applications within the Utilities folder.

TABLE 7.1

Applications Included with Mac OS X

Name	Description
Address Book	Contact management.
Automator	Automates repetitive tasks.
Calculator	An on-screen calculator.
Chess	A chess game with multiple difficulty settings.
Dashboard	An application used to display other small applications (called *widgets*) on the screen.
Dictionary	A comprehensive dictionary and thesaurus browser. Also contains a full dictionary of Apple-related terms and built-in access to Wikipedia (an online encyclopedia).
DVD Player	An application used to play video DVDs.
Font Book	An application used to preview, add, and manage fonts used by Mac OS X.
Front Row	A full-screen display application for browsing music, movies, and photographs

(continued)

TABLE 7.1	(continued)
Name	**Description**
iCal	A calendar application with a built-in task manager.
iChat	An instant messaging (IM) application. Used for sending instant text messages, plus audio and video chatting.
Image Capture	An application for downloading images from your digital camera, iPhone, or iPod Touch, and for importing images from a scanner.
iTunes	A versatile application used for playing and recording music CDs, and managing digital music, audiobooks, podcasts, movies, and TV shows. Also used for purchasing online movies, music, and applications from Apple's iTunes store. iTunes is also used to sync content from your Mac to an iPod or iPhone.
Mail	An e-mail application. Supports multiple accounts and uses contact information from Address Book.
Photo Booth	A program for taking snapshot pictures from the Mac's iSight camera. Comes with a range of built-in effects such as mosaic, glow, and stretch to enable customization of pictures.
Preview	An application used for viewing a wide range of graphics files and PDF (Portable Document Format) files. Also used by a range of Mac OS X applications to create print previews.
QuickTime Player	Apple's application to play a wide range of video and audio files.
Safari	A Web browser.
Stickies	An application that creates notes that appear on the desktop.
System Preferences	An application providing access to the various control panels for adjusting a wide range of Mac OS X preferences.
TextEdit	A surprisingly comprehensive word processor. Uses information from the Dictionary application for spell-checking and a thesaurus. Capable of opening, and saving, files in various Microsoft Word formats.
Time Machine	A backup utility.

TABLE 7.2	

Utilities Included with Mac OS X

Name	**Description**
Activity Monitor	A utility that displays processor, system memory, disk activity, disk usage, and network activity. Displays currently running processes, and enables users to terminate processes.
AppleScript Editor	A utility used to create scripts.
AirPort Utility	A utility used for setting up, and adjusting settings for, an AirPort base station or Time Capsule device.

Name	Description
Audio MIDI Setup	A utility that routes audio and MIDI files, such as for audio recording.
Bluetooth File Exchange	A utility used to create connections between Mac OS X and a device connected via Bluetooth.
Boot Camp Assistant	A utility used to facilitate the installation of a Windows operating system, on a second partition alongside Mac OS X.
ColorSync Utility	A utility that creates ColorSync International Color Consortium (ICC) profiles. These are used to synchronize color input and output between different devices attached to Mac OS X (typically a printer with your display).
Console	A utility that displays a window to the Unix log for Mac OS X. This window provides a log of information based upon system activity. It's primarily useful for programmers and system administrators looking to troubleshoot Mac OS X activity. The reason it is a Unix log is because a Unix-based operating system is behind the Mac OS X GUI.
Digital Color Meter	A utility that presents color information for the pixel under the pointer.
Directory	A utility that provides access to directory services (supplies a separate Open Directory server, such as those running Apple's Mac OS X Server), such as to look up shared address books or verify access permissions to file servers.
Disk Utility	A utility used for formatting, verifying, and repairing disk volumes. Also used to burn optical disks and create disk images.
Exposé	A utility that temporarily rearranges all the windows displayed in the Finder. Used to quickly move between applications, and quickly access the desktop.
Grab	A utility used to take pictures of the screen (either the whole screen or individual windows) and save them as image files.
Grapher	A utility used to create 2-D and 3-D graphs from equations.
Java Preferences	A utility that enables users to check and switch between versions of Java installed and used by Mac OS X.
Keychain Access	A utility used to store and manage passwords, certificates, keys, and secure notes; and throughout Mac OS X to access Web sites, wireless networks, volumes, and so on.
Migration Assistant	A utility used to transfer files, applications, and settings from one Mac to another.
Network Utility	A wide collection of tools used in relation to networking and the Internet.
Podcast Capture	A utility used to create audio, or video, podcasts and distribute them by using Mac OS X Server's Podcast Producer.
RAID Utility	A utility that enables configuration and management of disk arrays from multiple disks, using Apple's RAID card.
Spaces	A utility for navigating up to 16 virtual desktops.
System Profiler	A utility that lists the hardware inside your Mac system, and reports on how it is configured. It also reports on what software is installed. This is a useful tool for getting to know your system, as well as tracking down problems.
Terminal	A command line interface (CLI) used to control the Unix underpinnings of Mac OS X.
VoiceOver Utility	A text-to-speech utility used by Mac OS X to speak various interface elements. Useful for users with limited visual ability.

Installing applications

As you've seen, Mac OS X comes with a huge array of preinstalled applications. However, it is almost certain that at some point you will want to install a custom application. Installing additional applications is a great way to get the most out of your computer, and applications can achieve a myriad of tasks, and create or design virtually anything.

Installing these other applications is fairly easy, although there are a few different methods available. Typically, most applications are delivered on a volume. Often this volume is a CD or DVD, but increasingly it is a digital file known as a *disk image* (its filename extension is .dmg, so some people call them *DMG files*). You can download these disk image files via the Internet, and double-clicking them opens a volume on the desktop. In practice, this disk image is indistinguishable from an optical disc, such as a CD or DVD.

Typically, inside the root folder of the CD or DVD, or inside the disk image, you will find a text file called Read Me or Installation Instructions. No matter how many times you've installed a program to your Mac, it's always worth taking a look at any installation instructions before installing one.

Inside the root folder of the CD, DVD, or disk image, you will also find the installation files. Typically, there are two principal methods of installing new programs on your Mac. The first method, which is by far the most common, is the drag-install method, whereby you drag the application from the installation volume to your Applications folder; the second is via a dedicated installer that places the appropriate files in the correct locations on your startup disk.

You do not get to choose which method you use; each application has its own installation method as determined by the manufacturer. Typically, the window that the installer file opens in displays the installation method (see Figures 7.1 and 7.2). If you have any confusion as to which installation method is being used, read any supporting material or the manual. Don't worry, if you accidentally double-click and open a drag-installation program, it usually opens and runs directly from the CD; in this case, simply quit the program and perform a drag-install.

Installing a program via the drag method

The drag method is commonly used when installing an application from a downloaded disk image, although it's increasingly being used to install programs from removable media (CD, DVD, and so on). If a drag installation is required, it is usually indicated via a message in the window. Typically, it says something along the lines of "drag this file to your hard disk to install" (see Figure 7.1).

Often, the installation file includes a shortcut alias to the Applications folder and an indication (either an arrow or another message) explaining that dragging the file to this shortcut will install the program. You can identify the shortcut by the small arrow in the bottom right of the folder. If such a shortcut folder exists, the quickest way to install the application is to click and drag the application icon over the shortcut alias, and then let go of the mouse button. This copies the file directly from the disk image to the Applications folder on your hard disk.

The alternative is to drag the application icon from the installation volume to the Applications folder in the Finder. Although you can drag the application to any part of the Finder, the Applications folder makes the most sense.

Double-clicking the file opens it. If you downloaded the application from the Internet, a warning appears (see Figure 7.2). Click Open to run the program. You only see this warning the first time you install the application. This warning is a security measure designed to confirm that you downloaded the program and are comfortable that the application's origin is one you can trust. (See Chapter 23 for more information on Mac OS X security.)

Drag-installed applications typically do not require your Mac to restart before they run. You may, however, be prompted to type in a serial number or be prodded to enter your registration details before the program runs. Increasingly, programs use the Internet to activate online, asking an online server to confirm that they are legitimate, licensed copies.

FIGURE 7.1

Drag-installations are often clearly labeled inside the window. Drag the application to the Applications folder to install it.

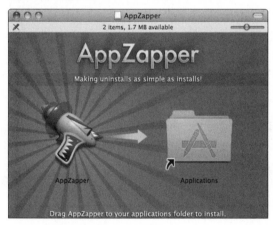

FIGURE 7.2

If an application has been downloaded from the Internet, you will see this message upon running it for the first time.

Tip

If a disk image has an application, but no shortcut to the Applications folder, you'll need to locate the Applications folder in the Finder. A quick way to do this is by using the shortcut in the Finder window's Sidebar, but for some reason disk image volumes open without the toolbar or Sidebar showing. If you click the Show Toolbar button in the top right of the window, the toolbar and Sidebar both appear. Now you can just drag the file to the Applications shortcut in the Sidebar.

Installing from a dedicated installer program

The second way to install programs onto your Mac is more traditional: using an installer application. Typically, this install application file is called Install or Setup, and it appears when you open the installation volume (see Figure 7.3). Double-clicking the file runs an installation program that will prompt you for various bits of information, and provide some options, before copying the necessary files to the appropriate part of the Finder. Typically, you are required to agree to a software-usage license agreement and enter any accompanying serial numbers before the installation can take place.

Although it's easy to dismiss installer programs as the older, more traditional means of installation, they do often serve a useful purpose. Typically, they are used to install a suite of software tools, comprised of multiple programs (such as Adobe Creative Suite and Microsoft Office). The installer often provides the means to fine-tune the installation and install only the programs you require, thus not filling up your hard disk with unused programs.

FIGURE 7.3

A typical volume containing an installer program; double-clicking the file runs the installation process.

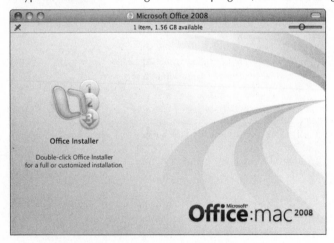

Removing applications

Sooner or later you may decide that you no longer want an application on your Mac. It may have only been a trial application that you have decided not to purchase, or you could have realized that you no longer use the program and want to reclaim the space it takes up on the hard disk.

Removing applications from Mac OS X couldn't be easier. Simply locate the program in the Applications folder and drag it straight to the Trash in the Dock. After emptying the Trash (choose ⬦ Empty Trash), the application is gone for good. As with trashing any item you don't want, be sure that you no longer want to use it before emptying the Trash.

Most applications place other small files in various places on the Mac. Typically, they place files in the Library folder. Subfolders such as Application Support and Preferences are good places to look for support files to delete after you've removed the main application files. These support files are typically small, and only used by the application, so leaving them on your Mac isn't typically considered a bad thing (at least not by Apple). You can hunt down these files and move them to the Trash, although you should be careful not to empty the Trash until you're sure that all your other programs run correctly.

Tip

There's a good reason for leaving the support files for a deleted application in the Library folder: If you ever decide to reinstall the program, all your preferences will be retained.

Note

Some programs, such as Microsoft Office, also come with uninstaller programs that remove all the files associated with an application. If a program has a dedicated uninstaller, run that instead of dragging the files directly to the Trash. If you are uninstalling your software to reinstall it on another Mac (or install a clean copy of Mac OS X) and that software uses activation to discourage use of pirated copies (such as Adobe Creative Suite and QuarkXPress), be sure to deactivate the software before uninstalling it; otherwise you may lose the ability to have the software work when you reinstall it.

Tip

If you install a lot of programs, and like to keep a clean system, you should invest in a program that specializes in removing the associated clutter created by program installation. Programs like AppZapper (www.appzapper. com) track the files installed by applications, and remove them when you delete a program.

Opening Applications and Documents

When you want to work with an application, you start, or open, the program. This process is also known as *launching* an application. When you open an application, you can view or edit its contents, or you can create new content from scratch.

Often the content you create in an application can be saved as a document. For example, you can open an application like TextEdit and use it to write a letter in the blank window; you can then save that letter as a document. You can then close the application, shut down the Mac, and come back another day and reopen the document to continue working on it.

There are numerous ways to open applications and documents, and often the two occur simultaneously (opening a document often opens the corresponding application). In this section, we explain the different ways of opening applications and documents.

Launching an application

There are many different methods for launching an application:

- **Applications folder.** Locate the program's icon in the Applications folder. Double-click it to launch the application. Alternatively, Control+click or right-click the icon and choose Open from the contextual menu, or you can select the icon and choose File ⇨ Open or press ⌘+O.

- **Dock.** Many applications have a shortcut to them placed in the Dock (you can add application shortcuts to the Dock, as Chapter 2 explains). Click the Dock icon to launch the application, or Control+click or right-click it and choose Open from the contextual menu.

- **Apple menu.** Choose ⌘ ⇨ Recent Items and choose an item from the Applications section of the menu.

- **Spotlight.** Type the name of the application in the Spotlight search (see Chapter 3), and choose the corresponding application from the list of results.

When an application launches, a bouncing icon usually appears in the Dock, indicating that the application is launching. After it has launched, the icon stops bouncing. (If the application's icon was already in the Dock, that icon usually begins to bounce when you launch the application.) The application icon has a glowing blue-and-white sphere underneath, to signify that it is an open application and not a shortcut. (You can turn off the bouncing-icon effect for program launch, as Chapter 2 explains.)

Opening items from the Finder

In Chapter 2, we cover how to open files and folders; you use the same methods to open a document and its corresponding application. The methods are as follows:

- Locate a document in the Finder and double-click it to open the document.

- Select the document and choose File ⇨ Open or press ⌘+O.

- Select the document and choose File ⇨ Open With and select an appropriate application. Use this method to open the document in an application other than the default (such as opening a Word file in TextEdit rather than in Microsoft Word).

- Control+click or right-click a file and choose Open from the contextual menu.

- Control+click or right-click a file and choose Open With from the contextual menu, then choose a compatible application from the submenu.

- Drag a document onto a compatible application icon in the Dock.

- Drag a document onto a compatible application icon in the Applications folder.

- Click a document icon in the Dock, or one residing inside a Stacks folder in the Dock (see Chapter 2).

- Choose ⌘ ⇨ Recent Items and choose an item from the Recent Documents section.

If the default application associated with that document isn't already open, it launches and opens with the document ready to be worked on. If the application is already open, the application comes to the foreground and the document opens within it.

If there is no corresponding application for a file (because the file type is unknown to Mac OS X), you see an error message, as shown in Figure 7.4. (We look at setting default applications for file types later in this chapter.)

Opening multiple file types is easy, even if they are different file types. Simply select the documents and double-click, or use one of the Open commands. If the documents are handled by different applications, multiple applications launch and open the documents.

FIGURE 7.4

If you try to open a document that does not have an associated application, you receive this error message.

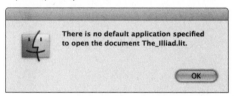

There is no default application specified
to open the document The_Illiad.lit.

OK

Using the Recent Items Menu Option

You can access documents and applications by using the Finder feature, Recent Items. Choosing ➪ Recent Items displays a submenu with three sections: Applications, Documents, and Servers. The Recent Items submenu enables you to quickly reopen an application or document you recently used, as well as access again a server that you recently accessed.

Suppose, for example, that you recently opened iTunes and quit the program. Rather than navigating to the Applications folder and clicking the iTunes icon to launch iTunes, you can choose ➪ Recent Items ➪ iTunes. (The figure shows the Recent Items menu).

Although it's useful for applications, the Recent Items menu is even more important for recently accessed documents. This is because your documents are less likely to be stored in a single location; instead, they are distributed throughout your disks and folders. (Also, people tend to add their favorite applications to the Dock instead of using the Recent Items submenu.)

The Recent Items submenu in Mac OS X keeps track of the 10 most recent items by default. But you can set the number of items displayed to any amount between 5 and 50 items. Use the Appearance system preferences to set the number of items that appear in the Recent Items submenu, as explained in Chapter 21.

continued

continued

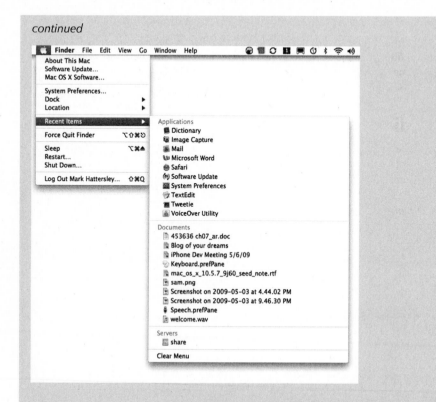

The Clear Menu option appears at the bottom of the Recent Items submenu. Choosing it removes all the items from the Recent Items submenu, leaving it a blank slate. This doesn't affect the actual items on your disks; it merely removes them from the Recent Items submenu.

Opening documents within an application

As you work with documents, you may find yourself inside an application looking to open a previously created document. Some standard methods for opening a document from within an application include:

- **Open dialog box.** Choose File ⇨ Open, or press ⌘+O, and use the Open dialog box to navigate to the desired file. Highlight the document and click Open.

- **Open Recent menu.** Choose File ⇨ Open Recent and choose a document recently used by the application. (Note that not all applications have this menu option.)

Some applications may also offer further options for opening documents. Adobe applications, for example, have a menu option called Browse (choose File ⇨ Browse) that opens a dedicated application called Bridge to browse and open documents used by various Adobe applications.

Note

When you open documents from within an application, you aren't restricted to documents created by that application. You can open any file type supported by that application, no matter what application was used to create it. The document's filename extension, explained in Chapter 2, tells Mac OS X — and thus the application — what the document's file type is.

The Open dialog box

When you choose File ⇨ Open in a Mac OS X application, you get the Open dialog box shown in Figure 7.5. (Most applications also let you press ⌘+O to open the Open dialog box.) The Open dialog box has the same navigation controls as a Finder window and by default shows the Columns view mode. You can switch the view among Columns, Icon, View, and List modes by using the iconic buttons in the top left of the dialog box.

FIGURE 7.5

The Open dialog box has the same navigation options as a Finder window. You use it within applications to locate and open documents.

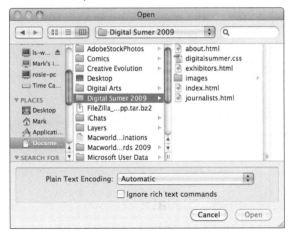

You navigate in the Open dialog box just as you do in a Finder window through the folder structure of your hard disks and other volumes. In the default Columns view, each column shows the contents of a folder, and clicking a folder opens up the contents of that folder in the column to the right. You scroll left to see folders higher up the folder hierarchy, and you scroll right to move to the currently selected folder. In icon view, double-clicking folders takes you inside that folder, and you use the navigation buttons or popup menu to navigate back up the folder structure. In list view, you use the disclosure triangles to reveal the contents of folders.

To the left of the Open dialog box is the Sidebar, which also includes the same items as a Finder window. You use it to access different volumes and common areas on the Mac (such as the desktop and Documents folder). You can also quickly navigate to any volume or folder displayed in the Finder by dragging it into the Open dialog box.

Initially, the Open dialog box displays two columns. You can resize the columns by dragging the handle at the bottom of each column divider. You can also click and drag the handle on the bottom right of the Open dialog box to resize it. Although the Open dialog box lacks Close and Minimize iconic buttons, it has a Zoom iconic button you can click to maximize the size of the Open dialog box. You can move the dialog box around by clicking and dragging the title bar.

As you move around the Open dialog box, you will notice that some files are in black text, while others are grayed out. The black text indicates that the application can be opened; files with grayed-out text cannot be opened by the current application.

Tip

You can also use Spotlight within the Open dialog box. Type a search term in the text field at the top right of the dialog box to use Spotlight technology to search Mac OS X for that term. (Chapter 3 covers Spotlight in detail.)

Two buttons appear at the bottom of the Open dialog box:

- **Open.** Click this button and the application opens any selected files in the Open dialog box.
- **Cancel.** Click this button to close the Open dialog box without opening any file.

Many applications also offer a selection of customized options at the bottom of the Open dialog box. Microsoft Word, for example, has two popup menus: The Enable popup menu lets you narrow down the file choices based on file type, and the Open popup menu provides three options — Original, Copy, and Read-Only — that enable you to open the file in any of these modes. Figure 7.6 shows Word's Open dialog box.

Setting a new default application

Documents types are linked to specific applications depending upon the file type of the document. For example, text files are likely to open with TextEdit, movie files with QuickTime, and PDF files with Preview. As you install new applications, they may assume control of these document types. Microsoft Word may decide to take control of some text file types, and Adobe Reader will take control of PDF documents, and so on.

Mac OS X enables you to determine which application will open a document when you double-click it (or choose an Open command). You can change this setting for the individual document, or for all documents that share a common file extension (such as all PDF documents).

FIGURE 7.6

The Open dialog box often includes options in addition to the standard Open and Cancel buttons. In Microsoft Word, these options enable you to narrow down file choices by file type (the Enable popup menu) and to control how the selected files are opened (using the Open popup menu's Original, Copy, and Read-Only options).

To change the default application used to open a document type, select a document in the Finder and choose File ⇨ Get Info, press ⌘+I, or Control+click or right-click it and choose Get Info from the contextual menu. This opens the Info window (see Figure 7.7), covered in Chapter 2. Now locate the Open With area of the Info window to see a popup menu containing the name of the application currently associated with that file. The popup menu contains a list of all applications that can be used to open that particular kind of file. Choose an application option from the list and that document will be associated with that application, and opening the document will open that applicationIf the application you desire is not included in the popup menu, choose the Other option at the bottom of the list and the Other settings sheet opens (see Figure 7.8). The Other settings sheet is similar to the Open dialog box; however, it lists items in the Applications folder. (You can navigate to applications stored elsewhere in the Finder.) Highlight the application that you want to associate with the document and click Add.

The Other settings sheet includes the Enable popup menu. By default, the option in this menu is Recommended Applications, and with this option chosen, you can only select compatible applications. If you choose All Applications from this menu, you will be able to associate any application.

FIGURE 7.7

You can use the Info window to determine which application opens by default when you double-click a document.

Below the popup menu in the Open With area is a Change All button. If you have selected a different application to associate with the document, clicking the Change All button changes the settings for all similar documents. So if you select a text file (these are files with a .txt filename extension), choose Microsoft Word from the Open With popup menu, and click Change All, all text documents found in Mac OS X Finder will now open with Microsoft Word instead of the default application (in this case, TextEdit).

After you select a new application to associate with a document type, the icon for that document changes. And if you click Change All, the icons for all the similar documents will change; they will now reflect the associated parent application. If you accidentally select the wrong application, it is easy to rectify your mistake: Select the file, open the Info window, and choose the original application in the Opens With popup menu. The first item in the menu will be the original application that was associated with the document, followed by the word "(default)." Selecting this always takes you back to where you began.

FIGURE 7.8

You can use the Other settings sheet to associate any application with a document.

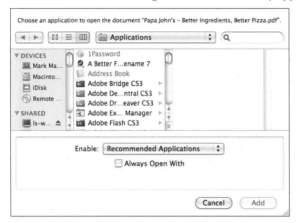

Using Quick Look to view documents

In Mac OS X 10.5 Leopard, Apple introduced a new technology called Quick Look. Amazingly, it enables you to view the contents of a document without launching any application at all. To use Quick Look, Control+click or right-click any item in the Finder and choose Quick Look from the contextual menu. A gray translucent window appears in the middle of the screen displaying the contents of the file.

If you select another document file while Quick Look is open, the view inside the Quick Look window changes to display the contents of that document. Press the spacebar to close the Quick Look window, or click the Close iconic button (the circular X icon) in the top left of the Quick Look window. Figure 7.9 shows the Quick Look window displaying an image document.

Although Quick Look doesn't launch the supporting application for the selected document, it does need a supporting application installed on your Mac. Fortunately, most documents can be viewed by using the Preview and QuickTime Player applications that come with Mac OS X. Sometimes installing an application enables Quick Look to display the contents of that file, for those document formats not supported by Preview or QuickTime Player. But not always: Adobe InDesign and Illustrator documents, for example, cannot be displayed in Quick Look, even if you have installed InDesign and Illustrator.

The number of file types covered by Quick Look is impressive. It can display documents, movies, audio files, saved Web pages, PDF files, and so on. If a document takes more room than fits in the Quick Look window, a scroll bar appears to the side enabling you to scroll through the contents. Quick Look displays the contents of a file the same way that an application would. If you use Quick Look on a music track, Quick Look displays any associated cover art, the song title, artist, album, length of track; and it plays the track. It even has a scrubber enabling you to move through the audio. All of this is the same information that would be used in iTunes.

FIGURE 7.9

Quick Look browses through the contents of a document without opening an application.

Tip

The quickest way to access Quick Look is to select an item in the Finder and press the spacebar. This brings up a Quick Look window and is much faster than using any menu options.

Managing Multiple Open Applications

As you learned in Chapter 1, Mac OS X has *preemptive multitasking*. Multitasking means that the operating system can run more than one process at a time, which although handy is hardly a novel feature in this day and age. The preemptive part was introduced in Mac OS X, and it means that Mac OS X dynamically parcels out chunks of time to the various open applications, so no application can hog up all the resources.

Multitasking is such a central feature of a modern operating system that it can be distressing to imagine a time before such a feature existed. Imagine if one program stopped running when another one began; for example, if you were playing music in iTunes, it would stop when you began working in Word, and Mail would only be able to check for new e-mail messages if you had the program open and active at the time.

But the ability to run multiple programs at once can be disorientating. A stray mouse click can take you from one program to another, bringing its windows to the front and putting the application you were working on to the back. To a complete newcomer, it may appear as if a program has disappeared completely, leaving the user confused as to whether the system has crashed or not. Of course, most computer users these days are used to the concept of using multiple programs at once, and Mac OS X makes the process as straightforward as possible. Even so, you must get used to having multiple layers of programs and documents open at once; these can lay on top of each other on the desktop, like different paper documents laying on top of each other on your desk.

Fortunately, Mac OS X provides many methods to switch among documents and applications. And Mac OS X features such as Exposé and Spaces (covered in Chapters 8 and 21) offer you a quick means to organize and access documents and applications on your Mac. Plus you can quickly hide open documents and bring them back in an instant.

As we mention in Chapter 2, a key difference between Mac OS X and Microsoft Windows is that only one application in Mac OS X can control the menu bar at any one time. The application currently in control is known as the *active application*, and you can tell which one it is by looking at the menu bar — the menu option next to the menu is the name of the active application. If you click on the desktop, this active application is the Finder; when you switch to any other application, the name Finder in the menu bar changes to the name of that application.

Switching among applications

As we mention earlier, all open applications display an icon in the Dock. When you have an application open, you can switch to that application by clicking on its icon in the Dock, making it the active application. This is the most straightforward and commonly used method of switching among open applications.

Using the Dock isn't the only method of moving among applications. You can also move from one application to another by clicking in any visible window belonging to that other application. You can also move from one application to another by clicking its minimized window in the Dock — assuming the application has been minimized, as Chapter 2 explains. Of course, opening up a new document switches to the application associated with that document (launching it, if necessary, as outlined earlier in the chapter).

Another way to switch among applications is to use the application switcher (see Figure 7.10). This appears over the desktop as a translucent gray window with icons for each running application. Here's how to use the application switcher:

1. **Press ⌘+Tab.** The application switcher window opens, with the current application's icon at the far left and the next application in the list selected.

2. **Continue holding ⌘.** Now, with each additional press of Tab, the selection moves to the right. You can also use the → and ← keys or the mouse to move through the applications instead of pressing Tab (but keep holding ⌘).

3. **Release ⌘.** When the application you want to switch to is selected, release the ⌘ key. The selected icon's application becomes the active application.

If you decide not to switch to a different application, press Esc and then release ⌘.

Owners of MacBooks with Multi-Touch trackpads can use a four-finger gesture on the trackpad to access the application switcher. Here's how to use the trackpad to switch applications:

1. **Place four fingers on the trackpad.** Now move all four fingers to the left or right without taking your hand off the trackpad. This brings up the application switcher.

2. **Select an application.** You can select an application by moving to it, using the trackpad. Click one of the icons to make its application the active one. Alternatively, you can use the Tab, ←, and → keys to select an application. Press the Return key when you have decided which application to make active.

If you decide not to switch to a different application, press Esc or simply click anywhere on the screen other than on an icon in the application switcher. Or repeat the four-finger swipe used in the first step.

FIGURE 7.10

The application switcher appears over the screen and enables you to switch from one application to another.

When you switch from one application to another by using the application icon in the Dock or by using the application switcher, all the windows associated with that application come forward as a group, with one window active (meaning you can work in it). The exception is for document windows that are minimized in the Dock; they remain in the Dock. But if all document windows for an application are minimized in the Dock, one of the windows opens as the application comes forward.)

If you switch to an application by clicking one of its windows in the desktop or in the Dock, that window becomes active, along with the application. When you have multiple applications open, the windows from different applications may be stacked on top of each other on the desktop. You can bring all windows from an application to the front by clicking the application in the Dock.

Note

Some applications also feature a Bring All to Front menu command: Choose Window ⇨ Bring All to Front. This brings all the windows associated with that application to the front, placing them all above windows from other applications.

Using Hide to reduce window clutter

Modern computers can run many applications simultaneously, without suffering any noticeable reduction in performance. This is great, of course, but it does mean that a lot of application windows start to clutter up your screen.

One way of getting rid of the clutter is to use the Minimize iconic button (as covered in Chapter 2). This places a small icon of the document window in the Dock. However, there is another option available called Hide. The Hide option distinguishes itself from the Minimize command by *not* placing an icon in the Dock. When you hide an application, all its open windows vanish from the desktop and no items are placed in the Dock. This reduces screen clutter, and also prevents the Dock from being cluttered if you have a lot of windows open in a particular application. You can hide all the windows of an application by using any of these methods:

- Press ⌘+H.
- Choose Hide *applicationname* (such as Hide Word) from the application menu.
- Control+click or right-click the icon in the Dock and choose Hide from the contextual menu.
- Option+click anywhere on the desktop.

Related to Hide is another Mac OS X command called Hide Others. This does the exact opposite of the Hide command: It keeps the currently active application on-screen but hides all the windows belonging to other applications. You can hide windows belonging to all other applications by using any of the following methods:

- Press Option+⌘+H (note: This command works on all applications other than the Finder).

- Choose Hide Others from the application menu.

- Control+click or right-click the application's icon on the Dock and hold down the Option button; now choose Hide Others from the contextual menu.

- Option+⌘+click the application's icon on the Dock. (If that application is not already active, it becomes the active application.) This technique can be a great way of switching applications that have lots of windows open at the same time.

To restore any applications that have hidden windows, click their icons in the Dock. You can always tell which applications are open because they have the small glowing white circle underneath the application icon.

Tip
You can hide windows belonging to all applications other than the Finder, by Option+⌘+clicking the desktop. And you can show all applications by choosing Show All from the active application's application menu.

Knowing when an application wants your attention

As we've mentioned, one of the great advantages of the multitasking operating system is that applications can run in the background while you work in another application. This is great for long tasks (such as video rendering) because it means you can leave one application running in the background while you work on something else.

However, occasionally an application running in the background needs your attention. It might be to notify you that it has finished its task, or there may be a dialog box that needs your attention; either way you're best to switch to the application, find out what it wants, and deal with it. It may be that a program is quitting, and Mac OS X is asking you if you want to save a document first, or iCal might be trying to inform you about an important event that you set an alert to.

Mac OS X has a particular way of attracting your attention (one that has as many fans as detractors). When an application wants your attention, it bounces up and down in the Dock, like an excitable kid in class. It bounces, then sits in the Dock for a moment, then bounces again. Even if the Dock is minimized, the icon bounces fairly high so it's hard to miss. Ignoring this bouncing Dock icon requires a Herculean effort, and you're better off just dealing with the precocious application, as there's usually a good reason to interrupt you. Figure 7.11 shows an icon bouncing in the Dock.

FIGURE 7.11

If you see an application icon bouncing up and down in the Dock (and let's face it, you can't miss it), this is your sign that a Mac OS X application needs your attention.

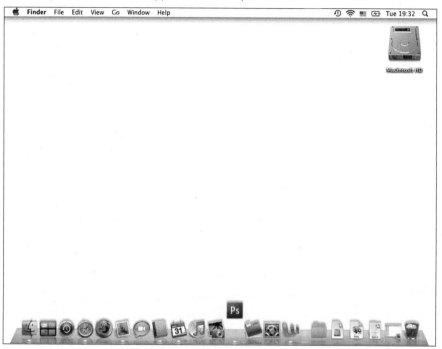

Creating Documents

So far we have only looked at working with documents that already exist, but you won't always be working with files already on your Mac. Sooner or later, you'll need to create something from scratch, and when this time comes, you'll need to create a new document.

Many applications save you the trouble by creating a new document whenever you open the program; Microsoft Word and TextEdit are examples of such programs. However, some applications do not automatically open a new document; Adobe Photoshop is one such example. Even if an application opens a new document by default when you launch the program, there are times when you are running the program and want to create a new document. Some applications may have their own unique way of doing things, but most Mac OS X applications enable you to create a new document by using one of the following methods:

- Choose File ➪ New.
- Press ⌘+N.
- Control+click or right-click the application icon in the Dock and choose New Document from the contextual menu.

Creating a copy of a document

You can also create a new document by copying an existing file in the Finder. This method is especially useful if the document has content that you want to use, such as a letterhead or some stock text. The easiest way to make a copy of a document is to select it in the Finder and choose File ➪ Duplicate or press ⌘+D. Alternatively, you can press and hold Option and drag a document from one the desktop or a Finder window to another location (release Option when your mouse is in the new location). Chapter 2 has more information on duplicating documents.

In Mac OS X, you can also use the Copy and Paste commands to duplicate files. Select an item in the Finder and choose Edit ➪ Copy or press ⌘+C, then navigate to another part of the Finder and choose Edit ➪ Paste Item or press ⌘+V. Note that you cannot use the Cut command rather than Copy to move the document to a new location; you can only put a duplicate the item in the new location. The Cut, Copy, and Paste commands are outlined in further depth later in the chapter.

Creating documents with stationery pads (templates)

If you have a document that often serves as a base for creating other documents, you can create a *stationery pad*. Most applications call these *templates*, but Apple still refers to these in its own applications as stationery pads. When you open a stationery pad, the preformatted content and settings appear. For example, you could have a text document with a company logo, address, phone number, e-mail, and basic text, all of which you preformatted. It's like tearing a sheet off an endless pad of preprinted stationery, which is where the name comes from.

You create stationery pads by using the Info window (see Figure 7.12). Follow these steps to turn an ordinary document into a stationery pad.

1. **Select the file you want to use as a stationery pad in the Finder.**
2. **Choose File ➪ Get Info, press ⌘+I, or Control+click or right-click it and choose Get Info from the contextual menu.** This opens the Info window, as described earlier in the chapter.
3. **Select the Stationery Pad option so that it is checked.** This turns the document into a stationery pad.

Using stationery pads is almost the same as using a regular document. You open the document, as outlined earlier in the chapter. Doing so usually has the application create a duplicate of the file in the same location in the Finder (with the same filename plus "copy" amended to the end). If the application does not understand stationery pads, it simply opens the document as if it were a regular file. In some cases, the stationery pad document opens in a document window and is named Untitled, and when you save the file you are prompted to give it a name; this prevents the original stationery pad from being overwritten.

Some applications enable you to save documents as stationery pads, or templates. We look at saving documents later in the chapter.

You use the Finder's Info window to turn a regular document into a stationery pad.

259

If you create a stationery pad, then decide at a later point that you want to go back and make changes, you need to revisit the Info window for the document and deselect the Stationery Pad check box. This returns the stationery pad to a regular document. You can now open it, edit it, and save it as you would a normal document. When you have finished making your changes, use the Info window to convert it back to a stationery pad.

Saving Documents

After creating a new document, or while editing a document, you need to save your progress. Saving is an essential part of working with documents, committing the document you are working on — in its current state — to the disk. If you didn't save your progress while working on a document, you would need to create the document from scratch every time you worked on it. When you are working on documents for a length of time, we strongly advise you to save at periodical intervals to protect your work in case of any problems.

Make sure that the document you are working on is in the currently active window, and save your progress by choosing File ➪ Save or pressing ⌘+S. The Save command automatically updates the file on the disk with the contents of the new one.

If you are working on a new document that has not already been saved, choosing the Save command instead performs a Save As command. This opens a dialog box (see Figure 7.13) that enables you to name and select a location for the new document. The document and its contents are then stored in a file on that location.

FIGURE 7.13

The simple version of the Save As dialog box enables you to enter a name and location for a new document to be saved on your computer.

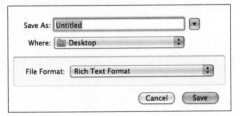

You can use the Save As command at a later date to save the current document as a new file. Simply choose File ➪ Save As or, in many applications, press Shift+⌘+S. This enables you to save the changes you have made to a document without replacing the original file you were working on, such as to have different versions of the document.

Note

Note that the Save As dialog box's option and layout can vary from application to application, just as the Open dialog box can. In some applications, the Save As dialog box is actually a settings sheet attached to the window of the document you're currently working on; in others it is a dialog box that you can move by dragging the title bar.

The Save As dialog box comes in two flavors: simple and expanded. The simple version (shown in Figure 7.14) enables you to give a name to your document and choose from a preset list of destinations in the Where popup menu. You may also get some options regarding the file type to save to. In TextEdit, for example, you can choose between Rich Text Format, Rich Text Format with Attachments, Web Page, Web Archive, OpenDocumentText, Word 2007 Format, Word 2003 Format, and Word 97 Format.

This simple version of the Save As dialog box is fine for most purposes, although there may come a point where you want to select a more detailed location for your file. When this happens, you need to use the expanded Save As dialog box. To access the expanded Save As dialog box, click the down-pointing arrow iconic button to the right of the Save As text field (see Figure 7.14). Note that the button's icon changes to an up-pointing arrow; click it again to access the simple Save As dialog box.

FIGURE 7.14

The expanded Save As dialog box offers a wider range of options for saving files.

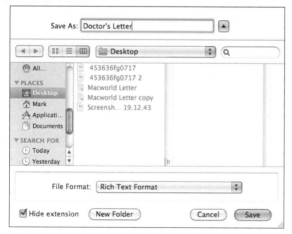

The expanded Save As dialog box has a location browser similar to that in the Finder window for navigating the Mac's folder structure. This enables you to select a specific disk and to save your document in it. As with the Open dialog box, the Save As dialog box displays the folder hierarchy in Columns view mode by default; you choose between Icon, List, and Columns view modes by using the iconic buttons in the top left of the window.

The unnamed popup menu offers the list of standard documents, plus a list of recent places to choose from. The Sidebar to the left of the Save As dialog box enables you to navigate to the devices, volumes, places, and smart folders found in a Finder window.

There is also a Spotlight search function in the Save As dialog box. Although it makes little sense to search for items while saving a document, you can use the Spotlight search box to search for folders you know the name of, but not their exact locations. Enter a term into the Spotlight search box and folders matching the search term appear in the Save As dialog box. Double-click a desired folder to make it the save location.

Another option you have in the expanded Save As dialog box is the ability to create a new folder while saving a document. Click New Folder and a dialog box appears asking for a name for the folder. Enter the desired name and click Create. The new folder appears as the save location in the Save As dialog box. Figure 7.15 shows a Save As dialog box in the expanded view, being used to create a new folder.

Another way of choosing a location for the file is to drag a folder from the Finder to the Save As dialog box. This changes the save location to that area.

FIGURE 7.15

You can create new folders on your Mac while saving a document.

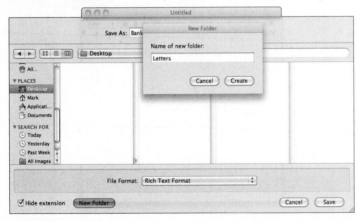

Tip

You can resize the Save As dialog box. If you're having difficulty navigating the Save As dialog box, then drag the resize handle at the bottom right of the dialog box.

Either before or after choosing the file's location, you need to give it a name. Do so in the Save As text field at the top of the dialog box.

Tip

You can use the Cut, Copy, and Paste commands while using the Save As dialog box. This method enables you to copy (or cut) a part of the document for use as the new filename before using the Save As option; then paste it into the Save As text field at the top of the dialog box. You can use the Edit menu, or any of the keyboard shortcuts outlined earlier, to cut and paste text into the dialog box.

When you have selected a name and location for the document, click Save.

Saving a Stationery Pad

In some applications, you can use the Save As dialog box to specify that the document is a stationery pad, or template. Depending on the application, the capability to save a document as a template can vary. Some applications offer this choice via radio buttons or a check box in the Save as dialog box; others, such as Microsoft Word, offer it via a popup menu. In the case of Microsoft Word, the menu option is Word Template (.dotx). The figure shows the Microsoft Word template option.

Closing Documents

When you've saved a document and no longer want to work on it, you can close the document but leave the application running. The easiest way is to click the Close iconic button (the red X icon) in the upper left of the document window. You can also choose File ➪ Close or press ⌘+W. Some applications have a Close All command, accessed by choosing File ➪ Close All or pressing Option+⌘+W.

If you quit an application (as described later in this chapter), its document windows are closed as well.

If you close a document window whose document has unsaved content, an alert dialog box appears, giving you a chance to save the changes. This is covered in the section on quitting applications later in this chapter.

Moving Documents

After you have created and saved a document, you may well decide to move it from its original location. Moving documents in Mac OS X is straightforward: Simply locate the file in the Finder, and click and drag it to a new location. You can drag a document to any folder or volume displayed in the Finder; you can also drag it to the Sidebar of any Finder window, to the Dock, to any folder displayed in the Dock, to the desktop, or to the root level of your hard disk. Chapter 2 outlines moving files around in more detail.

Working with a Document's Content

When an application is active and a document window is on the screen, you can generally tinker around with its content.

Whether you are creating a new document or editing an existing one, you can add content to a document, move existing content around, and even move content from one document to another document.

Each application works with at least one content type, and many use their own content type. For example, Microsoft Word works with text, RTF, and Word document file types; Adobe Photoshop works with Photoshop, TIFF, JPEG, PNG, GIF, and many more file types; iMovie with MPEG-4 video and iMove project file types; and so on. For in-depth details on working with just about every major application that runs on Mac OS X, consult Wiley Publishing's excellent books on them.

Although applications work on a great range of documents and have many specific controls for them, there are standard techniques that work commonly across many applications, regardless of the type of data created and how it is managed by the application. A good example is the Cut, Copy, and Paste commands. They are a universal concept used to shuffle content around in a document. For example, in Word, you use them to move blocks of text around a document (or to another document) and in Adobe Photoshop, you use them to move around parts of images. Additionally, many programs enable you to drag content from one part of a document to another — or by holding down the Option key, copy content from one spot and duplicate it in another.

Using Cut, Copy, and Paste

One of the first things any computer user learns is how to perform cut, copy, and paste operations. This is a universal computer technique that works identically in many operating systems. Indeed, it's hard to imagine any part of the computer world that is more universally recognized. Essentially, you select a part of a document and either remove it (cut) or duplicate it (copy), and then insert it elsewhere (paste).

Select part of a document and Choose Edit ➪ Cut or press ⌘+X (if you want move the data) or Edit ➪ Copy or press ⌘+C (if you want to duplicate the data in another location). Either of these actions places the data on the Clipboard, which is a temporary storage area in the Mac OS's memory for data being moved or copied.

Now that you have the content in the Clipboard, you can place it somewhere else. Typically, items are pasted at the point where the cursor is, although the paste location can differ depending on the application. Select where you want the data to be placed and choose Edit ➪ Paste or press ⌘+V.

Pasting does not remove data from the Clipboard, so you can paste the same data multiple times in different locations. The data remains in the Clipboard until it is overwritten with new data (typically when you next use the Cut or Copy commands). This means that you only get to paste one set of data at a time, and when you cut, or copy another set of data, the original data is removed from the Clipboard. So if you want to go back and paste the first set of data again, you locate it and use Cut or Copy to place it in the Clipboard again.

Tip

Although Mac OS X only enables users to cut, or copy, one item at a time, plenty of applications extend the Clipboard and enable users to paste multiple different sets of data without having to repeatedly use the Cut or Copy commands. One popular choice is a free program called PTHPasteboard (http://pth.com/prod-ucts/pthpasteboard/). **Some applications, such as Microsoft Office, also allow multiple items to be stored in the Clipboard, but only for use within those applications.**

You can cut, copy, and paste within a single document, among multiple documents in use by a single application, or among the documents of different applications. These applications include the Finder, so you can cut, copy, and paste text to and from filenames, for example. Using the Cut, Copy, and Paste commands rapidly becomes second nature — especially if you use the keyboard shortcuts:

- Cut. ⌘+X
- Copy. ⌘+C
- Paste. ⌘+V

Unlike most keyboard shortcuts, these are not all named logically after letters they begin with (although Copy is based upon C). Instead they are in a line on the bottom row of the keyboard. (It can help to think of X as "X out," as a synonym for cut, and to think of V as an insertion wedge, such as is common in copy editing.) The V, X, and C shortcut keys used for the Cut, Copy, and Paste shortcuts are a universal standard found on most operating systems.

Using drag and drop to move data around

Mac OS X also provides another quick way to move around text, graphics, and other material, called *drag-and-drop editing*. This technique works only with applications designed to take advantage of it, but fortunately this includes most applications found in Mac OS X.

Using drag and drop in a document

To use drag and drop in a document, first open it and select the text, graphics, or other data you want to move. Next, position the pointer inside the selected area, and press and hold the mouse button down. Drag the mouse; you'll see a lightened image of whatever data you are dragging appear under the mouse, so you know the intended selection is being dragged. (Figure 7.16 shows some data being dragged around in the TextEdit application.) Typically, an insertion point appears in the document as you drag the mouse around, indicating the exact position that the data will be copied to. Release the mouse button to move the data from its original position to the new one.

As you can see, drag and drop is the functional equivalent of cut and paste. If you want to copy the data and leave the original rather than move it, press and hold down the Option key before, or while, dragging the data from one part of the document to another. This copies the data and leaves the original source material in place. (A small green + icon appears near the mouse pointer, so you know you're copying the data instead of moving it.)

FIGURE 7.16

With drag-and-drop editing, you can move data around a document.

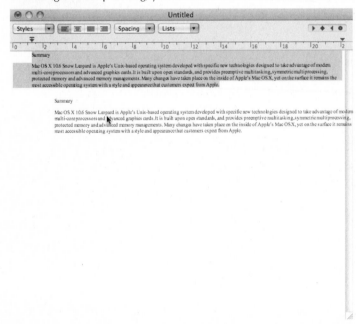

Tip

Drag and drop can be a surprisingly tricky maneuver to master at first. If you find yourself continuously select-ing new data instead of dragging data, you are probably clicking and moving too quickly. Try holding down the mouse button, without moving the mouse, for a moment before moving the mouse. This pause signifies to Mac OS X that you are performing a drag-and-drop operation.

Using drag and drop between two documents

You can also use drag and drop to move material from one document to another. To do this, first open both documents and make sure both are visible on the screen. Also make sure that the desti-nation that you want to drag material to is visible, because it is difficult to navigate to a document while performing a drag-and-drop procedure. Now select the text, graphic, or other source mate-rial and click on it with the mouse to start the drag-and-drop procedure. Drag the selected material from the first document to the desired insertion point in the second document.

As you drag, a lightened image of the selected material follows the pointer. When you drag the pointer into a new window, a small green + icon appears and an insertion point shows you where the item will be inserted when you release the mouse button (see Figure 7.17). Unlike the regular drag-and-drop pro-cedure within a document, the data isn't moved from one document to another, but copied. This is the same as if you had held down the Option key when moving material within a document. The only requirement is that the destination document be capable of handling the type of material you're dragging.

FIGURE 7.17

You can move text, images, and other data among documents by using the drag-and-drop method.

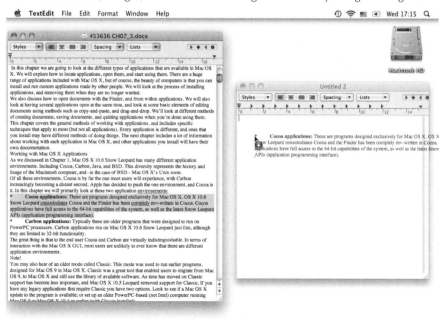

Whether you prefer drag-and-drop editing, or cut-and-paste commands, is largely a question of personal taste. Most people find themselves using whichever technique is at hand: If you're using the mouse, drag and drop lets you keep using the mouse, while if you're using the keyboard, cut and paste lets you keep using the keyboard.

Tip

Drag-and-drop editing does not wipe the content of the Clipboard, as copy and paste does. So it's a good method to use when you have a Clipboard containing important data that you want to leave in the Clipboard but still want to move something else around. You can use the drag-and-drop method for that something else, then continue pasting whatever is in the Clipboard.

Using drag and drop to create clippings

Another technique related to drag and drop is called *clip editing*. This is where you use the drag-and-drop technique outlined previously, except instead of dragging an item to another location within a document, you drag it directly to the desktop or another location within the Finder. This creates a clipping of the file with an icon similar to that of a regular document, except that it has the curl on the bottom-left corner rather than the usual top-right corner (see Figure 7.18). Clipping files can contain text, pictures, QuickTime movies, or sound, but a single clipping file can only contain one kind of data.

When you open a clipping file in the Finder, it appears in its own window (see Figure 7.19). This window offers a preview of the contents, but you cannot select content in a clipping window. To copy the contents of a clipping window into a document, you drag the clipping file itself from the Finder into a document. As with drag-and-drop copying from a document, an insertion point shows where the contents will be inserted. Releasing the mouse inserts the contents of a clipping document.

The great thing about clipping files is that they can be stored on Mac OS X and used again and again. For example, you could keep a clipping document of your address and drag it to a document every time you wanted to insert it.

FIGURE 7.18

A clipping file icon created from a selection of text taken from Text Edit

Open GL-Open GL
(Open Comput

FIGURE 7.19

You can view the contents of a clipping file in a window in the Finder, but you cannot select, copy, or adjust any of the content within this window.

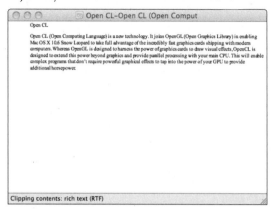

Sharing Documents with Other Users

Mac OS X is a multiuser operating system, so it is possible that the account you are working in is running alongside many other user accounts on the same Mac. While different users share the Mac OS X volumes and many of the system files, the elements of each user account (including the personal documents) are available only to the user who is currently logged in. The process of setting up and managing different accounts is covered in detail in Chapter 20.

While you are logged in to your account, you cannot access the files stored on another user's portion of Mac OS X, unless they've given you file-sharing access to their folders, as explained in Chapter 13. To get at the files on another user's account, you need to log out and then log back in as that user. Of course, this means that you won't be able to access the documents in your account (or copy any files from that user's account to your own).

However, you can share files with other users by means of the Drop Box. This standard folder exists for each user account and is used for other users to place (or *drop*) files into. (Only the Drop Box's owner can see what's in the folder, although any user can put files into it.) It is metaphorically like the drop boxes that sit on people's office desks.

Mac OS X delivers a warning message when you place an item into a Drop Box (see Figure 7.20). Note that dragging a file to a Drop Box doesn't move the file; it copies it to the new location and the original file remains in its current location.

Picking up a file that has been placed in the Drop Box is easy. Go to the Drop Box in the Public Folder in your Home folder. Any files other users have placed in your Drop Box are located here. You can then copy the files from the Drop Box to any location in your disks or other volumes.

Cross-Ref

Chapter 13 has detailed information regarding setting up file sharing in Mac OS X, enabling multiple users on different machines to access, and work on, the same documents.

FIGURE 7.20

When you move a file to another user's Drop Box, this warning message appears.

Quitting Applications

When you've finished working with an application, you can quit it, which stops Mac OS X from running it. This frees up some system resources, enabling Mac OS X to run other programs more efficiently. Mac OS X offers several methods for quitting an application. Some are for typical situations, whereas others are for when a program stops responding.

Quitting from within an application

Mac OS X provides a uniform way to quit applications: by choosing File ⇨ Quit or pressing ⌘+Q in the active application.

If you have any documents with unsaved data, Mac OS X displays an alert dialog box for each unsaved document (see Figure 7.21). This is the same dialog box that appears if you try to close a document before saving its content. You can click one of three buttons:

- **Don't Save.** This option quits the application without saving your document. Any changes that you have made to the document are discarded.
- **Cancel.** This option cancels the quit process, returning you to the document window.
- **Save.** This option saves the document, then quits the application.

FIGURE 7.21

When you quit an application, you are asked if you want to save any documents with unsaved data.

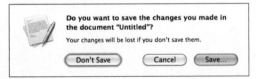

Quitting an application from the Dock

You can also quit an application via its Dock icon. Control+click or right-click the application icon in the Dock and choose Quit from the contextual menu. This method is useful for quitting applications that are running in the background, because you don't have to switch to it first to choose File ➪ Quit or press ⌘+Q.

If you quit an application while it is in the background, it may cause the icon in the Dock to bounce up and down. This is to alert you that it has an unsaved document that requires your attention. Switch to the application to deal with the unsaved document.

Tip
A quick way to quit multiple applications is to use the application switcher (outlined earlier in this chapter). Press ⌘+Tab to bring up the application switcher. As described earlier, select the desired application, but press Q instead of releasing the mouse button. This quits that application. You can now repeat this process for other applications, quitting them one at a time. Release the ⌘ key when you're finished.

Quitting by logging out, shutting down, or restarting

One method of quitting all open applications is to end your computer session. Logging out, shutting down, or restarting your Mac (see Chapter 2) causes all open applications to quit. A dialog box asks if you are sure that you want to quit all applications and log out, restart, or shut down (as the case may be). Any applications with unsaved data interrupt the logout, restart, or shutdown process and display alert dialog boxes where you can decide whether to save the unsaved documents. Mac OS X quits the applications when you have dealt with all the unsaved documents, then proceeds to log out, restart, or shut down. Figure 7.22 shows a dialog box asking if you want to quit all applications and log out; Mac OS X acts similarly for restarting or shutting down your Mac.

FIGURE 7.22

One method of quitting all open applications is to log out of your Mac OS X session.

Using the Force Quit command

Although it's increasingly rare, there may come an occasion when your application freezes or becomes unresponsive to any input commands. You may see the spinning colored ball whenever you try to use the application, and the Quit command is no longer accessible from the menu (or the application does not respond to any command to quit). In these situations, you need to use a Force Quit command, which will almost certainly quit the application and enable you to carry on with your computing session. You can force an application to quit in several ways.

Using the Force Quit dialog box

Choose ⇨ Force Quit or press Option+⌘+Esc to bring up the Force Quit dialog box (see Figure 7.23). It displays a list of all currently running applications. Choose the one that you want to quit and click Force Quit.

FIGURE 7.23

The Force Quit dialog box makes applications quit, even when they are unresponsive.

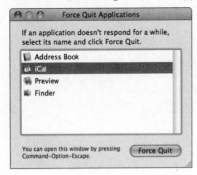

Using the Dock

You can force applications to quit from the Dock. Control+Option+⌘+click the application icon in the Dock; now choose Force Quit from the contextual menu.

Using the Activity Monitor

Another option for forcing an application to quit is to use a utility called Activity Monitor. It is located in the Utilities folder, which is inside the Applications folder (`/Applications/Utilities`). (In the Finder, choose Go ⇨ Utilities or press Shift+⌘+U to open or go to the Utilities folder quickly.) Activity Monitor lists all the active processes, which includes the currently active applications (see Figure 7.24). Select an application in the list and click Quit Process, or you can choose View ⇨ Quit Process or press Option+⌘+Q.

Caution

Forcing an application to quit skips any alerts to save unsaved documents, so any unsaved changes you have made will be lost. Sometimes this is unavoidable, but if you can save a document first, and quit it the standard way, that's the best course of action.

The Activity Monitor lists all the processes currently active in Mac OS X. This includes all the applications. Select a process and then click the Quit Process button, press Option⌘+Q, or choose View ⇨ Quit Process to force a process to quit.

Summary

Mac OS X comes with dozens of applications and utilities, but you can also install applications from other companies to do even more things with your Mac.

In this chapter you discovered how to open applications in Mac OS X through the Finder, Dock, and by using the Recent Items submenu. You also learned how to install new applications in Mac OS X. Installing applications is usually a simple operation of dragging the application files from the installation volume onto your Applications folder, but some applications require that you use an installation program. Uninstalling applications is usually as simple as dragging them to the Trash or running their uninstaller applications.

This chapter covered a variety of techniques used to manage the display of applications and documents on-screen. One method is to minimize document windows to the Dock, so they are out of the way but still accessible. Another method is to use the Hide or Hide Other commands. You can also switch among applications by using the Dock or the application switcher.

You also discovered how to edit documents. When working with documents, you can move or copy contents within and across documents by using the standard Cut, Copy, and Paste commands. You can also drag and drop contents within and across documents. And you can create clipping files by dragging contents from a document to the desktop or to a Finder window, then drag that clipping file into other documents; clipping files make great repositories of frequently used content snippets, such as your address or company logo.

You can convert documents into stationery pads, Apple's name for templates. When opened, a copy of the stationery pad document is automatically created, so your stationery pad document remains untouched for future use. Many applications have their own mechanism for creating templates.

There are also several methods for saving documents, though the most common is to choose File ⇨ Save or press ⌘+S in the active application. The first time you save a document, you get the Save As dialog box, in which you specify the filename and its location. There are two versions of the Save As dialog box, one with limited options for where to save files and one with the same navigation capabilities as in a Finder window; you can switch from one version to the other within the Save As dialog box. You can also use the Save As dialog box at any time, to create a copy of the document with a new name, such as to keep before and after copies of an edited document.

Finally, you discovered the process of quitting an application. This is usually a simple matter of pressing ⌘+Q or choosing Quit *applicationname* from the application menu, but you can also quit applications from the Dock or the application switcher. (If the application has any unsaved documents, you are given a chance to save them before quitting.) Applications are also quit automatically when you log out, restart, or shut down the Mac.

Working with Mac OS X Applications, Utilities, and Widgets

M ac OS X 10.6 Snow Leopard is much more than an operating system. It's chock-full of tools that enable you to do all sorts of things, from managing your address book to taking photographic snapshots. These tools come in three forms: applications, utilities, and widgets.

What distinguishes the three types of tools from each other comes down essentially to complexity. Technically, all three types are software programs. However, an *application* usually is software that you use to perform a task unrelated to managing your computer, such as surfing the Web or playing DVDs. A *utility* usually is a tool to manage the computer itself, such as one that manages color profiles or formats disk drives. And a *widget* usually is a very simple program that gives you quick access to a feature, such as translating text or weather information.

But these are arbitrary distinctions, and Apple may have classified some tools differently in Mac OS X than you might have. In the end, what really matters about the labels application, utility, and widget is where you find the tools on your Mac. Mac OS X stores them, respectively, in the Applications folder, the Utilities folder, and the Dashboard (for widgets). All three locations have tools that Apple includes with Mac OS X 10.6 Snow Leopard; you can also add your own.

Note

You can move tools from the Applications folder to the Utilities folder, or vice versa, if you want. You might do so to organize your tools in a configuration that's more logical to you. Just drag them to the desired folder. However, you cannot move widgets into these folders, nor can you move applications or utilities into them. And note that moving applications or utilities can cause issues such as Software Update not being able to update them.

IN THIS CHAPTER

How applications, utilities, and widgets differ

Mac OS X's built-in applications

The utilities that come with Mac OS X

The widgets included with Mac OS X

Cross-Ref

The fourth kind of built-in program in Mac OS X is a service. Services are functions that you can use within your applications, such as converting text between the two forms of Chinese, Googling text, or taking a screen shot. Chapter 16 explains how to use them.

Touring the Applications Folder

The Applications folder has the most preinstalled tools, and it is where software you download or buy is typically installed, as Chapter 7 explains in more detail. The easiest way to get to the Applications folder is to open a Finder window (just double-click any disk or folder icon in the Finder); you'll see the label Applications in the resource list at left, under the Places category. Click it to display the Applications folder's contents. You can also get to the Applications folder by opening your startup drive; you'll see a folder called Applications that you then double-click to open. Figure 8.1 shows the Applications folder.

Tip

Should you delete your Mac's included applications, such as when recovering your system from a crash, you can reinstall them from your Mac OS X 10.6 Snow Leopard installation DVD. After opening the DVD, open the Optional Installs folder, double-click `Optional Installs.mpkg`, then select the Applications option, press Continue, and follow the prompts. You can choose individual applications by expanding the Applications option and selecting the desired suboptions.

Note

New Macs include a copy of Apple's iLife software, which includes GarageBand, iMovie, iPhoto, and iWeb. (The newest version, iLife '09, costs $79 if you have an older version on your Mac or no version on your Mac at all.) For details on the iLife applications, check out iLife '09 Portable Genius by Guy Hart-Davis, published by this book's publisher, Wiley Publishing.

Address Book

The Address Book holds information on your contacts, such as names, mailing addresses, phone numbers, and e-mail addresses. It's easy to add contacts; just click the + button under the Names list, then fill in the fields in the contact's "card," as Figure 8.2 shows. Use the Preferences dialog box (choose Address Book ➪ Preferences or press ⌘+, [comma]) to customize how your Address Book displays contact information, as well as determine other preferences.

Tip

To change the picture associated with a person, double-click the square to the left of the person's name. You will then get a dialog box that enables you to choose an image from your Mac, as well as resize it and apply special effects to it.

But that's just the beginning. The Address Book works with other Mac OS X tools. For example, it synchronizes with the Mail e-mail application's contacts, so as you add contacts to either program, they are available to both. It also syncs with the iCal calendar application, so you can choose attendees to calendar events from your address book and even e-mail calendar invitations to people in your address book.

FIGURE 8.1

The Applications folder

FIGURE 8.2

The Address Book. Left: Updating a contact. Right: Setting preferences.

In the Preferences dialog box's Accounts pane, you can also set Address Book to synchronize contacts with Apple's MobileMe, Google's Gmail, and Yahoo's Yahoo Mail services, as well as with Microsoft Exchange 2007 servers commonly used for corporate e-mail, calendaring, and contacts. You can also invite other MobileMe users to share your address book, which is a handy way to maintain group contact lists for clubs or other groups. (Chapter 15 covers Apple's MobileMe service in depth.) You can also import contacts from a variety of sources by choosing File ➪ Import or pressing ⌘+O. Finally, Address Book can export contacts to the vCard format, which many other mail applications can import, as well as export a backup copy of your address book.

Chapter 11 covers Address Book in more detail, and Chapter 19 covers how to use Address Book with the Microsoft Exchange server.

Automator

Another way to automate work in Mac OS X is to use Automator. Automator differs from AppleScript in that it takes advantage of *workflows*, series of steps that are predefined within various applications. Automator enables you to combine these predefined workflows however you want to accomplish a repetitive task. (By contrast, the commands available in AppleScript are each one step, so it takes more work to combine them.) Chapter 25 covers Automator in detail.

Calculator

The Calculator application is actually three calculators — Basic, Scientific, and Programmer — as Figure 8.3 shows. Choose the one you prefer by using the View menu. Other View menu options include using reverse Polish notation (RPN), setting the preferred number of decimal places, and showing separators after thousands. There's also a Paper Tape option (choose Window ⇨ Show Paper Tape or press ⌘+T) that keeps a recording of all the calculations you've made; you can print this record by choosing File ⇨ Print Tape or pressing ⌘+P. Note that you don't need to display the paper tape to be able to print it.

The Calculator application also has a set of handy conversions, which you access from the Convert menu. For example, you can convert a result from acres to hectares or from dollars to euros by choosing the desired "from" and "to" measurements.

FIGURE 8.3

The three faces of the Calculator, from left to right: Basic, Scientific, and Programmer

 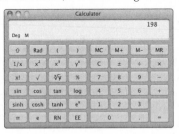 

Chess

If you need a break and like to play chess, use the Chess application to match your skills against those of Mac OS X 10.6 Snow Leopard. Among the options in this man-versus-machine game is the capability to have the Mac speak its moves to you, as well as to change the appearance of the chess board and pieces.

Dashboard

The Dashboard (also available by pressing the keyboard shortcut assigned to it, which by default is the F4 key) is where you access widgets, the set of quick-access tools that comes with Mac OS X. When you open the Dashboard, the widgets superimpose themselves over your desktop; to get back to what you were doing, just click anywhere outside a widget or press the keyboard shortcut assigned to Dashboard.

We cover the Dashboard interface and the included widgets later in this chapter, in the section "Touring the Widgets."

Dictionary

The Dictionary application combines the New Oxford American English dictionary, the Apple dictionary of computer terms, the Oxford American Writers thesaurus, the Wikipedia online encyclopedia, and a dictionary of information technologies terms, as well as a Japanese dictionary, Japanese-to-English translation dictionary, and a dictionary of Japanese synonyms. (The three Japanese dictionaries and the information technologies dictionary don't display by default; turn them on in the Dictionary's Preferences dialog box.)

To use the Dictionary, select which dictionary you want to look in (or click All to search them all), then enter a search term in the Search box. Figure 8.4 shows an example.

FIGURE 8.4

The Dictionary application and sample results

Mac OS X's Application "Suites"

With so many included applications and utilities in Mac OS X 10.6 Snow Leopard, it can be hard to see what you really have available. Therefore, it can be helpful to mentally group some of these applications as virtual suites.

For example, you can think of TextEdit, Dictionary, Address Book, and iCal as your "business suite." You can think of DVD Player, Front Row, iTunes, and QuickTime Player as your "entertainment suite." You can think of Image Capture and iSync as your "file-syncing suite." And you can think of Mail, iChat, iCal, and Address Book as your "collaboration suite."

DVD Player

The DVD Player application does exactly what you would expect it to do: play DVDs on your Mac. Mac OS X 10.6 Snow Leopard sets DVD Player as the default player for video DVDs, so when you insert a DVD into your Mac's SuperDrive, DVD Player launches automatically. Its controls include setting the screen size for video playback, navigating to specific chapters, and enabling closed captions. There are also familiar iconic controls to play, rewind, fast-forward, and pause, plus a slider that enables you to move to any point in the video, as Figure 8.5 shows.

You can set DVD Player to not play a DVD automatically by deselecting Start Playing Disc in the Preferences dialog box (choose DVD Player➪Preferences or press ⌘+, [comma]). And you can set a different program as the default player by using the CDs and DVDs system preference (covered in Chapter 21).

Tip

Your Mac can play DVDs on an HDTV monitor or TV set, not just on a computer monitor, at resolutions as great as 1280 × 1024 dpi. That is, if your HDTV unit has a computer input jack and you have the right connector cables for your Mac.

Do note that DVD Player does not play Blu-ray or HD DVDs, even if you connect a compatible drive to your Mac — at least not in the initial version of Mac OS X 10.6 Snow Leopard. If you run Windows on your Mac (see Chapter 18), you can play such discs on a compatible external drive with Windows' DVD player. Or you can use a third-party program such as Roxio's Toast Titanium ($99, www.roxio.com) that adds Blu-ray support to the Mac OS (if you have a Blu-ray drive, of course).

FIGURE 8.5

DVD Player has controls resembling a handheld remote.

Font Book

From its very first version in 1984, the Mac OS has supported high-quality type fonts. The Font Book application enables you to manage these fonts, so you can selectively enable and disable them, as well as group them into sets. The more fonts that are enabled, the more memory is used, so if you have lots of fonts, managing which ones are enabled can help you keep your performance fast. Chapter 22 explains how to use Font Book in more detail.

Front Row

It's no secret that Apple is into audio and video big-time, what with iTunes, the Apple TV, and its video-enabled iPods and the iPhone. Front Row is a portal to audio and video content on your Mac and on the Web via the iTunes Store, letting you watch movies and theatrical trailers, TV episodes, photo albums, and more using the remote control that comes with many Macs. Chapter 9 covers this application in more detail.

iCal

Managing your schedule is easy with iCal, the Mac's built-in calendar application. You get all the calendar functions you expect, such as recurring events, configurable alarms, to-do lists, multiple calendars (to keep work and personal events separate, for example), and multiple calendar views (such as daily, weekly, and monthly), plus a few cool additions, such as the capability to set the time zone for the meeting (handy if you work across time zones) and attach documents to a calendar event.

iCal also integrates with other applications, such as Address Book and Mail, so you can invite people in your Address Book to a meeting and send reminders and invites via Mail. iCal also checks Mail automatically to see if you've gotten any new meeting invitations. In a group setting, you can connect to other calendars over the Web by using a technology called WebDAV (Web-based Distributed Authoring and Versioning) to enable a calendar server that multiple people can access. The Availability Panel (choose Window ⇨ Availability Panel or press Shift+⌘+A) helps find when multiple people are available for a meeting — if you are using a shared calendar.

Chapter 11 details how to use iCal, while Chapter 19 covers how it works with Microsoft Exchange.

iChat

With the built-in instant messaging (IM) iChat application, you can chat with almost anyone. That's because iChat supports AIM (AOL Instant Messenger), Google Talk, Jabber, .Mac, and MobileMe accounts. (Sorry, Yahoo's Messenger and Microsoft's Windows Live Messenger IM systems are not supported.) You log into whichever account you have; you can configure multiple accounts in the Accounts pane of the Preferences dialog box (choose iChat ⇨ Preferences or press ⌘+, [comma]). You can also chat with people on your local network by using the Mac OS X's Bonjour technology, even if they don't have IM accounts.

iChat's capabilities include videoconferencing, saving chat transcripts, sending SMS messages to mobile users, support for Bluetooth headsets, and sharing documents with chat participants.

Chapter 11 explains how to use iChat in more detail.

Image Capture

Many people use Apple's iPhoto software (part of the iLife software package) to work on their images, and they transfer images from digital cameras, iPods, and scanners there. So they tend not to know about Image Capture, an application that comes with Mac OS X. Image Capture enables you to bring in images from almost any device, whether connected to your Mac via a cable, over the network, or wirelessly over Bluetooth or Wi-Fi. (Click the globe iconic button at the bottom left of the Image Capture window to hide or show network-connected devices; it acts as a toggle.) Unlike iPhoto, Image Capture enables you to see previews of your images before you bring them into your Mac.

Image Capture is easy to use. Any supported device shows up in its list at left when connected. Select the desired device, and Image Capture will show the images available to transfer to your Mac. Figure 8.6 shows an example for a connected iPod Touch that has a bunch of screen grabs on it. Just select the images to transfer and click Download, or click Download All to bring them all into your Mac.

FIGURE 8.6

Image Capture showing images available for transfer from a connected iPod Touch

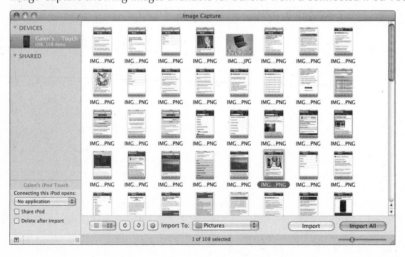

Image Capture can also control scanners that support the nearly universal Twain protocol. Figure 8.7 shows the Advanced view of the Image Capture controls for one of our scanners. (By default, the Simple view displays; click Advanced to see the Advanced view. The Advanced button changes to Simple, which if clicked returns you to the Simple view.)

FIGURE 8.7

Image Capture showing the controls to operate a connected scanner

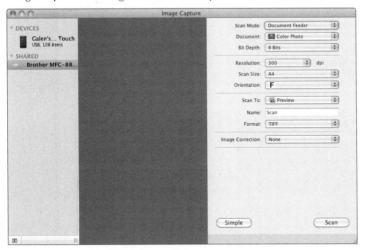

You can tell Image Capture whether to load automatically when a supported device is connected to your Mac by clicking the arrow-in-a-box iconic button at the bottom left of the Image Capture window. You'll get a list of applications such as iPhoto and Image Capture, as well as No Application. Choose the one you want to launch for the selected device, or choose No Application if you want to manually choose what application to use each time.

iSync

Although the iPhone and iPod Touch are the coolest, most useful handhelds around, they're not the only ones. The iSync application enables you to synchronize contacts, calendar entries, and other such information from non-Apple PDAs and smartphones such as the Palm Treo and Research in Motion (RIM) BlackBerry, as well as many phones from Motorola, Nokia, and others. It can synchronize over Bluetooth connections as well over USB (Universal Serial Bus) connections. (You synchronize iPhones and iPods by using iTunes.) Figure 8.8 shows iSync set up for a Motorola Razr phone; the options differ from device to device, based on the capabilities of each.

Mail

Apple's Mail application does much more than let you read your mail, though it does that too. It reads RSS (Really Simple Syndication) feeds and enables you to set up reminder notices and to-do lists, synchronizing any items to iCal. Chapter 11 details how to use Mail to read, send, and manage e-mail. Sure, you can use e-mail applications like Microsoft Entourage and Mozilla Thunderbird, but Mail works just as well and automatically integrates with other Apple applications such as iCal and Address Book.

FIGURE 8.8

The iSync application enables you to synchronize data between the Mac and some non-Apple handheld devices and phones, such as the Motorola Razr shown here.

New Feature

Mac OS X 10.6 Snow Leopard adds native support for Microsoft Exchange 2007, an e-mail, calendar, and to-do notes server popular in business. That means that Mail (as well as Address Book and iCal) can connect to Exchange 2007 servers easily (see Chapters 11 and 19). Mail continues to support the POP and IMAP e-mail protocols used by nearly every e-mail server out there, including Microsoft Exchange 2003 and earlier, IBM Lotus Notes, Novell GroupWise, and Web-based systems such as Google Gmail, MSN Hotmail, and Yahoo Mail.

Photo Booth

The Mac comes with a built-in camera, called an iSight, that is quite handy for videoconferencing and for taking pictures. You can use Photo Booth to take those pictures, whether you use the built-in iSight or other digital camera attached to your Mac. The application is simple: Launch Photo Booth, then choose the three photo options by using the iconic buttons at the bottom left of the screen: single photo, a rapid-succession ("burst") series of photos, and a movie clip. You can also apply various effects to the photos, using the controls at the bottom right of the screen.

The still photos are stored in the Web-friendly JPEG format, whereas the movie clip is stored in Apple's QuickTime Movie format. You'll find the images stored in the Photo Booth folder inside your Mac's Pictures folder. And you'll see them in a slider at the bottom of the Photo Booth application; click a thumbnail image to display it at a large size. You can then click Email to send someone the image, the iPhoto button to send the image to the iPhoto application (part of Apple's iLife suite), the Account Picture button to make the current image the one that displays for your account (such as when choosing who to log in as and in your personal card in the Address Book), and the Buddy Picture button to make the current image the one that displays when you use iChat. The camera button turns the camera back on so you can take more pictures.

Figure 8.9 shows Photo Booth in action.

Preview

There are few applications as useful as Preview, a tool you'll use all the time — often without even thinking about it. Preview enables you to open a variety of image files, so you can see what an image is without waiting for a slow-loading application like Adobe Photoshop to open. Even better, Preview launches automatically for any image formats that another program hasn't "claimed" as its own. (Remember, applications will associate various file formats to them, so when you double-click the file, the associated application launches automatically.)

FIGURE 8.9

The Photo Booth application enables you to take photos or movie clips by using an iSight camera, then apply effects to them.

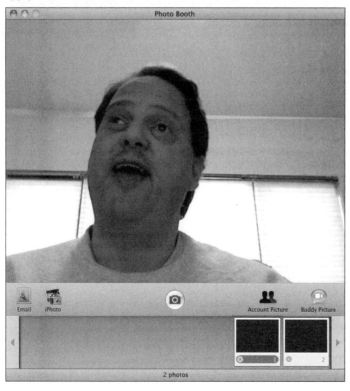

Opening filesWhat does Preview open? A lot:

- **EPS.** The Encapsulated PostScript format that helped launch the desktop publishing revolution in the mid-1980s. Although Adobe PDF (Portable Document Format) has largely supplanted it, EPS files exist by the millions on people's hard drives and servers.

- **GIF.** The Graphics Interchange Format widely used on the Web.

- **ICNS.** The Apple icon format used to display the icons on your Mac, such as for applications in the Dock and files in the Finder.

- **JPEG.** The Joint Photographers Expert Group format widely used on the Web and in digital cameras, plus the JPEG-2000 variant that's less used.

- **Microsoft BMP.** The native image format on Windows PCs.

- **Microsoft Icon.** The icon format used by Windows to display application and file icons in the Explorer and Start menu.

- **Open EXR.** A high-definition video-image format created recently by Industrial Light & Magic (which does special effects for tons of movies, starting with the original *Star Wars* effects) for use in its special effects work.

- **PDF.** Adobe's Portable Document Format, which has become a nearly universally used file format to distribute documents of all sorts.

- **Photoshop (.psd).** Adobe's native format for bitmap images, and one that is widely used by artists and publishers.

- **PNG.** The Portable Network Graphics format that most Web browsers support.

- **TIFF.** The Tagged Image File Format, a longtime standard image format still widely used by publishing and photo-editing applications.

Tip

Many Adobe Illustrator native files are actually EPS or PDF files, so you can usually open the Illustrator .ai files in Preview as well.

New Feature

Preview no longer opens or saves in the PICT, SGI, and TGA formats supported by previous Mac OS X versions. But the support for the ICNS and Microsoft Icons formats is new to Mac OS X 10.6 Snow Leopard.

Capturing images

Shown in Figure 8.10, Preview does much more than just let you open images for preview. It enables you to capture your computer screen as an image (choose File ⇨ Take Screen Shot), e-mail the image being previewed (choose File ⇨ Mail Selected Image), bookmark images for easy access later (in the Bookmarks menu), and import images from a connected iPod, iPhone, or digital camera (choose File ⇨ Import Image).

Plus, Preview can convert opened images to another supported format (choose File ⇨ Save As or press Shift+⌘+S). Note that it can save images in all the formats it can open, except for EPS.

New Feature

In Mac OS X 10.6 Snow Leopard, Preview now can import files directly from an attached scanner (choose File ⇨ Import from Scanner) or iPhone or iPod Touch (choose File ⇨ Import from _devicename_). Also, the File ⇨ Take Screen Shot menu command had been File ⇨ Grab in previous versions of the Mac OS.

Adjusting images

Preview lets you make all sorts of adjustments to images, using the controls in the Tools menu: Adjust Color, Adjust Size, Rotate Left, Rotate Right, Flip Horizontal, Flip Vertical, Crop (you must first use the mouse to select part of the image before you can crop it), and Assign Profile (to apply a color profile to the image for proper color conversion when printing).

When you adjust the color, a dialog box appears with sliders for various color adjustments, including Exposure, Contrast, Temperature, Saturation, Tint, and Sharpness. New to Mac OS X 10.6 Snow Leopard, this dialog box now shows a histogram of the image, which many people familiar with professional editing tools such as Adobe Photoshop use to understand the effects of their color adjustments.

Working with PDF files

If you work with a lot of PDF files, you can annotate them in Preview. (Click the Annotate button that appears at the top of the image window, choose View ⇨ Show Annotations Toolbar, or press Shift+⌘+A, and then use the annotation tools that appear at the bottom of the screen.) You can also choose Tools ⇨ Annotate and choose the desired annotation from the submenu. This annotation capability means you don't have to use Adobe's own free Reader application to do such work with PDF files. (Note that people who use Reader or Acrobat Professional will be able to see the annotations you make in Preview.)

Other PDF capabilities include the ability to rearrange pages in a PDF document, to add and edit bookmarks, and to open multiple PDF files in the same Preview window (as long as you open them all at the same time).

New Feature

The ability to view multiple PDFs at once is new to Mac OS X 10.6 Snow Leopard. (You could open multiple images, but not PDFs, in the same Preview window in previous versions of the Mac OS.) the Annotate button at the top of the image window is also new.

Also, Preview now lets you correctly select text in multicolumn PDF files. Before, Preview couldn't tell that there were columns, so it would select text from across multiple columns as you used to mouse to select text.

Managing display options

Preview has several controls to manage the display of images. For example, by choosing View ⇨ PDF Display, you get several suboptions for how PDF files display, such as in a continuous scroll or as two-page spreads.

Choose View ⇨ Slideshow or press Shift+⌘+F to have Preview create and play all open images as a slideshow.

FIGURE 8.10

The Preview application does much more than let you quickly open images to see what they look like. It also enables you to convert images from one format to another.

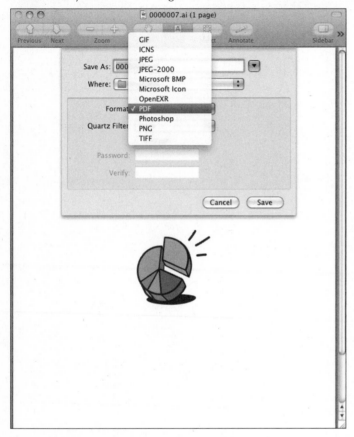

You can also display or hide the Sidebar in the Preview window by choosing View⇨Sidebar⇨ Show/Hide Sidebar, clicking the Sidebar iconic button at the top of the window, or pressing Shift+⌘+D. The sidebar contains thumbnail images of whatever is open in that Preview window. If you have opened a PDF file, the Sidebar shows thumbnails of each page. You can toggle between thumbnail, annotations, and table-of-contents views by using the options in the View⇨Sidebar submenu. (These Preview window view options existed in previous versions of the Mac OS but were accessible only through the Thumbnails iconic popup menu in the Sidebar. That iconic popup menu has been replaced in Mac OS X 10.6 Snow Leopard with a row of iconic buttons at the bottom of the Sidebar.)

The Contact Sheet option in the View⇨Sidebar submenu (you can also press Option+⌘+1) places one or more row of images or pages in the current Preview window, acting like the Finder's grid view so you can see all images in one window at a reasonable size. While the contact sheet is displayed, you cannot see full view of any page or image, as you can in thumbnails view.

If you are working with images or PDF files that you plan to print or display on another device, you can preview how they will look at the destination printer or other device by choosing View ⇨ Soft Proof with Profile and then choosing the output device's color profile from the submenu.

The View menu also has the standard controls to zoom in and out, and to display the image or PDF at actual size. Plus, you can have Preview automatically resize the display as you resize the window, by choosing View ⇨ Automatically Resize or pressing Shift+⌘+R. Preview also lets you toggle the background display of images and PDF files by choosing View ⇨ Show Image Background or pressing Option+⌘+B. (Some images have transparent or other backgrounds that Preview normally converts to white to improve the on-screen display; this command lets you turn off that display conversion; the actual image is unaffected.)

New Feature

The new buttons for thumbnail and other views in a preview window, the Contact Sheets capability, the ability to see soft proofs, and the automatic resizing are all new to Mac OS X 10.6 Snow Leopard.

QuickTime Player

The QuickTime Player application does just what it says: plays QuickTime movies. Like Preview, QuickTime Player launches automatically if no other program is associated with the QuickTime movie format (.mov files). QuickTime Player can open both movie files from your computer or connected network server and movie files on the Web. (Chapter 9 covers the QuickTime Player.)

Safari

The Safari browser is perhaps the most-used application that comes with the Mac OS X. It's your gateway to the Web, and it is just as capable as its principal competitors, Mozilla Firefox and Opera. (People who pick something other than Safari typically do so because they like another application's user interface better; for example, Safari is not so great at keeping bookmarks accessible, while Firefox is. And there's no reason you can't run multiple browsers on your Mac.) Chapter 10 covers Safari in detail.

Stickies

Many people are addicted to using Post-It notes as reminders, covering their workspaces with them. You can do the same on your virtual desktop with the Stickies application. After launching Stickies, choose File ⇨ New Note to create a note. You can type in, copy in, or import text, format it by using the controls in the Stickies menu bar, and even drag or paste in graphics. To add hyperlinks to Web content, choose Edit ⇨ Add Link. The Window menu enables you to control the display of notes, as well as navigate through them. You can also have Stickies spell-check your notes and speak them to you.

System Preferences

The System Preferences application is where you set up much of the Mac OS X's behavior, such as the desktop background, security settings, and time zone. Chapter 21 covers the various system preferences in detail.

TextEdit

The TextEdit application is a lightweight word processor in which you can write, edit, format, and even spell-check text. Although you'll likely use a full-fledged word processor such as Microsoft Word or Apple iWork Pages for reports, flyers, and the like, you'll find that you can do a lot of editing work in TextEdit, from instruction sheets to letters. It's also a handy tool to edit the Web's HTML pages when you don't need the WYSIWYG and specialty features of a program such as Adobe Dreamweaver. TextEdit can open text-only (ASCII), Microsoft Word, and Rich Text Format (RTF) files, as well as save files in the text-only, PDF, RTF, Word 97, Word 2003 XML, and Word 2007 formats. (HTML files are really text-only files, but TextEdit is smart enough not to replace the .html or .html filename extension on Web pages with the text-only format's .txt filename extension when it saves them.)

Note

To get the option to save in file formats such as PDF or Word 97, your TextEdit document must be a rich-text document. Choose Format➪Make Rich Text or press Shift+⌘+T. In a rich-text document, you can apply formatting such as boldface, italics, specific fonts, and text sizes.

So just how much can you use TextEdit as a word processor, rather than a just a quick-and-dirty text editor? The short answer is "quite a bit." Figure 8.11 shows an example document in TextEdit.

In the Format menu, you'll find controls to add tables and lists (both bulleted and numbered), enable automatic hyphenation, and set basic text attributes such as font and size. There's also a control to save the file as plain text, stripping out all the fancy formatting (saving the file as a text-only file has the same effect). You can also apply styles, which are collections of text attributes such as font and size, that you can apply all at once to selected text. At the top of the TextEdit window are controls to apply paragraph alignment, lists, styles, and line and paragraph spacing. You can also set tabs and indents by using the tab bar right above the document window.

These formatting controls provide the basics that most documents need, though TextEdit doesn't do paragraph styles where the style is applied to the entire paragraph; TextEdit's styles apply only to selected text. Plus, unlike the style function in traditional word-processing programs such as Microsoft Word, TextEdit's styles don't update the text that uses them when you edit the styles.

The Edit menu provides the other editing features that most people use routinely, such as features for inserting page breaks and other special characters; spell- and grammar-checking the document; inserting hyperlinks; automatically formatting dates, phone numbers, and other types of data formats (this feature is called Data Detectors); turning on and off typographic dashes and "curly" quotes; changing the text case; and even changing the text order between right-to-left (as in European languages) and left-to-right (as in Middle Eastern languages). There's even a control to have the Mac speak your document's text.

New Feature

Mac OS X 10.6 Snow leopard adds a few text-editing capabilities to TextEdit. One is the Edit➪Transformations menu command and its suboptions: Make Upper Case, Make Lower Case, and Capitalize (which capitalizes the first letter of each word). Another is the Text Replacement in the Edit➪Substitutions menu command, which enables any text substitutions you set in the Text pane of the Language & Text system preference (see Chapter 21).

FIGURE 8.11

The TextEdit application provides basic — but not unsophisticated — word-processing capabilities.

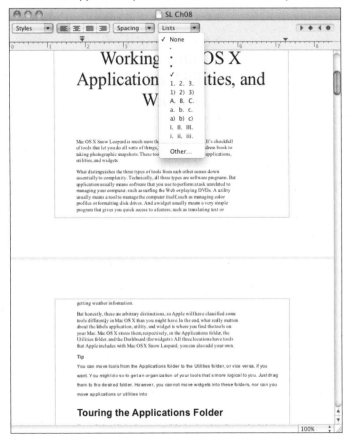

What TextEdit can't do is create and manage paragraph styles, generate tables of contents and footnotes, track changes, add comments, insert mailing addresses, insert and create embedded graphics and text boxes, or other such professional features found in iWork Pages and Word.

Time Machine

Backing up files and applications is something everyone is supposed to do, but that few people actually do it with any regularity. Part of the problem is that backup software has been clunky for years. Apple's Time Machine application revolutionized backup software when it was introduced in Mac OS X 10.5 Leopard by making backing up easy and powerful at the same time. Chapter 4 covers in detail how to use Time Machine.

Touring the Utilities Folder

Utilities are small apps that you use infrequently, usually to adjust the behavior of the Mac OS or to do very specific functions such as using the Grapher utility to generate and print graphs. Let's take a look at the ones that come with Mac OS X 10.6 Snow Leopard.

New Feature

The Directory utility is gone in Mac OS X 10.6 Snow Leopard; its functions are set up when you set up an Exchange 2007 account in Address Book, iCal, or Mail. If you don't use Exchange, you can set up a non-Exchange directory by using the Configure LDAP button in Mail's Preferences dialog box, in its Compose pane.

Also gone in Mac OS X 10.6 Snow Leopard is the ODBC Administrator utility, which had been used for central management of Open Database Connectivity, a standard way to let computers access ODBC-compatible databases on servers. You must now install separate ODBC drivers in Snow Leopard.

Activity Monitor

If you're having performance slowdowns or simply curious about how your Mac resources are being used, use the Activity Monitor utility to see what is running on your Mac, as well as the CPU, memory, disk, network, and other resources used to run them. You'll get a list of processes — this means both applications and operating system tasks — that are running. You can filter the list by using the popup menu at the top of the screen, as well as stop a process or get more information on it by using the buttons at the top. Figure 8.12 shows the Activity Monitor.

Tip

Note that stopping an operating system process can make the Mac OS X unstable, so do so with care. It's more common to stop applications that may have frozen or are stealing the Mac's resources from everything else, though it's easier to do so by pressing Option+⌘+Esc to open the Force Quit Applications dialog box, selecting the unresponsive or troublesome application, and clicking Force Quit.

AirPort Utility

AirPort is Apple's brand of Wi-Fi wireless routers. And AirPort Utility enables you to manage any AirPort that you have on your network, such as setting access permissions, security levels, and the AirPort's public ID. But this utility will not work with other companies' wireless routers, even though your Mac can connect to them.

AppleScript Editor

The AppleScript Editor enables you to create and edit scripts, which are a powerful way to automate tasks. You can write your own scripts or record actions and have the sequence stored as a script. Chapter 25 covers AppleScript in detail.

New Feature

The AppleScript Editor, previously called just Script Editor, has been moved from the Applications/AppleScript folder to the Applications/Utilities folder.

FIGURE 8.12

The Activity Monitor utility enables you to see what is running on your Mac and what resources are being consumed.

Audio MIDI Setup

The Mac has long supported music, way before the iPod existed. It did so with high-quality input and playback of sound and support for the MIDI (Musical Instrument Digital Interface) standard that enables you to bring sound in from musical instruments and use the Mac as a sound-mixing studio-in-a-box. The Audio MIDI Setup utility enables you to manage how the Mac handles incoming and outgoing audio connections. Figure 8.13 shows the utility controls for headphone output.

The utility has built-in controls for microphone, line in, and headphone connections — something that all Macs support. You can adjust the volume, sound quality (the Format options), and loudness settings. If you have other sound equipment to bring audio into the Mac or to receive audio from the Mac, plug it in to the Mac, then click the + iconic button at the bottom right of the Audio MIDI Utility dialog box. (Most devices plug in to the line in and headphone jacks, but some will use USB, FireWire, or other connections, so check with the device's manual. You may also need to run an installation utility that adds the device's setup options to the Audio MIDI Utility's controls.) If the Mac recognizes the device, it will add it to the list at left, and when you select that added item, you'll see the available controls for it in the main window of the dialog box. (Use the – iconic button to remove a selected device. Use the Action iconic popup menu (the gear icon) for additional controls, such as setting up a device as the default input or output channel for the Mac.

FIGURE 8.13

The Audio MIDI Setup utility enables you to control the settings for your audio inputs (microphone, line in, and musical instruments) and output (headphones, speakers, and recording devices).

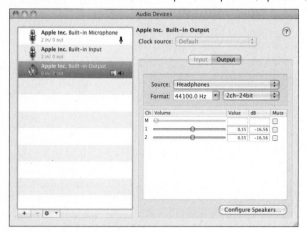

Bluetooth File Exchange

If you have set up a Bluetooth device by using the iSync application covered in the section "Touring the Applications Folder," use the Bluetooth File Exchange utility to send or receive files on such devices.

When you launch Bluetooth File Exchange, you'll be asked to select a file, then asked to choose which Bluetooth device to send it to. If you want to download a file from a Bluetooth device instead, click Cancel, and then choose File ⇨ Browse Device or press Shift+⌘+O, select the desired Bluetooth device, and click Browse. You'll get a list of files, from which you can select the ones to copy to the Mac.

Cross-Ref

Chapter 12 covers the basics of Bluetooth networking, Chapter 13 covers Bluetooth file sharing in detail, and Chapter 21 covers Bluetooth setup in detail.

Tip

You can send and receive files without launching this utility. Instead, click the Bluetooth icon in the Apple menu bar and choose Send File or Browse Device instead. Doing so runs the Bluetooth File Exchange utility. These same controls exist in the utility's File menu.

Boot Camp Assistant

When Apple began using Intel's processor chips in 2006, it opened up the possibility that Macs could run Microsoft Windows, not just Mac OS X. Shortly after making the switch, Apple provided a utility called Boot Camp that enables you to format part of your Mac's internal drive as a Windows disk, install Windows on it, and then install the drivers that enable Windows to take advantage of the Mac's hardware. The result is a Mac that can switch between Mac OS X and Windows, with users choosing which one they want when they start the Mac.

The Boot Camp Assistant utility does the setup work for your Mac. (You need to supply your own copy of Windows.) Chapter 18 covers working with Windows in more detail.

Tip

Boot Camp works well if you want to run either Mac OS X or Windows, but it doesn't let you run both at the same time. To do so, you can use either Parallels' Desktop or EMC VMware's Fusion application. Both create a virtual drive for Windows that you can run from the Mac OS X, and both let both Mac and Windows applications run simultaneously and share files, hardware, and other Mac resources.

ColorSync Utility

A hallmark of the Mac has been its support for graphics and publishing, which is why the Mac remains the dominant computer used for publishing, photography, and film production. A key issue in dealing with visual media is ensuring correct color as images pass from one device to another, such as from camera to scanner to Mac to printer. Each device handles color differently, so color profiles are used to map devices against each other, and color is adjusted appropriately as it passes among the devices. You use ColorSync Utility to adjust those mappings for the various devices you use.

ColorSync Utility starts with a profile (an ICC, or International Color Consortium, file) assigned to each device. Mac OS X comes with ICC profiles for common devices, and various devices' installation programs typically add any special ICC profiles they need. That means you usually don't have to do anything special with ICC profiles other than make sure that your image-editing and layout applications (such as Adobe Photoshop, Adobe InDesign, and QuarkXPress) are set up to know which profiles to apply to which images so they have the right color source defined. You can see a list of installed profiles in the Profiles pane of the utility.

But if you want to adjust these color profiles, you can do so with ColorSync Utility, shown in Figure 8.14. Do be careful, as these changes require a highly technical set of skills to avoid screwing up the color your Mac presents. The simplest adjustments are to assign different profiles to your devices, or to assign profiles to those that don't have them installed. To assign a profile, go to the Devices pane and click the triangle-icon popup menu to the right of Current Profile, and choose Other to navigate to the new profile. (If you click Open to the right of the profile name, you can see the specific technical settings.)

If you're really advanced, use the Filters pane to adjust and add color adjustments for the selected profile and the Calculator pane to calculate the various color values in different color models. (A color model describes the physical capabilities of different color production techniques, such as a monitor's light-based pixels versus printed inks.)

FIGURE 8.14

Use ColorSync Utility to adjust how colors are adjusted by various devices.

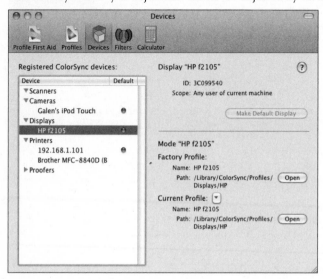

Console

Behind the scenes, applications, utilities, and the Mac OS send messages to each other to communicate instructions, changes, and status. The Console utility enables you to monitor and filter these messages. Hardly anyone uses Console; it's really designed for support technicians to troubleshoot a malfunctioning Mac and for software developers to diagnose issues in the programs they are creating.

DigitalColor Meter

The DigitalColor Meter utility measures the color being sent to your monitor. You can select the color model you want the measurements in, then move the mouse pointer across your screen. The measurements for wherever your mouse pointer happens to be will display; you can also save them as text or as an image. The DigitalColor Meter utility calibrates your monitor's color accuracy. You can compare these values of what the Mac "thinks" it is producing to the values that an external color-measuring device, called a *colorimeter*, registers. If the values don't match, you know you need to run the Displays control panel (see Chapter 21) or third-party software to adjust the Mac's color settings.

Disk Utility

Of all the utilities that Apple includes with Mac OS X 10.6 Snow Leopard, Disk Utility, shown in Figure 8.15, is probably the one you'll use the most. Disk Utility does several things, all related to managing your disk drives. Among its capabilities are formatting disks, checking (verifying) and repairing disks, mounting and unmounting disks, converting disks into disk images, and recording ("burning") disk images to CDs and DVDs.

Note

Mounting means making the disk appear in the Finder; unmounting means making it invisible but still connected (compare that to ejecting, which disconnects the disk, so you can unplug it. A disk image is a file that contains all the contents of a disk, so you can move it to another drive or to a removable medium such as a recordable DVD.

Note

In the Sidebar at left of Disk Utility, the drives are shown aligned to the far left, while the disks (for a multiple-disk drive) and partitions for each drive are listed indented below the disk name. Note that you may see the term volume used to refer to disks; a volume is a general term for any type of storage container, such as a disk, a partition, or a network file share. A partition is the part of a disk that appears as a single entity to the Mac; it can be the entire disk or a portion of it, and disks can have multiple partitions.

FIGURE 8.15

Disk Utility is where you manage disks, repair them, and burn their images to CDs and DVDs.

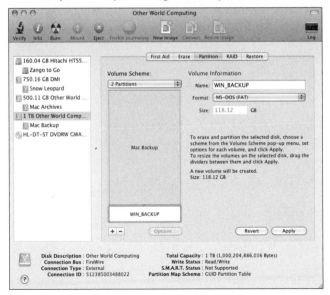

Fixing and restoring disks

The most-used part of Disk Utility is the First Aid pane, where you can check a disk's health and try to repair it. Select the disk (or individual partition) from the Sidebar, then click Verify Disk to check it or Repair Disk to check and repair it. You also have the options, on some disks at least, to verify and repair the disk permissions, which are used by the Mac OS to determine who can access what files: the operating system, the Mac's administrator, and/or individual users if the Mac is set up for multiple owners, as described in Chapter 20.

Caution

You cannot repair the disk you started the Mac from. So if you have a problem with the Mac's built-in disk (the one nearly everyone starts up from), you will need to instead start up from the Mac OS X installation DVD and run Disk Utility from it, or boot from a separate disk. We recommend you always have a backup disk for your files and that the disk be configured with Mac OS X so you can boot from it when repairs are necessary to your standard boot disk.

Disk Utility comes with a handy set of features to create and restore disk images. That means you can make a copy of an entire disk and store it as a single file on another drive or on a recordable DVD. This is a handy way to store drive backups and then reinstall them later, or transfer them to another Mac. To create an image, select the disk, partition, or drive, then click the New Image iconic button at the top of the Disk Utility window. (You can also open the disk image by choosing File⇨ Open Disk Image or pressing Option+⌘+O.) To put the contents of a disk image on a disk, go to the Restore pane and click Image to select the source disk image. Drag the disk you want to write the disk image onto from the list at left into the Destination field. If you want to erase the target disk's contents, enable the Erase Destination option. Click Restore to begin the restoration process.

Tip

You can copy a disk by using the Restore pane without first creating a disk image for it. Simply drag the source disk into the Source field of the Restore pane, then drag the target disk into the Destination field and follow the restoration instructions previously described.

Tip

You can burn a disk or a disk image to CD or DVD by selecting it in the disk list, then clicking the Burn iconic button.

Sometimes, you need to convert disk images for their destination. To do so, open the disk image by choosing File⇨Open Disk Image or pressing Option+⌘+O, then click the Convert iconic button. In the dialog box that appears, you can choose the disk image's new location, its image format (compressed, read-only, read/write, or CD/DVD master), and its encryption level (none, 128-bit, or 256-bit).

Adding, partitioning, and formatting disks

When you add a new hard disk to your Mac, you have to format it, which you do in Disk Utility. But you may also want to partition to disk, which means to divide it into several volumes, each of which appears in the Finder as if it were a separate disk. Disk Utility enables you to do this as well. Figure 8.15 shows Disk Utility partitioning an external disk into a Mac disk and a Windows disk. A disk must have at least one partition.

When adding a disk, it displays in the Disk Utility's Sidebar. Select it, then go to the Partition pane to set up the partitions. (Use the + and – iconic buttons to add and delete partitions. You can enter the size for each in the Size field or simply drag the bottom of each partition up or down to change the size.)

A key decision is how to format the partition. You have four variations of Mac OS Extended (called *HFS+* on some older versions of Mac OS X) to choose from: regular, journaled, case-sensitive, and case-sensitive journaled. Usually, you should pick Mac OS Extended (Journaled), as that keeps a list, or journal, of all changes made, making recovery easier in the case of a failure. But journaling makes your disk run more slowly, so it can be problematic if you run high-performance applications frequently, such as video-rendering tools. The case-sensitive options are best suited if you are running Linux or Unix on the disk, as those operating systems treat words that are capitalized differently in different instances as separate words.

Note

You don't have to partition a disk to format it. If you select a disk and go to the Erase pane, you can also format the disk. In this case, one partition is created for the whole disk.

The MS-DOS (FAT) formatting option creates a Windows-compatible disk, which the Mac can also read. (Note that FAT means File Access Table, the name of the Windows directory structure used to locate files.) If you install Windows on a separate partition by using the Boot Camp utility, that partition will be formatted as MS-DOS. You might create an MS-DOS disk for use as an external disk that you want a Boot Camp partition or a Parallels or Fusion virtual machine to be able to access. (See Chapter 18 for more on using Windows with Mac OS X.)

You can erase (format) a partition or disk at any time by using the Erase pane. Of course, doing so wipes out all the data and applications on it, so be careful.

Cross-Ref

Chapter 4 covers backup and Disk Utility in more detail.

Using RAID

For servers and other critical uses where you need information available all the time, a major enemy is disk failure. Should something go wrong in the disk itself, you can lose all the data stored on it. Using a backup utility such as Mac OS X's Time Machine (see Chapter 4) can help you get back up and running, but you will lose any data saved after the last backup. RAID, which stands for redundant array of independent disks, is a technology meant to better protect your data in case of failure. Basically, RAID writes the data to multiple disks, so if one fails, the information is still available on the other disks. That also means that there's no downtime, as the data remains accessible. (You would repair or replace the broken disk, but you can usually do so without taking the Mac offline.)

To create a RAID system you need two disks of equal capacity. Go to the RAID pane and drag the disks into its central area. Give the RAID set a name in the RAID Set Name field, specify its formatting type, using the Volume Format popup menu, and choose Mirrored RAID Set from the RAID Type popup menu. Then click Create.

Caution

There are two other options in the RAID Type popup menu: Striped RAID and Concatenated RAID Set. Neither stores your data redundantly, so if one disk fails, you will lose all your data. These two options are meant to combine several physical disks as if they were one big "logical" disk — you're essentially fooling the Mac to think the multiple disks are just one big one. (The striped and concatenated options use different technical approaches to accomplish the same result.) It's fine to use these RAID options to pool together several disks, but don't think it will make your data safer.

Exposé

Easily accessible by pressing F3 on newer Macs (and F9 on others), Exposé takes all running applications and open Finder windows and makes them fit on your screen so you can easily switch among them. Just click the application or window you want to go to, and Exposé puts that one on top of the others. (Chapter 21 covers the Exposé & Spaces system preference in more detail.)

Tip

Another way to switch among running applications is to press ⌘+Tab. But, unlike Exposé, pressing ⌘+Tab does not switch among Finder windows. You can also switch among applications by using the Dock; if you minimized any Finder windows, they display in the Dock as well (see Chapters 2 and 7 for more details on using the Dock).

New Feature

In Mac OS X 10.6 Snow Leopard, Exposé is integrated into the Dock. If you have an application running with multiple windows open, click and hold the application's icon in the Dock. Exposé shuffles all the windows so you can click one to switch to it. Chapter 2 covers the Dock in detail.

Exposé had been in the Applications folder in previous versions of Mac OS X. In Snow Leopard, it is found in the Utilities folder.

Grab

The Grab utility captures whatever is displayed on your monitor, saving it as an image file. Use the Capture menu to determine what to capture: the entire screen, a selection of the screen (you draw a rectangle by using the mouse), or the selected window. These are the Screen, Selection, and Window options, respectively, in the Capture menu. There's also an option called Timed Screen that gives you ten seconds to arrange what's displayed before the display is captured.

A window appears with your screen grab. You can save it by choosing File ➪ Save or pressing ⌘+S. You'll be asked to supply a filename and choose the folder to store the file in. Note that screen grabs are saved as TIFF files. You can also copy the image to the clipboard for pasting in other applications by choosing Edit ➪ Copy or pressing ⌘+C. Likewise, you can print a screen grab by choosing File ➪ Print or pressing ⌘+P.

Tip

You can get information about a screen grab's size and color bit depth by choosing Edit ➪ Image Inspector or pressing ⌘+1.

Note

The Grab utility may sound familiar to you. That may be because you've seen it as an option in the Preview application: Choose File⇨Grab there to launch Grab, saving you a trip to the Utilities folder.

A fast way to use Grab is via keyboard shortcuts:

- Press Shift+⌘+3 to grab the whole screen.

- Press Shift+⌘+4, then drag the mouse to create a selection area (a marquee) of what you want to grab. If you press and hold Option when moving the mouse, the initial mouse location becomes the center of the marquee. Release Option to grab the selected area. (Press Esc to cancel the grab.)

- Press Shift+⌘+4, then press and hold the spacebar. As you move the mouse, Grab automatically creates a marquee to fit whatever window or dialog box the mouse passes over. Release the spacebar to grab the selected area. (Press Esc to cancel the grab.)

Grapher

If you're a scientist, engineer, or mathematician, you'll find the Grapher utility quite handy. It enables you to create 2-D and 3-D graphs based on mathematical formulas. The key is to understand the math to be able to create the formulas that generate the graphs. Grapher helps by including many examples of common equations. After you create your graph, you can save it and its underlying equations, as well as export the graphic itself in your choice of EPS, JPEG, PDF, and TIFF formats. Figure 8.16 shows an example graph.

Java Preferences

The Java Preferences utility enables you to configure how the Mac handles Java applications, which are a common way to deliver functionality over the Web or through a browser (though Java applications can run directly on the Mac as well).

The default settings work for most people, but if you want to change them, use this utility to do so. The General pane lists the versions of Java installed and lets you determine the version you want to run by default, both for applications (which run in the Mac OS) and applets (which run in your browser). Java Standard Edition, Version 6 for 64-bit operating systems (Java 6 SE 64-bit) is the default in Mac OS X 10.6 Snow Leopard, though Apple will likely update that as new Java versions are released over time. You can also change that version preference if you install a newer version of Sun Microsystems' Java on your Mac.

Use the Security pane to determine whether Java applets are kept after they are used (faster but less secure), to delete unwanted files, and to set the Keychain settings (described later in this section) to store passwords used by Java applications. You can also set the level of compression for Java resource (.jar) files, though that's about saving disk space more than about enhancing security.

Use the Advanced pane to set default behaviors, such as when to prompt the user to accept to let a new Java applet run and what type of security certificates to accept. These settings should look familiar, as most browsers offer the same controls over Java applets that they run.

FIGURE 8.16

The Grapher utility enables you to display scientific equations as graphs.

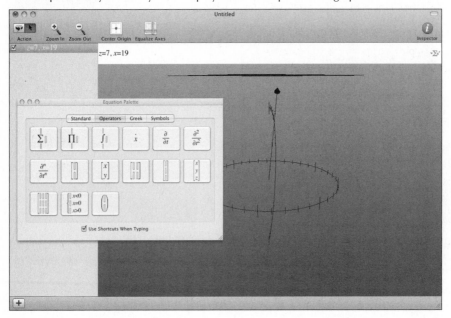

New Feature

Although Mac OS X has long included the Java Runtime Environment that lets Java applications and applets run, Mac OS X 10.6 Snow Leopard introduces an improved version. It runs much faster, so your Mac can better run the many Java applets now available on the Web. You won't see any differences in the Mac OS itself, just in Java performance.

Keychain Access

When you tell an application or a Web browser to store your password or login information, where is it stored? Often, it is stored in the Mac's Keychain, a system for managing passwords and related security settings. (That's why you're often asked if you want to save the password or access settings [such as digital certificates] in the Mac Keychain.) You use Keychain Access to manage those saved passwords and related security settings.

Within Keychain Access, you can specify how you want passwords to be handled, as Figure 8.17 shows. Double-click the item you want to manage from the list in the center of the screen, then go to the Access Control pane to set the options. The options include letting any application access the password, requiring confirmation to use the stored password, and requiring the user to type your Keychain master password first.

Caution

The beauty of the Mac Keychain is that you have to remember just one password (to open Keychain), and Keychain then remembers the specific password needed for the current application or password. The ugly side of Keychain is that if someone else knows that master password, he or she has access to all your passwords, such as those you use for online banking and purchasing goods at, say, Amazon.com. So when you set up Keychain (see Chapter 23), pick a hard-to-guess password.

FIGURE 8.17

Use Keychain Access to manage your stored passwords, digital certificates, and other stored access controls.

Migration Assistant

The Migration Assistant utility will move the applications, data, security settings, and preferences from one Mac to another. You typically use it when you get a new Mac and want to transfer everything from your old Mac to it. To use this utility, you need to have both Macs up and running, connected to each other via a FireWire cable or via Ethernet connections through a local area network (LAN). (A MacBook Air requires the use of a USB-to-Ethernet adapter to connect to a LAN.) If the old system has an older Mac OS X version such as 10.5 Leopard, don't worry: The utility is smart enough to keep Mac OS X 10.6 Snow Leopard on the new system.

After you select the source computer (the old one whose information you want transferred), the utility will walk you through the necessary steps, which will include restarting the Macs, so be sure that no other applications are running.

Caution

After you transfer your old Mac, some applications will need to be reenabled by entering a license key as a way to reduce software piracy, so be sure you have those handy. (They're usually on the install disk or in the accompanying manual.) Others (such as those from Adobe Systems) need to be deactivated on the original computer and reactivated on the new one; it's best to deactivate them on the old system before you migrate them to the new Mac, so if something goes wrong, you aren't stuck with an activated license you can't actually use. And in some cases, you may need to reinstall an application; that's typically due to the application using a copy-protection scheme that Migration Assistant doesn't recognize.

Network Utility

The Network Utility provides a whole suite of tools to monitor your network. Most users won't need to use it, but it's a great utility for a network administrator or support technician.

Info

Figure 8.18 shows the utility's Info pane, which shows the status of the Mac's network adapters: the IP address (the Internet Protocol-format address on the network), MAC address (the Media Access Control identifier that is unique to each device), information on the equivalent itself, and information on the recent data traffic through it.

You choose which network connection, called the *network interface*, to monitor by using the popup menu. Most Macs have three built-in network interfaces: en0, the Ethernet jack; en1, the wireless radio; and fw0, the FireWire jack. If you install other network interfaces on your Mac, such as a 3G wireless broadband card, they'll show up as well.

FIGURE 8.18

The Network Utility provides a suite of tools for checking the Mac's network connections, as well as other activity on the network.

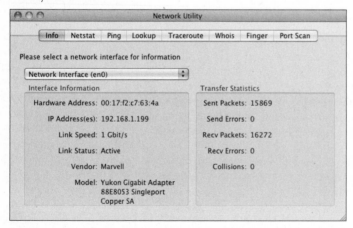

Netstat

This pane enables you to explore detailed network settings. Check one of the four options — the network routing table, protocol statistics, multicast information, or state of all socket connections — and click Netstat to get the results. Note that it can take the Mac several minutes to gather the results.

Ping

Use the Ping pane to see if a network device responds. It's the network version of poking someone to see if they're awake or alive. Enter the IP address or Web address (URL), then click Ping. The pane will show whether the device responded to the ping.

Lookup

The Lookup pane asks a Web site or other network resource for information about itself. (You can choose what information you want by using the Select Information to Look Up popup menu.) Enter the IP address or URL, then click Lookup.

Traceroute

The Traceroute pane discovers all the servers that a connection goes through between your Mac and that server. When you enter an IP address or URL in your browser and click Trace, the Internet sends that request through a bunch of servers, each handing off the request to the next one available. (Some may be your own servers.) The response comes back the same way, often through a different route. You use Traceroute to look at these paths to see if any problematic servers are used, such as those that have trouble delaying traffic.

Whois

The Whois database stores the ownership information for every Web address. So if you want to know who owns a Web domain or who is using a specific URL, enter it in this pane and click Whois. You should get a response listing the ownership information, including the domain registrar and the Web host used. If you don't get a response by using the default whois.internic.net database, try some of the other databases listed in the popup menu or type in one not listed that you prefer to use.

Finger

The Finger pane is where you can look up information about a specific user at a specific Web address. Enter both the username and the Web address, then click Finger. Note that many servers deny finger requests, and will respond with a "connection refused" message.

Port Scan

Use the Port Scan pane to see what services are available (open) at a specific URL or IP address. Enter the IP address or URL and click Scan. For example, if you are having trouble transferring files via FTP or accessing an e-mail, you can scan the device's ports to see whether the relevant service is available. In the case of FTP, using Port Scan should show that the FTP is open on port 21. If it does not show up as open, you know that the FTP service is not enabled, and if it shows up on a different port, you know that it is configured nonstandardly and that you either need to adjust your access settings to it from the Mac or fix its settings at the server.

Podcast Capture

The server version of Mac OS X comes with an application called Podcast Producer that enables you to convert audio and video into podcasts for distribution over the Internet and via iTunes. The Podcast Capture utility on Macs enables you to use the built-in microphone and iSight camera (and/or FireWire- or USB-connected devices) to record audio and video, then upload the files to Podcast Producer for conversion into podcasts. The Podcast Capture utility will not work unless you have Podcast Producer running on a Mac OS X Server; you need to also connect your Mac to that server by using the Podcast Capture utility before you can capture any audio or video for use by Podcast Producer.

You can produce podcasts from your Mac without using Podcast Producer and Podcast Capture, but you'll have to use third-party applications to do so.

RAID Utility

The RAID Utility works only if you have an Apple RAID card installed in an Intel-based Apple Xserve or Mac Pro system. You use the utility to configure the RAID settings, much as you would for a non-Apple RAID in Disk Utility, as described earlier in this section.

Remote Install Mac OS X

The MacBook Air got a lot of attention for its superthin design, but it was so thin only because it had no DVD drive. That makes it hard to install a new version of Mac OS X on an Air! Apple provided two solutions: a USB DVD drive for the Air that Apple and others sell separately, and the Remote Install Mac OS X utility that lets any networked Mac, or PC, offer the services of its CD or DVD drive.

First, make sure both the installation Mac and the MacBook Air are connected to the same network. (You can use a wired or wireless connection from your installation Mac.) Then insert the Mac OS X install disc in the installation Mac and run the Remote Install Mac OS X utility. Follow the prompts, and the utility will install the Mac OS X on the Air over its wireless connection by using the DVD in your installation Mac's drive.

Spaces

The Spaces application enables you to group applications so you have less clutter on your desktop, even when many applications are open. You set up which spaces each application belongs to, then as you switch from one space to another, only the applications running associated to the current space display on-screen. So you might have one space to which your business programs are associated (like Microsoft Excel and Apple iWork Pages); a second space for your creative applications, such as Adobe InDesign and Apple iPhoto; and a third space for your communications applications, such as Apple Mail and Yuuguu. (You can set up to four spaces.) Applications that you always want accessible, such as Safari and TextEdit, would be associated to every space.

With your spaces defined, all you have to do is hold Control and use the arrow keys to switch from one space to another, use the keyboard shortcuts you set in the Exposé & Spaces system preference, or use the Spaces menu that appears in the menu bar to select a desired space.

To set up Spaces, use the Exposé and Spaces system preference, as described in Chapter 21. After Spaces is set up, you can also add an application to any space from the Dock by Control+clicking or right-clicking the application icon and choosing Assign Application To from the contextual menu that appears.

New Feature

The ability to assign an application to a space in the Dock is new to Mac OS X 10.6 Snow Leopard. Also, Spaces had been in the Applications folder in previous versions of Mac OS X; it is now found in the Utilities folder.

System Profiler

You can check the configuration of your Mac easily, using the System Profiler utility. It gives you detailed information on every aspect of your hardware, network, software, and system settings. After opening the utility, select the aspect of your Mac that you want information on from the list at left, and the utility will show the results in the main window. Figure 8.19 shows an example. Note that you can also access this utility by choosing ➪ About This Mac and clicking More Info.

Tip

Choose View ➪ Refresh or press ⌘+R to have System Profiler update the information to the current state; this is especially handy for network and application information that can change while you have System Profile open.

Tip

If the information presented is overwhelming, use the options in the View menu to reduce their level of detail: Choose View ➪ Mini Profile or press ⌘+1 to get the least detail, and choose View ➪ Basic Profile or press ⌘+2 for a medium level of detail. Choose View ➪ Full Profile or press ⌘+3 to display everything possible.

FIGURE 8.19

The System Profiler utility displays an incredible amount of information on every aspect of your Mac's settings and configuration. Shown here are battery and power details.

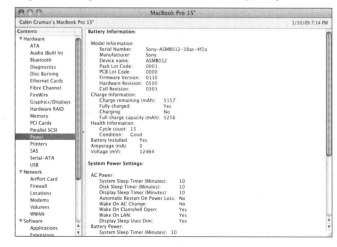

Terminal

It's easy to forget that Mac OS X is a version of the Unix operating system best known for cryptic commands that must be entered precisely to work. But Unix runs under the graphical interface that makes the Mac OS so easy to use, and the Terminal utility is your way into that part of the operating system.

When you run Terminal, you get a plain window where you type your commands and see the responses, as Figure 8.20 shows. Chapter 26 explains how to use Unix, but there are a few tips worth sharing here about configuring Terminal.

FIGURE 8.20

The Terminal utility is your gateway to the command-driven Unix foundation of the Mac OS.

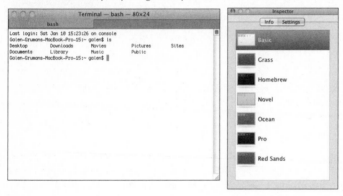

First, you can change its visual appearance by using the Preferences dialog box (choose Terminal ⇨ Preferences or press ⌘+, [comma]) to change the color scheme, font, text size, cursor style, window size, and more by using the controls in the Settings pane. For a faster but less exhaustive way to change Terminal's visual settings, choose Shell ⇨ Show Inspector or press ⌘+I, then choose the desired appearance in the Settings pane, as Figure 8.20 shows.

Second, you can have multiple Terminal windows open at the same time; choose Shell ⇨ New Window ⇨ appearance name. Or press ⌘+N to open a new window using the Basic appearance. Being able to choose a specific appearance is handy for visually distinguishing the Terminal windows, so you can more easily keep track of what you are doing in each. Plus, you can save a set of windows as a group that you can reopen all at once later: Choose Window ⇨ Save Windows as a Group to create the group, and choose Window ⇨ Open Window Group to open the group. Note that if you enable Use Window Group When Terminal Starts when creating a group, that group will open automatically when you launch Terminal.

Third, you can save all the commands and responses for offline review and archiving from a Terminal session by choosing Shell ➪ Export Text As or pressing ⌘+S.

New Feature

In Mac OS X 10.6 Snow Leopard, you can have multiple Terminal sessions running in the same Terminal window, so you can switch among sessions from one location. Choose Window ➪ Split Pane or press ⌘+D to open a new pane for a new session in the Terminal window. (You can open as many as you like.) To close a pane, be sure it is the active pane, then choose Windows ➪ Close Split Pane or press Shift+⌘+D.

VoiceOver Utility

VoiceOver Utility is where you set the conditions for when and how the Mac speaks what is on-screen. It is intended for visually impaired users. With the utility, you can specify dozens of conditions, such as whether content in Web pages is spoken, whether captions are also displayed, how punctuation symbols are spoken, and whether other sounds are muted. Figure 8.21 shows the utility. Chapter 6 covers the VoiceOver functionality in detail.

Note

VoiceOver must be turned on via the Universal Access system preference, as described in Chapters 6 and 21. You can access this utility from the system preference as well as from the Utilities folder.

FIGURE 8.21

VoiceOver Utility provides rich controls over how screen contents are spoken to visually impaired users.

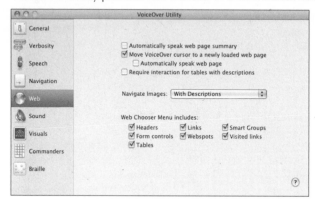

X11

As mentioned earlier in this section, Mac OS X is built on Unix, and thus supports the Unix X11 Window System interface. You use the X11 utility to run such applications. Chapter 26 covers X11 in more detail.

Touring the Widgets

Since Mac OS X 10.4 Tiger, Macintosh users have been able to run lightweight applications called widgets. As described in the "Touring the Applications Folder" section of this chapter, these widgets are available through the Dashboard application, which you can easily open by pressing F4 on most Macs. Figure 8.22 shows the Dashboard window, which overlays your entire screen when open. By default, four widgets show up in the Dashboard: Calculator, iCal, Weather, and World Clock.

Note
You can change the keyboard shortcut for opening and closing the Dashboard, as well as set up a "hot corner" on your Mac's screen to open and close it by using the Exposé & Spaces system preferences, as described in Chapter 21.

Managing widgets

To add other widgets to the Dashboard, click the large + icon at the bottom left of the Dashboard window to get a scrolling bar of the other available widgets. Just drag into the Dashboard window those widgets you want to display when you open the Dashboard. Or just open the widget by clicking it in the scrolling widget bar. Either way, the widgets appear in the window each time you open the Dashboard until you explicitly remove them. And you can drag any widget anywhere you want in the Dashboard window to arrange the widgets to your tastes.

You can remove any of these widgets from the Dashboard window by clicking the Close iconic button (the X icon) in the widget's upper-left corner. But these X icons appear only if the scrolling widget bar is visible, which means you need to have clicked the large + icon at the bottom left of the Dashboard window. Because any widget you open stays in the Dashboard window, that window can get cluttered very easily. So you'll occasionally have to open the scrolling widget bar so you can clean up the Dashboard window.

Note
To close the scrolling bar and display just the Dashboard window, click the large X that appears at the bottom left of the screen.

You can also use the Widgets widget to remove and add widgets. To access it, click either the Widgets iconic button in the scrolling widget bar or click the Manage Widgets button. (You can see the Widgets widget in the lower left of Figure 8.22.)

Widgets themselves often come with preference controls. Look for the **i** icon (the international symbol for information), usually in one corner of the widget's window, to open its preferences.

Using the widgets that come with Mac OS X

Mac OS X 10.6 Snow Leopard comes with 21 preinstalled widgets from Apple and other providers, covering a wide variety of functions, from information display to calculators.

FIGURE 8.22

The Dashboard is where you access widgets. Shown here are the four default widgets, plus the Widgets widget to manage widgets (at lower right) and the scrolling widget bar (at bottom).

Address Book

The Address Book widget enables you to quickly search the Address Book application. Type all or part of the name, and the widget will display the contact information for that person. You can also scroll through Address Book entries by using the arrow buttons that appear at the bottom of the widget, but only after you have found one entry through the search function.

Business

The Business widget is essentially a Yellow Pages search tool. It uses your ZIP code (which you provided when you registered your Mac) to search entries in the Directory Assistance business directory, and it also has categories of businesses you can choose if you don't have a specific business name you are searching for. If you click a result, the Directory Assistance Web page opens up in your browser with more details on that business. Note that this widget requires an active Internet connection to get the data it displays.

The Business widget can be awkward to use. For example, there's no easy way to navigate through large lists of results. And the category listings don't include many businesses that you can find if you type their name instead. You can customize the widget's search settings (ZIP code, distance away from that location to include in the results, and number of results to display per page) by clicking the preferences icon at the bottom left of the widget.

Calculator

The Calculator widget is a simple arithmetic calculator — not nearly as powerful as the Calculator application. If you need to use a calculator a lot, you'd do better to add the Calculator application to your Dock for easy access. (Chapter 2 explains how to manage the items in the Dock.)

Dictionary

The Dictionary widget works like the Dictionary application, except that it provides less information than the application does. It's great for a quick lookup, but no more. Note that you can use the popup menu or arrow icons at the top of the Dictionary widget to move among the Oxford New American dictionary, Apple dictionary, and thesaurus results for your search term; the Oxford dictionary results are displayed by default. (The Wikipedia and Japanese dictionaries available in the Dictionary application are not available in the widget.) Keep in mind that this widget requires an active Internet connection to get the data it displays.

ESPN

Use the ESPN widget to get the latest news and scores for the sport of your choice. The widget has a News tab and a Scores tab, which you switch between by using the News and Scores buttons. Clicking a headline opens the related story at the ESPN Web site in your browser. To choose which sport's information appears in the ESPN widget, use the widget's preferences. Note that this widget requires an active Internet connection to get the data it displays.

Flight Tracker

The Flight Tracker widget is a handy way to find out what flights are scheduled today between the cities of your choice and to track a specific flight's status. Figure 8.23 shows both the schedule and tracking views in the widget. First enter the origin and destination, plus the specific airline if you want, in the widget, then click Find Flights. A list appears at right; click the desired flight and then click Track Flights to see its status. Note that this widget requires an active Internet connection to get the data it displays.

FIGURE 8.23

The Flight Tracker widget is a handy way to search for flights (left) and track their status (right).

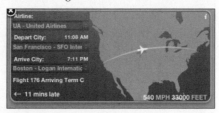

Google

The Google widget is very simple: Enter a search term and press Enter (or click the Search iconic button). A Google search page opens in your browser with the results. Note that this widget requires an active Internet connection to get the data it displays.

iCal

The iCal widget offers a very simple view of the information in the iCal application. It displays the current date and month, and enables you to move among months by using the arrow buttons at the top of the widget window. If you click the name of the month at the top of the widget, the widget displays the current month instead — a quick way to return to the current month.

If you click the big numeral at left for the current date (or the name of the day above it), a pane slides out listing calendar events for that date. If you click the date number again, the widget collapses so only the date is shown; one more click and the month view slides back out. Note that you cannot see the events for any day other than the current date.

iTunes

The iTunes widget does nothing other than open if the iTunes application is not running. But if iTunes is open, it provides quick controls to play, pause, rewind, and fast-forward your music, as well as to turn on shuffle and repeat play. Via the widget's preferences, you can select which playlist to play.

Movies

If you're looking for a theatrical movie to watch, this widget can help. Based on your city or ZIP code (which you enter in its preferences), it will show a list of all current movies playing, as well as at what theaters and at what times, as Figure 8.24 shows. If tickets can be bought online via Fandango, a button to buy them becomes available. You can watch the film's trailer, if available, by clicking Trailer. Note that when you first open the Movies widget, you get what appear to be poster-style ads for current movies. Click any poster to enter the widget and look up listings. Note that this widget requires an active Internet connection to get the data it displays.

People

The People widget enables you to search people in a White Papers-type utility. Note that you have to enter a city and state, and that it misses a lot of smaller cities in its database. Honestly, it does a poor job of finding people, so it's not one you'll likely use. Note that this widget requires an active Internet connection to get the data it displays.

Ski Resort

If you like to ski and want to know the conditions at your favorite resort, this is the widget for you. Enter your a ski resort name in the preferences, and the widget displays the snow and other conditions for that resort. Note that the widget displays major resorts but may not have details for smaller ski areas available. Also note that this widget requires an active Internet connection to get the data it displays.

FIGURE 8.24

The Movies widget enables you to see what movies are playing nearby, as well as at which theaters and at what times. You can also view a trailer and buy tickets in some cases.

Stickies

The Stickies widget works very much like the Stickies application, though all you can do is add text, choose the sticky note's color, and choose the note's font and size; there are none of the fancy options available in the Stickies application. The one potential caveat to the Stickies widget is that the notes appear only when the Dashboard window is open, so it's really useful only when you have widgets open.

Stocks

The Stocks widget enables you to quickly see how your favorite stocks, mutual funds, and stock indexes are doing, with the latest closing prices and a configurable graph for past performance for the selected stock, fund, or index, as Figure 8.25 shows. You can add and remove entries by using the widget's preferences, as well as set the stock price-change display to show as percentages rather than as dollars. (If you have an iPhone or iPod Touch, you'll instantly recognize this widget, which is almost identical on those devices as on the Mac.) Note that this widget requires an active Internet connection to get the data it displays.

Tile Game

The Tile Game widget displays a leopard image as a series of adjacent squares, or tiles, that it then scrambles. The game's objective is to figure out how to restore the image to the unscrambled version. Click inside the game to start the random scrambling and click it again to stop the scrambling. Then double-click a tile adjacent to the blank tile to move it into that blank tile's location. Keep moving tiles until you figure out the solution — or close the widget and reopen it to start again. (If you close the Dashboard but don't remove the Tile Game widget from the Dashboard screen, you can pick up the game where you left off.)

FIGURE 8.25

The Stocks widget tracks the performance of the stocks, mutual funds, and stock indexes.

Translation

The Translation widget does what you'd expect: translate words and phrases between the two languages you select by using the popup menus. The languages available for translation are Han (traditional) Chinese, Simplified Chinese, Dutch, English, French, German, Greek, Italian, Japanese, Korean, Portuguese, Russian, and Spanish. Note that this widget requires an active Internet connection to get the data it displays.

Enter the term to translate and press Enter; the result will appear. If you change the destination language, the new translation appears automatically. There's an iconic button to the left of the destination language that swaps the source and destination languages; this makes it easy to switch from, say, translating English to French to translating French to English.

Unit Converter

There are all sorts of measurement systems in place that vary from country to country or discipline to discipline. The Unit Converter widget makes it easy to convert among such measurement systems. In this simple widget, you choose the type of measurement you want to convert: Area, Currency, Energy, Length, Power, Pressure, Speed, Temperature, Time, Volume, and Weight. You'll get a popup menu for the "from" and "to" values within each of those categories, such as the currencies you want to convert if you choose Currency or the types of measurements such as inches, feet, and meters if you choose Length. Enter the "from" value and press Enter; the widget will display the result. Change the "to" value's measurement from its popup menu and the new value appears automatically. Figure 8.26 shows two examples. Note that for the currency conversions, this widget requires an active Internet connection to get the data it displays.

Weather

You can get a quick look at a six-day weather forecast by using the Weather widget. It will show the basic predictions (snow, rain, cloudy skies, and so on) using graphics, and the predicted high temperatures for each day. Through the widget's preferences, you can change the city whose weather you want to predictions for, as well as set the widget to also display the predicted low temperatures for each day. Note that this widget requires an active Internet connection to get the data it displays.

FIGURE 8.26

The Unit Converter widget converts measurements in 11 categories. Shown here are example currency (left) and power (right) conversions.

 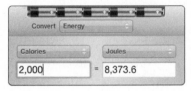

Web Clip

A Web clip is a widget created from part of a Web page. Launching this widget simply opens the Safari Web browser, where you can select and save the Web clip. (For more details, see the section in this chapter on adding widgets from other sources.)

Widgets

The Widgets widget enables you to manage what widgets display in the scrolling widgets bar. Simply deselect the widgets you don't want to display, or reselect them to make them visible again. If you added non-Apple widgets (described in the "Adding widgets from other sources" section of this chapter), you'll notice a red – symbol to the right of their names; clicking that icon deletes the widget not only from the Dashboard window but also from your Mac.

You can also use the Widgets widget to sort the widgets by name or date. And you can use it to go to the Apple Web site page, where you can download additional widgets via your browser: Just click More Widgets.

World Clock

The World Clock widget simply displays the current time at whatever location you choose in its preferences.

Adding widgets from other sources

You can have more widgets than what Apple provides with Mac OS X. Figure 8.27 shows two such widgets, one for the Fetch FTP utility and one created from a Web page.

FIGURE 8.27

Two example widgets that don't come from Apple: The Fetch FTP widget (left) and a Web clip of headlines from infoworld.com (right)

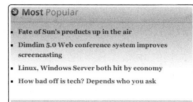

There are three ways to get additional widgets:

- **Download widgets from the Web.** An easy way to do so is to click More Widgets in the Widgets widget to open a page at the Apple Web site in your browser that lists third-party widgets you can download to your Mac. You can also get there by going to `www.apple.com/downloads/dashboard/`. You can also find such downloadable widgets at other Web sites, such as `www.google.com/macwidgets/` and `www.widgets.yahoo.com/download/`. Do a Web search for "Mac widgets" to find other sources. (If you download a widget with Apple's Safari browser, Safari asks if you want it to install the widget for you. If you use a different browser, double-click the downloaded file to begin installation.)

- **Install widgets automatically.** Some applications install widgets — either automatically or as an option — for quick access to some of their features. Intego's security software, for example, installs a dashboard widget so you can monitor the security of your system, such as antivirus status. And the Fetch FTP utility's installation gives you the option of installing a widget, as another example.

- **Create a Web clip.** In Safari, go to a Web page that has a component you want to use as a widget and choose File ➪ Open in Dashboard. You'll see a marquee that you can move over the part of page you want to turn into a widget, as Figure 8.28 shows. Click Add when done (the button appears near the top right of the Safari window). The Safari-based widget — called a Web clip — now appears in your Dashboard window and can be managed like any other widget.

FIGURE 8.28

To create a Web clip in Safari, you choose File ⇨ Open in Dashboard, then move the marquee over the part you want to turn into a widget, then click Add.

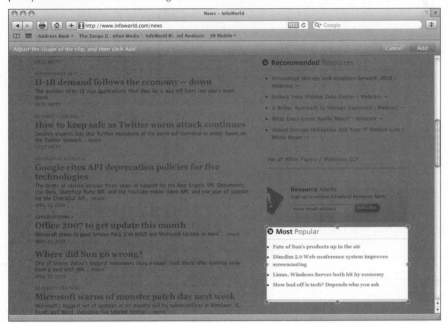

Summary

Mac OS X 10.6 Snow Leopard comes with dozens of applications, utilities, and widgets, each stored in different places. The distinction between applications and utilities is somewhat artificial; applications tend to be more complex and used for purposes beyond managing the Mac itself.

Widgets have very specific functionality, and, therefore, are less capable than applications and utilities; furthermore, they are available only from the Dashboard. When you are using widgets, you cannot also use applications and utilities at the same time; instead you must close the Dashboard to use applications and utilities. A special type of widget, called a Web clip, is a snippet from a Web page that you can create by using the Safari browser.

In addition to the applications, utilities, and widgets that come with Mac OS X, you can add your own, typically by buying them (though some are free).

Playing Music and Videos

W ho needs a CD player, radio, DVD player, or TV when you have a Mac? The Mac OS's capability to become an entertainment center is simply amazing, thanks to its support of audio and video formats and to the iTunes and DVD Player software that come with the Mac. Sure, you'll likely still have a traditional home entertainment center in your living room, but your Mac can handle the job in the other rooms of your house — and in dorm rooms, small apartments, and other quarters, it can be your home entertainment center if you attach a large-enough monitor and good speakers to it.

Everyone knows that Apple revolutionized the music industry with its iPod. But it's actually iTunes that makes the iPod revolution possible. iTunes is not just the Mac's built-in music player but also its built-in radio and podcast player. It's also your direct connection to buying music, TV shows, and movies that you play back on your Mac. Plus it enables you to manage all your media for both your Mac and your iPod. Oh, and if you have an iPhone or iPod Touch, it also acts as the gateway for keeping your calendars, e-mail, and mobile applications in order.

Before we get into the details of music and video on your Mac, there are a few things you need to remember:

- **The MP3 format is the most common format for music on computers, and many programs can play this format, including iTunes and the Safari browser.** Other music formats that iTunes supports include AAC (Advanced Audio Coding; also called MP4 audio), AIFF (Audio Interchange File Format), Apple Lossless, Audible audiobook, and WAV (the name comes from the `.wav` filename extension Microsoft used for its Windows audio format). The AAC format gives you the highest quality, so it's the best to use for music you import from your music CDs into iTunes.

- **The MPEG-4 (MP4) format is the most common format for video on computers, and iTunes, Safari, and other applications that come with Mac OS X 10.6 Snow Leopard can handle it.** But there are many other formats you may encounter, including Silverlight, Flash (.flv), Windows Movie (.wma and .wmv), and QuickTime Movie (.mov). iTunes can play MPEG-4 and QuickTime Movie formats. To play the other formats, you need a separate playback utility or a plug-in for your browser. When you try to play such files in your browser, you usually get a prompt asking if you want to download the associated helper file, which you should do. For Windows Movie files, you'll need the free Flip4Mac (www.telestream.net).

- **Apple updates iTunes on a different schedule than it updates Mac OS X, so the version of iTunes running on your Mac when you read this may be newer than the 8.2 version that Mac OS X 10.6 Snow Leopard initially included.** You may see new capabilities or interface changes in your version of iTunes compared to what this chapter describes.

- **Don't steal music or videos.** It's perfectly legal to import the CDs you bought into iTunes for playback on your Mac and iPod. It's perfectly legal to buy music and videos from the iTunes Store and other online music and video sites. It's *not* legal to copy music, videos, or other media from your friends' CDs, unlicensed sharing sites such as BitTorrent, or from commercial DVDs by using extraction software such as Mac the Ripper — when you get such "free" media, you're taking money away from the people who make this stuff, which makes it harder for them to make more.

Using iTunes As Your Music Library

iTunes is your Mac's music hub, the application that you use to manage and play your music. You'll spend a lot of time in iTunes, which works best if you also have an Internet connection so you can buy music and get album covers that display in your iTunes music library.

Setting music preferences

The first thing to do on a new Mac is set up iTunes' music preferences. (If you're upgrading your Mac OS to 10.6 Snow Leopard, your previous iTunes settings are retained.)

Import settings

Start by choosing iTunes ⇨ Preferences or pressing ⌘+, (comma) and then going to the General pane. Here you tell iTunes how to import music files from your music CDs. Use the When You Insert a CD popup menu to control iTunes' behavior when you insert a music CD into your Mac. The options are Show CD, Begin Playing, Ask to Import CD (the default), Import CD, and Import CD and Eject. Show CD simply displays the CD in the left pane of iTunes but does nothing with it. Begin Playing plays the CD automatically, which can be handy if you want to listen to a friend's CD without making an illegal copy.

Tip

If you're loading your music collection into your Mac, choose the Import CD and Eject option from the When You Insert a CD popup menu to make the import process simple and fast: As you insert a CD, iTunes automatically imports the songs and then ejects the CD when done so you know it's time to pop in another. After you have your music collection on your Mac, change the option to either Ask to Import CD (so if you insert a new CD you're asked whether to add its music to the library or just to make it available for play in iTunes as long as it is inserted in your Mac) or Show CD (so nothing happens, under the assumption you don't want to import it or play it, as you already have the music on your Mac).

Before you begin importing music files, it's critical to set your desired audio conversion settings, which you do by clicking Import Settings in the General pane of the Preferences dialog box. The default settings are the best for music CDs: AAC Encoder as the Import Using option and iTunes Plus as its Setting option. This option imports your music in the high-quality AAC file format, which both iTunes and the iPod and iPhone can handle, but AAC-format music files won't play on many MP3 players or on the Web. So if your music is destined for the Web or non-Apple music players, choose MP3 in the Import Using popup menu and 192 Kbps in the Setting menu (to get the highest quality available to MP3). The other options are only useful in special circumstances, such as choosing the WAV format for use in a Windows music player (though most can also handle MP3).

In the Playback pane (shown in Figure 9.1), you can control how iTunes plays music:

- **Select Crossfade Songs and choose a crossfade duration from the slider to get that deejay effect of overlapping music, with a new song fading in as another ends and fades out.**

- **Select Sound Enhancer and adjust the slider to boost the volume of both the treble and bass (or lower them) across all songs.** Use this setting to compensate for weak or overly strong speakers.

- **Select Sound Check to have iTunes control the volume of songs so they all play at the same level of loudness.** This helps get rid of variations in the recordings, but note that it can make intentionally quiet songs play too loudly and intentionally noisy songs play too softly.

Tip

To make iTunes the default audio player for audio you open in your Web browser, go to the Advanced pane of the Preferences dialog box and click the Set button that appears to the left of Use iTunes for Internet Playback.

Sharing settings

iTunes can access music and other media on other Macs and Windows PCs, as well as make your Mac's music accessible to others, as long as all the computers are on the same network and using iTunes. Use the Sharing pane to control what is shared. Selected by default, the Look for Shared Libraries option scans the network for other iTunes libraries. Any detected appear in the Library list in the Sidebar at the left side of the iTunes window.

FIGURE 9.1

The Playback pane of iTunes' Preferences dialog box

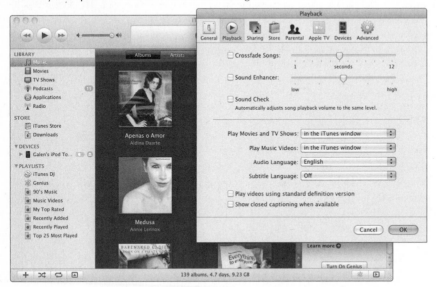

If you want to share your music and other media, select the Share My Library on My Local Network option, then choose either Share Entire Library or Shared Selected Playlists (and then select from the list the types of Media — Music, Podcasts, Movies, and/or TV Shows — plus any specific music playlists you want to share). You can require a password for someone to access your library by selecting Require Password and entering the password in the adjacent text field. (This is handy if you use a wireless network and don't want outsiders tapping into it to access your library, or if visitors are connected to your wired network.)

Parental settings

There's a lot of media content you may not want your kids to access, perhaps because of obscene language or sexual content. iTunes enables you to apply parental controls to the media it presents; go to the Parental pane in the Preferences dialog box.

In the Disable section, choose which media sources you want to block access to. Choices include Podcasts, Radio, iTunes Store, and Shared Libraries.

After choosing your country's ratings system in the Ratings For popup menu, in the iTunes Store section, select what kind of ratings you want to limit iTunes Store purchases to. Choices include movies, TV shows, and games. There's also the Restrict Explicit Content option that applies to all media types.

To keep your kids from overriding your iTunes parental controls, click the lock iconic button at the lower left of the Parental pane and enter your password. (See Chapter 20 for more details on setting up user accounts, passwords, and parental controls.)

Importing music files

For iTunes to be your music hub, it needs to have music. There are two ways to get music files into iTunes, in addition to getting them from an online music store:

- **If you already have music files on your Mac or in a computer-friendly format such as MP3 on a disk, choose File ➪ Add to Library or press ⌘+O, then select the disk or folder that contains the music files.** iTunes copies them to its music library folder. (Music in any subfolders is copied as well, as are any iTunes-supported media such as images and video files.)

- **If your music is on a music CD (or DVD), insert the disc into your Mac.** Depending on the option you chose in the When You Insert a CD popup menu in the General pane of the iTunes Preferences dialog box, iTunes may automatically import the disc's music, ask you if you want to import the music, play the disc, or just display its contents. If iTunes simply plays the disc or displays its contents, you can import the music by clicking Import CD at the bottom right of the iTunes window, as Figure 9.2 shows. (Note how iTunes displays the disc's contents; if it does not, click the disc's name in the left pane of the iTunes window, in the Devices list.)

That's all there is to it!

FIGURE 9.2

The contents of a CD we are about to import the music from

Buying music online

Apple was the first independent company to get the recording industry to agree to legal online sales, and its iTunes Store has become one of the world's biggest sellers of music online. It's easy to get music from iTunes Store: Click iTunes Store in the Sidebar at the left side of the iTunes window and then browse the store's offerings by genre or artist, or search by artist, album, or song. As Figure 9.3 shows, you can buy whole albums or individual songs.

Tip

To listen to a song in the iTunes Store before you buy it or the album, just double-click the song.

If you're not signed in to the iTunes Store, you are asked to do so before you can actually buy the music. You can also sign in by clicking Sign In in the iTunes Store or choosing Store ⇨ Sign In in the iTunes program. (If you don't have an account, you can create one in the sign-in window that appears.) After you sign into the iTunes Store, iTunes remembers your sign-in information and signs in automatically each time you use it. To sign out (perhaps you're using a friend's computer or don't want your kids charging music against your credit card), choose Store ⇨ Sign Out.

Note that the music you buy from the iTunes Store can be kept on as many computers as you like. But until late 2008, you were limited to keeping copies of music files on up to five computers (Macs and Windows PCs) for playback. (That five-computer limit still applies to all video and apps.) Any music files bought when Apple restricted playback to five computers remains limited to five computers unless you paid in iTunes to upgrade them to unlimited usage. Thus, to play such music (as well as to access videos and apps downloaded from the iTunes Store), you need to authorize each computer to your iTunes Store account by choosing Store ⇨ Authorize Computer and entering the sign-in information. To disable a computer for the playback of pre-late 2008 music (and video and apps) bought with your iTunes sign-in, choose Store ⇨ Deauthorize Computer. (An iPod or iPhone doesn't count as a computer, since an iPod's or iPhone's music library is "tied" to a specific computer's library and can sync only to that one library.)

Of course, iTunes Store is not the only source of online music. You can buy music from other venues, such as Amazon.com. These online stores typically download an MP3 file to your Mac, perhaps even into your iTunes library. As far as iTunes is concerned, the music you bought from them is the same as if you imported it from a CD.

Tip

In grid view, you can switch between album, artist, genre, and composer views by using the buttons at the top of the iTunes window. If more than one album matches an artist, genre, or composer, slide your mouse sideways within the icon to see the various albums that match. To get a detailed view of the results in grid view, just double-click an album cover for album, composer, and artist views, and the genre icon for the genre view to get all the matching songs, arranged by album. Also, you can adjust the size of album covers in grid view by using the slider at the upper right of the window.

FIGURE 9.3

Searching for music on the iTunes Store

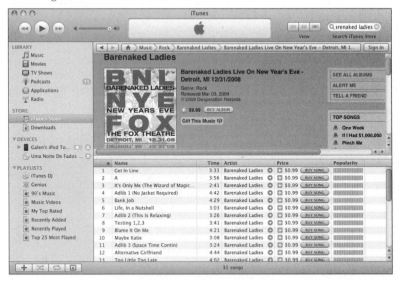

Managing your music

When you import or buy music, iTunes automatically organizes it by the artist and album; if you have an Internet connection, it can look up the related information. If you have an iTunes Store account, it also downloads the album artwork automatically for music you import from disc. (Choose Advanced ➪ Get Album Artwork to retrieve the album covers for music you've imported from CDs or other sources outside the iTunes Store if you see that some album covers are blank.)

Controlling music display

You can easily peruse your music by using iTunes' three view modes: List, Grid, and Cover Flow; using the iconic View buttons near the top of the iTunes window; or by choosing View ➪ As List, View ➪ As Grid, or View ➪ As Cover Flow. Figure 9.4 shows the three views.

Note in the various views that display songs the check boxes to the left of each song title. Any song that is selected will play if you play that album, and any selected song will be synchronized to your iPod or iPhone if you select Sync Only Checked Songs and Videos in the Summary pane for a selected device, as Figure 9.5 shows.

iTunes' Iconic Controls

Many of iTunes' controls are available as iconic buttons. The figure below shows what they do.

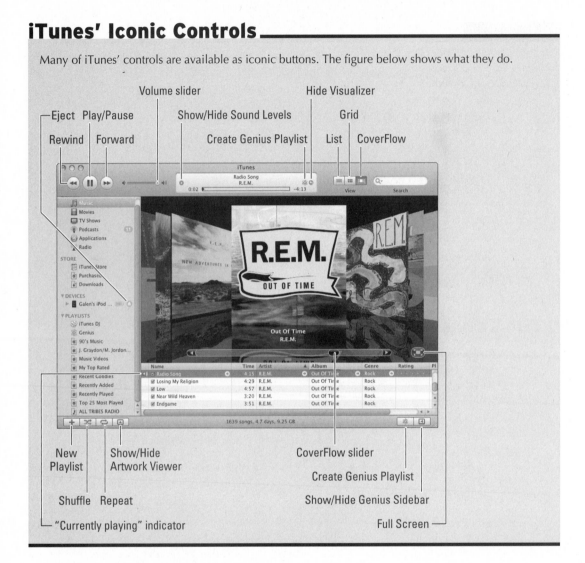

Volume slider

Hide Visualizer

Eject Play/Pause

Show/Hide Sound Levels

Grid

Rewind Forward

Create Genius Playlist

List CoverFlow

New Playlist

Show/Hide Artwork Viewer

CoverFlow slider

Create Genius Playlist

Shuffle Repeat

Show/Hide Genius Sidebar

"Currently playing" indicator

Full Screen

Syncing with iPods and iPhones

When you connect an iPod or iPhone to your Mac and open iTunes, the device shows in the Devices list in the Sidebar at the left of the iTunes window, as you can see in Figure 9.5. If you select a device and click Sync, iTunes copies all music and other iTunes media supported by that device to the device, as well as removes from that device any media files that had been removed from iTunes. This is how you keep your iPod or iPhone updated on your music and other media files. But a device can be associated to only one copy of iTunes (to prevent media piracy). So if iTunes doesn't recognize an iPod or iPhone, it will ask if you want to replace all its contents with the contents of the iTunes library — thus, if you connect your iPod to a friend's Mac and say yes, you will lose all the contents of your iPod and have it replaced with your friend's iTunes library.

FIGURE 9.4

iTunes' music view modes: The Cover Flow view (top left) enables you to scroll through your albums, list view (top right) shows songs in lists sortable by the column headers, and grid view (bottom left) shows album covers side by side. In grid view, double-click an album to get this view of its songs (bottom right).

Note

To prevent music (and videos) from syncing to your iPod or iPhone, select Manually Manage Music and Videos in the Summary pane for the selected device. When you sync the device, no music, podcasts, or video files will be copied or removed to reflect the current state of the iTunes library. You might use this when updating your iPod on a friend's computer to get, say, an iPod software update but not have your music and videos replaced. This can be handy if you are on vacation or otherwise away from your Mac for a long time. You might also use it to sync your iPhone or iPod Touch to a work computer to keep your calendar and other data (in the Info pane) synced without losing your music and video in the process. But note that any applications for an iPhone or iPod Touch are deleted from the device when synced via a "foreign" iTunes — there is no manual management option for applications in the version of iTunes that initially shipped with Mac OS X.

The Summary pane is not the only pane that controls what is synced to your iPod or iPhone. Other panes will appear based on your device's capabilities, with options to determine what exactly is synced. (Your settings are retained until you change them.) The panes can include any of the following: Music, Movies, TV Shows, Podcasts, Photos, Info, and Applications. When connected, all iPods show the Music and Podcasts panes in iTunes. When connected, video-capable iPods show the Movies, TV Shows, and Photos panes. The Info and Applications panes display only if an iPhone or iPod Touch is connected.

Tip

If you bought music on your iPhone or iPod and want to transfer it to an authorized computer, do so by choosing File ⇨ Transfer Purchases from "devicename".

FIGURE 9.5

The Options section in the Summary pane for a selected device enables you to control how music is synchronized to an iPod or iPhone.

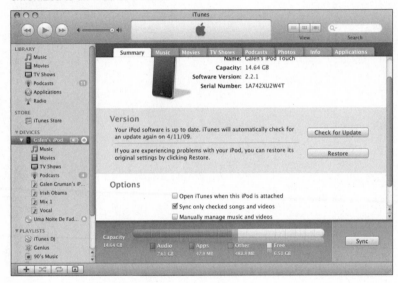

Working with playlists

A *playlist* is simply a collection of songs — like a mix tape. There are two kinds of playlists in iTunes: regular playlists and smart playlists.

A regular playlist contains whatever songs you add to it. To create the playlist, click the + iconic button at the bottom left of the iTunes window, choose File ⇨ New Playlist or press ⌘+N. The center part of the iTunes window shows an empty list, and an untitled playlist name appears at the bottom of the Playlist group at the left of the iTunes window. Click the untitled playlist name so you can name it something meaningful. Then click Music from the left side of the iTunes window to display your music. Drag the songs you want added to your playlist to the playlist's name. If you click the playlist name, you'll see all the songs in it. You can drag them within the list to control the order in which they play.

A smart playlist is built on rules, so its contents change automatically based on those rules. For example, you might create a rule that says to include only music added to iTunes in the last 60 days that is not part of a compilation album, and that is rated at least three stars. Thus, you get a playlist of your current favorites that stays automatically updated as you add music and as you rate the music you have.

To create such a smart playlist, choose File ➪ New Smart Playlist or press Option+⌘+N. You get the dialog box shown in Figure 9.6, in which you add the rules and their parameters. (The rules in Figure 9.6 create the "current favorites" playlist described previously.) After you click OK to save the playlist, it appears in the Playlist group; click its name to rename it if desired.

Note

Smart playlists are indicated by a purple page icon with a gear in it, while regular playlists are indicated with a blue page icon with a musical note in it.

Tip

You can create a CD of a selected playlist by clicking Burn Disc (at the bottom right of the iTunes window) or by Control+clicking or right-clicking the playlist name and choosing Burn Playlist to Disc.

FIGURE 9.6

Creating a smart playlist

Working with Genius

In 2008, Apple introduced a feature called Genius to iTunes that categorizes music by how it sounds and then can group music accordingly. Primarily meant as a way for Apple to recommend additional music you may want to buy, Genius can also be used to select music for playback — think of it as a playlist based on how the music actually sounds. For example, if you are throwing a dance party, you would select one or more dance songs in your library and then turn on Genius so iTunes plays only similar dance songs, regardless of their genre, album, or artist. Of course, this feature can lead to a monotonous selection (because it's designed to find music that sounds similar to your selection), so you probably won't want to leave it on as your regular listening mode.

To turn on Genius, choose Store ⇨ Turn on Genius. You need to sign in to your iTunes Store account or create one. Genius then goes through all your music and builds "sounds like" profiles for each song, then matches those profiles against the music in the iTunes Store — a process than can take quite some time when you first turn on Genius. (The Genius Sidebar — turn it on and off by choosing View ⇨ Show/Hide Genius Sidebar or by pressing Shift+⌘+G — displays the songs that iTunes recommends you buy that are similar to your currently selected song.)

After Genius has processed all your music, you can tell Genius to automatically create smart play-lists. Just select the song you want to use as the "sounds like" master, then click the Genius iconic button (the atom icon) at the bottom right of the iTunes window. If you click the Genius smart playlist in the Sidebar at the left side of the iTunes window, you can hear the songs Genius has decided are a good acoustical match.

Rating music

If you look at your songs in list view, you'll see a Rating column. By default, songs have no ratings, but you can assign your own ratings to them on a scale of zero to five stars. Click a song and then choose File ⇨ Rating and then the number of stars to assign. You can now sort your songs in list view by rating, which enables you to play music based on your rating — chances are, you'll use this to easily select and play just your top-rated music.

Playing your music

Playing music is easy in iTunes. Select Music from the Library list in the Sidebar at the left of the iTunes window, then select the album, artist, composer, genre, or composer by using the View controls described earlier in this section to choose what you want to play.

Tip

You can select multiple albums, composers, genres, or songs for playback by ⌘+clicking individual selections or Shift+selecting a range.

You can narrow down your musical selections by using the iTunes browser; choose View ⇨ Show Browser or press ⌘+B to open the view shown in Figure 9.7, where you can narrow your choices by genre, artist, and then album.

Tip

To quickly find music in iTunes, you can enter a term in the Search box at the upper right of the iTunes window and press Return or click the Search iconic button (the magnifying glass icon).

Music plays in the order displayed, so if you use list view you can control the order of play by title, artist, album, genre, or rating.

Or you can choose a playlist from the Playlists list at the bottom-left side of the iTunes window.

Note

If you select no music, iTunes plays your entire library.

FIGURE 9.7

The iTunes browser enables you to narrow your song (and other media) choices.

After you've selected your music, click the Play iconic button at the upper left of the iTunes window to play the music. (Or, for a single song, just double-click it.) You can use the Rewind and Forward iconic buttons to move back and forth among your song selections. Information about the currently playing song appears at the top of the iTunes window.

Note

There's a volume slider near the Play iconic button that controls how loudly iTunes plays the music. But this control does not change the Mac's overall volume; you control that by using the volume slider in the menu bar or by using the Sound system preference (see Chapter 21). So, if the Mac's volume is set to halfway, putting iTunes' volume slider to maximum means that iTunes will play songs at that halfway point (that is, at the maximum level set for the Mac). The reason iTunes has a separate volume control is so you can adjust the volume based on the music you're playing relative to the Mac's overall sound volume.

Just like a stereo, iTunes also has controls that enable you to mix it up a bit. Click the Shuffle iconic button (it looks like two crossed arrows) at the bottom left of the iTunes window to play the selected music in random order. Click it again to play music in the order of the tracks in the original album. (If the button's icon is black, shuffling is off; if it is blue, shuffling is on.) You can also choose Control ⇨ Shuffle to more precisely control how the shuffling occurs by using the submenu options By Song, By Album, and By Group.

You can also click the Repeat iconic button (its icon is made of two arrows forming a loop) to play the selected items over and over again in a loop. (If the button's icon is black, Repeat is not on; if it is blue, Repeat is on. If it is blue and the numeral 1 appears in the lower-left corner, Repeat plays your selection twice — that is, repeats it once — and then stops playing.) The same controls are available by choosing Control ⇨ Repeat.

Note

You can also play music in a variety of file formats by using the QuickTime Player application that comes with Mac OS X; choose File ➪ Open or press ⌘+O to select the desired music file. However, you can open and play only one song at a time. Also, you can listen to MP3 files in your Web browser from a Web page that provides a link to the file — a handy way to listen to music or podcasts provided on the Web site. (You can't open an MP3 file on your Mac for playback in your browser.)

Using iTunes for Podcasts

At its core, a podcast is simply an audio file. Typically, a podcast is a lot like an episode of a radio program — a newscast, an interview, advice, a deejay's current faves, a comedy routine, and so on — that you listen to on your iPod, iPhone, or Mac. Typically, a podcast is part of a series that you subscribe to. Lots of radio programs, for example, are now available as podcasts, so you can listen to them at your convenience. And many Web sites offer their own podcasts, often the equivalent of audiobooks for their textual content.

iTunes enables you to access and play podcasts, as well as synchronize them to your iPod or iPhone. To access podcasts, click the Podcasts option in the Sidebar at the left of the iTunes window. A window with any podcast subscriptions appears. To add podcast subscriptions, click Podcast Directory to open the iTunes Store and peruse its list of podcasts. (They are usually free.) You can also add podcasts to iTunes directly at many Web sites. Look for a Subscribe or iTunes button; clicking these buttons typically adds the podcasts to your iTunes podcast list with no further ado.

After you have a subscription set up, an icon for it appears in the main part of the iTunes window whenever you click Podcasts. Double-click the icon to see all the individual podcast episodes available, as Figure 9.8 shows. As with songs, you can select and deselect them, play them, and delete them. (If you downloaded an individual podcast to iTunes and want to subscribe to the whole series, just click the Subscribe button.)

You can also manage the subscription by clicking Settings, which opens the dialog box shown at the bottom of Figure 9.8. Here, you can set how many episodes are kept, how often iTunes checks for new episodes, and which episodes iTunes should download.

Tip

If you have the URL for a podcast subscription, a quick way to subscribe to the podcast is to choose Advanced ➪ Subscribe to Podcast, paste the URL into the Subscribe to Podcast dialog box that appears, and click OK.

FIGURE 9.8

The episodes available for a subscribed podcast, plus (at the bottom of the window) the subscription management controls

Listening to Internet Radio

The Web and iPods may well kill radio — who needs to listen to the endless blather and commercials on most stations, anyhow? — but it also may reinvent radio. That's because radio itself is moving to the Web. Podcasts are one example of how radio is adapting to the Web and to the iPod. But radio is also available in its "live" form as streaming audio — instead of its signal coming to you over the radio, it comes to you over the Internet.

In the Sidebar at the left side of the iTunes window, click Radio to get a list of genres. Click the disclosure triangle to the left of a genre to get a list of available streams. Now double-click the desired stream to hear what is currently playing. Just like radio!)

Tip

Drag a stream to the Playlists list in iTunes' Sidebar to add a shortcut to it, for easy access later.

Of course, you don't need iTunes to listen to Internet radio. You can go to any Internet radio "station" in your Web browser and listen to its stream through the browser. Many regular radio stations offer such audio streams from their Web sites (look for a link with a name like "Listen Now" or "Internet Radio" or "Streaming Audio"); as an example, check out `www.kqed.org/radio/listen/`. If you're into college radio's eclectic programming, you'll be pleased by the wealth of college radio stations available as audio streams. Plus some organizations have created their only-on-the-Web radio "stations," such as Shoutcast.com and AOL Radio.

Tip

If you have the URL for an Internet radio "station," a quick way to listen to it in iTunes is to choose Advanced ⇨ Open Audio Stream or press ⌘+U, paste the URL into the Open Audio Stream dialog box that appears, and click OK.

Using iTunes for TV Shows and Movies

iTunes plays a lot more than audio. It can display video as well, such as TV shows and movies in the MPEG-4 format that you download to your Mac or create on it by using tools such as Apple's iMovie. The process for managing and watching video in iTunes is very much like that for music files, as covered earlier in this chapter.

Setting video preferences

There's very little in the way of preferences that you need to set for playing back video. In the Preference dialog box's Playback pane (see Figure 9.1 earlier in this chapter), you can control video playback:

- Use the Play Movies and TV Shows popup menu to determine where TV and movie videos play: in Artwork Viewer, in the iTunes Window, in a Separate Window, Full Screen, or Full Screen (With Visuals). Note that the artwork viewer is the small preview box at the bottom of the iTunes window's Sidebar; you need to click the Show Artwork Preview iconic button — the up-facing-triangle-in-a-box icon — to see the preview box. Also note that the Full Screen (With Visuals) option displays animated graphics when you're playing music; it can be fun at a party where your Mac is being used as your stereo.

- Use the Play Music Videos popup menu to determine where music videos play. The options are the same as for the Play Movies and TV Shows popup menu.

- Use the Audio Language popup menu to choose the default language for your videos. Note that this option has an effect only if the videos support multiple language audio tracks and if the video has the audio track in the language chosen here. (If it does not, iTunes plays the audio in the language that matches the Mac OS X's default language, as set in the Language & Text system preference covered in Chapter 21.)

- Use the Subtitle Language to choose the default language for the subtitles in your videos (typically available in foreign-language videos). As with the Audio Language popup menu, iTunes uses Mac OS X's default language if the video's subtitles are not available in the language chosen here.

- Select the Play Videos Using Standard Definition Version if you want iTunes to play the standard (SD) video instead of the high-definition (HD) video in a file that has both formats. You might choose this if your Mac has a small screen that can't benefit from the extra detail of HD video.

- Select the Show Closed Captioning When Available option to have iTunes display closed captions — the subtitles meant to help the hearing impaired — for videos that have them (not many do).

Importing and buying videos

If you have MPEG-4 (.mp4) video files available — perhaps home movies you created in iMovie or videos downloaded from the Web — choose File⇨Add to Library or press ⌘+O, then select the disk or folder that contains the video files. iTunes copies them to its video library folder.

You can also buy movies and TV shows from the iTunes Store — it works the same way as buying music and podcasts, as described earlier in this chapter. Note that the video files purchased from iTunes have the filename extension .m4v.

In both cases, the videos appear in the central iTunes window if you click TV Shows or Movies (as appropriate) from the Library list at the left of the iTunes window.

Note

Apple restricts playback of videos bought or rented through the iTunes Store to five computers: the one you downloaded it to plus four others of your choice. To choose other computers, you need to authorize each computer to your iTunes Store account by choosing Store⇨Authorize Computer and entering the sign-in information. To disable a computer, choose Store⇨Deauthorize Computer. (An iPod or iPhone doesn't count as a computer, because an iPod's or iPhone's video library is "tied" to a specific computer's library and can sync only to that one library.)

Managing your videos

iTunes provides few management controls for videos. Just as with music files, you can change the view to help you peruse them via the three view modes — List, Grid, and Cover Flow — using the View iconic buttons near the top of the iTunes window or by Choosing View⇨As List, View⇨As Grid, or View⇨As Cover Flow.

Watching Videos with DVD Player

iTunes can't play video DVDs as it can music CDs. But DVD Player can play DVDs. If you insert a DVD into your Mac, DVD Player automatically begins playing it full screen. Press Esc to get to the menu bar and other controls. (You can set DVD Player to *not* play a DVD automatically by deselecting Start Playing Disc in the Preferences dialog box: Choose DVD Player⇨Preferences or press ⌘+, [comma].)

The player offers iconic controls over playback (such as Rewind, Forward, Play, Pause, and Stop, plus volume settings, chapter navigation, playback speed, and closed captioning) in a control designed to look like the kind of remote control (shown here) that came with your physical DVD player. You can also control DVD Player by using the menu bar's various menu options; the menu bar includes a few more options than the virtual remote control, such as the capability to set the playback window size.

Do note that DVD Player does not play Blu-ray or HD DVDs, even if you connect a compatible drive to your Mac — at least not in the initial version of Mac OS X 10.6 Snow Leopard.

You can also use the iTunes browser (choose View⇨Show Browser or press ⌘+B) to select your videos based on genre, show, and season.

You also can control whether videos are synced to a connected iPhone or video-capable iPod by selecting Manually Manage Music and Videos in the Summary pane for the selected device. As with music, videos are synced to iPhones and video-capable iPods when you sync unless the Manually Manage Music and Videos option is selected.

But iTunes' other management capabilities for music — playlists, ratings, and Genius — are not available for videos.

Playing your videos

As with songs and podcasts, the easiest way to play an individual video in iTunes is to double-click it. Or select the videos to watch and click the Play iconic button. The other playback controls such as Rewind and Forward are also available via iconic buttons. However, you cannot set videos to shuffle or repeat, as you can for music.

Tip
To watch a video in full screen — even if that's not the playback preference you set in the Preference dialog box's Playback pane — click the Full Screen iconic button at the center right of the iTunes window.

Using iTunes with the iPhone and iPod Touch

Although iTunes is generally designed for managing and playing music and videos, it also acts as the central manager for other information in the iPhone and iPod Touch: e-mail accounts, calendars, contacts, and Safari bookmarks, as well as for any mobile applications on your iPhone or iPod Touch. (Of course, the controls for music, podcast, video, and photo syncing available to other iPods work the same way with the iPhone and iPod Touch.)

When you connect an iPhone or iPod Touch to your Mac and select the device from the Devices list in the Sidebar at the left side of the iTunes window, the Summary pane appears. You also see a list of tabs for other panes. The Info pane controls how iTunes manages information on your iPhone or iPod Touch when you sync. Figure 9.9 shows the Info pane.

The Info pane offers the following sets of controls:

- **Contacts.** Select the Address Book Contacts option and then select either All Contacts or Selected Groups so the contacts in your Mac's Address Book and in the iPhone's or iPod Touch's Address Book remain synchronized. The Put New Contacts Create on the iPod into This Group option, if selected, puts any contacts added on the iPhone or iPod Touch into the group you specify in the adjacent popup menu. You might use this option to separately track contacts you enter when using your mobile device. Also, you can have iTunes sync Yahoo and Google contacts to your iPhone or iPod Touch by selecting the desired service and clicking Configure to set up the specific mappings.

- **Calendars.** Select the Sync iCal Calendars option and then select either All Calendars or Selected Calendars so the appointments in your Mac's iCal and in the iPhone's or iPod Touch's Calendar are kept synchronized. (Note that if you use Microsoft Exchange's calendar and want it to be synchronized to your iPhone or iPod Touch, you need to create a calendar in iCal called Entourage.) You also have the option of limiting calendar syncing to appointments by selecting Do Not Sync Events Older Than __ Days and then entering the number of past days you want to limit syncing to.

- **Web Browser.** There's just one option in this section: Sync Safari Bookmarks. If selected, the bookmarks in your Mac's Safari browser remain synced with those in your iPhone's or iPod Touch's Safari browser.

- **Mail Accounts.** To sync your mailboxes' account information in Apple's Mail application — not the e-mails themselves but the connection and other settings — with the iPhone's or iPod Touch's Mail application, select the Sync Selected Mail Accounts and then select the accounts you want to keep synchronized (if you have more than one account set up in Mail).

- **Advanced.** If you want to clear information from your iPhone or iPod Touch and replace it with the information from your Mac, select the desired option in this section: Contacts, Calendars, Bookmarks, and/or Mail Accounts. The next time you sync, iTunes deletes the specified information from your iPhone or iPod Touch and replaces it with the information on your Mac, rather than synchronizes the two. Note that these options are automatically deselected after you sync, so regular syncing resumes for later syncs.

FIGURE 9.9

The Info pane that controls syncing with iPhones and iPod Touches

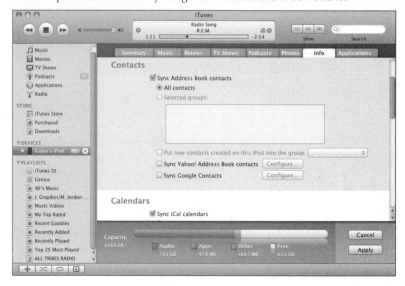

The Summary pane shows an additional option if your iPhone or iPod Touch runs the version 3 iPhone OS: Encrypt iPod Backup. If selected, this option secures the backup of your device on your Mac using encryption, so if someone gains access to your Mac, he or she cannot read the contents of the backed-up data. Click the adjacent Change Password button to set the password needed to decrypt the backup file.

Cross-Ref

For more on using iCal, Address Book, and Mail, see Chapter 11. For details on the MobileMe service that can also synchronize to iPhones and iPod Touches outside of iTunes, see Chapter 15.

Caution

If your iPhone or iPod Touch has applications previously synced to another copy of iTunes, such as on a different Mac, all the applications on your iPhone or iPod Touch are deleted and replaced with just the ones in the current copy of iTunes — just as when you sync music and videos from a "foreign" iTunes.

There's another iTunes pane specific to iPhones and iPod Touches: Applications. This keeps a list of the mobile applications you've synced to iTunes. If you select the Sync Applications option, iTunes updates your iPhone or iPod Touch with the ones stored on your Mac. You can sync all applications or selected ones; if you select specific applications to sync, only those are kept up-to-date on both your Mac and the mobile device.

You can manage your mobile applications in iTunes by clicking Applications in the Library list in the iTunes Sidebar. As Figure 9.10 shows, a grid of installed mobile applications appears. (There is no list or Cover Flow view available for mobile applications.) You can check to see if any of the applications have updates available by clicking Check for Updates; if iTunes has detected available updates, the option changes to *x* Updates Available. Either way, clicking it opens the iTunes Store, shown in Figure 9.11, from which you can choose which application updates to update. The next time you sync the iPhone or iPod Touch, the updated application is transferred to it.

Note

An iPhone or iPod Touch can also detect application updates when connected to the Internet via a 3G or Wi-Fi wireless connection, and you can install the updates wirelessly from the device. If you do, the next time you sync the device to iTunes, the update is copied over to iTunes so it remains updated as well.

The Preference dialog box's Devices pane has two iPhone- and iPod Touch-specific controls:

- **Disable Automatic Syncing for iPhones and iPods.** Normally, when you sync an iPhone or iPod Touch to your Mac, iTunes backs up any applications, calendar entries, and other data on the device as a safety measure. But this can slow down your syncing considerably. Select this option to disable the automatic backups. (A list of the most recent backup for each device you sync appears in above this option. You can select a backup and click Delete to get rid of it.) If you do disable automatic backup, Control+click or right-click your device in iTunes's Sidebar and choose Backup from the contextual menu to manually back it up — we recommend you do so occasionally as a safety measure.

- **Look for iPhone and iPod Touch Remotes.** If your device has the Remote application installed, it can control iTunes wirelessly, essentially turning your iPhone or iPod Touch into a remote control for your Mac's iTunes. Deselect this option to prevent that remote control capability (so, for example, party guests can't take over your iTunes surreptitiously).

FIGURE 9.10

Selecting the Applications item in the Library list displays installed mobile applications

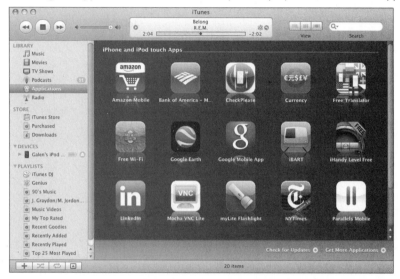

FIGURE 9.11

You can download updates available for your iPhone or iPod Touch applications from the iTunes Store within iTunes.

Using iTunes with Apple TV

The Apple TV device enables you to get audio and video to your stereo and TV so you don't have to listen or watch it on your Mac. But Apple TV can work with your Mac, so you can synchronize its media contents with your Mac's, which makes your Mac's music and video library available to your stereo and TV through Apple TV.

When set up and connected to your home network, your Apple TV should be detected by iTunes and show up in the Devices list in the iTunes Sidebar. You sync to it as if it were an iPod, using the Summary and other panes to control what is synced.

You can control Apple TV syncing in the Apple TV pane of the Preferences dialog box. Selected by default, the Look for Apple TVs option adds any detected Apple TV devices to your iTunes Devices list.

 You can remove an Apple TV from the Devices list by clicking the Eject iconic button to the right of its name, or select the Apple TV on the Apple TV pane of the Preferences dialog box and click Remove Apple TV.

If you don't want iTunes to sync to the Apple TV at all, select the Disable Automatic Syncing for Apple TVs.

Working with QuickTime Player

The QuickTime Player does more than play media files; it lets you record your own and convert media files for use in iTunes, MobileMe, and YouTube. But QuickTime Player does not substitute for DVD Player and iTunes (both covered earlier in this chapter); you cannot play DVDs with it, for example.

New Feature

Mac OS X 10.6 Snow Leopard has a restyled QuickTime Player playback dialog box, plus it plays files from the Web faster than previous versions did and provides a new Panoramic playback mode for videos. It also now includes functions that you used to have pay $35 for (in the form of the QuickTime Player Pro application): the ability to export movies, record media (audio, video, and screencasts) from your Mac, and trim media files. Finally, Apple has boosted the video processing speed by using its new QuickTime X engine, so media files — especially Web-based ones — should load faster and play with fewer pauses and quality compromises. Gone in the Snow Leopard version of QuickTime Player are the A/V controls that let you adjust screen color, speaker settings, and so forth — you now must do these using the Sound and Displays system preferences.

Playing media files

QuickTime Player's most basic capability is to play supported auto and video formats, which include Apple's QuickTime movie (.mov) format, the MPEG-4 (.mp4) video format, the MP3 audio format, and Apple's AAC audio format. To play a supported file on your Mac or on an attached drive, choose File ➪ Open File or press ⌘+O, then select the file from the Open dialog box and click Open. You can also open media files from the Web by choosing File ⇨ Open URL or pressing ⌘+U; enter the URL in the dialog box that appears or choose a previously opened URL from the Movie URL popup menu.

In either case, you'll get a playback dialog box with the filename in its title bar, as the lefthand side of Figure 9.12 shows.

Click the Play iconic button to play the file (it turns into the Pause iconic button), and click and hold the Rewind and Fast Forward iconic buttons to navigate through the file — much like any on-screen player. You can also drag the time bar's thumb to move to a desired point in the video or audio file. For audio, and for video that has audio, you'll also get a volume slider to the left of the playback window.

The playback dialog box for video files has two additional options:

- The Options iconic popup menu (the arrow-coming-out-of-a-box icon) opens the menu shown in Figure 9.12 that has options to prepare the file for iTunes, MobileMe, and YouTube, as well as to trim the file (both capabilities are covered later in this chapter).

- The Screen Toggle iconic button (the opposing-arrows icon) toggles the playback display between full-screen view and the dialog box. You can also resize the dialog box to any size you want by dragging its lower-left corner.

Tip
To see details about an open media file, choose Window ⇨ Show/Hide Media Inspector or press ⌘+I. The Media Inspector dialog box displays information such as the file location, format, frames-per-second (fps) rate, data rate, and size.

QuickTime Player also has controls for the video playback in its View menu:

- Choose View ⇨ Enter Full Screen or press ⌘+F to toggle to full-screen view.

- Choose View ⇨ Actual Size or press ⌘+1 to see the video at actual size.

- Choose View ⇨ Fit to Screen or press ⌘+3 to fit the video to screen proportionally.

- If you are viewing a video in full-screen mode, you can choose View ⇨ Fill Screen or press ⌘+4 to fill the screen with the video (this may distort or crop the video if the video's ratio is different from the screen's), or choose View ⇨ Panoramic or press ⌘+5 to make the video fill the screen height and compress the sides if they won't otherwise fit; you can then pan (scroll) the video to decompress one side (which compresses the other side even more) to change the area of focus. You would use the Panoramic option if you want to watch a wide-screen (16:9 ratio) video at full height on a standard-width (4:3 ratio) monitor and still be able to pan to the cut-off portions (which you could not do with the Fill Screen option).

- Choose View ⇨ Increase Size or press ⌘+= to zoom in the video, or choose View ⇨ Decrease Size or press ⌘+– to zoom out the video.

- For videos that have language options, you can choose View ⇨ Show Closed Captioning or press Option+⌘+T, choose View ⇨ Languages and then choose an available language from the submenu, and/or choose View ⇨ Subtitles ⇨ On/Off.

- For videos that have chapters, choose View ⇨ Show/Hide Chapters or press ⌘+R to display the chapter-navigation controls in the video playback dialog box.

- Choose View ⇨ Loop or press ⌘+L to have the video playback loop (replay) the video endlessly.

FIGURE 9.12

The playback dialog boxes for video and audio (left) in QuickTime Player. At right, the trim controls for video and audio.

Editing media files

You can edit media files — essentially, cut pieces out, or *trim* them — using the controls in QuickTime Player. To do so, choose Edit ⇨ Trim or press ⌘+T. For video files, you can also click the Options iconic popup menu and choose Trim. The time bar changes to the trim slider, which show a sequence of stills for video and the sound waves for audio, as the righthand side of Figure 9.12 shows.

Drag the trim slider's thumbs on either the left or right side to trim from the beginning or end, respectively, of the file. You can start with one side and then move onto the other side. For audio files, you can also choose Edit ⇨ Select All But Silence or press Shift+⌘+A to exclude the silent part of the file (this moves the trim sliders to exclude silence at the beginning and/or end of the file, but it leaves silence inside the file). Click Trim to complete the cut. (You can choose Edit ⇨ Undo Trim or press ⌘+Z to cancel the trim.)

When done, choose File ⇨ Save As or press Shift+⌘+S to make the changes permanent in a copy of the original file permanent. (If you want to overwrite the source file, you choose File ⇨ Close or press ⌘+W, then when the warning dialog box appears asking if you want to discard your changes, click Save to save the original file with the changes.

Creating media files

Although it's called a player, QuickTime Player can also create media files: movies, sound recordings, and screencasts ("movies" of what occurs on your Mac's screen, such as for how-to guides). The process for all three is similar:

- **Movie recording.** Attach a video camera to your Mac or use its built-in iSight camera. Then choose File ⇨ New Movie Recording or press Option+⌘+N. The Movie Recording dialog box opens. As Figure 9.13 shows, the dialog box has controls for video and audio sources, quality levels, and recording destination; click the Choose iconic popup menu to select the desired options. The key control is the Record iconic button (the big-red-circle-with-a-white-circle-inside icon). Click it to start recording; it changes to the Stop iconic button (the big-red-circle-with-a-white-square-inside icon), which you click to end the recording and make the playback dialog appears so you can see what you just recorded. The dialog box also has the same volume settings and Screen Toggle iconic button as the playback dialog boxes. Note that if no camera is attached (or, if you're using an iSight camera on a laptop, if the laptop case is closed), the Movie Recording dialog box displays the message "The camera is off."

- **Audio recording.** Choose File ⇨ New Audio Recording or press Control+Option+⌘+N. The Audio Recording dialog box opens. As Figure 9.13 shows, the dialog box has controls for audio sources, quality levels, and recording destination; click the Choose iconic popup menu to select the desired options. The key control is the Record iconic button (the big red circle icon). Click it to start recording; it changes to the Stop iconic button, which you click to end the recording and make the playback dialog appears so you can hear what you just recorded. The dialog box also has the same volume settings as the playback dialog boxes.

FIGURE 9.13

The Movie Recording dialog box (left) and Audio Recording dialog box (right)

- **Screen recording.** Choose File ➪ New Screen Recording or press Control+⌘+N. The Screen Recording dialog box opens. The dialog box has just two controls: the Choose iconic popup menu for audio sources, quality levels, and recording destination, and the Record iconic button (the big red circle icon). Click Record to start recording; a settings sheet appears and asks you to confirm that you want to record the screen. The settings sheet notes that you can click the Stop iconic button in the menu bar or press Control+⌘+Esc to end the recording and make the playback dialog appear so you can see what you just recorded. Click Start Recording to begin the screen recording, or click Cancel to not record the screen.

Exporting video files

QuickTime Player makes it easy to share video files with others, such as through iTunes, MobileMe Gallery, and YouTube. Use the Sharing menu to export the video files at the appropriate size, resolution, frame rate, and format for any of these three services. You can also choose one of these three export options from the Options iconic popup menu in the video playback dialog box.

If you select iTunes, you get three options in the dialog box that appears: iPhone and iPod, Apple TV, and Computer (some may not be available based on the format of the video file being converted). Select one and click to Share to export the video for the desired playback service. QuickTime Player adds the video file to your iTunes library when it's done.

If you select MobileMe Gallery, a dialog box opens that lets you provide details on the video to display in your MobileMe account's Gallery window (see Chapter 15), which lets you share files with others via the Web. Enter the video title you want displayed in the Title field and any descriptive text you want displayed in the Description field. If you want an iPhone- and iPod Touch-compatible video to also be available for mobile users of MobileMe, select the Include a Movie Compatible with iPhone and iPod Touch option. You can control access to the video on MobileMe by using the two Access options: Hide Movie on My Gallery Home Page, and Allow Movie to Be Downloaded. Click Share to export the file and upload it to your MobileMe Gallery. (You will need an Internet connection for the file to be uploaded to MobileMe.)

If you select YouTube, a dialog box appears in which you enter your YouTube username and password; enter that information and click Sign In to begin the export and upload process. (If you want your Mac to remember these settings, select the Remember This Password in My Keychain option before clicking Sign In.) Note that YouTube has both a 1GB file size limit and a 10-minute duration limit. (You will need an Internet connection for the file to be uploaded to YouTube.)

Note

Some video exports can take many minutes to complete. To monitor the progress of your video exports, choose Window ➪ Show Export Progress or press Option+⌘+P.

Using Front Row

Mac OS X includes yet another media playback application: Front Row. It's essentially a front end to iTunes that lets you play video and audio in full-screen mode without ever seeing the standard

Mac OS Finder (once it's running, anyhow). Front Row is designed to let you control your Mac as if it were a TV, so you can connect your Mac to a digital TV or large monitor and control it using the Mac's infrared remote control (as well as using your keyboard, if you want).

Figure 9.14 shows the Front Row screen. Use the ↑ and ↓ buttons on the remote control, or on your keyboard, to navigate from one option to the next, and click the remote control's Play/Pause button or press Return on the Mac's keyboard to select an option.

If you select Movies, TV Shows, Music, Podcasts, or Photos, Front Row shows a list of compatible files from your iTunes library. Navigate to the desired file and press Play/Pause on the remote control or press Return on the Mac's keyboard to begin playback.

Press Menu on the remote control to go back a level in the menu hierarchy. When you are in the main menu, pressing Menu exits Front Row. (You can also press Esc on the Mac's keyboard to quit out of Front Row at any time.)

Front Row's Settings option brings you to a screen where you can turn on or off the screen saver and the program's sound effects. The program's Sources option shows you what media sources are connected to your Mac, if any; your Mac displays as a source as well.

FIGURE 9.14

The main Front Row screen.

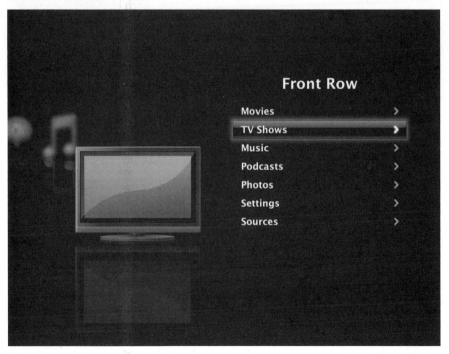

Summary

iTunes is your Mac's central tool for managing and playing music and videos. It not only maintains your library of media files, but also manages file synchronization with devices such as iPods, iPhones, and Apple TV. Plus, it enables you to share music and videos with other computers and to access their music and videos.

You can import music from your CDs, converting them into digital files that work in iTunes and iPods — even on the Web. iTunes can also import MPEG-4 video files that you may have created in a program such as iMovie or downloaded from the Web. You can also buy music, TV shows, and movies from the iTunes Store, as well as from other online stores.

iTunes enables you to sort and search your music, plus create playlists — collections of music you put together or that you create the rules for, telling iTunes what to put together. The Genius feature tells iTunes to create a playlist of songs that sound like the currently selected song. For videos, iTunes only enables you to sort and search them.

When playing music, you have all the controls you'd expect from a stereo, including shuffle and repeat. iTunes offers just the basic playback controls for video, such as Play, Pause, Rewind, and Forward, but when you play DVDs in the separate DVD Player application, you get the full set of controls you'd expect from any physical DVD player's remote control.

You can also subscribe to podcasts for playback in iTunes and for synchronization to iPhones and iPods so you can listen to them on the go. iTunes' support for Internet radio gives you access to a wealth of programming from hundreds of traditional radio stations and online-only Internet radio "stations."

iTunes also acts as the central manager for iPhones' and iPod Touches' non-media content, such as contacts, appointments, Safari bookmarks, and mobile applications.

The QuickTime Player utility does much more than play several video and audio formats. It lets you trim video and audio files, such as to take out silence in audio files, as well as export video for use in iTunes, MobileMe Gallery, and YouTube. QuickTime Player also lets you record your movies, audio, and screencasts.

The Front Row application is another way to play video and audio on your Mac, using a full-screen interface. Think of it as a front end to iTunes that you can use on a large monitor as if it were a TV.

Part II

Networking and the Internet

Connecting to the Web

The World Wide Web — known as the *Web* for short — has transformed society. The Web was created in the 1990s as a way to use the Internet — a global network originally created so military commands and other government entities could communicate in the aftermath of a nuclear war — for researchers and others to communicate more richly than just via the exchange of text messages. Quickly, the Web became widely used for other purposes, such as transmitting e-mail, transferring files, and providing real-time chat. Scientists at the European Center for Nuclear Research (known by its French acronym CERN) created a language that let people create pages with text, images, and hyperlinks to other pages and resources. The Hypertext Markup Language (HTML) language to create these pages and the Hypertext Transfer Protocol (HTTP) to connect users to these pages became the basis for the Web we know today.

To access Web pages, you use something called a *Web browser*, the first popular version of which was invented at the University of Illinois at Champaign and called Mosaic. It evolved into the popular Netscape Navigator browser, which later became the foundation for the Mozilla Firefox browser. Today, however, the Microsoft Internet Explorer browser is the most popular way to access the Web from Windows PCs because it comes preinstalled on these computers. Apple soon came up with its own browser, Safari. It is preinstalled on the Mac OS, making it the predominant Web browser for Mac users.

Regardless of the browser you use, the Web has also become much more sophisticated than what CERN and Mosaic first delivered. You can use the Web as a computer, running applications in it, storing data in it, and doing so much more. And browsers like Safari have more than kept up, becoming sophisticated applications that for many users are the most-used software on their Macs.

Connecting to the Internet

Before you can use the Web, you have to connect to the Internet, because the Internet is the global network through which Web pages are accessed. And how you connect to the Internet from your Mac depends on several factors.

Chapter 21 explains the key facility in Mac OS X 10.6 Snow Leopard to set up access to both the Internet and any local networks you have access to: the Network system preference. But before you even get to the Network system preference, you have to understand the physical connection you're using to connect to the Internet.

Using Internet connection devices

In a home environment, it's very likely that you have a cable modem or a DSL modem that connects your home to the Internet over what is commonly called a *broadband connection*. Your Mac may plug directly into it via an Ethernet cable, or there may be a router device that your Mac connects to and that then connects to the cable modem or DSL modem. Some cable and DSL (Digital Subscriber Line) modems include a router, so multiple computers and other networked devices such as printers all connect to it and thus to each other, as well as to the Internet. (These routers typically have a port labeled WAN, for *wide area network,* used to connect to the Internet, and several ports labeled LAN, for *local area network,* used to connected devices within your home or office to each other as well as to the Internet.)

Note

Modem means modulation/demodulation, a fancy way of saying a device that translates the analog sound waves (such as on a phone line or in wireless radios) into a computer's digital signals and back again. Although a cable modem or DSL modem is called a modem, it often nowadays connects to an all-digital network, so doesn't have to do the analog-digital conversion. But the "modem" name has stuck.

Cross-Ref

Chapter 13 explains how to share files with others over a local area network.

Many people use an older technology called a dial-up modem that uses the phone line as the connection to the Internet. In this case, the Mac has a modem either built into it as a card inside the box or attached as a small hardware device, typically to a USB (Universal Serial Bus) port.

It's also possible that your Mac (and other devices) use a wireless technology called Wi-Fi (technically, the IEEE 802.11a/b/g/n family of standards) to connect to the cable or DSL modem or to a router or wireless access point that is connected to that cable or DSL modem. In some cities, there's an alterative to DSL and cable modems that uses one of several wireless technologies to connect to the Internet; these wireless devices are typically called *wireless broadband routers* but yours may have a different name.

In all these cases, the basic setup is that an Internet service provider such as your phone or cable company provides a box or other means to connect to the Internet, and your Mac and other devices connect to that device so they can access the Internet through it.

In a business environment, the basic approach is the same, though a more powerful Internet router that can handle lots of simultaneous user connections is used in place of a cable or DSL modem in larger organizations. There's likely a more complex network between your Mac and the Internet router as well.

For your Mac to connect to the Internet, your cable or DSL modem — or whatever Internet connection device you're using — must be properly set up. The steps to do this vary from device to device and manufacturer to manufacturer, so check your documentation. Most require that you enable something called DHCP (Dynamic Host Configuration Protocol), which assigns your Mac and any other device connected to the network a unique identifier so the network knows how to route traffic to and from each device.

Tip

Having a connection to your DSL modem, cable modem, wireless access point, or router (wired or wireless) does not mean you are connected to the Internet. It just means you are connected locally. If you're not sure you have an Internet connection active, launch the Network Utility, go to the Ping pane, enter `apple.com` (or any Web site's URL) in the Ping field, and click Ping. If you get an error message saying the destination was unavailable (or something similar), you're not connected to the Internet. Chapter 8 explains the Network Utility in more detail.

Setting up connections manually

After the Internet connection is set up, you can connect your Mac to that device. Usually, if you plug your Mac into a DSL modem, cable modem, or router by using an Ethernet cable, the Internet access happens automatically, thanks to the magic of DHCP. In the Network system preference, the Ethernet item in the list at left shows a green dot indicating a connection, as Figure 10.1 shows. If you select Ethernet, you'll see a pane, also shown in Figure 10.1, that provides details about the connection.

Using an AirPort (Apple's name for Wi-Fi) connection usually is almost as easy: Turn on AirPort in the Network system preference, and your Mac will see your wireless access point or router and connect to it. It should ask you for a password. (If it does not, your wireless network is not secure, and you should enable the WPA [Wi-Fi Protected Access] or other available security settings in your wireless access point or router following the manufacturer's instructions.) If there are multiple wireless networks available — common in home environments because your neighbors likely have their own wireless networks whose signals might penetrate into your home — you'll see a list of available networks if you click the AirPort menu bar iconic popup menu or if you select AirPort in the Network system preference and open the Network Name popup menu. Select the name of your wireless network (called an SSID [Service Set Identifier] in most wireless access points' and routers' setup instructions). Again, the AirPort item in the list at the left of the Network system preference pane shows a green dot when the connection is active, and selecting AirPort displays a pane of connection details.

New Feature

A radio-wave icon next to a wireless network's name indicates its signal strength (the more waves, the stronger the signal). Mac OS X 10.6 Snow Leopard now shows the signal strengths for all visible wireless networks in the AirPort menu bar iconic popup menu and in the Network Name popup menu in the Network system preference.

Note

A lock signal next to a wireless network's name means that a password is required to connect to that network.

FIGURE 10.1

The Network system preference is where you set up Internet and local area network connections. The Ethernet pane is the default pane; switch to other panes by using the connection list at left. The current status for each network connection also appears in that list.

For a dial-up connection, go to the External Modem pane (click External Modem in the list at the left of the Network system reference), then enter the phone number, your username, and your password in the appropriate fields. You may need to set additional configuration information by clicking Advanced; check with your dial-up provider's instructions. After your modem is set up, click Connect to make the connection. (Or use the connection software that came with your dial-up service, if such separate software was provided.) If the modem is connected, a green dot appears next to External Modem in the list at left of the Network system preference.

Setting up connections with assistance

If you're not comfortable manually setting up a connection, you can use the Mac OS's Network Setup Assistant utility. In the Network system preference, click Assist Me, then click Assistant in the dialog box that appears. The Network Setup Assistant launches, and its first dialog box asks you to name the connection; enter anything that makes sense to you, such as **Home DSL** or **Wireless Internet**, then click Continue.

Note

You will need the connection settings from your Internet service provider (ISP) to complete the setup.

The next dialog box asks you for the type of connection you are trying to set up. You have the following choices:

- **I Use AirPort to Connect to the Internet Wirelessly.** If you choose this item and click Continue, the next dialog box shows a list of available wireless networks; select the one you want to connect to, enter the password (if any) in the password field, and click Continue.

- **I Use a Telephone Modem to Dial My ISP.** If you choose this item and click Continue, the next dialog box asks for the dial-up configuration information: account name, password, ISP's dial-up number, a number to get an outside line (such a 9 or 8 in an office or hotel), and an option to select whether you have call waiting service on the phone line. Click Continue to get the next dialog box, which shows the brand of modem that Mac OS X detects (you can change it by choosing a different model in the unnamed popup menu), then click Continue again to get a dialog box that confirms your setup. Click Continue to try the connection.

- **I Use a DSL Modem to Connect to the Internet.** If you choose this item and click Continue, the next dialog box tells you that it will try to connect you automatically when you click Continue. If it cannot connect you, a new dialog box appears that asks you to enter PPPoE settings (Point-to-Point Protocol over Ethernet, the most common type of DSL connection) and click Continue or to select the More Choices option and click Continue; you are then asked for the DHCP or static IP address provided by your ISP, which you should enter and then click Continue.

- **I Use a Cable Modem to Connect to the Internet.** If you choose this item and click Continue, the next dialog box tells you that it will try to connect you automatically when you click Continue. If it cannot connect you, a new dialog box appears that asks you to enter either PPPoE settings or DHCP settings, as specified by your ISP, and click Continue.

- **I Connect to My Local Area Network (LAN).** If you choose this item and click Continue, the next dialog box tells you that it will try to connect you automatically when you click Continue. If it cannot connect you, a new dialog box appears that asks you to enter the IP address, subnet mask, router address, and DNS (Domain Name Service) host settings, as specified by your ISP or network administrator, and click Continue.

No matter what method you use, if the connection is successful, you get a dialog box saying so; click Continue to complete the connection. Otherwise, you get an error message and can either click Diagnose to run the Network Diagnostic Assistant to try to detect the reason for the failed connection, or click OK to close the error message. (You'll have to edit the connection settings in the Network system preference to try again.)

Disconnecting from the Internet

When you use a broadband connection such as a cable or DSL modem, you tend to stay connected to the Internet as long as your Mac is running. When you're idle with these connections, there's no load on the Internet connection, so there's no harm (unless you're paying by the minute or hour, which is rare for such connections). But because the connection is open, a hacker might try to break into your Mac though this is rare unless you use what's called a static IP address to connect your Mac directly to the Internet.

Cross-Ref

Chapter 23 explains how to protect your Mac from hackers.

If you use a dial-up connection, you typically pay by the hour or minute so you don't want to stay connected when you're not using the Internet.

Here's how to disconnect from the Internet (as well as any local area network you're attached to):

- **Dial-up connection.** If you're using a dial-up modem, click Disconnect from the External Modem pane in the Network system preference, or choose Disconnect from the Modem iconic popup menu in the menu bar if you've enabled that icon by selecting the Show Modem Status in Menu Bar option in the External Modem pane of the Network system preference.

- **Wi-Fi connection.** If you're using a Wi-Fi connection, click Turn AirPort Off in the AirPort pane of the Network system preference, or choose Turn AirPort Off from the AirPort iconic popup menu in the menu bar if you've enabled that icon by selecting Show AirPort Status in Menu Bar option in the AirPort pane of the Network system preference.

- **Wired connection or Bluetooth network.** If you're using a wired connection (DSL modem, cable modem, FireWire, or local area network), or if you're using a Bluetooth network, go to the Ethernet, FireWire, or Bluetooth pane, as appropriate, in the Network system preference, and choose Off in the Configure IPv4 popup menu.

Browsing the Web with Safari

Now that you're connected to the Internet, you can take advantage of all sorts of Internet-enabled services, such as e-mail, instant messaging, and the Web. Chapter 11 explains how to use e-mail and instant messaging, so let's focus on the Web here.

Apple provides its Safari 4 browser with Mac OS X 10.6 Snow Leopard. After you launch Safari, you can go to any Web page simply by entering its URL (Uniform Resource Locator, the technical name for a Web address) in the field at the top of the browser window. Figure 10.2 shows the result for the URL `http://zangogroup.com/bookpkg.html`.

The figure also shows the navigation buttons that help you move among Web pages, plus the menu commands at the very top and the row of bookmarks below the navigation buttons.

New Feature

Mac OS X 10.6 Snow Leopard includes the newest version of Safari: Safari 4. (Mac OS X 10.5 Leopard came with Safari 3.) Safari 4 may or may not be new to you, depending on whether you downloaded it to your Mac before you got Mac OS X 10.6 Snow Leopard. Among its new features are the tabs bar at the top, the Cover Flow display in the bookmarks and History windows, the ability to search the Web-visits history, and the slideshow-like Top Sites window.

FIGURE 10.2

The Apple Safari browser and its main controls

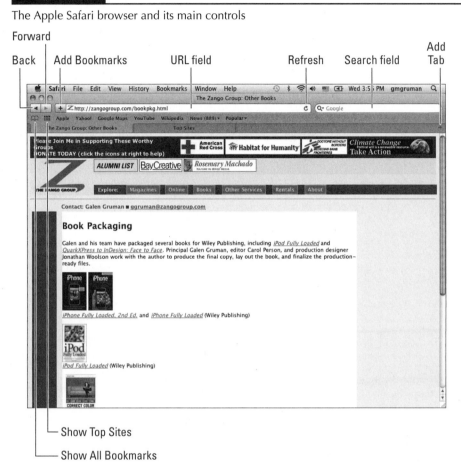

Forward

Back   Add Bookmarks   URL field   Refresh   Search field   Add Tab

Show Top Sites

Show All Bookmarks

Navigating the Web

Entering the URL for every page you want to visit is a lot of work, plus it requires you to know the URL of every page you want to visit — a highly unlikely situation. That's why the Web has multiple navigation mechanisms. Entering the URL is just the basic way, and it's a fast way to go some place new. For example, if you hear about a new Apple product, typing `apple.com` in the URL field is easy to do.

Using hyperlinks

When you're at a site such as Apple's, you'll notice *hyperlinks*, or highlighted text and images that when clicked open a different Web page. Hyperlinked text is usually displayed in blue and underlined, while hyperlinked pictures usually have a blue border around them. But the highlighting of a hyperlink can be different from page to page and site to site — and they don't even have to be highlighted. What you can count on is that the mouse pointer will change when it is over a hyperlink, as Figure 10.3 shows.

FIGURE 10.3

The regular mouse pointer (left) and the mouse pointer when you hover over a hyperlink (right)

Using bookmarks

If you find yourself repeatedly going to a Web page, you can *bookmark* it — meaning save the page in a list that you can then go back to and click desired pages from any time you want. To save a page as a bookmark in Safari, choose Bookmark ➪ Add Bookmark or press ⌘+D.

Tip

The fastest way to bookmark a page is to click the + iconic button to the left of the URL.

You'll get a dialog box that asks you to name the bookmark (by default, the bookmark's name is the same as the Web page's title) and to specify where to add the bookmark. The default location is the bookmarks bar, the list of bookmarks below the URL field. But that can become full very fast, so you can also choose Bookmarks Menu, which adds the bookmark to the Bookmarks menu. Or you can choose a folder within the bookmarks bar or a folder that is saved in the bookmark collection list.

In Safari, the bookmarks bar displays under the URL field. If you see a down-pointing triangle next to a bookmark, that means it's a bookmarks bar folder, and clicking the arrow displays a popup menu of all the bookmarked links in that folder.

You can also see all bookmarks saved, including those saved folders outside the bookmarks bar's folders, by clicking the Show All Bookmarks iconic button (the open-book icon). Or choose Bookmarks ➪ Show All Bookmarks or press Option+⌘+B.

Tip

You can toggle between the Bookmarks list and your Web page by clicking the bookmark icon. It switches between the two views each time you click it.

Figure 10.4 shows a page being bookmarked; on the left is the bookmarks list you would get by clicking the Show All Bookmarks iconic button (the open book icon), which includes in the Bookmarks list various bookmarks added and imported. The Collections list gives you access to the entries stored in the bookmarks bar and Bookmarks menu, as well as to the browser history (the previously viewed pages), any RSS feeds you subscribe to (covered in the "Using RSS in Safari" section of this chapter), any URLs in your Address Book, and any URLs saved in the Mac's Bonjour network list (such as printers; Chapter 12 explains Bonjour networking).

Note in Figure 10.4 how Safari shows a preview in the Cover Flow presentation style for any selected bookmarks. Over time, Safari will fill in the Web site images, so when you first use Safari, the Cover Flow previews will all start out as dark folder icons emblazoned with the Safari logo.

FIGURE 10.4

When you add a bookmark in Safari, you can store it in any of several locations. On the left is the full bookmarks list that you've built over time. To the right is a preview of the currently selected bookmark item.

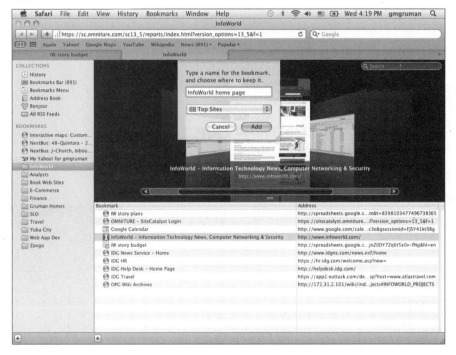

And you can see a slide show-like preview of your favorite Web pages — determined by what you visit the most — by clicking the Top Sites iconic button (the grid icon) in the bookmarks bar. You get a set of Web page previews, such as those shown in Figure 10.5, in what Safari calls the Top Sites window.

Note

When you are in the Top Sites window, the search field at bottom right is labeled Search History. Entering a term and pressing Return or clicking the magnifying glass icon will not search the Web but will display your history of Web pages visited.

Click Edit to change the Top Sites window's selections (and note that the Search History field disappears, replaced by the Small, Medium, and Large buttons):

- Click the Close iconic button (the X icon) that appears over a preview to remove that preview.
- Click the Retain iconic button (the thumbtack icon) to keep that preview in place, rather than replace it later with a more-visited site. (The thumbtack icon turns blue if you've clicked it to keep the preview in place.)
- Drag previews within the Top Sites window to rearrange them.
- Click the Small, Medium, or Large buttons to change the previews' size.

When you're finished, click Done to go back to the regular view, in which you can click a preview to open the Web page.

FIGURE 10.5

In the Top Sites view, Safari builds a slide show of Web page previews based on the sites you visit most often; clicking the grid icon in the bookmarks bar displays the clickable previews. In edit mode, shown here, you can choose which pages to keep permanently by clicking their Retain iconic buttons (the thumbtack icons).

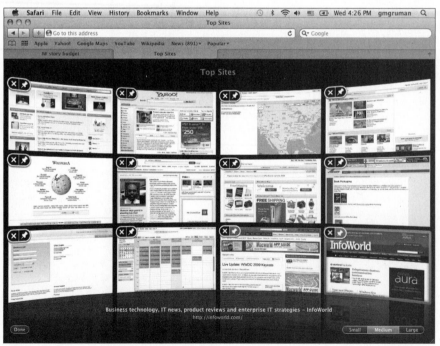

You can export your Safari bookmarks to an HTML file by choosing File ⇨ Export Bookmarks. You can import that bookmark in another browser (not just in Safari, and not just on the Mac), which is a handy way to keep your home and work computer in sync when it comes to bookmarks. You can also import bookmark lists generated by other browsers by choosing File ⇨ Import Bookmarks.

Using history

Safari keeps track of the pages you visit, saving them in what it calls History. You can see the pages you visited on specific dates by choosing History and then the specific date from the menu. Choosing History ⇨ Show All History opens the History window (which has the same look as the unnamed bookmarks window, as shown in Figure 10.4) of what you've recently visited.

Tip

You can quickly switch to the History window from the bookmarks window by clicking History in the bookmarks window's Collections list.

Note

When you are in the Top Sites window — not in the History window as you would expect — you can search for Web pages previously visited by entering a term in the Search History field and then pressing Return or clicking the Search iconic button (the magnifying glass icon).

Other History menu options include:

- **Reopen Last Closed Window.** This option is handy when you accidentally close a window and want to get back to it quickly.

- **Reopen All Windows from Last Session.** This option opens the windows that were open when you last quit Safari.

- **Clear History.** This option removes all the history bookmarks, so no one can see what you were browsing (a favorite of teenagers).

Using navigation buttons

As Figure 10.2 shows, the Safari toolbar has iconic navigation buttons. These help you move across pages accessed in your current browser session for the current tab or window:

- **The Home iconic button.** Opens your home page (which you set in Home Page field of the General pane of the Preferences dialog box for Safari); this page opens automatically whenever you launch Safari. You can also choose History ⇨ Home or press Shift+⌘+H to go to your home page.

- **The Show the Previous Page iconic button (usually called simply Back).** Moves to the previous page you visited, letting you retrace the sequence of pages you've visited. You can also choose History ⇨ Back or press ⌘+[.

- **The Show the Next Page iconic button (usually called simply Forward).** Moves to the next page you've visited, letting you retrace the sequence of pages you've visited. (Forward only has an effect if you first moved back to a previous page you visited.) You can also choose History ⇨ Forward or press ⌘+].

- **The Show RSS iconic button.** Opens the current Web page's RSS feed. If there is no RSS feed attached to this page, the Show RSS iconic button does not appear.

- **The Reload the Current Page iconic button (usually called simply Reload or Refresh).** Reloads the current page to ensure its contents are current, something you might do for pages whose information changes frequently, such as pages containing the latest news and stock prices. You can also press View ⇨ Reload Page or press ⌘+R.

- **The Search field.** Enables you to search for Web pages by using the Google search engine; simply type in your term and press Return or click the Search iconic button (the magnifying glass icon). You can also choose Edit ⇨ Find ⇨ Google Search or press Option+⌘+F.

Using window and tab controls

Normally, when you open Safari and load a Web page, it replaces any Web page previously loaded. But what if you want to look at several Web pages at once? You can, using either or both of two approaches.

The first method is to open a new window for the new Web page to display in. Choose File ⇨ New Window or press ⌘+N. Then use the Window menu to switch among windows (the open windows are listed at the bottom of the Window menu.)

To close the current window, choose File ⇨ Close Window, press Shift+⌘+W, or click the red circle icon in the upper left of the window.

The second method is to open a new tabbed pane (called just *tabs* by most people) in the current window for the new Web page to display in. Initially, Safari shows no tabs, just a window containing a single Web page. To open a new tab, choose File ⇨ New Tab, press ⌘+T. Doing so opens a new tabbed pane, indicated by a row file folder-like tabs that appears below the toolbar (as you can see in Figures 10.3 and 10.5). Adding a tabbed pane also adds the Add Tab iconic button (the + icon) to the far right of the tabs row. You can now click the Add Tab iconic button to add new tabbed panes (choosing File ⇨ New Tab or pressing ⌘+T continue to work.) Click a tab to switch to its pane.

To close a tabbed pane, hover the mouse over its tab until the Close iconic button (the X icon) appears, as shown in Figure 10.6; click the Close iconic button (the X icon) in the tab. (You can also choose File ⇨ Close Tab or press ⌘+W.) If you hold Option when clicking the Close iconic button, all tabbed panes *except* the one with the Close iconic button are closed.

You can have multiple windows open, and each can contain tabbed panes or not, depending on how you want to move among the various Web pages. Safari also provides a series of controls over tabbed panes, all of which appear in the Window menu:

FIGURE 10.6

The row of tabs below the toolbar contains all open tabbed panes. This row enables you to open multiple Web pages in the same browser window. To close a pane, hover the mouse over its tab until the Close iconic button (the X icon) appears, as in the second tab here.

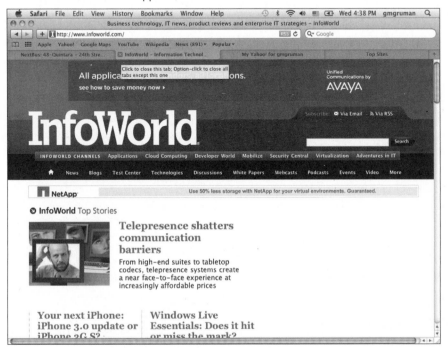

- Choose Window ⇨ Select Next Tab or press Control+Tab to move to the next tabbed pane in the current window.

- Choose Window ⇨ Select Previous Tab or press Control+Shift+Tab to move to the previous tabbed pane in the current window.

- Choose Window ⇨ Move Tab to New Window to convert a tabbed pane into a separate window.

- Choose Window ⇨ Merge All Windows to convert all open windows into individual tabbed panes into a single window.

You can also use shortcuts to quickly open new windows and tabbed panes from hyperlinks on a Web page:

- **⌘+click.** Opens a link in a new tabbed pane, leaving the current pane visible.

- **Shift+⌘+click.** Opens a link in a new tabbed pane and switches to that new pane.

- **Option+⌘+click.** Opens a link in a new window, leaving the current window visible.

- **Option+Shift+⌘+click.** Opens a link in a new window and switches to that new window.

As explained in the "Setting Safari preferences" section, you can change these shortcuts so ⌘+click and Shift+⌘+click open new windows and Option+⌘+click and Option+Shift+⌘+click open new tabbed panes.

Configuring the Safari Toolbar

Safari's toolbar is fairly spare, with no controls for features such as printing and zooming. Unless you add them, that is. Safari lets you customize the toolbar to add or remove any of more than a dozen iconic buttons. To do so, Control+click or right-click in the toolbar and choose Customize Toolbar from the contextual menu, or choose View⇨Customize Toobar. The Customize Toolbar settings sheet appears, as shown in the figure. Drag the desired buttons from the sheet into the toolbar at your desired location. (To remove an item, drag it out of the toolbar into the sheet. You can also Control+click or right-click it in the toolbar and choose Remove Item from the contextual menu when the Customize Toolbar sheet is not open.) To reset the toolbar to the defaults, drag the default set into the toolbar. Click Done when done.

Figure 10.11 later in this chapter shows a Safari browser window using a customized toolbar.

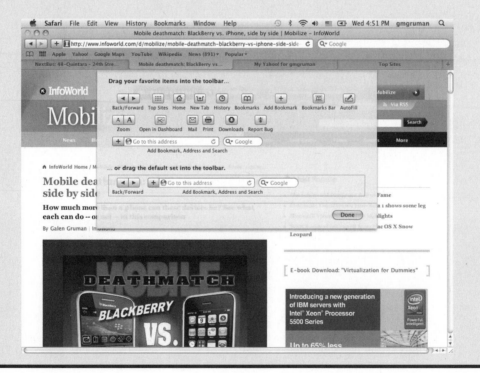

Using view controls

To help see text and images more clearly, Safari offers two zoom controls:

- **Zoom In.** Makes the Web page bigger (useful when the text is small), enlarging the view. Of course, less of the page can fit in the window when you zoom in, so you'll likely have to scroll more to see the rest of the contents. Choose View ⇨ Zoom In, press ⌘+=, or click the Zoom In iconic button (the magnifying glass icon with the + symbol) in the toolbar (if you customized your toolbar to include it).

- **Zoom Out.** Makes the Web page smaller, reducing the view and making more of the page fit in the window. Of course, the text will get smaller and may become hard to read. Choose View ⇨ Zoom Out, press ⌘+–, or click the Zoom Out iconic button (the magnifying glass icon with the – symbol) in the toolbar (if you customized your toolbar to include it).

Tip

If you choose View ⇨ Zoom Text Only, the Zoom In and Zoom Out controls affect only the Web page's text. This can result in some awkward displays for Web pages, but it also keeps the layout more in line with the creator's intent and requires less scrolling than zooming in for everything does. You can also choose View ⇨ Actual Size or press ⌘+0 (zero) to see the Web page at its normal, default size.

Using sharing controls

When you visit a Web page, you often want to tell someone else about it, or make a printout so you can refer to it later or show others. Safari has several controls to help do so:

- Press ⌘+P to print the current page to the printer of your choice. You can also click the Print This Page iconic button (known simply as Print) in the toolbar (if you customized your toolbar to include it) to print the current page.

- Choose File ⇨ Mail Contents of This Page or press ⌘+I to send the Web page as an HTML attachment to other people via Apple Mail.

- Choose File ⇨ Mail Link to This Page or press Shift+⌘+I to send the URL for the current page to other people via Apple Mail.

Using interface controls

Safari gives you some controls over what displays on-screen:

- You can hide or show the bookmarks bar by choosing Show/Hide Bookmarks Bar or pressing Shift+⌘+B.

- You can hide or show the toolbar by choosing Show/Hide Toolbar or pressing Shift+⌘+\.

- You can hide or show the status bar by choosing Show/Hide Status Bar or pressing ⌘+/. The status bar shows the names of page destinations as you hover your mouse over the hyperlinks to them.

- You can change what appears in the Safari toolbar, such as the navigation buttons and other controls — by choosing View➪Customize Toolbar, as the sidebar "Configuring the Safari Toolbar" explains.

Using specialty controls

Safari has several other controls that defy easy categorization but are often useful:

- Safari's popup blocker can eliminate many of the annoying windows that pop up from ads trying to intrude into your view while you're viewing a Web page. Choose Safari➪Block Pop-Up Windows or press Shift+⌘+K to toggle popup blocking. (If the menu item has a check mark to its left, popup blocking is turned on.)

- Safari can save the current Web page to a file on your Mac; choose File➪Save As or press ⌘+S. You have two save options in the dialog box that appears: Web Archive, which saves the HTML page plus the graphics on the same page to the folder of your choice, and Page Source, which saves just the HTML page to the folder of your choice. Click Save after you've decided what to save and where to save it.

- The Downloads dialog box (choose Window➪Downloads or press Option+⌘+L) shows all recently downloaded files, so you can find them in Finder, resume any whose downloads were paused, see the status of those currently being downloaded (and halt any you don't want to keep downloading), and clear the list of recent downloads.

- The page search box (choose Edit➪Find➪Find or press ⌘+F) opens the Find banner right above the Web page so you can search for text on that page. Enter the text in the Find banner's search field and press Return or click the Search iconic button (the magnifying glass icon). Use the Back and Forward iconic buttons in the Find banner to search for other occurrences of the search term on that page. Click Done to close it, choose Edit➪Find ➪Hide Find Banner, or press Shift+⌘+F. You can quickly search for any text selected on the page by choosing Edit➪Find➪Use Selection for Find or pressing ⌘+E.

- If you want to see the HTML code used for the current page, such as to help you re-create something for one of your own pages, choose View➪View Source or press Option+⌘+U to open a new window that displays the HTML code.

- The Open in Dashboard control (choose File➪Open in Dashboard) enables you to select any part of the Web page as a module that is stored in the Mac's Dashboard as a widget (see Chapter 8), so you can open just that piece of the Web page in the Dashboard later. An example is if you want to save the sports scores box on a news page and see just that score box in the Dashboard.

- The Auto Fill control (choose Edit➪AutoFill Form or press Shift+⌘+A) looks at any forms on the Web page and fills in anything it can find appropriate from your Address Book or from previous forms you've filled out.

- The Report a Bug control (choose Safari➪Report Bugs to Apple) opens a form in which you can report errors on the current Web page to Apple.

Using Search Engines

The Safari browser uses the Google search engine to find content on the Web. Google is by far the most popular search engine available, but it's not the only one. If you want to use a search engine other than Google in Safari, you need to go to its Web page yourself. Alternative search engines include Ask (`www.ask.com`), Microsoft Bing (`www.bing.com`), and Yahoo (`www.search.yahoo.com`).

Google also offers a range of specialty search tools, not available through the Google search field in Safari, that you might want to explore at `www.google.com/advanced_search`, including tools for news, code, and books, as well as options for narrowing your search based on various criteria.

Setting Safari preferences

There are lots of preferences you can set for Safari. Here are the key ones. To go to the Preferences dialog box, choose Safari ⇨ Preferences or press ⌘+, (comma).

The General pane and the Security pane, both shown in Figure 10.7, have many of the critical preferences.

The General pane's options are:

- **Default Web Browser.** This popup menu determines which browser is opened by default when you click a hyperlink in another program. If you have other browsers installed on your Mac, they will display in the popup menu's options. Safari is the default choice.

- **New Windows Open With.** This popup menu enables you to choose what appears in new windows: the home page (the default), nothing, the same page as in the current window, the bookmarks window, or a tab folder that you choose (this opens all its tabs).

- **New Tabs Open With.** This popup menu enables you to choose what appears in new tabs: the home page, nothing (the default), the same page as in the current tab (or window if no tab is open), or the bookmarks window.

- **Home Page.** This field is where you enter the home page for your browser, if you want one. Click Set to Current Page to make it the home page. Delete the entry to have no home page.

- **Remove History Items.** This popup menu enables you to specify how long visited items are available in the History menu and list. Your choices are After One Day, After One Week (the default), After Two Weeks, After One Month, After One Year, and Manual (which means they remain until you choose Safari ⇨ Empty Cache or press Option+⌘+E). To prevent Safari from tracking your Web page visits, choose Safari ⇨ Private Browsing; if a check mark appears to the left of this menu option, it is enabled.

- **Save Downloaded Files To.** This popup menu determines where downloaded files are stored. The default option is the Downloads folder; you can also choose Other to select a different folder.

- **Remove Download List Items.** This popup menu controls how long downloads stay in the Download dialog box's list: Manually (the default), When Safari Quits, and Upon Successful Download.

- **Open "Safe" Files After Downloading.** This option, if selected, makes the Mac OS open downloaded files automatically. Safari tries to determine which are safe to open, to reduce the chances of a virus or other malware being installed onto your Mac without you being aware (see Chapter 23). But the chance remains, which is why we recommend not selecting this option, so the decision to open a downloaded file is one you consciously make each time.

- **Open Links from Applications.** This option enables you to select how links in other programs are opened in Safari: in a new window or in a new tab (if no window is open, then new window is opened even if you selected the new tab option).

FIGURE 10.7

The General pane (left) and Security pane (right) of the Safari Preferences dialog box

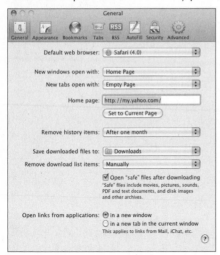

The Security pane's options are:

- **Fraudulent Sites.** This option, if selected, displays a warning when you are visiting a site that appears to be a scam. For example, if a link purports to be to www.apple.com but is to another site, Safari displays a warning. A common trick, called *phishing*, to steal users' identities is to send e-mails allegedly from their banks or credit card agencies asking them to click a link to update information. The link's text may look like a legitimate URL, but the actual hyperlink is to a different site where the thief hopes you enter all your account information so he can go steal your account's funds. This feature tries to detect such phishing expeditions. (See Chapter 23 for more on protecting yourself from identity theft.) This option is selected by default.

- **Web Content.** The four options here determine what actions Safari takes with common Web content. If selected, Enable Plug-Ins lets plug-ins such as Flash and Adobe Reader run in Safari. If selected, Enable Java lets Java-based Web applications run in Safari. If selected, Enable JavaScript lets JavaScript run in Web pages that are often used to deliver special features in Web pages such as recognizing you as a registered user). If selected, Block Pop-Up Windows prevents Web pages from opening new windows on their own (selecting this option is the same as choosing Safari ➪ Block Pop-Up Windows or pressing Shift+⌘+K.) All four options are selected by default.

- **Accept Cookies.** The three options here determine how Safari handles *cookies*, which are small files placed on your Mac by Web pages to store information such as your name or account status. Select the Always option to have all cookies stored. Select the Never option to prevent all cookies from being stored. (Many Web pages won't work if cookies are blocked.) Select the Only from Sites I Visit (the default) option to allow cookies from Web pages you visit but not from other pages that these pages may link to (such as marketers' and advertisers' sites). Click Show Cookies to see what cookies are stored on your Mac; you can delete the ones you don't want to keep from the list that appears.

- **Database Storage.** This popup menu determines how much database content from Web pages can be stored on your Mac before you are asked to allow more storage. The options are 1MB, 5MB (the default), 10MB, 50MB, 100MB, 500MB, and None. Click Show Databases to show any stored Web databases on your Mac; you can delete any unwanted ones from the list that appears.

- **Ask Before Sending a Non-Secure Form from a Secure Web Site.** If selected, this option will cause Safari to display a warning when a secure Web page (one whose URL begins with `https://`) sends for data to an unsecured Web page (one whose URL begins with `http://`). Such a situation could indicate a hacked Web site, or simply sloppy Web page design.

As shown in Figure 10.8, the Appearance and Advanced panes control display-oriented preferences.

The Appearance pane's options are:

- **Standard Font.** This area shows the current font used for regular text. You can change it by clicking Select and choosing a different font and/or size.

- **Fixed-Width Font.** This area shows the current font used for text used to display code snippets and other such typewriter-like displays. You can change it by clicking Select and choosing a different font and/or size.

- **Display Images When Page Opens.** If selected, this option displays the images on a Web page. Deselect this option so images don't display (something that can greatly speed up page load times and is very helpful for dial-up users).

- **Default Encoding.** This popup menu sets the language and character set defaults for Web pages in case the Web page doesn't say what language characters it uses. (Whatever the Web page specifies as its language encoding overrides this popup menu's settings.) If you open a Web page whose language isn't specified and that doesn't match your Default Encoding setting (it will look like gobbledygook), you can choose an encoding for that page by choosing View ➪ Text Encoding and then the language encoding that you think it is.

FIGURE 10.8

The Appearance pane (left) and Advanced pane (right) of the Safari Preferences dialog box

The Advanced pane's options are:

- **Universal Access.** In this section, select the Never Use Font Sizes Smaller Than option and choose a size in the adjacent popup menu to prevent type from being displayed at a smaller size than chosen. This is helpful to keep pages readable even when the designers chose tiny type, but it can make some pages' text wrap incorrectly or even run into other text, especially if you choose larger text sizes as the minimum. If you're over 40 years old, you'll want this option selected, which it is by default, though probably at a larger size than the default 9 points.

  Also in the Universal Access section, select Press Tab to Highlight Each Item on a Webpage to be able to press Tab to move among items on a Web page. Normally, you would press Option+Tab to do so, but that can be hard for people with arthritis or other physical handicaps.

- **Style Sheet.** If you want to impose your own style sheet (fonts, colors, sizes, and so on) on all Web pages, choose Other and then select the CSS (cascading style sheet) file you want to use. Otherwise, leave this set at the default of None Selected.

- **Proxies.** Click Change Settings if you want to open the Proxies pane in the Network system preference to change how your Mac accesses specialized Web services such as Gopher. Only an advanced user familiar with networking protocols should adjust these settings.

- **Show Develop Menu in Menu Bar.** This option, if selected, adds the Develop menu to Safari's menu bar. The Develop menu has various options that helps a Web page developer find errors in Web pages he or she is previewing in Safari, as well as enables the developer to turn various features on or off while testing the pages.

The Bookmarks and Tabs panes, shown in Figure 10.9, provide controls over access to Web pages in Safari.

The Bookmarks pane's options are:

- **Bookmarks Bar.** Use the three options here to determine if the Top Sites iconic button (the grid icon) appears in the toolbar, as well as whether Bonjour network links and/or Web pages from your Address book display in the bookmarks bar. The Include Top Sites option is selected by default, whereas the Include Bonjour and Include Address Book options are deselected by default.

- **Bookmarks Menu.** Use the three options here to determine if the bookmarks bar, Bonjour, and Address Book URLs appear in the Bookmarks menu. By default, the bookmarks bar is selected, which adds the Bookmarks Bar option to the Bookmarks menu; the Bookmarks Bar menu option has a submenu that lists all the URLs bookmarked in the bookmarks bar.

- **Collections.** Use the two options here to determine what appears in the Collections list in the bookmarks window. By default, both Address Book and Bonjour are selected and thus listed in the Collections list.

- **Synchronize Bookmarks Using MobileMe.** If selected, this option synchronizes this Mac's Safari bookmarks with other Macs that share the same MobileMe account. Click MobileMe to open the MobileMe system preference. (Chapter 15 covers MobileMe in depth.)

FIGURE 10.9

The Bookmarks pane (left) and Tabs pane (right) of the Safari Preferences dialog box

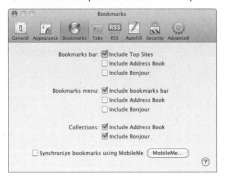
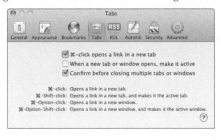

The Tabs pane has these options:

- **⌘+Click Opens Link in a New Tab.** If selected (the default), ⌘+clicking or Shift+⌘+clicking a hyperlink opens it in a new tabbed pane. If deselected, these actions open the hyperlinks in a new window instead. This option also affects the shortcuts for opening hyperlinks in new windows. If selected, Option+⌘+click and Option+Shift+⌘ open new windows; if deselected, they open new tabs instead.

- **When a New Tab or Window Opens, Make It Active.** This option, if selected, automatically switches the browser to a new tabbed pane or window. By default, this option is deselected, so new windows and tabbed panes open in the background, leaving the current window or pane visible.

- **Confirm Before Closing Multiple Tabs or Windows.** If selected (the default), Safari displays a warning when you close multiple windows or tabbed panes at once. For example, when you close a window, all its panes are closed with it, so when this option is selected, Safari asks if you really meant to close just the window's active tabbed pane (in other words, if you clicked the window's Close button instead of the tab's by mistake). Similarly, if you close all open windows at once (by pressing Option+⌘+W), Safari asks if you really meant to close just the current window (in other words, if you pressed Option by mistake).

The remaining two Preference dialog box's panes are unrelated, though both are shown in Figure 10.10: AutoFill and RSS.

The AutoFill pane has one set of options called AutoFill Web Forms. The three options, if selected, determine where Safari looks for data to fill in Web forms automatically: the Address Book, your username and passwords you've used in Safari for Web pages, and forms you've previously filled out from Safari. If you click Edit next to the Address Book option, the Address Book application launches so you can edit its contacts (see Chapter 11). In the other two cases, you can remove specific entries by clicking the Edit button next to the option.

FIGURE 10.10

The AutoFill pane (left) and RSS pane (right) of the Safari Preferences dialog box

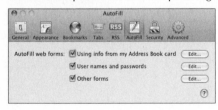
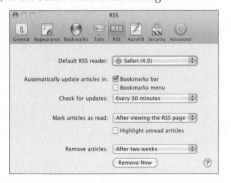

The RSS pane has these options (RSS is covered in the next section of this chapter):

- **Default RSS Reader.** This popup menu determines what program automatically is used to open and display RSS feeds. Safari is the default option, though you could select Mail or choose another Web browser, RSS-capable mail application, or a stand-alone RSS reader program that you have installed on the Mac.

- **Automatically Update Articles In.** There are two options here: Bookmarks Bar and Bookmarks Menu. Safari automatically updates the RSS feeds for any feeds that are bookmarked in the selected options' locations.

- **Check for Updates.** This popup menu determines how often Safari looks to see if an RSS feed has been updated: Every 30 Minutes, Every Hour, Every Day, or Never. If you choose Never, you must open the RSS feed manually, such as by going to its bookmark.

- **Mark Articles as Read.** This popup menu determines how Safari knows you've seen an RSS feed item: After Viewing the RSS Page (the default) or After Clicking Them. The first option assumes that simply seeing the list of entries counts as having read them; the second options makes you actually click the link before the RSS entry is counted as having been read.

- **Highlight Unread Articles.** If selected, articles that have not been read are highlighted in bold. By default this option is deselected.

- **Remove Articles.** This popup menu determines how long RSS feed items are retained in the feed list. Safari deletes the entries based on which option you choose: After One Day, After One Week (the default), After Two Weeks, After One Month, or Never. Click Remove Now to delete all RSS feed entries, whether read or not.

Using RSS in Safari

RSS, which stands for Really Simple Syndication, is a way of sending content directly to a browser, e-mail program, or stand-alone RSS reader program. A Web browser enables you to go to content, RSS brings the content to you, and as new content is added to a specific RSS feed, it shows up in your list of RSS articles.

Web browsers like Safari can subscribe to RSS feeds, treating them essentially as Web pages that you open through bookmarks. When you go to a Web page that offers RSS feeds, look for an RSS icon or the word Subscribe. Open the RSS page as you would any Web page. Then choose Bookmarks ⇨ Add Bookmark or press ⌘+D to bookmark this RSS feed. Figure 10.11 shows an RSS feed being bookmarked.

Tip
Safari 4 can detect whether a Web page has an RSS feed associated to it. If it finds such an RSS feed, a steel-blue RSS icon appears on the right-hand side of the URL field; click it to open the RSS feed in Safari.

As with a Web page (see the section "Using bookmarks" earlier in this chapter), you can place the bookmark in the bookmarks bar, the Bookmarks menu, or in a folder. But, unlike with Web page bookmarks, you also get to choose Mail as a bookmarking option, which if selected has Apple Mail subscribe to the RSS feed. (Both Safari and Mail can subscribe to the same feed.)

Cross-Ref

Chapter 11 covers using Mail to read RSS feeds.

When you add an RSS feed, the All RSS Feeds option appears in the Collections list in the bookmarks window, plus All RSS Feeds now appears in the Bookmarks menu so you have quick access to a list of all your RSS feeds. You can access the RSS feeds from the list of all RSS feeds or from the location you bookmarked it to, such as the bookmarks bar. If you also bookmarked the RSS feed to Mail, you can see the feed entries there as well, as Figure 10.12 shows.

Based on the settings in the RSS pane in Safari's Preferences dialog box (see the previous section), Safari will keep the entries for your bookmarked RSS feed up to date.

FIGURE 10.11

Adding an RSS feed to Safari is no different than bookmarking a Web page.

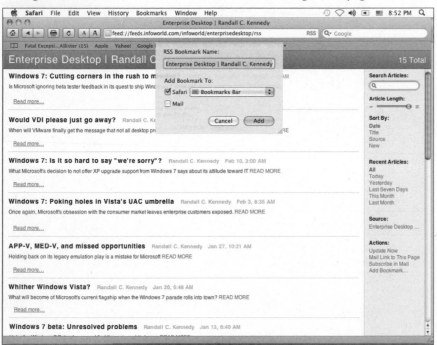

FIGURE 10.12

Viewing an RSS feed in Apple Mail

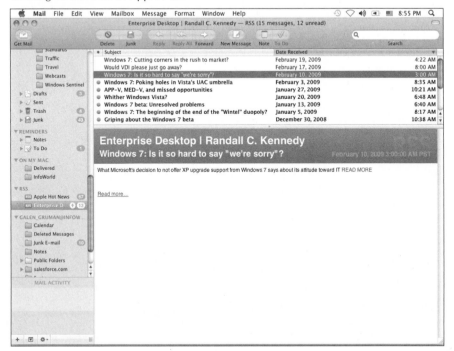

Using Other Browsers

Safari comes with Mac OS X 10.6 Snow Leopard, but it's not the only browser available for your Mac. And it may not be the best one for you, either. Two other mainstream browsers worth considering are Mozilla Firefox (www.mozilla.com) and Opera (www.opera.com). You can have multiple browsers on your Mac, and even run them at the same time, so it's not an either/or proposition.

Why would you consider a different browser than Safari? The two biggest reasons are:

- **Security.** Safari is one of the least secure popular browsers available. Firefox and Opera are more secure, according to security experts, with better protection against phishing and other hacking attacks. Also, both Firefox and Opera let you set a password to open them (in the Security pane of Firefox's Preferences dialog box and in the Advanced pane of Opera's Preferences dialog box), so someone can't just fire up Firefox or Opera and connect to all your accounts for which you have enabled autofill. Safari can't do that, so anything that is set to autofill can be accessed by anyone who has access to your user account.

- **User interface.** Safari's handling of bookmarks can be awkward: You either need to group bookmarks in a folder accessible from the bookmarks bar, which requires more planning, or open the bookmarks window, which takes over your entire screen. Many people prefer the bookmarks sidebar that Firefox and Opera offer to keep your bookmarks easily accessible but not in the way. And both Firefox and Opera have more controls over Web pages' content, such as Firefox's capability to manage plug-ins individually and Opera's preference to silence audio on Web pages.

Figure 10.13 shows the Web page from Figure 10.2 in Firefox, while Figure 10.14 shows the same Web page in Opera. We suggest you try them both to see if one would be better as your default Web browser than Safari or work well as an additional browser on your Mac. Don't get us wrong: Safari is a good browser, and popular in its own right. But it's not always the best choice, so we hope you'll explore other options as well.

FIGURE 10.13

The Mozilla Firefox browser

FIGURE 10.14

The Opera browser

Summary

Before you can use the Web to access content and services, you need to connect your Mac to the Internet. Typically, you connect to the Internet through a broadband Internet connection, such as through a DSL or cable modem, wireless router, or dial-up modem using a service from an ISP.

The Network system preference is where you establish the settings that connect your Mac to the broadband Internet connection device, as well as to other computers and devices on your local area network. The Network system preference offers the Network Setup Assistant to help guide you through the setup for wired and wireless broadband connections, as well as for dial-up modem connections.

Mac OS X 10.6 Snow Leopard comes with Apple's Safari browser preinstalled, so it's the default browser for many Mac users. Like all browsers, Safari lets you enter URLs to go to a specific Web address, as well as use hyperlinks on those pages to jump to other pages and use bookmarks to save favorite pages in lists that you can later click to go directly to them. Safari also enables you to see the history of your Web visits, so you can go back to Web pages you've recently visited. The Bookmarks menu, bar, and page all provide access to bookmarked pages and visited-page histories. There are also toolbar buttons that enable you to navigate back and forth among the pages you've visited in the current browser session.

Safari can display Web pages in tabs or separate windows, or both. It offers a variety of controls to create, delete, and otherwise manage the tabs and windows. In Safari, you can print and mail Web pages to other people, as well as save Web pages to your Mac and view the HTML source code used in the Web pages you view. If you're a Web page developer, the optional Developer menu provides controls to check for coding errors and turn various controls on and off for testing.

Safari enables you to search for text on a Web page you're visiting, as well as use the Google search engine to find information on the Web at other pages. You can also go directly to other search engines if you prefer not to use Google's search engine.

Safari's many preference options enable you to set security, such a blocking popups and preventing some potentially dangerous Web technologies from running in your browser. The Preferences dialog box also lets you establish user interface standards such as the default font, font size, and language for Web pages, plus how new tabs and windows open by default.

Safari can read RSS feeds, as well as bookmark them for easy access later. It also provides controls on whether RSS feeds' entries are automatically updated and, if so, how often they are updated and their contents retained. You can bookmark RSS feeds not only in Safari but also in Apple Mail, in case you prefer to read RSS feeds there.

Mac users have two main alternatives to Safari: Mozilla Firefox and Opera. Both have better security controls, and many people prefer their capability to show a list of bookmarks on the side of the screen instead of relying solely on menus or a window of bookmarks that obscures any Web page you're viewing. With Mac OS X, you can install and run multiple browsers, so you can use any combination of Safari, Firefox, Opera, and other browsers as you prefer.

Collaborating and Communicating

J ust as accessing the Web is a major use of the Mac, and a reason that Apple has put so much care into its Web applications such Safari and Web-based technologies such as iTunes and MobileMe, communicating with other people is a key reason people use a Mac — and again a key area that Apple has focused its applications on.

Communication is a fundamental human activity. People love to talk to each other. All sorts of new technologies have changed how we communicate — e-mail, online chat boards, instant messaging, feeds like Twitter, social network sites like Facebook, and so on — but what's constant is that we are still talking to each other, just over greater distances than ever before possible.

Collaboration — working together — is what enables people to do so many great things, bringing together skills, intuition, and physical labor, along with the energy created by coming together. You can't collaborate if you can't communicate, so the Mac's communication capabilities are key. Other capabilities, such as file sharing, enable you to build on that communication to accomplish actual work.

The two core communications applications that Mac OS X 10.6 Snow Leopard provides are Mail and iChat. Mail is Apple's e-mail client, which enables you to send and receive e-mails. iChat is Apple's instant messaging client, which enables you to send instant messages so you can chat in real time with other people no matter where they are.

Two other Mac OS applications supplement Mail and iChat, helping you manage the collaboration: Address Book, which stores your contact information, and iCal, which tracks your meetings, appointments, deadlines, and other such items. Both can also be shared in a workgroup.

Cross-Ref

Chapter 8 covers iTunes, Chapter 10 covers Safari, and Chapter 15 covers MobileMe. Chapter 13 covers sharing files with other people.

Setting Up Apple's Mail

Apple's Mail application is, simply put, world-class. Most people can use it as their regular e-mail client, rather than use a separate one such as Microsoft Entourage or Mozilla Thunderbird. You can manage multiple e-mail accounts, have your mail automatically sorted, and even access RSS (Really Simple Syndication) feeds in your e-mail list.

But before you do any of that, you need to set up Mail. If you've upgraded your Mac to Mac OS X 10.6 Snow Leopard, your existing Mail accounts will be ready for you in the Snow Leopard version of Mail. If you have a new Mac, you need to set up your Mail accounts. Either way, you can also import your existing e-mail accounts from other programs so they're all available in Mail.

New Feature

Mail (as well as iCal and Address Book) now natively works with the Microsoft Exchange 2007 e-mail server commonly used in business, using Microsoft's ActiveSync technology so your e-mail, calendar, contacts, and notes are immediately updated between the Exchange server and your Mac. Chapter 19 covers how to take maximum advantage of this new ActiveSync support and work with Exchange.

Setting up new e-mail accounts

If you have no e-mail accounts set up in Mail, the program walks you through a series of steps to set up your e-mail account when you first run it.

If you already had an e-mail account set up (such as because you upgraded your Mac to Mac OS X 10.6 Snow Leopard) and want to add an additional account, first choose File ➪ Add Account.

Whether you are creating your first e-mail account or adding a new one, the process is the same: In the dialog box that appears, enter the name you want people to see in the From field when they receive e-mails from you, as well as your e-mail address and the password for that e-mail account. Click Continue.

Mail tries to connect to the e-mail server automatically. If it cannot, it displays the dialog box shown in Figure 11.1, where you need to choose the e-mail server type (the Account Type popup menu) and server address (the Incoming Mail Server field) and then enter your username and password for the e-mail account. (The Description field is optional, and provides a description in Mail to help you remember the account's purpose, such as Work, Home, or Shopping Address.) There are three server types:

FIGURE 11.1

If Mail can't connect to your e-mail server based on your e-mail address, it asks you for the connection details in this dialog box.

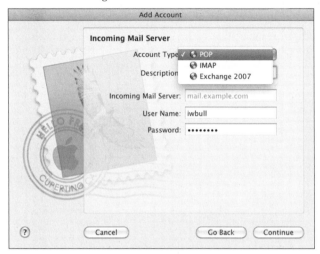

- **POP, which stands for Post Office Protocol.** This is the most common type of server account. Note that by default, POP assumes you have just one computer accessing e-mail, so it downloads the messages to your Mac and then deletes the messages from your e-mail server — which makes those e-mails unavailable if you check e-mail from a different computer later. You can change this default, as we explain in the "Accounts preferences" section later in this chapter. POP is typically the e-mail server type used by free e-mail services such as Gmail and Hotmail, by e-mail accounts you set up with most Web hosts, and in the e-mail accounts that come from your Internet service provider (such as your cable company or telephone company).

Tip

Typical POP server addresses take the form pop.domain or mail.domain, such as `pop.apple.com` or `mail.apple.com`. Sometimes, it's just the domain name, such as `apple.com`. If none of these work, check your documentation or ask your IT support staff.

- **IMAP, which stands for Internet Mail Access Protocol.** This server type is less common but makes it easier to use e-mail from several computers because it leaves the messages on the server by default so they're still there when you access e-mail from a different computer. Typically, businesses set up IMAP e-mail access for their employees. Note that IMAP is the standard that Microsoft Exchange 2003 and earlier use to let Mac users access mail both within a corporate network and over what it calls an Outlook Web Access (OWA) connection for access over the Internet.

Tip

Typical IMAP server addresses take the form `mail.domain`, such as `mail.apple.com`. Sometimes, it's just the domain name, such as `apple.com`. For Exchange 2003 and earlier, the form is often owa.domain, such as `owa.apple.com`. If none of these work, check your documentation or ask your IT support staff.

- **Exchange 2007.** This server type — new to Mac OS X 10.6 Snow Leopard — provides a direct connection to Microsoft Exchange 2007 servers (but not to earlier versions) using Microsoft's ActiveSync technology. If you choose Exchange 2007 as the server type, you get two additional options: Address Book Contacts and iCal Calendars. Select either or both to have Exchange 2007 synchronize your Mac's contacts and/or schedules with the Exchange address book and calendar you use at work so you have one master set of records. Note that Exchange leaves all messages, calendar entries, and contacts on the server, so they're always accessible from any computer you log in from.

Cross-Ref

Chapter 19 covers using Mail with Exchange in more detail.

Click Continue. Mail tries to connect to the server with your new settings. If it cannot, get your tech support to tell you the correct settings and try again. Click Cancel if you want to try again later after you've had a chance to get the correct settings.

When setting up an e-mail account, you may get an error message that asks you to verify the identity of the server you are connecting to, as Figure 11.2 shows. This typically happens when you use a Web host, a company that lets you set up a Web site and e-mail addresses on its servers. In this case, the Web host's actual domain won't be the same as for your e-mail server, and Mail notices that difference. Because providing fake domain names is a common trick of identity thieves, Mail asks you to verify that you are connecting to the correct server, as opposed to a scammer's server who is hoping to get your username and password to then use to access your information elsewhere. You can see the details by clicking Show Certificate, as we did in Figure 11.2. If you're confident that the server is legit, click Connect; otherwise, click Cancel and verify the server information with your tech support or documentation. (And if you're setting up multiple e-mail accounts on this Mac to this server, select the Always Trust option so you're not asked again about this mismatch.)

After Mail has made a connection, it will ask you for the setting so it can send out e-mail. Typically, a Web host or business uses a different server to send out e-mail than to receive it. Here are the options for outgoing e-mail configuration:

- **Outgoing Mail Server.** This is the server that takes the e-mail from Mail and sends it to the Internet for delivery to your addressees. The typical outgoing server uses a technology called SMTP (Simple Mail Transfer Protocol); therefore, the server's address usually takes the form smtp.*domain*, such as `smtp.apple.com`. Sometimes, it's mail.*domain* or just the domain name, such as `mail.domain.com` or `apple.com`. For Exchange 2003 and earlier, the form is often owa.*domain*, such as `owa.apple.com`. If none of these work, check your documentation or ask your IT support staff.

- **Use Only This Server.** Select this option if you want all outgoing mail to go through the same server. Otherwise, you can specify a separate server for each e-mail account. If you have, for example, your work and personal e-mail accounts on the Mac, you may want your personal e-mail to go through its own server and not pass through your company's server (where it can be monitored). Or your company may insist that all e-mail go through its servers to ensure you're not sending out confidential data.

- **Use Authentication.** Select this option if the outgoing server requires you to authenticate yourself — prove you are who you say you are. Then enter your username and password in the adjacent fields. (Note that the authentication username and password may differ from the one you use to check your e-mail.) More and more Web hosts and companies are requiring authentication so spammers can't send e-mails through their servers.

- **Description.** Enter a brief description in this optional field to help you remember what this server is, such as Home, Joe's House, or Office.

Click Continue; Mail tries to make a connection. It may open a new dialog box asking you to enable outgoing mail security. If your Internet service provider (ISP) or Web host requires such security, select the Use Secure Sockets Layer (SSL) option and then choose the appropriate option from the Authentication popup menu: None, Password, Kerberos Version 5 (GSSAPI, which stands for Generic Security Services Application Programming Interface), NTLM (which stands for Windows NT LAN Manager), and MD5 (Message-Digest algorithm 5) Challenge-Response. Your tech support or documentation should tell you which option to use. Click Continue, then review the settings in the next dialog box. If they're correct, click Create. (If you want to connect immediately, select the Take Account Online option first.) Otherwise, click Go Back to change your settings or Cancel to stop (none of your settings are saved if you click Cancel).

FIGURE 11.2

If Mail sees a mismatch between your e-mail account's server name and that of the server that claims to host your e-mail, it provides this warning. The mismatch could be harmless, such as when you use a Web host to provide your e-mail server, or it could indicate someone is trying to scam you by collecting your username and password.

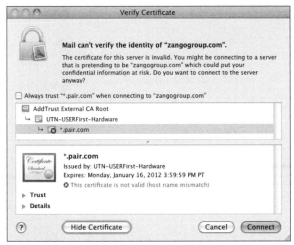

Sending E-Mail While Traveling

You're at a hotel, a friend's or in-law's home, a café with a Wi-Fi hot spot, or other temporary location. You try to send your e-mails but keep getting "cannot connect" error messages. Yet your e-mails send fine from your home or the office. What's the culprit?

Because spammers send billions of messages each year through other people's e-mail servers to make their scamming messages look like they came from legitimate sources, more and more Internet service providers (ISPs) and Web hosts are disallowing use of their servers by strangers. For example, when you use an e-mail address provided by your cable company and you send messages from home over your cable service's broadband connection, your cable company sees that you're sending a message from inside its network and that your outgoing server is on the same network, so it lets your messages through. But when a friend visits and tries to send e-mail, her computer is using, say, her phone company's outgoing e-mail server. The phone company sees her try to send messages through its servers but notes that she's not connected via the phone company's broadband connection, so it blocks her messages from going into its servers.

There's no one answer to addressing this issue for sending your legitimate e-mail. But chances are that one of the following methods will work. Check with your ISP or Web host to see what method they're using to let you send e-mail when traveling.

- **Use authentication to enter your username and password, either in your e-mail account or when prompted by Mail.** Some ISPs will accept e-mail coming from foreign networks if there's a valid authentication attached to the message. Try selecting SSL as the authentication method if the username and password isn't accepted. Also, try checking your e-mail before sending, then try to send; some Web hosts let you send from a foreign location after you've read your e-mail (and established a legitimate connection) for a set time (such as for 45 minutes after making that initial connection).

- **Set up an outgoing server in Mail using the settings for the location you're in**. (A friend might let you use her settings, but chances are small that a hotel or other business will.) It's also possible that your ISP has a separate outgoing mail server address to use when customers travel, so check with it. To add a server, choose Mail ➪ Preferences or press ⌘+, (comma), go to the Accounts pane, and select your account from the list at left, as shown here at left. In the Outgoing Mail Server (SMTP) popup menu, choose Edit SMTP Server List. Click the + iconic button in the window that appears to add a new outgoing server, as shown on the right-hand side of the figure. Double-click in the Description column to give the new outgoing server setting a name and double-click in the Server Name column to provide its server address. Go to the Advanced pane and select the appropriate options for the outgoing server. Click OK when done. You're now back in the Accounts pane. Using the Outgoing Mail Server (SMTP) popup menu, choose the new outgoing server to send your e-mails through it. Use the Accounts pane in Mail preferences to switch among outgoing servers as needed.

- **Change the outgoing port to get around blocks set up at some hotels and other facilities.** Sometimes, the issue is not with your ISP but with the ISP serving the location you're working from. Some block the standard SMTP ports (25 and 587). You can try to get around this block by changing the SMTP port to 465. To do so, go to the Accounts pane of the Preferences dialog box and choose Edit Server List from the Outgoing Mail Server popup menu. In the sub-dialog box that appears, go to the Advanced pane, select Use Custom Port, and enter **465**. Click OK, then close the Preferences dialog box. When you're back at your home or work location, repeat these steps, except select Use Default Ports.

Importing existing e-mail accounts

If you have e-mail accounts already set up in another copy of Apple Mail (such as in a different user account on this Mac or in a folder from an old user account) or other e-mail program, you can import the account and its e-mail messages into Mail by choosing File ➪ Import Mailboxes. In the Import dialog box that appears (see Figure 11.3), choose the e-mail program you want to import from and Click Continue. For most of the options, Mail opens a dialog box asking you to locate the mailbox folder and then click Continue to transfer the settings and mail to Mail. For Entourage, it launches Entourage and then imports the settings and e-mail messages. Click Done when the import is completed.

Setting Mail's preferences

There are many settings you can configure in Apple Mail to manage both overall preferences such as fonts and mailbox layout and mailbox-specific settings such as how to store e-mail, how often to check for e-mail, and the like. To access these preferences, choose Mail ➪ Preferences or press ⌘+, (comma).

When importing e-mail accounts, Mail asks which program the account is associated to so it knows how to import its settings and messages.

General preferences

The General pane, shown in Figure 11.4, has a grab bag of settings:

- **Default Email Reader.** Choose the e-mail program that should launch automatically when you click a mail link on the Web or other application. The Default is Mail, but if you have other e-mail programs installed, they will appear in the popup menu as well. No matter what your default e-mail program is, you can use any of them by launching them when desired.

- **Check for New Messages.** Choose how frequently you want Mail to look for new messages. You choices are Manually, Every Minute, Every 5 Minutes (the default), Every 15 Minutes, Every 30 Minutes, and Every Hour. If you choose Manually, you must choose Mailbox ⇨ Get New Mail and then choose the desired mailbox to check, or choose Mailbox ⇨ Get All New Mail or press Shift+⌘+N to check all accounts for new messages.

- **New Message Sound.** By default, Mail plays the New Messages sound when it detects new messages. You can change that sound to one of the standard Mac OS X sounds in this popup menu, choose your own sound (choose the Add/Remove option), or turn off the audio notification (choose None). Select the Play Sounds for Other Mail Actions options if you want Mail to provide audio feedback, such as when sending messages.

FIGURE 11.4

The General preference pane in Mail

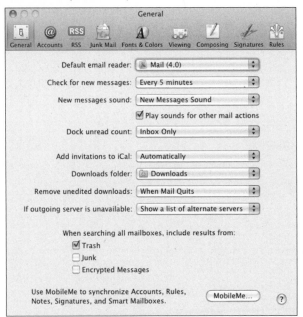

- **Dock Unread Count.** Choose how you want the Mail icon in the Dock to display the number of unread messages available. The Inbox Only option shows the count for messages only in the main inbox, which is where all accounts are placed by default. (You can change their locations, as described in the "Working with e-mails" section later in this chapter.) The All Accounts option shows the count for all accounts, whether or not they are in the main inbox, as well as any messages in the Draft folder and any unread messages in the Trash folder, but not unread messages in the Junk Mail folder. The None option disables the new-message display in the Dock.

- **Add Invitations to iCal.** If you receive an e-mail with an invitation attached (as an .ics file), choosing Automatically in this popup menu (the default) adds the item to your iCal calendar automatically. (If you accept the message in your e-mail, it displays in iCal as an appointment; if you don't act on the invitation, the invitation itself appears in iCal, where you can accept or decline it.) If you choose Never, the invitations are not added to iCal.

- **Downloads Folder.** This option determines where attachments in your messages are downloaded to when you save them. The default is the Downloads folder, but you can use an alternative location by choosing Other and then navigating to the desired folder.

- **Remove Unedited Downloads.** This option determines when Mail deletes attachments that you have not saved to your Mac or that you have not modified (such as by editing the message in Mail and saving it). The options are When Mail Quits, After Message Is Deleted (the default), and Never.

- **If Outgoing Server is Unavailable.** The default option is Show a List of Alternate Servers, which has Mail ask you to choose a different outgoing mail sever if available (see the side-bar, "Sending E-Mail While Traveling," for details on setting up these alternate servers). Your other option is Automatically Try Sending Later.

- **When Searching Mailboxes, Include Results From.** This option determines where the search feature in Mail looks when you are searching across all e-mail accounts. You can select any or all of the Trash, Junk, and Encrypted Messages options.

- **MobileMe.** Click this button to open the MobileMe system preference for synchronizing mail and other information across multiple Macs if you have a MobileMe account. Chapter 15 explains MobileMe in depth.

Accounts preferences

In the Accounts pane, shown in Figure 11.5, you can configure your e-mail accounts after you've set them up. At left is a list of existing accounts; select the one you want to modify. Then go through the three subpanes.

FIGURE 11.5

The Accounts preference pane in Mail. Shown at left is the Mailbox Behaviors subpane; shown at right is the Advanced subpane.

Note

After you make changes in the Accounts pane and close the Preferences dialog box, Mail will ask you to save your changes or cancel them. Changes made to other panes are automatically saved, but not changes to accounts because accidental changes could cause Mail not to access those accounts correctly.

The Account Information subpane is where you can modify the basic defaults for the account, such as the e-mail address, the name that appears in messages you send, the Description for this account, the incoming and outgoing mail servers, and the username and password for the account (if any). The sidebar "Sending E-Mail While Traveling" explains how to set up outgoing mail servers, as well as shows this subpane.

The Mailbox Behaviors pane is where you set how mail is retained, as well as how notes are handled, on your Mac. The following settings are available:

- **Drafts.** Available only for IMAP accounts; select the Store Draft Messages on the Server option to keep draft messages (those you are composing and have saved but not sent) on the server instead of on your Mac's local folder. But note that IMAP servers handle this feature unreliably, so messages can be lost because they don't end up being stored on the server as expected.

- **Notes.** Select the Store Notes in Inbox option to have Mail keep track of the notes and to-do items you've set in services such as Microsoft Exchange.

- **Sent.** In the Delete Sent Messages When popup menu, choose when (or if) you want Mail to delete sent messages from your Mac. Your options are Never (the default), One Day Old, One Week Old, One Month Old, and Quitting Mail (immediately after you quit Mail). Deleting messages can save disk space but it also means you can't find old messages when you want them.

  For IMAP and Exchange 2007 accounts, you also get the Store Sent Messages on the Server option; if selected, all e-mails you sent are stored on the IMAP server and are thus accessible from any computer or iPhone.

- **Junk.** In the Delete Junk Messages When popup menu, choose when (or if) you want Mail to delete sent messages from your Mac. Your options are the same as for Delete Sent Messages. As there's little reason to keep junk mail, the default is One Week Only (so you have a little while to review them in case legitimate mail is inadvertently flagged as junk).

  For IMAP and Exchange 2007 accounts, you also get the Store Junk Messages on the Server option; if selected, all e-mails flagged as junk are stored on the server and are thus accessible from any computer or iPhone.

- **Trash.** If you are working with a POP or IMAP account, select the Move Deleted Messages to the Trash Mailbox if you want to keep deleted messages at least briefly (so you can recover any accidentally deleted ones). If this option is deselected, messages are permanently deleted when you delete them from the inbox.

  For POP and IMAP accounts, if you select the Move Deleted Messages to the Trash Mailbox option, you can choose when they are permanently deleted by using the Permanently Erase Deleted Messages When popup menu, whose options are the same as for Delete Sent Messages When popup menu. (The Permanently Erase Deleted Messages When popup menu is also available for Exchange 2007 accounts, even though the Move Deleted Messages to the Trash Mailbox option is not available for them.)

  If you are working with an IMAP or Exchange 2007 account, you have the Store Deleted Messages on the Server option, which keeps deleted messages on the server when deleted from your Mac so they are accessible from any computer or iPhone.

The Advanced pane controls how Mail interacts with your e-mail server:

- **Enable This Account.** Select this option for Mail to connect to the account's server to check for new mail in and send mail from this account. If an account is disabled, it disappears from the list of inboxes, but it will not be deleted.

- **Include When Automatically Checking for New Messages.** Select this option for Mail to check for new messages on the schedule you set in the General preferences pane. If deselected, you must manually check for new mail by choosing Mailbox⇨ Get New Mail and choosing this account from the submenu.

- **Remove Copy from Server After Retrieving a Message.** This option, available for POP accounts only, determines how long messages are retained on the server after you've read them. We recommend you choose After One Week, so if you have multiple computers you check e-mail from, they all get a chance to download the message before it is deleted from the server. Your options in the adjacent popup menu are Immediately, After One Day, After One Week, After One Month, and When Moved from Inbox. Click Remove Now to delete all messages stored on your e-mail server, such as to make space in a server that is running short on storage capacity.

  The When Moved from Inbox menu option for Remove Copy from Server After Retrieving a Message can be useful if you have just one Mac you check e-mail from and you create folders in to keep messages sorted; if this option is selected and you move a message, it is deleted from the e-mail server, presumably because you've read it and no longer need to keep a copy. But if you have mail filtering rules (covered in this chapter's "Working with e-mails" section), they typically move mail into specified folders, and that action also deletes the message from the e-mail server even if you haven't actually read it yet.

- **Prompt Me to Skip Messages Over __ KB.** This option, available only for POP accounts, makes Mail ask you whether to download messages (including any attachments) larger than the size you specify here. (Leaving it blank downloads all messages without asking.) That's handy if you are using a slow connection (either at your main location or when traveling).

- **Keep Copies of Messages for Offline Viewing.** This popup menu, available for IMAP and Exchange 2007 accounts, determines which messages are copied to your local folder so you can read them when not connected to the server. The options are All Messages and Their Attachments (the default), All Messages But Omit Attachments, Only Messages I've Read, and Don't Keep Copies of Any Messages.

- **IMAP Path Prefix.** This field, available only for IMAP accounts, is where you put in a server address as provided by your network administrator to ensure a proper connection to the IMAP server. Leave it blank unless given such an address.

- **Root Path.** This field, available only for Exchange 2007 accounts, is where you put in a server address as provided by your network administrator to ensure a proper connection to the Exchange 2007 server. Leave it blank unless given such an address.

- **Port.** This option should rarely be changed. Mail automatically uses standard ports — addresses at e-mail servers that are used to handle specific requests such as checking e-mail or sending out e-mail. Sometimes, a network administrator uses nonstandard ports to thwart hackers; in that case, enter the correct port number here.

- **Use SSL.** Select this option to enable SSL authentication for this account. Note that if you select this option for an e-mail server that does not support SSL, you may not be able to connect. Conversely, some servers require that you enable SSL to connect. If SSL is enabled, choose the appropriate authentication method for your server by using the Authentication popup menu.

- **Authentication.** Use this popup menu, available for IMAP accounts only, to choose the authentication method for your IMAP server: Password (the default), MDS Challenge-Response, NTLM, or Kerberos Version 5 (GSSAPI).

- **Use Idle Command If the Server Supports It.** This option, available for IMAP accounts only, enables what is called *push messaging*. This lets the IMAP server send you new e-mail on its own, rather than wait for you to click the Get Mail button in Mail to retrieve mail or for your scheduled e-mail check interval to occur.

Junk Mail preferences

More than half of all e-mail sent today is junk, unsolicited ads, or scams typically relating to (real or fake) business, drugs, vacations, health insurance, pornography, and more. You can reduce the amount of junk mail that actually makes it into your inbox by selecting the Enable Junk Mail Filtering option in the Junk Mail pane, as shown in Figure 11.6.

If junk mail filtering is enabled, you have the following options:

- **When Junk Mail Arrives.** Select how you want Mail to handle mail it determines to be junk: Mark as Junk Mail but Leave It in My Inbox, Move It to the Junk Mailbox (the default), or Perform Custom Actions (this makes the Advanced button accessible).

- **The Following Types of Messages Are Exempt from Junk Mail Filtering.** Select the kinds of e-mails that are never treated as junk: Sender of Message Is in My Address Book, Sender of Message Is in My Previous Recipients (people you've received e-mail from before and not flagged as junk), and Message Is Addressed Using My Full Name (such e-mail typically comes from a person who has your full name in his or her address book because he or she replied to one of your e-mails, which reduces the chance it's a junk message from a spammer sending to random e-mail addresses).

FIGURE 11.6

The Junk Mail preference pane in Mail (left) and the sheet in which you create your own junk-filtering rules (right)

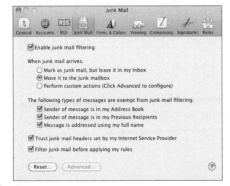 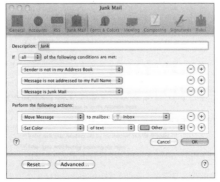

Tip

To see and edit who's in your Previous Recipients list, choose Window ⇨ Previous Recipients.

- **Trust Junk Mail Headers Set by My Internet Service Provider.** Select this option (the default) to treat any messages marked as junk by your ISP or Web host as junk. The only reason to deselect this option is if your ISP or Web host is so aggressive in flagging messages as junk that many legitimate e-mails are being flagged and thus diverted to the Junk Folder in Mail.

- **Filter Junk Mail Before Applying My Rules.** This option, selected by default, filters out junk mail before applying any message-filtering rules you've set up (see the "Working with e-mails" section in this chapter).

- **Reset.** Click this button to reset the junk mail settings to Mail's recommended defaults.

- **Advanced.** Click this button to specify more rules on how to handle potential junk mail. (For this button to be clickable, you must have selected Perform Custom Actions as the option for When Junk Mail Arrives in this pane.) In the sheet that appears, you set up a series of rules to detect possible junk mail. These rules work just like the message-filtering rules explained in the "Rules preferences" section later in this chapter.

Fonts & Colors preferences

In the Fonts & Colors pane, shown in Figure 11.7, you can customize the appearance of your mail's text. To change the font and size of messages and other text in Mail, click the Select button that appears to the right of the type of text you want to change: Mailbox font (the list of mailboxes at the left of the Message Viewer), Message List Font (the list of messages for a selected inbox), Message Font (the text within a message itself), Note Font (the font used for text in notes), and Fixed-Width Font (the font used for plain text [unformatted] messages or for HTML [Web-formatted] messages that use tags such as `<code>`). To apply fixed-width font to non-HTML messages, you must select Used Fixed-Width Font for Plain Text Messages option.

FIGURE 11.7

The Fonts & Colors pane (left) and Viewing pane (right) in Mail's Preferences dialog box

Select the Color Quoted Text option and then choose the desired colors for the three levels of indentation for quoted text in messages. Quoted text is the original message retained in a reply, and the entire thread is available in the message (so you don't have to find the previous messages to remember what was written).

Viewing preferences

The Viewing pane, shown in Figure 11.7, controls how various details are displayed in and for messages:

- **Show Header Detail.** This popup menu enables you to determine what header appears in your e-mail messages received. The default option is Default, which shows the From, Subject, Date, To, Cc, and attachments information for each message. The None option hides all header information Choose Custom to select which information you want to display in mail headers by selecting options from a list. The All option shows all the detail, including the servers through which the message passed on its way to you. (This can help show a spam message by using a forged From address.)

- **Show Online Buddy Status.** This option, which is selected by default, adds the Buddy Availability column (labeled with the quote-balloon icon) to your message lists and, if a buddy who sent you an e-mail is online, an icon appears in the Buddy Availability column next to any e-mail from that buddy. A buddy is someone you have added in iChat (covered later in this chapter) *and* for whom you have entered instant messaging (chat) information in Address Book.

- **Display Unread Messages with Bold Font.** This option, which is selected by default, boldfaces any message in an inbox's message list so you know you haven't read it yet.

- **Display Remote Images in HTML Messages.** This option, which is selected by default, displays any images linked from within the e-mail message. To see the images, you need a live Internet connection.

- **Use Smart Addresses.** This option, which is selected by default, shows only the sender's name in a message's To, From, Cc, or Bcc field if the message contains the name or your Address Book does. (If the name is unknown, the e-mail address appears instead.) If this option is deselected, the message displays both the sender's name (if known) and the e-mail address in these fields. If you're concerned about ensuring that e-mails really come from the people the names indicate, deselect this option.

- **Highlight Related Messages Using Color.** This option, which is not selected by default, highlights any message related to the currently selected one in an inbox's message list with a colored background. (Click the color swatch to change that highlight color.) Mail looks at the recipients and message headers to determine related messages, so the accuracy of the results can vary.

Composing preferences

The Composing pane, shown in Figure 11.8, controls how new and reply messages are formatted, addressed, and routed:

FIGURE 11.8

The Composing pane in Mail's Preferences dialog box

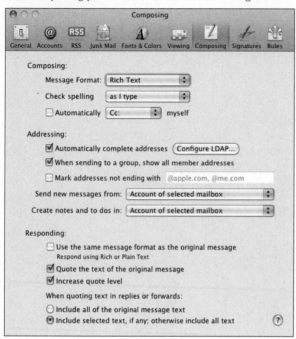

In the Composing section, you have three options:

- **Message Format.** Choose either Rich Text (the default) or Plain Text. The Rich Text option formats the e-mail in the Web's HTML format, so formatting such as boldface, indentation, and fonts are transmitted with the text so the recipient sees the same formatting on his or her end (if his or her e-mail application supports such formatting, of course, which most today do). The Plain Text option removes all formatting.

- **Check Spelling.** Your choices are As I Type, When I Send, and Never. If you choose As I Type, Mail indicates possible misspellings by using dotted red underlines; if you choose When I Send, it alerts you to any misspellings and gives you a chance to correct them before sending the message.

- **Automatically __ Myself.** If you select this option, Mail will either Cc (carbon copy) or Bcc (blind carbon copy) you on all messages you send, depending which option you pick in the popup menu. Note that recipients won't see any addresses that you Bcc'd on the message in the message header. They will see anyone you Cc'd the message to.

In the Addressing section, you have five options:

- **Automatically Complete Addresses.** If selected, this option tells Mail to look up potential addressees as you type their names in the To, Cc, or Bcc fields in a new or reply message. As you type, it looks for names that contain the characters typed so far in your Address Book, in e-mails you've previously sent or received, and in your LDAP (Lightweight Directory Access Protocol) directory, if you use one. (LDAP is used by some business networks to store employee information such as for a shared company address book. To use LDAP, you must first click the LDAP button and then add each LDAP server you want to check addresses against in the sheet that appears. Click the + iconic button to add an LDAP server, then enter the LDAP settings for it; you'll need to get those settings from your network administrator. You can have multiple LDAP servers configured to check against.)

- **When Sending to a Group, Show All Member Addresses.** Mail can access groups set up in Address Book, as explained in the "Working with Address Book" section later in this chapter. If this option is selected, when you send a message to a group, each group member's name or address appears in the message's To, Cc, and Bcc fields.

- **Mark Addresses Not Ending With.** This option makes all addressees appear in red unless their e-mail addresses end with the domains specified in the adjacent field. For example, if you enter `@apple.com` in the field, any addresses in new and reply messages' From, To, Cc, and Bcc fields that don't end in `@apple.com` will be red, while the `apple.com` addressees will be in black. To enter multiple domains, separate them with commas, such as `@apple.com, @infoworld.com`. You would use this feature to quickly tell when you are sending e-mails to people outside your organization, for example.

- **Send New Messages From.** This popup menu enables you to choose the "from" account for e-mails you send. The default is Account of Selected Mailbox, which means that if you have multiple e-mail boxes, the current one is where messages will be sent from (so you end up replying from the same account where you received a message, for example). You can also choose any account set up in Mail, so all messages come from that one e-mail address, no matter which account they were sent to.

- **Create Notes and To Dos In.** This popup menu enables you to define where notes and to-do items are stored in Mail. The default option is Account of Selected Mailbox, which adds any notes or to-do items to the current mailbox (if it supports these items; typically only Exchange and MobileMe accounts do). You can also choose an account that supports such items or On My Mac, which stores them in iCal.

The Responding section controls the formatting of reply messages (including those forwarded to others):

- **Use the Same Message Format as the Original Message.** If selected, the reply will be in HTML (rich text) if the original message was that format and in plain text if the original message was in that format. If this option is deselected (the default), the reply will be in whatever format you chose in the Message Format popup menu.

- **Quote the Text of the Original Message.** This option, which is selected by default, includes the original message in your reply.

- **Increase Quote Level.** This option, which is selected by default, makes the current reply the top level of the quote, meaning the text being replied to is indented one level in from the reply. Each previous reply in the message is indented a further level, with greater indentation for the older portions of the reply to help keep the history of the replies clear. (The original message is thus indented the most.)

- **When Quoting Text in Replies or Forwards.** There are two options: Include All of the Original Message Text and Include Selected Text If Any; Otherwise Include All Text. If you select the latter option and select a portion of the original message when replying, only that selection is included in the reply.

Signatures preferences

In the Signatures pane, shown in Figure 11.9, you can automatically add signatures to the messages you send. These signatures typically contain your name and business-card-style information such as your company, address, phone number, and so on. It might also include a saying or other personalized text.

You can have multiple signatures and apply one or more to each mail account you have, though it's typical to have one signature per account.

To start, click the + iconic button. A new signature appears in the middle column of the Signatures pane, named Signature #1. (The next new one is named Signature #2 and so on.) Double-click the name to change it. Then enter the signature text in the field at right. You can format text by selecting it and choosing the desired formatting options from the Format menu. Options include fonts, colors, indentation, and alignment. If you select the Always Match My Default Message Font option, your signature will ignore any font and size applied here, though the rest of the formatting is retained.

FIGURE 11.9

The Signatures pane in Mail's Preferences dialog box

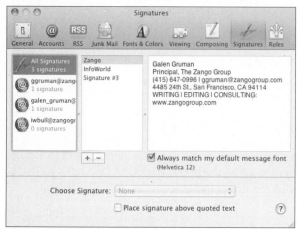

After you've created your signatures, you associate them to e-mail accounts. Select All Signatures in the list at the left of the pane to see all defined signatures in the middle column. Drag each signature onto the account that you want to use that signature, then release the mouse button. (You can associate multiple signatures to one account.)

The next step is to enable the signatures for each account. Select an account; the signatures associated to it display in the middle column. The Choose Signature popup menu at the bottom of the Signatures pane also becomes active. By Default, it is set to None, which means no signature is used. Choose the desired signature from the popup menu, or choose At Random or In Sequential Order to have Mail choose the signature for you. (If only one signature exists for an account, all options but None use that sole signature.)

Tip

Normally, a signature appears at the very bottom of the message. But if you select the Place Signature Above Quoted Text option, when you reply to or forward a message, the signature appears before any quoted text from the original message. (This assumes you selected the Quote the Text of the Original Message option in the Composing pane.)

To delete a signature associated to an account, select that account; only the signatures for that account appear in the middle column. Select the signature to delete, then click the – iconic button.

To edit a signature, select it in any account that uses it or from the All Signatures "account," then modify it in the right-hand field; all instances of it are updated.

Rules preferences

Mail lets you set up filtering rules that it applies to new messages as it loads them. (You can also apply these rules to existing messages). The typical reason to set up rules is to manage large volumes of e-mail. If you set up folders within your inboxes, such as for individual projects at work, you can set up rules that automatically move messages to specific folders based on their subject or who they came from. Other controls include deleting messages and marking them as read.

Figure 11.10 shows the Rules pane. Any existing rules are listed, and any rules whose Active options are selected are applied to incoming messages automatically. To delete a rule, select it from the list and click Delete. To duplicate a rule, select it from the list and click Duplicate. To edit a rule, select it from the list and click Edit. To add a rule, click Add Rule.

Tip

Drag rules within the list to change the order in which they execute. The topmost rule runs first, followed by the second rule, and so on.

When adding or editing a rule, a window appears that lets you select the criteria to filter messages with (what Mail calls *conditions*) and the actions you want to apply to those that match the criteria. As Figure 11.10 shows, you can have multiple criteria per rule, as well as multiple actions.

FIGURE 11.10

The Rules pane (left) and the window that appears to create and edit rules in (right)

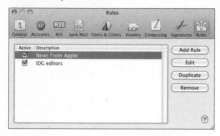
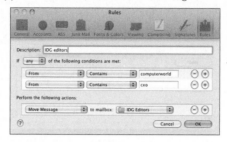

Note

If you do use multiple criteria, be sure to choose either Any or All from the If __ of the Following Conditions Are Met popup menu. If you choose Any, only one of the criteria needs to match for the rule to be applied; if you choose All, every one of the criteria you set need to match for the rule to be applied.

The first step is to give the Rule a name, which you do in the Description field. Then set up the criteria. Choose the criteria from the rightmost popup menu. There are 26 criteria to choose from, such as To, Subject, Date Sent, Sender Is Not in My Address Book, Message Content, and Priority Is High.

If there are options for the selected criterion, choose it from the adjacent popup menu that appears. If a criterion is based on text, such as matching part of a sender's name, enter that text in the adjacent field. For each criterion, these adjacent popup menus and text fields will appear only if needed. For example, if you choose Date Sent, a popup menu appears with two options: Is Less Than and Is Greater Than. Choose the appropriate option, then enter a number in the Days Old field that appears. If you choose Is Less Than and enter **10**, the rule will find all messages that were received in the last 10 days.

With the criteria set, you cannot set the actions to be applied to messages that meet your criteria. There are 13 such actions, including Move Message, Delete, Forward Message, Mark as Read, and Run AppleScript.

Click the + iconic button to add a criterion. Select a criterion and click the − iconic button to delete it. If the selected action has additional options, a popup menu with them appears next to the action. One action merits special attention: Stop Evaluating Rules. If you choose this action, any rules in the Rules pane that come after this rule will *not* execute.

Click OK to save the rule, or Cancel to not save it.

Managing E-Mail Accounts and Mailboxes

With your e-mail accounts set up, you're ready to send and receive e-mail messages. But first take a few more minutes to understand how to manage your e-mail accounts and the mailboxes that contain the messages so you don't get overwhelmed with the huge number of messages that are sure to collect in Mail. If you have multiple e-mail accounts set up in Mail, knowing how to manage those accounts is even more crucial to keep everything straight.

Some management controls reside in the Mail Preferences dialog box, those over which accounts are active (the Accounts pane), what accounts messages are sent from by default (the Composing pane), which signature is associated to each account (the Signatures pane), and how messages are filtered (the Rules pane). Refer to the details on those sections in the "Setting Mail's preferences" section in this chapter.

The rest of the account management, as well as your mailbox management, happens in the Message Viewer, which Figure 11.11 shows. In the Sidebar is a list of the active e-mail accounts, with the status of each indicated through a series of icons.

FIGURE 11.11

Each active account's mail is stored in a mailbox folder within the Inbox list in the left section of the Message Viewer window. Other mailbox folders are listed as well.

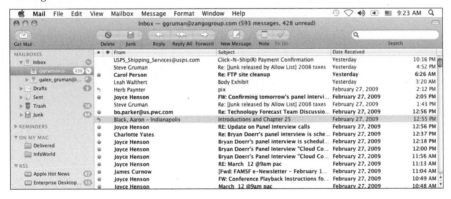

Note

Apple's Mail uses the terms account and mailbox. Technically, a mailbox is a folder for messages, RSS feeds, notes, and to-do items. An account is a set of connection settings for an e-mail address and the messages associated to that address. Mail uses the term mailbox to refer to the message, RSS, and notes folders stored locally on your Mac, as well as the messages associated to an account. So deleting an account's mailbox does not delete its account — you have to do that in the Accounts pane of the Preferences dialog box (as explained in the "Accounts preferences" section of this chapter).

Understanding mailbox folders

All e-mail accounts appear as folders within the Inbox. The Inbox contains the mailboxes for all e-mail accounts that are active, meaning they connect to the e-mail server to receive and send messages. As we explain later in this section, you can create additional mailboxes that are stored locally on your Mac, not connected to an e-mail server; these appear in the On My Mac list instead.

Tip
The Sidebar in Mail is reorderable, so you can arrange your accounts and inboxes in whatever order you prefer by dragging them to the desired locations.

If the account mailboxes have folders, you see a disclosure triangle to the left of the mailbox name; click it to expand the folder list (as you can see was done for the On My Mac list in Figure 11.11).

An oval to the right of the account mailbox shows the number of unread messages in that account or folder. Note that draft messages — those you haven't sent yet — are considered new messages.

There are several standard folders in the Mailboxes list, in addition to the Inbox: Drafts, Sent, Trash, and Junk. These four folders contain e-mails from all your accounts. You can switch to these folders by choosing Mailbox ➪ Go To and then choosing the desired folder from the submenu.

The Inbox folder also collects all mail from all accounts; to see just the mail for a specific account, click that account from the Inbox's account list (if they do not display, click the right-pointing triangle to the left of Inbox to expand the list of accounts).

As Figure 11.12 shows, the message list in these five folders displays which account the e-mail is associated to. This means you have one place to store your draft (unsent) messages, junk mail (to see if any legitimate mail got put there), sent messages, and deleted messages (in the Trash folder). If you want to view these folders' messages by the account, click the Mailbox column header in the message list to have Mail sort the message by account (mailbox) name. (You can sort messages by any of the columns displayed.)

FIGURE 11.12

The Drafts, Sent, Trash, and Junk folders contain messages from all e-mail accounts, so the account for each message is displayed in the Mailbox column.

Turning accounts on and off

In the accounts list, a ~ symbol within an oval indicates the account is offline, meaning that Mail is not checking messages for it. You might take an account offline when you know the server is down or you are not connected to the Internet (such as when working on an airplane) so you don't get connection error messages. To take an account offline, Control+click or right-click its name in the Inbox list, and choose Take "*account*" Offline in the contextual menu. To bring it back online (so it sends and receives messages), Control+click or right-click its name and choose Take "*account*" Online.

Tip

To quickly put accounts online or offline, choose Mailbox ⇨ Take All Accounts Online or Mailbox ⇨ Take All Accounts Offline. You can also take any individual account offline or online by choosing Mailbox ⇨ Online Status and choosing the desired account from the submenu. The submenus are toggles, so if an account is currently offline, the menu displays Take "account" Online; if an account is currently online, the menu displays Take "account" Offline.

Note that taking an account online, or offline, is not the same as enabling, or disabling, an account in the Advanced subpane of the Accounts pane in Mail's Preferences dialog box (see the "Accounts preferences" section earlier in this chapter). If an account is enabled, it displays in the Mailboxes list; if it is disabled, it does not.

You can also delete accounts. Select the account in the Inbox and either choose Mailbox ⇨ Delete Mailbox or Control+click or right-click the account and choose Delete Mailbox from the contextual menu. This deletes the account and all its associated messages from Mail.

Using smart mailboxes

Chances are you get lots of e-mails, and you have various folders set up to store messages related to a specific project or task — whether your volunteer work at the PTA, your vacation planning, or a project at the office. You can use rules (see the "Rules preferences" section earlier in this chapter) to have Mail automatically put mail that matches specific criteria into folders. This lets you put all e-mails whose subject has keywords related to the project plus all mail from specific people, for example, in one folder. Using rules is a great way to sort your mail for projects.

But there's another way: *smart mailboxes*. A smart mailbox is essentially a special kind of rule. What makes it special? Two things:

- All the messages that match the criteria are put in a folder placed in the accounts list at the left of the Message Viewer. A new category named Smart Mailboxes then appears in that left column, listing any smart mailboxes you set up.

- A smart mailbox does not remove the messages from their accounts or folders in those accounts. A smart folder is really a view that brings all those messages together no matter where they are stored in Mail. (It's like a playlist in iTunes.) This means that you can use both smart mailboxes and rules, and when you delete a smart mailbox, you don't affect the messages in their account and folders.

To create a smart mailbox, choose Mailbox ➪ New Smart Mailbox. You'll get a dialog box such as the one shown in Figure 11.13. It works very much like the dialog box you use to create rules (see Figure 11.10). You choose a criterion from the popup menu, adding any parameters appropriate for that criterion. Click the + iconic button to add additional criteria. Also select whether you want the smart mailbox to apply All or Any criteria by using the second popup menu in the Contains __ That Match __ of the Following Conditions. But there are a few controls for smart mailboxes that differ from those for creating rules:

- In the first popup menu in Contains __ That Match __ of the Following Conditions, you can make the smart mailbox contain either — but not both — e-mail messages or notes and to-do lists.

- To determine whether the smart mailbox contains messages sent to the Trash or Sent folders, you select the Include Messages from Trash and Include Messages from Sent options.

Click OK to save the smart mailbox, which will appear in the left column of the Message Viewer.

You can edit a smart mailbox by Control+clicking or right-clicking it in the accounts list, then choosing Edit Smart Mailbox in the contextual menu; or select the smart mailbox and choose Mailbox ➪ Edit Smart Mailbox. You can duplicate a smart mailbox (to use it as a template for a new one) by Control+clicking or right-clicking it in the accounts list, then choosing Duplicate Smart Mailbox in the contextual menu; or select the smart mailbox and choose Mailbox ➪ Duplicate Smart Mailbox. You can delete a smart mailbox by choosing Delete Mailbox through either means. (Deleting a smart mailbox does *not* delete the messages or notes items from Mail.)

A related feature is the smart mailbox folder, which you create by choosing Mailbox ➪ New Smart Mailbox Folder. Give it a name and click OK. The folder appears under Smart Mailboxes in the left column of the Message Viewer. A smart mailbox folder is just a folder that you can use to contain smart mailboxes (simply drag them into it). For example, if you are a PTA volunteer who works on several committees, you might create a smart mailbox folder called PTA and then have separate smart mailboxes you store in that folder for each committee so you can keep the e-mails or notes items separate for each committee.

FIGURE 11.13

Setting the criteria for a smart mailbox

Maintaining mailboxes

Mail provides several additional controls that perform maintenance work on your accounts and mailboxes. Unless otherwise indicated, you can access these controls from the Mailbox menu, by Control+clicking or right-clicking an account or mailbox and choosing from the contextual menu, or by clicking the Action iconic popup menu (the gear icon) at the bottom of the left column.

- **You can force Mail to look for new mail by choosing Mailbox ⇨ Get All New Mail, pressing Shift+⌘+N, or clicking Get Mail in the toolbar.** Or get new mail for a specific account by choosing Mailbox ⇨ Get New Mail and then choosing the desired account from the submenu.

- **If you use Microsoft Exchange as your e-mail server, you can synchronize what's on your Mac with what's on the Exchange server by choosing Mailbox ⇨ Synchronize "*account*".** (Only Exchange accounts will display in the menu.) Exchange synchronizes with Mail periodically on its own, so you would choose this option only when you want to synchronize outside of that regular schedule.

- **Choose Erase Deleted Items to force Mail to permanently delete messages from the Trash folder before the time set in the Mailbox Behaviors subpane of the Accounts pane in Mail's Preferences dialog box (see the "Accounts preferences" section earlier in this chapter) — or if you set Mail to not automatically delete messages from the Trash folder at regular intervals.** If you choose this option from the Mailbox menu, you can choose in a submenu to delete all messages in the Trash folder, or just those associated to a specific account. If you choose this option through the contextual menu, you delete only messages for that account.

- Choose Erase Junk Mail to force Mail to permanently delete messages in the Junk folder before the time set in the Mailbox Behaviors subpane of the Accounts pane in Mail's Preferences dialog box — or if you set Mail to not automatically delete messages from the Junk folder at regular intervals. If you choose this option from the Mailbox menu or press Option+⌘+J, you can choose in a submenu to delete all messages in the Junk folder, or just those associated to a specific account. If you choose this option through the contextual menu, you delete only messages for that account.

- Choose Archive Mailbox to save all messages onto your Mac or an attached local or network drive. This way you can delete the messages from your server and/or your Mac's Mail folders to save on storage space while still having the messages available in an archive should you need to access them later.

- Choose Edit "*account*" to open the Accounts pane of Mail's Preferences dialog box (see the "Accounts preferences" section earlier in this chapter).

- Choose Rename Mailbox to change the name of a mailbox. Note that you cannot change the names of account mailboxes, just local mailboxes (those listed in the On My Mac section of the left column in the Message Viewer) and folders within account mailboxes.

- Choose Use This Mailbox For (available only from the Mailbox menu) to have Mail use a local folder you created (in the On My Mac section) for Drafts, Sent, Trash, or Junk, as chosen in the submenu, instead of the default folders.

- Choose Rebuild (available only from the Mailbox menu) to clean up the mailbox folder stored on your Mac. Doing so can make the mailbox respond more quickly, such as when you select messages. But note that if you change the default folders for Junk, Sent, and so on for an Exchange account, those changes will be lost and the default folders will be used instead.

- From the contextual menu for an account mailbox, choose Get Account Info to see the server status for the account, as Figure 11.14 shows. You can switch to another account by using the popup menu in the Account Info dialog box. The dialog box's display depends on the type of account. The Account Info dialog box has several panes:

  - Quota Limits (for IMAP and Exchange accounts only). Shows what is stored on the server and whether it exceeds the storage limits set by your e-mail administrator.

  - Messages on Server (for POP accounts only). Displays all messages stored on the e-mail server and enables you to delete selected messages from the server. Using the Show Messages popup menu, you can view all messages on the POP (Post Office Protocol) server, those that have been downloaded to your Mac, and those that have been removed from your Mac but are still on the server.

  - Mailbox Behaviors. Provides access to the Mailbox Behaviors subpane in the Accounts pane of the Preferences dialog box.

- **Subscription List (for Exchange accounts only).** Shows all RSS and newsgroup feeds subscribed to from the Exchange server and enables you to manage those subscriptions.

- **Summary.** Provides a summary of your account settings.

FIGURE 11.14

The Account Info dialog box for an e-mail account

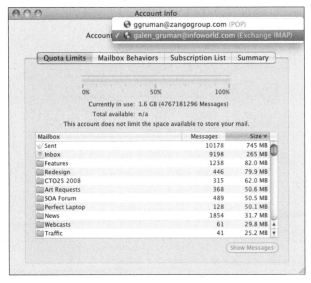

Working with E-Mails

Most of the time you're in Mail, you're working with individual e-mail messages, reading them, responding to them, or writing new ones. Figure 11.15 shows the message list available for each e-mail account you have, as well as for the folders you may have set up to help manage those messages.

Reading messages

By default, Mail lists messages in the order they are received, with the most recent message at the bottom, and all unread messages listed in boldface. You can change the sort order by clicking any of the columns in the message list, such as by sender or subject. When you click a column to sort it, a triangle appears to the left of the column name. If it points down, the column is sorted in reverse alphabetical order (Z to A) or in reverse chronological order (latest first); if it points up, the column is sorted in alphabetical order (A to Z) or in chronological order (earliest first). Note that for the Subject column, Mail ignores the Re: and Fwd: prefixes in subjects that indicate replies and forwarded messages, so all messages with the same subject are kept together (as opposed to having all replies and forwards grouped together regardless of subject).

You can change the columns displayed by Control+clicking or right-clicking the column row and selecting the desired columns (and deselecting the undesired ones) from the contextual menu, as shown in Figure 11.15. The Sort By menu option has the same effect as clicking a column to sort it. Or you can choose View ⇨ Columns or View ⇨ Sort By to change the displayed columns and the default sort order.

FIGURE 11.15

The message list for a mailbox

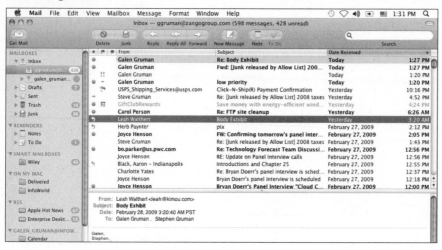

You can search your messages by entering a term in the toolbar's Search field and pressing Return or clicking the Search iconic button (the magnifying glass icon). As Figure 11.16 shows, when you search in Mail, you get a set of controls above the message list to narrow the search — similar options to what you get when searching in the Finder. You can select a specific mailbox or All Mailboxes, as well as narrow the search to Entire Message, From, To, or Subject. You can also save the search for later use by clicking Save; this creates a smart mailbox based on your search.

Tip

You can open multiple Message Viewer windows by choosing File ⇨ New Viewer Window or pressing Option+⌘+N. You might do this so you can switch quickly between different mailboxes.

Tip

To add a message's sender to your Mac's Address Book, choose Add Sender to Address Book or choose Shift+⌘+Y.

Mail's search options appear above the message list.

When you click on a message in the message list, you see part of the message in the preview pane below the message list. If you double-click the message, a separate window opens, as shown in Figure 11.17. It displays the sender, subject, send date, recipients, and any attachments included, as well as the actual message text.

In the message window's toolbar, you can delete the message by clicking Delete, mark it as junk by clicking Junk, print it by clicking Print, or send it to someone else by clicking Reply, Reply All, or Forward (as explained in the "Replying, forwarding, and redirecting messages" section later in this chapter).

Mail provides special controls for file attachments in messages you read:

- **It shows in the message header how many files are attached.**
- **Click the adjacent Save button to save the attachments to your Mac.** If you click and hold the mouse button, the Save button acts as a popup menu, letting you choose a specific attachment to save.
- **Click Quick Look to see the attachments in a Quick Look window.** If there are multiple attachments, the first attachment is previewed. Hold Option to change the Quick Look button to Slideshow, which then previews the attachments in a single Quick Look window that displays each attachment in turn.
- **If you click the disclosure triangle to the left of the attachments list, you see icons for each attachment, as Figure 11.17 shows.** You can double-click an icon to open it. For example, double-clicking a calendar invitation (an .ics file) adds it to iCal, while double-clicking a PowerPoint file opens it in either Microsoft PowerPoint or Apple iWork Keynote, based on what is set as your default application for this file type.

Using a technology called *data detectors*, Mail scans your messages for dates (including relative dates such as "tomorrow"), times, names, phone numbers, and other contact information. If you hover the mouse over such information, it is highlighted as a popup menu. Click the popup menu to get relevant options, such as Create New Contact, Add to Existing Contact, Create New iCal Event, or Look up Date in iCal.

FIGURE 11.17

An open message, with the file attachments expanded

New Feature

In Mac OS X 10.6 Snow Leopard, Mail can automatically identify flight numbers and provide a popup menu over the flight number to take you directly to the Dashboard's Flight Tracker widget (see Chapter 8) to get current flight information.

Writing messages

To send someone a message, click New Message in the toolbar, choose File ➪ New Message, or press ⌘+N. The New Message dialog box appears, as shown in Figure 11.17.

Addressing the message

In the To field, type in the e-mail address for the person you want to send the message to. As you type, Mail displays a list of people in your Address Book whom you've sent messages to previously, or who are in your company's server address book; choose the desired e-mail address rather than continuing to type it. Type a comma between e-mail addresses to send the message to multiple people.

Tip

An easy way to add recipients to the To, Cc, and Bcc fields is to click in the desired field and click Address Book in the toolbar. That opens the Addresses panel, from which you can click a person to have his or her e-mail address inserted. (You can also open this panel by choosing Window ➪ Address Panel or pressing Option+⌘+A.) Note that the Addresses panel includes any contacts in the Mac's Address Book for which you have e-mail addresses.

Mail's Message Indicators

At the very left of the message list, Mail places icons that indicate message status. A blue circle indicates an unread message. A left-pointing circular arrow indicates a message you've replied to, while a right-facing straight arrow indicates a message you've forwarded; click the arrow to open the reply or forwarded message.

If you enable the Flags column (labeled with the flag icon), you see three other iconic indicators: !! indicates a high-priority message (as determined by the sender), ! Indicates a normal-priority message (as determined by the sender), – indicates a low-priority message (also as determined by the sender), a flag indicates a message you've flagged (to find easily later), and a gold mailbag indicates a message flagged as junk.

Figure 11.15 shows all the icons but !.

Mail also uses typographic effects in the message list to help you quickly navigate your e-mail. Boldface messages have not been read, while gold-colored messages are flagged as junk.

You can also enter addresses in the Cc field, which copies the message to the people in that field. (*Cc* means carbon copy, from the days when secretaries used carbon paper to make copies of memos and indicated in the memo who was sent a carbon copy.) As Figure 11.18 shows, you can use the menu iconic popup menu to add a Bcc field into which you can blind-copy (*Bcc* originally meant blind carbon copy) the message to recipients. Anyone who gets the message sees the addresses in the To and Cc fields, but not the recipients (other than themselves) in the Bcc field.

Tip

To delete a recipient, put the text cursor after the name and press Backspace.

In the Subject field, enter a subject or description for your message. If you leave the Subject blank, Mail asks you when you send the message if you're sure you want to send the message without a subject.

Entering the message itself

Enter your message in the main section of the dialog box. You can format the text by using the options in the Format menu if you've set your account to send Rich Text e-mail, as explained in the "Composing preferences" section earlier in this chapter. Select the text and then choose the desired font, color, alignment, and so on from the Format menu. You can also click the Fonts and Colors buttons in the toolbar to choose fonts and colors.

Note

To change your spelling and grammar settings, apply capitalization transformations, or adjust text substitutions, you must first create a new message. Otherwise, these options are grayed out as unavailable.

FIGURE 11.18

The New Message dialog box

Mail also gives you controls over your text, such as spell checking and automatic substitution. Choose Edit ➪ Spelling and Grammar, and then choose the desired submenu option.

The key submenu option to set is Check Spelling, which has three choices: When Typing, Before Sending, and Never. If you choose When Typing, potential errors are highlighted with red dotted underlines. If you choose Before Sending, the Spelling and Grammar dialog box appears, in which alternative words are suggested for you to choose from, in which you can type in your own corrected text, or in which you can tell Mail to ignore the spelling. (You can see the Spelling and Grammar dialog box at any time when composing a message by choosing Edit ➪ Spelling and Grammar ➪ Show Spelling and Grammar or pressing ⌘+: [colon].)

The three other submenu options are:

- Check Document Now (press ⌘+; [semicolon]), which spell-checks the message immediately.

- Check Grammar with Spelling, which checks your message's grammar along with its spelling. (If a checkmark appears to the left of this option, it is enabled.) Note that potential grammatical errors are indicated through green dotted underlines.

- Correct Spelling Automatically, which makes Mail correct any misspellings it detects as you type. (If a checkmark appears to the left of this option, it is enabled.) Be careful with this option: Mail may "correct" words it does not recognize, even though they are in fact correct.

Mail also has controls to change the capitalization of selected text. Choose Edit ➪ Transformations and then the desired option: Make Upper Case, Make Lower Case, and Capitalize (which capitalizes the first letter of each word).

You can also have Mail automatically replace text with other text as you type. To do so, choose Edit ➪ Substitutions, then select the suboption for what you want to have automatically substituted: Smart Quotes (which replaces keyboard quotes with their curly, typographic versions), Smart Dashes (which replaces two consecutive hyphens with an em dash), and Smart Links (which converts Web and e-mail addresses into clickable hyperlinks). Note that if a suboption has a checkmark to its left, it is enabled.

There are three other suboptions available when you choose Edit ➪ Substitutions:

- Smart Copy/Paste, which ensures that spaces are added and deleted as necessary when you paste text between words.
- Text Replacement, which enables any text substitutions you set in the Text pane of the Language & Text system preference (see Chapter 21).
- Show/Hide Substitutions, which displays or hides the Substitutions dialog box shown in Figure 11.19. This dialog box lets you turn on or off the various substitution settings, as well as access the Text pane of the Language & Text system preference (by clicking the Text Preferences button).

New Feature

The transformation and substitution controls are new to Mac OS X 10.6 Snow Leopard.

FIGURE 11.19

The Substitutions dialog box

Using other mail composition controls

To add one or more files as attachments to your message, click Attach in the toolbar, choose File ➪ Attach Files, or press Shift+⌘+A.

If you have multiple e-mail accounts, you can choose which account sends the message by using the From popup menu. Likewise, if you have multiple outgoing mail servers set up (see the "Accounts preferences" section earlier in this chapter), you can choose which outgoing mail server to use from the adjacent popup menu. You can also choose which signature to use for the message by using the Signature popup menu (see the "Signatures preferences" section earlier in this chapter).

Depending on which options you've enabled in the Menu iconic popup menu, there may be additional controls in the New Message dialog box:

- **The Bcc field enables you to blind-copy recipients, so no other recipients know they received the message.** You can also display this field by choosing View ➪ Bcc Address Field or pressing Option+⌘+B.

- **The Reply To field enables you to put in an e-mail address to which all replies to this message will be sent, instead of to your e-mail address.** (An assistant might use this field when sending messages on behalf of his or her boss, for example.) You can also display this field by choosing View ➪ Reply-to Address Field or pressing Option+⌘+R.

- **The Priority popup menu enables you to choose the messages priority level: low, normal, and high.** Depending on the recipient's e-mail client, the priority may display as an icon in their message list (that's what Mail does if you've enabled the Flags column), apply a color to the message, or use some other highlighting. You can also set priority by choosing Message ➪ Mark and choosing the desired priority level from the submenu.

Mail lets you apply fancy formatting to your messages; click Show Stationery and pick one of the options from the preview area that appears above the area you type the message text in. Note that these messages use embedded images and fonts that may not display on recipients' e-mail programs.

The toolbar also has the Photo Browser button. Click it to see photos stored in iPhoto or in Photo Booth. Drag a photo over a person's name in the To, Cc, Bcc, or Reply To fields to attach their photo to the message. Someone with a compatible e-mail program will see the photo in those fields when reading the message.

Sending and saving messages

When you're ready to send your message, click Send in the toolbar, choose Message ➪ Send, or press Shift+⌘+D. If you want to save the message so you can work on it later, click Save as Draft in the toolbar, which stores the message in the Drafts folder. Note that clicking Save as Draft does not close the New Message window, so you can keep working on the message and click Save as Draft again to update what is saved in the Drafts folder. Close the message without sending it by clicking the Close button (the X icon) in the New Message dialog box.

Replying, forwarding, and redirecting messages

There are multiple ways to send messages you've received from others, whether you've selected the message in the message list or have the message open. Reply sends a response to the person who sent you the message, Reply All sends the response to anyone who received the message, and Forward sends the message to anyone you choose. In all three cases, you can enter your own message, as well as edit the original message included. You can also change who gets the reply or forwarded message by adding or deleting e-mail addresses in the To, Cc, and Bcc fields.

Cross-Ref

To set what part of the original message is included in your reply or forward, use the options in the Composing pane of Mail's Preferences dialog box, as explained in the "Composing preferences" section earlier in this chapter.

You reply to a message by clicking Reply in the toolbar, choosing Message ⇨ Reply, or pressing ⌘+R. To reply to all recipients, click Reply All, choose Message ⇨ Reply All, or press Shift+⌘+R. If the sender is in your iChat buddy list (see the "Using iChat" section later in this chapter), you can send an instant-message response via iChat by choosing Message ⇨ Reply with iChat or pressing Shift+⌘+I.

To forward a message to someone else, click Forward in the toolbar, choose Message ⇨ Forward, or press Shift+⌘+F. Choosing Message ⇨ Forward as Attachment sends the e-mail as an attachment within an e-mail message; note that that not all e-mail programs will be able to open that attachment.

You can also *redirect* a message to another e-mail account by choosing Message ⇨ Redirect or pressing Shift+⌘+E. The difference between forwarding and redirecting is that forwarding shows the message as being sent by you, while redirecting shows the message as being sent by the original sender (not you).

Tip

If you get e-mail from spammers or people you don't want to get e-mail from, consider choosing Message ⇨ Bounce or pressing Shift+⌘+B. This sends a reply to the sender saying your e-mail account does not exist; often, spam software, newsletter- and ad-sending software, and individuals will remove your e-mail account from their mailing lists when they get your bounced-message reply.

Deleting, moving, and junking messages

You can select one or more e-mails (⌘+click each to select multiple e-mails) and delete them all by clicking the Delete button in the toolbar, or send them to the Junk folder by clicking Junk in the toolbar. (If you are in the Junk folder, you can mark messages as not junk by clicking the Not Junk button in the toolbar; the messages are moved back to the Inbox.)

To move a message to a folder, simply drag it into the desired folder in the left column of the Message Viewer. Or select it from the message list and choose Message ⇨ Move To and then the desired folder from the submenu. You can also copy messages by holding Option when dragging them to a folder or simply by choosing Message ⇨ Copy To and then the desired folder from the submenu. To create a folder, select the mailbox or folder that you want to create the folder in, then click the + iconic popup menu under the Message Viewer's left column and choose New Mailbox from the menu.

Cross-Ref

You can set up rules that automatically move, copy, delete, forward, or mark as junk messages that meet the criteria you set, as explained in the "Rules preferences" section earlier in this chapter. You can apply rules to selected messages by choosing Message ⇨ Apply Rules or pressing Option+⌘+L.

Using RSS Feeds in Mail

RSS feeds are an easy way to stay up-to-date on sports scores, news headlines, or other information that is frequently updated. When you subscribe to such a feed, Mail checks periodically to see if there are new entries, which it stores in the RSS list in the Message Viewer. Each RSS feed you sub-scribe to displays in this list; click the feed name to get a message list that shows all the entries. You read entries just as you would e-mail messages.

You can delete, mark as junk, or print the RSS entries. And you can erase deleted items, mark them as read, archive the feed, delete the feed from the RSS list in Mail, or manually update the feed by Control+clicking or right-clicking the RSS feed name and choosing the desired option from the contextual menu, or clicking the Action iconic popup menu (the gear icon) at the bottom of the Message Viewer's left column and choosing the desired options from the menu.

Cross-Ref

You can view RSS entries in Mail and/or Safari. Chapter 10 explains how to subscribe to and view RSS feeds in Safari.

To add feeds to Mail, click the + iconic button and choose Add RSS Feeds. The dialog box shown in Figure 11.20 appears. Here you can select RSS feeds subscribed to in Safari or enter the feed URL manually.

FIGURE 11.20

The window for adding RSS feeds to Mail

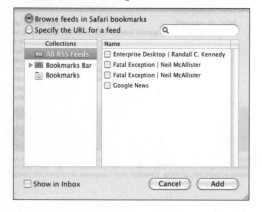

The Preferences dialog box (choose Mail ➪ Preferences or press ⌘+, [comma]) has three sets of RSS options in its RSS pane:

- **Default RSS Reader.** Choose the RSS reader that RSS feeds are automatically added to when you subscribe to an RSS feed. Choose Mail, Safari, or Select to choose an application you've installed to read RSS feeds.

- **Check for Updates.** Choose how often you want Mail to update the RSS feeds it displays: Every 30 Minutes, Every Hour, or Every Day.

- **Remove Articles.** Choose how RSS entries are deleted from Mail: Manually, After One Day, After One Week, After Two Weeks, After One Month, or After One Year.

Working with Notes and To-Do Items in Mail

You can add notes in Mail by clicking Note in the toolbar, choosing File ➪ New Note, or pressing Control+⌘+N. Enter your text, format it as desired by using the Fonts and Colors buttons or the Format menu, add any attachments by using the Attach button, and click Done to save the note. You can also send the note to someone else by clicking Send, which creates a new e-mail message by using the Notes stationery and whatever you've entered into the note.

To create a to-do item, click To Do in the toolbar, choose File ➪ New To Do or press Option+⌘+Y. Figure 11.21 shows a to-do item being created. (If you are entering a note, you can convert it to a to-do item by clicking To Do in the note's toolbar.)

FIGURE 11.21

Creating a to-do item

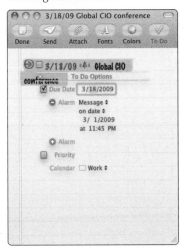

To set the due date for a to-do item, click the right-pointing arrow icon that appears to open the To Do Options list. Select the Due Date option, press Tab to move the text cursor among the date fields, and adjust the month, day, and year. To set a reminder alarm, click Alarm and choose the options from the popup menus that appear. To set a priority, select the Priority option and then choose the priority level from the popup menu that appears. Choose the calendar to add the to-do item to by choosing it from the popup menu to the right of Calendar.

Note

To-do items are saved in iCal or, if you choose your Exchange e-mail account or Entourage as the calendar, in Exchange.

Any to-do items you create are displayed in the Reminders section of the Message Viewer's left column. Notes are displayed separately from to-do items. Furthermore, both notes and to-do items are listed based on which account they are created in: On My Mac (which means in iCal) or in a specific Exchange e-mail account. Notes and to-do items appear in the message list, where you can read and delete them.

Note

To delete a to-do item as you are creating it, click the Close button (the X icon) that appears when you hover the mouse over a to-do item. Otherwise, delete it from the Message Viewer. Notes can be deleted only from the Message Viewer.

Using iChat

E-mail is a great way to send lengthy messages or messages to multiple people, but it can be cumbersome for quick messages between two people. Instant messaging, also called *chat*, is a simpler, faster way to "talk" to someone else over computers using text. To help you chat, Mac OS X 10.6 Snow Leopard comes with the iChat application.

Setting up iChat

With iChat, you can chat with people who have Apple MobileMe/Mac.com addresses, AOL Instant Messenger (AIM), GoogleTalk, and Jabber accounts, as well as with other people on your local network (using what Apple calls its Bonjour technology).

Tell iChat what services you have accounts for in the Preferences dialog box's Accounts pane, shown in Figure 11.22. (Choose iChat ➪ Preferences or press ⌘+, [comma] to open the Preferences dialog box.) Click the + iconic button to select a service, then provide the login information for that account. If you have multiple accounts, add the login information for each.

Note

You must have an account on the same service as the people you want to chat with. iChat cannot connect users from different chat services.

FIGURE 11.22

The Accounts pane in iChat's Preferences dialog box

For each account, you have three subpanes to set:

- **Account Information.** This subpane lets you enable the account, automatically log into this account when iChat launches, have new buddies you chat with automatically added to your buddies list, and — if the chat service permits — allow multiple simultaneous logins so you can have multiple chats at the same time.

- **Security.** This subpane lets you block others from seeing that your account is idle, determine your privacy level (who can see that your account is logged in), and — for services that support this capability — encrypt chat messages.

- **Server Settings.** If your network blocks standard chat sessions, you may be able to get around that by entering proxy server settings in this subpane. Check with your network administrator.

In the Messages pane, you can set the visual display of chat text, set a keyboard shortcut to switch to iChat if you are working in another application, automatically save chat transcripts, and choose to collect all chats in a single window rather than keep each chat in its own window.

In the Alerts pane, you tell iChat how to alert you to various events, such as logging in, a buddy becoming available, sending a message, receiving a chat invitation, or getting a file transferred to you. Your alert options include choosing a sound, having the iChat icon bounce in the Dock, running an AppleScript, or speaking a message.

The Audio/Video pane lets you choose an external camera (if attached to the Mac) and microphone (including Bluetooth headsets) to use for audio and video chats. You can also limit how much bandwidth the chat can take on your network connection so as not to slow down other network operations, to open iChat when a video camera is attached, and play a ringing sound when invited to a chat conference (a multiuser chat).

Chatting with people

Before you can chat, you have to have people to chat with. You can set up *buddies*, people who you can easily chat with by clicking their names in your chat window. Add a buddy by choosing Buddies⇨Add Buddy or pressing Shift+⌘+A. In the dialog box that appears, enter the buddy's account name and what chat service he or she uses (only services for which you have set up in the Accounts pane of the Preferences dialog box appear in this list). You can choose a group to add the buddy to, as well as enter the buddy's first and last names. (Create a group by clicking the + iconic popup menu at the bottom of the chat window and choosing Add Group.)

In your buddy list, Control+click or right-click a buddy you want to chat with and choose the type of chat you want to initiate, as Figure 11.23 shows. You can also block specific users from chatting with you. Or select a buddy and click one of the chat buttons at the bottom of the window: text, audio, video, or screen share. Or to start a text chat, select a buddy and choose Buddies⇨Send Instant Message or press Shift+⌘+M.

FIGURE 11.23

Initiating a chat (here, to someone using the AIM chat service)

Tip

If you have several chat accounts, or want to use the Bonjour chat with people on your local network, you can open a chat window for any chat account you have in the Window menu.

Tip

If you're not available to chat, you can simply quit iChat so you show as not available in your buddies' chat windows. Or you can choose an away status from the popup menu under your name.

If you want to chat with someone not in your buddy list, choose File ➪ New Chat or press ⌘+N, then enter their chat address. If you have more than one chat account, choose the one you want to chat from. You can also choose the type of chat you are initiating: text, audio, video, or screen sharing. Click OK to send the invitation. If the person accepts your invitation, a chat window opens. People may also initiate a chat with you the same way; click Accept to chat with them, or click Block to prevent them from chatting with you.

When you've connected to someone else for a chat, the dialog unfolds at the top of the window, as Figure 11.24 shows. Enter your text in the window at bottom and click return to send it. If you want to attach various smiley face-type icons — called *emoticons* — select them from the popup menu to the right of the text-entry field. You can also choose Edit ➪ Insert Smiley and choose the desired icon from the submenu.

FIGURE 11.24

Chatting with someone else (here, to someone on the local network) via text (left) and via video (right)

Using audio and video

In addition to chatting via text, you can initiate an audio chat by clicking the Start an Audio Chat iconic button (the phone icon) at the bottom of the chat window. Both parties need to have a way to hear the conversation (such as using headphones or speakers) and to be heard (such as using a microphone) to be able to participate in the chat. (A headset addresses both needs.) Participants also need to configure the Audio/Video pane in iChat's Preferences dialog box to use those devices. After the connection is made, you just start talking. Note that the audio quality may be inferior to a telephone connection.

Similarly, click the Start a Video Chat iconic button (the movie-camera icon) to start a video chat, as shown in Figure 11.24. Both parties need to have an external camera or a built-in iSight camera, as well as a microphone and headphones or a speaker, or a headset, set up. A participant without a camera can still join the chat but only has access to the audio portion.

Another form of video chat is what Apple calls iChat Theater. This enables you to share photo albums from iPhoto or files of any sort in a video window.

One way to initiate a "theater" session is to choose File ⇨ Share iPhoto with iChat Theater to share a selected iPhoto album, and choose File ⇨ Share a File with iChat Theater to share selected files. Either way, click Share to set up the "theater." Then invite a person to a video chat. The person you are chatting with sees a slide show that you control on his or her video chat window.

You can also start by inviting someone to a video chat and, when he or she is connected, click the + iconic button at the bottom of the video chat window, then choose Share iPhoto with iChat Theater or Share a File with iChat Theater, select the desired iPhoto album or files, and click Share.

New Feature

Mac OS X 10.6 Snow Leopard's iChat looks the same as in previous versions, but Apple has tweaked it under the hood so it can handle video using a third of the bandwidth as in previous versions, so people with slower Internet connections can now use video chat. iChat now also can handle more types of network routers automatically, overcoming connection difficulties that users experienced in previous versions. And "theater" chats can now run as large as 640-by-480-pixel resolution.

Using screen and file sharing

You can share screens across iChat. Click the Start Screen Sharing iconic button (the two rounded rectangles icon) at the bottom of the chat window to initiate a screen sharing session. The button opens a popup menu with two options: one to invite the person to share his or her screen with you and one to accept your shared screen. The other party will get a dialog box asking if he or she agrees to the screen sharing chat. The person can accept the invitation, block you, or send you a text reply. If the screen sharing chat is accepted, the screen sharing window then opens on the Mac that is viewing the shared screen. People can initiate a screen sharing chat with you the same way.

You can send someone you're chatting with a file by choosing Buddies ⇨ Send File or pressing Option+⌘+F when in the text field of a chat. Choose the desired file and click Send. You can also send a file simply by dragging it into the text box at the bottom of the iChat window. Either way, when you press Return in the text field, the file is sent along with your text message. People can send you files the same way.

New Feature

You can now use Mac OS X's Quick Look feature to preview the contents of files send to you via iChat before opening them. Chapter 2 explains Quick Look in detail.

Cross-Ref

Chapter 13 covers file sharing and screen sharing in more depth.

Using Address Book and iCal

Keeping track of contacts, notes, to-do items, and meetings is an important part of collaborating, which is why Mac OS X 10.6 Snow Leopard comes with the Address Book and iCal applications to help you track these items.

Working with Address Book

The Address Book, shown in Figure 11.25, is a simple application that stores your contacts with whatever detail you want to provide.

Adding and editing cards

To add a person, creating an address book card, choose File ➪ New, press ⌘+N, or click the + iconic button at the bottom of the Name column in the Address Book window. A card form appears in which you enter the person's name, contact information, and any notes. Leave blank any fields you don't want to fill out.

FIGURE 11.25

The Address Book with a card displayed

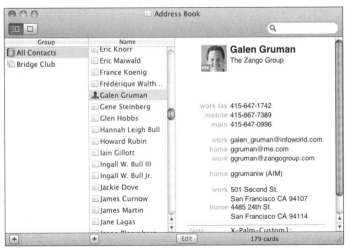

To associate a photo or other image to that card, drag the image file onto the square with the person's silhouette in the card. Or select the card and choose Card ⇨ Choose Custom Image or press Option+⌘+I. (To delete an image from a card, select the card and choose Card ⇨ Clear Custom Image.

Tip

Address Book assumes the new contact is a person, but if it is a company, select the Company option; this changes the name fields to the company's name. You can change a card from a company to a person later by selecting Company when editing the card, or by choosing Card ⇨ Mark as a Company or pressing ⌘+\. Deselect the Company option when editing the card, or choose Card ⇨ Mark as a Person or press ⌘+\.

Some fields, such as those for e-mail addresses and phone numbers, are popup menus that enable you to choose the type of contact you are providing, such as home fax or work phone. If a green circle with a plus sign appears next to an entry, click it to add an additional contact of the same type, such as a second work e-mail address. Some fields will have a minus sign in a red circle next to them; click it to delete that field's contents.

Tip

You can add field options to cards by choosing Card ⇨ Add Field and then choosing the desired field from the submenu.

To edit an existing contact, select it in the list of contacts, then click Edit at the button of the Address Book window, choose Edit ⇨ Edit Card, or press ⌘+L. Click a field you want to edit and change the information as desired. When done, click Edit again.

Working with groups

You can group contacts so you can send one e-mail to the group and know everyone in that group will get it. To create a group, choose File ⇨ New Group, press Shift+⌘+N, or click the + iconic popup menu at the bottom of the Group column in the Address Book window and choose New Group. A group named untitled group appears in the Group column; change the name to one that makes sense for the group, then drag the contacts from the Name column into that group to add them.

You can also create smart groups, which are kept updated automatically based on the criteria you select. First create the smart group by choosing File ⇨ New Smart Group or by clicking the + iconic popup menu at the bottom of the Group list in the Address Book window and choosing New Smart Group. Give the smart group a name, then choose the first criterion from the first popup menu, such as Card or Name. In the second popup menu, set the condition, such as Contains or Is Set (meaning this field has information in it). In the adjacent text field, add the text for the condition. Add conditions by clicking the + iconic button at the end of the condition. Delete them by selecting a condition and clicking the – iconic button. Click OK when done.

Managing cards and groups

To delete individual contacts (cards) or groups, select them and then choose Edit ⇨ Delete Card or Edit ⇨ Delete Group. To rename a group, just click its name in the Group list; you can also select it and choose Edit ⇨ Rename Group.

Other card management options available include the following; note that one or more cards should be selected:

- To find cards, enter the search text in the Search field and press Return or click the Search iconic button (the magnifying glass icon).

- To send an e-mail to contacts with your updated card, select the groups and/or individuals you want to send the update to and choose File ⇨ Send Updates.

- If you have multiple cards for someone, select them and choose Card ⇨ Merge Selected Cards or press Shift+⌘+\.

- You can find duplicate cards by choosing Card ⇨ Look for Duplicates.

- To mark a card as your own, select it and choose Card ⇨ Make This My Card.

Setting Address Book preferences

To set Address Books preferences, choose Address Book ⇨ Preferences or press ⌘+, (comma). There are five panes:

New Feature

The LDAP and Sharing panes from previous versions of Address Book have been merged into the new Accounts pane.

- **General.** Here you set whether the card displays as *lastname, firstname* or as *firstname lastname*. You also choose how cards are sorted: by first name or last name. In the Address Format popup menu, choose the country for which the cards' addresses should be formatted. You can also change the text size by choosing Small, Medium, or Large from the Font Size popup menu.

- **Accounts.** Address Book can sync with a CardDAV Address Book Server (running on a Mac OS X Server), a Microsoft Exchange 2007 server, an LDAP server, a Google account, or a Yahoo account. If you use any of these servers, click the + iconic button at the bottom left of the Accounts pane and choose the supported server and complete its sign-in information.

  All Macs have an On My Mac account, which if selected displays two subpanes In the Accounts pane: Account Information and Sharing. In the Account Information subpane, you can specify that Address Book should sync with MobileMe, Yahoo, and/or Google accounts. In the Sharing subpane, you can set up sharing with MobileMe users, as explained in Chapter 15. You subscribe to Address Books that someone else has shared by choosing File ⇨ Subscribe to Address Book or pressing ⌘+U.

  If you have an LDAP or CardDAV account, there is only the Account Information subpane, in which you specify the account and server access information provided by your network administrator. If you have an Exchange 2007 account, you specify the account information in the Account Information subpane and the server information in the Server Settings subpane.

New Feature

Support for Exchange 2007 is new to Mac OS X 10.6 Snow Leopard. See Chapter 19 for details on using Address Book with the Microsoft Exchange server and the Microsoft Entourage e-mail program.

- **Template.** If you find yourself adding the same fields over and over again to your cards, you can add them permanently to all cards by choosing them in the Add Field popup menu in this pane. Fields in the popup menu that are checked are added; those not checked are not in the cards. To remove an added field from a card, select it so the check mark disappears.

- **Phone.** Here you set your preferred display for phone numbers from a list of six common conventions; you can also create your own.

- **vCard.** Here you set the format for vCards generated by Address Book, as well as control whether notes and photos are included. A vCard is a standard for exchanging contact information across applications, and these settings tell Address Book how to exchange card data with vCard-compatible applications. If you don't want your personal card shared, be sure to select the Enable Private Me card option.

Working with iCal

iCal is Mac OS X 10.6 Snow Leopard's calendar application. Figure 11.26 shows its month view. You can change view to Day, Week, or Month by using the View menu, or simply click Day, Week, or Month in the toolbar. To see the current month at a glance, no matter what view is chosen for the main window, click the View or Hide the Mini Calendar button (the calendar icon) below the Calendars column, or choose View ➪ Show/Hide Mini Calendar.

FIGURE 11.26

The iCal application, displaying the month view

You can show or hide the To Do Items column at right by clicking the View or Hide To Do Items iconic button (the thumbtack icon) at the bottom right of the iCal window, or by choosing View ➪ Show/Hide To Do List or pressing Option+⌘+T.

Working with iCal accounts

Although when you use iCal it may appear to be a single calendar, the truth is that iCal can hold multiple calendars. You can create local calendars, as explained in the next section, and you can create accounts that let iCal work with CalDAV, Google, Yahoo, and Microsoft Exchange 2007 accounts.

To add an account to iCal, go to the Accounts pane of the Preferences dialog box (choose iCal ➡ Preferences or press ⌘+; [comma]), and click the + iconic button at the bottom of the left column. The Add an Account sheet appears, as Figure 11.27 shows. Leave the Account Type popup menu set to Automatic, and enter the e-mail address and password for the account you want to synchronize iCal to. iCal will try to determine its settings for you automatically. If it can't choose one of the options from the Account Type popup menu — CalDAV (an iCal server), Exchange 2007, Google, or Yahoo — and complete the requested account information. Then click Create. The account will display in the iCal Sidebar along with any calendars in that account.

Figure 11.27 shows an Exchange account and its Mail To Do calendar in the Sidebar below the local calendars.

New Feature

Support for Exchange 2007, Google, and Yahoo calendar synchronization is new to Mac OS X 10.6 Snow Leopard.

FIGURE 11.27

Adding an account to iCal to synchronize server-based calendars with your Mac

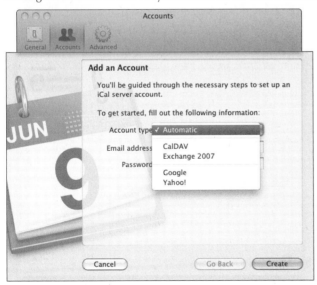

Managing calendars

Note the list of calendars in the iCal Sidebar in Figure 11.26. You can show and hide their appointments in the main calendar window by selecting and deselecting them in the Calendars column. Home and Work are there by default, while Entourage was added in the figure automatically by Microsoft Entourage 2004 to support synchronization with that application. Likewise, for the figure, Apple's Mail added the IMAP calendar to support synchronization with a Microsoft Exchange server. Thus, the calendar that various appointments appear in determine whether they sync with other applications — and which applications. The Mail To Do to-do list was also added by Mail as part of an Exchange 2007 account.

Note

Entourage 2004 does not sync notes and to-do items with iCal, but Exchange 2007 does.

Cross-Ref

See Chapter 19 for details on using iCal with the Microsoft Exchange server and the Microsoft Entourage e-mail program.

You can add your own local calendar by clicking the + iconic button below the Calendars column and giving the new calendar a name. You can also choose File ➪ New Calendar ➪ On My Mac to add a local calendar.

To add a calendar to an Exchange or IMAP account (if you have one set up in Mail), click and hold the + iconic button below the Calendars column, then choose the desired account from the popup menu that appears. You can also choose File ➪ New Calendar ➪ *account* to add a calendar to an Exchange or IMAP account.

Tip

To add calendars created by other people, such as those with federal holidays or phases of the moon, choose Calendar ➪ Find Shared calendars. Your Web browser will open, displaying a page of such calendars available for download (some free, some not).

You can also add a calendar group by choosing File ➪ New Calendar Group or pressing Shift+⌘+N. Drag calendars into the group so you can display or hide them all at once. To name or rename the group, click it and then enter the (new) name.

Working with events

It's easy to add an event such as an appointment or meeting to your calendar: Select the desired calendar from the Calendars column, then Control+click or right-click in the date or time slot you want to add the event and choose New Event from the contextual menu. Now type in the event. To edit an event, click it. To get a detailed view of event options, whether when adding or editing it, double-click it to get the expanded entry form shown in Figure 11.28. If you don't see the full form, click Edit on the shortened form to get it.

FIGURE 11.28

Filling in an event's details

Fill in the relevant fields: the event title (labeled New Event by default), Location, URL, and Note. Select All-Day if the event runs the entire day, such as a birthday. Otherwise, choose the start and end days and times by using the From and To fields. The Time Zone popup menu defaults to your current time zone, but you can choose another time zone here. Choose the calendar to put the event in, using the Calendar popup menu.

Tip

You can set the current time zone in the Time & Date system preference for all applications on your Mac, as Chapter 21 explains. To change just iCal's time zone, such as when you are traveling, click the current time zone's popup menu at the upper right of the iCal window, and choose a new time zone. If the desired time zone is not listed, choose Other to open a dialog box where you can click on a world map or choose from a list to select a new time zone.

In the Repeat popup menu, you can set the event as a recurring event: Every Day, Every Week, Every Month, Every Year, or Custom, which lets you choose multiple days, such as every Tues and Thursday every week, or on specific dates, such as the 17th of every month or on the third Wednesday of the month. In the Alarm popup menu, you can set an alarm — a sound, e-mail, or popup alert — or open a file at a period before the event you specify.

Click Add File to attach a file to the event.

You can add attendees by clicking the Attendees field; as you begin typing names, a menu of matches from Address Book and Mail appear that you can select from; enter a tab between names. After you add an attendee, you can click it to get a list of options, such as mailing the event to that person, marking the person as an optional attendee, and editing the attendee.

If you added attendees, the button at the bottom right is named Send; click it to send each of them an invitation to the event. If you add attendees later, the button is named Update instead, so only the new attendees are invited. If no attendees are added, the button is named Done. In all three cases, clicking the button saves the event.

To invite someone to an event outside of the Attendees field, Control+click or right-click it and choose Send Event. The Mail application opens with an .ics calendar invitation attached. Add the addresses and type in any message you want, then send the invitation via e-mail.

If you have outstanding calendar invitations from Exchange (in the .ics format), either via Entourage or Mail, they appear below the Calendars column in the iCal window, as shown in Figure 11.26. You can decline, accept, or tentatively accept (the Maybe option) the appointment. You can view or hide this Notifications window by clicking the View or Hide Notifications iconic button (the envelope icon) or by choosing View ⇨ Show/Hide Notifications.

Working with to-do items

To create a to-do item, choose File ⇨ New To Do or press ⌘+K. Or Control+click or right-click the To Do Items column and choose New To Do from the contextual menu. (Click the View or Hide To Do Items iconic button [the thumbtack icon], choose View ⇨ Show To Do List, or press Option+⌘+T if the To Do Items column is not visible.)

Type in the to-do item's text. To provide more detail, double-click the to-do item to open a dialog box similar to the one shown in Figure 11.28. The options for a to-do item are:

- **Completed.** Select this option when you've done the task.
- **Priority.** Set a priority in the Priority popup menu.
- **Due Date.** Select this option if the to-do item has a due date, then set the date.
- **Alarm.** Use this popup menu to issue an alert at a user-specified interval before the due date.
- **Calendar.** Choose which calendar to associate the to-do item to, using this popup menu.
- **URL.** Enter a URL in the URL field, such as a related document on the Web.
- **Note.** Add a note in the Note field if desired.

Note

To edit an existing to-do item, simply double-click it.

You can sort the To Do Items column by selecting the To Do Items popup menu; the options are Sort by Due date, Sort by Priority, Sort by Title, Sort by Calendar, and Sort Manually. (This option lets you drag the to-do items in any order you want.) If Hide the Items After the Calendar View is selected (a check mark appears by the option), only to-do items whose calendars are selected in the Calendar column appear; otherwise, all to-do items appear. If the Show All Completed Items is selected, all items appear in the To Do Items column; otherwise, only noncompleted ones appear.

You can work on to-do items by Control+clicking or right-clicking them to get a contextual menu. The options are straightforward: Cut, Copy, Paste (if one or more events was previously cut or copied), Duplicate, Select All, and Get Info. You can also sort them by choosing Sort By, change an item's priority by choosing Priority, change the calendar an item belongs to by choosing Calendar, and mail the item by choosing Mail To Do.

Navigating the calendar

Beyond changing the view as explained in the beginning of the "Working with iCal" section, you can also move through the calendar several ways. Click the left-facing triangle in the toolbar, choose View⇨Previous, or press ⌘+← to move to the previous day, week, or month (depending on the current view), and click the right-facing triangle, choose View⇨Next, or press ⌘+→ to move to the next day, week, or month. Click Today in the toolbar, choose View⇨Go to Today, or press ⌘+T to go to the current date's entry. Choose View⇨Go to Date or press Shift+⌘+T to enter a specific date to go to.

Type text in the Search field and press Return or click the magnifying glass icon to find events or to-do items that contain specific text.

As you navigate the calendar, double-click an event or to-do item to get basic details on it. You can then click Edit to change the item and Done to close the details.

New Feature

To get more details, open an Info window for a selected item by pressing ⌘+I, choosing Edit⇨Get Info, or Control+clicking or right-clicking the item and choosing Get Info from the contextual menu. The Info window is new to Mac OS X 10.6 Snow Leopard; previous versions of the Mac OS used these commands to display the basic details.

New Feature

To get details of whatever item your mouse is hovering over, open the Inspector window by choosing Edit⇨ Show Inspector or pressing Option+⌘+I. The Inspector window is new to Mac OS X 10.6 Snow Leopard.

Publishing and subscribing to calendars

iCal can publish its calendars and subscribe to others people's published calendars.

To publish a calendar, select it in the calendars column and choose Calendar⇨Publish. You'll be asked whether to publish it via MobileMe (see Chapter 15) or on a private server. Other settings include having the published calendar updated automatically as it changes, including to-do items, attachments, and alarms. After publishing the calendar, iCal displays a dialog box that provides the URL for the calendar, as well as provides the Visit Page button to open the calendar in your Web browser and the Send Mail button to send an e-mail containing the link to other people.

A published calendar will have a radio-wave icon to its right in the Calendars column (the icon looks somewhat like the AirPort menu bar icon). You can send e-mails to people and provide its URL by selecting the calendar in the Calendars column and then choosing Calendar⟶Send Publish E-Mail, which opens Mail with the calendar's URL entered into the message body. To unpublish a calendar, select it in the Calendars column and then choose Calendar⟶Unpublish.

You can subscribe to published calendars by choosing Calendar⟶Subscribe and entering the calendar's URL.

Setting iCal preferences

iCal has only a few preferences set in its Preferences dialog box, which you access by choosing iCal⟶Preferences or pressing ⌘+, (comma). Figure 11.29 shows the General and Advanced panes of the Preferences dialog box.

In the General pane, you have the following options:

- **Days Per Week.** This popup menu enables you to choose how many days display per week: 7 or 5.

- **Start Week On.** This popup menu enables you to select the first day of the week as displayed in iCal.

- **Scroll in Week View By.** This popup menu has two options: Day and Week. If you choose Day, clicking the triangle buttons in the toolbar moves the calendar display one day at a time; if you choose Week, it moves the calendar display one week at a time.

- **Day Starts At.** This popup menu enables you to set the time that appears at the top of the iCal week and day views. (Earlier times are grayed in the display.)

- **Day Ends At.** This popup menu enables you to set the time that indicates the end of your business day. (Later times are grayed in the display.)

- **Show __ Hours at a Time.** This popup menu determines how many hours display on-screen in the day and week views.

- **Show Event Times in Month View.** If selected, this option puts the event times when you view the calendar in month view; note that this can be hard to read.

- **Show Birthdays Calendar.** If selected, this option adds a calendar called Birthdays to the Calendars column.

- **Add a Default Alarm to All New Events and Invitations.** If selected, you can enter a number of minutes that will set an alarm for every new event at that time interval.

- **Synchronize iCal with Other Computers and Devices Using MobileMe.** If selected, this option enables iCal to sync with other devices by using your MobileMe account, as Chapter 15 explains. Click the MobileMe button to set up MobileMe.

FIGURE 11.29

The General pane of iCal's Preferences dialog box (left); the Advanced pane (right)

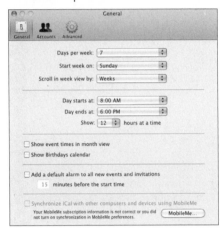
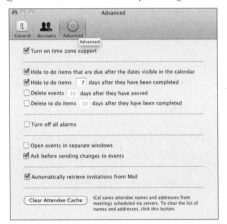

The Advanced pane has the following options:

- **Turn On Time Zone Support.** This option, which is selected by default, enables you to set up an independent time zone for iCal, such as when traveling, as explained in the section earlier in this chapter on working with events.

- **Hide To Do Items That Are Due After the Dates Visible in the Calendar.** This option, which is selected by default, shows only to-do items that fall within the current calendar view (day, week, or month).

- **Hide To Do Items __ Days After They Have Been Completed.** This option, which is selected by default, hides completed to-do items after the specified number of days have passed; 7 is the default setting.

- **Delete Events __ Days After They Have Passed.** If selected, this option automatically removes events from your calendar after the specified number of days have passed; 30 is the default.

- **Delete To Do Items __ Days After They Have Passed.** If selected, this option automatically removes to-do items from your calendar after the specified number of days have passed; 30 is the default.

- **Turn Off All Alarms.** If selected, this option disables all alarms.

- **Open Events in Separate Windows.** If selected, this option opens a new window for each event you open; otherwise, opening an event closes the previously open event.

- **Ask Before Sending Changes to Events.** This option, which is selected by default, displays an alert when changes to events occur, asking you if you want to update the attendees with the new information. If no attendees are selected for an event, this alert does not display.

- **Automatically Retrieve Invitations from Mail.** This option, which is selected by default, automatically detects calendar invitations in Mail and asks you to accept or decline them in iCal.

- **Clear Attendee Cache.** This button, if clicked, deletes from your Mac's attendee list the names and addresses of any attendees in calendar events scheduled from servers (whether from iCal server, Exchange, or MobileMe). It does not delete the attendees from the events but does remove them from the list of potential matches that appears when you begin typing attendee names in an event.

Summary

Mac OS X has two main collaboration applications focused on communications (Mail and iChat), plus two applications that help manage your collaboration activities (Address Book and iCal). You can import your settings and e-mail messages from other e-mail programs, as well as from previous versions of Mail.

Apple's Mail is a full-featured e-mail application that works with all common e-mail systems, including Web-based services such as Google Gmail, POP-based services commonly provided by Web hosts, and both IMAP-based and Microsoft Exchange e-mail services common in business. Mac OS X 10.6 Snow Leopard features native support for Microsoft's ActiveSync technology, which allows instant synchronization of e-mail, newsfeeds, contacts, to-do items, and calendar entries between the Exchange collaboration server and Mac OS X's Mail, iCal, and Address Book.

Mail provides a rich set of controls over how messages are checked, displayed, organized, and filtered. It also lets you access multiple e-mail accounts at the same time. Mail's smart folders feature lets you create playlist-like folders that contain all messages that meet whatever criteria you specify, without moving the original messages from their standard locations in Mail's folders.

When creating and sending e-mails, you can add attachments, apply visual templates, and automatically append a default signature for yourself, as well as control how the original message you are replying to or forwarding is quoted in that reply or forward. When replying to an e-mail, you have the option of replying via iChat instead of Mail if the sender is one of your instant messaging buddies.

Mail can display RSS feeds as if they were mail messages, as well as let you manage your RSS feeds. You can also see and manage your RSS feeds in Safari.

For IMAP and Exchange accounts, Mail displays to-do items and notes. These items are also synchronized to iCal.

The iChat instant messaging service works with several popular IM services, including AOL Instant messenger, GoogleTalk, Jabber, and MobileMe, plus any Mac on your local network. You can set up buddy lists that contain the contact information for people you chat with often, for easy chat connections, but strangers can also ask to chat with you (and you can ask to chat with strangers, if you know their instant message addresses).

iChat supports not only text chat, but also audio chat (essentially, Internet-based phone calls), video chat (Internet-based videoconferencing), and screen sharing chat (where you can observe or control the other person's screen, or let them control yours). You can enclose files in your text chats to easily exchange files with your chat buddy.

The Address Book lets you manage your contacts, and it works with Mail, iChat, and iCal to make it easy to fill in and contact people listed in the Address Book. Address Book can sync with Exchange 2007, Google, and Yahoo accounts.

iCal lets you create and track appointments, to-do items, and meetings, as well as invite other people to them via e-mail notifications. It supports .ics invitations that can be sent via e-mail; the recipient can accept the invitation either in Mail or iCal and have a confirmation sent to the originator.

In addition to syncing invitations with others, you can set up shared calendars in iCal, accessible via the Web or the local network. And iCal can sync calendars with your Exchange 2007, Google, and Yahoo accounts.

Setting Up a Network

L ongtime Mac users know that Apple practically invented the network. Sure, computer networks existed before the Mac, but the early Macs were the first personal computers that regular human beings could connect to each other. No high priests of IT required. To make this possible, Apple invented a technology called AppleTalk that enabled you to connect Macs to each other over cables so they could communicate, and a technology called Apple Filing Protocol (AFP) that enabled them to exchange files. It was truly revolutionary.

Fast-forward 25 years to today and networking is not so special. Even at home, a network of several computers and a printer or two is not uncommon. The world has caught up to the Mac. Well, mostly. Mac OS X stays a step ahead by connecting to several kinds of networks, not just Apple's own standard. So the Mac can easily fit into all sorts of network situations, while most PCs cannot.

In practice, that means that you can easily set up a Mac-only local network, connect to a Windows network, create a mini-network around your Mac with Bluetooth devices, and — oh, yes — connect to computers of all types that use the ubiquitous Internet Protocol.

This chapter looks at setting up local networks where there is no dedicated server that makes applications, file repositories, and other central resources available to everyone. In this case, each computer acts as both a server and a client, providing information to others and accessing information directly from them in what's known as a *peer-to-peer network*.

Note

If you're setting up a network that uses a dedicated server, you are working in what's known as a *client/server environment*. (The server provides and manages the access to the centrally stored information and other resources used by the clients, meaning your Macs, PCs, and network-attached printers.) This chapter does not cover dedicated-server setup, as that requires having specialized skills for the specific server you're using (typically, Linux, Mac OS X Server, Unix, or Windows Server). In a client/server environment, Mac uses whatever protocol you specify on that server to connect: Apple's AFP or Windows's SMB (Server Message Block). When setting up the Macs as clients of dedicated servers, just enable networking as explained in this chapter for AFP and in Chapter 18 for SMB, and set up file sharing as explained in Chapter 13, and you're ready to network.

So what is a local network? Technically, it's a small network of less than a dozen devices connected to a server, often referred to as a LAN (for *local area network*). But the practical definition, and the one this chapter uses, is a network of a handful or two of computers and devices that have no central server. Instead, each system is set up to "serve" (deliver) its data up to everyone else, in more of a collaborative, peer-to-peer setup than the traditional "one server, many clients" client/server approach to networking where everything goes through that central server.

Caution

Being part of a network can expose your Mac to serious dangers, such as data theft and viruses. Be sure to use the Mac OS's security controls, as explained in Chapter 23, to reduce that risk.

Creating a Physical Network

Before you can have your Mac and other devices communicate, you need first to connect them physically so the communication can happen. There are two ways to do this:

- Connect two Macs directly to each other via a cable (Ethernet or FireWire) or via a wireless connection.

- Connect multiple computers and other devices through a router, switch, or hub by using an Ethernet cable or wireless connection (or both). If you're using a router, it can also connect to the Internet, giving all the devices Internet access as well as access to each other. This is the most common way to network.

Figure 12.1 shows the three most common configurations: a direct connection, a home network, and an office network.

Note

A router can connect multiple networks, both internal ones such as your LAN and external ones such as the Internet. A switch (called an access point on a wireless device) connects devices within a local network, routing traffic just to the intended device. A hub connects devices within a local network and sends all data to all devices, letting each device figure out what data is intended for it. Thus, home networks use routers, while office networks may use a mix of routers and switches. (They rarely use hubs these days because of their inefficient data delivery.)

Cross-Ref

Chapter 10 explains how to connect your Mac or the network it's on to the Internet, including details on router configuration and connections via dial-up modem.

FIGURE 12.1

The three typical network setups: direct connection (top), home (middle), and office (bottom)

Direct connection

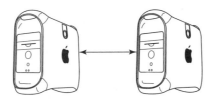

Typical home network

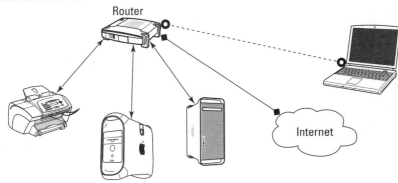

Typical office network

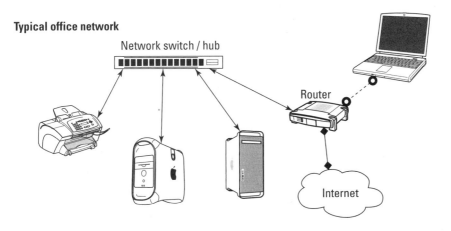

Wired connections

Nearly every Mac comes with an Ethernet (RJ-45) port, which lets you plug in the standard Ethernet cable. An exception is the MacBook Air, which requires a USB-to-Ethernet dongle (a type of adapter) to connect to an Ethernet cable. Every Mac built in the last four years supports the fastest form of Ethernet, called gigabit Ethernet because it can transmit data as fast as 1 gigabit per second (1 Gbps), which is about 125 million characters per second. To get that speed, your network cables and your router, switch, and/or hubs need to support that speed. Otherwise, you'll get a slower speed, such as the former 100 megabits per second (100 Mbps) standard or the now-ancient 10 Mbps. Don't worry so much about the speed: 100 Mbps and up is fine. And keep in mind that these speed ratings are maximum speeds; typical speeds are about a third to half the maximum.

Note

If you want to connect two Macs directly via Ethernet, you may need a special form of Ethernet cable called a crossover cable. It looks like a regular Ethernet cable, except that the wires inside are ordered differently to provide a direct connection. If your Mac was built before 2002, it likely needs a crossover cable to make a direct Mac-to-Mac connection; if it was built in 2002 or later, it can usually direct-connect by using either a regular cable or a crossover cable. Apple has a list of specific models' requirements at its Web site (`http://support.apple.com/kb/HT2274`).

You can also network two (and only two) Macs together by using a FireWire cable. FireWire cables come in three connector types: 6-pin 400 Mbps, 4-pin 400 Mbps, and 800 Mbps. Each type of connector plugs into a corresponding jack type on a Mac. Most Macs have the 6-pin 400 Mbps jack (called IEEE 1394a or alpha). Newer Macs have the 800 Mbps jack (called IEEE 1394b or beta); many Macs built since 2003 have both, while some Macs built in 2009 (such as the MacBooks) have just 800 Mbps jacks. No Macs have the 4-pin 400 Mbps jack, which is typically used in digital camcorders and portable hard drives. Despite the different connector and jack types, you can buy adapters to connect Macs with FireWire jacks. The FireWire 800 jack, for example, supports the older 6-pin and 4-pin FireWire 400 connectors by using an adapter.

Wireless connections

MacBooks and most desktop Macs come with wireless networking built in; exceptions include the Mac Pro line and many Power Mac models, for which you need to buy Wi-Fi adapters. (Apple calls this wireless networking technology AirPort, but most people call it 802.11a/b/g/n or Wi-Fi.) Wi-Fi comes in four types: 802.11b, which runs at up to 11 Mbps; 802.11a, which runs at up to 54 Mbps but uses a different radio band than the other versions of Wi-Fi, so it's less compatible; 802.11g, which runs at up to 54 Mbps; and 802.11n, which runs at up to 100 Mbps. In practice, you'll get a fifth to a third of the maximum speed. A Wi-Fi connection can reach as far as about 300 feet, assuming there are no obstructions — metal and other dense materials can weaken or even block the signal and thus the range.

Note

On most routers, the slowest device on the wireless network makes all other devices run at the same speed. Some recent wireless routers can isolate such slower devices so they don't slow down the rest.

Another form of wireless networking is Bluetooth, which most Macs built in the last five years support. Bluetooth is a short-range wireless technology (usually limited to about three feet for headsets and cell phones and 10 feet for other devices such as printers and Macs) and a fairly slow technology as well (1 Mbps to 3 Mbps). Bluetooth is typically used to connect headsets, cellular phones, and PDAs to a Mac.

Setting Up a Mac for a Local Network

With the physical (including wireless) connections in place, you need to configure your Mac to communicate across the network. You do so in the Network system preference, as shown in Figure 12.2.

FIGURE 12.2

The Network system preference, with an Ethernet connection active

The left side of the Network system preference shows the different possible network connections. Active ones have a green dot plus the message "Connected"; inactive ones have a red dot plus either the message "Off" or "Not Configured," as the case may be; and ones that are set to be active but are not connected have a yellow dot and the message "Not Connected" — in other words, the ones that are having problems.

Click one of the connections in the list at left to see the status details in the main part of the pane, as shown for the Ethernet connection in Figure 12.2. You can also change a network connection's settings in the main part of the pane by clicking the Advanced button, which opens a configuration pane. Figure 12.3 shows the configuration pane for an Ethernet connection.

FIGURE 12.3

The Ethernet settings pane in the Network system preference

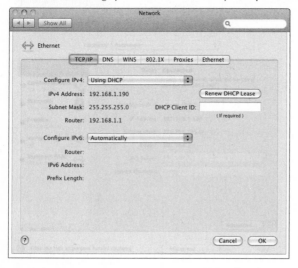

Tip

If you're not very familiar with networking, try clicking the Assist Me button in the Network system preference to have the Mac walk you through the settings in a friendly Q&A approach.

Tip

If you use your Mac in multiple places, you can store separate settings for each. In the Location popup menu in the Network system preference, choose Edit Locations to create a new set, give it a name, and click Done. (Use the Action iconic popup menu [the gear icon] to rename or duplicate an existing location.) Use the Location popup menu to switch to a different set. Most of the time, though, Automatic works just fine, figuring out the network settings where possible for you.

Setting up Ethernet connections

For an Ethernet connection to work, your Mac must have an Internet Protocol (IP) address, which is a unique ID for your Mac that enables other Macs and network devices to differentiate it from other devices they're connected to.

If you're using a router or a switch, chances are it uses a technology called Dynamic Host Control Protocol (DHCP) that has it issue the IP address for every connected device (so you don't have to worry about it). If not, you will need to give your Mac its own IP address, one that must be unique on your network.

When an Ethernet connection is selected in the Network system preference, the Configure IPv4 popup menu is typically set to Using DHCP, which tells the Mac to get its IP address from the router or switch each time it connects. Choosing DHCP automatically fills in the IP Address, Subnet Mask, and Router (the router's IP address, so the Mac knows where to look to get its own IP address) information. And it also usually fills in the DNS (Domain Name Service) Server and Search Domains information used to connect your Mac to the Internet as well. You might choose Using DHCP with Manual Address if you need to give your Mac a permanent address but want the router to manage the rest of the settings.

The other IPv4 menu options are:

- **Using BootP.** Your router may use a different IP-assignment technology than DHCP called Bootstrapping Protocol (BootP). If so, select this option.

- **Manually.** You must enter the IP address, subnet mask, router, DNS server, and search domains information yourself. Check with your network administrator for the correct settings.

- **Off.** This turns off the Ethernet connection on your Mac.

- **Create PPPoE Service.** Some DSL-based Internet service providers use a technology called Point-to-Point Protocol over Ethernet (PPPoE) to handle connections to the Internet. If your Mac is directly connected to the DSL service, as opposed to through a router, choose this option and fill in the information provided by the Internet service provider (ISP). Typically, if you set up PPPoE on your Mac, you are not part of a local network. Less frequently, it means that you're on a local network but only your Mac has an Internet connection.

Typically, you just need to choose Using DHCP and you're now on the network. But your network may require other settings, which you access by clicking Advanced to open a settings sheet. For Ethernet, the sheet has six panes of settings: TCP/IP, DNS, WINS, 802.1x, Proxies, and Ethernet:

- **TCP/IP.** This pane has the same IPv4 popup menu as the main Network system preference does. (TCP stands for Transmission Control Protocol, which handles how IP addresses are managed within a network.) If your Mac can't connect to its IP address, click Renew DHCP Lease; sometimes another device gets assigned the IP address your Mac had and the Mac doesn't realize it's now competing for that old address; clicking Renew DHCP Lease forces the router to assign you a free IP address. Enter a DHCP Client ID only if your network administrator requires it; some networks use these when there are multiple DHCP servers or to block unauthorized users from getting an address. You can also tell the Mac to automatically or manually set an IPv6 address if the router supports it, or to turn off this feature. An IPv6 address is a longer version of an IP address that is slowly replacing the IPv4 addresses we all use today (because we're running out of addresses, we need longer addresses; they do to IP addresses what the ZIP+4 addition did to ZIP codes).

- **DNS.** In this pane, you can add DNS server addresses and search domains. Typically, your router fills them in for you, but if you're not using DHCP or BootP (perhaps when traveling), you can add your own. Click the + iconic button at the bottom of the DNS Server column to add a DNS server address, and click the + iconic button at the bottom of the Search Domains column to add a search domain. To delete an entry, select it and click the – iconic button at the bottom of its column.

- **WINS.** If you're on a Windows-based network, enter an ID for your Mac (if there's not one there automatically), choose or enter a Windows network name, and add any Windows servers (click the + iconic button). Your network administrator should provide these settings.

- **802.1x.** IEEE 802.1x is a standard for authenticating that users are who they say they are, to help keep snoops out of the network. If your network is set up to use 802.1x, click the + iconic button to add one or more of the three 802.1x methods — user profile, login window profile, and system profile — and then provide your username and password, select the appropriate authentication options from the list, and if your network uses authentication certificates, click Configure Trust to load the certificates. Your network administrator should provide these settings.

- **Proxies.** Your network may handle certain Internet or network services for you, such as Web access and FTP file transfer. If so, select these proxy servers and enter their network address (in the long text field) and port number (in the short one after the colon); if a password is required, select Proxy Server Requires Password and fill in the Username and Password fields. Two options are different: Auto Proxy Discovery has the Mac look for proxy servers on its own, and Automatic Proxy Configuration has you enter the IP address for a file that will configure all these settings for you. Select the Exclude Simple Hostnames option to bypass proxy servers for services that appear to be local; typically, doing so helps a wireless connection see a resource on your local network that it might otherwise not see. Also, in the Bypass proxy Settings for these Hosts & Domains field, enter any hosts and domains in the same local network as your Mac, to reduce network traffic out to and back through a proxy server for something accessible locally. Finally, select the Use Passive FTP Mode (PASV) option to allow File Transfer Protocol connections (see Chapter 13) even if your Mac is protected by a firewall.

- **Ethernet.** This pane controls how your Ethernet port functions. Usually, you leave the Configure popup menu set to Automatically so the Mac OS can figure out the rest for you. But if you change it to Manually, you can select the network speed in the Speed popup menu, the type of flow control in the Duplex popup menu, and the delay between "conversations" with other devices in the MTU popup menu. (If your Mac "talks" too fast, other devices might not "understand" it. The MTU, or maximum transmission unit, setting controls the "talk" speed.) Your network administrator should provide any such settings.

New Feature

Gone from the Ethernet configuration panes (and from the AirPort ones as well) is the AppleTalk pane. Over the last decade, Apple has been slowly moving AppleTalk's features — providing a unique ID for each Mac and discovering other network resources — into the standard IP service and into its Bonjour technology used to connect printers and other peripherals. In Mac OS X 10.6 Snow Leopard, that transition is complete, and AppleTalk is no longer needed. So now it's gone.

Note

Other devices you want to connect to the network will have similar settings as Mac OS X's Network system preference, though they may not be as elaborate. Also, in some cases, you configure a device by entering its IP address in your browser to get a configuration screen, while in others you may use settings available through its setup screen, and in still others you may need to connect them to your Mac via a USB cable and run a setup utility for them on your Mac.

Understanding IP Addresses

An IP address is composed of four sets of numbers, called *segments,* in the form xxx.xxx.xxx.xxx. Within a local network, you use four ranges of addresses, called *private IP addresses:* 10.0.0.0 through 10.255.255.255, 172.16.0.0 through 172.31.255.255, and 192.168.0.0 through 192.168.255.255. Only one device within a network can use any of the numbers, though it's fine if devices on different networks use the same numbers. (Note that the largest permitted number in any IP address segment is 255, not 999.)

Most home-oriented routers are preconfigured to use the address 192.168.0.1, 192.168.1.1, or 192.168.2.1, and thus the devices that connect in the local network are assigned private addresses that start with 192.168.0., 192.168.1., or 192.168.2., respectively. But you can change that router address to anything in those supported ranges.

A subnet mask helps the router manage traffic across several linked networks by indicating what parts of the IP address must be the same for devices to be on the same network: 255.255.255.0 means the first three segments of the IP address must be the same (255 means "must match" and 0 means "don't need to match") — so the devices whose IP addresses are 172.28.5.15 and 172.28.5.75 will be on the same network, but not the device whose address is 172.30.5.16 nor the device whose address is 172.28.74.9, because not all first three segments match as the subnet mask says they must.

The other IP addresses — called *public IP addresses* — are assigned to Web and Internet resources, such as Web sites, and must be unique on the Internet. When you sign up for a domain, such as apple.com, the domain registry assigns you a unique public IP addresses. When a user enters **apple. com**, the router looks up its public IP address and routes the request to it. So Web addresses are really aliases to public IP addresses.

How does the Mac know where to look up these aliases when it sends e-mail or goes to a Web site? Through a DNS server. The DNS Server entry in the Network system preference thus tells your Mac where to find the public IP addresses. Your ISP typically provides its own DNS server, and the router looks it up for you, so usually you don't need to tell the Mac what the DNS server is.

Setting up Wi-Fi connections

For wireless (AirPort) networking, the Network system preference's main pane is simpler: There's the Network Name popup menu where you can select what available wireless network to connect to, where you can turn off wireless network by clicking Turn AirPort Off, and where you can select the Show AirPort Status in Menu Bar to get an iconic popup menu that lets you select an available network or turn AirPort on or off without needing to open the Network system preference. The Ask to Join New Networks option, if selected, displays a window when the Mac detects a new wireless network and asks if you want to join it if you're not already connected to a wireless network.

By clicking the Advanced button, you get a settings sheet with seven panes. Six panes are the same as for Ethernet networking: TCP/IP, DNS, WINS, 802.1x, Proxies, and Ethernet.

The one special pane (see Figure 12.4) is for wireless configuration in AirPort, which enables you to save and manage login connections to various wireless networks. (Mac OS X calls these saved connections *preferred networks.*) Click the + iconic button to add a Wi-Fi connection. If you know the wireless network's name, or *SSID* (Service Set Identifier), enter it in the Network Name field, or click Show Networks to have the Mac OS find available networks so you can select one. Using the Security popup menu, select the wireless network's security protocol, then enter the password in the field that displays. If you select the Show Password option, you can see the password as you type it; otherwise, you see a row of bullets (•). Click Add to add the new Wi-Fi connection. You also have the option Remember This Network; if selected, the Mac automatically connects to the network the next time it sees it and you are not connected to a different Wi-Fi network.

You can also manage your Wi-Fi connections in this pane:

- Select a connection and click the – iconic button to delete it.
- Select a connection and click the Edit iconic button (the pencil icon) to edit its settings.
- Drag Wi-Fi connection names to reorder them; the Mac will connect to the topmost wireless network it sees from the list.
- The Select Remember Any Network This Computer Has Joined option, which is selected by default, adds Wi-Fi networks to the preferred network list automatically as you log in, including their passwords, so you can connect automatically in the future.
- The Disconnect from Networks When Logging Out option, if selected, drops any Wi-Fi connections if you log out as the current user, so the user who logs in next must establish a new Wi-Fi connection. (Wi-Fi connections are always disconnected when you shut down or restart the Mac.)
- The Require Administrator to Control AirPort option, if selected, requires that the user enter the administrator password to control the wireless connections (so the kids can't log on to a Wi-Fi hot spot without your okay).

FIGURE 12.4

The AirPort settings pane in the Network system preference

Setting up a Bluetooth network

The principles of setting up Bluetooth networking are the same as for Ethernet and Wi-Fi networking. But the actual process is more complicated because there are many kinds of Bluetooth devices that have different capabilities. (Be sure to read each device's documentation as to its capabilities and how to set it up.) And the Bluetooth technology uses a concept called *pairing*, which means that devices are configured to work with other specific devices. So you have to first pair a Mac and a Bluetooth device for them to communicate. You don't get the same kind of automatic connection that you do with Ethernet and Wi-Fi.

Cross-Ref

Several parts of this book cover the many aspects of Bluetooth. Chapter 8 covers the iSync application used to synchronize data between the Mac and Bluetooth-connected devices. Chapter 21 covers how to tell the Mac which Bluetooth devices may connect to it, using the Bluetooth system preference. Chapter 13 covers the Bluetooth File Exchange utility that enables you to share files with Bluetooth devices.

In Mac OS X, you set up Bluetooth networking in two places: the Bluetooth system preference and the Network system preference. Chapter 21 covers how to pair Bluetooth devices to the Mac by using the Bluetooth system preference. This chapter covers how to use Bluetooth for local network of devices, not simply for paired connections.

With Mac OS X 10.6 Snow Leopard, you can create what's called a Bluetooth PAN (personal area network). This enables your Mac to use a Bluetooth connection to connect to the Internet through a compatible cellphone. (The cellphone connects to the Internet through its 3G radio.) Essentially, the cellphone acts as the router for the Mac and other Bluetooth devices. But there's a catch: The phone has to support PAN Network Access Point technology. In the Bluetooth system preference, each device shows its supported capabilities under its name, so you can check for PAN support very quickly.

If your cellphone supports Bluetooth PAN, you configure it in the Network system preference by selecting the Bluetooth PAN connection. The options are the same as for Ethernet connections.

Tip

If Bluetooth PAN does not display as a connection in the Network system preference, click the + iconic button beneath the list of connections, then choose Bluetooth PAN from the Interface popup menu, give the connection a name, and click Create.

Note

You can also use Bluetooth as a modem for your Mac to give it Internet access. That doesn't create a local network, but does let the Mac access the Internet. Select the Bluetooth (not Bluetooth PAN) connection, and enter the phone number, account name, and password for the Bluetooth phone. You may need to click Advanced to set up the modem's configuration (in the Modem pane) and/or the Point-to-Point Protocol configuration (in the PPP pane) that manages how the Internet connection is managed.

Connecting Macs Directly

Sometimes, you don't need a whole network, just a way to exchange files and other services directly between two Macs in what's called an *ad hoc network*. There are four ways to do that. In all cases, after you've established the network connection, you should be able to share files as explained in Chapter 13.

Ethernet direct connection

You can connect two Macs directly to each other via an Ethernet connection. (As noted earlier in this chapter, you may need to use a crossover Ethernet cable to do so.) When connected, go to the Network system preference in each, select the Ethernet connection, and assign them a manual IP address. The first three segments should be the same for both, while the final segment should be unique. For example, you might use 192.168.1.101 and 192.168.1.102.

FireWire direct connection

If you have a FireWire cable, connect the two Macs with it. When connected, go to the Network system preference in each, select the FireWire connection, and assign them a manual IP address. The first three segments should be the same for both, while the final segment should be unique. For example, you might use 192.168.1.101 and 192.168.1.102.

Wi-Fi direct connection

You can use Wi-Fi to connect two Macs when there's no wireless router or access point available; instead, you set one of the Macs to act as the access point. In one Mac, go to the Network system preference, select the AirPort connection, and click Turn AirPort On. In the Network Name popup menu, choose Create Network. The dialog box shown in Figure 12.5 appears. If you want to require a password, select the Require Password option and then enter one. Click OK to start this ad hoc wireless network.

The other Macs connect to this Mac as they would to any wireless router or access point: Choose it from the wireless list in the AirPort menu bar or in the Network name popup menu in the Network system preference.

Note
You may have to change the wireless channel assigned to the ad hoc network in the Channel popup menu when creating the ad hoc wireless network, if other wireless networks nearby use the default channel (11).

FIGURE 12.5

Creating an ad hoc wireless network

Bluetooth direct connection

If both Macs have Bluetooth, you can use it to establish a direct connection.

First, go to one Mac and enable Bluetooth Discovery Mode in the Bluetooth system preferences (see Chapter 21) and turn on Bluetooth File Sharing (see Chapter 13) in the Sharing system preference.

On the second Mac, go to the Bluetooth system preference and click the + iconic button to search for a Bluetooth device (if asked, choose Any Device as the device type). When that second Mac finds the first Mac, select the first Mac's name in the device list and click Continue. You will be asked to provide a pairing code; enter any number and press Return.

On the first Mac, a dialog box appears asking you to enter the same number you entered on the second Mac. Do so and press Return. You will get a confirmation of the connection and can press Quit to exit the Bluetooth setup.

Summary

The Macintosh was the first computer to make networking easy, and today it provides the greatest amount of built-in networking support so Macs can easily join both Mac and Windows networks.

A network of computers and other devices typically is created by cabling the devices through a router or other central device, although wireless connections can be used instead of cables as well.

The Network system preference is where you configure a Mac to participate in a network, providing its unique ID (its IP address) and specifying other settings that help it access the Internet in addition to local servers, computers, and devices.

Bluetooth networks require the use of a cellphone or similar device that supports PAN to act as a router for your Mac and other devices to network through. Setting up a Bluetooth device requires first pairing it with your Mac, which you do in the Bluetooth system preference before setting up the networking settings in the Network system preference.

You can connect two Macs directly to each other to exchange files by using either a crossover Ethernet cable or a FireWire cable. In either case, you set a manual IP address for each Mac. You can also set a Mac to act as a wireless router so other Macs can connect to it wirelessly, and you can use Bluetooth to enable one Mac to connect to another wirelessly.

Sharing Files and Other Resources

I f you work with other people — and who doesn't? — you're going to share files and perhaps other resources. Sure, you can exchange files via e-mail, file servers (including Internet-based services such as Apple's MobileMe, as explained in Chapter 15, and FTP [File Transfer Protocol] servers, as explained in Chapter 14), or various media such CD-R (Compact Disc-Recordable) discs and flash drives. But the Mac OS also makes it easy to directly share files and other resources by providing you with access to other peoples' Macs and enabling them to access yours.

This direct sharing has been a hallmark of the Mac since shortly after the first Mac shipped. Since then, Apple has extended its capabilities so you can control other Macs and share a Mac's directly connected resources such as printers and Internet connections.

The key to direct sharing is to be able to access each other's Macs over the same local wired or wireless network (see Chapter 12) or over the Internet (see Chapter 15). You can also set up sharing with Bluetooth devices by using the Bluetooth system preference, as Chapter 21 explains. If you've enabled this access, the actual sharing is easy. (See Chapter 18 for details on sharing files with Windows users.)

But be warned: Opening your Mac for sharing can make you a target for evil-doers, so be sure to secure your Mac, as Chapter 23 explains.

Enabling File and Other Sharing

Even if your Mac is connected to a network or to the Internet, people can't share its files and resources unless you set up sharing. And anyone you want to connect to for sharing has to enable sharing on his or her Mac.

There are just two places to set up sharing: the Sharing system preference and the MobileMe system preference.

Setting up the Sharing system preference

The Sharing system preference, shown in Figure 13.1, is where you do most of the setup work. Twelve types of sharing controls in the system preference appear in the list on the left: DVD or CD Sharing, Screen Sharing, File Sharing, Printer Sharing, Scanner Sharing, Web Sharing, Remote Login, Remote Management, Remote Apple Events, Xgrid Sharing, Internet Sharing, and Bluetooth Sharing.

FIGURE 13.1

The Sharing system preference's Screen Sharing pane

Here's what each pane configures, in order of how it appears in the Sharing system preference's list:

- **DVD or CD Sharing.** If selected, this option enables other users to access any DVDs or CDs mounted on your Mac. The only configuration setting is the Ask Me Before Allowing Others to Use my DVD Drive option.

- **Screen Sharing.** If selected, this option enables other users to see what's on your screen. You can choose to allow all users to see your screen or specify specific users, using the Allow Access For controls. The Computer Settings button, if clicked, shows a sheet with two additional options: one that lets anyone ask for permission to control (not simply observe) the screen and another that lets remote users connected via a VNC (virtual network computing) remote-control application control the screen if they enter the password you specify here. Note that if Remote Management is enabled, it takes over screen sharing and disables the options in the Screen Sharing pane. Figure 13.1 shows the pane.

- **File Sharing.** If selected, this option enables people to share files with your Mac. You specify which folders to share in the Shared Folders window; click the + iconic button to add a share folder, and click the – iconic button to remove a selected share folder. You then specify in the Users window which users can share the selected share folder and the degree of permissible sharing — Read & Write, Read Only, and Write Only (Drop Box) — for that user. (You add and delete users by using the familiar + and – iconic buttons.) Figure 13.2 shows the pane.

Tip

You can also enable file sharing for a disk or folder by selecting that item and pressing ⌘+I to open an Info window. Select Shared Folder to add the disk or folder to the Shared Folders window in the File Sharing pane of the Sharing system preference. The Sharing system preference need not be active when you do this, but you will need to have it open at the File Sharing pane to change the sharing permissions for any disks or folders you make sharable via an Info window.

FIGURE 13.2

The File Sharing pane of the Sharing system preference

Where Are Shared Files Kept?

When you give someone permission to put files in your Drop Box — by providing Write Only (Drop Box) file-sharing permission — just where are those files? They're in the Drop Box folder inside your Public folder, which is inside your Home folder. The path is `/Users/username/Public/Drop Box`.

So what is the Public folder for? Any files stored in the Public folder are accessible to any other user you've given Read Only or Read & Write file-sharing permission. Note that if any user on your Mac sets up file sharing, anyone with access to the Mac, whether a user logged into the Mac or a user who has file-sharing permissions to access to Mac over the network, can see the contents of *all* users' Public folders.

- **Printer Sharing.** If selected, this option enables people to use printers attached to your Mac. This is a great way to share a non-networked printer with other users on your network. A list of available printers appears on the left of the pane. If you enabled sharing for a printer in the Print & Fax system preference, it will be selected here; otherwise, select it here to enable sharing. Select a shared printer and add or remove users from the window at right by using the familiar + and – iconic buttons. You can give each user one of two permissions: Can Print and No Access. (Note that if you want to configure a printer, click the Open Print Preferences button as a shortcut to opening it.)

- **Scanner Sharing.** If selected, this option enables people to use scanners attached to your Mac. It works like the Printer Sharing pane.

New Feature
Scanner sharing is new to Mac OS X 10.6 Snow Leopard.

- **Web Sharing.** If selected, this option enables users on your network to see the Web pages you place in the Sites folder in each user's Home folder, as well as the Web pages you've stored in the `/Library/WebServer/Documents` folder. There are no configuration settings for Web Sharing: It's simply on or off. (Chapter 14 explains Web sharing in more detail.)

- **Remote Login.** If selected, this option enables other users on your network to take over your Mac by using the Terminal (see Chapter 26). You can select who those users are through the Allow For Access controls. Note that the Remote Login pane also tells you the Unix command that these remote users will need to be able to log in via the Terminal.

- **Remote Management.** If selected, this option enables other users to take over your Mac by seeing your screen on theirs and then using their mice and keyboards to run your Mac remotely. You can select who those users are through the Allow For Access controls. For each user, you set exactly what they can control by clicking Options, which opens a sheet of options, as Figure 13.3 shows: Observe, Control, Show When Being Observed, Generate Reports, Open and Quit Applications, Change Settings, Delete and Replace Items, Start Text Chat or Send Messages, Restart and Shut Down, and Copy Items. The Computer Settings button, if clicked, shows a sheet with four additional options: one that lets anyone ask for permission to control (not simply observe) the screen; one that lets remote users connected via a VNC remote-control application control the screen if they enter the password you specify here; one that puts a remote status indicator in your menu bar, so you get a visual indicator if someone is remotely managing your Mac; and a set of four text fields that lets you add descriptions about your computer that are included in any reports that are generated (typically something that your Mac administrator would set up).

Note

People can use the Screen Sharing utility on their Macs to control or observe your Mac if Remote Management is enabled, as explained later in this chapter. For complete remote management of your Mac, such as to install software, do live troubleshooting, and generate reports on the Macs' activity, they must have the Apple Remote Desktop software, which is a separate purchase.

FIGURE 13.3

The options for remote-control sharing in the Sharing system preference's Remote Management pane

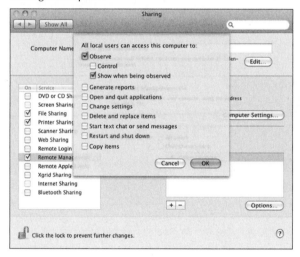

- **Remote Apple Events.** If selected, this option enables your Mac to accept commands and other information from other Macs, typically used for applications to collaborate with each other. Click Options to open a sheet where you set a password for such events to submit and to enable Apple Events generated in Mac OS 9. You can select who those users are through the Allow For Access controls. (Note that this type of sharing is not common, so you should have a specific reason to turn it on.)

- **Xgrid Sharing.** If selected, this option enables your Mac to share its processing capabilities with other Macs, in what is known as *grid computing*: Each Mac does a task — a part of the computation — and the results are then all combined, which helps speed up processing and takes advantage of the fact that most PCs are idle most of the time. In the Xgrid Sharing pane, use the Authentication popup menu to control access to your Mac via a password or single-sign-on certificate (or have no authorization). Click Configure to open a sheet where you set which controllers (systems that distribute the Xgrid tasks) your Mac should accept tasks from, as well as whether your Mac should accept a task at any time or only when it is idle.

- **Internet Sharing.** If selected, this option enables other users on the network to access the Internet through your Mac. Use the Share Your Connection From popup menu to determine which network connection your Mac must be using for its Internet connection to be shared: AirPort, Ethernet, FireWire, or Bluetooth. Use the To Computers Using options to determine which network connections the others users' Macs must be using to connect to your Mac. Note that you can make your Mac act as a wireless router so other computers can connect directly to it, even if there is no wireless network that you're all connected to. Selecting AirPort Options opens a sheet where you set up the password these users must use to connect to Mac wirelessly.

- **Bluetooth Sharing.** Select this option to enable file sharing with other Bluetooth-enabled devices. You control exactly what can be shared and with whom by using the several options in this pane. The When Receiving Items popup menu enables your Mac to accept and save files received, accept and open them, ask you what to do with them, and not accept (Never Allow) files. Select the Require Pairing option to force the other device to "pair" with your Mac, as explained in the Bluetooth system preference section earlier in this chapter. Use the Folder for Accepted Items popup menu to select where these received files are deposited. The When Other Devices Browse popup menu enables the Mac to automatically deny or allow — or ask you what to do — each time a Bluetooth device tries to browse your Mac's files to see what you have. You can also require pairing for browsing, as well as set up which other folder — just one, note — users can browse. If you want to set up your Bluetooth preferences, click Bluetooth Preferences to jump to the Bluetooth system preference. Figure 13.4 shows this pane.

FIGURE 13.4

The Bluetooth Sharing pane of the Sharing system preference

Setting up the MobileMe system preference

If you subscribe to Apple's MobileMe service, you can set up both file sharing that enables you to place files on the Web for others to access using the iDisk utility and screen sharing and remote control using the Back to My Mac feature that works over Internet connections (rather than just on the local network).

Chapter 15 explains how to use the MobileMe service and the iDisk utility. To enable Back to My Mac, open the MobileMe system preference and go to the Back to My Mac pane. Click Start to turn on this feature. All computers that share a MobileMe account that have this feature turned on can share screens and allow remote control among each other.

Accessing Files and Other Resources

With sharing enabled, you can now actually share stuff. Mac OS X makes it easy to do so.

Sharing files with other Macs

The most common type of sharing is the sharing of files with other Macs. If all is well, you'll see the other Macs in any Finder window, in the Shared section of the list at left — whether they're connected over Ethernet, FireWire, Wi-Fi, Bluetooth, or Back to My Mac. Click the Mac's name and, if the Mac requires you to log in, click the Connect As button near the top right of the window and enter your username and password, as shown in Figure 13.5.

If the shared Mac does not appear in the Finder window's Shared list, choose Go ⇨ Connect to Server or press ⌘+K and click Browse to scan the network for shared Macs, then double-click them to get the login shown in Figure 13.5.

If the connection is successful, you'll see the other Mac's shared disks and folders as if they were any other folder on your Mac, as Figure 13.6 shows. The shared Mac also appears as a network drive icon on your desktop, so you can simply double-click it to open it while you remain connected.

Note

When you open a disk or folder on your Mac that you've allowed to be shared with others, Mac OS X will display "Shared Folder" at the top of the window, above the list of items in the disk or folder. That provides a handy reminder of what others have access to.

FIGURE 13.5

Logging into a Mac that has enabled file sharing

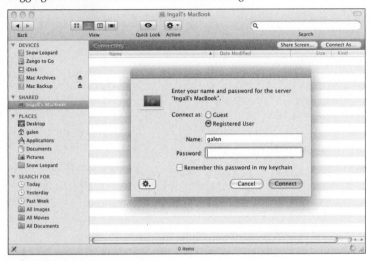

FIGURE 13.6

When connected to a Mac, its shared disks and folders appear as regular folders that you access like any other disk or folder on your Mac.

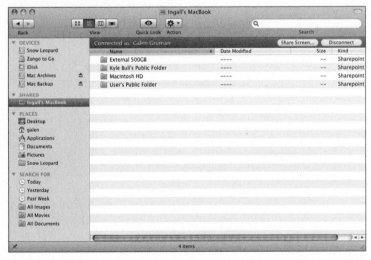

Sharing files with Bluetooth

If you're sharing with other Macs via a Bluetooth connection, as explained in Chapter 12, those Macs appear in the Finder window's Shared list like any other Macs shared over the network. But if you're sharing files with a Bluetooth-connected device such as a smartphone, you use a different method to share files.

If the Bluetooth icon is in the menu bar, choose Send File in its menu to select the files you want to transmit, then click Send to get the dialog box shown in Figure 13.7. You can also Control+click or right-click an item and choose Send File in the contextual menu. (Otherwise, enable this iconic menu in the Bluetooth system preference. Or use the Bluetooth File Exchange utility.) Select the device you want to send the file to, then click Send to transmit the files. The file will be placed in whatever location that device has set up for receiving files.

To get files from a Bluetooth device, choose Browse Device from the Bluetooth iconic popup menu, choose the device, select from it the files you want, and click Get. (You can also click Send to choose files to send to the device.)

Cross-Ref
See Chapter 21 for the details on connecting to Bluetooth devices.

FIGURE 13.7

Sending a file to a Bluetooth device (left); browsing a Bluetooth device to get or send files (right)

Sharing screens

When you connect to a Mac as explained in the "Sharing files with other Macs" section earlier in this chapter, you have the option to share that Mac's screen by clicking Share Screen (see Figure 13.5) to launch the Screen Sharing utility. If that Mac has enabled screen sharing, you can connect to it to see its screen or even control it based on the settings in that Mac's Screen Sharing pane in its Sharing system preference. Based on those settings, you may be asked for a password, or the person you are trying to observe may get a dialog box asking him or her whether you should have access. You can let people share your screen the same way.

Tip

Another way to access screen sharing is via your browser. Enter `vnc://ip_address` **in the URL field (replace ip_address with the Mac's actual IP address, such as 192.168.1.2). The browser then launches the Mac's Screen Sharing utility (or it may ask you choose it or another VNC utility you may have installed, then use the selected application). You can also run Screen Sharing directly by double-clicking it in its folder:** `/System/Library/CoreServices/Screen Sharing`.

While Screen Sharing is trying to connect to the other Mac, you'll see a status dialog box, as shown in Figure 13.8. You can also change Screen Sharing's preferences by choosing Screen Sharing ⇨ Preferences or pressing ⌘+, (comma), as also shown in the figure. There are three sets of settings:

- **When Viewing a Computer with a Larger Screen.** You can choose to shrink the window to fit in your screen (the Scale to Fit Available Space option), or to scroll through the other Mac's screen (the Show Full Size option).

- **When Controlling Computers.** You can choose Encrypt Passwords and Keystrokes Only (Faster) or Encrypt All Network Data (More Secure).

- **When Displaying Remote Screens.** You can choose Adapt Quality to Network Connections (Faster) or Show the Screen at Full Quality (More Detailed).

FIGURE 13.8

The Screen Sharing utility's Preferences dialog box appears on the left. The status window as Screen Sharing tries to make a connection appears on the right.

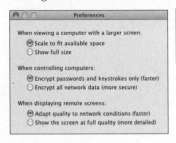

After the screen sharing connection is made, the Screen Sharing utility opens, as Figure 13.9 shows. If you have the ability to control that Mac, your mouse movements and clicks, as well as keyboard entries, give you the same abilities as if you were physically at that Mac. If you can observe only, you will see whatever the other user is doing.

FIGURE 13.9

Sharing another user's screen

Sharing other resources

If you've enabled other types of sharing in the Sharing system preference, they're generally accessible as if they were local to your Mac, using the same methods you would use for devices attached to your Mac:

- **CDs and DVDs.** Another Mac's shared DVD drive should appear in the Devices section in the Sidebar of any Finder window, as if it were a drive connected directly to your Mac.

- **Printers.** Another Mac's shared printer will display in the Default pane when you click the + iconic button to add a printer in the Printers & Fax system preference (see Chapter 17).

- **Scanners.** Another Mac's shared scanner will appear as a device in the Image Capture utility on your Mac.

- **Internet.** Macs connected to your Mac via Ethernet, FireWire, Wi-Fi, or Bluetooth will have Internet access without having to do anything on their end. But your Mac may experience some slowdown if others use the Internet heavily through it.

- **Web.** Other Macs connected to your Mac can access the Web pages in your Sites folder through their browser, as explained in Chapter 14.

Summary

If your Mac is accessible to other Macs via the local network, you can set it up to share files over Ethernet, FireWire, Wi-Fi, and Bluetooth connections, as well as over the Internet for users who share a MobileMe account with you. You can share files with other users over the same connections.

You can also share your DVD drive, connected printers, connected scanners, and Internet connections with users you provide sharing access to. Mac OS X also enables you to observe and control other Macs via its Screen Sharing utility.

Serving Web Pages and Files from Your Mac

I f you run a Web site, chances are that you have a dedicated Web server at your facility or, more likely, managed for you by a Web host. These commercial-grade servers can handle the network load and have someone who makes sure that everything is running 24/7. From that server, you make your Web site available to the world. Likewise, you might have an FTP server set up at your facility or offered by your Web host to share files with clients and co-workers, using the File Transfer Protocol.

But your Mac can be that server, either to the entire Web or to people within your local network, thanks to the Mac OS's Web serving and FTP serving capabilities.

We don't recommend using your Mac as a server connected to the Internet — that can open you up to all sorts of hacking problems, as Chapter 23 explains. Plus, you need a continually available high-speed Internet connection to that Mac, which must be left on 24/7. You'll be hard pressed to find an Internet service provider (ISP) that offers such connections for home-based users.

Sure, if you're a network whiz, you can put the Mac outside the local network, using a business-class Internet connection so your internal users aren't at risk. But if you have that capability, you're better off using a server operating system such as Mac OS X Server, Linux, or Windows Server to offer your Web site and FTP to the entire world, given they're designed to do so with greater management and security capabilities.

IN THIS CHAPTER

Using your Mac as a Web server

Understanding Web home page names

Using your Mac as an FTP server

Note

If you do host your own Web site from your Mac, it will need its own public IP (Internet Protocol) address, as Chapter 12 explains. And you'll need to register a domain with a domain registry service or with a DNS (Domain Name Service) provider that then maps to your public IP address so, for example, when a user types www.apple.com, **he or she is sent to the correct IP address for the server hosting the site.**

But within your network, Mac OS X's capability to act as a Web server and FTP server makes it very convenient as a way to share project information and mock-ups to your colleagues without needing to set up a separate server. Or you can use a Mac as a simple server for departmental Web and FTP sharing, instead of going the more complicated route of using a server operating system.

Serving Web Pages from Your Mac

Mac OS X comes with a built-in Web server, the open source Apache server software that the vast majority of Web sites also use, commercial or not. But you don't need to learn Apache to use it on the Mac; Mac OS X 10.6 Snow Leopard does the behind-the-scenes work for you.

There are two kinds of Web sites you can host on your Mac: personal Web sites and a common Web site. Each user of your Mac can have his or her own personal Web site in the home folder's Sites folder. There's also a common folder — /LibraryWebServer/Documents/ — that you can use as a main Web site.

To make any or all of these Web sites available to others on your local network, put your Web site's files in the appropriate folders. Then turn on Web sharing on your Mac by launching the Sharing system preference and selecting the option to the right of the Web Sharing label in the list of sharing services at left. If you click Web Sharing, the Web Sharing pane opens and displays the IP addresses your local network users will need to enter in their browsers to access your Web sites, as Figure 14.1 shows.

Caution

Note that if you have multiple users on your Mac, and one of them turns on Web sharing within his or her account, Web sharing is turned on for all accounts.

The common Web site's IP address (which users need to enter to access the site) is the same as for your Mac, followed by the folder indicator (/), such as 192.168.1.190/. The personal Web site's IP addresses start with that main IP address and then add the username, such as 192.168.1.190/~galen/.

FIGURE 14.1

The Web Sharing pane of the Sharing system preference

The Basics of Web Pages

Of course, you need Web pages available in your site for people to see them. You can create the Web pages in all sorts of applications: Microsoft Word and Apple iWork Pages can save their files in HTML format, for example, and then there are professional Web site creation applications such as Adobe Dreamweaver (www.adobe.com) and Karelia Software's Sandvox (www.karelia.com).

The home page for a Web site should be named index.htm or index.html (it doesn't matter which). If a user types the URL without a page name, such as 192.168.1.190/~galen/, the Apache server delivers index.html or index.htm automatically, if that page exists in the folder. If you don't use this filename, then the user must type in the full URL to get to the page, such as 192.168.1.190/~galen/books.html.

The folder comes with a bunch of prebuilt index pages, as shown in the figure here. Their names all start with index.html. and add a code for the language they're written in, such as fr for French and pt for Portuguese. (The index.html.en file is in English, and if you don't create your own index.htm or index.html file in this directory, people will see the prebuilt English page automatically when they enter your Mac's URL in their Web browser, if Web Sharing is turned on.)

continued

continued

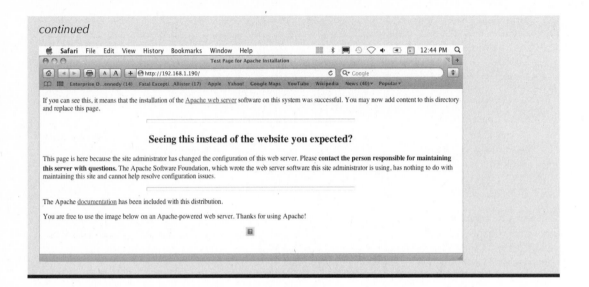

Providing FTP Access from Your Mac

The File Transfer Protocol (FTP) is an Internet standard for letting people upload and download files to and from other computers. In a local network, the Mac's built-in file sharing (see Chapter 13) is a better option for exchanging files, but if you are working with non-Mac users, you might want to enable FTP access so they can exchange files with you.

To enable FTP on your Mac, go to the Sharing system preference's File Sharing pane, as shown in Figure 14.2. Click Options to open the settings sheet and select Share Files and Folders Using FTP. Users can connect to your Mac with an FTP application such as Fetch Softworks' Fetch (`www.fetchsoftworks.com`) and Panic Software's Transmit (`www.panic.com`).

To connect to your Mac, users will need the Mac's IP address, an account name, and a password. That means you need to set up at least a Sharing Only user account for people to exchange files with your Mac via FTP. (Chapter 20 explains how to create these Sharing Only accounts.) You don't need a user account for each user you want to enable FTP access for, just an account whose username and password you give out to all such users.

In the File Sharing pane of the Sharing system preference, add the folders you want to make available via FTP by clicking the + iconic button under the Shared Folders list. Select a folder to be shared via FTP and then give the Sharing Only user account the desired privileges for file exchange in the Users list: Read & Write (download and upload), Read Only (download from your Mac), or Drop Box (upload to your Mac). When the user connects via FTP, he or she will be restricted to that folder. Note that you can provide FTP access (as well as Mac file-sharing access and/or Windows SMB file sharing — whatever is selected when you click Options to open the settings sheet in the File Sharing pane) for multiple user accounts, and can enable such access to more than one folder. But we recommend that you set up a single folder and single user account for all FTP access.

Note

You cannot set FTP access for just specified user accounts or folders. If you enable FTP access, all shared folders are accessible via FTP for all user accounts that are given sharing permissions. If you want to set FTP-only access to specific folders or users, you need to get a separate FTP server application for your Mac, such as the open source FileZilla Server (`http://filezilla-project.org`) or Jscape's Secure FTP Server (`http://jscape.com`).

Tip

You might use a Web-based file-sharing service, such as the iDisk service that comes with Apple's MobileMe service (see Chapter 15), instead of using your Mac as an FTP server. Such services are more secure and don't require your Mac to always be on. If you have an external Web host, chances are it also offers FTP server options that address these two issues.

If the people use an FTP application, it typically has them enter the IP address, account name (they'll typically refer to this as the *username*), and password. If they're using their Web browsers' FTP capabilities, they should enter `ftp://username:password@ip_address`, such as `ftp://galengruman:bayarea@192.168.1.190` (the account name here is `galengruman` and the password is `bayarea`).

FIGURE 14.2

The dialog box in the File Sharing pane of the Sharing system preference that enables FTP access

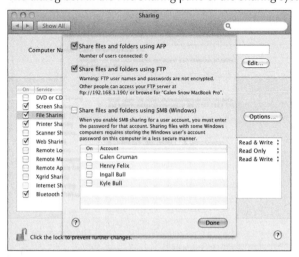

There are some dangers with enabling FTP access on your Mac, in addition to the general danger of opening up the Mac to outsiders:

- The Mac's FTP server is great for handling text-only files but not for many other types of files that use a file-encoding mechanism known as *binary files*. In fact, binary files can get corrupted during transmission. A commercial FTP server automatically detects binary files and properly transmits them; the Mac OS's FTP server does not. Therefore, you should compress any file you want to make available via FTP to others by using the Mac OS X's built-in compression utility. (Select the files, Control+click or right-click them, and choose Compress from the contextual menu to create a Zip archive file.) People sending files to your Mac via the Mac's FTP server should also compress their files before sending them. (To decompress an archive, just double-click it.)

- Account names and passwords sent via FTP are not encrypted, so someone who can snoop your network can discover the user account and password being used. (This is why it's important to set up a Sharing Only user account and limit its access privileges to one folder so if the username and password are discovered, the hacker can only mess with that one location on your Mac.)

Tip

There is a form of FTP called Secure FTP (SFTP) that is more secure to use because it uses encryption. And Mac OS X supports SFTP through its Unix Secure Shell (SSH) capability. Chapter 26 provides more information on SSH. To use SFTP, you need to enable Remote Login and tell people to use an SFTP client that goes through SSH. Because using SFTP requires more technical knowledge and special software, it can be impractical to require its use. Plus SFTP is slower than regular FTP because of the processing overhead required to handle its encryption capabilities.

Summary

Macs can act as Web and FTP servers to any computer connected to your Mac, whether on a local network or over the Internet.

Although technically the Mac can host Web sites accessible over the Internet and provide a central FTP file-exchange location, security and performance issues make this a less-than-ideal option. But within a network, for access by other users in your organization or home, the built-in Web and FTP server capabilities can be useful.

The Mac OS enables each user account to have its own personal Web site, plus you can set up a common Web site. The Web pages and associated materials for personal Web sites are stored in each user's Sites folder, while the common Web site's files are stored at /LibraryWebServer/Documents/.

Mac OS X's FTP capabilities work like the Mac's file sharing, except that users can use FTP software or their Web browser's FTP capabilities instead of (or in addition to) standard Mac file sharing. Plus non-Mac users gain access to file exchange via FTP. But the Mac's FTP service can corrupt files during transmission, so you may want to use commercial-class FTP server software or an external FTP server (such as from your Web host or Apple's MobileMe service) instead.

Working with MobileMe

When you work with multiple computers, it's easy to get inconsistent information in your calendars and address books. And it's easy to forget to copy a file from one to the other, such as from your desktop Mac to your MacBook. (Windows PCs can be part of the mix as well.) Add the iPhone or iPod Touch to the mix, and it can get impossible to keep everything synchronized and accessible.

If that's a frustration you experience, you may want to use Apple's $99-per-year MobileMe service ($149 for a family pack with one master account and four additional family members all sharing the same online storage space). Mac OS X 10.6 Snow Leopard and the iPhone OS both provide built-in support for it.

MobileMe has several components to help you keep your information automatically synchronized, as well as provide other connection advantages:

- **The synchronization service.** The service itself keeps calendars, contacts, notes, Safari bookmarks, and e-mail up-to-date across the computers and devices you specify. It also can synchronize basic Mac settings across multiple Macs, such as dashboard widgets, Dock items, keychains (saved passwords), and system preferences; and Mail settings, such as signatures, smart mailboxes, and message filtering rules.

- **The MobileMe Web-based apps.** These let you manage your e-mail, contacts, and calendar from a Web browser, so even if you don't have your MobileMe-enabled Mac, PC, or iPhone with you, you're still in touch and in control.

- **The iDisk service.** This service provides a Web-based virtual hard drive to which you can upload files, making them accessible to not only to yourself but also anyone you give permission to. Thus, you can easily share files with others, as well as have a file folder in the Internet from which you can access chosen files from any Internet-connected Mac or PC.

- **The Gallery Web app.** This application enables you to create photo libraries you can share with friends and family. You can upload photos to it several ways, including via Publish to Gallery functions in Apple iPhoto '09 or Apple Aperture 2. Friends and family can also add their own photos through the Web or via e-mail.

- **A MobileMe e-mail address.** You can use this address as a personal or business e-mail from any computer or device that supports either of the standard e-mail connection protocols, POP3 (Post Office Protocol 3) or IMAP (Internet Message Access Protocol).

- **The Back to My Mac service.** This service enables you to connect Macs across a network or the Internet so you can remotely control them, such as to connect to your work Mac from home or to help a relative who lives out of the area figure out an issue on their computer by seeing what they are doing on your Mac and taking over if necessary.

Note

Before Apple enhanced it to support the iPhone, MobileMe was available under a different name: .Mac.

The MobileMe service is separate from Mac OS X 10.6 Snow Leopard, even though Mac OS X comes with support built in. That means that Apple may change the features and operations of MobileMe before the next new version of Mac OS X. Therefore, some of the instructions here may not be valid in the future, even though they were correct when this book went to press. If Apple does change how MobileMe operates, you can expect it to provide a free update to Mac OS X that gives you those changes.

Setting Up MobileMe

The first step in using MobileMe is to set up an account. You can do so from your Mac's Mobile Me system preference by clicking Learn More to open a Web page in which you sign up for a 60-day trial account. You need an Internet connection and a valid credit card to sign up.

After you've signed up for MobileMe, you need to sign in to MobileMe on each Mac you will use with it. You do that in the same MobileMe system preference on each Mac, filling in your Member Name and Password and then clicking Sign In. (Sign in using the same credentials on every Mac that you want to synchronize through this MobileMe account.) Figure 15.1 shows the MobileMe system preference.

Cross-Ref

Chapter 21 covers the system preferences, including the MobileMe system preference, in detail.

Caution

If your MobileMe account expires, all your data stored only on MobileMe is deleted. Any data that also resides on your Macs is retained, of course.

The MobileMe system preference is where you initially sign up for the service and then sign in after you have an account.

Settings on a Mac

After you've signed in on your Mac, you see four panes: Account, Sync, iDisk, and Back to My Mac. The Account pane shows your current settings, such as the expiration date for your MobileMe subscription and how much storage space you have left for file and e-mail storage. If you click Account Details, a Web page opens that enables you to manage your account settings such as password, credit card information, and time zone. Figure 15.2 shows that Web page's password pane.

The Sync pane is where you turn synchronization on or off, as well as decide what information is to be synchronized, see which computers were last synchronized and when, and decide whether to remove a computer from being synchronized to this account. Figure 15.3 show the Sync pane.

The iDisk pane is simpler, showing you how much file storage space has been used, as well as letting you enable a public folder (and assign a password to it if you want) and have MobileMe automatically keep a local copy of the iDisk folder on this computer so its information remains available to you when you don't have an Internet connection.

The Back to My Mac pane enables you to turn on and off the capability to have other Macs using this MobileMe account control this Mac. (Chapter 21 explains each of the Sync, iDisk, and Back to My Mac panes' settings in detail.)

FIGURE 15.2

The MobileMe Web site enables you to manage account information such as your billing information and password. (The password pane is shown here.)

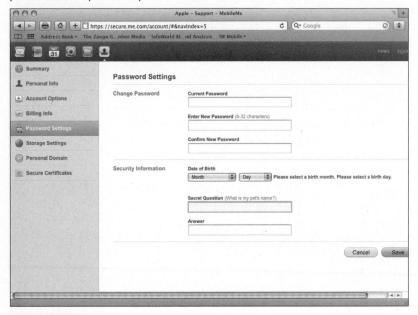

FIGURE 15.3

The MobileMe system preference's Sync pane enables you to control specifically what is synchronized and how often.

In addition to synchronizing your own information across multiple Macs, Windows PCs, iPod Touches, and/or iPhones, you can also use MobileMe to synchronize contact information with other MobileMe users. (Sorry, there's no equivalent feature for calendar sharing.) The secret is to enable sharing in your Mac's Address Book with other MobileMe users. To do so, follow the instructions in the sidebar, "Sharing Contacts with Other People," later in this chapter.

Settings on the Web

As previously mentioned, you go to the Web to manage your overall MobileMe account settings, such as your billing information and password (see Figure 15.2). You can get there by clicking Account Details in the Accounts pane of the MobileMe system preference, or simply by going to me.com from a Web browser.

Tip

If you log in to the your MobileMe account and don't see the account settings — perhaps you logged in to use one of the Web tools such as Mail — you can go to the account options by clicking the button at the top of the screen that is the silhouette of a person's head. Enter your password when requested to do so.

After you sign in, you get the various account options, as shown in the list on the left of Figure 15.2:

- **The Summary pane.** Shows you when your subscription expires and how much storage you've used. You can jump to the Storage Settings pane by clicking Settings. And you can jump to the Account Options pane by clicking Options.

- **The Personal Info pane.** Enables you to change your name, preferred language, time zone, and alternative e-mail address, as well as turn off or on getting marketing notices related to MobileMe from Apple.

- **The Account Options pane.** Enables you to convert a trial account to a paid one, cancel an account, or renew an account.

- **The Billing Info account.** Enables you to update your credit card information, as well as the billing address for the designated card.

- **The Password Settings account.** Enables you to update your password and the secret questions used to validate your identity if you forget your password.

- **The Storage Settings pane.** Enables you to determine how much of your 20GB of MobileMe online storage is allocated to e-mail and to files. By default, 10GB is allocated to each. To change the default, choose a new value for your online e-mail storage from the Mail popup menu. MobileMe will allocate the rest of your 20GB to your online file storage.

- **The Personal Domain pane.** Enables you to connect a Web domain that you own — such as ilovemymac.com — to Apple's iWeb application (which is part of Apple's separately sold iLife '08 or iLife '09 software). This enables you to create and update your Web site within iWeb and have the changes automatically uploaded to the Web site. This Web site is hosted — stored and made publicly available by — the MobileMe service. Note that space taken by your Web sites counts against your file storage limit.

- **The Secure Certificates pane**. As shown in Figure 15.4, the pane enables you to cut off access to Back to My Mac and secure iChat sessions (see Chapter 11) if your Mac is lost or stolen. You revoke the security certificate, which means that the various computers you've set up with MobileMe accounts can't use Back to My Mac or join your secure iChat sessions.

Tip

Immediately after revoking the certificate, you should change your password as well, so whoever has the lost or stolen Mac can't just log in from that Mac into your MobileMe account, figure out your password, and lock you out first. After you've revoked the certificates and changed the password, generate a new secure certificate by using the instructions in the Secure Certificates pane, then have all MobileMe account users update their passwords, turn off Back to My Mac on their Macs in the MobileMe system preference, and then turn it back on. Doing so gives them — and only them — the new certificate.

FIGURE 15.4

The MobileMe options on the Web let you revoke the security certificates for Back to My Mac and secure iChat sessions in case your Mac is lost or stolen.

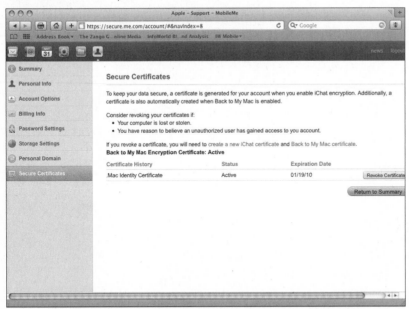

Settings on an iPhone

You won't find a MobileMe icon on your iPhone's (or iPod Touch's) Home screen, but that doesn't mean the device can't be part of a MobileMe shared environment. When you set up your MobileMe e-mail account on your iPhone, you get the synchronization for the calendar and contacts as well. Here are the steps:

1. Tap the Settings button, then the Mail, Contacts, Calendars option.

2. Tap Add Account and then tap MobileMe from the list of supported e-mail services.

3. **Complete the setup information by keying in the Name, Address, Password, and optional Description fields.** Note that all the Address field needs is your MobileMe username; it will add the @me.com part automatically. Then tap Save.

4. **You now set up what you want to synchronize in the pane that appears (see Figure 15.5).** Slide the switches to On for the information you want synchronized between your iPhone and the other computers and devices using this MobileMe account: Mail, Contacts, Calendars, and Bookmarks. Tap Done when done.

You can change these settings any time by tapping your MobileMe account in the Accounts list for Mail, Contacts, Calendars.

FIGURE 15.5
_____

After you've added a MobileMe e-mail account to your iPhone or iPod Touch, you can select what other MobileMe data to synchronize.

Settings on a Windows PC

To use MobileMe to keep Windows PCs' data synchronized with your Mac and/or iPhone, you need to be running Windows XP or Vista (and the forthcoming Windows 7 should work, too, because it's just a version of Vista), as well as iTunes 8.01 or later and the MobileMe control panel (find the link for it at www.apple.com/mobileme/features/pc.html). After you install the MobileMe Preferences control panel (a control panel is the Windows version of a system preference), you sign in to MobileMe from it by using your username and password.

Tip

To find the MobileMe Preferences control panel, choose Start ⇨ Control Panel ⇨ Network and Internet in Vista or Start ⇨ Control Panel ⇨ Network and Internet Connections in XP, then double-click the MobileMe icon. If you have Classic Views enabled in either version of Windows, just choose Start ⇨ Control Panel and then double-click the MobileMe icon. Finally, if you are running XP in the Classic Start Menu mode, choose Start ⇨ Settings ⇨ Control Panel and then double-click the MobileMe icon. (Note that the MobileMe icon may not be visible in the control panel window until you scroll down to see more of the available control panels.)

You'll see three panes in the control panel, as Figure 15.6 shows:

- **Account.** This pane provides the same controls as in the Mac's MobileMe system preference's Account pane.

- **Sync.** This pane is similar to the Sync pane on the Mac, except that you can select only three types of things to share: Contacts, Calendars, and Bookmarks. Also unlike the Mac version, you can choose which applications to sync for each. The options will depend on what you have installed, but typical choices for Contacts are Google Contacts, Yahoo Address Book, Windows Contacts (on Vista) or Windows Address Book (on XP), and Outlook. For Calendars, the only option is Outlook. For Bookmarks, the supported browsers are Internet Explorer and Safari (but not Chrome, Firefox, or Opera).

Note

The Outlook options appear only if you've properly configured Outlook to connect to an Exchange server. If MobileMe detects that you have Outlook running but it can't connect to Exchange, MobileMe will ask for your Outlook login information. After MobileMe has connected successfully with Outlook, Outlook does not have to be running on your PC for synchronization to occur.

The Show in System Tray option is the Windows equivalent of the Mac's Show Status in the Menu Bar option — it puts a quick-access icon to MobileMe in the Windows system tray, which is the set of one-click launch icons in the Start bar. One unique option for Windows is the Warn When More than __% of the Computer's Data Will Change option. If selected, you'll get an alert when MobileMe replaces more than the chosen percentage of information. The Mac doesn't have this option because it automatically detects major changes and presents them in the Conflict Resolver dialog box covered in the next section of this chapter.

- **iDisk.** This pane has the same options as in the Mac's MobileMe system preference.

FIGURE 15.6

The MobileMe Preferences control panel's Sync pane in Windows.

Synchronizing Data

If you set up synchronization on your Mac, Windows PC, and/or iPhone, MobileMe will keep the devices synchronized based on the selections and schedule you chose. (If you chose Automatically in the Sync pane of the MobileMe system preference, the synchronization typically happens within 15 minutes, assuming the devices are connected to the Internet.)

For the most part, you set your sync options and let MobileMe take it from there. Of course, MobileMe will occasionally discover that you have conflicting data across your various devices. In that case, you get the Conflict Resolver dialog box shown in Figure 15.7. The dialog box shows you the MobileMe information and the information from your Mac, and asks you to choose which is correct. Click Review Now to go through these conflicts one by one, then click the correct data. Click Next to move on to the next conflict, if there is one, and click Done when done. You then get an alert, also shown in Figure 15.7, that enables you to update MobileMe with your selections (click Sync Now), wait until the next scheduled sync (click Sync Later), or cancel your conflict resolutions (click Cancel).

Note

When you sync to MobileMe, note that the Mac will also try to sync with any other device you've set up via iSync (see Chapter 8), such as your non-Apple cellphone or PDA. These devices aren't affected by the MobileMe sync settings, and instead will sync directly to your iCal, Mail, and Address Book, depending on which they support.

FIGURE 15.7

If MobileMe synchronization detects inconsistent information, it will ask you to resolve the conflict.

Notes if you're using an iPhone

The Mac uses iTunes as its normal synchronization tool to keep calendars, contacts, and bookmarks synchronized between a Mac and an iPhone (or iPod Touch) connected via a USB cable. MobileMe removes the need for this physical tethering and use of iTunes as the synchronization mechanism, so you can keep your iPhone updated over a Wi-Fi or 3G connection.

Caution

When you first sync your MobileMe account on your iPhone, all the contact and calendar information on your iPhone is deleted and then replaced with the information stored in the Internet-based master data for your MobileMe account. Thus, to avoid losing that data permanently, you should first synchronize your iPhone and your Mac, then your Mac to MobileMe so that master data has all that information. Then when MobileMe replaces the iPhone's data, you know it will put back all the data that had been on the iPhone originally, as well as the other data synchronized from your other computers.

Cross-Ref

Chapter 19 explains how to use Microsoft Exchange with a Mac. Chapter 11 shows how to set up the Mail application that comes with Mac OS X to access e-mail servers. On an iPhone, follow the instructions in the previous section for setting up a MobileMe account, but tap Microsoft Exchange instead of MobileMe.

Sharing Contacts with Other People

In addition to synchronizing data among your own computers and devices, you can also share the contacts in your Mac's Address Book with other MobileMe users, as well as let them share your Address Book contacts. You can even let them edit your contacts.

To set up contacts sharing, launch Address Book and go to the Sharing pane in its preferences dialog box (choose Address Book➪Preferences or press ⌘+, [comma]). Select Share Your Address Book, and then click the + iconic button to enable sharing with the MobileMe users you choose. People must have a MobileMe account (meaning an e-mail address that ends in @me.com) as one of their e-mail addresses for the OK button to become active so you can add them to the list. Be sure to select the Allow Editing option for each user that you want to be able to update your contacts.

To access another MobileMe user's Address Book, launch Address Book and choose File➪Subscribe to Address Book and then enter that person's MobileMe e-mail address and click OK. Anyone who wants to access your shared Address Book must do the same on their Mac.

Notes if you're also using Exchange

If you use a Microsoft Exchange server at work (using Entourage on your Mac or Outlook on your Windows PC) and MobileMe for personal and family information, note that synchronization may not work as you expect.

That's because any calendar items displayed in the Entourage calendar in iCal will not be synchronized via MobileMe. And any calendar items displayed in calendars other than Entourage will not synchronize via MobileMe. MobileMe and Exchange essentially leave each other's data alone. Any Mac that is set up to synchronize to both Exchange and MobileMe will show current calendar entries for both, but you can expect them to update at different times.

Note that e-mails are also handled independently, so they too will update separately. Chapter 19 covers how to work with Exchange servers in more detail.

Using iDisk to Access Files over the Internet

iDisk is an example of what's called a *cloud service* — using the Internet as a repository for data and virtual computer to run applications, which access over an Internet connection from any computer. iDisk is essentially a file folder you access over the Internet.

After you've set up your MobileMe account as described earlier in this chapter, your iDisk storage folder is available directly from your Mac and through your browser (on any computer).

Using iDisk from a Mac

On the Mac, you'll see iDisk listed in the Devices list in Finder windows when you open a folder or drive. Click iDisk to switch to it. Figure 15.8 shows an iDisk window into which files are being copied.

Figure 15.9 shows the other way to open an iDisk: Choose Go ➪ iDisk from the Finder. As the figure shows, there are three suboptions: My iDisk, Other User's Disk, and Other User's Public Folder. If you choose Other User's Disk, you need to enter a valid MobileMe account and password for that iDisk; you would use this option to access your iDisk from another person's Mac. If you choose Other User's Public Folder, you enter that person's MobileMe e-mail address; if a password is required, you'll be asked for that later.

iDisk folders look like regular Finder folders, and they work like regular Finder folders, too. Just drag files into and out of them, to copy them from and to your Mac, as well as from and to each other to move them within iDisk.

FIGURE 15.8

You can access iDisk folders from the Finder like any other folder.

FIGURE 15.9

You can connect to your iDisk folder as well as other people's iDisk folders by using the Finder's Go menu.

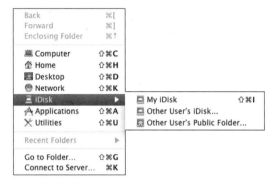

Tip

Because iDisk stores your files on Apple's servers via the Internet, copying files to and from iDisk can be slow — much slower than copying files across disk drives or even drives on your local network. We suggest that because of this slowness, you copy any desired files to your Mac before trying to open them; opening them over the Internet and saving subsequent changes can be excruciatingly slow.

Using iDisk through a browser

The other way to access iDisk is through your browser. The fastest way to get to your iDisk folders is to go to the Web address www.me.com/idisk/. (If you're not on your computer, type your username at the end of that address.) Or you can go to www.me.com, sign in to your MobileMe account, and click the folder icon at the top of the window to go to the iDisk folders. Figure 15.10 shows the Web page for iDisk.

Although iDisk in a browser looks like iDisk on your Mac, it doesn't work the same way. While you can drag files among the folders on iDisk, you cannot upload files by dragging them from your Mac onto an iDisk folder. Nor can you download files by dragging them from the iDisk folder onto your Mac. Instead, you must use the Upload and Download iconic buttons.

When you click the Upload button, which shows an upward-pointing arrow in a circle, you get a dialog box in which you choose the files (sorry, no folders) that you want to upload. Click Choose, then select the files to upload, and click Select. The files will upload into whatever iDisk folder is selected in your browser.

When you select files in an iDisk folder on your Web browser and click the Download button, which shows a downward-pointing arrow over an inbox, iDisk first compresses them into a Zip file, then downloads that to the Downloads folder. (You can see the Downloads folder in the Dock, as well as in your Home folder.) iDisk does the same compression action if you select one or more folders. If you select just one file for download, it does not compress the file; and if that file is an image, it automatically opens it in Preview after the download is complete.

In addition to the Download button, iDisk offers the Share File button when you select files in an iDisk folder on your Web browser. Clicking this button lets you share large files with others by sending them an e-mail with a link from which they can download the file. It also has an option to password-protect the shared files as well.

When you access iDisk through a Web browser, as shown here, you have to use Download and Upload iconic buttons to transfer files to and from your Mac.

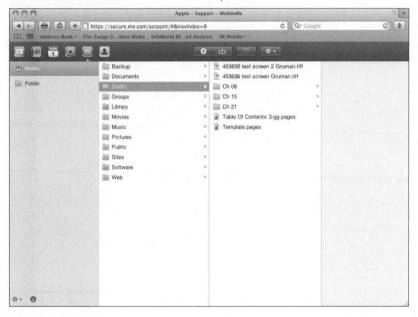

iDisk on the Web also provides some extra controls for files and folders, which you access through the List of Actions iconic popup menu (the gear icon). The options are self-explanatory: New Folder, Rename, Duplicate, Delete, Compress, Decompress Archive, and Preferences. There's just one preference, an option to turn on simple iDisk folders, which removes from display the folders the Mac OS, iLife, and MobileMe uses: Backup, Library, Sites, Software, and Web.

There's also a Delete iconic button (the red slashed-circle icon) that enables you to quickly delete selected folders and files.

The Public folder is where you place files you want to be available publicly. (As noted earlier in this chapter, you can password-protect this public folder in the MobileMe system preference's iDisk pane.) For people to access this public folder from the Web, they would go to `public.me.com/username` in their browser, replacing `username` with your MobileMe account name.

When people go to your public folder, they see a window like the one in Figure 15.11, where all public files are listed. The available controls depend on whether you allowed Read Only access or Read and Write access in the MobileMe system preference's iDisk pane, as described in Chapter 21's section on the MobileMe system preference.

If you set the public folder as Read Only, a person can only select the desired file to download and click the down-pointing arrow icon to the filename's far right to transfer a copy to his or her computer. Note that he or she can download only one file at a time.

If the public folder is set as Read and Write, the other options are available, including the ability to delete a selected file (using the slashed-circle iconic button), upload personal files one at a time (by clicking Upload), and create new folders (by clicking New Folder). The iDisk Home button lets users return to the main folder from any subfolders they are in.

FIGURE 15.11

A public iDisk folder

Using Back to My Mac for Remote Control

The Back to My Mac feature can make it really easy to remote-control your computer or get files from it remotely — if it works. The idea is that you can enter your MobileMe username and password on one computer and gain access to another computer that has the same account, such as a second Mac you own or a family member's Mac.

The available Mac will appear in the Sharing section in a Finder window's Sidebar, and you get the option to access its files or to control it (the Screen Sharing option). Back to My Mac is similar to the Mac's built-in file sharing feature, except that it doesn't require the same permissions setup (see Chapter 13). And it provides remote-control capabilities via Screen Sharing, which you otherwise would need a separate VNC-based remote-control application for. (VNC is a standard for remote-controlling computers.)

But — and this a big but — Back to My Mac often won't work. It's very picky about the types of connections you have between the two Macs, requiring the routers involved to let the initiating Mac's control request pass through, rather than block it as a potentially dangerous intruder. (If you can adjust your routers' settings, you want to enable UPnP and NAT-PMP, if available. But there's no guarantee that doing so will let your Back to My Mac session work.) So you may find that even though your Mac can technically run Back to My Mac, it won't work. Instead, you'll get an error message after a few minutes when you try to connect to the Mac.

If you do get a connection, what you see is the remote Mac listed in the Sharing section of a Finder window's Sidebar, with two buttons at the top of the window, as Figure 15.12 shows: Share Screen and Connect As. (If asked to enter a username and password, do so; this would be set up by the owner of the other Mac and be a different username and password than the ones for your MobileMe account.) After a connection is established — and this can a few minutes — you should see the contents of the remote Mac's drives just as you would any disk's contents. You can move, copy, delete, and create files and folders on that remote Mac, as well as copy files to and from it, as you would with any disk.

FIGURE 15.12

A remote Mac available via Back to My Mac will appear in a Finder window Sidebar's Sharing section. When connected, its contents will appear as if it were another drive attached to your Mac.

To control the remote Mac, enable screen sharing by clicking Share Screen. This button disappears if you begin working with the remote Mac's files; to get it back, just click the remote Mac's name in the Finder window Sidebar's Sharing section again.

Depending on how the other Mac set up the Sharing system preference's Screen Sharing pane (see Chapters 13 and 21), you are asked for a username and password, asked to ask the other person for permission to remote-control her Mac, or both. Figure 15.13 shows the dialog box where you are asked how you want to proceed; it also shows the prompt the remote user gets if you ask for permission. When connected, you can observe and work with the computer's files and applications based on the preferences established in the Sharing system preference, again as explained in Chapters 13 and 21. Figure 15.14 shows one Mac sharing another's screen.

FIGURE 15.13

At the top, the dialog box the controller may get when trying to connect to another Mac. At the bottom, the alert the controlled Mac's user may get when someone tries to control it.

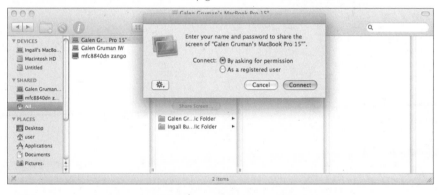

FIGURE 15.14

Sharing the screen of a remote Mac via Back to My Mac

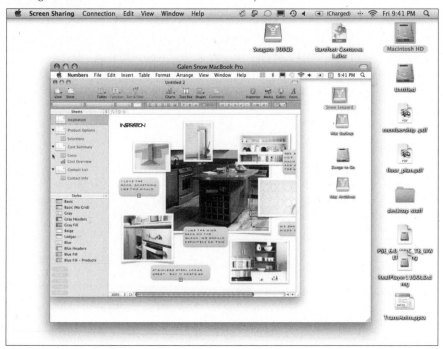

Running MobileMe Applications on the Web

When you go to MobileMe via your browser, you have more applications available to you than just iDisk, covered earlier in this chapter. You can also work with your calendar, contacts, e-mail, and photo albums. Figures 15.15 and 15.16 show two of these Web applications.

Just as the Contacts application works just like the Mac's Address Book, the Calendar application works like the Mac's iCal. The Mail application works only with your MobileMe e-mail account, unlike the Mac's Mail application, which supports multiple e-mail accounts.

The Gallery application enables you to create picture albums composed of GIF, JPEG, and PNG images, as well as enable synchronization with iPhoto and your iPhone and set whether others can add their own photos or download them. Each album has its unique Web address, as shown in Figure 15.16, that you can share with others so they can peruse, and perhaps contribute to, your albums.

FIGURE 15.15

MobileMe's Web-based Calendar application

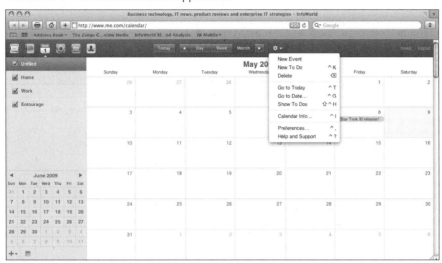

FIGURE 15.16

MobileMe's Web-based Gallery application

Summary

With a MobileMe subscription, you can set up automatic synchronization for a variety of information across Macs, including calendar entries, e-mails, contacts, system preference settings, mail rules and related settings, Safari bookmarks, and Dock settings. iPhones, iPod Touches, and Windows PCs can also have some of this information synchronized with them.

MobileMe also provides a feature called iDisk that enables you to store files on the Internet so they can be accessed by any computer that has the username and password. You can make some files open to the public in a separate folder.

The Back to My Mac component of MobileMe enables you to access files and even control the screen of a remote Mac that is signed in to the same MobileMe account — but network configurations at either end of the connection can prevent Back to My Mac from working.

MobileMe's Web applications let you manage your calendar, contacts, MobileMe e-mail, and image gallery directly from the Web.

Part III

At Work with Mac OS X

Working with Services

I t's amazing just how much software comes with Mac OS X 10.6 Snow Leopard. Chapter 8 details the several dozen applications, utilities, and widgets. But there's another kind of software in Mac OS X beyond these: helper applications called *services*.

A service can be specific to an application or general purpose (meaning it's available for several applications). The services available at any moment depend on which application (including the Finder) is running. Apple includes a bunch of services in Mac OS X, and individual applications can add their own (Opera and Skype both do, for example), some of which other applications can use as well (depending on how they are designed).

To find out what services are available, choose Services from your application's menu. For example, choose Finder ⇨ Services, or Pages ⇨ Services, or Excel ⇨ Services.

Understanding Service Availability

The services are displayed contextually based — not only based on the application that is running but also based on what is selected. For example, iWork Pages shows the Look Up in Dictionary, Make New Sticky Note, Send Selection, and Search in Google menu options only when text is selected. And both Numbers and Keynote show Look Up in Dictionary, Make New Sticky Note, Capture Full Screen, Capture Screen Region, Capture Timed Screen, Send Selection, and Search in Google when text is highlighted.

Figure 16.1 shows the services available in the Finder: Look Up in Dictionary, Make New Sticky Note, Send Selection, Open, Reveal, Show Info, and Search in Google. Figure 16.2 shows the services available for Safari on a Chinese-language Web site; notice the Chinese text conversion option.

FIGURE 16.1

The services available in the Finder

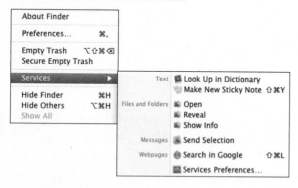

FIGURE 16.2

The services available in Safari for a Chinese-language Web site

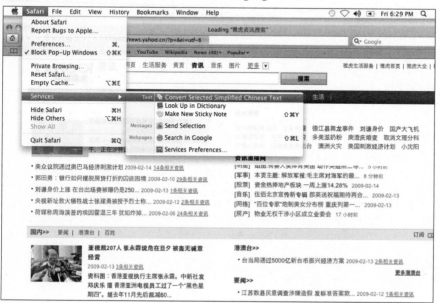

New Feature

New to Mac OS X 10.6 Snow Leopard, the Mac OS categorizes the available services based on the applications they are designed to work with, as Figure 16.1 shows. This keeps the services list uncluttered with irrelevant options, as could happen in previous versions of the Mac OS.

New Feature

Also new is the Services Preferences menu option, which lets you control which services appear in the Services menu, as explained later in this chapter.

A Tour of the Common Services

Although the services are contextual, so you may not come across them all, Mac OS X supplies 37 services that are commonly available, organized in seven groups.

Tip

Some services are also available if you Control+click or right-click a text selection or other element in an application. These services will display at the bottom of the contextual menu that appears.

Development services

Five services may appear in the Development group in the Services submenu. They do the following:

- **Create Service.** This option lets you create a service from a series of actions via Automator.

- **Create Workflow.** This option lets you create an Automator workflow. (See Chapter 25 for more details on Automator.)

- **Get Result of AppleScript.** This option runs the select text as an AppleScript and presents any results as text. (See Chapter 25 for more details on AppleScript.)

- **Make New AppleScript.** This option launches the AppleScript Editor and places the selected text in it.

- **Run as AppleScript.** This option runs the selected text in the AppleScript Editor.

Files and Folders services

Five services may appear in the Files and Folders group in the Services submenu. They do the following:

- **Open Selected File in TextEdit.** This option opens the selected file in TextEdit.

- **Folder Actions Setup.** This option lets you set up a series of folder actions (see Chapter 3).

- **Open.** This option opens the Open dialog box.

- **Reveal.** This option opens the folder in which the selected files reside (handy if you've selected an alias).

- **Show Info.** This option displays the Get Info window, as Figure 16.3 shows. (Chapter 2 covers Get Info in detail.)
- **Send File to Bluetooth Device.** This option sends the selected file to a Bluetooth device, if any are available, that you select.

Internet services

Just one option is in the Internet group:

- **Open URL.** If you select a Web address (a URL), the Open URL service will open it in your default Web browser.

FIGURE 16.3

The Show Info service opens a Get Info window for each selected item.

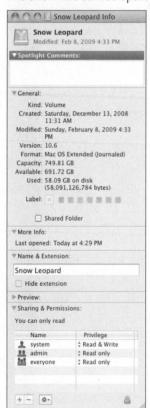

Messaging services

There are four default message-oriented services. They do the following:

- **New Note from Selection.** This service creates a note in Apple's Mail program (see Chapter 11) from the selected text.

- **Send File.** This service sends a file to the destination of your choice via Apple's Mail program.

- **Send Selection.** This service opens Mail and places the text selection in the message body. If no text is selected, the service simply opens Mail. Note that the Send Selection service does *not* attach to the message any files you may have selected, as you might expect.

- **Send To.** If you select an e-mail address, this service opens Mail and addresses an e-mail to that address.

Pictures services

Five options are in the Pictures group. The options do the following:

- **Capture Full Screen.** As you would expect, this option takes an image of the entire screen.

- **Capture Screen Using Timer.** This option gives you a ten-second delay before the entire screen is captured, so you can move the mouse, start a process, or do any other last-minute activity you want captured.

- **Capture Selection from Screen.** This option enables you to use your mouse to draw a rectangular area that you want captured.

- **Import Images.** This option lets you import images into the current application.

- **Set Desktop Picture.** This option sets the currently selected image as the desktop's background image.

Note
The Capture Full Screen, Capture Screen Using Timer, and Capture Selection from Screen options all run the Grab utility covered in Chapter 8, which saves an image of your screen as a PNG file.

Tip
You can always press Shift+⌘+3 to capture the full screen at any time and Shift+⌘+4 to capture a screen region at any time. Press Shift+⌘+4 and then press the spacebar to get a camera icon that you click in a window to capture just that window.

The Missing Services

Previous versions of Mac OS X had several services not available in Mac OS X 10.6 Snow Leopard. But their functionality perseveres, although through other means.

For example, gone are services that ran components of standard Mac OS X applications such as Finder, Font Book, Preview, and TextEdit.

The spell-checking function remains available within Apple applications (such as Mail, Pages, Script Editor, and TextEdit) through their standard menus but not via the Services submenu.

And the services to start and stop text-to-speech speaking (see Chapter 6) are handled through keyboard shortcuts.

Searching services

There are three options in the Searching group. Here's what they do:

- **Look Up in Dictionary.** This option opens the Dictionary application (see Chapter 8) and looks up the first word in the selected text, displaying any results found. Figure 16.4 shows an example result.

FIGURE 16.4

The Dictionary displays the result of looking up the first word in a text selection if you use the Look Up in Dictionary service.

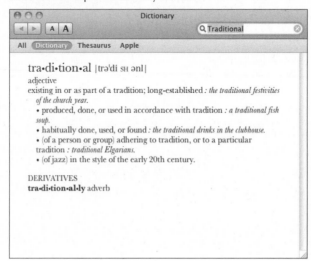

- **Search with Google.** As you would expect, choosing Search in Google opens the Safari Web browser to Google's search page and searches for that selected text, so you see the results instantly.

- **Spotlight.** This option searches for the selected text on your Mac and in Spotlight-compatible applications such as Address Book and Mail; Chapter 3 coves Spotlight in detail.

Text services

The greatest number of built-in services is in the Text grouping. Here's what they do:

- **Add to iTunes as a Spoken Track.** This option converts the text to an audio file and adds it to your iTunes library.

- **Convert Selected Simplified Chinese File and Convert Selected Traditional Chinese File.** The two Chinese-text options convert the selected text file not to English but between the two forms of Chinese: simplified and traditional. If the selected file's text is in traditional Chinese script, you get the option to convert it to simplified script. If the selected file's text is in simplified Chinese script, you get the option to convert it to traditional script.

- **Convert Selected Simplified Chinese Text and Convert Selected Traditional Chinese Text.** The two Chinese-text options convert the text selection not to English but between the two forms of Chinese: simplified and traditional. If the selected text is in traditional Chinese script, you get the option to convert it to simplified script. If the selected text is in simplified Chinese script, you get the option to convert it to traditional script. Figure 16.5 shows an example of traditional text converted to simplified text. You can see the greatest number of change in the rightmost five ideograms, although others are changed as well.

FIGURE 16.5

At top is a headline in traditional Chinese script, and at bottom is the same headline in simplified Chinese script, courtesy of the Convert Selected Traditional Chinese Text service.

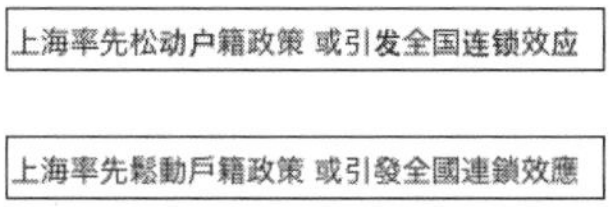

上海率先松动户籍政策 或引发全国连锁效应

上海率先鬆動戶籍政策 或引發全國連鎖效應

- **Create Collection from Text.** This option creates a font collection based on the fonts used in the selected text.

- **Create Font Library from Text.** This option creates a font library based on the fonts used in the selected text.

- **Make New Mail Note.** This option creates a new note in Mail containing the selected text. Chapter 11 covers the Mail application in detail.

- **Make New Sticky Note.** This option creates a new on-screen note containing the selected text. Chapter 8 covers the Stickies application in detail. (If you use the Make New Sticky Note service in the Finder, such as when highlighting part of a filename, it will create a new note but not include the selected text.)

- **New TextEdit Window Containing Selection.** This option opens a new document window in TextEdit containing the selected text.

- **Show Address in Google Maps.** This option opens Google Maps in Safari and shows the selected location.

- **Summarize.** This option summarizes the text selection into a more concise version.

Changing Services Preferences

If you choose Services Preferences from the Services submenu, the Keyboard Shortcuts pane of the Keyboard & Shortcuts system preference opens, as shown in Figure 16.6. Although the pane is named Keyboard Shortcuts, if you click the Services option in the list at left, you gain control over which services appear in the Services submenu.

In the Services subpane, the available services from both Mac OS X and individual applications display, grouped by the categories that display in the Services submenu. Click a disclosure triangle to expand the list of options for a category. Select any options you want to appear in the Services submenu, and deselect any options you don't want to appear.

Note
Even if you select a Services submenu option, it displays only in applications for which that service makes sense.

FIGURE 16.6

The Services subpane of the Keyboard Shortcuts pane in the Keyboard & Shortcuts system preference is where you determine which services are available in the Services submenu.

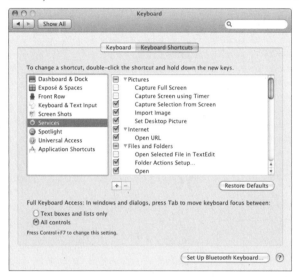

Summary

Mac OS X 10.6 Snow Leopard comes with 37 services that are available in the Services menu option in the Finder's and in applications' menus. The default services fall into seven groupings: Development, Files and Folders, Internet, Messaging, Pictures, Searching, and Text. Services display contextually, based on what application they were chosen from and what is selected. Most work with text and, therefore, require that text be selected to become available.

Some services are also available when you Control+click or right-click text within an application.

Mac OS X 10.6 Snow Leopard has removed a few services in its Services submenu, making them available within applications or by other means instead. This reduction, combined with the new contextual display, greatly simplifies the Services submenu options.

You can control which services are available in the Services subpane of the Keyboard Shortcuts pane in the Keyboard & Keyboard Shortcuts system preference.

Printing and Faxing

I n an era of electronic documents, there's still a place for printed ones. When it's time to print a document, or send someone a fax copy, you need to ensure that your Mac is properly set up for the printers and fax modem you have.

Mac OS X 10.6 Snow Leopard manages both printing and faxing from a common system preference: Print & Fax, as shown in Figure 17.1. Note that fax options won't appear unless you have a fax modem attached; Macs do not include built-in fax modems as some Windows PCs do.

You can have multiple printers and faxes configured for your Mac. Sometimes you have multiple devices connected to your Mac, sometimes you use different printers and faxes at different locations and want your Mac to be set up for them, and sometimes both situations apply. Your Mac will recognize a printer or fax it's configured for when that device is available, but you must have it connected to be able to set it up in the first place.

Setting Up Printers

You can connect your printer to your Mac in any of several ways, depending on your printer's capabilities. These include using USB, FireWire, wired network (Ethernet), wireless network (Wi-Fi), and Bluetooth wireless connections. If your printer uses any of the wireless or Ethernet settings, refer to its manual to see how to set it up so your Mac can see it, such as specifying its IP address if it's an Ethernet or Wi-Fi printer or making it discoverable if it's a Bluetooth printer. Printers that connect directly to the Mac via a USB or FireWire cable usually need no special setup on the printer itself.

Your printer may have come with an installation CD or instructions for downloading its installation software from the Web. You typically need to run this software before the printer is connected to copy over the drivers the Mac needs to properly work with your printer. But in some cases, you need to run this software after the printer is connected. Again, check your printer's setup instructions.

Mac OS X also comes with printer drivers for common Canon, Epson, Hewlett-Packard, and other printers, so your Mac may already have the proper drivers installed.

New Feature

Mac OS X 10.6 Snow Leopard no longer installs all of its included printer drivers when you install the OS, as previous versions did. Instead, it installs drivers for any printers used previously on that Mac (if you are upgrading from a previous version) or that it detects (if you are installing Mac OS X for the first time on a drive). That saves disk space. If you later add a printer and have an Internet connection, Mac OS X 10.6 Snow Leopard will see if Apple has the appropriate drivers and download them for you automatically if it does. You can also manually install printer drivers from the Mac OS X install DVD by double-clicking `Optional Installs.mpkg` in the Optional Installs folder. Expand the Printer Drivers option and select both the Printer Drivers of Many Popular Printers and the Printer Drivers of Many Other Printers options; then click Continue and follow the prompts.

New Feature

Just as Mac OS X 10.6 Snow Leopard now automatically downloads drivers for new printers from the Internet, it also now updates your printer drivers automatically — as long as you have an Internet connection.

Just to confuse matters further, some of these setup programs will handle the entire setup job for you, so when done you see the printer in the Print & Fax system preference. Others install just the driver and require you to complete the setup yourself, as outlined next.

FIGURE 17.1

The Print & Fax system preference

Adding printers

After you know when (or even whether) to install printer-specific software, you're ready to go. Connect your printer, open the Print & Fax system preference, and click the + iconic button at the bottom left of the window. The dialog box shown in Figure 17.2 will appear, showing a list of detected printers in its Default pane.

If your new printer is listed, select it to see its settings. You typically can edit its Name and Location information; the Location field is typically used in an office to say in what part of the building the printer is located. If your Mac has the correct driver, it displays in the Print Using popup menu. If you want to override that choice, or if no driver appears, choose Select a Driver to Use to choose a driver already installed on your Mac. A list then appears for you to choose from. If your Mac doesn't have the correct driver, choose Other to select it from a disk or folder on or attached to your Mac. Click Add when done. Your printer is now ready.

FIGURE 17.2

The Mac OS autodetects printers that it recognizes when you tell it to add a new one.

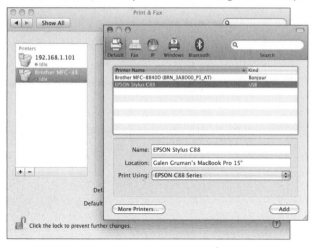

If your new printer is not listed, go to the IP, Windows, and Bluetooth panes to try to find it.

- If you know your printer is a Bluetooth printer, for example, go to the Bluetooth pane, which will then scan for Bluetooth devices within range (usually up to 20 feet) and set as discoverable.

- Use the IP pane for printers attached via an Ethernet or Wi-Fi network. Most such printers use the Internet Printing Protocol, so choose that from the Protocol popup menu. Exceptions include many Hewlett-Packard printers, which instead use HP JetDirect. The third protocol option, Line Printer Daemon, is no longer common. No matter what the protocol is, enter the printer's IP address, as shown in Figure 17.3. The Mac OS will try to find the correct driver for it; change the setting in the Print Using popup menu if it can't find the right driver or chooses the wrong one. Change the Queue field only if your printer's documentation or network administrator tells you what the Queue information should be.

- Use the Windows pane for printers attached via a local Windows share network if you are using one.

- Click More Printers to open a separate dialog box that enables you to install Epson IP and Epson FireWire printers; for Epson IP you'll need to provide the printer's network address.

In all cases, you can change the Name and Location fields to your liking. Click Add when done.

Tip

To delete a printer you no longer use, select it in the Print & Fax system preference, then click the – iconic button below the printer list.

Tip

If you have multiple printers, such as in an office, you can help distribute the load by pooling them. Pooling treats multiple printers as if they were one printer, and the Mac automatically figures out which one to send a job to based on availability. To create a printer pool, select the printers in the Print & Fax system preference (click the first one, and ⌘+click the others). Now click Create Printer Pool and give that pool a name. If you select that pool's name in the Print dialog box's Printer popup menu, the Mac will automatically choose which printer to use. You can do the same with fax modems.

FIGURE 17.3

Entering the network address for a printer not autodetected by the Mac OS

Managing printers

If you have multiple printers connected, choose which one you want to be the default printer by using the Default Printer popup menu. You can also set the default paper size by using the Default Paper Size popup menu.

To make a printer available for use by other users on your local network, select it from the printer list and then select the Share This Printer with Other Users on This Network option. (You typically share local printers, such as those connected via a USB cable to one Mac; network printers are already shared with everyone on the network.) Note that your Mac must have Printer Sharing enabled in the Sharing system preference, as shown in Figure 17.4. If Printer Sharing is not enabled, you'll see an alert in the Print & Fax system preference; click Set Permissions to jump to the Sharing system preference to turn Printer Sharing on, then select which printers to share. You can set separate controls for different users, with two options for each: Can Print and No Access.

Note
A printer must not be powered down or asleep if you want it available to be shared.

FIGURE 17.4

The Printer Sharing pane of the Sharing system preference

Clicking the Options & Supplies button opens a dialog box that enables you to change Name and Location fields (in the General pane), change the printer driver (in the Driver pane), and check on ink or toner and paper supply levels (in the Supply Levels pane). The supply levels display only for printers that can communicate this information to the Mac. The General pane may also show an Open Printer Utility button for those printers that offer a utility to do things like clean their print heads and change the ink saturation.

Tip

Another way to manage your printers is via a Web browser, if you have administrator privileges (which means you have an administrator account's username and password). Enter `http://localhost:631/admin` **as the URL to get the Mac's Unix-based printer management tool. Click Manage Printers to configure your printers; the controls are essentially the same as in the Print & Fax system preference and in the print queue, though here they are all available in one place.**

Using Printers

Using a printer is typically easy: Choose File ⇨ Print or press ⌘+P from the application you want to print from. Sometimes, the application may have an iconic print button as well in a toolbar. After you select any options for your print job and click Print, the Mac works with the printer behind the scenes so you can get back to work.

Tip

A very easy way to print a document is to drag its file onto the printer icon onto your desktop or into a Finder window. To get the printer icon in any of these places, open the Print & Fax system preference, select the desired printer or fax (including print and fax pools), then drag it to the desired location: the desktop or into an open Finder window. To add it to the Dock, Control+click or right-click the printer icon when you are printing and choose Keep in Dock from the contextual menu. You can put the printer icon into multiple locations. Double-clicking the printer icon opens its print queue. The same techniques apply to fax modems as well. (The print and fax queues are covered later in this chapter.)

The Print dialog box

When you print, you'll get a Print dialog box, such as that shown in Figure 17.5. The basic layout is the same for most applications, though you may see some slight layout and visual differences.

At left is often a preview of what you are printing, with controls to go through previews of each page. At top right are usually the controls to choose which printer to use, how many pages to print, how many copies of those pages, and whether to print collated and/or two-sided pages.

The unnamed popup menu in the center right of the dialog box contains more controls, which when selected change the options in the bottom right of the dialog box. The standard popup menu options are:

- **Layout.** Enables you to print multiple thumbnails (smaller versions of your pages) onto a single sheet of paper, add a border to your printed page, enable two-sided printing, and flip the page output.

- **Color Matching.** Enables you to apply a color profile to your output to help it reproduce as accurately as possible.

- **Paper Handling.** Enables you to choose to print all pages, even pages, or odd pages; print front to back or back to front; and scale the page to fit the paper size.

- **Paper Feed.** Enables you to select which paper tray to use for the printing, including using a different tray for the first page (such as for stationery).

- **Cover Page.** Enables you to print a cover page before or after the document and even fill in a billing code.

- **Scheduler.** Enables you to set the time at which to print a document (such as holding large print jobs until after hours).

- **Summary.** Enables you to review all the settings in one place.

Note

The unnamed popup menu may show more options than listed here. Most are installed by the printer driver to make its specific functionality available. And many applications add their own menu option for any special printing functions they offer.

The last option is the PDF popup menu at the bottom left of the Print dialog box. Its choices include creating a PDF file from your document, faxing or e-mailing that PDF, opening a PDF preview in the Preview application, and saving a PDF to a specific folder (such as iPhoto and Web Receipts). The Edit Menu option in the PDF popup menu enables you to hide some of these options.

Note

The PDF options in the Print dialog box produce decent-quality results, but they don't provide the same quality and other options as if you used Adobe's Acrobat Standard or Professional software. If you use Acrobat, you will see it listed as a printer in the Printer popup menu. The PDF menu options won't use Acrobat, even if you have it installed, to generate the PDF files.

FIGURE 17.5

An application's Print dialog box

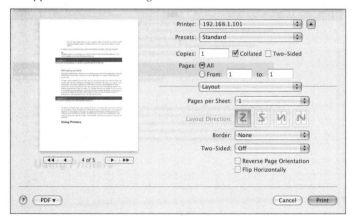

Managing the print queue

After you click Print, the Mac creates the necessary data for the printer, often storing that data on your hard drive until the printer can accept it, in a process called *spooling*.

While the Mac is spooling the print job, you have some control over it, such as pausing the job or canceling it. When you print, the printer's icon shows up in the Dock; Control+click or right-click it to see the options available, as shown in Figure 17.6. The key ones are the printer name, Pause Printer, and Printer Setup. Choosing Pause Printer suspends printing; the option changes to Resume Printing. Choosing Printer Setup opens the General pane you get when clicking Options & Supplies in the Print & Fax system preference.

Choosing the printer name from the contextual menu — or simply clicking the printer icon in the Dock — opens the print queue shown in Figure 17.7. The print queue shows the status of all print jobs in process or waiting to be sent. You can select any print job listed and click Delete to end its output or Hold to pause it. Other print jobs are unaffected. Click Pause Printer to suspend all print jobs, even if none are currently in process; the button changes to Resume Printer when clicked.

The print queue also has several menu options that are useful. The Printer menu's options include Customize Toolbar (to change what buttons display), Make Default (to make the current printer the default one), Print Test Page, and Network Diagnostics. Some multifunction devices may also show an Open Scanner Utility option. The Jobs menu enables you to hold, delete, and get details on print jobs, which you can also do from the print queue's buttons; but it also has the very handy Show Completed Jobs and Show Everyone's Jobs that give you a complete printing history and way to see where various print jobs came from, respectively.

Tip
After you print, the printer may stay in the Dock and its print queue remains open. If you don't want the print queue to remain open, Control+click or right-click the icon to get its contextual menu, then choose Auto Quit in that menu. If Auto Quit is checked, the print queue will close any print job that is done. The printer icon will also remove itself from the dock when the print job is complete. To keep the printer icon in the Dock permanently, choose Keep in Dock.

FIGURE 17.6

The contextual menu options for a printer in the Dock

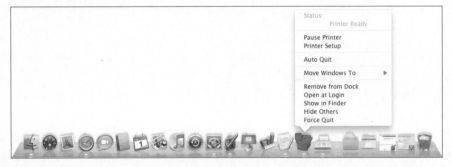

FIGURE 17.7

The print queue for a selected printer enables you to manage individual print jobs, as well as the printer itself.

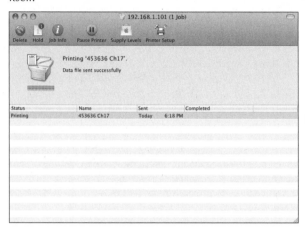

Setting Up and Using Fax Modems

You set up fax modems in the Print & Fax system preference the same way you set up printers, as explained earlier in this chapter, with one difference: Go to the Fax pane to see which fax modems are connected. Select the fax modem to use, and click Add, as Figure 17.8 shows. When added, the fax modem displays in the Print & Fax system preference, where you can then set its preferences, as Figure 17.9 shows. The settings are:

- In the Fax Number field, enter the phone number you're using to fax from. (This is a federal requirement meant to discourage junk faxes.)

- Select the Show Fax Status in Menu Bar option to get a phone icon in the menu bar that will display the status of any faxes being sent or received, as well as let you cancel them.

- Select the Share This Fax with Other Users on the Network option to let other Mac users send faxes from your Mac's fax modem.

- Click Receive Options to get the dialog box shown in Figure 17.10, where you set up whether and how your Mac's fax modem should handle incoming faxes. You can turn receipt on or off (note that your Mac must be turned on and attached to a phone line to receive faxes), as well as set how many rings to wait for before the fax modem answers and what to do with the incoming faxes: Save them to a folder of your choice, print them to a printer of your choice, and/or e-mail them to an e-mail address of your choice.

Note

When you connect a fax modem to your Mac, you may see an alert in the Network system preference saying that the external modem is not configured. Don't worry about that; it has no effect on your ability to use the modem for faxing. The Network system preference sees the fax modem as a dial-up modem, so it expects you to fill in the dial-up and related information so it can use the fax modem, to connect to an Internet service. If you're not using a dialup Internet service, you don't need to configure the external modem.

The Open Fax Queue button in the Print & Fax system preference opens a window identical to the print queue window shown in Figure 17.7, except that fax jobs are displayed instead of print jobs. You have the same options to delete and hold individual fax jobs and to suspend or resume the fax modem.

Tip

The default printer drivers that Mac OS X 10.6 Snow Leopard installs when it finds a new printer usually do not include the fax modem or scanner drivers for multifunction printers that offer fax and/or scan capabilities. Therefore, be sure to install the drivers from the disc that came with the multifunction printer or go to the manufacturer's Web site to download the drivers for your Mac.

FIGURE 17.8

The Fax pane when adding a fax modem to the Print & Fax system preference

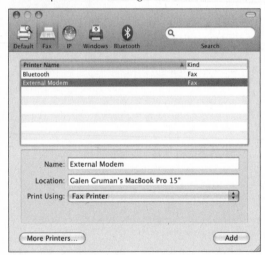

FIGURE 17.9

The Print & Fax system preference when a fax modem is selected

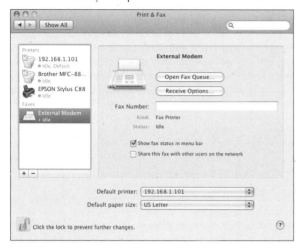

FIGURE 17.10

The Receive Options dialog box for a fax modem

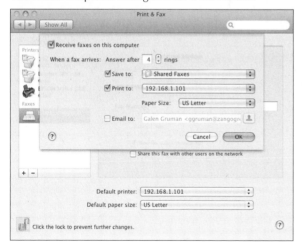

With your fax modem set up, using it is easy: From any application that can print, choose File➪Print or press ⌘+P to get the Print dialog box. Choose the fax modem from the Printer popup menu, as shown in Figure 17.11, and fill in the fax information, such as fax number to send to and the information for the cover page in the bottom right of the Print dialog box. Click Fax when you're ready to send the fax.

FIGURE 17.11

The Print dialog box when you choose to fax a document rather than print it

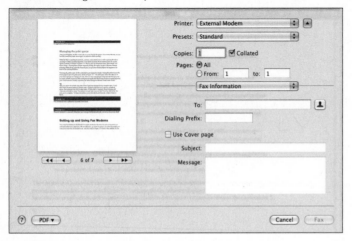

Note
As with printers, fax modems appear in the Dock when you fax (see the icon to the right of the printer icon in Figure 17.6). You have the same controls with the fax icon as you do with a printer icon.

Summary

The Mac OS lets you connect one or more printers and fax modems (or fax machines) so you can print or fax documents. You typically can connect printers and fax devices via the USB, FireWire, Ethernet, or Wi-Fi connections, though FireWire-capable devices are uncommon.

Although the Mac OS has drivers for some printers preinstalled and can set these up automatically, you should always run the printer setup utility that comes with your printer (on a disc or available from the manufacturer's Web site). For fax devices, you must install the appropriate drivers from the manufacturer. Note that multifunction printers that have fax and/or scan capabilities require the manufacturer drivers to be installed for your Mac to access those fax and scan features, even if the Mac has the drivers built in for the printer services.

The Print & Fax system preference contains the management controls for printers and fax devices.

To use a printer or a fax device, open the Print dialog box by choosing File ⇨ Print or pressing ⌘+P. You'll see a variety of configuration options, such as page side, duplexing, and quality level; these options vary from printer model to printer model. For faxing, you also use the Print dialog box, but choose the fax device from the Printer popup menu. The Print button then changes to Fax.

When you click Print to start the print job, the instructions that are destined for the printer are first spooled to a disk file on your Mac, then sent onto the printer. This lets you continue working on the document while it is printing. Because the Mac stores these print-job files, you can manage them by opening the printer icon in the Dock. You see a list of all open print jobs and their status; you can delete, reorder, pause, or resume each job.

Using a technique called *pooling*, the Mac can send print and fax jobs to any available printer or fax device. The advantages are that jobs are sent first to idle devices, speeding output; the disadvantage (at least for printing) is you don't know which printer's output tray has your document.

Integrating with Windows

T here's no question that the Mac is special. Many people believe it to be the best personal computer ever developed, thanks mainly to the Mac OS. But although the Mac is indeed special and brilliant, it is also a minority choice in the world of computing. Most people use Microsoft Windows — Windows XP, Windows Vista, or, not long after this book appears, Windows 7. Dealing with Windows is a reality for Mac users. And Mac OS X 10.6 Snow Leopard helps make it easy to work with the wider Windows world while staying firmly on the luxury Mac island.

Mac OS X integrates with Windows at many levels. It supports Windows disk formats, such as for CDs and hard drives. It works with Windows networks. And it can even run Windows and, therefore, Windows programs that have no Mac version available.

So the question for a Mac user is not "Can I integrate with Windows?" but "How should I integrate with Windows?" There's no one right answer to this question because it depends on your circumstances. But two basic levels of integration usually determine how you integrate with Windows:

- If you mainly need to share files with Windows users, you'll find that most common Windows file formats are supported on the Mac. Plus, many standard Windows programs, such as Microsoft Office, are available on the Mac, and most Mac-only programs can usually export to a Windows-friendly format. So you can usually open files you get from Windows users as is, and they can open the files you give them. Usually, you can exchange files via e-mail or a server, but because your Mac reads from and writes to Windows disks, you can exchange files this way as well.

- If you need to run Windows programs that are not available on the Mac because you're part of a Windows-based company or workgroup, you're in luck. Any Intel-based Mac can actually run Windows XP, Vista, or 7. The Mac OS comes with the software that enables it to run Windows (you need to buy Windows yourself), so you can boot between Windows and Mac OS as needed, while being able to access all the files on your Mac no matter which operating system is running. And two inexpensive programs (EMC VMware's Fusion and Parallels' Desktop) let you run Windows and the Mac OS at the same time, so you don't have to reboot the Mac to switch from one operating system to another.

Now we'll show you exactly how this all works.

Working with Windows Files

The most basic way to integrate with Windows is by sharing files. The Mac OS makes it easy to do so via drives, networks, and e-mail.

Software that has versions on both Windows and Mac OS X almost always uses the same file format for both systems, so exchanging files is a snap. Microsoft Office, Adobe Creative Suite, and FileMaker Pro are just a few examples. And many media formats are the same across platforms, such as MP3 files, QuickTime Movies, and MPEG-4 videos, as well as the EPS, GIF, JPEG, PNG, and TIFF graphics formats.

For file formats that aren't cross-platform, you can usually rely on DataViz's $80 MacLinkPlus for Mac or $50 Conversions Plus for Windows software (www.dataviz.com) to convert them to a supported format. And if you want to play Windows Media Files on your Mac, the free Flip4Mac Player from Telestream (www.telestream.com) nicely does the job; for editing and otherwise working with WMV files beyond playback, Telestream also offers the $30 WMV Player Pro.

Before you begin sharing files with Windows users, though, you need to be aware of a few issues.

Dealing with filenames and filename extensions

The most noticeable difference between Windows and Mac is the file-naming convention, but with the advent of Mac OS X a decade ago that difference is no longer as great. To be cross-platform-compatible, restrict your filenames to 250 characters (including the filename extension), always use a filename extension, and do not use the following characters as part of the filename: : / | . * " < > ? / \. These restrictions conform to the Mac OS X standards but Windows users will need to make a couple of compromises:

- They can't use the full Windows filename size of 255 characters. (250 is the maximum on the Mac.)
- They can't use the : / | . * " < > ? / \ characters in their filenames because Mac OS doesn't support them, even though Windows supports all of them but :.

Although Mac OS X supports filenames as long as 250 characters, you may have trouble copying Windows files to the Mac if the Windows filenames exceed 31 characters and you use the AppleTalk networking protocol to connect your Macs and PCs. That's because of limits in some of the programs to make these cross-platform connections, which enforce pre–Mac OS X filename conventions on all files. It's easy enough to test whether your software is limiting you to 31 characters: Just transfer a file and see if the software shortens the name or refuses to transfer the file. In either case, it's time to upgrade your networking software or switch from AppleTalk to a protocol like IP (the Internet Protocol). In fact, with Mac OS X 10.6 Snow Leopard, you can no longer use AppleTalk.

Both Windows and Mac OS X use filename extensions to identify the file type. For example, a Microsoft Word file has the filename extension .doc or .docx (depending on the version), a TIFF file has the extension .tif or .tiff (some applications prefer one over the other but "see" both), an iWork Pages file has the extension .pages, and an MP3 music file has the extension .mp3.

But filename extensions are typically not displayed to the user in the Finder, so you may not know what kind of file you're dealing with. Here's how to make filename extensions visible:

- **Mac OS X.** Choose Finder ⇨ Preferences or press ⌘+, (comma). (You have to be using the Finder, not be in an application, to see the Finder menu.) In the Preferences dialog box that appears, go to the Advanced pane, select the Show All Filename Extensions option, and close the dialog box.

- **Windows XP.** Open any folder and then choose Tools ⇨ Folder Options. (You have to have a disk or folder open to have the View menu.) In the Folder Options dialog box that appears, go to the View pane. Deselect the Hide Extensions for Known File Types option, and then click OK.

- **Windows Vista or Windows 7.** Choose Start ⇨ Computer, then choose Organize ⇨ Folder and Search Options in the dialog box that appears. Go to the View pane and select the Show Hidden Files and Folders option, and then click OK.

Using Fonts Across Platforms

Three types of font formats are in common use today: TrueType (filename extension .ttf), PostScript Type 1 (these have two files for each font, a .pfb and a .pfm file), and OpenType (.otf). Mac OS X natively supports all three, as do Windows XP, Vista, and 7.

If you use the same font file on both Windows and Mac OS X, you get the same characters, even though Windows and Mac applications may not be able to show you all the same characters in the font. So the files transferred across platforms will display correctly on both.

But if you install a Mac version of a font on the Mac and a Windows version on the PC — a common scenario for PostScript fonts, but an occasional issue as well for TrueType and OpenType fonts, especially those that come with applications — you likely will discover that their special characters (accented letters, foreign characters, math symbols, and so on) don't always match, and some characters may not appear in Windows that appear on the Mac (or vice versa). Even when the characters are the same, their size and spacing might differ slightly, causing text to take more or less room as it moves from one platform to another.

continued

continued

Note that the developer of PostScript Type 1 fonts, Adobe Systems, began phasing out that format in 1999, so it's hard today to buy new PostScript Type 1 fonts. However, users tend not to replace their old PostScript fonts with the OpenType format that Apple, Adobe, and Microsoft all settled on as a joint standard, so chances are very high that you'll deal with PostScript Type 1 fonts. After all, it can cost thousands of dollars to upgrade your font collection. (The TrueType font format was developed by Apple, and Microsoft quickly signed on to use it, which is why it is also very commonly used.)

So favor TrueType and OpenType fonts where possible, and use the same font files on both your Macs and PCs, not just ones whose font names are the same.

Using drives and media

Mac OS X reads Windows CDs, DVDs, and hard drives without any effort on your part. These drives show up in the Finder like any other drive, and you can work with them as if they were Mac drives; copying, deleting, renaming, and creating files as desired. If you use another kind of external drive, such as a floppy drive, memory card, or thumb drive, it almost always is supported by the Mac directly; sometimes you may need to install a Mac OS driver that the hardware maker provides.

When you format a hard drive by using the Mac OS's included Disk Utility (see Chapter 8), you can choose to format it as an MS-DOS (FAT) drive, which makes it work on any Windows PC. (FAT stands for File Access Table, a method for tracking a disk's files.)

What Mac OS X cannot do on its own is write or copy to hard drives formatted as NTFS, the Windows NT File System that Windows NT, 2000, XP, Vista, and 7 all support. (Mac OS X can read and copy *from* NTFS drives.) NTFS is a better disk format than MS-DOS because it stores data more efficiently. To write to NTFS drives from the Mac means buying a driver, such as Paragon Software's NTFS for Mac OS X ($30; www.paragon-software.com).

On the Windows side, it's not so easy to use Mac media. Windows and Mac OS X use the same formats for DVDs and memory cards, so you can pass these back and forth as is. But you'll need Mac drivers installed in Windows for other kinds of media and drives. Two companies have long offered such software, which not only let Windows PCs read Mac media but also write to them: MediaFour's MacDrive ($50; www.mediafour.com) and Acute Systems' TransMac ($54; www.acutesystems.com).

Sharing through servers

If your Mac is on a network, it's very easy for it to access files on servers that Windows users also access files through. Your IT department has to set up the servers so they are accessible to both Mac and Windows users, of course.

When the servers are ready for use, you need to connect to the server, which mounts it as a drive in the Finder. To connect a file server, use one of the following techniques:

- Choose it from the Sharing section in a Finder window's Sidebar.
- Choose Go ⇨ Connect to Server or press ⌘+K from the Finder, and then click Browse to find the desired file server.
- Use your browser to enter a Web or IP address for the file share. Whoever set up the file share will need to provide you with that address.

When connected, simply drag files between it and your Mac to copy them. Chapter 13 explains in detail how to connect to networks and their files shares.

Another option is to use Microsoft SharePoint, a collaboration server that enables Microsoft Office users to work together on project files and share contacts, calendars, and so on. However, SharePoint uses a proprietary technology called ActiveX that Microsoft has not made available to the Mac OS, so Mac users have limited capabilities as part of a SharePoint environment. For example, you can't edit files directly in Microsoft Office for Mac; instead you must download them to your Mac, edit them there, and upload the changed versions back. You also can't connect to shared Outlook calendars from Entourage. Furthermore, the Windows SharePoint servers must implement a technology called WebDAV for the Macs to be able to see them on the network.

Note
Microsoft has said that around the time this book is published, it will provide a free upgrade to Office 2008 for Mac users that enables them to connect natively to SharePoint 2007 servers, reducing or perhaps even ending these compatibility woes. But the planned fix will not help Mac Office 2004 users, nor will it help Mac Office 2008 users trying to connect to SharePoint 2003 environments.

Connecting to PCs directly for file sharing

You can share files directly with a Windows user over a network by using the Windows equivalent of file sharing. The key is to have the PC user set up file sharing for whichever folders she wants to make accessible to you. You also need her IP address so you know where to connect. With the IP address, you simply enter smb:// followed by the IP address — such as smb://172.18.12.136 — as the address in the Connect to Server dialog box (choose Go ⇨ Connect to Server or press ⌘+K in the Finder), then click Connect, as shown in Figure 18.1. When prompted, enter the username and password provided by the Windows user.

Note
The smb:// tells the Mac to use Microsoft's Server Message Block protocol as opposed to Apple's own Apple Filing Protocol (afp://), the File Transfer Protocol (ftp://), or the Web's Hypertext Transfer Protocol (http://). A protocol essentially is a "language" that defines how devices and computers connect through networks.

FIGURE 18.1

Enter the Windows PC's address that has the desired share folder in the Connect to Server dialog box.

To get the PC's IP address:

- The Windows XP user chooses Start ⇨ Run.

- The Windows Vita and 7 user chooses Start ⇨ All Programs ⇨ Accessories ⇨ run.

Then no matter the version of Windows, the user types cmd and presses Enter; then in the Command Prompt window that appears, the user types ipconfig and presses Enter. The IP address (called IPv4 in Windows Vista and 7) is then presented. (The Windows user then types exit and presses Enter to close the Command Prompt window.)

To set up the file share, the Windows user should first display the folder to be shared in the Windows Explorer (the Windows equivalent of the Finder), then right-click it to display the contextual menu. The next step depends on which version of Windows the user has:

- **Windows XP.** Choose Sharing and Security to open the Sharing pane shown in Figure 18.2. Select the Share This Folder option. Then click Permissions to open the Share Permissions dialog box in which you add users and set their permissions (Full Control, Change, and Read). Click OK to save the Share Permissions settings and click OK again to save the Sharing settings.

- **Windows Vista.** Choose Share to open the File Sharing dialog box; in Vista, choose Share With ⇨ Specific People. Choose the Mac user to be allowed to share the folder or choose Create a New User from the unnamed popup menu to add a user through the User Accounts control panel that then appears. (Here's how the User Accounts control panel works: Click Manage Other Users to open the Manage Accounts dialog box, click Add a User, give the user a name, close the dialog boxes, and navigate back to the folder to share and select the new user from the Unnamed popup menu.) Now click Add to give that user permission to share the folder, and choose the level of access, using the Permission Level popup menu to the right of the user's name. (The Reader permission level grants read-only access, Contributor grants read and write privileges, and Co-owner grants full control of the folder.) Click Share to turn sharing on for the folder.

Figure 18.2 shows the two sharing dialog boxes.

FIGURE 18.2

The Windows XP Sharing dialog box (left) and the File Sharing dialog box used by both Windows Vista and 7 (right)

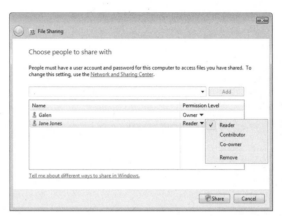

Letting Windows users connect directly to your Mac

The Mac OS comes with the Samba open source version of the Windows SMB network protocol built in, but it is only available for those users you specify. For a Windows user to access your Mac's shared files over a network, you need to first set up an account with Standard privileges — not Sharing Only privileges — for that user in the Accounts system preference (see Chapter 21), as Figure 18.3 shows.

Next enable file sharing for the folders you want Windows users to share, as explained in Chapter 13. (Any folders you've already enabled file sharing for can also be shared with Windows users.)

Then enable SMB sharing in the Sharing system preference. First, select File Sharing from the list at left and then select the folder to be shared with in the Shared Folders list. If the user's account doesn't already appear in the Users list, click the + iconic button to add the user. (Select the user from the list that appears and click Select.) Then click Options in the lower right of the Sharing system preference. A sheet appears with additional options. Select the Share Files and Folders Using SMB and make sure that every user who should have SMB access is also selected in the user list, as Figure 18.4 shows. (You need to know their passwords to enable SMB access.)

Caution

The password protection in the SMB protocol is less secure than in other protocols, so only enable SMB sharing for Windows users.

FIGURE 18.3

Set up a Standard user account for Windows users you want to be able to access shared folders.

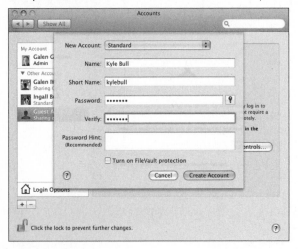

FIGURE 18.4

Enabling SMB file sharing for Windows users in the Sharing system preference

The final step is to make sure that all the computers use the same Windows domain; otherwise, they only see those with the same name. By default, PCs are set with the Windows domain Workgroup, as are Macs. To change the domain in Windows, the Windows user should follow these steps:

1. **Choose Start ⇨ Control Panel and click Switch to Classic View if it is not already enabled.** Double-click the System icon to open the System Properties dialog box.

2a. **In Windows XP, go to the Computer Name pane and click Change.**

2b. **In Windows Vista and 7, click Change Settings and then click Change in the Computer Name pane that appears.**

3. **In all three versions of Windows, select Workgroup and enter the workgroup name in the field below, then click OK.** Click OK again to save the settings and close System Properties.

4. **Restart Windows for the changes to take effect.**

On the Mac, go to the Network system preference and click Advanced. In the sheet that appears, go to the WINS pane and enter the correct domain name in the Domain field and press Return. (WINS stands for Windows Internet Name Service.) Click OK and then click Apply to save the changes.

The Windows user now has access to any folder to which you provided that specific user access. To access that shared folder, the Windows user does the following:

- **Windows XP.** Choose Start ⇨ My Network Places and click View Workgroup Computers.
- **Windows Vista.** Choose Start ⇨ Network.
- **Windows 7.** Choose Start ⇨ Computer, then click Network in the sidebar.

In all three cases, the Windows user double-clicks the Mac whose folder is shared to open it.

Alternatively, the Windows user can map the shared folder itself as a network drive:

- **Windows XP.** Choose Start ⇨ My Computer and choose Tools ⇨ Map Network Drive.
- **Windows Vista and 7.** Choose Start ⇨ Computer, then click Map Network Drive at the top of the window.

The Windows user then enters the full address for the folder, in this form: `\\192.168.1.100\Users\name\folder\folder`. Make sure backslashes, not forward slashes, are used. The address starts with `\\` and is followed with your Mac's IP address. Then the full path to the folder follows, separated by `\` characters. As an example, if you had the folder Working Files on your Mac's desktop, the address might be `\\122.18.12.140\Users\yourname\Desktop\Working Files`. (Your Mac's name is what appears to the right of the house icon in the Places list in a Finder window.)

Note

The Windows user may need to click Different User Name in Windows XP or select Connect Using Different Credentials in Windows Vista or 7 to be able to enter the username and password you provided.

Note

If the folder-sharing Mac does not show up in the Windows network, there are many potential causes, all of which need a network administrator to figure out.

Sharing via e-mail, FTP, and Web services

If you're not on a network (or not on one that enables Windows PCs and Macs to exchange files) and aren't physically close enough to share disks, you can use the Internet as a big server to exchange files with almost anyone, no matter what kind of computer that person uses.

The easiest way is to attach files to an e-mail that you send to another person. The person saves the files on his computer and open them with his applications, assuming his applications can work with the file format you're using. The reverse also holds: He can send you files via e-mail that you then save on your Mac and open with your compatible applications.

Tip

When sharing files across platforms via e-mail, it's a good idea to first compress the files into a Zip archive. This not only reduces the size of your attachment — so it takes less time to upload, transmit, and download — but also eliminates the possibility that the recipient will not be able to open the files. Most e-mail programs are smart enough to recognize Mac files and deliver them properly to Windows users, but some are not. Those badly behaved (usually Windows-based) e-mail programs end up stripping out a key part of the Mac file in transmission, making them unusable by a Windows user. Sometimes they strip out this information when they receive the file, and sometimes they do so only when they forward the file to someone else. Some of these applications offer an option in their preferences to send files in the AppleDouble format; if so, use that option to eliminate the problem.

Another way to create a network file share via the Internet is to set up an FTP folder on a Web server, and then provide everyone with the FTP address, a username, and a password to access that folder. (FTP stands for File Transfer Protocol, a standard for uploading and downloading files via the Internet.) You can then upload and download files from it in a way that 's very similar to using file sharing on a local network. You need a Web server, or a Web host that offers FTP capabilities, to set up this kind of Internet-based shared folder, and then an FTP client such as Fetch Softworks' excellent Fetch application ($25; www.fetchsoftworks.com) to handle the uploading and downloading on the Mac. Figure 18.5 shows Fetch. Windows users might consider an FTP program such as SmartSoft's Smart FTP Home ($37; www.smartftp.com), Ipswitch's WS_FTP Pro ($55; www.ipswitch.com), or the free FileZilla (www.filezilla-project.org).

You can also use Internet file-sharing services such as the iDisk component of Apple's MobileMe service (see Chapter 15) to exchange files with both Mac and Windows users.

FIGURE 18.5

The Fetch FTP application. Here, we're dragging a file from the list of files stored at the FTP server on the Internet onto a Mac's desktop (at upper left).

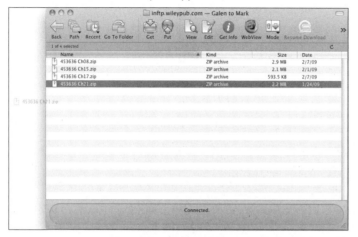

Running Windows on Your Mac

One of the most remarkable capabilities of the Mac is that it can double as a Windows PC, thanks to the use of Intel's processor chips beginning in 2006. Any Intel Mac — but not the PowerPC-based Macs that preceded the Intel-based generations — can run Windows XP, Vista, or 7. (Some users have also been able to run Windows 2000, though that is not officially supported.) Mac OS X comes with the Boot Camp tools to set up Windows on your Mac as a separate environment, so you can choose to boot into Mac OS or Windows when you start up your Mac.

Two other companies, Parallels and EMC's VMware subsidiary, provide inexpensive virtualization software (about $80) that lets you run Windows and Mac OS X at the same time. (They also let you run the Linux and Unix operating systems.) If you use Windows applications routinely, we recommend you use one of the virtualization options instead of Boot Camp because they make it so much more convenient to use Windows without making you stop using your Mac applications. They install Windows in what is called a *virtual machine*, a disk file that Windows "thinks" is a computer.

Boot Camp's big advantage over these virtualization options is clear when you are running PC games or video-editing software, which run more slowly and can have degraded display and video quality when running through a virtualization application.

Of course, you can have your cake and eat it, too, by setting up a Boot Camp partition and also installing Parallels Desktop or VMware Fusion. When you need the full Windows speed, you boot into Windows via Boot Camp. When you don't, you can run Windows via Parallels or VMware and keep the Mac OS running at the same time.

Note

No matter which option you choose to run Windows, you need to supply your own licensed copy of Windows.

Caution

Because of its popularity, hackers and other ne'er-do-wells target Windows with viruses, Trojan horses, spyware, scams, and other malware. Although such malware (so far) doesn't cross over to the Mac OS, your Windows partition or virtual machine is just as vulnerable as a Windows PC, so be sure to get security software for it as you would for a "real" PC.

Setting up Boot Camp

In the Application folder's Utilities folder, you will find the Boot Camp Assistant, which sets up a partition on your Mac's hard drive to hold Windows.

Caution

If you are installing Windows XP, you must install the Service Pack 2 (SP2) or Service Pack 3 (SP3) version. You cannot install a pre-SP2 version and later update it to SP2 or SP3.

Also, you must have a USB keyboard and mouse connected to your Mac (or use a MacBook's built-in keyboard and trackpad) when installing Windows. That's because Windows loads Bluetooth late in its startup sequence, so your wireless keyboard and mouse won't be available to enter the necessary settings when you install Windows.

Make sure you have enough hard disk space to hold Windows; 25GB is a minimum size for Windows XP and 32GB for Windows Vista or 7 if you plan on running a few Windows applications. If you plan on doing video-to-DVD work with programs like Roxio Creator or Adobe Premiere Elements on your Windows partition, you'll need at least 15GB more for the DVD source image, cache, and target image. Also note that you must install the Boot Camp partition on your Mac's startup disk; you cannot install it on an external disk. Then double-click the Boot Camp Assistant to launch it.

The first thing Boot Camp Assistant does is provide a dialog box with the Print Installation & Setup Guide button. Be sure to print the 25-page guide for guidance on the various options. Then click Continue to begin the setup.

You're then asked how to *partition* your Mac's startup disk, which means to divide it into separate areas for the Mac OS and Windows. (If you have more than one internal disk, you can select any of them for the Windows partition.) Boot Camp starts with 5GB for Windows; click the dot between the Mac partition and the Windows partition and slide it to the left to increase the Windows partition size. When the maximum free disk space has been used, you can't slide the dot any farther to the left. Slide the dot to the right to decrease the Windows partition size. Figure 18.6 shows the dialog box.

You can also click Use 32GB to set the Windows partition to 32GB. And you can click Divide Equally to divide your hard disk space equally between the Mac OS and Windows. But if the Mac OS uses more than half your disk space already, clicking Divide Equally makes the remainder available for Windows. When you're satisfied with your partition size, click Partition. Then go get a cup of coffee or tea; it can take many minutes to partition the disk, and your Mac is essentially unusable while the partitioning occurs.

Caution

After you partition the internal drive, you can't resize the Boot Camp Windows partition if you didn't give it enough space or if you gave it too much. You must delete the partition and start over. To delete the Boot Camp partition, run the Boot Camp Setup Assistant, click Continue, then select the disk that has Boot Camp on it, select the Restore to a Single Mac OS Partition option, and click Continue.

Tip

Well, there is an alternative to deleting a wrong-sized partition and creating a new one: Coriolis Systems' iPartition software enables you to resize the Boot Camp partition easily ($50; www.coriolis-systems.com). And Paragon Software (www.paragon-software.com) plans to offer CampTune software that does the same for an undetermined price.

FIGURE 18.6

Boot Camp Assistant enables you to select how much hard disk space to allocate to Windows.

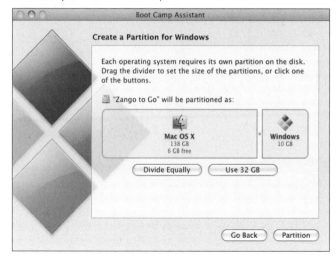

After the partitioning is complete, you get a screen with two options: Quit & Install Later and Start Installation. If you're ready now, click Start Installation. If not, click Quit & Install Later; then run the Boot Camp Assistant when you are ready to install Windows, select Start the Windows Installer, and click Continue. Either way, you need to insert your Windows installation CD or DVD. Your Mac restarts and runs the Windows installation disc.

The first choice to make when installing Windows is a critical one. The wrong answer can wipe out your Mac's data. You're presented a list of disk partitions on which to install Windows. Choose the one whose name includes Bootcamp. (The other partitions contain your Mac's data, which you do *not* want to install Windows over.) In Windows XP, use the ↑ or ↓ key to move among them; then press Return (called Enter in Windows). In Windows Vista or 7, use your choice of the mouse or keyboard to choose the Bootcamp partition, then click Next.

You are then asked to format the partition:

- **Windows XP.** You see a list of options. First, decide what kind of formatting you want for your partition: FAT or NTFS. Note that the FAT option appears only if your Boot Camp partition is 32GB or smaller in size. We believe that NTFS is a better formatting choice because it is more stable and provides faster file access than FAT. When you've decided which format to use, choose one of the Format options for your chosen format type (the "quick" ones are fine) by using the ↑ or ↓ key to move among them and press Return (called Enter in Windows).

- **Windows Vista and 7.** Click Drive Options (Advanced), then click Format, and then click OK. Your Windows partition is formatted as NTFS.

Note

The Mac OS can read and copy from NTFS-formatted disks, including the Boot Camp partition. But it can't write or copy to such disks unless you buy software such as Paragon Software's NTFS for Mac OS X ($30; www. paragon-software.com). If you want to access your Windows files on the Boot Camp partition from the Mac OS, you'll need this software.

After Windows is done formatting the partition, it begins installing Windows, which can take 30 to 45 minutes. You are asked a series of questions on your preferred Windows settings, just as if you were installing Windows on a PC.

When Windows is finished installing itself, you need to install the drivers that tell Windows how to work with your Mac's hardware. To do so, first eject the Windows installation disc (choose My Computer, Control+click or right-click the optical drive (D:), and choose Eject This Disk. Now insert your Mac OS X 10.6 Snow Leopard installation DVD. After a few seconds, it should automatically begin installing the necessary drivers; if not, double-click the optical disc (D:) in My Computer and then double-click setup.exe in the Boot Camp folder. Either way, if you get an error message saying that the software has not passed Windows testing, click Continue Anyway. Also, do not click any Cancel buttons that appear in the sequence of dialog boxes that will open and close. Windows will restart and may display some wizards for updating your software drivers (follow their prompts if so).

Install any Windows software you want. We suggest you install MediaFour's MacDrive ($50; www. mediafour.com) or Acute Systems' TransMac ($54; www.acutesystems.com) so you can access files on the Mac OS partition from the Windows partition.

You're done!

Using Windows via Boot Camp

With Windows installed, you can boot into it any time you want. When you start (or restart) your Mac, press and hold Option until a set of disk icons appears. Use your mouse or the ← and → keys to move among them, selecting the Windows disk (really the Boot Camp partition) when you want to boot into Windows and the Mac OS X disk (partition) when you want to boot into the Mac OS.

To set which partition to boot into by default, in the Mac OS choose ⬇ System Preferences and click Startup Disk. Select the startup disk (partition) you want the Mac to boot into by default. The next time you start the Mac, it will boot into that disk unless you press and hold Option to choose which disk (or partition) to start from.

You can also make this default startup choice in Windows. Click the Boot Camp icon in the system tray, then choose Boot Camp Control Panel from the menu. Select the startup disk you want to use by default and click OK. (You can also access the Boot Camp control panel by choosing Start ⬇ Control Panel, selecting Classic View (if it's not already selected), and then double-clicking the Boot Camp icon.

Tip

A quick way to boot back into the Mac from Windows is to click the system tray's Boot Camp icon and choose Restart in Mac OS X, though note that this option changes the default start disk to the Mac OS X as well.

Keep these tips in mind when using Windows in a Boot Camp partition:

- **You won't be able to get Windows' special startup options, such as Safe Mode, by pressing F8 if you use a Bluetooth keyboard.** That's because Windows doesn't load the Bluetooth drivers until much after these options are no longer available. Use a USB keyboard or, if you have a MacBook, its built-in keyboard when you need these options.

- **Be patient when using a Bluetooth keyboard or mouse.** Windows doesn't load the Bluetooth drivers until the very end of the startup process, after your Windows desktop, system tray, and so on have appeared. It may seem that Windows is frozen because it does not respond to your wireless input, but give it a bit more time before giving up.

- **If you have a MacBook that supports gestures on the touchpad, you can use the standard Mac gestures for Window-supported features.** These include holding two fingers on the trackpad and clicking the trackpad button to right-click (the Windows equivalent to Control+click), as well as dragging two fingers to scroll. (See Chapter 21 for more details on setting trackpad gesture preferences for the Keyboard & Shortcuts system preference and Chapter 2 for details on the various Macs' supported gestures.)

- **The Mac's Control key acts as the Windows Ctrl key, the Option key as the Alt key, and the ⌘ (Command) key as the ⊞ (Windows) key.** Table 18.1 shows other key mappings.

TABLE 18.1

Boot Camp's Key Assignments for Windows and Mac Keyboards

Windows Key	Apple USB Keyboard	MacBook Built-in Keyboard and Apple Bluetooth Keyboard
Alt	Option	Option
AltGr	Control+Option	Control+Option

continued

TABLE 18.1 *(continued)*

Windows Key	Apple USB Keyboard	MacBook Built-in Keyboard and Apple Bluetooth Keyboard
Backspace	Delete	Delete
Ctrl	Control	Control
Ctrl+Alt+Delete	Control+Option+Delete ⊠	Control+Option+Delete
Delete	Delete ⊠	Fn+Delete
Enter	Return	Return
Keypad Enter	Enter	Enter*
Insert	Fn+Enter *or* Help	Fn+Enter
Num Lock	Clear	Fn+F6*
Pause/Break	F16	Fn+Esc
PgDn	Page Down	Page Down
PgUp	Page Up	Page Up
Print Screen (PrtScr)	F14	Fn+Shift+F11
Print Active Window	Option+F14	Fn+Shift+Option+F11
Scroll Lock (ScrLock)	F15	Fn+F12
⊞ (Windows)	⌘ (Command)	⌘ (Command)

*Not available on all MacBooks' built-in keyboards or in Apple Bluetooth wireless keyboards

New Feature

When you work in Windows from a Boot Camp partition, Mac OS X 10.6 Snow Leopard now lets Windows see your Mac OS partition, so it can read files on it and copy them to the Windows partition. However, you cannot save files on the Mac OS partition or copy files to it. But you can open, save, and modify your Windows partition's files from the Mac OS.

Using Windows virtual machines

When Parallels first released its Parallels Desktop virtualization software for the Mac ($80; www. parallels.com), it changed the rules about letting Macs fit into Windows-dominated environments. Now that a Mac could run Windows simultaneously with the Mac OS, people quickly began adopting Macs, knowing that it was both a safe and convenient choice given the Windows support. EMC's VMware subsidiary followed up with its similar product, Fusion ($80; www. vmware.com), so Mac users now have a choice. The capabilities are nearly identical, so either is a good choice.

Unlike Boot Camp, Parallels Desktop and VMware's Fusion don't need a fixed amount of space for Windows. Each can grow its virtual machine's file size as needed, so you're not stuck with a partition that's too small. Each also enables you to save your virtual machines on any disk accessible to the Mac, such as to an external FireWire disk. You can even move these virtual machines by moving their folder to a new location.

Tip

It's best to use a FireWire disk rather than a USB disk for running a virtual machine. Most Macs have several USB devices connected to them, so the Windows disk must compete for the connection's bandwidth, which can really slow it down. This is particularly an issue if you are also running Time Machine and backing up to a USB disk — performance slows to a crawl when that occurs. FireWire is much faster and devices connected through it are much less likely to be competing with so many other devices.

Both Parallels Desktop and VMware Fusion automatically install their own drivers in Windows to make sure the Mac's capabilities are available to Windows, much as Boot Camp does. But they offer more capabilities, such as the capability to drag and drop files between Windows and Mac OS X and the capability for Mac OS X and Windows to see each other's disks as network file shares. The preferences settings in Fusion, as shown in Figure 18.7, show the types of options available for both programs.

FIGURE 18.7

VMware Fusion's preferences indicate the kinds of capabilities available in both Fusion and Parallel Desktop.

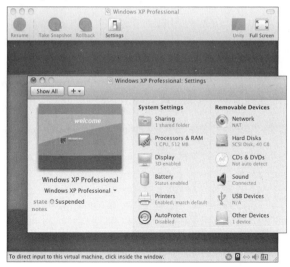

Both programs also enable you to set up how networking works: You can have the Windows virtual machine use the same network address as the Mac (called *shared networking* in Parallels and *NAT*, short for *network address translation*, in Fusion) or appear on the network as if it were a separate PC (called *bridge networking* by both programs). The use of bridge networking can be handy if you use a Mac at work, where the Windows virtual machine is the "official" system supported by the company and the Mac is tolerated as long as it is not on the network.

Note

Parallels Desktop sometimes behaves badly when it comes to file shares. You may get a message asking you to provide a username and password for \\.psf. That's the Home folder on your Mac (the .psf filename extension indicates a Parallels shared folder, which is its connection to an actual Mac folder or disk), which Parallels needs to access if you want to drag files back and forth or cut and paste information across the two operating systems. It shouldn't ask you for that password, so if it does, try choosing Devices ⇨ Shared Folders ⇨ Disconnect All, letting Windows log out and back in, choosing Devices ⇨ Shared Folders ⇨ Connect All, and letting Windows log out and log in again. This often clears out the issue.

They both give you the option of having the Windows My Pictures, My Documents, Desktop, and My Music folders in Windows be mapped to your Pictures, Documents, Desktop, and Music folders in the Mac OS so any files placed in these folders are automatically available to both operating systems in their familiar locations. That also means you don't need to duplicate the files in these folders across the operating systems. Figure 18.8 shows the preference to set up this mapping in Parallels Desktop.

FIGURE 18.8

Mapping Windows folders to their Mac OS equivalents in Parallels Desktop

You can run both Parallels Desktop and VMware Fusion so that Windows appears in a separate window (as shown in Figures 18.9 and 18.10), in full-screen mode (where you switch back and forth with the Mac OS by using a keyboard shortcut), or so your Mac OS and Windows active programs appear at the same time in what Parallels calls *Coherence mode* and what Fusion calls *Unity mode*. Figures 18.11 and 18.12 show these "melded" Mac OS/Windows modes that make Windows applications appear to be Mac applications.

Tip

If you use Coherence or Unit mode, we recommend that you move the Windows taskbar (where the Start logo appears) to the top of the screen so it doesn't get covered up by the Mac Dock at the bottom of the screen. (Or move the Mac Dock to one side of the screen and the Windows Start bar to the other side.) To move the Windows taskbar, click and drag it to the new location (you may have to right-click the bar first and choose Unlock the Taskbar). In the Mac OS, choose ➪ Dock and then the desired location from the submenu.

FIGURE 18.9

Parallels Desktop with Windows in a window

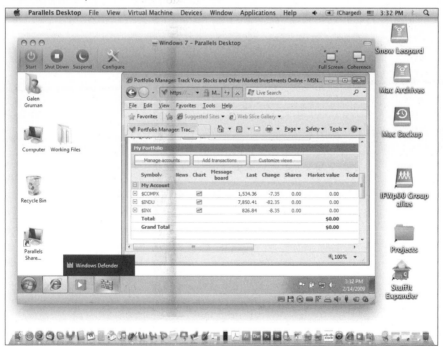

529

FIGURE 18.10

VMware Fusion with Windows in a window

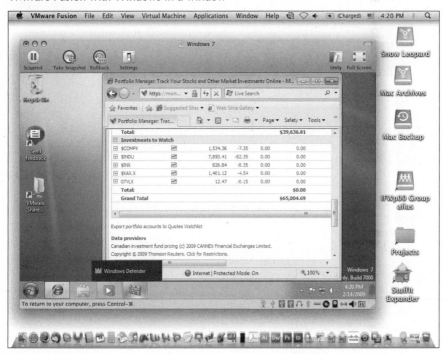

Both Parallels Desktop and VMware Fusion have an array of menu options, like any Mac application, where you can enable and disable various features, such as associating the DVD drive to Windows (or disassociating it so the Mac can use it) and choosing the network type. Both also have iconic popup menus at the bottom of the screen when you run Windows in a window; those popup menus let you enable, disable, and enable various aspects such as attached disks, networking, and attached USB devices. You can see these iconic popup menus at the lower right of the Windows windows in Figures 8.9 and 8.10.

Both programs also let you have multiple virtual machines set up, and both provide a list of them to choose from. You can even run multiple virtual machines simultaneously, though that quickly eats up your Mac's processing capabilities.

Finally, both can import Windows, its settings, and its applications from actual PCs, so you can move your PC onto your Mac and get rid of that PC box.

Parallels Desktop with Windows in Coherence mode

Sometimes, it makes sense to use both a Boot Camp Windows partition and either Parallels Desktop or VMware Fusion as well. One reason would be to run Windows in Boot Camp for processor-intensive activities, or those that require dedicated video memory, such as some video-editing software, and to use Parallels or Fusion the rest of the time when you want to run both Windows and Mac apps at the same time. Both programs let you use a Boot Camp partition from the Mac OS.

When you want to have Parallels use a Boot Camp partition, when you create a new virtual machine, be sure to select Custom as the installation type. When asked for the virtual hard disk option, choose Boot Camp and click Continue, and then follow the rest of the prompts. In Fusion, you'll see your Boot Camp partition already listed as an available virtual machine in the list that appears when you start Fusion — as long as your Mac OS account has administrator privileges.

FIGURE 18.12

VMware Fusion with Windows in Unity mode

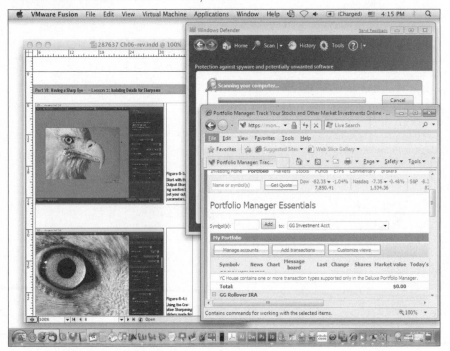

Summary

The Mac OS is built to integrate with Windows environments though file exchange, network compatibility, and even the capability to run Windows.

For file exchange, it can read and write to many PC-formatted disks, including CDs, DVDs, flash drives, and FAT-formatted hard disks. It can read NTFS-formatted disks but not write to them unless you buy extra software to do so. Windows is not so fluent, requiring extra-cost software to read Mac hard drives and older media such as floppy disks.

Because both PCs and Macs use filename extensions to identify what type a file is, it's a good idea to have both Windows and Mac OS display these extensions. That way you can figure out what the file type is in case you receive a file format that Windows or the Mac does not recognize.

Modern professionally produced fonts are identical on Mac and Windows, so you can be sure they have the same characters and identical output, but older fonts — especially PostScript Type 1 ones — can vary even if their names are the same.

File servers and Internet-based file-exchange methods such as FTP and e-mail make it very easy to exchange files between Mac and Windows users. You can also have Macs and Windows PCs directly share files through a network connection, though there is significant setup to be done on both ends, and Windows can't always see the Macs' shared folders.

Mac OS X comes with a utility that enables you to reserve (partition) part of your Mac's startup disk so you can install Windows on it. You can then boot between Mac OS and Windows based on which operating system you need at the moment. You can use various file-sharing techniques to exchange files between them.

If you use Windows applications frequently, you should buy either Parallels Desktop or EMC VMware's Fusion. They enable you to run Windows and its applications simultaneously with the Mac OS X and its applications, so you don't have to switch back and forth. Plus you can share your drives and files — even copy and paste across operating systems — as if everything were on the same operating system.

For those times you need a separate partition for Windows, such as to get the necessary performance or video support for some applications, both programs let you keep your Boot Camp partition and boot into it. When you don't need such dedicated Windows usage, they make your Boot Camp partition available from the Mac OS so you can run Windows programs from it while using the Mac OS.

Working with Microsoft Exchange

Mac OS X 10.6 Snow Leopard comes with a great e-mail application (Mail), calendar application (iCal), and contacts manager (Address Book). But many people in the business world use Microsoft's Exchange products to handle all three functions, with Exchange Server on the back end managing everything and Entourage on the Mac (called Outlook in Windows) providing users with access to their e-mail, calendars, and contacts from the Exchange Server.

Microsoft has long made its Entourage application available for the Mac, so users have been able to work with Exchange for more than a decade. But Mac OS X 10.6 Snow Leopard now integrates the Microsoft ActiveSync technology, making it even easier to work in an Exchange Server-based business, especially if your business uses the newest version of that server, Exchange Server 2007.

That means you can continue to use Entourage as your e-mail, contacts, and calendar applications alongside Address Book and iCal, or you can drop Entourage and use Mail, Address Book, and iCal exclusively and still be a "native" participant in your business's Exchange environment.

New Feature

Native support for ActiveSync and Exchange Server 2007 is new to Mac OS X 10.6 Snow Leopard.

Cross-Ref

Chapter 11 explains how to set up and use Mail, iCal, and Address Book, both for Exchange and other servers.

How Exchange Works

Microsoft Exchange is a server application that stores and routes several kinds of information to users that connect to it through a *client application* such as Entourage, Outlook, or Mail. Exchange handles e-mail, contacts, calendar entries, to-do items, RSS (Really Simple Syndication) feeds, and newsgroup feeds. By managing these types of information in a central location (the Exchange Server), Exchange makes it easy to share and collaborate, such as being able to check a colleagues' calendar to see if he or she is available, or to send e-mails to people you select from a corporate directory (rather than having to have entered their e-mail addresses manually or have them stored in your Mac's Address Book).

Note

Microsoft Exchange is not the only server application you might use for communication and collaboration. IBM's Lotus Notes and Novell's GroupWise are also used by many businesses, and they come with a Mac client application to allow access to their e-mail, contacts, and calendar information. But Mac OS X 10.6 Snow Leopard does not support them natively, so they don't integrate as well with Mail, iCal, or Address Book as Exchange does.

There are several versions of Exchange Server in use: 2000, 2003, and 2007. Exchange Server 2003 is the most widely deployed, but Exchange Server 2007 is steadily replacing 2000 and 2003 installations as businesses upgrade to the latest version. It's important to know which version of Exchange Server your business uses because how your Mac works with Exchange Server varies based on the server version your business has.

If your business runs Exchange Server 2000 or 2003, you won't get much of the benefits of Mac OS X 10.6 Snow Leopard's newfound support for Exchange 2007. That's because if you're using Mail, it interacts with Exchange Server 2000 or 2003 through an IMAP (Internet Message Access Protocol) connection, which gives it access to just e-mails and the corporate address book. And iCal and Address Book won't synchronize to Exchange Server 2000 or 2003 directly; you must use Entourage 2003 as the go-between, as explained later in this chapter. (Chapter 11 explains how to set up Mail through an IMAP connection if you are using Exchange 2000 or 2003, or Lotus Notes or Novell GroupWise.)

Note

Your network administrator must set up Exchange Server to support IMAP connections, such as through a virtual private network (VPN) or Outlook Web Access (OWA), for your Mac to connect outside your corporate network. Inside a corporate network, IMAP or OWA must be enabled for Exchange Server 2000 or 2003 if you want to access Exchange through Mail instead of through Entourage. (By contrast, you can connect natively with Exchange Server 2007 from Mail, iCal, and Address Book.)

If your business runs Exchange Server 2007, you'll get much better integration with your Mac, to the point where you don't need to run Entourage any longer if you don't want to. That's because Mail, Address Book, and iCal can talk directly to the Exchange 2007 server, synchronizing e-mail, contacts, and calendar entries (as well as RSS feeds, to-do items, and newsgroup feeds). Plus, with the ActiveSync support, this synchronization happens instantly, not on a scheduled basis as with IMAP.

Because Exchange processes and stores all e-mails, contacts, and calendar items centrally, then distributes the relevant items to each user, by default you always have a copy of your e-mail, contacts, and calendar items on the server. So, if you access Exchange from another computer (or from your iPhone or iPod Touch), you have access to all the same information as from your "regular" Mac. And if your Mac crashes or you accidentally delete messages, the messages are likely to still be available on the Exchange server. You can configure for how long these messages are stored on the server in Mail's Preferences dialog box (choose Mail ➪ Preferences or press ⌘+, [comma]), in the Accounts pane, as Chapter 11 describes.

Note

Typically, Exchange copies your messages, calendar items, and contacts to your Mac as well as keeps copies on the Exchange Server, but sometimes Exchange Server is configured not to allow local copies to be kept. For example, some industries have high standards to safeguard information and thus make employees keep everything only on servers so their data can't get stolen if their Mac is lost or stolen.

Using Mac OS X's Mail with Exchange

Mail is the Mac OS X application that you're likely to use the most with Exchange, because people typically spend much more time in e-mail than in their address books or calendars. Plus, you can update Address Book within Mail and accept calendar invitations within Mail. How Mail interacts with Exchange depends on the version of Exchange Server you use.

Cross-Ref

To set up Mail, follow the instructions in Chapter 11. The details here are specific to using Exchange, but most of the setup is the same no matter which e-mail server you use.

Setting up Mail for Exchange 2007

When setting up an e-mail account in Mail, you have the option of setting up Address Book and iCal at the same time for an Exchange 2007 e-mail account. As Figure 19.1 shows, when asked for the incoming mail server information, there are two options not available for other types of e-mail accounts: Address Book Contacts and iCal Calendars. If you select Address Book Contacts, your Exchange contacts list is synchronized automatically with Address Book on your Mac; if you select iCal Calendars, your Exchange calendar and to-do items are synchronized automatically with iCal on your Mac.

When you create an Exchange e-mail account, you can set how long messages are kept on the Exchange server in the Accounts pane of the Preferences dialog box (choose Mail ➪ Preferences or press ⌘+, [comma]), as Chapter 11 describes. If you are using Exchange 2007, you have slightly different options than had been available in previous versions of Mac OS X (before you had to make an IMAP connection to Exchange 2000, 2003, and 2007; now you need to make an IMAP connection only to Exchange 2000 and 2003).

When configuring Exchange 2007-based e-mail accounts, you can also synchronize Address Book and iCal with Exchange using the Also Configure options.

Figure 19.2 shows the two subpanes whose options differ for Exchange 2007 from the IMAP options used in Mac OS X 10.5 Leopard and earlier: Mailbox Behaviors and Advanced. Here's what's different:

- **Mailbox Behaviors.** In Trash options, gone is the Move Deleted Messages to the Trash Mailbox option, given that deleted e-mail is automatically moved to the server's Trash folder.

- **Advanced.** The Root Path field enables you to put in a server address as provided by your network administrator to ensure a proper connection to the Exchange 2007 server. Leave it blank unless given such an address.

When set up, Mail syncs to Exchange 2007 immediately, so both are always kept up-to-date. With previous versions of Exchange, Mail syncs periodically as set in the Check for New Messages popup menu in the General pane of Mail's Preferences dialog box.

Setting up Mail for Exchange 2000 or 2003

If your company uses Exchange Server 2000 or 2003, set up your e-mail account as standard IMAP connection (called Exchange IMAP in some dialog boxes), as Chapter 11 explains.

FIGURE 19.2

For Exchange 2007 accounts, the Mailbox Behaviors subpane (left) and Advanced subpane (right) differ from the IMAP options provided for Exchange 2007 and earlier in previous versions of Mac OS X.

Working with an Exchange e-mail account in Mail

Apple's Mail works very well with Exchange 2000, 2003, and 2007. When you create an account for an Exchange e-mail account, Mail accesses not only its e-mails but also its notes and to-do items and any RSS and newsgroup feeds set up on that server.

Cross-Ref

For the details on how to use Mail, see Chapter 11. This chapter covers just Exchange-specific functions.

You can force Exchange and Mail to sync by choosing Mailbox ➪ Synchronize "*accountname*", or by Control+clicking or right-clicking the account in the left column of the Message Viewer window and choosing Synchronize "*accountname*" from the contextual menu. If you're using Exchange 2007, you rarely need to force synchronization, as ActiveSync maintains a continuous synchronization; but in earlier versions of Exchange, forcing a sync is a handy way to get new mail before the best scheduled sync takes place (such as when your boss says he or she just sent you a message and needs an immediate answer).

In the Mail Message Viewer window's Sidebar, you'll see your Exchange e-mail account listed below the RSS section. You click the disclosure triangle to the left of the Exchange account's name to expand the mailbox and see all the folders set up at your Exchange sever. In addition to the usual Drafts, Junk E-Mail, and Trash, you'll see any other folders stored in Exchange, such as Calendar (which contains your Exchange appointments), Notes (which includes your Exchange notes), Public Folders (which contains shared folders set up by your e-mail administrator), and any other folders set up by your e-mail administrator.

Control+click or right-click your Exchange account mailbox and choose Get Account Info from the contextual menu to see all messages and folders stored for your account on the Exchange server, whether you've exceeded your storage quota limits, and to manage subscriptions to RSS and newsgroup feeds provided through the Exchange server.

Any to-do items you create in Mail are displayed in the Reminders section of the Message Viewer's Sidebar. Notes are displayed separately from to-do items. Furthermore, both notes and to-do items are listed based on which account they are created in: On My Mac (which means in iCal) or in a specific Exchange e-mail account. Notes and to-do items appear in the message list, where you can read and delete them.

Note

To-do items are saved in iCal or, if you choose your Exchange e-mail account or Entourage as the calendar, in Exchange.

Note

One thing you cannot do with Mail is set up an away notice on an Exchange server, which sends an automated reply to people letting them know when you are on vacation or otherwise unavailable. (In Entourage 2008, you can set up such a notice by choosing Tools ⇨ Out of Office.) Note that this "away notice" capability does not exist in Entourage 2003, either.

Using iCal with Exchange

The process for setting up iCal differs notably, depending on whether you use Exchange 2007 or an earlier version of Exchange.

Setting up iCal for Exchange 2007

If your business uses Exchange Server 2007 and you selected the iCal Calendars option in the Accounts pane of Mail's Preferences dialog box (choose Mail ⇨ Preferences or press ⌘+, [comma]) — as shown in Figure 19.1 — appointments and to-do items you set in iCal are synced to your Exchange calendar and vice versa.

You can also set up iCal itself to work with Exchange 2007, rather than do so through Mail. Go to the Accounts pane in iCal's Preferences dialog box by choosing iCal ⇨ Preferences or pressing ⌘+, (comma). Add your account information in the Account Information subpane, as shown in Figure 19.3, and the server connection information in the Server Settings subpane. (These should match the Account pane's settings in Mail's Preferences dialog box.)

Cross-Ref

For details on how to use iCal, see Chapter 11. This chapter covers Exchange-specific functions only.

The Accounts pane in iCal for setting up synchronization with Exchange 2007

Setting up iCal for Exchange 2000 or 2003

If your business uses Exchange 2000 or 2003, you need to use Entourage as the way station between Exchange and iCal. To do so in either Entourage 2004 or Entourage 2008, go to Entourage's Preferences dialog box (choose Entourage ⇨ Preferences or press ⌘+, [comma]), then go to the Sync Services pane. As Figure 19.4 shows, select the Synchronize Events and Tasks with iCal and .Mac option to set up the Entourage calendar in iCal and have events and to-do items sync automatically.

Note

You must choose either to sync your local Entourage calendar or the Exchange server calendar; you cannot sync both to iCal.

In iCal, you now have a calendar called Entourage, as Figure 19.5 shows. Any appointments and to-do items you add to the Entourage calendar in iCal are synchronized to Exchange (the others are not), and any Exchange calendar items are synced to the Entourage calendar in iCal.

FIGURE 19.4

To sync calendar and contacts between Exchange 2000 or 2004 and the Mac OS's iCal and Address Book, use the Sync Services pane of the Preferences dialog box in Entourage 2004 (shown here) or Entourage 2008.

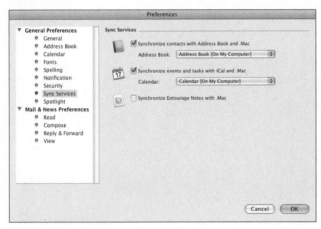

FIGURE 19.5

The Entourage calendar (in the list at the left side of the window) is created by Entourage to allow calendar synchronization between iCal and Exchange 2000 or 2003.

Using iCal with Exchange 2007

Once iCal is set up to sync with Exchange 2007, you can do several things you can't do with earlier versions of Exchange:

- When you open an event in iCal, click in the Location field to get a list of available meeting rooms to schedule the meeting in (if meeting-room availability is enabled in your Exchange 2007 server's Global Address List).

- Likewise, you can check the availability of attendees invited to the event, by choosing individuals in the Invitees field.

Cross-Ref

See Chapter 11 for details on the iCal functions that work with all versions of Exchange, such as sending meeting invites.

Using Address Book with Exchange

The process for setting up Address Book also differs, depending on whether you use Exchange 2007 or an earlier version of Exchange.

Setting up Address Book for Exchange 2007

If your business uses Exchange Server 2007 and you selected the Address Book Contacts option in the Accounts pane of Mail's Preferences dialog box (choose Mail ➪ Preferences or press ⌘+, [comma]) — as shown in Figure 19.1 — contacts you add and modify in Address Book are synced to your Exchange address book and vice versa.

Using Entourage with Exchange

There's no law that says you have to give up the Microsoft Entourage client application just because Mac OS X 10.6 Snow Leopard adds native Exchange 2007 compatibility. If you prefer Entourage over Mail, keep using Entourage. You can still have Address Book and iCal sync straight to the Exchange 2007 server if you want to use these Mac OS X applications (because they do sync to other, non-Exchange products you may be using).

And if your business uses Exchange Sever 2000 or 2003, you're essentially forced to use Entourage if you want to sync Address Book and iCal to Exchange. If you don't care about that, you can use Mail instead of Entourage, configured as an IMAP e-mail account — or stick with Entourage because you prefer it or are familiar with it.

There's no special trick to setting up or using Entourage on Mac OS X 10.6 Snow Leopard. After installing the software, you should be asked to enter your account information the first time you launch Entourage. If not, or to change your settings later, choose Entourage ➪ Account Settings and either click the New button to create a new account or double-click an existing user account to change it. Follow the prompts for a new account; when changing an existing account, note that the Account Settings and Advanced panes hold the account and server information needed to connect to Exchange. (Your network administrator should provide the server settings to you.) To synchronize Entourage with Mac OS X's iCal and Address Book, follow the previous instructions in this chapter for your version of Exchange Server.

You can also set up Address Book itself to work with Exchange 2007, rather than do so through Mail. Go to the Accounts pane in Address Book's Preferences dialog box by choosing Address Book⇨ Preferences or pressing ⌘+, (comma). Add your account information in the Account Information subpane, as shown in Figure 19.6, and the server connection information in the Server Settings subpane. (These should match the Account pane's settings in Mail's Preferences dialog box.)

Cross-Ref

For the details on how to use Address Book, see Chapter 11. This chapter covers just Exchange-specific functions.

Setting up Address Book for Exchange 2000 and 2003

If your business uses Exchange 2000 or 2003, you need to use Entourage as the way station between Exchange and iCal. To do so in either Entourage 2004 or Entourage 2008, go to Entourage's Preferences dialog box (choose Entourage⇨Preferences or press ⌘+, [comma]), then go to the Sync Services pane. As Figure 19.4 shows, select the Synchronize Contacts with Address Book and .Mac option to sync contacts with Address Book automatically.

FIGURE 19.6

The Accounts pane in Address Book for setting up synchronization with Exchange 2007

Using an iPhone or iPod Touch with Exchange

It was the iPhone OS 2.0 in summer 2008 that brought Microsoft's ActiveSync technology to the Apple world, giving iPhone and iPod Touch users the ability to directly connect their devices to

Exchange servers rather than following the tortured path of synchronizing through iTunes on their Mac, which in turn would sync to Address Book and iCal, which would in turn synchronize to Exchange through Entourage. (And you had to use Mail to access your Exchange e-mail if you wanted iTunes to sync it your mobile device.)

If you set up your iPhone or iPod Touch to sync directly with Exchange, and you set up Entourage, Mail, iCal, and/or Address Book to sync to Exchange (directly via Exchange 2007 or through Entourage for earlier versions of Exchange), your Mac and your mobile devices will stay in sync with each other and with the Exchange server.

Note

You can use Apple's MobileMe service to sync your Mac to your iPhone or iPod Touch and to other computers if you don't use Exchange, as Chapter 15 explains. Likewise, if you use IBM's Lotus Notes 8.5, IBM offers the iNotes Web-based application for iPhones and iPod Touches to sync e-mail, and Novell supports Web-based access to GroupWise 8.

Note

If you use a mobile device such as a RIM BlackBerry or a Windows Mobile device, you need to use a special utility to sync to the Mac, such as the free PocketSync Manager for the BlackBerry (www.blackberry.com) or Mark/Space's $40 Missing Sync (www.markspace.com) for Windows Mobile devices.

Setting up the iPhone or iPod Touch to access Exchange Server 2000, 20003, or 20007 is easy:

1. **Tap Settings to open the Settings application, then tap Mail, Contacts, Calendars to set up (or modify) an account.**

2. **Tap Add Account to get a list of supported e-mail servers.** Tap the Microsoft Exchange logo and follow the prompts to set up your account.

3. **You're asked for your e-mail address and password; if the iPhone or iPod Touch can figure out the rest of the settings for you, it will.** Otherwise, it will ask you for the server address and any security settings (which your network administrator should provide to you).

4. **You're asked whether you want to sync mail, contacts, and/or calendars.** If you set any of these to On, they will sync wirelessly to the Exchange server. If you set any of these to Off, you must sync them through iTunes, as explained later.

5. **When set up, Exchange will start loading your messages, calendar items, and/or contacts onto your iPhone or iPod Touch. In the device's Mail application, you will see a list of your Exchange e-mail folders.** If you tap any folder to open it, Exchange begins loading its messages. (Exchange loads new messages into your inbox automatically, but loads messages in other folders only when you open them.) Any messages you send are automatically copied to Exchange's Sent Items folder, so they can be synchronized with your Mail's or Entourage's Sent Items folder on your Mac.

To modify your Exchange settings, go to the Settings application, tap Mail, Contacts, Calendars, tap the account to change (you can have multiple e-mail accounts set up, but only one Exchange account), and then change the desired settings. Figure 19.7 shows the series of screens to set up and modify your Exchange settings on an iPhone or iPod Touch.

FIGURE 19.7

Left: The pane to select the type of e-mail account to set up on an iPhone or iPod Touch. Center: The pane in which you enable or disable what Exchange syncs to your iPhone or iPod Touch. Right: The account and server settings you can modify for Exchange.

If you don't want to synchronize your contacts or calendar with Exchange — perhaps you want to keep personal items off your company's Exchange Server — disable synchronization on the iPhone or iPod Touch, as shown in Figure 19.7. You can still sync such items between your Mac and mobile device through iTunes.Chapter 9 explains how to do so.

Summary

Mac OS X 10.6 Snow Leopard comes with Microsoft's ActiveSync technology, which enables direct connections between Microsoft's Exchange Server 2007 e-mail, calendar, and contact application and the Mac OS's Mail, iCal, and Address Book applications. If you use an earlier version of Exchange Server, you can still sync Mail to it via an IMAP connection, and sync iCal and Address Book to it by using Microsoft's Entourage client application as a way station.

When you configure Mail for an Exchange 2007 e-mail account, you can use a few different settings available in previous versions of Mac OS X relating to how files are stored on the Exchange server.

If you use an iPhone or iPod Touch, you can set it to synchronize wirelessly to an Exchange server, rather than synchronize through iTunes to Mail, iCal, and Address Book.

Part IV

Maintaining Your Mac with Mac OS X

Managing User Accounts

T he Mac is a personal computer, so the idea of having, much less managing, a user account on your Mac may seem like a bizarre concept. After all, you're the user and it's your Mac, so why do you need an account?

If you are truly the only user of the Mac, then the idea of an account can seem unnecessary. Except that it isn't. And if more than one person uses your Mac, you definitely need to set up and manage the accounts, so each user's data, applications, and so on are kept separate for privacy, security, and stability reasons.

First, let's assume you're truly the only user of the Mac. Why bother knowing about, much less managing, a user account? The basic reason is that your Mac has an account for you whether you know it or not. And the benefit of managing that account is to set up security so if anyone else tries to use your Mac — particularly a thief — he or she is blocked by the need to enter a password to use that Mac. Passwords are tied to user accounts, so you need the user account. Plus, the user account is what Mac OS X 10.6 Snow Leopard uses to save some of your preferences, such as the login items (the applications and utilities that start up automatically when your Mac starts up).

Now let's look at why you might have multiple user accounts. In a business setting, your IT department will need an account that enables it to administer your Mac, so the IT staff can keep the Mac updated and otherwise work on it when you're not around. Plus this account gives IT access to your Mac if you leave the company, so IT can ready it for a new employee.

In a home setting, chances are other family members — as well as guests such as the babysitter and your visiting friends — will want to use your Mac, at least occasionally. You don't really want them to have access to all your applications and data, do you? Or be able to install and remove applications, right? If you create user accounts for those other people, you can make it as if they have their own separate Mac, keeping your part of the Mac safe and secure.

Plus, you can apply parental controls to some of those accounts, so you can restrict your kids' activities, such as the hours they can use the Mac or the Web sites they can visit. Even if you don't let your kids use your Mac, you'll want to use the parental controls to control their Macs, essentially making you the IT administrator with full access from your user account on their Mac and limiting their access within their user accounts.

Cross-Ref

For more on Mac OS X 10.6 Snow Leopard's security controls, see Chapter 23. For details on file sharing, see Chapter 13.

Setting Up User Accounts

When you install Mac OS X 10.6 Snow Leopard — or first use it on a new Mac — a default user account is set up for you, giving you full rights to the Mac and to change other user's accounts — something called *administrator privileges*.

You can modify those default settings, as well as create new user accounts, in one place: the Accounts system preference. (Choose ⇨ System Preferences and click the Accounts icon to open the Accounts system preference.) Figure 20.1 shows the initial pane in that system preference, the Password pane. At left is the list of user accounts, which initially shows your user account and the Guest user account. In the list of accounts, the currently logged-in account is at top under the My Account label and other configured accounts are under the Other Accounts label.

Note

If the Lock iconic button (the bronze padlock icon) at the bottom left of the Accounts system preference is closed, you must unlock it to make most changes. Click it, and enter your password when requested, then press Return or click OK. The Lock iconic button changes to an open one, indicating that the system preference is unlocked. Click the Lock iconic button again to lock it.

FIGURE 20.1

The Password pane of the Accounts system preference is where you set basic user account settings.

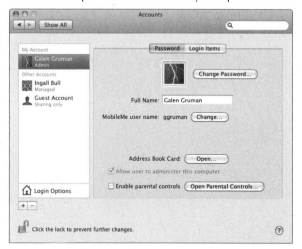

Adjusting personal settings

The Accounts pane has three groups of settings related to your user account and how it functions. The Password pane is where you set your password, select the picture used to identify your account, and set up other personal settings. The Login Options button at the bottom of the user accounts list in the Password pane opens a new, unnamed pane that enables you to determine how you log in to the Mac at startup. The Login Items pane is where you set which applications open when your Mac starts up.

Name, password, and related settings

The most commonly used settings are visible in the pane itself, controlling your name and password. Here are the key controls for setting these personal settings:

- **Full Name.** Enter your username in the Full Name field; this is the name that shows up as your Mac's name when you log in. (Note that the name of your Mac on the network, such as if you enable file sharing, is set elsewhere: in the Sharing system preference, as Chapter 13 explains.)

- **MobileMe User Name.** If you have a MobileMe account, you enter the MobileMe name in the text field. (You will later need to enter your MobileMe password in the MobileMe system preference.) If you've previously set up a MobileMe account, click Change to enter a different username. If you change the username, the MobileMe system preference opens. (MobileMe is covered in detail in Chapter 15.)

- **Address Book Card.** Click Open to open the Address Book application (see Chapter 11) to set up your address book card, which can include your name, address, e-mail, and other information that you can have several Mac applications use, such as to share your electronic business card with other users.

- **Picture.** Click the picture to choose a different image to represent yourself from Apple's image library, or choose Edit Picture at the top of that library to open a settings sheet in which you can take a new picture by using a camera attached to the Mac (such as the iSight camera built into many Macs); click the camera iconic button to take that photo. You can use an existing picture you have stored on your Mac by clicking Choose below the camera iconic button and then navigating through your disks and folders to that desired picture. Or use the Recent Pictures popup menu to choose a picture previously used. Use the slider to zoom in or out of your chosen picture, and drag the picture within its preview rectangle to crop it to your liking. (*Crop* means to cut off one or more sides of an image.) Figure 20.2 shows an imported photo being cropped. Click Set when done.

- **Change Password.** Click Change Password to open a settings sheet where you can change your login password (or set one up if you don't have one). Chapter 23 covers the password options in detail.

Note

By default, the account that is set up when you install Mac OS X Snow Leopard, or that is set up for you on your new Mac, has administrator privileges. Thus, the Allow User to Administer This Computer option is already selected. It's also grayed out for the default user because at least one account has to have administrator privileges.

FIGURE 20.2

Crop the image you want to use to represent your user account by dragging it within the cropping box; use the slider to enlarge or reduce the image.

Login items

When you install some programs, they set themselves automatically to load when your Mac starts up (or restarts). Examples include iTunes, which loads a function to look for music CDs and iPods when inserted so it can open automatically when they are detected, and antivirus applications, which begin running immediately upon startup to catch possible threats to your Mac. But you can also set your user account so any application loads at startup; this way the apps you always use are ready to go after the Mac has started. You might, for example, have your mail program set to launch at startup.

As Figure 20.3 shows, the Login Items pane displays all applications and utilities set to launch at startup, and it's where you add applications to the automatic startup list. The controls are simple:

- **To add an item for automatic startup, click the + iconic button, then locate the application or utility you want to launch automatically.** (Chances are it will be in the Applications folder or the Utilities folder, both of which are covered in Chapter 8.)

- **To remove an item for automatic startup, select it in the list and click the – iconic button.**

- **To display an item after automatic startup, select the Hide check box to the left of the application name.** (The Hide option is selected by default when you add applications to the automatic startup list.) The application will be visible on-screen after the Mac starts; for example, if you make Apple Mail a startup item, you see the window with your e-mail after startup.

- **To hide an item after automatic startup, deselect the Hide check box.** It will run minimized, so its dialog boxes and so on will not display on-screen. You, of course, can display the application in full by clicking its icon on the Dock. (Chapter 2 covers the Dock in detail.)

That's it!

FIGURE 20.3

The Login Items pane of the Accounts system preference

Login options

There's another set of personal settings for your account that you control by clicking Login Options at the bottom of the user accounts list. When you click Login Options, the Mac OS displays the untitled pane shown in Figure 20.4.

Note

The login options affect all user accounts on the Mac, which is why the Password and Login Options panes disappear when you are changing login options.

Here you can set the Mac to automatically log in to a specific user account by choosing that account in the Automatic Login popup menu, rather than requiring the user to sign in each time you start up the Mac. Choose Off to require that a user be chosen at startup.

Note

The Automatic Login popup menu may be grayed out. If so, that means automatic login is disabled in the Security system preference, as Chapter 23 explains.

Using the Display Login As options, you can control how the list of accounts appears when you start or restart the Mac. The List of Users option shows each username (and associated image), so a user clicks the desired name and then enters the password for that user. The Name and Password option requires the users to enter their usernames and passwords. This second option is more secure, as it forces users to remember their usernames (something a thief is not likely to know), not just their passwords, but because it requires them to remember their usernames, it can be a pain to deal when users repeatedly forget their usernames.

FIGURE 20.4

The login options in the Accounts system preference

Other options for the login screen are:

- **Show the Restart, Sleep, and Shut Down Buttons.** If selected, this option controls whether these buttons are displayed at the login screen.

- **Show Input Menu in Login Window.** If selected, this option enables users to switch to a different language's keyboard from the login screen — great for a Mac that is used as a public terminal, such as a store or dorm rec room, or if you have family or perhaps an exchange student who speak languages other than English.

- **Show Password Hints.** If selected, this option shows the password hint for each account; you set that password hint in the Password pane when you set up the account's password.

- **Use VoiceOver in Login Window.** If selected, this option makes the Mac read aloud the options in the login screen for visually impaired users (see Chapter 6).

- **Show Fast User Switching Menu As.** If selected, this option adds an option to the menu bar that enables you to quickly log out of your current account and log in to another one. The best part is that the previous user's applications are not closed, so they continue to run while the user is logged out and thus can keep doing their work. There's a popup menu with this option that has three options to control what is displayed in the menu bar: Icon, which shows the icon of a person's head; Name, which shows the user account name (such as `Galen Gruman`); and Short Name (such as `galen`), which shows the user's short name established when you first created the user account, as explained in the "Managing additional user accounts section" later in this chapter.

- **The Join button.** When you click this button (to the right of the Network Account Server label), you can set the directory services to use to determine who can log in to various services, applications, and databases on the network and what their settings are; this option enables a business to manage these settings from a central location. Clicking this button opens a settings sheet. Here, you choose a server from the Server popup menu or enter a server name in the Server text field, as shown in Figure 20.5. Or click the Open Directory Utility button to open the Directory utility where you choose what directory services protocols are enabled (ActiveDirectory, BSD [the Berkeley Software Distribution version of Unix], LDAP [Lightweight Directory Access protocol], and Local) and then to edit their settings to communicate properly with the specified directory server on the network).

New Feature

The Join button had been called Directory Services in previous versions of the Mac OS. And the settings sheet has been greatly simplified, so all you have to enter now is the server name.

FIGURE 20.5

Specifying a server for directory services through the Accounts system preference's login options

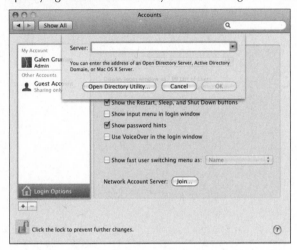

Managing additional user accounts

As noted in this chapter's introduction, many Macs have — or should have — more than one user account set up.

In a business environment, the IT staff should have an administrator account on all Macs so they can manage them. And you might want to set up user accounts on Macs used by several people, such as contractors or employees who work in different shifts on the same Mac (such as customer support staff or sales clerks).

In a home environment, even if you have several computers, you'll very likely want at least a guest account for babysitters and other visitors. You'll also want to have your own administrator-type account on your kids' Macs. And you likely want to set up accounts for individual family members on a Mac accessible to everyone, such as one in the family room or one you take on family vacations.

Adding accounts

To add additional user accounts to your Mac, click the + iconic button at the bottom of the user accounts list on the left of the Password or Login Items pane in the Accounts system preference. The controls and options are nearly the same as described in the previous sections of this chapter. But there are a few differences and additions to note.

When you create an account, you fill out the unnamed pane shown in Figure 20.6. Most of its options match the options you see in the Password pane for an existing account. But some are unique to creating an account:

- **New Account popup menu.** This menu enables you to determine the type of account: Administrator, Standard, Managed with Parental Controls, Sharing Only, and Group. An administrator has full access to the Mac OS and can manage other users' accounts. A standard user can manage only his or her own account and access any information available to all users. An account with parental controls is restricted in what it can do, as explained in the "Using Parental Controls" section later in this chapter. A sharing-only account can only access files over the network if file sharing is enabled, as described in Chapter 13. A group is a way of giving multiple user accounts a common set of settings, as described in the section "Using account groups" later in this chapter.

Tip

You can change a user's account type to Administrator, Standard, or Managed with Parental Controls after you create the account. Just select or deselect the Allow User to Administer This Computer option in the Password pane to change the type to or from an Administrator type, and just select or deselect the Enable Parental Controls option to change the type to or from a Managed with Parental Controls type. An account that has both options deselected is a Standard type.

Note

You cannot change a Sharing Only account to a different type later, nor can you change one of the other account types to a Sharing Only account later.

- **Short Name.** This text field lets you set a short name (or nickname) for the user; this name is used as the name of the Home folder.
- **Turn on FileVault Protection.** This option, if selected, encrypts the user's home folder and all its contents, making it harder for a hacker to gain access to it, as Chapter 23 explains. Note that this option is available only for the Administrator, Standard, and Managed with Parental Controls user account types.

Caution

If you create an account without providing a password, Mac OS X 10.6 Snow Leopard asks if you're sure you don't want a password set and lets you cancel the creation so you can enter a password. Remember that any user account that has no password can be a conduit for a thief or hacker to access the Mac, as Chapter 23 explains.

FIGURE 20.6

The settings when creating a new user account

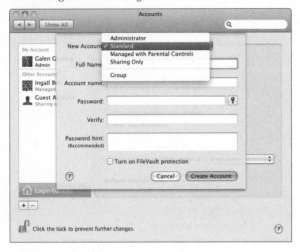

Managing accounts

After you create a user account, you won't see the Password or Login Items panes. Instead, there's just the Accounts system preference window with the user accounts list and one pane with the user picture, Reset Password, Name, MobileMe User Name, and — for the Administrator, Standard, and Managed with Parental Controls types only — the Allow User to Administer This Computer and Enable Parental Controls options.

You must start up or log in to the user accounts to modify their Address Book Card settings and to access the Password and Login Items panes.

Note
Multiple user accounts can have administrator privileges, giving them equal control over the Mac.

Deleting accounts

You can delete a user account by selecting it from the list and then clicking the – iconic button. You are then asked what to do with the user's home folder and all the applications and files stored within it: Save them as a disk image file, move them to the Users folder's Deleted Users subfolder, or delete them.

A disk image compresses everything into one file that you then have to double-click to see the various individual files inside; it's handy when you want to move the files to an archive disk for storage. The Deleted Users subfolder makes all the files easily accessible but takes more room, so it's ideal if you think you'll need access to the various files for a while. Of course, you could also move this folder to an archive disk.

Using guest accounts

Mac OS X comes with a predefined Guest Account, which is meant for use by occasional users that you don't want to set up individual user accounts for. This is the perfect account for the babysitter, your visiting nephews and nieces, and your kids' after-school friends. Figure 20.7 shows the pane that appears when you click the account.

To enable the guest account, select the Allow Guests to Log In to This Computer option. Note that a guest account does not require a password, so anyone can log in to it from your Mac's login screen. (But no one can log in to your Mac remotely over the network by using this account.) And note that when a guest user logs out (or restarts or shuts down the Mac), all the files in the guest account's home folder are deleted.

You can further restrict what the guest account can do when logged in through these two options:

- **Enable Parental Controls.** Select this option to restrict when access is permitted, what applications and Web sites can be accessed, and so on, as described in the "Using Parental Controls" section later in this chapter.

- **Allow Guests to Connect to Shared Folders.** Deselect this option so guests cannot access the files in the Users folder's Shared subfolder; that keeps these files accessible just to people who have individual user accounts.

FIGURE 20.7

The settings for the Guest Account automatically created by Mac OS X

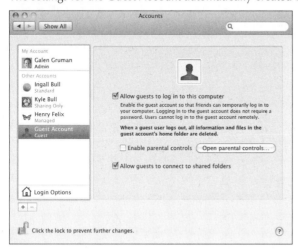

Using account groups

As noted in the "Adding accounts" section earlier in this chapter, you can create account groups. After creating a group, the label Groups appears in the user accounts list. Click the disclosure triangle to see the list of groups. Then select a group to add individual user accounts to it. You get a list of user accounts; simply select the users you want in that group, as shown in Figure 20.8.

The reason to set up a group is to simplify file sharing. When you set up file sharing (see Chapter 13), you can give permission to specific groups to access various disks, folders, and files. It's easier to select a group when giving such permissions than to select every individual user who should have access. Plus, when you add and delete users from a group, the file-sharing permissions don't need to be changed to reflect the changes in users — whoever is a member of the group that has file-sharing permission has access to those shared resources only as long as he or she is a member of that group.

FIGURE 20.8

Adding users to a group in the Accounts system preference

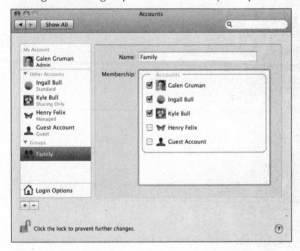

Switching among accounts

When you start up the Mac, you log in as a specific user. But restarting the Mac to switch users is time consuming, plus it closes applications you may want to keep running, such as e-mail or file downloading.

You could log in and out between users by choosing ⌘ ⇨ Log Out *username* or pressing Shift+⌘+Q to log out the current user and then log in as a different user via the Mac's login screen. But, just as with restarting, this closes all active programs.

There's a faster way to switch users when you have several people using a Mac over a short period of time, such as during the course of an evening. When you do this *fast switching*, all the accounts remain logged in as you switch to other users — and all applications remain running — but only one user is active at any time.

But you can fast-switch among accounts only if you selected the Show Fast User Switching Menu As option, as explained in the "Login options" section earlier in this chapter. When that option is selected, an icon or name appears in the menu bar that enables you to select a user to switch to, as Figure 20.9 shows. All logged-in users display a white check mark in an orange circle to the left of their names.

FIGURE 20.9

Logging in as a different user when fast user switching is enabled

Tip

If your Mac is logged in to a Standard or Managed with Parental Controls account, you can still make many Administrator-only changes, such as adjusting system preferences where the Lock iconic button displays the closed-padlock icon. Clicking the Lock iconic button prompts the Mac to ask for an administrator's username and password. If you enter such a username and password for an administrator user account set up on this Mac, you have full administrator privileges until you close the lock (which may happen automatically when you exit the system preference or utility or switch to something else).

Using Parental Controls

Kids, teenagers, and some adults tend to do dangerous or stupid things when using a computer. They might snoop in your personal or financial files. They might accidentally delete your work files. They might install applications — perhaps unwittingly from a Web site that promises games or other innocent-seeming downloads — that contain viruses, spyware, or other malware. They might go to Web sites that contain pornography, extreme violence, or other inappropriate material. Or they stay up all night playing games and surfing the Web instead of sleeping or doing their homework. Or they spend their weekends online instead of visiting friends or participating in out-door activities.

If you log in as an administrator, you can restrict the ability to do these unwanted things. You do so by using the Mac OS's parental controls.

The first step is to set these users' accounts as Managed with Parental Controls in the Accounts system preference. When you create a new account you want to manage by using parental controls, choose Managed with Parental Controls in the User Account popup menu. If you didn't do that, select the Enable Parental Controls option in the Accounts system preference's Password pane for each user account you want to restrict.

After you have set these user accounts to the Managed with Parental Controls type, you need to specify what the restrictions are. You do so in the Parental Controls system preference, as shown in Figure 20.10. The system preference opens automatically to the System pane.

FIGURE 20.10

The Parental Controls system preference's System pane

On the left of the Parental Controls system preference is a list of users who have either a Standard or Managed with Parental Controls account type. If you select the Guest Account or a Standard user account, the system preference asks you whether you want to turn on parental controls for that account, essentially converting it to a Managed with Parental Controls account type.

When you select a Managed with Parental Controls account, you have five panes that you can configure restrictions in: System, Content, Mail & iChat, Time Limits, and Logs.

System pane

In the Parental Controls system preference's System pane, you set the following options:

- **Use Simple Finder.** If this is selected, it directs the Mac to use the Simple Finder, a stripped-down version suited for smaller children. Figure 20.11 shows an example of the Simple Finder. Instead of showing users disks and folders, it simply provides three folders in the Dock — Applications, Documents, and Shared — that users access applications and files from. When opened, these folders have a simple, standard display, with none of the options that Finder windows typically have.

- **Only Allow Selected Applications.** If this option is selected, the Mac restricts the user to the applications listed below. The list has several categories preestablished: iLife, Internet, Widgets, Others, and Utilities. (Other compatible applications, such as iWork, appear in the list if you have installed them.) You can enable and disable a group by selecting or deselecting the check box to the group's left. To enable or disable individual applications in a group, expand the group by clicking the disclosure triangle to the left of its name to get a list of all applications in it. Then select or deselect the applications as desired. (Note how the group's check box changes to – when it contains a mix of enabled and disabled applications. To quickly find a specific application, enter some or all of its name in the search box above the right-hand side of the applications list.

- **Can Administer Printers.** If selected, the user can add or change printers and fax modems.

- **Can Burn CDs and DVDs.** If selected, the user can create CDs or DVDs by using the Mac's drives.

- **Can Change Password.** If selected, the user can change his or her own password to log in. (You can always override the password if desired as explained in Chapter 23.)

- **Can Modify the Dock.** If selected, the user can change what appears in the Dock in his account. (This option does not affect the Dock for other users.)

Tip

If you want to control access to the Web, e-mail, and instant messaging, be sure to disable any Web applications other than Safari, any e-mail applications other than Apple Mail, and any instant-messaging applications other than iChat. That's because Mac OS X 10.6 Snow Leopard has parental controls for Web, e-mail, and instant messaging access only for these three Apple programs that come with Mac OS X.

FIGURE 20.11

An example of Simple Finder, which provides a limited set of Mac OS X capabilities suited for small children and other inexperienced users

Content pane

In the Content pane of the Parental Controls system preference, you have the following options, as shown in Figure 20.12:

- **Hide Profanity in Dictionary.** If selected, profane ("dirty" or "swear") words are hidden in the information displayed in the Dictionary application (see Chapter 8).

- **The Website Restrictions area of the Content pane.** This provides controls over limiting access to Web sites that contain sexual, profane, and other "adult" content, as follows:

  - **Allow Unrestricted Access to Websites.** By selecting this option, you are letting the user access any site on the Web — that is, imposing no restrictions.

  - **Try to Limit Access to Adult Websites Automatically.** By selecting this option, you can set the Mac to automatically filter Web sites that it detects inappropriate content on. (Note that there's no guarantee that it will block all such sites, and it may also mistakenly block legitimate sites.) If you select this option and click Customize, you can add sites that you will always allow access to and those you will not allow access to, regardless of the Mac's own "judgment").

- **Allow Access Only to These Websites.** By selecting this option, you can restrict the account to specific Web sites that you specify. Click the + iconic button and then enter the URL for the approved site. (To make it easier to enter the URLs, we suggest you open a bookmark list in your browser or in TextEdit and copy each URL in turn into the list). Mac OS X provides a starter list of sites that Apple suggests are suitable for children. You can remove any you don't approve of by selecting them one at a time and clicking the – iconic button.

Caution

The Content pane's Web filtering works only with Apple's Safari browser, so you should disallow access to other browsers in the System pane of the Parental Controls system preference.

FIGURE 20.12

The Parental Controls system preference's Content pane

Mail & iChat pane

In the Mail & iChat pane, you can specify whether to limit the user's ability to exchange e-mail and instant-messaging chats with the addresses you specify. First, specify what you are limiting by selecting the Limit Mail and/or Limit iChat options at the top of the pane.

Then click the + iconic button to add a user, then enter the first name, last name, and address, as Figure 20.13 shows. You can add several e-mail, AIM (AOL Instant Messenger), and/or Jabber addresses for each user: Enter the address in the field, select the type of address in the adjacent popup menu, and then click the + iconic button to open a new row for a new address. (To delete one address for an approved person, select it and click the – iconic button.) Click Add when done.

Note

You cannot modify an approved person's entry once added. Instead, you must delete it by selecting the person in the list and clicking the – iconic button; then create a new entry for that person by clicking the + iconic button and reentering all the information.

By entering an e-mail address in the Send Permissions Requests To text field, you tell the Mac OS to automatically send you an e-mail when this restricted user tries to contact someone not on the approved list.

Caution

The Mail & iChat pane's Web filtering works only with Apple's Mail and iChat programs, so you should disallow access to other e-mail and instant-messaging applications in the System pane of the Parental Controls system preference.

FIGURE 20.13

Adding an approved person for e-mail and chatting in the Parental Controls system preference's Mail & iChat pane.

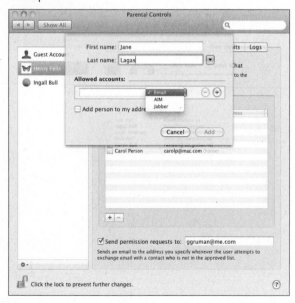

Time Limits pane

In the Time Limits pane, you can make sure your kids, or other users, aren't using the computer instead of sleeping or doing other activities. Figure 20.14 shows the options:

- **Weekday Time Limits section.** In this section, select the Limit Computer Use To option to have Mac OS X stop this user account from working after the amount of time you specify in the adjacent slider is reached. Note that the Mac OS tracks the total time used each day, even if the user logs in and out throughout the day.

- **Weekend Time Limits.** In this section, select the Limit Computer Use To option to have Mac OS X stop this user account from working after the amount of time you specify in the adjacent slider is reached.

- **Bedtime.** In this section, select the School Nights option to set the times during which the Mac cannot be used (typically, when you want your child to be asleep) from Sunday night through Thursday night. Use the adjacent time fields to select the specific times. Select the Weekend option and its adjacent time fields to set when during Friday and Saturday nights that the Mac cannot be used.

Note

The Bedtime settings can be used for any time periods you choose, not just nighttimes. So if you don't want your kids to use the computer during the days on weekends, you could restrict the times to, say, between 10 p.m. and 6 p.m., so the user could use the Mac only on weekend evenings.

FIGURE 20.14

The Parental Controls system preference's Time Limits pane

Logs pane

In the Logs pane, you can track the user's Web site, application, and chat activity, as Figure 20.15 shows. Use the Show Activity For popup menu to control how much of the user's activity is displayed. Use the Group By popup menu to choose how the activity is organized in the display, by date or application.

To get details on specific activities, select which of the four types of activities you want to see the logs for by selecting it in the Log Collections list: Websites Visited, Websites Blocked, Applications, and iChat. The details for that collection appear in the Logs pane. To get details on which type of activity — such as for each application — was used, expand the log by clicking the right-facing triangle icon, as shown in Figure 20.15.

If you decide that an activity is inappropriate — for example, if the user is chatting too much — you select the item in the log and click Restrict to turn off access to the application used for that activity. If you want to see what that application's state is, such as to read e-mails in Mail or see what music and videos are in iTunes, select the application in the log and click Open to launch it.

FIGURE 20.15

The Parental Controls system preference's Logs pane

Settings management

There are several options for managing parental control settings by using the accounts list at the left of the Parental Controls system preference.

If you are setting similar restrictions for multiple user accounts, select the first user account for which you have completed the settings, then click the gear-shaped iconic popup menu and choose Copy Settings for "*username*". Then select the user account you want to copy these settings to, click the gear-shaped iconic popup menu, and choose Paste Settings to "*username*".

You can set Mac OS X 10.6 Snow Leopard to let you manage parental controls remotely from another Mac that has access to this one over the network. To do so, select the Manage Parental Controls from Another Computer option. This option enables a parent to adjust parental controls or monitor activity from work while the child is home, for example, or check on the computer in a child's bedroom from her Mac in the family room.

This option is available in three locations:

- When you first open the Parental Controls system preference, before any user account is selected, the Manage Parental Controls from Another Computer option displays in the main pane. Select it.

- Select a Managed with Parental Controls user account, click the Action iconic popup menu (the gear icon), and choose Allow Remote Setup.

- Select either the Guest Account or a Standard user account to see it. The main pane in the system preference will indicate that parental controls are not on for this account, and provide an option to turn it on. Don't do so, but do select the Manage Parental Controls from Another Computer option.

However you turn on this option, you're enabling the remote control for all Managed with Parental Control user accounts.

Finally, you can disable parental controls for a selected user account by clicking the Action iconic popup menu (the gear icon) and choosing Turn Off Parental Controls for "*username*". (This is the same as deselecting Enable Parental Controls option in the Accounts system preference's Password pane.)

Summary

The Mac OS supports multiple user accounts. This enables businesses to give IT staff administrator privileges on all Macs, as well as enables parents to establish separate accounts for their kids, guests, and others at home. Each account can be given different privileges and access rights, controlling access to files, applications, and Internet services such as e-mail, Web pages, and instant messaging.

The default user account has administrator privileges, giving it control over all other accounts. The default user should establish password protection on his or her account, as well as other users' accounts, to prevent misuse of the Mac by unauthorized users.

Users can adjust personal settings, such as the images used to represent them, as well as set up the applications that launch when they start or log in to their user accounts on the Mac.

User accounts can be one of several types, including Administrator, Standard, Managed with Parental Controls, and Sharing Only. The Mac's administrator — and there can be several — can change any other user's settings. A Standard user can manage only his or her account's settings. A Managed with Parental Control user's permissions are determined by an administrator using the Mac OS's parental controls. The special Guest Account automatically deletes all files saved in that account when the user logs out, making it ideal for occasional users such as babysitters and your kids' friends; its privileges can also be restricted by using parental controls.

A Sharing Only user can only connect to file shares as determined through the Mac OS's file-sharing controls. You can also set up account groups, which makes file sharing easier to manage for all types of users.

There are several ways to switch among user accounts, including restarting the Mac into a different account, logging out of the current account and logging into a different account, and using the fast-switch capability to let a new user log in while keeping previously logged in users' accounts active. In this third approach, applications continue to run for logged-out users.

The Parental Controls system preference enables administrators to restrict the applications that other accounts can use, as well as set time limits and restricted use hours for the Mac on a per-user basis. These controls also enable the administrator to decide how much control each account has over printers, the Dock, CD and DVD creation, and its own password.

The parental controls also can restrict access to specific Web sites or Web sites deemed inappropriate for children, as well as restrict who the user can correspond with via e-mail and instant messaging. But these three controls work only with Apple's Safari, Mail, and iChat applications, not with alternative products.

Administrators can monitor the activities of accounts to which parental controls have been applied, such as seeing the data and times for accessed applications, Web sites blocked, and logs of chat sessions. Administrators can also open applications used by the parentally controlled users to see their state, such as the e-mails sent and received and the music and video downloaded.

To ease the management of parental controls, administrators can apply settings from one user to other users, as well as allow access to the Mac's parental controls from a remote Mac. This enables a parent to adjust parental controls or monitor activity from work while the child is home, for example.

Setting System Preferences

T he Mac is ready to run out of the box, but you need to adjust anything with as many capabilities as Mac OS X 10.6 Snow Leopard to
the peculiarities of your equipment, software, environment, and, yes,
personal preferences. You use the System Preferences window to do this customization work.

Mac OS X has 26 system preferences you can adjust. And each system preference has multiple settings within it, so you can make hundreds of customization decisions. That's a lot, and attests to the Mac OS's flexibility, but
don't worry about facing so many options. You can adjust system preferences
at any time, choosing which you want to adjust — and leaving alone the
ones you don't want change.

There are several other Mac OS preferences you can adjust that are not found
in the System Preferences window. You can adjust what displays in the
Finder windows, as well as adjust the access permissions and other attributes
of your Mac's drives, both of which are covered later in this chapter. You can
also adjust the fonts available to your applications, as explained in Chapter
22, plus you can add and remove applications from the Dock, as explained
in Chapter 2.

Adjusting System Preferences

To change system preferences, you open the System Preferences application
by choosing ➪ System Preferences. You get the window shown in Figure
21.1. The 26 standard Mac OS system preferences appear, as do any system

preferences installed by any of your applications or hardware. (For example, Mac notebooks have the Trackpad system preference, while desktops do not. If you connect a pen-based tablet to your Mac, you'll see the Ink system preference. And if your Mac has FibreChannel storage drives, you'll see the FibreChannel system preference.)

New Feature

Gone in Mac OS X 10.6 Snow Leopard is the QuickTime system preference. The Internal system preference has been renamed Language & Text, and the Keyboard & Mouse system preference has been split into two system preferences: Keyboard and Mouse.

By default, the system preferences are organized by category: Personal, Hardware, Internet & Network, System, and Other. (Other is where your non-Apple system preferences are stored, and this category appears only if you have non-Apple system preferences installed.) To get an alphabetical arrangement of your system preferences, choose View ➪ Organize Alphabetically.

When you are in a system preference, it may not be clear how to go back to the System Preferences application window. The easy way is to click the Show All button at the top of the window, or click the left-facing arrow iconic button. (Those arrow buttons let you move backward or forward through the system preferences you've opened, like the Back and Forward buttons in a Web browser.) You can also Control+click or right-click the System Preferences icon in the Dock to get a popup menu of all system preferences, or choose the desired system preference from the System Preference application's View menu; these two approaches are especially handy when the System Preferences application window is obscured on-screen by other windows.

You can also just start typing the function you are looking for while in the System Preferences application window; doing so activates the search window and highlights the system preferences most likely to have what you are looking for.

Tip

In each system preference's window, click the Help iconic button (the ? icon) to get basic help on the system preference's settings.

Note

Many system preferences — Accounts, Date & Time, Energy Saver, Network, Parental Controls, Print & Fax, Security, Sharing, Startup Disk, and Time Machine — require that you provide your account login password to change them. If the Lock iconic button (the bronze lock icon) at the system preference window's lower left is closed, click it; you'll be asked for your account password to allow changes to this system preference. The Lock iconic button displays an opened lock, so you know you can make changes; click it again to require a password for further changes.

FIGURE 21.1

The System Preferences application window

Personal preferences

The group of personal preferences focuses mainly on preferences about how you like to work, such as the language you use, what Finder features, such as Spaces, you want active; what the desktop background and is, and so on. But the best way to distinguish personal preferences from the others is that these preferences are stored as part of a user's profile, so if you have set up your Mac for use by multiple users (what the Mac OS X calls *accounts*, as explained in Chapter 20), each user can have separate personal preferences. The other preferences affect all users.

Appearance

Use this system preference to customize the appearance of the Finder and other windows. Figure 21.2 shows the Appearance system preference. The options are largely self-explanatory, with options to change the color of buttons and highlighted text, to determine the placement of the arrow iconic buttons on windows' scroll bars and determine other scrolling behaviors, to determine how many recent applications and other items display in the Recent Items list (accessed by choosing ➪ Recent Items), and to manage how text is displayed on LCD monitors.

We prefer to place the scroll arrows together because that makes it easier to switch between scrolling up and down — no need to move the mouse great distances to switch between them. Note that smooth scrolling looks nicer but can slow down your Mac when you scroll documents and file lists, so you might want to leave it deselected.

The Use LCD Font Smoothing When Available option really does make the text on an LCD monitor look nicer, so we recommend you keep that setting. Do note that some applications, notably those from Adobe Systems, have their own font-smoothing options, but enabling both does no harm.

FIGURE 21.2

The Appearance system preference

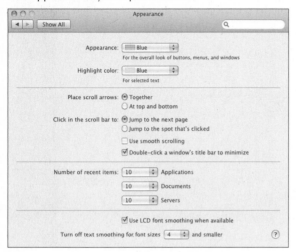

Desktop & Screen Saver

People love to show off pictures, and their computer screen is often used as a really big frame for doing so. Knowing this about people, Apple includes several dozen desktop backgrounds that give your Mac's screen a distinct look — and you can add your own images as well.

In the Desktop pane (shown in Figure 21.3), select from any of the images in the list at left. Each of the six Apple folders — Desktop Pictures, Nature, Plants, Black & White, Abstract, and Solid Colors — has an assortment of backgrounds you can use. Just click the desired image within its folder.

Or you can use your own images. To access images in the Pictures folder, click the disclosure triangle next to the Folders label in the Sidebar, then click Pictures. Add images from elsewhere on your Mac by clicking the + iconic button below the list, then navigate to the desired image. If you select a folder that contains images, the folder will be added to the Folders list, making all its images available. (Select an image or folder, then click the – iconic button to delete the image or folder from the list. Don't worry: The actual file or folder is not deleted from your Mac.)

Use the untitled popup menu above the thumbnail images in the Folders list to determine how the selected image is displayed. The best option is the default, Fill Screen, which makes the image fit the screen without distorting it, though some of the image may not display if one dimension — height or width — is greater than the corresponding dimension on the Mac's display. (By contrast, the Stretch to Fill Screen option distorts the image but does not cut any part out.) The other options are Fit to Screen, which fits the image as best it can but can leave gaps on the sides; Center, which displays the image at actual size and leaves a solid background around the four sides; and Tile, which repeats the image in a grid to fill the desktop (usually the ugliest option).

You should know about a few other controls in the Desktop pane as well:

- **The Change Picture option.** If this option is selected, the Mac OS X automatically replaces the desktop picture with the next one in the list. It will cycle through every image available, based on the schedule you select in the Change Picture popup menu.

- **The Random option.** This option is available only if Change Picture is selected, and the pictures change in random order, not in the order they appear in the list at left.

- **The Translucent Menu Bar option.** This option enables some of the desktop background to appear behind the Apple menu bar. This can be distracting if you have a dark image under that bar, so you may want to disable this option in that case.

FIGURE 21.3

The Desktop & Screen Saver system preference, with its Desktop pane at left and its Screen Saver pane at right

 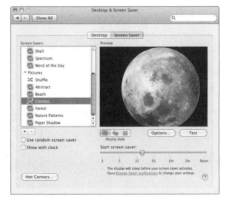

You use the Screen Saver pane (also shown in Figure 21.3) to set what happens to your screen display after the computer is idle. Screen savers began as a way to prevent *burn-in*: An image would etch itself into your screen after several hours, leaving a ghostly imprint over your display. A screen saver uses either a changing series of images, or a single image that moves across the screen, to prevent this. Burn-in was a hazard of early CRT monitors, but has not been an issue in years. Today, a screen saver is more a fashion statement and a way to let colleagues who come to your desk when you're not there know you've been away for a while.

You choose your desired screen saver image from the list at left, which includes several images from Apple. Note that if you use the Shuffle option, you are presented a list of Apple-provided screen savers; select the ones you want the Mac OS X to pull from as it shuffles the images. If you double-click an item in the list, you get various display options such as Cross-Fade between Slides, Message, and Delay; these options vary based on the type of screen saver selected. (You can also click the Options button instead to get these options.)

As with the Desktop pane, use the + and – iconic buttons to add and delete sets of images from the list. You can bring in a folder of images, subscribe to an RSS feed, or go to an Apple Web site page that enables you to buy image sets.

In the pane, you have several options for your screen saver:

- **Select the Use Random Screen Saver option to have the Mac OS X choose images randomly from the image list.**

- **Select the Show with Clock option to have Mac OS X place a clock on the screen saver display.**

- **Use the Start Screen Saver sliders to select how long the system must be idle before the screen saver begins.** If this setting will start the screen saver after the Energy Saver system preference has put the monitor to sleep, the Mac OS displays a note to that effect under the slider, with a link that opens the Energy Saver system preference. If you don't adjust the Start Screen Saver slider and/or the Energy Saver system preferences so the screen saver starts before the monitor is put to sleep, the screen saver simply won't turn on — the display sleep setting "wins" over the screen saver setting.

- **Click Hot Corners to associate a command with each of the four corners of the screen.** Then when you move the mouse all the way into that corner, that command executes. This feature is identical to the controls in the Exposé & Spaces system preference, so we cover the settings there.

- **Click the Options button to open a sheet of options specific to the selected screen saver.** These options vary widely, from setting the speed of an effect to choosing an RSS feed source. Note that some screen savers have no options, so the Options button is grayed out in these cases.

- **Choose from the three Display Style iconic buttons to determine how the screen image displays.** (Note that these options are available only if you select a picture from the Screen Savers list.) Slideshow presents each image in the set in order. Collage creates a collage dynamically from the images. And Mosaic creates a grid of images from the set.

Click Test to see how your screen saver will display with the options you've selected.

Note

The Screen Saver system preference does not reduce your display's power consumption when idle. Use the Energy Saver system preference to turn your monitor off while it is idle to reduce your power usage.

Dock

The Dock system preference, not surprisingly, controls the Dock that provides quick access to applications. Its options are straightforward:

- Use the Size slider to set the size of the Dock's icons.

- Select the Magnification option and then adjust its slider to make the Dock item that your mouse is hovering over larger (so you know your mouse is over it).

- Select the Left, Bottom, or Right option in the Position on Screen control to determine at which edge of the screen the Dock will display.

- Use the Minimize Window Using popup menu to determine how an open application's window shrinks into the Dock when you minimize it (by clicking the yellow – icon in the window's upper left). Your choices are Scale Effect and Genie Effect; try each to see which effect you prefer.

- Select Animate Opening Applications to make their Dock icons bounce as they are loading (so you know they are loading).

- Select Automatically Hide and Show the Dock to make the Dock disappear while you are not using it. (To open it, move your mouse to the very edge of the screen where it displays, as you selected via the Position on Screen control.)

Exposé & Spaces

The two panes in this panel — Exposé and Spaces — determine how these two Mac OS X applications work. Figure 21.4 shows the system preference.

Let's start with the Exposé pane. Your first set of options is Active Screen Corners. Here, you set what action occurs when you place your mouse all the way in the selected corner. There's a popup menu for each corner, set by default to –, which means no action. For each corner, your options are All Windows, Application Windows, Desktop, Dashboard, Spaces, Start Screen Saver, Disable Screen Saver, and Put Display to Sleep.

In the Exposé area, you set the keys and mouse button clicks that trigger the various Exposé display options. The left-hand popup menu sets the key, while the right-hand popup menu sets the mouse click. The All Windows option toggles the display of windows for all running applications and open folders, the Application Windows option toggles the display of windows for the currently active application, and the Show Desktop option toggles between showing the desktop only and the open applications and folders.

In the Dashboard area, you set which key and mouse button hide and show the Dashboard (see Chapter 8).

If any of your choices conflict with other key or mouse button assignments, a yellow !-in-a-triangle icon appears next to the affected option.

You use the Spaces pane to control the display of spaces, which let you group applications and then toggle among them to keep screen clutter down when you have lots of applications running. To turn Spaces on, select Enable Spaces; to see an icon in the menu bar of which space is currently active, select Show Spaces in Menu Bar.

By default, Spaces is set to allow four spaces, but you can change that by clicking the + and – iconic buttons in the Rows and Columns area to increase or decrease the number of spaces.

FIGURE 21.4

The Exposé & Spaces system preference, with its Exposé pane at left and its Spaces pane at right

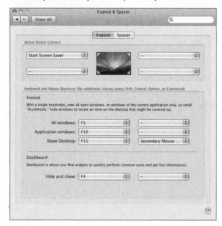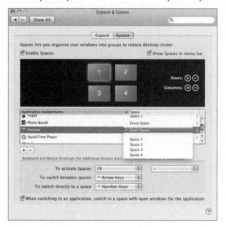

In the Assignments area, you choose which applications belong to which space. If an application does not show up in the Assignments list, click the + iconic button to add it. To remove an application from the list, select its name and then click the – iconic button. To actually assign an application to a space, select the application and then use the adjacent popup menu to select a specific space or Every Space (so it is always displayed).

In the Keyboard and Mouse Shortcuts area, you can set keyboard shortcuts to control the display of Spaces. The To Activate Spaces option enables you to set both a keyboard's shortcut and a mouse button click to toggle Spaces off and on. (Spaces must be enabled for this to work.) The Switch Between Spaces popup menu enables you to choose which key to hold to navigate through the spaces by using the arrow keys; your choices are Shift, Option, and ⌘. If you choose ⌘, you would press and hold ⌘ and then press the arrow keys to move among the spaces. Similarly, the Switch Directly to a Space popup menu enables you to choose which key you hold — Shift, Option, or ⌘ — in combination with a number key to select a specific space to jump to. For example, if you choose Option, pressing Option+3 jumps to space 3.

There's one more option to know: When Switching to an Application, Switch to a Space with Open Windows for the Application. When you open an application from the Dock or Finder, this tells the Mac OS X to open the space in which that application has open windows. The idea is that the space where an application has open windows is the one you are actively using.

Language & Text

The Language & Text system preference deals primarily with language settings, but also deals with associated attributes such as calendars and currencies. As Figure 21.5 shows, it has four panes.

New Feature

The Language & Text system preference had been called the International system preference in previous versions of Mac OS X.

In the first pane, Language, you select the languages available to the Mac OS. At left is a list of all available languages; drag a language to change the order in which it appears in the language lists the Mac OS may present to you in various settings. To edit what languages appear, click Edit List and in the sheet that appears, deselect any languages you don't want to appear, and select any languages you do want to appear.

At the right-hand side of the pane is the Order for Sorted Lists popup menu. This menu enables you to choose the sort order — the alphabetization order or equivalent — for sorted lists.

In the second pane, Text, you control several aspects of text entry. Note that these features work only with applications designed to use them, including Apple's TextEdit, iWork, iChat, and iMovie. But expect more applications to support these new features over time.

New Feature

The Text pane is new Mac OS X 10.6 Snow Leopard. Its Word Break popup menu had resided in the Language pane in previous versions, and now has additional options. The symbol and text substitution options, as well as the Spelling and Smart Quotes popup menus are new to Mac OS X 10.6 Snow Leopard.

Using the Symbol and Text Substitution pane, you can tell Mac OS X what text to automatically substitute with other text, such as automatically replacing (c) with ©. Mac OS X comes with several substitutions predefined; those that are selected in the On column are active, meaning that when you type the text in the Replace column, Mac OS X automatically substitutes the text in the With column. You can add your own substitutions by clicking the + iconic button at the bottom of the pane, then entering the "before" and "after" text in the Replace and With columns, respectively. To delete a substitution, select it and click the – iconic button. To disable but not delete a substitution, just deselect it. Click Restore Defaults to undo all changes you've made to the Symbol and Text Substitution pane and return to the Mac OS X defaults.

On the right-hand side of the pane are the rest of the text-control options:

- **Spelling.** This popup menu lets you override the spelling dictionary used by compatible applications. The default option — Automatic by Language — uses the spelling dictionary for whatever language you have selected in the application for the text you are working on or, for applications that don't let you choose a working language, that is at the top of the list in the Language pane of the Language & Text system preference. The Spelling popup menu lets you select a specific language and force the use of its spelling dictionary no matter what language you are working in.

- **Word Break.** This popup menu lets you select how the Mac OS determines where words break, so when you double-click text it knows what to select. For most people, the default option of Standard should be kept. Two of the menu options — Greek and Japanese —

are useful when you work primarily in another language despite what is set as your primary language in the Language pane. The other available option — English (United States, Computer) — modifies the normal English rules of using patterns of spaces and breaks (such as paragraph returns) to determine where words break to also handle some of the unique conventions in programming languages. For example, in a programming language, the text *aKey:aValue* is considered to be two words (*aKey* and *aValue*), with the colon indicating where the word break is. But in normal English, *aKey:aValue* is considered to be one word, so double-clicking it selects the entire string. Thus, a programmer would choose English (United States, Computer) as his or her Word Break option.

- **Smart Quotes.** These two popup menus let you choose what quotation marks are used when you type " and ' on the keyboard around words. In English, the standards are *"abc"* and *'abc,'* respectively, but this popup menu lets you choose the standards for other languages, such as *«abc»* and *‹abc›* used in continental French for quotations.

FIGURE 21.5

The Language & Text system preference, with its Language pane at upper left, Text pane at upper right, Formats pane at lower left, and its Input Sources pane at lower right.

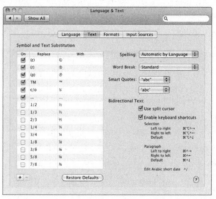
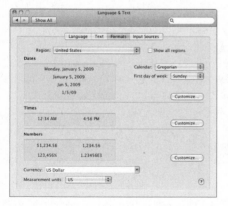

In the third pane, Formats, you choose the basic formats for dates, time, numbers, and money. When you choose your region or country from the Region popup menu, Mac OS X chooses the standards for that region or country. (By default, a list of common regions displays; select Show All Regions to see the complete list.)

You can override the defaults for your chosen region by using the controls below the Region popup menu. For example, if you're in the United States but use a different calendar than the standard Gregorian calendar, choose that new calendar in the Calendar popup menu. You can customize the calendar display, such as always abbreviating months' names, by clicking the Customize button. There's a Customize button for time display as well (such as how to display a.m. and p.m.), and one for numbers (such as whether thousands are separated by commas).

There are also two popup menus that control the measurement systems for money (the Currency popup menu) and whether the Mac OS X's default units are English, such as feet and pounds, or metric, such as meters and kilograms (the Measurement Units popup menu).

The fourth pane, Input Sources, tells the Mac OS what keyboards and equivalent input sources to use. Check the input sources for each language you use; note that some languages have different keyboard options and may have multiple versions to choose from. You can select as many input options as you want.

New Feature

The Input Sources pane in Mac OS X 10.6 Snow Leopard had been called Input Menu in previous versions, and now has several new controls. Also, the Character Palette is now called the Character Viewer (but is otherwise unchanged).

Note that the language you chose as your primary language when you installed Mac OS X is at the top of the language list, enabled and grayed out, so it is always active and cannot be turned off. If you select one or more additional input sources to the primary one, the Input Source iconic popup menu appears in the menu bar, displaying the flag of your primary input's country. This menu also includes an option to open the Language & Text system preference.

Do note the Keyboard & Character Viewer option at the top of the input sources list. It adds to the Input Source iconic popup menu options to open the Character Viewer and Keyboard Viewer panels for access to special characters (see Figure 21.6 and Chapter 22). It also adds a menu option to open the Keyboard system preference.

Note

If you select the Keyboard & Character Viewer option — but do not select additional input sources — the Input Source iconic popup menu uses the Character Viewer icon (an asterisk in a box).

If you have a tablet attached to your Mac, you also have the Ink Server option at the top of the input sources list; you use this the Ink Server input source for handwriting recognition in pen-based tablets. (If you have such a tablet connected to your Mac, you'll also have a system preference called Ink that enables you to configure the handwriting recognition.)

FIGURE 21.6

The Character Viewer (left) and Keyboard Viewer (right) are two of the on-screen input sources you can use for accessing special characters.

New Feature

How Mac OS X determines the icon and menu options in the Input Source iconic popup menu has changed in Mac OS X 10.6 Snow Leopard and is now based on the selections in the Input Sources pane. Also, the bidirectional text capabilities in the Input Sources pane display only if you have chosen at least one left-to-right language (such as English or French) and at least one right-to-left language (such as Hebrew or Arabic) from the list of input methods, as Figure 21.5 shows. (These options also used to be on the Language pane in previous versions of Mac OS X.)

New Feature

In Mac OS X 10.6 Snow Leopard, the Ink Server input source now appears only if a pen tablet is connected to the Mac, and the Japanese Kana Palette is now handled as part of the Character Viewer. If you have a Multi-Touch trackpad, you get the Trackpad Handwriting option, as the sidebar "Touch-based Chinese Handwriting" in Chapter 22 explains.

The Input Source Shortcuts section of the pane shows the keyboard shortcuts that let you navigate among language input sources: ⌘+spacebar to go to the next input source and Option+⌘+spacebar to go to the previous input source. If you have selected multiple language input sources, the Keyboard Shortcuts button becomes available so you can change these defaults; clicking it opens the Keyboard system preference's Keyboard Shortcuts pane.

Use the Input Source Options radio buttons to choose whether the current input source applies to all open documents or whether you want to assign different input sources to each document.

Finally, if you have selected both a left-to-right language (such as in Western languages like English and French) and a right-to-left language (such as Arabic, Hebrew, and Persian) as input sources, the Bidirectional Text section (shown in Figure 21.5) appears with these options:

- **Use Split Cursor.** This option for bidirectional text, if selected, displays a split cursor that indicates a boundary between text using left-to-right reading order and right-to-left order. When moving the cursor through documents that contain both left-to-right and right-to-left text, the cursor changes where the reading order changes, so you can choose which direction to go at the boundary.

- **Enable Keyboard Shortcuts.** This option for bidirectional text, if selected, enables shortcuts for moving within text selections and among paragraphs, as well as for editing the Arabic short date format. (The shortcuts are visible in Figure 21.5.)

Security

Use the Security system preference to control access to your Mac and the data stored on it. The system preference has three panes: General, FileVault, and Firewall.

In the General pane, you control how to wake up the computer when it is asleep or its screen saver is active. Select Require Password __ After Sleep or Screen Saver Begins to reduce the chance of someone walking by your idle Mac and start using it. Use the popup menu within this option to select how much time must elapse before a password is required; the default option is Immediately.

New Feature

The ability to set a delay for requiring a password to wake the Mac from screen saver or sleep mode is new to Mac OS X 10.6 Snow Leopard.

Most of the other options in the General pane are self-explanatory: Disable Automatic Login, Require a Password to Unlock Each System Preferences Pane, and Log Out After __ Minutes of Inactivity.

The Use Secure Virtual Memory option, if selected, protects information such as passwords that are usually stored in the Mac's memory but are sometimes written to disk in a temporary file when the memory is needed for other applications. That temporary file is called *virtual memory*, and because it is a file, it is available to programs that might be secretly installed on your Mac looking to snag your passwords. The Use Secure Virtual Memory Option protects that temporary file, but also slows down your Mac slightly; we recommend you use it.

If you deselect Disable Remote Control Receiver, you should pair the remote control that came with your Mac so only it can control your Mac. (Otherwise, any remote control can.) To do so, click Pair and follow the instructions in the sheet that appears. The button changes to Unpair; if you click it and do not select Disable Remote Control Receiver, any remote can control the Mac.

New Feature

Gone from this pane in Mac OS X 10.6 Snow Leopard is the Don't Allow This Computer to Wake for Network Access option. This is now handled exclusively in the Energy Saver system preference via its Wake for Network Access option.

The second pane, FileVault, encrypts the data stored in your Home folder (typically, the one with your name; it has a house icon next to it in the Sidebar's Places section when you open a Finder window) so no one else can read the data without your login password. (Encryption basically scrambles your data, so if someone copies it, he or she can't read it. You and the Mac can read it, because the Mac has the decryption, or unscrambling, key to use when you access the files.)

To enable FileVault, click the Turn On FileVault button. If you don't have a master password set for the computer, you are asked to create one. (You can also click Change to add one before clicking Turn On FileVault.) Before Mac OS X actually enables encryption, it displays a sheet with the Use Secure Erase, which deletes your Home folder's unencrypted contents after the encrypted version is created, so there's no old data to be snooped.

New Feature

When you enable FileVault you no longer have the Use Secure Virtual Memory option; FileVault now uses whatever you set for Use Secure Virtual Memory in the General pane.

Click Turn on FileVault to start the encryption process, which can take quite a bit of time. It also requires a lot of free disk space; if you don't have enough available, you get an error message that stops the process.

Caution

FireVault and Time Machine do not work well together, making it difficult to back up your Mac. Also, FileVault can notably slow down your Mac. Chapter 23 explains the pros and cons of FileVault in more detail.

The third pane, Firewall, protects your Mac from intruders who come from the Internet and/or your network to try to get into your Mac. Click Start to enable firewall protection; click Stop to disable it. To configure what the firewall blocks, click Advanced to open a sheet of options, as shown in Figure 21.7.

By default, Mac OS X allows all incoming connections that use Apple Filing Protocol (AFP), which permits other Macs and other computers that support AFP to connect to your Mac, subject to any restrictions you establish in the Sharing system preference.

New Feature

Mac OS X 10.6 Snow Leopard changes how the options in the Firewall pane are configured. Plus, it adds two new options: Automatically Allow Signed Software to Receive Incoming Connections and Enable Stealth Mode.

You block all incoming connections by selecting the Block All Incoming Connections option; this blocks even connections permitted in the Sharing system preference. But the name is misleading; this option does not block the services that Apple considers essential: the DHCP (Dynamic Host Configuration Protocol) connection used to give your Mac an address on the network, the Bonjour service used to connect to network printers and similar devices, and the IPSec (Internet Protocol Security) service used to protect the data your Macs sends to the network.

The settings sheet for the Security system preference's Firewall pane

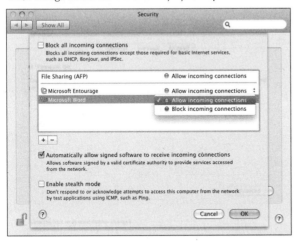

You can specify how to handle other connections, such as e-mail connections from a Microsoft Exchange Server, by adding them to the window in the middle of the sheet. Click the + iconic popup menu to add a service, choose the application that uses it (such as iCal or Microsoft Entourage) from the dialog box that appears, then set the permissions from the popup menu to the right of the application name. Your permissions choices for each application are Allow Incoming Connections and Block Incoming Connections.

The Automatically Allow Signed Software to Receive Incoming Connections option, if selected, can reduce the configuration effort for deciding what applications' incoming connections are permitted. This option lets applications that use a certificate accept connections even if not in the sheet's list. Such certificates are configured on the servers that handle the communications, typically by an IT department.

The Enable Stealth Mode option, if selected, essentially hides the Mac from applications that use the Internet Control Message Protocol (ICMP) to find computers, printers, and other devices on a network. This protocol is handy to help network administrators monitor their networks, but it can also be abused by hackers to find poorly protected computers. (Chapter 23 covers security techniques in more depth.)

Spotlight

Spotlight is the Mac's internal search function — that field in the upper-right of the Finder window preceded by a magnifying glass icon. The Mac searches its files for whatever text you type there. In the Spotlight system preference's Search Results pane, you select the types of files that you want Spotlight to search, and deselect those you don't want it to search. You can also change the order in which Spotlight displays its search results by dragging the categories within the list; the order of the list is the order in which the results will display in the Spotlight results.

The Privacy pane enables you to tell Spotlight what folders and disk drives not to search. Click the + iconic button to add folders and drives; select a folder or drive from the list and click the – iconic button to remove it from the Privacy list (and thus make it searchable).

Both the Search Results and Privacy panes also let you assign keyboard shortcuts to begin a Spotlight search and to open a Finder search window.

Hardware preferences

You can manage the Mac's hardware by using hardware system preferences. Note that two hardware system preferences — Ink and Trackpad — appear only if you have the compatible hardware installed (a pen-based tablet and a trackpad, respectively).

CDs & DVDs

Use the CDs & DVDs system preference to set up the Mac's default behavior when you insert a CD or DVD into its drive. There are five conditions you can configure the default behavior for, using the following popup menus:

- When You Insert a Blank CD
- When You Insert a Blank DVD
- When You Insert a Music CD
- When You Insert a Picture CD
- When You Insert a Video DVD

In each case, you have the following options:

- **Select the Ask Me What to Do menu option to have the Mac prompt you as to what to do when the condition occurs.** This option is available only for the When You Insert a Blank CD and When You Insert a Blank DVD menu options.

- **Select one of the preferred applications listed to handle the specific condition, such as choosing iTunes as the option for When You Insert a Music CD.** This way, iTunes automatically opens when you insert a music CD.

- **Assign your own application for the condition by choosing Open Other Application, which then enables you to navigate through the Applications folder to choose the default application for that condition.**

- **Have the Mac run a script, instead of an application, by choosing Run a Script.** This enables you to navigate through the Mac (it starts in the Public folder) to choose the default AppleScript for that condition.

- **Have the Mac do nothing, by choosing Ignore.**

Displays

You use the Displays system preference to adjust how your monitors display their images. Figure 21.8 shows the system preference's Display and Arrangements panes.

The system preferences vary if you have more than one monitor connected to your Mac; the Arrangements pane won't appear if you have just one monitor. And if you have multiple monitors, a separate Displays system preference window opens for each one. Whether you have one or more monitors attached, each Displays system preference shows the name of the monitor. (Color LCD is the name for a Mac laptop's built-in LCD screen.)

Note

If you have a Mac laptop with an external monitor connected, and you've closed the laptop lid, the built-in LCD screen turns itself off. In that case, when you open the Displays system preference, you won't see any controls for that LCD screen — the Mac OS essentially thinks it's disconnected. If you open the laptop lid, the Mac OS will detect the built-in LCD screen and provide the controls for it in the Displays system preference.

FIGURE 21.8

The Displays system preference's Display pane (left) and Arrangement pane (right)

 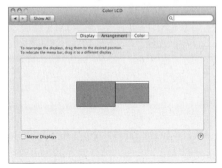

The Display pane enables you to set the resolution for the monitor's display by selecting one of the options in the Resolutions list at left. The higher the resolution, the more information is crammed into the screen, which of course makes each element smaller. Typically, you should leave the resolution set to the default resolution because it usually provides the best balance between readablity and workspace amount; the Mac OS autodetects the default resolution when you first connect a monitor.

Use the Colors popup menu to change the depth of color available: Millions is the default, but you can also choose 256 Colors and Thousands. It's been years since monitors could not display millions of colors, so this control is pretty much irrelevant today.

Likewise, the Refresh Rate popup menu is a legacy control you can usually ignore. First, LCD monitors only support one refresh rate (60 hertz), so the control is irrelevant for any LCD monitors. Second, if you do have an old-style CRT monitor, chances are that it runs at the maximum 75 hertz setting (which provides the most stable image) and can be left at that setting; only very old CRTs can't run at that rate. In the case of a Mac's built-in LCD screen, the Refresh Rate popup menu grays out and displays n/a; that's because the Mac knows that screen's refresh rate settings cannot be changed.

Use the Rotation popup menu to rotate the entire screen display. You use this option rarely, such as when you want to physically turn a monitor so it's standing higher than wider and rotate the display accordingly, turn the display upside down so someone standing in front of you can read the display, or use the monitor with an old-style projector that inverts the displayed image.

If you have multiple monitors connected to your Mac (and turned on), a separate Displays window appears for each, with the name of the monitor in each window's title bar. Often, each monitor shows the Displays window for itself. If you want all the Displays windows to be brought together onto one monitor, go to the Displays window for the monitor you want them all to display on and click Gather Windows in its Display pane.

If you want to manage basic monitor settings without opening the Displays system preference, select the Show Displays in Menu Bar option; you see a monitor icon in the menu bar from which you can change screen resolution and open the Displays system preference. (The Number of Recent Items menu option enables you to choose how many recently used screen resolutions display in the selection list.)

If your monitor supports remote control from the Mac, you see the Brightness slider, which enables you to increase or decrease the monitor's brightness instead of using the brightness controls built into the monitor itself. And if your monitor has a built-in iSight camera — standard on a Mac laptop or iMac — you may also see the Automatically Adjust Brightness as Ambient Light Changes option (depending on your Mac model); select it to have the Mac automatically adjust the screen brightness based on the available light. In a dark room, for example, this setting reduces the screen's brightness, while in a brightly lit room, it increases the brightness to help the image not be washed out by that ambient light. This setting is very helpful if you work in a place that is lit by natural light, given that light changes throughout the day and based on the weather.

Click Detect Displays if the Mac doesn't automatically recognize a monitor you've connected to it.

In the Arrangements pane, you tell the Mac how your multiple monitors are physically arranged, so it can arrange the display properly across them. The monitor with the white bar at the top is the "main" monitor, the one in which the Dock and System Preferences will appear; you can drag that to any monitor to make it the "main" monitor. You change monitor arrangements by dragging them around until their arrangement matches their physical arrangement on your desk or wall. You can arrange monitors side by side and/or top to bottom.

If you want to mirror the displays — typically when you have connected a monitor for a presentation to others but still want to use your laptop's screen to run the presentation — select the Mirror

Displays option to have the Mac superimpose a number on each connected monitor, so you can see what order they are arranged in. This matters because the Mac has no idea what the physical arrangement of your monitors is, and makes a guess on how they are arranged and then displays the screen across them. If it guesses wrong, you could move the mouse off the right-hand side of one monitor only to see it appear on the monitor to its left, not the one to its right. (You rearrange the way the Mac tiles the screens in the Arrangements pane.)

Note

If you use an Apple Cinema Display monitor, you get a unique pane — Options — in the Displays system preference. In the Options pane, you can turn off or on two buttons on these displays: the Power button and the Display Preferences button.

The other pane in the Displays system preference is the Color pane. Here you choose which color profile to use for the monitor, as well as view the profile settings. (You need to be a color expert to make any sense of those settings.) For the most accurate color display, be sure to use the color profile specific to your monitor; in some cases, you may need to install this profile from a CD or download a file provided by the manufacturer, while in other cases, Apple supplies the profile with the Mac OS.

Over time, monitors drift away from their profile's color settings, and what they display no longer precisely matches what the Mac "thinks" they are displaying based on their profiles. This is particularly true of old-style CRT monitors. There's another cause for such display drift: The lighting in your environment can wash out the colors you see, or having strongly colored walls can confuse your brain and distort the accuracy of the colors you see, even if the monitor is displaying them in a technically correct way. No matter what might be making what you see different than what the Mac "thinks" it's displaying, you can use the Display Calibrator Assistant utility to make what you see and what the Mac "thinks" you're seeing closer.

To do so, click Calibrate in the Displays system preference's Color pane. The Display Calibrator Assistant opens. Follow its instructions; when you're done, the utility generates a new profile for your monitor that makes it display colors accurately in your specific environment. You might want to run this utility once a year or when you make significant changes to your workspace's lighting or color scheme. Figure 21.9 shows some of the adjustments the utility helps you detect and then make.

New Feature

Long-time Mac users may notice that the screen looks a bit brighter in Mac OS X 10.6 Snow Leopard. That's because it's set to display more vividly; Apple has changed the default gamma setting from 1.8 to 2.2. (A gamma setting sets the color range and thus the vividness of the monitor.) If you prefer the old setting, run the Display Calibrator Assistant and change the gamma setting to 1.8 in the Native Gamma pane.

FIGURE 21.9

The Display Calibrator Assistant utility generates a color profile for use in the Displays system preference's Color pane that helps increase the color accuracy of your monitor. Shown here are two of the steps in that calibration process.

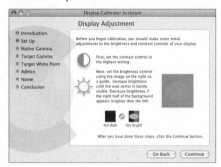
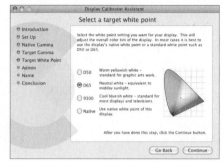

Energy Saver

Electronic equipment can suck down power, which is costly both in terms of money and also in terms of environmental damage. The Energy Saver system preference, shown in Figure 21.10, enables you to reduce your energy usage. If you have a Mac laptop, you'll get two panes — Battery and Power Adapter — so you can set the energy usage settings independently, with settings for when you are plugged in and ones for when you are running on battery power. For desktop Macs, you get just one pane.

For desktop Macs and for the Power Adapter pane for laptops, you have the following options:

- Use the Computer Sleep slider to determine how many minutes of inactivity put the entire Mac to sleep.

- Use the Display Sleep slider to determine how many minutes of inactivity puts the monitor — often the greatest user of power for computers — to sleep. If you make this value larger than the Computer Sleep value, the Energy Saver panel automatically adjusts the Computer Sleep setting to match the Display Sleep setting.

- Select the Put Hard Disk(s) to Sleep When Possible option to let the Mac save energy whenever it can when the disk drives are inactive. Because drives can restart very quickly, selecting this option rarely makes your Mac feel sluggish.

- Select the Wake for Network Access option so your IT administrator or a network device can wake your Mac over the network, such as to change settings or back up your files remotely.

- Select the Automatically Reduce Brightness Before Display Goes to Sleep option to have the Mac OS turn down the screen brightness when it has been idle for a while but before the Display Sleep idle time has been reached. This saves power but makes the screen turn back on faster in that "twilight" idle time.

- **Select the Start Up Automatically after a Power Failure option if you want the Mac to restart if the power goes out.** You would choose this if you were running the Mac unattended, such as for use as a server. (If you are running an application unattended, the application won't relaunch after that startup unless it's in your Login Items list, as set in the Accounts system preference.)

If you don't like your settings and want to start over, or are unsure what settings to use, click the Restore Defaults button to undo your settings changes and have Apple's recommended settings used instead.

Tip

A laptop Mac switches automatically to its battery if the power goes out, which could drain the battery if the laptop is left unattended. You may want to remove the battery when you leave your Mac laptop running unattended for more than an hour or so to prevent that from happening.

Note

One energy-saving option not available in the Energy Saver system preference is available in the Keyboard system preference's Keyboard pane: the ability to turn off the backlighting for the keyboard (on Macs that have such illumination).

On a laptop, the Battery pane has the same options, with the following three exceptions:

- **There is no Wake for Network Access option.** This is because you're not likely to be on the company network when running on battery power.

- **There is no Restart Automatically after a Power Failure option.** This is because the only power failure that would occur when running on battery power is that the battery runs out of power, in which case it can't restart the Mac.

- **There is an additional option: Slightly Dim the Display When Using This Power Source.** This option both saves power and gives you a visual cue when you are working on battery power (handy if the power cord has been pulled out and you don't realize it).

If your have a laptop Mac, the Energy Saver system preference also provides an option to display the battery status in the menu bar.

Typically, you would set the Computer Sleep and Display Sleep times to be smaller for the Battery pane's energy-saving savings to minimize unnecessary power usage.

The Energy Saver system preference offers one more control, and it is one that can help save energy but also provides convenience: the capability to schedule when the Mac turns on and off (or goes to sleep and wakes up). Click Schedule to get a sheet of options, as shown in Figure 21.10. To set a startup or wakeup time, select Start Up or Wake, then choose what days (Every Day, Weekdays, Weekends, or a specific day) and at what time to start up or wake up at. To turn off a Mac or put it to sleep at a scheduled time, select the option preceding the second row, and then choose the desired action in the adjacent popup menu: Sleep, Shut Down, or Restart; set the days and times for the desired action as well. Click OK to save the schedule. To disable the schedule, deselect the options.

The scheduling options in the Energy Saver system preference

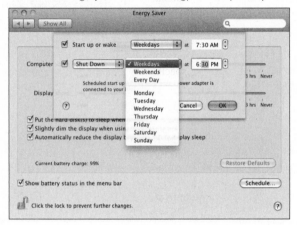

The capability to schedule the Mac's on/wake and off/sleep times can save energy by turning off computers that employees leave on when they go home. It also can have their — or your — Macs up and running when they — or you — arrive at the office (or while you are pouring your coffee at home or getting the kids ready for school). What you can't do is set a complex schedule, such as separate startup and shutdown times for weekdays and for weekends.

Note that the schedule only takes effect when the Mac is plugged in, not when it is running on battery power. Also note that if you are using the Mac past its off/sleep time, you will get an alert and a chance to stop the Mac from being turned off or put to sleep.

FibreChannel

Available only if your Mac has FibreChannel drives attached (such as on a Mac Pro or an Apple Xserve), this system preference enables you to set the basic settings for your FibreChannel drives and the communication with a FibreChannel storage network, such as the connection setting (Automatic, Arbitrated Loop, or Point-to-Point).

Ink

If you connect a compatible pen-based tablet to your Mac, you should see the Ink system preference. It enables you to control pen input, such as whether to perform handwriting recognition and how to handle various pen strokes. The key control is Handwriting Recognition, which you can set to On or Off. The system preference itself has three panes:

- **General.** You use this pane to tell the Mac how closely spaced your handwriting is (to help it better decipher what you write), what language you are writing in, how to determine when you are switching from using the pen to write to using the pen as a mouse, and which fonts to use to display the converted handwriting.

- **Gestures.** You use this pane to set the special pen strokes used to indicate actions, such as cutting text, pasting text, entering a tab, or selecting all text.

- **Word List.** You use this pane to enter special words (such as technical terms) that the Mac OS X would not find in its own handwriting-conversion dictionaries.

Note that not all applications support handwriting; those that do typically will display an Ink toolbar that enables you to select special commands (such as clicking a button for the ⌘ key when using the pen) and perhaps require you to write your text in a specific area, reserving a separate area for the converted text for you to correct or accept.

Keyboard

It's easy to take the keyboard for granted, but when you look at the Keyboard system preference, you realize how much it actually does. This system preference has two panes: Keyboard and Keyboard Shortcuts.

In the Keyboard pane, shown in Figure 21.11, you'll likely want to set the Key Repeat Rate and the Delay Until Repeat rate sliders. When you hold a key, the Mac OS will keep "typing" that key for you. You set how many times per second it does so via the Key Repeat Rate, while you set how long it waits to begin repeating the key via Delay Until Repeat. If you tend to let your fingers linger on keys, you might want to move the Delay Until Repeat closer to the Long end of the slider to avoid inadvertent repeated keystrokes.

The Mac automatically assigns the function keys — those whose names begin with *F*, such as F1 and F12, and thus sometimes called F keys — to specific actions. (Some keyboards include symbols to indicate what those default actions are.) But you many want to save those function keys for other purposes — particularly if your Mac is acting as a terminal to a Windows, Unix, or other server that uses those F keys for other purposes. If you select the Use All F1, F2, etc. as Standard Function Keys option, the Mac will not do its normal actions when you press the function keys. (In that case, hold the Fn key when pressing those keys to get the default actions: for example, press Fn+F4 to open the Dashboard.)

If your Mac has automatic backlighting for its keyboard, turn that feature on by selecting the Illuminate Keyboard in Low Light Conditions option. To avoid wasting energy, use the slider below that option to tell the Mac how long to wait after the last keystroke to turn off that backlighting; it will turn back on as soon as you begin typing again.

The final option is Show Keyboard & Character Viewer in Menu Bar. If this option is selected, you can access these two quick-access panels to special characters from the Input Sources iconic popup menu in the menu bar. (These viewers are covered in the section on the Language & Text system preference in this chapter.)

At the bottom of the Keyboard pane are two buttons:

- **Set Up Bluetooth Keyboard.** Click this button to open a sheet from which Mac OS X scans for a Bluetooth keyboard. If it finds one, the keyboard's name appears in a list. Click Continue to establish a connection (called pairing) between the Mac and the keyboard.

- **Modifier Keys.** Click this button to open a sheet where you can change the behavior of the standard Mac modifier keys: Caps Lock, ⌘ (Command), Option, and Control. You can assign any of these four keys to any of those four purposes, as well as disable any of these keys by choosing No Action. Few people have a need to reassign these keys. If you have multiple keyboards, you can customize their modifier keys separately, by choosing a keyboard from Select Keyboard popup menu. (Laptop users are most likely to have multiple keyboards: the one embedded in the MacBook and an external keyboard kept on the desk.)

New Feature

The Set Up Bluetooth Keyboard button replaces the Bluetooth pane found on earlier versions of Mac OS X; the display of the keyboard's battery status that had been in that pane is now available only via the menu bar's Bluetooth iconic popup menu. The ability to set separate modifier key settings for different keyboards is also new to Mac OS X 10.6 Snow Leopard.

FIGURE 21.11

The Keyboard pane (left) and the Keyboard Shortcuts pane (right) in the Keyboard system preference

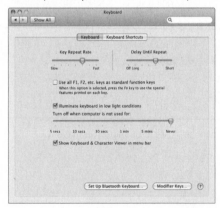

The second pane, Keyboard Shortcuts, enables you to turn on and off keyboard shortcuts used by the Mac OS, plus reassign existing shortcuts and create new ones. The left side of the pane has a list of shortcut types: Dashboard & Dock, Exposé & Spaces, Front Row, Keyboard & Text Input, Screen Shots, Services, Spotlight, Universal Access, and Application Shortcuts.

Select the desired group to get a list of its shortcuts in the right-hand part of the pane. Then select the check box for a shortcut to turn it on; deselect it to turn off a shortcut. To change a shortcut, double-click the shortcut itself from the list, then type the new shortcut. A yellow exclamation-mark-in-a-triangle icon appears if the shortcut is used elsewhere so you know you have more than one menu item using the same shortcut. (You can restore the default shortcuts by clicking Restore Defaults.)

New Feature

The grouping of shortcuts, as well as the inclusion of Services, is new to Mac OS X 10.6 Snow Leopard. So is the ability to assign new shortcuts to applications.

You can also add new shortcuts in this pane:

1. Click the + iconic button to open a sheet where you specify the new shortcut.

2. Using the Application menu, choose the specific application for which the shortcut should be available, or choose All Applications.

3. In the Menu Title text field, enter the exact name of the menu option you want the shortcut to invoke. For example, if you want to add a shortcut to Address Book's Delete Card menu option in its Edit menu), enter **Delete Card**.

4. In the Keyboard Shortcut text field, enter the shortcut you want to assign to this menu option.

5. Click Add.

Note that as you add shortcuts, they appear in the Applications set of shortcuts, which opens automatically as you enter a new shortcut. Any shortcuts available to all applications display under the All Applications heading, while shortcuts assigned to a specific application appear under that application's name. Use the disclosure triangle to open and close the shortcut lists under each header.

Also note that some applications don't support Mac OS X's capability to assign new shortcuts. Even if you add a shortcut for such applications in the Keyboard Shortcuts pane, they will not work. One way to tell if an application supports your new shortcut is to see if its menu displays the shortcut you added; if not, it likely does not support such shortcuts. (The reason could also be that you mistyped the menu option name.)

To delete a shortcut, select it and click the – iconic button.

New Feature

In Mac OS X 10.6 Snow Leopard, the Keyboard Shortcuts pane adds a column at left that lets you choose a category for the shortcuts you want to change. Note that one of those categories, Services, doesn't let you change shortcuts but instead lets you define what services appear in an application's Services submenu, as Chapter 16 explains.

When you're working in dialog boxes and similar containers of controls, the Mac OS enables you to press Tab to move among text boxes and lists; you use the mouse to access other controls such as popup menus ands check boxes. If you want to access all controls by using just the keyboard, change the Full Keyboard Access setting to All Controls. (You can also press Control+F7 at any time to switch between the two tabbing approaches.)

Mouse

You use the Mouse system preference, shown in Figure 21.12, to set basic mouse behavior. The two settings that most everyone should adjust to their personal preferences are Tracking Speed and Scrolling Speed, both of which provide sliders to adjust their speeds.

Tracking is the speed at which the on-screen mouse pointer follows the movements of the actual mouse on your desk or other surface. The faster it is set, the farther across the screen the mouse pointer moves, which is great if you have little space on your work surface in which to move the actual mouse — but not so great if you need precise control such as when drawing. You should experiment with the settings to see what feels right most of the time.

Scrolling is the speed at which pages and so on move as you use the mouse's wheel.

The other mouse options are less frequently adjusted and are as follows:

- **Use the Double-Click Speed slider to set how quickly you must double-click a mouse button for the Mac to register it as a double-click action instead of as two separate clicks.** Most people should leave this near the Fast side of the slider, but if you find yourself struggling to double-click fast enough, slow this setting down until it feels natural.

- **Select the Left or Right option as the Primary Mouse Button option to determine which button on your mouse is the "regular" button, the one that you use to click or double-click.** The other button is then treated as a secondary button, where it is either ignored or used as a shortcut for Control+clicking (which opens a contextual menu). The most common reason to use the Right button as your primary mouse button instead of the default Left button is if you use your left hand to control the mouse.

- **Select the Zoom Using Scroll Wheel While Holding option to have the Mac zoom when you both scroll the mouse wheel and hold down whatever key — Control, Option, or ⌘ — is specified in the adjacent popup menu.** Click the Options button to control how the zoom works. In the sheet that appears, you get three choices for how the screen image moves as you zoom: along with the mouse pointer's location, only when the mouse pointer reaches the edge of the image (the default), or so the mouse pointer remains at the center of the image. You can also select Smooth Images so as you zoom in and out, the image doesn't "jump" from one size to the next but instead grows or shrinks smoothly. This smoothing can slow down your Mac, which is why you can always press Option+⌘+\ to turn smoothing on or off, to activate it only when desired, or to deactivate it when the smoothing slows the Mac down too much.

FIGURE 21.12

The Mouse system preference

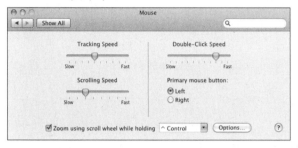

Print & Fax

Use the Print & Fax system preference, shown in Figure 21.13, to add printers and faxes to your Mac, as well as to set the default printer and paper size for all printers.

Select the Share This Printer with Other Users on the Network option to make the selected printer available to other users, but note that when they print to shared printers through your Mac, your Mac may operate more slowly as it processes the print job. You can restrict which printers are available and who may access them by clicking Set Permissions, which opens the Sharing system preference. (The Set Permissions button appears only if you have selected Share This Printer with Other Users on the Network.)

If you click Options & Supplies, you get a dialog box with three panes. The General pane enables you change the printer name and add a location label (handy in an office where you might add a location label such as "5th Floor South"). Some printers have their own management utilities; if so, the Open Printer Utility button may appear in the General pane to give you access to that printer's own management tool. The Driver pane enables you to choose which printer driver to use for the printer (typically because the printer was installed without the right driver available or because you want to use an updated version of the driver). The Supply Level pane shows information on the paper and toner available, but only if the printer communicates that information to the Mac.

Chapter 17 explains in detail how to set up printers and faxes, as well as how to work with the print queue.

FIGURE 21.13

The Print & Fax system preference

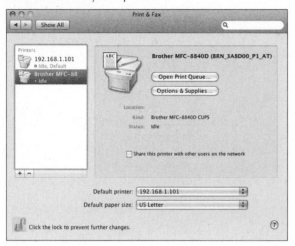

Sound

You use the Sound system preference to control the noises your Mac makes, as well as how it handles audio inputs and outputs. Figure 21.14 shows the Sound system preference. All three panes in the Sound system preference — Sound Effects, Output, and Input — have the Output Volume slider to control how loudly audio is played by the Mac (select the Mute option to turn off audio output altogether), as well as the Show Volume in Menu Bar option that, if selected, adds a slider to the menu bar that enables you to easily adjust output volume at any time.

The Sound Effects pane controls the alert and other feedback sounds the Mac makes. In the Select an Alert Sound area, select the sounds you want the Mac to make when it displays alerts. (Double-click a sound to hear it — be sure the Mac's volume is loud enough for you to hear it.) Use the Alert Volume slider to set how loud the alert sound plays relative to the Mac's overall output volume (which you set in the Output Volume slider).

Tip

To add your own sounds to the list of alert sounds, add them to the Library/Sounds folder for the current user — not to the Library folder at the root or System levels. The sounds must be in Apple's AIFF format, a format that the Garage Band application supports.

If the Play Alerts and Sound Effects Through popup menu is set to Selected Sound Output Device, the alert sounds will play through whatever audio output is currently selected. If you want to have these sounds always play through a specific device, choose it from the popup menu instead.

You can control several settings related to sound effects generated by the Mac:

- **Play User Interface Sound Effects.** Select this option to have the Mac use its special sounds for key activities such as emptying the trash or taking a screen shot by using the Grab utility (see Chapter 8).

- **Play Feedback When Volume Is Changed.** Select this option to have the Mac play a special sound when you increase or decrease the volume.

- **Play Front Row Sound Effects.** Select this option to have the Mac play the special sounds in the Front Row media player application.

FIGURE 21.14

The Sounds Effects pane (left) and Input pane (right) of the Sound system preference. (The Output pane, not shown, is very similar to the Input pane.)

 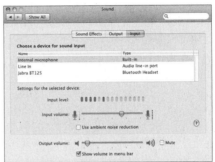

The Output pane lists all audio output devices available, such as speakers, headsets, and recording devices. Select a device from the list, and any controls appear below. Many devices offer a Balance slider, which enables you to adjust the balance between the right and left speakers.

You use the Input pane to control how the Mac receives and processes audio. Any connected audio inputs display in a list. Select the desired input to adjust its settings. In all cases, you see the Input Level indicator, which shows whether the input device is picking up any audio and, if so, at what volume, as Figure 21.14 shows. Use this indicator to make sure the audio device is receiving audio correctly. Practically every input device will also display the Input Volume slider, which you adjust as needed to get the sound level high enough to be heard clearly, while not being so loud that it overloads the sound processor and creates distortion. Some devices offer the Ambient Noise Reduction option that, if selected, tries to remove background noise from what the Mac "hears."

Trackpad

If you have a Mac laptop, or an external trackpad attached to your Mac, you will have the Trackpad system preference. It is similar to the Mouse system preference, with additional features specific to trackpads. The Tracking Speed, Double-Click Speed, and Scrolling Speed sliders and the Zoom While Holding option work identically to those in the Mouse system preference (covered earlier in this chapter).

Figure 21.15 shows the Trackpad system preference. Note that the Multi-Touch trackpad's gesture-related options appear only on Macs that support gestures, such as recent MacBooks and MacBook Pros.

New Feature

Mac OS X 10.6 Snow Leopard makes the gestures of second-generation Multi-Touch trackpads available to first-generation Multi-Touch trackpads. So you may see new options in the Trackpad system preference related to support gestures.

All trackpad-equipped Macs have these pre-Multi-Touch gesture options:

- **Use Two Fingers to Scroll.** If selected, you must use two fingers to scroll via the trackpad. This option prevents accidental scrolling if you have a finger resting on the trackpad and your finger drifts. If you select Two Fingers to Scroll, you can also enable horizontal scrolling (by selecting Allow Horizontal Scrolling) and set the scrolling speed via the Scrolling Speed slider.

- **Zoom While Holding.** If selected, this works the same as the Zoom Using Scroll Wheel While Holding option in the Mouse pane of the Keyboard & Mouse system preference.

- **Clicking.** If selected, you can tap the trackpad to act as a mouse click. Enabling this option also enables you to select Dragging, which enables you to double-tap the trackpad and then drag across the trackpad without lifting your finger to drag the current object. If you also select the Drag Lock option, you must tap the trackpad to stop dragging the object; otherwise, you just have to lift your finger off the trackpad. The reason to consider selecting Drag Lock is if you have to drag items far beyond where your finger can move on the trackpad. In such a case, you would lift your finger off the trackpad and then put it down and drag more.

- **For Secondary Clicks, Place Two Fingers on the Trackpad Then Click the Button.** If selected, you can use gestures to Control+click or right-click by putting both fingers on the trackpad and then clicking the trackpad button.

The other option available for all trackpads is Ignore Accidental Trackpad Input. If this option is selected, the Mac ignores small finger movements and light touches, assuming they aren't intentional actions.

New Feature

Gone in Mac OS X 10.6 Snow Leopard is the Ignore Trackpad When Mouse Is Present option, so you cannot have the trackpad disable automatically when a mouse is connected.

If your Mac has a Multi-Touch trackpad, you have more options:

- **One Finger.** In this section, select the gestures you want to do with one finger: Tap to Click, Dragging, and Drag Lock.

- **Two Fingers.** In this section, select the gesture you want to do with two fingers: Scroll, Rotate, Pinch Open & Close, Screen Zoom (which lets you hold down a modifier while swiping you hand up or down on the trackpad to zoom the entire display in or out), and Secondary Click (a right-click). The Options button next to Screen Zoom lets you change Screen Zoom's modifier key (by default it is ⌘), as well as specify under what circumstances the feature is available and whether to smooth the edges of images and text while zooming.

- **Three Fingers.** There's just one option in this section: Swipe to Navigate, which lets you page forward (swipe to the right) or backward (swipe to the left).

- **Four Fingers.** The Swipe Up/Down for Exposé gesture opens Exposé when you swipe up and closes it when you swipes down. The Swipe Left/Right to Switch Applications gesture lets you switch to other applications using the application switcher (see Chapter 7), but controlling it with gestures instead of the mouse or keyboard.

- **Video preview.** To the right of the gesture options is a preview window that plays a video of the selected gesture so you can see how it works.

New Feature

Mac OS X 10.6 Snow Leopard makes the three- and four-finger gestures of second-generation Multi-Touch trackpads available to first-generation Multi-Touch trackpads. So you may see new options in the Trackpad system preference related to these gestures.

FIGURE 21.15

The Trackpad system preference for non-Multi-Touch trackpads (left) and for Multi-Touch trackpads (right)

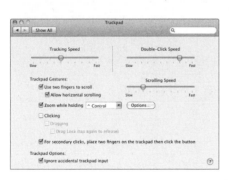

Mac OS X's Menu Bar Icons

Several system preferences install icons in your menu bar that provide shortcut access to various controls. The figure here shows the menu bar icons that various system preferences can install. Note that the Date & Time menu bar icon can be any of three choices: the time, the day and time, or a clock icon. Also note the Input Source menu bar icon displays as a flag if you have multiple languages selected as input sources in the Language & Text system preference, rather than displaying the Character Viewer icon as shown here.

To use one of these menu bar items, just click it and a popup menu of options appears. The system preferences offer an option to turn off or on the display of these menu bar icons; look for an option called Show *description* in Menu Bar in the relevant system preferences' panes. Selecting the option displays the menu bar icon, while deselecting it removes the menu bar icon.

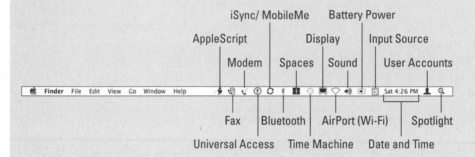

Note that other applications may install their own menu bar icons, which work the same way. But they may not have an easy way to remove them from the menu bar. Check the applications' preferences dialog box, as well as the menu bar icon's popup menu itself for an option to turn off their display.

Internet and network preferences

The Mac is a great control center for using Internet- and network-based services, and the four system preferences in this section are where you set the Mac up to work with the rest if the world.

Bluetooth

Bluetooth is a wireless data technology that enables devices to communicate over short distances, typically less than 15 feet. You see it mainly in hands-free headsets for cellphones, but Macs come with their own Bluetooth radio so you can wirelessly connect various devices, such as PDAs and smartphones for sharing information, headsets for use as a wireless headphone and microphone, wireless printers, GPS location devices, and wireless input devices such as mice and keyboards.

Caution

When turned on, Bluetooth can quickly drain a laptop's battery, so turn Bluetooth off when you are not using it.

Cross-Ref

Several parts of this book cover the many aspects of Bluetooth. Chapter 8 covers the iSync application used to synchronize data between the Mac and Bluetooth-connected devices. Chapter 12 covers setting up Bluetooth networks that enable your Mac to use Bluetooth devices as a modem, while Chapter 13 covers the Bluetooth File Exchange utility that enables you to share files with Bluetooth devices. Later in this chapter, we cover the Sharing system preference in which you set up the Bluetooth file-sharing preferences.

Use the Bluetooth system preference to manage how Bluetooth devices connect to your Mac. (To have your Mac connect to a Bluetooth device, such as to use a cellular phone as a modem, use the Bluetooth settings in the Network system preference, as detailed in Chapter 12.) Figure 21.16 shows the Bluetooth system preference with the detailed information for a configured device. For Bluetooth to work on your Mac, the On option must be selected in the Bluetooth system preference. Even then, nothing will happen until you've paired the Mac with a compatible Bluetooth device.

Tip

Be sure to select the Show Bluetooth Status in the Menu Bar option so you can tell at a glance whether Bluetooth is active on your Mac and whether devices are connected. In the menu bar, you see a stylized B iconic popup menu that shows you what is connected, provides submenus of configuration options and battery status for each connected device, and enables you to turn Bluetooth on and off.

Pairing means to establish a two-way connection, which you can do from either end of the connection. To have a device find your Mac and initiate pairing, your Mac must be *discoverable*, meaning it is broadcasting its name and availability. Select the Discoverable option in the Bluetooth system preference to make the Mac discoverable. More typically, though, you'll initiate the pairing from your Mac because you have the benefit of a screen, mouse, and keyboard to manage the pairing process.

Caution

Turning on the Discoverable option can pose a security risk, as it makes it easy for other devices to find and connect to your Mac via Bluetooth.

To pair a device, make sure it is set up as discoverable, then click the + iconic button in the Bluetooth system preference. The Mac searches for discoverable Bluetooth devices and lists those it finds in the Bluetooth Setup Assistant dialog box that appears; select the desired device and click Continue, following the instructions, which vary based on the device you're pairing. (If the device is not displaying but you know its device ID, you can enter it manually by clicking Specify Device.) When done, you are returned to the Bluetooth system preference, where your paired devices appear in the list at left, as Figure 21.16 shows.

Note

Click the – iconic button to delete a Bluetooth device's connection to your Mac.

You see device information, such as connection status, in the pane at right. If a device has a Connected status of Not Connected, you must tell the device to connect to your Mac; not all devices do this automatically, and the method for initiating a connection varies from device to device, so check your device manual.

FIGURE 21.16

The Bluetooth system preference showing detailed device information for a headset

You manage a paired Bluetooth device by selecting it in the list at the left of the Bluetooth system preference and then clicking the Action iconic popup menu (the gear icon), as Figure 21.16 shows. The options in this menu vary based on the device's capabilities and its connection status. But at the very least you'll see a Show More Info option, which provides deep detail as to the device's abilities and status. You'll typically also see a Disconnect option and either a Use device name or Do Not Use device name menu option, based on whether the device is in use.

If you select Show More Info, more options appear in the Action iconic popup menu (the gear icon), as shown in Figure 21.16, and the Show More Info menu options changes to Hide More Info. Two options are worth noting.

First, the Add to Favorites option enables the Mac to pair to a device in the future, because that device won't have to be discoverable for the Mac to find it again. (The Remove from Favorites option undoes that simplified re-pairing.)

Second, the Edit Serial Ports enables you to configure the connection to Bluetooth devices that support multiple capabilities or are designed for PC connections that the Mac needs to be set to emulate. (Be sure to read the device's manual to understand these settings before adjusting them.) There are two technical methods, called *serial ports*, that devices use to communicate — RS-232 and Modem — and you can select those here when you want to override the default connection settings established when you paired the device. Figure 21.17 shows the setup window that appears after you choose Edit Serial Ports for a hands-free headset. In this case, the device can be used as a hands-free microphone/headset combo or just as a headset, so we've set it up to use the

RS-232 serial port for use as a hands-free unit and to use the Modem serial port for use as a headset. Click the + iconic button to add such serial port configurations, then adjust the options shown in the window. (Click the – iconic button to delete a selected serial port configuration.) Click Apply when done to save the changes.

FIGURE 21.17

Configuring a Bluetooth device's serial port settings

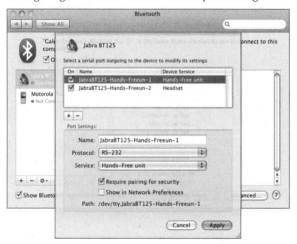

The Bluetooth system preference has two other sets of options of note.

First, click File Sharing Setup to turn on Bluetooth file sharing; this opens the Sharing system preference covered later in this chapter.

Second, click Advanced to open a sheet in which to set up the basic behaviors for Bluetooth on your Mac (for all devices):

- **Select the Open Bluetooth Setup Assistant at Startup When No Input Device Is Present option to have Mac OS X open the Bluetooth Setup Assistant when it can't find the wireless keyboard and mouse you previously set up.** (This way you know something's wrong and can correct it immediately).

- **Select the Allow Bluetooth Devices to Wake This Computer option to enable devices such as a keyboard and mouse to wake the Mac when it goes to sleep.** Otherwise, you'll have to connect a wired device to wake the Mac up, or open a laptop to use its built-in keyboard or trackpad. If selected, this option does not let other devices, such as a PDA or headset, wake the Mac up.

- **Select the Prompt for All Incoming Audio Requests option to force the Mac to alert you when a Bluetooth headset or other audio device tries to connect to it.** If you've set up your cellphone's Bluetooth headset to work with your Mac, you may want this option selected so the headset doesn't take over your Mac's audio when you didn't intend for it to do so (such as just because it happens to be in your pocket, for example).

- **Select the Share My Internet Connection with Other Bluetooth Devices option to enable Bluetooth devices to use your Internet connection.** This might make sense for a smartphone so you can bypass using your carrier's paid Web apps, but it can also let someone hijack your Internet connection.

- **Click the + iconic button to add additional serial ports for Bluetooth devices to use to connect to the Mac, and specify whether they use the RS-232 or Modem connection protocols.** You should add such serial ports to your Mac only if you have devices that require them. Select the On option for each serial port you want to make active, and select the Pair (key icon) option for each serial port that you want to require pairing for. To delete a serial port connection, select it and then click the – iconic button. (The default serial port is called Bluetooth-PDA-Sync and it can't be deleted.)

MobileMe

MobileMe is Apple's $99-per-year Web-based synchronization service, which enables you to synchronize files, data, and so on across multiple devices (Macs, Windows PCs, iPhones, and iPod Touches), as well as access that information from the Internet through a Web browser. For example, you can keep your calendars and address books synced across multiple computers and devices, and have files stored online (using the included iDisk service) so you can access them from any computer with an Internet connection. MobileMe stores all this data in a central location on the Internet that Apple manages; each time you sync a device, MobileMe copies new information to that central location, and then copies it to the other devices in your account as they sync to it. That way, all the devices end up having the same information, based on the master copy kept on MobileMe. (Chapter 15 covers how to use MobileMe in more depth.)

Note
MobileMe used to be called .Mac, so if you have a .Mac account, you have a MobileMe account.

You use the MobileMe system preference to set up how MobileMe works with your Mac. After signing into your MobileMe account, you get four panes in the system preference: Account, Sync, iDisk, and Back to My Mac.

The Account pane simply shows your account status, such as when your next annual renewal date is and how much capacity you have for storing e-mail in your MailMe e-mail box and how much storage you have available in your iDisk folder. You can also change account settings such as billing information and password by clicking the Account Settings button in this pane.

The Sync pane is the heart of MobileMe system preference, as shown in Figure 21.18. To enable syncing, select the Synchronize with MobileMe option and then choose how often you want the Mac to sync with the MobileMe service by choosing an option in the adjacent popup menu:

Automatically, Every Hour, Every Day, Every Week, or Manually. Click Sync Now to sync the Mac immediately, regardless of what the selected sync schedule is.

In the list of applications and data services, select those you want to sync across computers and devices. This determines what information is — and is not — synced, so go through the options carefully.

Tip

If you want to include an iPhone or iPod Touch in your MobileMe syncing, be sure that the device is already set up to sync to one of your computers via iTunes; then on your device, go to the Preferences app and add a new account in the Mail, Contacts, Calendars setting (select MobileMe as the account type). To include a Windows PC in your MobileMe syncing, be sure the PC has iTunes installed and that you have downloaded the MobileMe control panel from www.apple.com/mobileme/setup/pc/. (You also get the option to install it from the Apple Software Update utility that is installed on your PC with iTunes.) Click the Advanced button for additional controls that appear in an settings sheet.

- You will see a list of computers and devices being synced through this MobileMe account, as well as their last sync status. To remove a computer or device from the sync list (so it is no longer synchronized), select it from the list and click Unregister.

- Click Reset Data to override the synced data on the current Mac. You get a new dialog box. In its Replace popup menu, choose what data you want to replace: All Sync Info or one of the data sources selected previously. Then click ← to replace the information on the current Mac with whatever is stored at the MobileMe, or click → to replace the information stored at MobileMe with whatever is stored on the current Mac. Then click Replace to complete the data reset, or Cancel to leave the data alone.

FIGURE 21.18

The Sync pane of the MobileMe system preference

You use the iDisk pane to control the virtual disk drive that MobileMe provides, so you can place files on the Internet for access from all your MobileMe devices and even make them available for others to access. It can save you from not having a file you need because you left it on "the other machine." Figure 21.19 shows the iDisk pane.

The iDisk Usage indicator shows how much storage capacity you have on your virtual iDisk drive, so you know when it's time to start cleaning up files.

The Your iDisk Public Folder controls show you the Web address for your public folder, as well as enable you to set whether people can only read the files or can add their own (including replacing yours), and set what password must be used to access that public folder.

The final option is iDisk Sync, which enables you to keep a backup copy of the iDisk on your Mac so the files are accessible when you don't have an Internet connection, such as when you are in flight. Click Start to enable this local backup, and select Automatically or Manually to determine how often the iDisk backup is synced to your Mac.

FIGURE 21.19

The iDisk pane of the MobileMe system preference

The fourth pane, Back to My Mac, enables you to remote-control your Mac and access its data over a network or Internet connection from another Mac. Click Start to enable this feature. Every Mac that you want to control or control others from must have Back to My Mac enabled under the same MobileMe account.

With Back to My Mac enabled, you have to enable the controls you want to share, such as file sharing and screen sharing, in the Sharing system preference covered later in this chapter. You can jump to that system preference by clicking Open Sharing Preferences.

Caution

When Back to My Mac is turned on, some virtual private network (VPN) client software — usually used to connect remote workers to a business's internal servers — may not work. The Mac will usually give you an alert when a conflict occurs. In that case, switch off Back to My Mac when you need to use the VPN, then turn it back on when you are done with the VPN.

Network

To connect to the Internet or just other Macs and PCs, you need to be connected to a network. Use the Network system preference to manage your network settings. Most Macs have four separate network interfaces available, plus the ability to make dial-up connections to the Internet via a modem:

- **Ethernet.** This is the standard wired network connection, which uses a wider version of a phone connector called an RJ-45 jack. On the other end of the cable is typically a router, a box that manages all the traffic among the Macs and other devices such as PCs and printers. A special type of router — a DSL modem or a cable modem at home — also handles the connection between your network and the Internet. (There are also intermediary forms of routers called *hubs* and *switches*.)

- **AirPort.** This is Apple's brand name for the wireless networking technology known formally as IEEE 802.11a/b/g/n wireless and informally as Wi-Fi. It's basically a wireless version of Ethernet that is meant for sending lots of data to a wireless router that can be as far as 300 feet away.

- **External Modem.** This appears only if you've added an external USB modem to your Mac at some point in the past. You enter the phone number and other connection settings for that modem to connect to your dial-up service.

- **Bluetooth.** This is a short-range type of wireless network, typically used when you want to make your cellphone act as a modem for your Mac. Note that the Mac also uses Bluetooth to have other devices connect to it, such as headsets and printers; the settings for those kinds of Bluetooth connections are covered in the Bluetooth system preference section earlier in this chapter.

- **FireWire.** This is a wired connection (formally called IEEE 1394) typically used for attaching disk drives and video equipment that can also be used to create a network across Macs and PCs when you don't have a regular network to plug them into.

You can think of a network interface as a door through which connections are made.

Cross-Ref

Chapters 12 and 13 cover how to set up and manage networking on your Mac, so look there for detailed explanations of what the various Network system preference settings do. It also explains all those networking acronyms. Here, we stick to the basics. Also refer to Chapter 8's coverage of the Network Utility, which can help you troubleshoot your network and its connections to the Internet.

The Network system preference displays current information for each supported network interface, as Figure 21.20 shows. Click one of the connections in the list on the left to see the status in the main part of the pane. The Network system preference also enables you change the settings for each by clicking the Advanced button to get the settings sheet shown in Figure 21.21.

FIGURE 21.20

The Ethernet pane of the Network system preference

Most of the time, you can rely on the default settings for your network configuration, so chances are you will use the Network system preference only occasionally, such as when first setting up a connection in a new network. More likely, you'll use this system preference just to make sure that your network is functioning correctly, using the status indicators in its list of connections.

Tip

If you're not very familiar with networking, try clicking the Assist Me button to have the Mac walk you through the settings in a friendly Q&A approach.

Tip

If you use your Mac in multiple places, you can store separate settings for each. In the Location popup menu, choose Edit Locations to create a new set, give it a name, and click Done. (Use the Action iconic popup menu [the gear-shaped icon] to rename or duplicate an existing location.) Use the Location popup menu to switch to a different set. (You can also change locations at any time by choosing ⇨ Location; there's no need to go through the Network system preference.) Most of the time, though, Automatic works just fine for figuring out the network settings where possible.

But take a look at the four types of network connections to get an idea of what the Network system preference can do for you.

For Ethernet, you rarely have to adjust the settings because most networks use routers that manage the computers and other devices connected to them. The Configure IPv4 popup menu is typically set to Using DHCP, which tells the Mac to let the router manage its network connection. (DHCP stands for Dynamic Host Control Protocol, the technical standard for this management.) Choosing DHCP fills in the IP Address, Subnet Mask, and Router information, and it also usually fills in the DNS Server and Search Domains information as well — all of these ensure the Mac doesn't conflict with other network devices and that it is properly connected to those devices and to the Internet. If you choose one of the other options in the Configure IPv4 popup menu, you can manually set some or all of these settings — you'll need to get those proper settings from your network administrator. You can also choose Off to turn off Ethernet networking.

By clicking Advanced to get to the settings sheet, you can change even more settings in its six panes: TCP/IP, DNS, WINS, 802.1x, Proxies, and Ethernet.

FIGURE 21.21

The Ethernet pane in the Network system preference's settings sheet

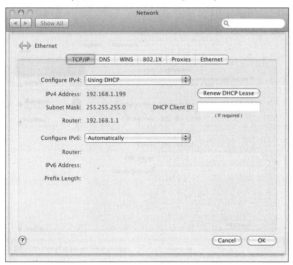

For wireless networking, the pane is simpler: There's the Network Name popup menu where you can select what available wireless network to connect to, where you can turn off the wireless network by clicking Turn AirPort Off, and where you can select the Show AirPort Status in Menu Bar option to get an iconic popup menu that enables you to select an available network or turn AirPort on or off without needing to open the Network system preference.

New Feature

In Mac OS X 10.6 Snow Leopard, the Network Name popup menu shows the relative signal strength for each available network, as does the AirPort iconic popup menu in the menu bar. The more radio waves in the icon, the stronger the signal. (You may also see a lock icon next to a network name to indicate wireless networks that require a password, though this is not new to Snow Leopard.)

By clicking the Advanced button, you get a settings sheet that has the same options as for Ethernet networking. The one special pane in this window is AirPort, which enables you to save and manage login connections to various wireless networks. (Mac OS X calls these saved connections *preferred networks* and lists them in its Network Names popup menu.) You can also determine the order in which the Mac tries to log in to these saved connections when it finds several available at the same time. (Click the + iconic button to add a saved connection, the – iconic button to delete the selected connection, and the Edit iconic button [the pencil icon] to edit the selected connection.) Other controls include having the Mac automatically add any network you establish a connection to the list of preferred networks, automatically disconnect from wireless networks when logging out a user account on your Mac, and require the administrator password to control the wireless connections (so the kids can't log on to a Wi-Fi hot spot without your okay).

For Bluetooth networking, the pane enables you to save and access connection settings (through the Configuration popup menu), plus enter the telephone number, account name, and password necessary to connect to a cellphone-based Bluetooth network. By clicking the Advanced button, you get a settings sheet that has many of the same panes as for an Ethernet connection, as well as the Modem pane in which you set up the specifics for whatever brand of cellphone you are using as a modem for your Mac.

Finally, for FireWire networking, the pane is identical to that for Ethernet networking; likewise, its settings sheet (which you access by clicking Advanced) has most of the same options as for Ethernet networking.

Three iconic buttons appear below the list of connections: + to add new network connections (also called *services* in the Network system preference, – to delete them, and Action (the gear icon) for other configuration options. Examples of network connections you would add would be a 3G cellular modem, a WiMax adapter, or a VPN connection to a corporate network.

Configuration options include duplicating services (so you can create a modified version of an existing one), renaming services, making services inactive, changing the preferred order of services (which dictates the order in which the Mac looks for active network connections to use), import and export configurations (so a Mac administrator can easily set up multiple Macs with the same settings), and create and manage virtual interfaces (meaning virtual LANs, or local area networks, which enables you to treat a network as if it were several networks, with different security and access settings for each virtual network on it).

Sharing

The Mac has long been a sharing-oriented computer, with the ability to share files, printers, and even access to the Internet with other Macs on your local network. Such sharing can be dangerous if it is not managed, especially now that people can come into your local network through the Internet and potentially access your computer without your knowledge. You use the Sharing system preference to control who gets access to what on your Mac.

Figure 21.22 shows four of this system preference's 12 panes. You select the desired pane from the Service list at left. You also enable which types of sharing are enabled by selecting the On check boxes in that list for those aspects you do want shared and deselecting those aspects you don't want shared. (Chapter 13 explains each of the sharing options in detail.)

FIGURE 21.22

The Sharing system preference, with four of its 12 panes. Top row: Printer Sharing (left) and File Sharing (right). Bottom row: Remote Management (left) and Bluetooth Sharing (right).

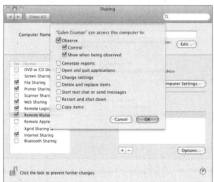
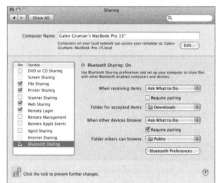

Caution

The Sharing settings open your Mac to anyone on your network. That is usually just someone in your home or office network. But it could be someone who's connected wirelessly over an unsecured wireless router. Or if you've given your Mac a static IP address that is available to the Internet through your router, then that network is available to anyone on the Internet. Be sure your network is secured, and that you know who has access to it so you can make the right choices in the Sharing system preference.

Note

In many cases, a Sharing pane will indicate an IP (Internet Protocol, or network) address for your Mac, so other users know what to connect to. The IP address is usually determined by your router, unless you set it up manually in the Network system preference. If set by the router, the IP address for your Mac can change over time, so you may need to double-check the address for your Mac in the Sharing or Network system preference and let those other users know when it has changed.

System preferences

The last group of Apple-supplied system preferences controls the behavior of the Mac OS's user interface.

Accounts

You use the Accounts system preference to set up user accounts for your Mac. In many cases, there is only one user (you), but you might set up multiple accounts on the same Mac for different family members so each member has his or her own independent space for files and applications. In a work setting, there might be a separate account for an administrator on each Mac.

The Accounts system preference has three main areas, as Figure 21.23 shows: the Password pane, the Login Items pane, and the list of user accounts on the left that appears in both panes.

In the list of accounts, the currently logged-in account is at the top under the My Account label and other configured accounts are under the Other Accounts label. If your account is set as an administrator — if Allow User to Administer This Computer is selected in the Password pane — you can modify the other accounts' settings; just select them to do so. Click the + and – iconic buttons to add and delete accounts, respectively. The list also includes two special items:

- **Guest Account.** This has its own settings that appear in an untitled pane. Select the Allow Guests to Log In to This Computer option so people can use your Mac without access to your files and any applications you've installed to your account only. You might do this for the babysitter so he or she can browse the Internet and play iTunes music, but not open your e-mail or work files. Select the Enable Parental Controls to further restrict what a guest can do by using the Parental Controls system preference covered later in this chapter (click Open Parental Controls to jump to those settings). By default, a guest may access any files in your shared folders, unless you deselect the Allow Guests to Connect to Shared Folders option.

- **Login Options.** This also has its own settings that appear in an untitled pane. Here, you can set the Mac to automatically log in to a specific user account (via the Automatic Login popup menu), rather than requiring the user to sign in each time he or she boots the Mac. You can also control whether the list of accounts in the sign-in list at startup displays a list of users that you click from or forces the user to type in her username and password. Other options for the login screen are Show the Restart, Sleep, and Shut Down Buttons; Show Input Menu in Login Window, which enables users to switch to a different language's keyboard; Show Password Hints, which shows the password hint for each account; Use VoiceOver in Login Window, which makes the Mac read aloud the options for visually impaired users (see Chapter 6); and Show Fast User Switching Menu As, which adds a menu to the menu bar that enables you to quickly log out of your current account and log in to another one. Finally, the Directory Services button enables you to set which directory services to use to determine who can log in and what the user's settings are; this option enables a business to manage these settings from a central location.

FIGURE 21.23

The Password pane of the Accounts system preference

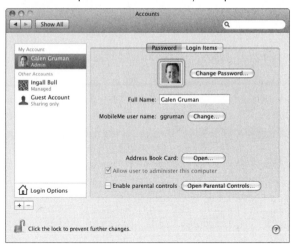

The Password pane contains the controls for the account's user. Click the picture to choose a different image to represent yourself from Apple's image library, or choose Edit Picture to take a new picture by using a camera attached to the Mac (such as the iSight camera built into many Macs), zoom in or out of the current picture, or select a previously used photo. Click Change Password to change your login password (or set one up if you don't have one). Enter your username in the Full Name field, as well as your MobileMe name and password (if you have a MobileMe account, as covered in Chapter 15). Click Open to open the Address Book application (see Chapter 11) to set up your address book card, which can include your name, address, e-mail, and other information that you can have several Mac applications use, such as to share your electronic business card with other users.

Select the Enable Parental Controls option to limit the user's capabilities (such as a child's) through the settings in the Parental Controls system preference, which you can jump to by clicking Open Parental Controls. To give this account the capability to establish and change settings for all users, select the Allow User to Administer This Computer option.

The Mac can automatically launch applications when it starts up. For example, you might want your browser and e-mail to launch automatically. Some applications set themselves to do so when you install them. Use the Login Items pane to determine what applications automatically launch when you start up your Mac. You'll see a list of any applications set to launch; you can add applications to the list by clicking the + iconic button, and delete a selected application by clicking the – iconic button. To the left of each application is a Hide option. If selected, Hide enables the application launch but does not open its windows, so it's not in your face when you start up. You'll see the application as active in your Dock, so it's ready whenever you want to go to it.

Cross-Ref
Chapter 20 explains the various types of user accounts.

Date & Time

To make sure your Mac is set to the right date and time, and displays that information the way you prefer, use the Date & Time system preference.

You set the date and time in the Date & Time pane, shown in Figure 21.24. Normally, you just ensure that the Set Date and Time Automatically option is selected; if you're connected to the Internet, the Mac will use the selected time server in the adjacent popup menu to get the current date and time. But you can override these by deselecting the option and changing the date and time fields below, or using the calendar and clocks to change the date and time. To change the calendar system you use (such as to Islamic or Buddhist) or change how dates and times display, click Open Language & Text to jump to the Language & Text system preference (covered earlier in this chapter) and then go to its Formats pane.

Use the Time Zone pane to set your current time zone. You'll see a map of the world, where you can click your approximate location to get the current time zone. Then choose your specific location from the Closest City popup menu; this option ensures that any local time-zone rules are followed on your Mac.

New Feature
In Mac OS X 10.6 Snow Leopard, there's a new option to set the time zone. If you select the Set Time Zone Automatically Using Current Location option, Mac OS X tries to figure out where you are by tracing your Internet connection, then selects your location based on that assessment. This comes in very handy if you travel, as it keeps your MacBook current in terms of time zone. (And if Mac OS X gets the time zone wrong, just deselect the option and manually choose your location.)

FIGURE 21.24

The Date & Time pane of the Date & Time system preference

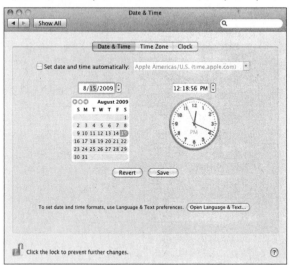

The Clock pane enables you to control whether and how the current date and time display in your Mac's menu bar. To display them, be sure that the Show Date and Time in Menu Bar option is selected. You can customize the display by selecting or deselecting the following options: Display the Time with Seconds, Flash the Time Separators (to make the colon flash), Use a 24-Hour Clock, Show AM/PM, Show Day of the Week, and Show Date. There's also an option to select whether the time displays in Digital or Analog format. (The Digital format shows the time using numbers, such as 12:15, and the Analog format shows a small clock with hour and minute hands.)

You can also set the Mac to announce the time out loud by selecting the Announce the Time option. Use the adjacent popup menu to select how often: On the Hour, On the Half Hour, or On the Quarter Hour. You can also choose which Mac voice to use by clicking Customize Voice.

New Feature

The ability to have the date display in the menu bar is new to Mac OS X 10.6 Snow Leopard.

Parental Controls

A Mac is a very powerful device, with access to the Internet and its riches and dangers, as well as access to applications, information, and media content that's not appropriate for everyone. Use the Mac OS's Parental Control system preference to help shield people — usually children — from sensitive applications and content on your Mac. Chapter 20 covers this feature in more detail, so we cover just the basics of the Parental Controls system preference here.

Any user account that has been set for parental controls (see the previous section on the Accounts system preference) will display in the list at the left of the Parental Controls system preference. Select the account to set the controls for; those controls appear on the right-hand side of the system preference, as shown in Figure 21.25.

FIGURE 21.25

The Parental Controls system preference

In the System pane, you set whether to have the Mac use Simple Finder, a stripped-down version suited for smaller children, and what applications the account can use. Other controls let you turn off or on access to printer management, CD and DVD burning, the capability to change the account password, and capability to modify the Dock.

In the Content pane, you can set whether to hide profane words in the Dictionary application's sources (see Chapter 8), as well as limit access to Web sites that contain sexual, profane, and other "adult" content. You can set the Mac to automatically filter Web sites. (You can also customize this filtering to add sites that you will always allow access to and those you will not allow access to, regardless of the Mac's own "judgment.") Or you can restrict the account to specific Web sites that you specify. (You'll need to know their URLs, so you might want to open a bookmark list and copy each in turn into the list.) Note that this Web filtering works only with Apple's Safari browser, so you should disallow access to other browsers in the System pane of the Parental Controls system preference.

In the Mail & iChat pane, you can specify whether to limit the user's ability to exchange e-mail and instant messaging chats with the addresses you specify. You can also tell the Mac to automatically send you an e-mail when the user tries to contact someone not on the approved list.

In the Time Limits pane, you can set a maximum number of hours of usage for both weekdays and weeknights, as well as times during the day that the user cannot use the computer (the Bedtime settings) — again, with separate weekday and weekend settings.

In the Logs pane, you can track the user's Web site, application, and chat activity.

Software Update

It seems that software is never finished; it either has flaws ("bugs") that need to be fixed or new features that the whizzes at Apple and other companies keep inventing. These days, companies such as Apple periodically create updates to fix the bugs and add new features, which they then distribute over the Internet. In the Software Update system preference, you can set your Mac to automatically get these updates for the Mac OS and other Apple software on a schedule of your choosing.

Figure 21.26 shows the Software Update system preference's Scheduled Check pane, where you set the update parameters. By default, the Check for Updates option is selected, and the adjacent popup menu is set to Weekly, so the Mac checks once a week for any updates. Deselect the option to stop automatic checking, or change the popup menu to Daily or Monthly to change the frequency. Also by default, the Mac is set to automatically download the updates so they're ready to install. (Deselect the Download Updates Automatically option to prevent automatic downloading.) When the Mac OS downloads an update, it displays an alert asking you for permission to install it.

Tip
You can have the Mac OS check for updates at any time by clicking Check Now in the Scheduled Check pane. But it's easier to choose ⇨ Software Update to do this.

The Installed Software pane of the Software Update system preference shows a list of previously installed updates in case you want to verify that you have a specific update.

FIGURE 21.26

The Software Update system preference's Scheduled Check pane

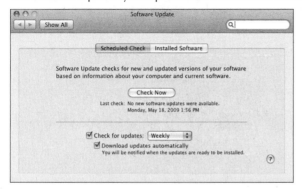

Speech

Your Mac can talk to you, and you use the Speech system preference to control when and how it talks to you. You can also talk to it by using the Speech system preference to help it recognize your words. (See Chapter 6 for more details on the Mac OS's speech features as they apply to the visually impaired.)

Use the Text to Speech pane to control how the Mac talks to you; the pane is shown in Figure 21.27. Choose your preferred system voice by using the System Voice popup menu, and the rate at which the voice speaks by using the Speaking Rate slider. You can hear how the voice and rate sound by clicking Play.

There are several alerts and announcements you can set the Mac to speak:

- **Announce When Alerts Are Displayed.** Select this option to have the Mac read any alerts that the Mac OS or your applications display. This can alert you to an issue if you're away from your computer. Click Set Alert Options to configure how the alerts are spoken; you can choose a different voice, set a delay of up to a minute for how long the alert is on-screen before the Mac speaks it, and choose (or create your own) alert phrase, such as "Alert!," "Pardon Me!," or "Zoinks!" (You'd have to create that last one by choosing Edit Phrase List in the Phrase popup menu in the window that appears after you click Set Alert Options.)

- **Announce When an Application Requires Your Attention.** Select this option to have the Mac verbally tell you that an application needs you to respond. This is the verbal version of the dancing icon in the Dock, which also occurs when an application is waiting for you to fill in a dialog box or respond to some other prompt.

- **Open Date & Time Preferences.** Click this button to jump to the Date & Time system preference, where you can set the Mac to announce the time every hour, half hour, or 15 minutes. (See the Date & Times system preference section earlier in this chapter.)

- **Open Universal Access Preferences.** Click this button to jump to the Universal Access system preference (covered later in this chapter), where you can turn on the Voice Over utility that helps the visually impaired by reading the screen to them, as Chapter 6 explains.

There's one more option in the Text to Speech pane: Speak Selected Text When the Key Is Pressed. Select this option to have the Mac read aloud whatever text you happen to have selected in your current application. To set the key combination that triggers this reading, click Set Key.

Note

The key combination you set to read aloud selected text also stops the Mac — when you press it — from speaking any alert or other announcement that is in progress. So it acts as a "shush" shortcut, not just a "read this" shortcut.

FIGURE 21.27

The Speech system preference's Text to Speech pane

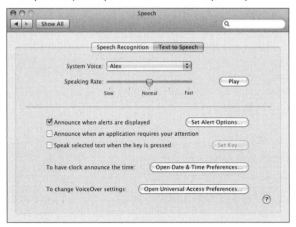

You use the Speech Recognition pane to configure the Mac to hear and interpret what you say to it. Figure 21.28 shows the pane. To enable speech recognition, turn it on by selecting the On option for Speakable items.

Whether speech recognition is on or not, you can configure its settings in the Settings and Commands subpanes. First take a look at the Settings subpane.

The Microphone popup menu enables you select which microphone the Mac should listen to, to interpret your speech. Most Macs have a built-in microphone, but you could also use an external microphone connected to the Line In jack or a wireless headset connected via Bluetooth (as explained in the Bluetooth system preference section earlier in this chapter). Whatever microphone you choose, help the Mac hear it correctly by clicking Calibrate. A dialog box appears after a few seconds that lists several phrases for you to speak so the Mac can make whatever adjustments are necessary in its processing of your voice to understand what you're saying.

Several controls determine how the Mac listens to you:

- **Change Key.** Click this button to open a sheet in which you type in the key you want to turn on and off the listening. The default is Esc, so you would press Esc before speaking a command, then Esc again when done so the Mac doesn't try to interpret anything else it hears as a command.

- **The Listening Method options.** Use this set of options to choose how the Mac listens for commands. Select Listen Only When Key Is Pressed to use the shortcut set up via Change Key to toggle listening off and on. Select Listen Continuously with Keyword to tell the Mac to listen all the tine, and when it hears a keyword you specify, to begin interpreting what you say next as a command — just like how the *Star Trek* starship *U.S.S. Enterprise* crew would say "Computer" before asking the computer a question. Set the keyword in the Keyword field; note that longer words or phrases are best (such as "Computer Command" or "Listen Macintosh") because they are easier to detect and less likely to be something you'd say in another context. In the Keyword Is popup menu, you can require the Mac to hear that keyword before each and every command, to not require it at all, to require it if at least 15 seconds have elapsed from the last command, or to require it if at least 30 seconds have elapsed from the last command. Those last two options are helpful if you typically issue many commands in sequence because they require you to say the keyword just at the beginning of that sequence.

- **Speak Command Acknowledgment.** Select this option if you want the Mac to make a noise when it understands your command correctly, so you know it did understand you properly before moving on. Choose that confirmation sound by using the Play This Sound popup menu.

You use the Commands subpane to tell the Mac what commands to listen for. Select as many of the commands sets that Apple provides for you that you want the Mac to do when you speak the commands: Address Book, Global Speakable Items (commands that all applications use), Application Specific Items (commands unique to it that the application supplies), Application Switching (commands to switch among applications, as well as launch and quit them), Front Window (commands for names of interface elements such as buttons and check boxes in the active window of an application), and Menu Bar (commands for the menu bar items running on your Mac).

To see what the actual speakable commands are, click Open Speakable Items Folder to see all the speech command files.

FIGURE 21.28

The Speech system preference's Speech Recognition pane, with the Settings subpane visible

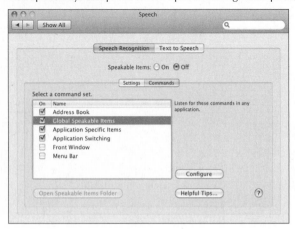

Note

You can configure two of the standard command sets by using the Configure button: Address Book and Global Speakable Items. If Address Book is selected, you can select which names in your address book you want to be able to speak as part of your commands; a sheet with a list of entries appears when you click Configure. If Global Speakable Items is selected, you can tell the Mac to listen for variations of common commands — so it understand "What is the time?" and "Tell me the time" as the same thing — instead of listening only for the actual command as written in the menu or dialog box; deselect Speak Command Names Exactly as Written in the window that appears when you click Configure.

Startup Disk

Most people have just one startup disk, but they still should know about the Startup Disk system preference, shown in Figure 21.29. For example, if you use Macs at your business and don't want to start from your local drive (perhaps you're lending the Mac to a contractor) — or can't because it is damaged — you would click the Network Startup icon and then click Restart so your Mac can run remotely by using a startup disk elsewhere on the network that your Mac administrator set up.

Or if you want to transfer lots of files to another Mac and you don't have a network connection that enables you to use file sharing, you can go to the Startup Disk system preference and click Target Disk mode, which makes the current Mac reboot so it appears to the other Mac as a hard drive. (The two need to be connected via a FireWire cable.)

If you have several startup disks, click the desired startup disk in the Startup Disk system preference. The next time you start the Mac, it will use that disk. (Click Restart to restart now.) This is a helpful option if you are testing applications or other configurations; you can set up the Mac OS X on an external drive for such testing and start from that disk, while still having your regular startup disk untouched.

FIGURE 21.29

The Startup Disk system preference

Tip

If you have multiple startup disks, or if you want to start up from your Mac OS X installation DVD, you can choose which startup disk to use when you start up: Just hold Option as the Mac starts, and after a few seconds, you'll see icons for each available startup disk. Use the arrow keys or mouse to move to the one you want, then press Return or click the ↑ iconic button that appears below the selected disk.

Time Machine

The Time Machine utility is an amazingly easy way to back up your Mac's files and restore them when needed, as Chapter 4 explains. To set up Time Machine, you start with the Time Machine system preference, shown in Figure 21.30.

The settings are straightforward: Turn Time Machine on or off with the Off/On toggle. Click Backup Disk to choose the drive to which you back up your data (or choose None to disable backup); you can also choose to back up to a Time Capsule, Apple's combo wireless router and wireless backup drive. Select the Show Time Machine Status in the Menu Bar option to get a visual indicator as to when Time Machine is backing up your Mac (it tends to slow down the Mac when it does, by the way), as well as to get an estimate of how much data remains to be backed up and to access a menu with the following options: Back Up Now, Enter Time Machine, and Open Time Machine Preferences.

After you've selected a backup disk, the Options button appears in the Time Machine system preference. Here, you can select what drives to not back up, tell the Mac whether to back up when your Mac laptop is running on battery power (backing up takes a lot of power), and tell you when Time Machine deletes old backups to make room for more. (It does so when your backup drive gets full.)

FIGURE 21.30

The Time Machine system preference

Universal Access

The Universal Access system preference helps users with various disabilities use the Mac. There are panes for visual appearance to help the visually impaired, for audio feedback to help the hearing-impaired, and for keyboard, mouse, and trackpad usage for the physically impaired. Figure 21.31 shows two of the five panes, and Chapter 6 covers each pane's settings in detail.

FIGURE 21.31

The Universal Access system preference's Seeing pane (left) and Mouse & Trackpad pane (right)

 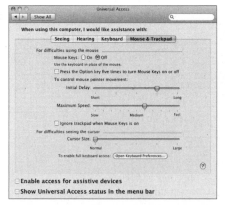

Summary

The Mac OS uses the System Preferences application to provide access to 26 sets of controls for standard Mac functions. Three additional system preferences — FibreChannel, Ink, and Trackpad — appear if you have the appropriate hardware attached to your Mac. In addition, non-Apple applications and hardware installation software may add their own system preferences.

You can view system preferences sorted alphabetically or by group. Using the View menu, you can switch to any system preference, or you can use the navigation buttons (Show All and the left- and right-facing triangles) in the System Preferences application window to move among system preferences.

Managing Fonts

When the Mac was first introduced in 1984, two things set it the most apart from the PCs of the day. One was the use of a mouse-driven graphical user interface. The other was the use of fonts (aka typefaces). Never before could you use typography in your documents, and the result was the desktop publishing revolution that ushered in the popularization of the media because anyone could produce good-quality publications. When the Web rose in the late 1990s, fonts were part of the basic mix of its presentation capabilities.

So the Mac has a long history of being font-oriented. Over the years, font technology has changed significantly, and the Mac OS has kept up with those changes. Mac OS X 10.6 Snow Leopard works with five kinds of font technologies, and it provides a management tool that enables you to control which fonts are active. (Because each font takes system memory, if you have a large font collection, you may not want them all loaded in memory at once.)

Exactly What Is a Font?

Technically, what computer users call a *font* is what typographers call a *typeface*: a set of characters available in one or more related stylistic variations. For example, the font/typeface Arial has the styles Arial Regular, Arial Italic, Arial Bold, Arial Bold Italic, Arial Black, and Arial Black Italic. In typographic terminology, that collection is a typeface and each stylistic variation is a font. In computer terminology, that collection is a font or font family and each stylistic variation is a style, typestyle, face, or typeface (depending on what program you're using). For consistency, this book uses the terms *font* for the set and *style* for the individual variations. Figure 22.1 shows a selection of fonts and their styles.

FIGURE 22.1

An assortment of fonts and their styles

American Typewriter Regular, Light, **Bold**, Condensed, Condensed Light, **Condensed Bold**

Arial Regular, *Italic*, **Bold**, ***Bold Italic***, **Black**

ITC Eras Book, Medium, **Demi**, Light, **Bold**, **Ultra**

Gill Sans Regular, *Italic*, **Bold**, ***Bold Italic***, Light, *Light Italic*

Helvetica, *Oblique*, **Bold**, ***Bold Oblique***

Hoefler Text Regular, *Italic*, **Black**, ***Black Italic***

Lucida Grande Regular, **Bold**

Marker Felt Thin, Wide

ITC Mendoza Roman Book, *Book Italic*, Medium, *Medium Italic*, **Bold**, ***Bold Italic***

Times New Roman Regular, *Italic*, **Bold**, ***Bold Italic***

Font Formats

Today, Mac OS X 10.6 Snow Leopard supports five font formats without the use of additional software: PostScript Type 1, PostScript Multiple Master, True Type, OpenType, and dfont.

Note

Many fonts are available in several of these formats. Despite having the same name, they may not offer the same characters, especially foreign-language characters and special symbols. Also, font makers add new characters over time to their fonts, so an older version of a font may have fewer special characters than the newer version. In either case, you can have a compatibility issue if you're sharing files with other people whose fonts may be a different version or a different format.

When the Mac debuted in 1984, there was just one font format, a bitmap format of fixed sizes. (A *bitmap* is a series of dots, or pixels, that combine to form a shape.) Each font's styles were rendered for each size as a series of pixels. That meant you could get 9-, 10-, and 12-point text, but not 11- or 13-point. Because the professional typesetting industry also used phototypesetting technology that rendered fonts at only specific sizes, that didn't feel like a limitation. But since then, the world of fonts has changed dramatically.

PostScript Type 1

The same year that the Mac debuted, so did a technology called PostScript, developed at Xerox by John Warnock and Chuck Geschke. They could not get Xerox to commercialize it, so they started their own company, Adobe Systems. Unlike the bitmap fonts of the original Mac OS, PostScript fonts were essentially mathematical equations that described fonts as a series of lines and curves (called *outline fonts*). A PostScript device could take those equations and, for any size, calculate the pixels needed to render it. That meant that font size was no longer set ahead of time but could be handled on the fly. In 1985, Apple saw the value of PostScript and adopted it in the Mac OS and in Apple's laser printers. That same year, a company called Aldus released PageMaker, the first desktop publishing program and one that used PostScript.

By 1986, the PostScript approach of outline fonts was the standard for professional-level desktop publishing. Mac OS X continues to support PostScript Type 1 fonts. Note that these fonts have two sets of files: printer files (the outlines) and screen files (bitmaps that Mac OS can use immediately to display text, rather than having to render the fonts at standard screen sizes, which can slow it down). Most PostScript fonts package these together in what are called suitcase files, but sometimes they are stored separately. The screen file has a short name such as `HelveBolIta`, while the printer file has a long name such as `Helvetica Bold Italic`. You need both for Mac OS X to use the Type 1 font.

Tip

Because PostScript Type 1 has essentially been superseded by the OpenType format, you should favor buying OpenType versions of fonts instead of PostScript Type 1 fonts, and consider replacing your older Type 1 fonts as you can.

TrueType

Over the years, new font formats emerged. Microsoft and Apple felt Adobe was charging too much for PostScript technology, so they created a competing outline font standard called TrueType that they both used in their operating systems (Windows and Mac OS X, respectively). Mac OS X comes with more than a dozen TrueType fonts, and uses TrueType as its primary font format.

Bitmap Fonts

For the 1980s and early 1990s, bitmap fonts survived as well because the Mac OS continued to support its original bitmap format. Adobe supported the bitmap technology as well for non-Apple computers, so it offered both PostScript Type 1 outline fonts and PostScript Type 3 bitmap fonts. The Type 3 fonts didn't really get much adoption, and bitmap fonts in general are rarely used any more in any operating system. Today, Mac OS X does not support bitmap fonts.

Microsoft relied on TrueType fonts for its Internet Explorer browser — which quickly became the standard browser on most computers — making TrueType fonts the de facto Web font standard. The Mac OS uses the same TrueType fonts as Microsoft does for Web display compatibility: Arial, Courier New, Georgia, Tahoma, Times New Roman, Trebuchet, and Verdana.

Note that TrueType fonts come in two file formats: TrueType (filename extension `.ttf`) and TrueType Collection (`.ttc`). A TrueType Collection file includes multiple styles in one file (such as `Baskerville.ttc`, which includes Regular, Italic, Bold, Bold Italic, Semibold, and Semibold Italic), while a "regular" TrueType file contains just one specific style (such as `CorsivaBold.ttf` containing just Corsiva Bold and `Corsiva.ttf` containing just Corsiva Regular).

PostScript Multiple Master

Adobe responded to the TrueType alliance with a "professional" variation of PostScript called Multiple Masters, where people used Adobe Type Manager software to create their own font variations. But few other programs provided support for Multiple Master fonts, and they have largely faded away. Even Adobe no longer produces new Multiple Master fonts.

However, today Mac OS X supports Multiple Master fonts (they all have "MM" in the filename), so you can use those that you have. But if you want to create your own variations, you'll need a font editor capable of doing so, such as FontLab Studio ($649; `www.fontlab.com`).

OpenType

Adobe, Microsoft, and Apple stopped competing over font standards after a few years, instead jointly developing the OpenType format that the recent versions of Mac OS X and Windows support natively. OpenType typically has many more characters available — for languages such as Russian, Greek, Hebrew, Arabic, and Japanese, as well as many specialized symbols for everything from currency to scientific expressions — than either PostScript Type 1 or TrueType. (To be fair, TrueType fonts released in recent years have increased the number of characters available in response to the OpenType fonts.)

Today, several of the fonts that come preinstalled in Mac OS X 10.6 Snow Leopard are OpenType fonts, such as Aquakana and Hiragino. (Both are Japanese-language fonts.)

dfont

Meanwhile, Apple developed a bitmap font format called the *dfont*, which it uses for its user interface, so it can guarantee that regardless of other font technologies active within the Mac OS, the menus, icon names, and so on will always display properly.

You can't buy dfont-format fonts, so the only reason to know they exist is so you know their purpose and don't mistakenly delete them.

Snow Leopard's New Fonts

Mac OS X 10.6 Snow Leopard comes with four new fonts: Menlo, Chalkduster, Heiti (with Korean, Japanese, Simplified Chinese, and Traditional Chinese variations), and Hiragino Sans GB (a Japanese font), shown here.

Menlo:
Snow Leopard may look like Leopard, but it's got a lot of hidden extras. *Italic.* **Bold.** ***Bold italic.***

Chalkduster:
Snow Leopard may look like Leopard, but it's got a lot of hidden extras.

Heiti:
Snow Leopard may look like Leopard, but it' s got a lot of hidden extras.
Light. K: 한국어. J: 日本語. SC: 简体中文. TC: 繁體中文.

Hiragino Sans GB:
Snow Leopard may look like Leopard, but it' s got a lot of hidden extras. J: 日本語.

Where Fonts Reside

Mac OS X stores fonts in several locations, which can be confusing. Here are the fonts locations and what is stored (or should be stored) in each:

- /Library/Fonts. This folder contains the fonts that come preinstalled with Mac OS X, as well as fonts installed *by a user with administrator privileges*, whether through Apple's Font Book application (covered later in this chapter) or simply copied to that folder. The fonts installed here are available to all users.

- /System/Library/Fonts. This folder contains the essential fonts needed by Mac OS X. You should never add or delete fonts in this folder. The fonts here are available to all users.

- /username/Library/Fonts. This folder contains fonts available to just that user, typically installed by a user *with or without* administrator privileges.

- /Network/Library/Fonts. If you're running Mac OS X over a network, this folder contains the fonts that the network administrator has installed for all network users to have access to.

The simplest way to install fonts is to copy or move the files to the appropriate font folder. The safest way is to use the Font Book utility that comes with Mac OS X, so you avoid the possibility of placing them in the wrong location or of deleting necessary files in those folders while you're there.

Managing Fonts in Font Book

To help you manage the fonts on your Mac, Apple provides the Font Book application. Why would you manage fonts? The key reason is that if you have lots of fonts, having them all loaded in memory can slow down your Mac's performance. Another reason is that if you have lots of fonts, you can be overwhelmed with font choices in your word-processing and page-layout software's font lists.

But Font Book also helps you deal with duplicate font files (which can confuse the Mac OS and applications) and corrupted font files (which can cause application and system crashes). Figure 22.2 shows Font Book, with a font highlighted that has a duplicate. Note how Font Book indicates problem fonts with a yellow triangle icon, as well as shows a detailed warning below its font preview window. (See the section on management options for fonts later in this chapter to learn how to deal with issues such as duplicate fonts.)

FIGURE 22.2

The Font Book application, with a duplicate font highlighted

Automatic font monitoring

Font Book tracks the state of your fonts and can update itself when fonts are added or deleted, if you tell it to in its Preferences dialog box (choose Font Book ⇨ Preferences or press ⌘+, [comma]). Note that Font Book tracks this status even when it's not running. There are two options to set:

- **Automatic Font Activation.** This option, which is selected by default, tells Font Book to automatically enable a font if you open a document that uses that font, even if you didn't previously enable it in Font Book. (But you must have installed the Font Book via Font

Book for it to be able to auto-activate it.) The Ask Me Before Activation suboption, which is not selected by default, tells Font Book to ask you whether to activate a disabled font when an application needs it.

- **Alert Me If System Fonts Change.** This option, which is selected by default, causes Font Book to display a notice that the system fonts have been updated or removed. This helps identify unexpected changes to your system's fonts.

Adding fonts

As is typical in Font Book, there are several ways to add fonts:

- Choose File ⇨ Add Fonts.
- Press ⌘+O.
- Click the second + iconic button at the bottom of the Font Book dialog box.
- Control+click or right-click within Font Book and choose Add Fonts from the contextual menu.

To navigate to the disk or folder that contains the fonts to be added, select those you want (you can select folders and individual font files), and click Open.

You can control how fonts are added in the Preferences dialog box (choose Font Book ⇨ Preferences or press ⌘+, [comma]), as Figure 22.3 shows. Your options are:

- **Default Install Location.** This popup menu enables you to choose where to install the fonts: User for the current user's /username/Library/Fonts folder, Computer for the /Library/Fonts folder, or (if you have any defined) a library. (See the "Working with font groupings" section in this chapter for details on libraries.)
- **Validate Fonts Before Installing.** This option, which is selected by default, has Font Book check the font files for corruption before installing, alerting you if the file contains errors.

FIGURE 22.3

The Font Book's Preferences dialog box

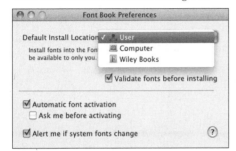

Previewing fonts

By default, Font Book shows you the alphabet in a pane on the right for whatever font is selected. You can change the size of this preview by selecting a font size from the Fit menu or using the slider at the far right.

To see all characters in the font, choose Preview⇨Repertoire or press ⌘+2. To see the alphabet and numerals, choose Preview⇨Sample or press ⌘+1. To see your custom text for the preview, choose Preview⇨Custom or press ⌘+3 and then type in the preview area whatever you want the preview to be.

You can disable this preview window by choosing Preview⇨Hide Preview or pressing Option+⌘+I. Reenable it by choosing Preview⇨Show Preview or pressing Option+⌘+I. And you can switch between that preview and the technical font details, as shown in Figure 22.4, by choosing Preview⇨Show/Hide Font Info or pressing ⌘+I. This information includes font format, languages supported, location on your Mac, and font file version.

Tip

If you Control+click or right-click a font in the Fonts list and choose Preview Font from the contextual menu or choose Preview Font from the Action iconic popup menu (the gear icon), a separate preview window appears. It includes a popup menu that enables you to switch easily among the various styles available for that font.

FIGURE 22.4

A font's technical details (at right)

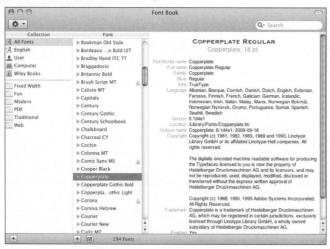

Working with font groupings

Font Book categorizes fonts several ways. At left, it displays groups of fonts under the Collections list. By default, Font Book displays several groupings:

- **All Fonts.** This group, if selected, displays all fonts available on the Mac in the Font list to its right.

- **English.** This group displays all Roman-based fonts.

- **User.** This group displays all fonts installed in the current user's `Library/Fonts` folder.

- **Computer.** This group shows all fonts displayed in the `/Library/Fonts` and `/System/Library/Fonts` folders.

- **Fixed Width.** This collection shows all default fonts whose characters are equally wide, such as typewriter and old-style computer terminal fonts: Andale Mono, Courier, Courier New, and Monaco.

- **Fun.** This collection shows the default fonts that Apple characterizes as whimsical: American Typewriter, Herculanum, Marker Felt, Papyrus, and Zapfino.

- **Modern.** This collection shows the default fonts that Apple characterizes as modern-looking, meaning simple and clean in appearance: Futura, Gill Sans, Helvetica Neue, and Optima.

- **PDF.** This collection shows the basic fonts that PDF files need to have available: Courier, Helvetica, Times, Symbol, and Zapf Dingbats.

- **Traditional.** This collection shows the default fonts that Apple characterizes as traditional-looking, meaning formal and old-fashioned: Baskerville, Big Caslon, Cochin, Copperplate, and Didot.

- **Web.** This collection shows the default fonts that are commonly used in Web pages: Andale Mono, Arial, Arial Black, Brush Script MT, Comic Sans MS, Georgia, Impact, Times New Roman, Trebuchet MS, Verdana, and Webdings.

A *collection* is more than a font grouping in Font Book. Other software — such as TextEdit and Apple's iWork Pages — can display these collections in their font lists, making it easy for users to choose from a subset of fonts organized on the basis of visual style or project standards. In both TextEdit and Pages, choose Format ➪ Fonts ➪ Show Fonts, as Figure 22.5 shows, to display the *font panel*. Users can add their own fonts to the font panel's Favorites collection by choosing Add to Favorites from the Action iconic popup menu (the gear icon), as well as add their own collections by clicking the + iconic button.

Another type of font grouping you can create is called a *library* (for an example, see the Wiley library in Figure 22.2). Its main difference from a collection is that it is not visible to programs such as TextEdit and Pages, so it's really meant for font management only within Font Book.

To create a collection in Font Book, click the gear-shaped iconic popup menu and choose New Collection, Control+click or right-click the Collections pane and choose New Collection, or click the + iconic button under the Collections list. To create a library, choose New Library instead. Now drag fonts from the Fonts list into the collection or library.

FIGURE 22.5

Font collections defined in Font Book are available in some applications, such as iWork Pages (shown here) and TextEdit.

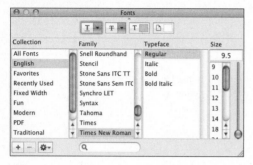

Note

If you select your new collection or library, you'll see in the Fonts list only the fonts within it. So select a different grouping to see available fonts in the Fonts list and drag the desired ones into the new collection or library.

So what can you do with collections and libraries within Font Book? Turn off or off entire sets of fonts, controlling their availability to the Mac OS and to applications; validate fonts (look for corrupt files); and remove the files from Font Book and the Mac OS.

Management options for fonts

There are several controls available via menus for fonts. There are three ways to get these menus:

- Control+click or right-click the grouping, font name, or style name.
- Select the grouping and click the Action iconic popup menu (the gear icon) and click the grouping, font name, or style name.
- Select the grouping and choose File or Edit to get various menu options.

Note that you can select multiple items by ⌘+clicking them.

Here are the management options available:

- Choose Disable "*fontname*" to turn off its fonts or Enable "*fontname*" to turn on its fonts. (This option is available in the Edit menu.)
- Remove "*fontname*" to remove the font files from both Font Book and the Mac OS (the font files are placed into the Trash). (This option is available in the File menu.)
- Validate Fonts to see if the font files are corrupt. (This option is available in the File menu.)

- Resolve Duplicates to disable duplicate copies of fonts. Duplicate fonts in the /user-name/Library/Font folder are disabled first, then those in the /Library/Font folder. (This option is available in the Edit menu.)

- Reveal in Finder to open the folder that contains the selected file (this option, available in the File menu, is not available for groupings).

Tip

Another way to enable or disable fonts is to select the grouping, font name, or style name and then click the third icon at the bottom of the dialog box. If it displays as a selected check box, selecting it turns off the grouping's fonts. If it displays as an empty check box, selecting it turns on the grouping's fonts.

The Edit menu has the Select Duplicated Fonts option to quickly find and select all duplicated fonts on your Mac. Then you can choose Edit ➪ Resolve Duplicates to deal with them in one fell swoop.

The File menu has a few extra options not available in the contextual menus:

- **Validate File.** This option enables you to check for corruption a font file not installed in Font Book.

- **Export.** This option copies the selected grouping, font, or style to a folder of your choice on the Mac.

- **Print.** This option prints the selected grouping, font, or style so you have an easy reference.

Finally, you search for fonts several ways in Font Book: Enter a font name in the search box at the upper right of the Font Book dialog box, choose Edit ➪ Find ➪ Font Search, or press Option+⌘+F. (Those last two options simply highlight the search box so you can begin typing immediately.) Note that the search looks at whatever fonts are displayed in the Fonts list, so be sure to select All Fonts or other grouping that is likely to contain your sought-after font.

Managing Fonts with Other Software

Although Mac OS X ships with Font Book for font management, other options available that do the same thing are available. But why even bother?

The most common reason is if you're working in a workgroup, where the fonts are centrally managed. Font Book doesn't support that multiuser scenario, whereas three other products do: Extensis's Universal Type Server (www.extensis.com), Inside Software's FontAgent Pro Server (www.insidersoftware.com), and Linotype's FontExplorerX Server (www.fontexplorerx.com).

You might also consider these vendors' font management tools for individuals — Extensis's Suitcase Fusion, Inside Software's FontAgent Pro, and Linotype's FontExplorerX Pro — to get a little more oomph in your Mac's font management. For example, they not only auto-activate fonts as needed, but also auto-deactivate them when you close an Adobe Creative Suite or QuarkXPress document that uses them (assuming no other open documents also use the temporarily enabled fonts). And they tend to offer more font preview options, as well as font-repair capabilities.

Accessing Special Characters

With your fonts installed and enabled, they're ready for use in your applications. Applications designed to work with fonts will have controls that let you apply fonts to text, typically through the Edit menu, but perhaps also elsewhere, such as in style sheets. What may be less obvious is how to access the special characters available in many fonts, whether foreign-language characters or special symbols. After all, they don't show up on your keyboard.

Using keyboard shortcuts

Symbols are commonly used in all sorts of documents, from legal symbols to scientific ones. That's why most fonts have a selection of popular symbols built in that you can access via keyboard shortcuts. Table 22.1 shows the shortcuts for common symbols for Macintosh fonts, and Table 22.2 shows the shortcuts for foreign characters such as accented letters.

TABLE 22.1

Shortcuts for Common Symbols

Character	Mac OS X Shortcut
Legal	
Copyright (©)	Option+G
Registered trademark (®)	Option+R
Trademark (™)	Option+2
Paragraph (¶)	Option+7
Section (§)	Option+6
Dagger (†)	Option+T
Double dagger (‡)	Option+Shift+T
Currency	
Cent (¢)	Option+4
Euro (€)	Option+Shift+2
Pound sterling (£)	Option+3
Yen (¥)	Option+Y
Punctuation	
Bullet (•)	Option+8
Ellipsis (…)	Option+; (semicolon)
Em dash (—)	Option+Shift+– (hyphen)
En dash (–)	Option+– (hyphen)

Character	Mac OS X Shortcut
Punctuation	
Open double quote (")	Option+[
Closed double quote (")	Option+Shift+[
Open single quote (')	Option+]
Closed single quote *or* apostrophe (')	Option+Shift+]
Measurement	
Foot (")	Control+"
Inch (')	Control+Shift+"
Mathematics	
Virgule (/ for building fractions)	Option+Shift+1
Infinity (∞)	Option+5
Division (÷)	Option+/
Root (√)	Option+V
Greater than or equal to (≥)	Option+>
Less than or equal to (≤)	Option+<
Inequality (≠)	Option+=
Rough equivalence (≈)	Option+X
Plus or minus (±)	Option+Shift+=
Logical not (¬)	Option+L
Per mil (‰)	Option+Shift+R
Degree (°)	Option+Shift+8
Function (*f*)	Option+F
Integral (∫)	Option+B
Variation (∂)	Option+D
Greek beta (ß)	Option+S
Greek mu (µ)	Option+M
Greek Pi (Π)	Option+Shift+P
Greek pi (π)	Option+P
Greek Sigma (Σ)	Option+W
Greek Omega (Ω)	Option+Z
Miscellaneous	
Apple logo ()	Option+Shift+K
Open diamond (◊)	Option+Shift+V

TABLE 22.2

Shortcuts for Western European Accents and Foreign Characters

Character	Mac OS X Shortcut
acute (´)*	Option+E *letter*
cedilla (ç)*	*see Ç and ç* (may be used with any letter)
circumflex (ˆ)*	Option+I *letter*
grave (`)*	Option+` *letter*
tilde (~)*	Option+N *letter*
trema (¨)*	Option+U *letter*
umlaut (¨)*	Option+U *letter*
Á	Option+E A
á	Option+E a
À	Option+` A
à	Option+` a
Ä	Option+U A
ä	Option+U a
Ã	Option+N A
ã	Option+N a
Â	Option+I A
â	Option+I a
Å	Option+Shift+A
å	Option+A
Æ	Option+Shift+'
æ	Option+'
Ç	Option+Shift+C
ç	Option+C
É	Option+E E
é	Option+E e
È	Option+` E
è	Option+` e
Ë	Option+U E
ë	Option+U e

Character	Mac OS X Shortcut
Ê	Option+I E
ê	Option+I e
Í	Option+E I
í	Option+E i
Ì	Option+` I
ì	Option+` i
Ï	Option+U I
ï	Option+U i
Î	Option+I I
î	Option+I i
Ñ	Option+N N
ñ	Option+N n
Ó	Option+E O
ó	Option+E o
Ò	Option+` O
ò	Option+` o
Ö	Option+U O
ö	Option+U o
Õ	Option+N O
õ	Option+N o
Ô	Option+I O
ô	Option+I o
Ø	Option+Shift+O
ø	Option+O
Œ	Option+Shift+Q
œ	Option+Q
ß	Option+S
∫	Option+B
Ú	Option+E U
ú	Option+E u
Ù	Option+` U
ù	Option+` u
Ü	Option+U U

continued

TABLE 22.2 *(continued)*

Character	Mac OS X Shortcut
ü	Option+U u
Û	Option+I U
û	Option+I u
Ÿ	Option+U Y
ÿ	Option+U y
Spanish open exclamation (¡)	Option+1
Spanish open question (¿)	Option+Shift+/
French open double quote («)	Option+\
French close double quote (»)	Option+Shift+\

* Enter the shortcut for the accent and then type the letter to be accented. For example, to get é, type Option+E and then the letter e.

Touch-based Chinese Handwriting

Mac OS X 10.6 has a new feature for users wanting to write the Chinese strokes called *trackpad handwriting*. This makes innovative use of the Multi-Touch trackpad found on newer MacBooks to input the complex array of strokes used in Chinese logographs (more commonly called *ideograms* or *characters*). (Chapter 2 covers the Multi-Touch trackpad in detail.)

To use trackpad handwriting, go to the Input Sources pane of the Language & Text system preference. In the list of input sources at left, select one or both of the Chinese languages: Simplified Chinese (used in mainland China) and Traditional Chinese (used in Taiwan). Each has several suboptions for different stroke styles, including the new Trackpad Handwriting option, which if selected enables stroke entry on a Multi-Touch trackpad. (If you don't see the Trackpad Handwriting option, your Mac's trackpad does not support this new feature.) The Show/Hide Trackpad Handwriting keyboard shortcut description also appears in the Input Source Shortcuts section at right.

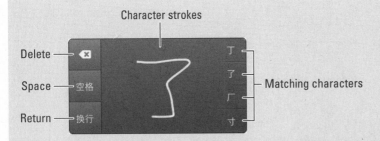

When working in the Finder or other applications, press Control+spacebar to bring up the Trackpad Handwriting window; any characters you input are entered at the current text cursor location. The interface appears on the lower half of the desktop, and in front of other all other windows (including the active window), as the figure shows. You can enter text in documents, filenames, or any other part of Mac OS X that would normally enter letters typed out on the keyboard.

In the Trackpad Handwriting window, there are virtual buttons on the left and right side of the trackpad, and the trackpad's central area is where you draw character strokes, using a single finger. As you draw, white strokes appear on-screen in the Trackpad Handwriting interface to match your movements. To the right of those strokes appear three possible ideogram matches, with the character at the top the one that Mac OS X believes to be closest match. To select a character, press the part of the trackpad that corresponds to its location on the Trackpad Handwriting window. On the left side of the Trackpad Handwriting window are three virtual buttons; from top to bottom, they are Delete, Space, and Return.

Note that you can still use the keyboard to enter characters at the same time as using the Trackpad Handwriting window. But, while the Trackpad Handwriting window is on-screen, you cannot control the mouse pointer. You toggle between using the Trackpad Handwriting window and using the track-pad or mouse pointer by pressing Control+spacebar.

Using other tools

Some applications come with tools to insert special characters not visible on the keyboard or accessible via keyboard shortcuts. For example, in Adobe InDesign, choose Type ➪ Glyphs or press Option+Shift+F11. In Microsoft Word, choose Insert ➪ Symbol. In iWork Pages and in TextEdit, choose Edit ➪ Special Characters.

But no matter which applications you're using, you can always rely on the two built-in tools in Mac OS X: the Keyboard Viewer and Character Viewer. The Keyboard Viewer gives you a visual quick reference to keyboard shortcuts, while the Character Viewer enables you to access any character available on your Mac, even those that have no keyboard shortcuts.

Both are available under the Input Sources iconic menu in the menu bar. Note that you might need to turn on the Input Source iconic menu by choosing ➪ System Preferences, and then going to the Language & Text system preference's Input Sources pane. Select the Show Input Menu in Menu Bar option. Also be sure the On check box is selected for the Keyboard & Character Viewer at the top of the Name list so the Keyboard Viewer and Character Viewer are available in the Input Sources iconic menu. Note that if you select Keyboard & Character Viewer, the Show Input Menu in Menu Bar option is automatically selected. (Chapter 21 explains this system preference in more detail.)

New Feature

In previous versions of Mac OS X, the Character Viewer had been called the Character Palette.

After you've opened the Keyboard Viewer, just hold the modifier keys such as Option and ⌘ to see what characters are available for each key, as Figure 22.6 shows. Now just press the key that gets you the special character you want.

FIGURE 22.6

Mac OS X's Keyboard Viewer

After you've opened the Character Viewer, first decide which type of character you're looking for by choosing an option in the View popup menu: Roman, Japanese, Traditional Chinese, Korean, Simplified Chinese, All Characters, Code Tables, Pi Fonts, and Glyphs. The Character Viewer's display changes based on your selection.

Note

All the displays include a Favorites pane that displays any characters you've tagged as a favorite by choosing Add to Favorites in the Action iconic popup menu (the gear icon) at the bottom of the palette.

If you choose one of the specific languages or All Characters, the Character Viewer looks like the left image in Figure 22.7, providing the By Category pane that enables you to choose from types of characters, such as Arrows or Phonetic Symbols, to help you quickly narrow your choices down. Select the desired character from the central pane and click Insert to place it in your document at the text cursor's current location. (The By Radical pane sorts Chinese ideograms based on their strokes.)

If you expand the Font Variation part of the palette (as shown in Figure 22.7), you can see all fonts in selected font collections, so you can choose the character in that specific font and have it inserted with the appropriate font formatting when you click Insert with Font. (The section "Working with font groupings" earlier in this chapter explains font collections.)

The Pi Fonts option enables you to pick a pi (also known as symbol) font by using the Font popup menu and see only its characters in the Pi Fonts pane. Note that this view shows only TrueType fonts, not pi fonts in PostScript Type 1 or OpenType formats, so its utility is limited. Select the desired symbol from the center pane and click Insert with Font; your document will have the character inserted at the text cursor's location and have the proper font applied to the inserted text.

The Glyph option's Glyph Catalog pane shows all the characters (also known as glyphs) for the font you choose from the Font popup menu and from its adjacent Style popup menu. Scroll through the characters in the central pane and click Insert with Font; your document will have the character inserted at the text cursor's location and have the proper font applied to the inserted text.

New Feature

As the sidebar "Touch-based Chinese Handwriting" explains, Mac OS X 10.6 Snow Leopard also lets you enter Chinese characters using the Multi-Touch trackpad on newer Mac laptops.

FIGURE 22.7

The full Character Viewer (left) with a language chosen in the View popup menu. At upper right is the core Character Viewer when Pi Fonts is chosen, and at lower right is the core Character Viewer when Glyph is chosen.

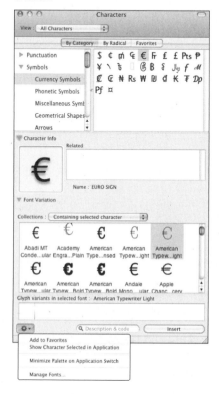

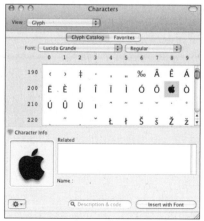

There are two other controls in Character Viewer worth noting, both options in the Action iconic popup menu (the gear icon):

- **Show Character Selected in Application.** This option has the Character Viewer show the first character of the text string selected in your currently open application. For example, if you selected $, you'll see $ highlighted in the Character Viewer.

- **Manage Fonts.** This option opens the Font Book applications.

You can also use a utility like Ergonis's PopChar X utility (€30, www.ergonis.com) to find and insert special characters. As Figure 22.8 shows, it grays out characters unavailable for the selected font.

FIGURE 22.8

The PopChar X utility

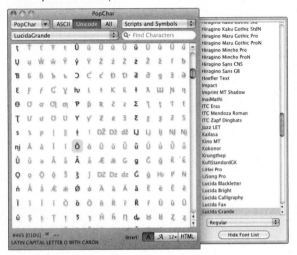

Summary

Mac OS X supports five font file formats: PostScript Type 1, PostScript Multiple Master, TrueType, OpenType, and dfont. TrueType and OpenType are the modern typographic standards, while the two PostScript formats are being phased out. The dfont format is internal to the Mac OS for use in menus and other user-interface elements, so you cannot buy fonts in that format.

Fonts can be stored in any of several locations, with /username/Library/Fonts used for fonts available only to a specific user, /Library/Fonts for fonts available for all users, and /System/Library/Fonts for system-required fonts.

The Font Book application enables you to both install and manage fonts, such as detecting and resolving duplicate fonts, detecting corrupt font files, and creating groups of fonts for easy activation and deactivation. Some groups, called *collections*, are available to other applications such as TextEdit and iWork Pages to give users easily navigated font sets. Font Book also enables you to preview fonts, plus it can auto-activate fonts that aren't enabled but needed by a document.

You can buy font managers to use instead of Font Book, which makes sense if you are managing fonts across a workgroup of users or if you need some of their specialized capabilities such as font repair.

To use the special characters, called *glyphs*, in fonts, you can use several methods, including keyboard shortcuts, the Keyboard Viewer and Character Viewer utilities that come with Mac OS X, or a separately purchased utility such as Ergonis's PopChar X. The new support for gesture-based Chinese handwriting on newer Mac laptops provides an additional input method for Chinese text.

Securing Your Mac

I t's a sad but true fact that there are people out there who steal or cause mischief. In the Internet Age, they now have incredible reach, able to damage thousands and even millions of computers by using all sorts of technology collectively known as *malware*: viruses, Trojan horses, worms, spyware, and more. Some of these folks even reach over the Internet or via other networks directly into your Mac to steal or damage data. And then there's the old-fashioned thief who simply steals your Mac, making all its private contents accessible — and some of that information could be valuable for identity thieves or business competitors.

Fortunately, there are many ways to protect your Mac. Mac OS X 10.6 Snow Leopard comes with some protection tools, and simply by setting various functions correctly, you can secure many parts of your Mac, as well. For those security areas not addressed within Mac OS X itself, there are applications available to protect you.

Identifying the Four Key Vulnerabilities

So what are the areas of vulnerability? There are four key ones:

- **The Mac itself.** Someone could steal your Mac (or you might lose it and it is never returned by the person who finds it) to get a free or salable computer and any installed applications.

- **Your personal data stored on the Mac.** This includes your passwords, account logins, and so on.

- **Your business, or other valuable data, stored on the Mac.** This data could be of interest to an unethical competitor or acquaintance. It could include sales lists, financial records, draft contracts, legal records, medical records, music and video files, or love letters.

- **The Mac environment.** This refers to the Mac, Mac OS X, and your applications. These can be hijacked to turn your Mac into a "zombie PC" that generates spam and other malware unbeknown to you, damaging other computer users — particularly your friends, colleagues, and family members listed in your Address Book contacts. Or your Mac can simply be hijacked to steal its resources to help run something unbeknown to you, whether for good or ill.

A very determined thief can probably get past all these defenses, but very few thieves are that determined (unless you work for the CIA or a similar type of organization). The key is to *layer* your security defenses: If someone gets past one layer, there's another one to get past as well. This will dissuade most thieves and hackers, who will move on. (So even if they have your Mac, they'll end up just wiping its data and selling it to someone else on the black market, with your data no longer available. Just be sure you regularly back up your Mac's data, as Chapter 4 explains.)

So how do you layer your security? The best approach is to tackle it in the order the previous list of key vulnerabilities appear, as the next four sections explain.

Securing the Mac itself

Because your Mac is a physical thing, there's nothing that the Mac OS can do to prevent it from being lost or stolen. You need to guard it as you would any other valuable property.

An easy way to do so is by using a security cable that attaches to the security slot on most Macs or that loops through the handle on older desktop Macs. (Be sure to get the right one for your model!) Kensington (www.kensington.com) sells a variety of these.

If you own a MacBook, putting it in a locked drawer when it's not in use is another easy way to secure it.

Should these not work, or you lose the Mac when traveling, you can make the Mac less valuable to a thief by using password security to render the Mac inoperable to anyone who doesn't know the password, as described in the "Using Password Protection" section later in this chapter.

Securing your personal data

It's amazing how many accounts and passwords you use every day on your Mac. You likely have usernames and passwords for online banking, Wi-Fi access, online shopping, and downloading music and more from the iTunes Store. Passwords are the first line of defense to securing your information, so it's critical that you ensure they are secure. Therefore, make sure you have passwords not only for your online accounts but also for your Web browser (so someone can't just view your passwords in it), for your Mac (ditto), and for documents that contain sensitive personal data (you can password-protect Microsoft Office and PDF files, for example).

A password should not be something simple or obvious, such as your middle name, pet's name, birth date, or other such easily discovered information. But it does need to be something you'll remember, so it should be personal but not widely known. You can enhance the password by making it at least eight characters long (that makes it harder for password-generation utilities to come up with a matching password). A good technique is to substitute some letters with other characters, to add an extra layer of challenge for password-guessers: You might replace O with 0, G with 6, L with 1, E with 3, and/or I with 1. (Just be consistent so *you* don't forget when to use the substituted character.)

Where possible, use one of three standard passwords to make it easy to remember what the password is likely to be. Too many passwords, and you'll forget. If you have just one and someone cracks it, all of your personal data can be compromised. You can use the Mac's Keychain Access utility to remember and retrieve passwords, as the "Using Password Protection" section later in this chapter explains.

Securing your files

If someone does get into your Mac, your data files are there for the taking. Passwords can slow the person down, but if you have sensitive data, a determined thief — a business rival, a determined soon-to-be ex-spouse, a conniving roommate — can use a software program that bypasses the password security and accesses the files.

So for such data, you want to add a type of security called *encryption* that scrambles the file's contents in a way that only it can later unscramble. So even if someone gets the file, he or she can't make any sense of it, password protected or not. As the "Using Encryption" section explains, Mac OS X comes with the FileVault encryption feature, and there are third-party encryption tools that offer even better protection should you need it.

Securing your Mac environment

The final area of vulnerability is the Mac's environment: your network and Internet connections, as well as the drives used to bring data and software onto your Mac. A hacker can see your Mac on the network and tunnel through it to get to your Mac's data or even install malware. Virtually weekly, you'll see a news story about a virus, worm, or Trojan horse threat in which a seemingly innocent download, Web link, or e-mail attachment infects people's computers and steals their information, turns their computers into "zombies" that start infecting other people, or damages their data, applications, and even operating system.

These security holes are many, but you can close some of them off by using the Mac's network settings and built-in firewall, as well as anti-malware applications. Just be aware that hackers know about these technology-based protections, so they are turning more and more to fooling people into taking an unsafe action, such as by sending a message allegedly from a person or business you know with what appears to be a legitimate attachment or link. You have to make sure that the message is real: Look closely at its sender, URL, and/or file attachment name. The "Plugging Security Holes" section later in this chapter explains the various techniques you can use to protect yourself.

Using Password Protection

You can set passwords for your Mac in several places — keeping in line with the concept of layered security. The first place is for your user account, which is what sets up the first barrier for a data thief. You can then set passwords for other layers of your Mac's security barrier, from application access to file sharing privileges.

Setting the user account

When you set up your Mac, you set up a user account. And you were asked to give it a password, this password is required to log in to the Mac, as well as to install software and make other changes that could compromise the Mac OS.

Whether you established a password or not, take a minute and think whether the password is strong enough to protect your Mac's contents should it get lost or stolen. If not, change it. To do so, go to the Accounts system preference, select your account, and click Change Password. You'll get a sheet in which you enter a new password (you have to enter the old one as well, to prove to the Mac OS that you're the rightful owner and not a thief trying to lock out the owner), as Figure 23.1 shows. You can also enter a password hint — just don't enter one so obvious that someone can use it to figure out your password. (How can a person get to this point if he or she doesn't have your password to log on to the Mac in the first place? Easy: If you left the Mac running, he or she doesn't have to log on.)

If you're not so good at inventing effective passwords, click the Password Assistant iconic button (the key icon) to get the Password Assistant dialog box, also shown in Figure 23.1. Use the Type popup menu to chose a type of password — Memorable, Letters & Numbers, Numbers Only, Random, FIPS 181 Compliant, and Manual — and then pick an option from the Suggestion popup menu. Choose More Suggestions if you don't like the first batch of suggestions. The strength of the chosen password displays in the Quality meter. Use the Length slider to increase or decrease the number of characters in the password. If you choose Manual, you can enter your own password and see how secure the Quality meter indicates it to be.

Note
The FIPS 181 Compliant option is designed to satisfy the Federal Information Protection Standard 181 used by government agencies and some businesses to produce secure, yet memorable, passwords.

You can change the password for other users, if your account has administrator privileges, by selecting the account and clicking Reset Password. You also can give or remove these users' administrator privileges and set parental controls for them. Administrator privileges gives the user wide access to your Mac's settings, including passwords, so don't give your kids, babysitter, or visitors such privileges. (Chapter 20 explains the parental control settings in detail; use them to restrict the activities that kids, babysitters, and guests have when using your Mac.) A user who has neither administrator privileges nor parental controls applied can change his or her password and access all of his or her files and applications, as well as files and applications made accessible to everyone, but that's it.

FIGURE 23.1

Use the Accounts system preference and, optionally, the Password Assistant, to set a secure password for your user accounts.

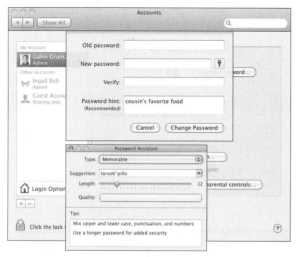

Note

Clicking Reset Password to change users' passwords does not change the password for their keychain, the file the Mac creates to store passwords for login. Keychains are covered later in this chapter.

You have one more option to think through in the Accounts system preference: Login Options. You can set an account to automatically log in. Note that doing so still requires that person to enter a password, so it's fine to use this option if you use the Mac most of the time. If your Mac is shared among several people, choose Off in the Automatic Login popup menu. (Chapter 21 covers the Accounts system preference in more detail.)

With a password set for all the user accounts, passwords are required to log in to the Mac and to make system-level changes such as installing applications, enabling file sharing, and changing system preferences. Figure 23.2 shows an example of a password request for such a change.

FIGURE 23.2

A prompt for a password for a system-level change (here, running Software Update)

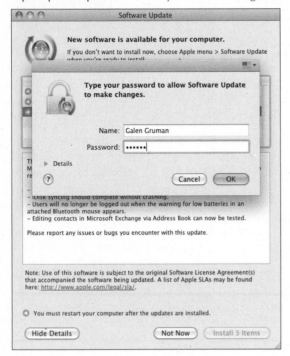

Overriding the Account Password

If you forget your login password for the Mac's administrator account, it appears as if you can't actually use your Mac any longer. Certainly you can't administer it. You may think your only choice is to reinstall the Mac OS, but there is in fact a way to override the administrator's (or anyone's) password.

First, start your Mac from your Mac OS X 10.6 Snow Leopard installation DVD. After selecting the language for the install disc to use, you will be asked for a disk on which to install Mac OS X 10.6 Snow Leopard. Don't select one. Instead, choose Utilities ⇨ Password. You are then asked to choose the disk containing the user account whose password you want to change. After selecting the disk, you can choose a specific user account on that disk. Enter the new password in the two text fields (the second one verifies that you typed it correctly) and click Save.

This trick does require that you have the Mac OS X installation DVD, so a thief who doesn't have such a DVD can't use it. But the fact that this trick is available shows why you need to protect your Mac at more than one layer; relying on just one layer of defense can leave you more vulnerable than you realize.

Enforcing password use

The next step is to make sure that passwords are required for sensitive operations, even after someone has logged in. After all, many people leave their Macs on when they're not using them, making them easy targets for someone who comes by when they're not around. You can require password use for several activities in the General pane of the Security system preference, shown in Figure 23.3.

The safest course is to make sure that all options are selected in the General pane. At a minimum, we recommend selecting Require Password and setting its popup menu to Immediately, so a password is needed as soon as the screen saver turns on. Just be sure to have the screen saver turn on after a relatively short time, such as five or ten minutes, in the Desktop & Screen Saver system preference's Screen Saver pane.

Selecting the Disable Automatic Login option overrides any automatic login set in the Accounts system preference, which is a way of discouraging another user with administrator privileges from automatically logging in, though because that person has admin privileges, he or she could simply deselect this option and turn automatic login back on. Still, it's a useful option to prevent those without admin privileges from automatically logging in.

Selecting the Require a Password to Unlock Each System Preferences Pane option means that the Lock iconic button (the brass padlock icon) at the bottom left of all system preferences is turned on, preventing the user from making any changes without supplying his or her password. This can be a pain when you're updating system preferences, but as you typically don't do so often, it's a good idea to enable this setting. If you know you're going to update a lot of settings, turn off the lock setting temporarily, change the settings, and then turn it back on.

Tip

If you see an open lock on a system preference, it means anyone logged in can change its settings. Click the lock to require the user to enter his or her password to make changes. This is a good idea for a Mac left in a public space such as a family room or office, where strangers could have access to it.

Selecting the Log Out After __ Minutes of Inactivity option is more secure than requiring a password to wake a sleeping Mac. By logging out the user, all the applications that were running are also closed, so there's less chance that an attack via the network can succeed, as nothing is running to latch on to.

Selecting the Use Secure Virtual Memory option encrypts the scratch space the Mac OS X uses when you are working, so a data thief can use it to find passwords or sensitive information. We recommend that this option be selected, as it is by default.

Tip

If you want the contents of your Trash securely deleted when you empty the Trash, choose Finder ⇨ Secure Empty Trash. You can make secure deletion the default by choosing Finder ⇨ Preferences or pressing ⌘+, (comma) and selecting Empty Trash Securely in the Advanced pane of the Preferences dialog box. Like using the Use Secure Virtual memory option, secure-deleting the Trash eliminates another place where stray information can be uncovered by data thieves.

Selecting the Disable Remote Control Infrared Receiver option means that someone can't control your Mac's iTunes or other media players via the remote control that comes with each Mac. Note that just not any remote control can access your Mac; you have to pair it first by clicking Pair and then pressing the remote control button to emit the infrared signal.

FIGURE 23.3

Use the Security system preference's General pane to determine when passwords are required by the Mac OS.

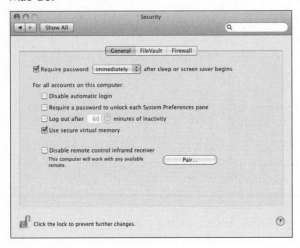

Preventing startup from other disks

One common way to get around having to know a login password is to attach an external disk to a Mac and then start from it. If that external disk's Mac OS X doesn't require a login password — or if it uses one the thief knows — then your startup disk's login password is useless.

Apple provides a way to tie your Mac's startup to a specific disk, one that requires a password to be able to choose a different startup disk. (After all, you may have a legitimate reason for choosing a different startup disk, such as to run the installation DVD or boot from the network for a contractor.)

You need an Intel-based Mac to tie Mac OS X to a specific default startup disk. And you need your Mac OS X 10.6 Snow Leopard installation DVD. Boot from that DVD, choose the language you want the installation DVD to use, and when the list of disks to install Mac OS X 10.6 Snow Leopard appears, don't choose one. Instead, choose Utilities➪Firmware Password Utility. In the dialog box that appears, click Change, select the Require Password option, and enter the password to use. (You need to enter it twice, to confirm you entered it correctly.) Click OK and restart the Mac.

The next time you try to start from a different disk — such as by holding Option, C, N, or T during startup to choose a disk, start from the CD or DVD drive, start from a network drive, or start in Target Disk Mode, respectively — a lock icon appears on-screen with a text field underneath. You must enter your firmware password and press Return or click the arrow icon to change the startup disk.

Tip

Here's a way to really secure your Mac when you leave it, such as during vacation: Use the Firmware Password Utility to tie startup to an external disk, and use a password that someone can't easily guess. Take the external startup disk with you, or leave it someplace else safe. Now someone who wants to access your Mac needs either that disk or your password, and is not likely to get access to either.

To disable this requirement, rerun the Firmware Password Utility, deselect the Require Password option, click OK, and restart the Mac.

Setting passwords for applications

We strongly recommend you set passwords on applications, such as your browser, that provide access to personal and sensitive information, such as bank accounts — especially if you use their features to remember passwords and automatically enter them for you. Talk about a treasure trove for an identity thief! Here is how to require a password for common applications:

- **Apple Safari.** There is no way to require a password for Safari, but you can choose Safari ➪ Private Browsing, which prevents Safari from storing any of your passwords, browser history, or download information, so a thief can't access them in the browser.

- **Mozilla Firefox.** Choose Firefox ➪ Preferences, go to the Security pane, and select Use a Master Password, then enter the password.

- **Mozilla Thunderbird.** Choose Thunderbird ➪ Preferences, go to the Privacy pane and then to its Password subpane, and select Use a Master Password to Encrypt Stored Passwords. You can change the master password by clicking Change Master Password. You can also view or change saved passwords by clicking Edit Saved Passwords.

- **Microsoft Entourage.** With a document open, choose Entourage ➪ Account Settings, double-click your user account, and go to the Account Settings pane. Either delete the password set in the Password text field or both enter the password in the Password text field and select Save Password in My Mac OS Keychain so Keychain Access manages the password's accessibility.

- **Microsoft Word.** With a document open, choose File ➪ Save As and click Options, then enter a password to open and/or modify the document (enter the password if requested for confirmation). (There's also an option to remove personal information from the document when it's saved; this information comes from the User Information pane in Word's Preferences dialog box.) Click OK and then save the document.

- **Microsoft Excel.** With a document open, choose File ➪ Save As and click Options, then go to the Security pane and enter a password to open and/or modify the document (enter the password if requested for confirmation). Click OK and then save the document.

- **Acrobat Professional.** With a document open, choose File ➪ Properties and go to the Security pane. Choose Password Security from the Security Method popup menu, then complete the form of options for what you want protected. Click OK until you are returned to the document (enter the password if requested for confirmation). When saved, the PDF file will have the security settings applied.

Note that there is no way to require a password to access Apple Mail e-mail accounts or Address Book contacts, nor is there a capability to require a password to open documents created in Apple iWork applications or in Microsoft PowerPoint. But a password is always required to purchase music, videos, and applications from the Apple iTunes Store.

Using Keychain Access

You may notice that the Mac OS sometimes asks you whether you want to save a password in a keychain; this prompt usually comes in the dialog box in which you are asked to enter a password. When you say yes, the Mac stores the password and fills it in for you the next time that password is requested by Mac OS X or an application. (Note that when Keychain Access asks you for permission to share the stored password with the requesting application, you can choose to allow it just that once or always.)

Note

Not all applications use the keychain, so you can't count on it as the central storage for all your passwords.

This keychain-based autofill of passwords is very convenient, but can make your Mac less secure. The key to enjoying the convenience of Keychain Access and not compromising your security is to have a good password for your user account. That's because by default, Keychain Access adds those passwords to your login keychain — a keychain is a set of stored passwords, security certificates, and other credentials — and then asks for your login password any time a specific password is required. In other words, it remembers your various passwords but needs you to remember just the master account password; when you tell it that, it tells the application the correct password for that application. So if your account password is weak, all your keychain-saved passwords are vulnerable.

Tip

If you want the login keychain password to differ from your account password, launch Keychain Access (it's in the Utilities folder in the Applications folder), select login in the Keychain list, and choose Edit ➪ Change Password for Keychain "login", then enter the new password. (You can change any selected keychain's password the same way.)

You can create separate keychains, not just use the login one established automatically when you create a user account. In the Keychain Access utility, choose File⇨New Keychain or press Option+⌘+N, give that keychain a name, and click Create. It's a very good idea to create a new keychain. Why? Because the login keychain is always open, making it less secure. A keychain you create is opened only when an application has stored a password in it, and then it closes after five minutes.

The trick is putting passwords in that new keychain. Whenever you are prompted to add a password to the keychain and answer yes, that password is placed in the login keychain, not in your other keychain. You have to manually move it in Keychain Access. Here's how:

1. Display the password list for the login keychain by selecting login in the Keychains list and then its passwords by selecting Password in the Category list, both at the left side of the Keychain Access dialog box.

2. Drag the desired password from the central pane onto the desired keychain, as shown in Figure 23.4.

3. Enter your account password (or login keychain password if different) to confirm that you want to move the password to the other keychain.

Tip

You can use the same technique to move other credentials; choose the desired credential type in the Category list and then drag the actual credential from the central pane to the desired keychain.

FIGURE 23.4

Drag a password from the login keychain to move it to another keychain.

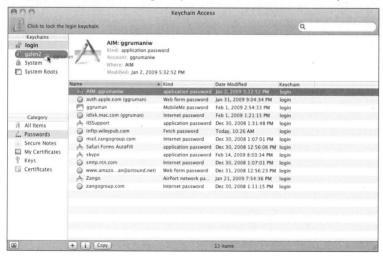

Note

Certificates are issued by Web sites to confirm their authenticity. Those in the My Certificates group are ones generated by the Mac such as for file sharing. Keys are used to access encrypted data. Secure Notes contain any text you want, so they are available for you later from the keychain, such as to store safe-deposit box combinations.

You can control how a password is used. To do so, double-click the password and then go to the Access Control pane, shown in Figure 23.5. If any application should have access, select Allow All Applications to Access This Item. Otherwise, select Confirm Before Allowing Access. If you want to force the user to enter the keychain password, also select Ask for Keychain Password. Select which applications may request the password by clicking the + iconic button; any applications that have permission appear in the Name list. You can remove an application's permission to use the password by selecting it and clicking the − iconic button. Click Save Changes when you're done.

FIGURE 23.5

Use the Access Control pane to determine exactly what applications may access a stored password.

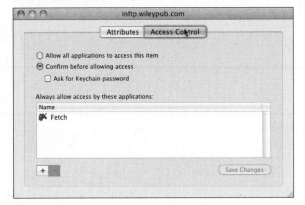

You can also use Keychain Access to look up passwords you've forgotten. To do so, double-click the password and go to the Attributes pane. (It should be open by default.) Select the Show Password option. You will be asked for your account or keychain password once or twice; after you've entered the account or keychain password, the item's specific password appears in the Attributes pane.

Two other Keychain Access options are worth noting:

- In the General pane of the Preferences dialog box (choose Keychain Access ➪ Preferences or press ⌘+, [comma]), select Show Status in Menu Bar so an icon with the keychain's current status displays. A locked icon means the keychain is locked; an unlocked icon means it is not. You can manually lock or unlock a keychain from the menu bar, or by choosing File ➪ Lock/Unlock Keychain "*keychainname*".

- If your keychain data gets corrupted, you can try to fix it by running Keychain First Aid (choose Keychain Access ➪ Keychain First Aid or press Option+⌘+A. You'll be asked for your password, and then can click Verify to see if the keychain has any issues or Repair to fix any issues.

Using Encryption

Your Mac may contain files that you want to do more than password-protect due to their confidential or sensitive information. We've all heard the stories about people losing thousands of financial records that were stored on a laptop that was lost. Had those laptops used encryption for those sensitive files, the risk of the loss would have been minuscule.

Mac OS X comes with an encryption utility called FileVault. You turn it on in the FileVault pane of the Security system preference: Just click Turn FileVault On. The FileVault process takes between 15 and 60 minutes to execute, and you can't do anything else while it is running — plus it logs you off and makes you log back in again, shutting down all open applications — so don't set up a FileVault unless you can do something else for a while.

Remember that turning FileVault on applies encryption just to the user account that sets it up, so each user with an account on your Mac should also set up FileVault to gain its protection.

If you have enough disk space — you need at least as much free space as your user's home account takes, and a Mac that's been in use for a while often does not — FileVault will convert your home user account so that any files stored in it are automatically encrypted. Any files stored outside of that account, such as on other drives or in other user accounts' Documents folders, are *not* encrypted.

Tip

If you don't have enough disk space to turn on FileVault, log in via another account (create another administrator account, if necessary, to do this), move your home folder's Documents, Music, and similar folders to an external drive to free up enough space, then turn on FileVault. Move the files back into the FileVault when done.

If your user account does not have a master password, you must set one before creating the FileVault. The master password can be different than the login password for this specific account. You'll need to know either one to be able to log in this user account or to be able to open files stored in the FileVault when it's opened from another user account or Mac. Click Set Master Password to set it. If you have such a password but want to change it, click Change.

After you ask Mac OS X to turn on FileVault, you get the Secure Erase option. If selected, this option deletes your original data after creating the encrypted copy in a way that it cannot be recovered through a file-recovery utility. If that scares you (and it should), leave the option unselected to make sure the FileVault copies are in good shape first. The original files will be deleted but recoverable through a utility such as those from Disk Doctors (www.diskdoctors.net), Prosoft Engineering (www.prosofteng.com), Stellar Information Systems (www.stellarinfo.com), and SubRosaSoft (www.subrosasoft.com).

After the FileVault operation is completed, your Mac will ask you to log back in. The Mac will appear unchanged, though the icon for your Home folder will have changed to the FileVault safe icon, as shown in Figure 23.6. You also won't be able to open that Home folder or see its contents in the Finder window's main pane. But you can access its contents in the Finder window Sidebar's Places section, as well as through applications' Open, Save As, and similar dialog boxes.

Mac OS X automatically decrypts and encrypts files as you work with them, so long as you are logged in with the correct password. You'll likely notice that the Mac runs a bit slower because of that automatic encryption and decryption. When you restart or shut down, you'll also see a message that the Mac is recovering disk space for your home folder, and notice a longer restart or shut-down time as a result of this cleanup operation.

Note
You can turn off FileVault by clicking Turn Off File Vault in the Security system preference's FileVault pane. As with creating a FileVault, this operation can take 15 minutes to an hour and will close your applications, log you out, and log you back in when done.

FIGURE 23.6

The icon for your Home folder changes to a safe icon if it is protected by FileVault.

Other user accounts on this Mac that have administrator privileges, as well as other computers that are connected to your Mac and have been given sharing access to it (see Chapter 13), won't see your user account's files and folders. Instead, they'll see a disk icon representing your FileVault. If they try to open that FileVault, they'll be asked to supply your login or master password to gain access, as Figure 23.7 shows. If they have a valid password, Mac OS X mounts your FileVault as if it were a new disk in the Finder.

FIGURE 23.7

Other users see your FileVault-protected Home folder as a secured disk and must provide a password to access its contents.

Tip

One limitation of Mac OS X's FileVault encryption is that it doesn't protect files not stored in the FileVault-protected Home folder. If you want to protect files stored elsewhere, you'll need a separate encryption utility, such as PGP Software's PGP Whole Disk Encryption ($119; www.pgp.com).

Caution

If you turn on FileVault, Mac OS X's Time Machine utility (see Chapter 4) will not work as expected. You won't be able to recover individual files by using the Time Machine software; you can only restore entire FileVault volumes with it. If you do want to just recover a specific file, you have to open it from the Time Machine backup drive, going through the various backup folders to find the file and then copy it back onto your Mac.

Plugging Security Holes

The most popularized threat today is malware: viruses, Trojan horses, worms, spyware, and other threats typically delivered via the Internet. These can come into your Mac from Web pages that run malicious code or have infected downloads, from e-mails that contain the same threats, or from hackers who find their way into your Mac through open ports on the network and on your broadband router (which connects you to the Internet).

There's little that Mac OS X can do about these threats, with one exception: its internal firewall, which helps secure your network's connections from attacks.

Protecting yourself from network attacks

If your Mac is exposed to the Internet, it could be a target for attack by a hacker. That's not too likely, as most Macs (and PCs) connect to the Internet through a router (such as a DSL or cable modem), and these routers should be set up to block traffic to nonstandard network ports, to prevent *pinging* from outsiders (pinging is how hackers see what's on your side of the router), and to enable firewall, stateful packet, and endpoint filtering to detect and block threats. But if your router is not set up to keep hackers out of your internal network, you could be at risk.

Of course, anyone on your local network can access your Mac, especially if you've turned on file sharing, Back to My Mac, screen sharing, or other sharing functions covered in Chapters 13, 15, and 21. Be sure that you don't provide more access than necessary with such functions; use the Mac's capability to restrict access to specified users and to require users to enter valid passwords.

Cross-Ref

Chapter 13 covers Mac OS X's file-sharing options. Chapter 15 covers the Back to My Mac remote-control function. Chapter 21's sections on the Bluetooth, MobileMe, and Sharing system preferences cover their security settings in detail. Chapter 3 also explains how to set file-sharing access for individual disks and folders.

Mac OS X offers its own firewall to protect it from attacks via the network, which is helpful if you fear attacks from someone who's broken into your network or if your Internet router's security is questionable. To set it up, open the Security system preference and go to the Firewall pane, shown in Figure 23.8. First click Start to turn on the firewall, then click Options to open the settings sheet to specify what is blocked and what is allowed through the firewall.

New Feature

Mac OS X 10.6 Snow Leopard changes how the options in the Firewall pane are configured. Plus, it adds two new options: Automatically Allow Signed Software to Receive Incoming Connections and Enable Stealth Mode.

In the settings sheet, you block all incoming connections by selecting the Block All Incoming Connections option; this blocks even connections permitted in the Sharing system preference. But the name is misleading; this option does not block the services that Apple considers essential: The DHCP (Dynamic Host Configuration Protocol) connection used to give your Mac an address on the network, the Bonjour service used to connect to network printers and similar devices, and the IPSec (Internet Protocol Security) service used to protect the data your Macs sends to the network.

You can specify how to handle other connections, such as e-mail connections from a Microsoft Exchange Server, by adding them to the window in the middle of the sheet. Click the + iconic popup menu to add a service, choose the application that uses it (such as iCal or Microsoft Entourage) from the dialog box that appears, then set the permissions from the popup menu to the right of the application name. Your permissions choices for each application are Allow Incoming Connections and Block Incoming Connections.

The Automatically Allow Signed Software to Receive Incoming Connections option, if selected, can reduce the configuration effort for deciding what applications' incoming connections are permitted. This option lets applications that use a certificate accept connections even if not in the sheet's list. Such certificates are configured on the servers that handle the communications, typically by an IT department.

The Enable Stealth Mode option, if selected, essentially hides the Mac from applications that use the Internet Control Message Protocol (ICMP) to find computers, printers, and other devices on a network. This protocol is handy to help network administrators monitor their networks, but it can also be abused by hackers to find poorly protected computers.

FIGURE 23.8

The settings sheet for the Security system preference's Firewall pane

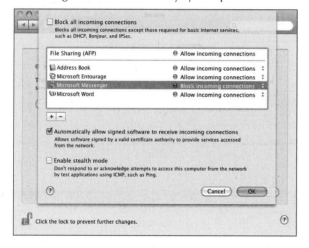

Note

Apple's approach to managing incoming connections is different than is typical for network administrators and Windows PC managers. They typically manage connections through network ports — addresses on a router that are typically assigned for specific connections. E-mail, for example, typically uses port 80. By shutting off ports whose associated service connections you don't want to allow in, you can block potential threats. But it requires knowing what each port is used for. By focusing on permissions for specific services and applications, Apple's firewall is easier for the average user to configure because it figures out what ports are affected.

If you think your Mac might be vulnerable, you can use the Network Utility to monitor its open ports, as Figure 23.9 shows. Launch the Network Utility (it's in the Utilities folder in the Applications folder) and go to the Port Scan pane. Enter your Mac's IP address (you can find this in the Network system preference; look for IP Address) to see what ports are open. You can also check your router by entering its IP address (also found in the Network system preference; look for Router). In fact, you can check for open ports for any computer, router, or Web site for which you have the IP address or URL. Your network administrator can tell you if any of the open ports are worrisome.

If you seriously want to understand what's happening with your network ports, Network Utility isn't the right tool. You'll need a network monitoring utility for your Mac instead, such as NetMonitor ($10; http://homepage.mac.com/rominar/net.html) or Digital Sentry ($20; www.koingosw.com). If you're on a network, your network administrator will, or should, have the right tools to monitor security for the entire network, not just for your Mac.

FIGURE 23.9

The Port Scan pane of the Network Utility

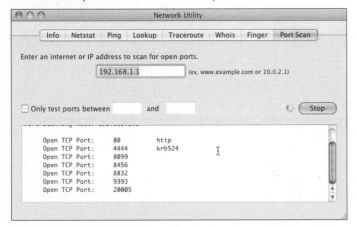

Keeping Mac OS X Up-to-Date

Apple very nicely provides an automatic update feature that periodically checks for updates to the Mac OS X and other Apple software, then downloads and installs that software. Not only do you get additional features from such updates, but you also get bug fixes and security patches that help protect your Mac from hackers and other ne'er-do-wells. You set the schedule for the automatic checking in the Software Update system preference, as described in Chapter 21. (The default schedule is weekly.)

Software Update runs automatically, but you can also make it look for updates whenever you want: Simply choose ⇨ Software Update and it looks for new updates.

When Software Update finds updates to install, it presents them in a list. It indicates any that require your Mac to restart. You can disable installation of any by deselecting the check box to the left of the update's description, or click Cancel to prevent the update from happening until the next check.

Protecting yourself from malware

To protect yourself from malware, the first line of defense is to be cautious in what you open on the Web or in an e-mail. Never open an attachment or go to a Web site from a link in an e-mail whose sender you do not know. Your bank, credit card issuer, or mortgage holder will not send you an e-mail with a link to verify your account; the links are to a thief's Web site, which collects the account numbers from the unwary who naively enter it. If you think such an e-mail might be legitimate, open your Web browser and type in the Web address you have on file or bookmarked, not the one that came in the e-mail. If there is a need to update your account, you'll be asked to do so when you log in to the account directly.

If you get a Valentine's e-mail from someone you don't know, or any message offering to share something interesting from a person you don't know, don't open it. The attachment is almost always malware. Yes, it's true that most malware is written for Windows PCs and won't work on your Mac, but there is some Mac malware, and there's no reason to think the Mac is somehow immune to attacks. It's not — it's just not the usual target. Note that if a friend's computer is infected, it may send you such links (it's been converted into a "zombie PC"); the hacker hopes you'll trust the friend's e-mail address and thus open the malware. Ask yourself if your friend would really send such a message — most are written in broken or legalistic English, a sign of a foreign hacker, and few sound like the actual person you know.

You should consider buying anti-malware software, especially if you have children or parents who might be naive about where they go in the Web and what e-mails they open. Intego's Internet Security Barrier X5 ($85; www.intego.com) and Symantec's Norton Internet Security for Mac ($80; www.symantec.com) both offer protection against viruses, worms, spyware, and Trojan horses — software that can take over your Mac, delete files, scan your contacts and send malware to them, and even record your passwords and account information and send it to the thieves who produced the malware. They also look for phishing attacks — those e-mails that have links to fake Web sites meant to steal your personal information — and other scams such as the e-mails falsely claiming to need your assistance to handle money on someone's behalf or the e-mails that ask you for money up front to process something (a pet adoption, a rent deposit, or account transfer are common ones) for someone without a local bank account in return for receiving your money back along with a fee "later."

E-mail programs — Apple Mail, Microsoft Entourage, and Mozilla Thunderbird — all have junk settings that also try to detect scams and phishing expeditions. Be sure you turn the junk detection features on. And if you manage your own e-mail server (directly or through a Web host), be sure to turn on its junk-mail detection features to reduce the amount of junk mail that actually makes it to your Mac. Ditto if you use an e-mail service such as Yahoo Mail or Google Gmail.

All of these programs do their job, but they don't catch everything, so human vigilance is still required.

Summary

Your Mac could be vulnerable in any or all of four areas: It could be physically lost or stolen, its stored personal data such as account information and passwords could be compromised, your files with sensitive data could be accessed, and it could be breached by an outsider and infected with viruses or other malware.

Your first line of defense is to secure the Mac itself, such as by locking it when not in use. You can reduce the chances of someone who steals or finds your lost Mac gaining access to its files by setting a login password, or even by tying startup to a specific drive.

Passwords should also be set for individual applications where possible, as well as to open files with sensitive data, which some popular programs support. You can also set the Mac to require passwords to make several kinds of system-level changes, as well as restrict what guests and other users have access to on your Mac through a combination of passwords and user-access privileges set in the Sharing system preference.

The Mac OS can store passwords for many applications for you in what's called a keychain, so all you have to remember is your keychain password instead of all your separate application and Web passwords. The Keychain Access utility lets you manage your passwords and other security credentials, as well as view them. Capabilities include choosing what passwords individual applications have access to and setting up separate keychains.

Mac OS X's FileVault encryption adds more protection to files stored in the home user's folders. Other users need a password to access the files, so they are protected even when file sharing is turned on. However, encrypted files cannot be restored from Time Machine backups without manual intervention.

Mac OS X offers a firewall capability to restrict access to the Mac's network connections to only approved services and applications. However, this should be used as an adjunct to, not a replacement for, the network's own firewall and other router-based security settings.

To protect yourself from malware such as viruses and spyware, you need to be careful as to what files you open and download, even if you are running anti-malware software.

Part V

Beyond the Basics

Enhancing Mac OS X with Utilities

A lthough Mac OS X 10.6 Snow Leopard comes with an amazing amount of utilities, as Chapter 8 explains, there are a few things the Mac OS doesn't do and a few things that benefit from enhancements. That's where third-party utilities come in. They fill the gaps and extend Mac OS X's native capabilities in cool ways.

This chapter surveys utilities you may want to bring into your Mac to either extend its current capabilities, or add new ones. And by "utilities," we don't mean full-fledged applications like Adobe Creative Suite, Microsoft Office, FileMaker, or Apple iWork that are used to do major work. Instead, we mean those little tools that make your life a little bit easier.

Of course, we don't mean to imply that everyone should get all of these utilities or only these utilities. Everyone's needs are different, and so there may be utilities not listed here that are perfect for you and ones listed here that you don't need. Our selections are meant to be utilities that *many* people should consider.

Utilities come from all sorts of sources, from major software providers to individuals who do it for the sheer joy of solving a problem. Many are free, and most of the rest are low cost (typically less than $25, though commercial wares tend to cost between $50 and $100). Some are sold in stores, but many more are available as downloads on the Internet.

Because of the volume and variety, it can be hard to know what's available and how to get it. Two good sources for tracking utilities are *Macworld* magazine (you can see its utility reviews at www.macworld.com/browse.html?type=3&cat=228) and the Version Tracker Web site (www.versiontracker.com/macosx/).

IN THIS CHAPTER

Utilities that extend Mac OS X capabilities

Utilities you can live without

Utilities that add new capabilities to Mac OS X

Extending Mac OS X

Consider these utilities to extend Mac OS X's own capabilities or provide better versions of what comes with Mac OS X.

Audio management

Rogue Amoeba (www.rogueamoeba.com) makes a variety of utilities that enhance how the Mac manages audio. Audio Hijack Pro ($32) enables you to capture sounds from any application or audio source on your Mac. Radioshift ($32) enables you to schedule recordings of Internet radio "stations" so you don't miss your favorite programs. (There's also a $10 version of Radioshift for the iPod Touch.)

Battery monitoring

Although Mac OS X shows you the state of your MacBook's battery's charge, it doesn't provide much information on how much charge your battery can hold (each time you recharge, you lose some storage capacity). CoconutBattery (free; www.coconut-flavour.com) gives you that precious information so you can see if your battery is working as it should.

Conferencing

You can hold audio and videoconferences with other Mac users by using iChat, as Chapter 11 explains, but iChat isn't up to the job of business-level conferencing, in which you can have multiple participants. The Yuuguu service and application (free for five simultaneous users, $9 per month for up to 30 simultaneous users; www.yuuguu.com) is easier to use, more flexible, and works — unlike many competing services — with Mac OS X, Windows, and Linux users equally well.

Disk management

Mac OS X's capability to search all attached drives quickly by name, attribute, and content (see Chapter 3) makes it very easy to find files when you need them. But they have to be on a disk attached to your Mac. What if your files are on CD or DVD, such as client archives or deliverables? DiskTracker ($30; www.disktracker.com) solves that problem, maintaining a catalog of offline disks' contents so you can still search for them and know what drive, CD, or DVD the actual files are on.

File synchronization

Apple's MobileMe (explained in Chapter 15) keeps your data (bookmarks, calendars, contacts, and so on) synchronized, and provides an online space called iDisk for storing files. A couple of really useful applications take iDisk a step farther, though, and are great for Mac users on the move. One, called DropBox (www.getdropbox.com) provides 2GB of free online storage, and pushes files to all your Macs with DropBox installed. You can pay $10 per month to get 50GB of storage. A more detailed utility called SugarSync ($5 to $25 per month; www.sugarsync.com) provides up to 250GB of storage and can sync any file or folder on your Mac to all your other Macs.

Font management

Although Mac OS X has the Character Palette to provide access to special characters (see Chapter 22), Ergonis's PopChar X (€30; www.macility.com/products/popcharx) does a better job more simply. It adds a menu to the menu bar that makes it easy to find and insert the characters not on your keyboard.

Media playback and delivery

Every Mac should have the basic media players installed to supplement QuickTime Player, iTunes, and Safari: Adobe Reader to read PDF files and Adobe Flash Player to play Flash animations and videos. You may also want to install the Adobe Shockwave Player to play 3-D games and presentations. All three utilities are free downloads at www.adobe.com.

If you deal with a lot of Windows video files (WMV), you know the Mac OS can't play them. But the Flip4Mac utility enables QuickTime Player, iMovie, and Final Cut Pro to work with WMV files. There's a free basic version at www.telestream.net, as well as a series of professional player and editor versions priced from $29 to $179.

If you stray into the world of DivX and other more obscure video formats, you should investigate a free program called VLC (www.videolan.org/vlc). This cross-platform media player works like QuickTime but can play just about any media file in existence.

Although Mac OS X can burn CDs and DVDs, anyone who records or copies lots of data and/or media discs will want Roxio's Toast ($100; www.roxio.com). It enables you to do all sorts of things with media files, such as send files from your Mac to TiVo digital video recorders, capture Internet audio and video streams, and stream your videos and music to your iPod or iPhone over the Internet, in addition to creating a variety of CD and DVD formats.

Remote access

Although Mac OS X allows screen sharing and remote control (see Chapter 13), it often does not work well across the Internet and even business networks. For two decades, Timbuktu Pro ($95 per computer; www.netopia.com/software/products/tb2) has provided reliable screen-sharing remote control, not only among Macs but also between Macs and Windows PCs (though only for Windows XP; at press time it did not support Vista or Windows 7). Timbuktu is expensive, it doesn't support the current versions of Windows, and the company was recently bought by Motorola, so its long-term future is unclear. But it does a great job.

Screen capture

Although you can take screen shots of your Mac by using the Grab utility (see Chapter 8), it's much easier to take screen images for books, manuals, and so on by using Snapz Pro X ($69; www.ambrosiasw.com). With Snapz Pro X you can be more selective about what you capture, as well as control the filenames as you take the screen captures, turn the mouse pointer on and off, and adjust image transparency and backgrounds. Plus, you can record sequences of actions as videos, so you can show people how to accomplish a series of steps.

Temperature monitoring

Modern processors run at a high temperature, and all Macs have built-in fans to dissipate the heat. Mac OS X does a pretty good job of controlling the internal temperature of a Mac, and it cranks up the fans and even turns off processor cores if things get too hot. In extreme circumstances, Mac OS X shuts down before allowing any damage to take place. Every Mac contains multiple heat sensors, and Marcel Bresink's Temperature Monitor and Temperature Monitor Lite (`www.bresink.de`) are free programs that display the temperature for each sensor in your Mac. MacBook users will particularly like them, as laptops can get very hot when placed on some surfaces that don't let heat dissipate.

Wi-Fi monitoring

The guy behind CoconutBattery also developed CoconutWiFi (free; `www.coconut-flavour.com`), which makes it easier to find Wi-Fi access points nearby. Mac OS X will show available Wi-Fi networks if you click the AirPort menu bar icon, but CoconutWiFi does that one better by showing you a green icon in the menu bar if there are unsecured Wi-Fi access points nearby and a yellow icon if there are secured ones available, as well as the number of access points available. That way you know immediately if there's a freely accessible access point you can connect to, or if only ones that require a login are available (chances are you won't have the passwords to these if you're casually looking for Wi-Fi access while on the road).

Utilities You May No Longer Need

Peruse any utilities directory on the Web, and you're sure to see lots of utilities. Many are specialized and of interest to some people. But some appear to be broadly useful, yet in practice are rarely necessary, mainly because Mac OS X now provides the utility features well enough on its own.

Perhaps the best example of this is file compression. There are dozens, perhaps hundreds, of utilities that compress and decompress files. But Mac OS X does this natively, creating Zip files (Control+click or right-click the files to be compressed and choose Compress x Items from the contextual menu) and opening Zip files (just double-click the file). For years, Aladdin Systems (now Smith Micro) offered StuffIt ($80; `www.smithmicro.com`), the flagship Mac compression utility that created a Mac-specific compression format (`.sit`) because there were no Zip utilities on the Mac. (Later on, StuffIt added Zip support.) But now that Zip is native to the Mac, there's no need for StuffIt's `.sit` format. And although StuffIt gives you more control over zipping and un-zipping (you can extract and add individual files, for example), it's not worth $80 to most people.

Another formerly popular class of Mac utility was the font manager, which enables you to collect all your fonts in one place and selectively turn them on and off as needed. The Mac's Font Book (see Chapter 22) has handled this task well since Mac OS X 10.5 Leopard for most users, so only professional users really benefit from the commercial utilities such as Suitcase Fusion ($100; `www.extensis.com`), FontAgent Pro ($100; `www.insidersoftware.com`), and FontExplorer X ($79; `www.fontexplorerx.com`).

The third class of utilities you probably don't need are disk utilities. The Mac's Disk Utility (see Chapter 8) enables you to format and repair disks, as well as create disk images and burn them to disc, while Time Machine (see Chapter 4) makes backup and file recovery a snap. So the need for disk-optimization and recovery utilities such as TechTool Pro ($98; www.micromat.com) isn't what it used to be. Such tools **are** essential for IT support in a workgroup or business, and if you have a serious home-based business or sole proprietorship, you may feel better having TechTool's capabilities in case it's needed.

Adding New Capabilities

Consider these utilities to add capabilities that most people should have but that Apple doesn't provide.

Application access

Although they could just as easily be considered applications instead of utilities, Parallels' Desktop ($80; www.parallels.com) or EMC VMware's Fusion ($80; www.vmware.com/products/fusion) — both are equally good — is a must-have for anyone who deals with Windows so you can run Windows applications on your Mac. (Chapter 18 covers these tools in depth.)

We recommend you install the Adobe AIR (free; www.adobe.com), which enables you to run desktop widgets that get data from the Internet. AIR widgets run like regular applications, so you don't have to switch to the Widgets window as you do with Apple's built-in widgets (see Chapter 8). Plus, AIR widgets can run in Windows, Linux, and Mac OS X, so they're great for companies, schools, clubs, and other groups whose people use different kinds of computers.

Communications

You can turn your Mac into a phone by using the Skype service and its Mac client (www.skype.com); pricing depends on where you are calling but is typically much cheaper than traditional phone services (there is a $10 minimum initial deposit). If you don't have a landline any more, it's a great way to make calls overseas without paying the ridiculously high international long-distance rates charged by cellular carriers. You can also make free computer-to-computer audio and video calls to other Skype users. Although theoretically you can use the Mac's built-in microphone and speakers, you'll want to get a USB headset for your audio calls. Your Mac's built-in iSight camera (if it has one) typically works well enough for the video calls. Just note that digital voice services like Skype don't support emergency-services numbers such as 911.

File transfer

If you manage a Web site — for your business, club, church, or family — or provide design or other services involving creating and distributing files, you'll benefit from a File Transfer Protocol (FTP) utility to make it easy to upload and download files to a Web-based server. There are two good ones to choose from: Fetch ($25; `www.fetchsoftworks.com`) and Transmit ($30; `www.panic.com/transmit`). There's also the free, open source FileZilla (`http://filezilla-project.org`) that is quite capable but not as user-friendly.

Security

Although the Mac is currently not a main target of hackers, so there aren't many viruses and similar malware threats for it; as it gains popularity, the chances of getting infected with malware will only increase. So rather than tempt fate, consider getting Intego's Internet Security Barrier X5 ($90; `www.intego.com`). For an antivirus-only tool, consider PC Tools' iAntivirus (`www.iantivirus.com`; free for home users, $30 for business users).

Summary

Although the Mac OS comes with many applications and utilities, you may find some features are missing, and others that could be more capable or easier to use. That's where utilities come in, filling in the gaps and improving some of what Apple has created. Hundreds of such utilities are available online in both commercial and hobbyist-created software for prices that range from free to more than $100.

Using AppleScript and Automator

Although computers have been touted for years as the ultimate tool to perform redundant tasks, you may feel as though they have generated new monotonous tasks. In previous chapters, you learned about technologies in Mac OS X 10.6 Snow Leopard that help you launch documents, edit text, manipulate multimedia, print documents, and perform hundreds of other tasks. And though you may be impressed by components in all those technologies; individually, the components don't do much by themselves — they tend to require user input. Scripting has long been a way to coordinate the different components of a task by enabling you to compose a script that plays back a set of commands in order.

The AppleScript scripting language is a simplified programming language that enables you to control your applications and perform tasks automatically. Scripts range from the simplest to the highly complex, depending on your skill at scripting, your knowledge of AppleScript's nuances, and the requirements of your task. This chapter contains enough information about AppleScript that even a scripting novice can get scripts up and running.

You begin by learning the underlying technologies that make AppleScript possible — messages and events. After you understand messages and events, it's on to an introduction of AppleScript and a look at the tools that enable you to run, modify, and create scripts of your own. Finally, you run through a few basic scripts, gaining an understanding of the AppleScript language as you go.

You also learn about Mac OS X's Automator application, which enables you to assemble script-like actions without programming skills and save them for reuse later.

Understanding Messages and Events

Macintosh applications perform tasks in response to events. Users originate events with the keyboard and mouse, and applications respond to the events by performing tasks. Similarly, an application can make other applications perform tasks by sending messages about events.

The events that applications send to each other in messages are called *Apple events*. AppleScript makes applications perform tasks by sending them Apple events.

When an application receives a message about an Apple event, the application takes a particular action based on the specific event. This action can be anything from performing a menu command to taking some data, manipulating it, and returning the result to the source of the Apple event message.

For example, when you choose ⇨ Shut Down or ⇨ Restart, Mac OS X sends an Apple event message to every open application saying a Quit event occurred. For this reason, applications quit automatically when you choose ⇨ Shut Down or ⇨ Restart.

When you drop document icons on an application icon, the Finder sends a message to Mac OS X saying this event happened, and the system sends the application an Apple event message that says an Open Documents event occurred. The Open Documents message includes a list of all the documents whose icons you dragged and dropped. When you double-click an application icon, the Finder sends the Mac OS a message that says this event happened, and the Mac OS sends the application an Open Application message. When you double-click a document, the application that created the document gets an Open Documents message with the name of the document you double-clicked.

Virtually all Mac applications respond to at least three Apple events: Open Application, Open Documents, and Quit Application. Applications that print also respond to the Apple event Print Documents. Only very old, very specialized, or poorly engineered Mac applications don't respond to these basic Apple events.

Applications that go beyond the three basic Apple events understand another two dozen core Apple events. These Apple events encompass actions and objects that almost all applications have in common, such as the Close, Save, Undo, Redo, Cut, Copy, and Paste commands. Applications with related capabilities recognize still more sets of Apple events. For example, word-processing applications understand Apple events about text manipulation, and drawing applications understand Apple events about graphics manipulation. Application developers can even define private Apple events that only their applications know.

Mac OS X provides the means of communicating Apple event messages between applications. The applications can be on the same computer or on different computers connected to the same network. To understand how Apple event messages work, think of them as a telephone system. Mac OS X furnishes a telephone for each application, as well as the wires that connect them. Applications call each other with messages about Apple events.

Apple events offer many intriguing possibilities for the world of personal computing. No longer does one application need to handle every possible function; instead, it can send Apple event messages to helper applications.

Introducing AppleScript

Apple event messages aren't just for professional software engineers. Macintosh enthusiasts with little technical training can use Apple event messages to control applications by writing statements in the AppleScript language. For example, suppose that you want to quit all open applications. Mac OS X doesn't have a Quit All command, but you can create one with AppleScript. You can use AppleScript commands to automate simple tasks, as well as to automate a more complicated series of tasks, as the rest of this chapter demonstrates.

The AppleScript language

With AppleScript you tell applications what to do, using natural language. This means simply that AppleScript is a programming language designed especially to make it easy for computer users, not computer engineers, to build their own solutions. (Actually, engineers use it, too.)

You tell applications what to do by writing statements in the AppleScript language. Although AppleScript is an artificial language, its statements are similar to sentences in a natural language such as English. You can look at many AppleScript statements and easily figure out what they're supposed to do.

The words and phrases in AppleScript statements resemble English, but they are terms that have special meanings in the context of AppleScript. Some terms are commands, and some terms are objects that the commands act on. Other terms control how AppleScript performs the statements.

A single AppleScript statement can perform a simple task, but most tasks require a series of statements that are performed one after the other. A set of AppleScript statements that accomplishes a task (or several tasks) is called a *script*. The term *script* is used because the computer follows the statements you put in order, much like an actor follows the script of a movie. A script can rename a batch of files, change an application's preference settings, copy data from a database to another application, or automate a sequence of tasks that you previously performed one at a time by hand. You can develop your own script tools to accomplish exactly what you need.

As an added boon, AppleScript can actually watch you as you work with an application and write a script for you behind the scenes. This process is called *script recording*.

Although AppleScript is designed to be a simple-to-understand language, it offers all the capabilities of a traditional programming language and won't frustrate programmers and advanced users. You can store information in variables for later use, write if ... then statements to perform commands selectively according to a condition that you specify, or repeat a set of commands as many times as you want. AppleScript also offers error checking and object-oriented programming.

Scripting additions

AppleScript has an expandable lexicon of terms. It knows meanings of basic terms, and it augments this knowledge with terms from other sources. Many additional AppleScript terms come from the very applications that AppleScript controls. We explore this source of AppleScript terms in greater detail later in this chapter.

Additional AppleScript terms also come from special files called *scripting additions*. AppleScript looks for scripting addition files in the following folders:

- ScriptingAdditions. Located in the Library folder of the System folder (path /System/Library/ScriptingAdditions/), it contains standard scripting additions from Apple that are available to all users of your computer. (This folder may also contain other files that are not scripting additions.)

- Scripts. Located in the main Library folder (path /Library/Scripts/), it contains more scripting additions that are available to all users of your computer.

Tip

If the ScriptingAdditions **folder doesn't exist in a Library folder where you want to put a scripting addition file, create a new folder and name it** ScriptingAdditions **(put no spaces in the name). Put your scripting addition file in this new folder.**

Introducing AppleScript Editor

For creating and editing AppleScript scripts, you can use the AppleScript Editor utility included with Mac OS X. AppleScript Editor can also run scripts, and it can make scripts into self-contained applications that run when you double-click them in the Finder. AppleScript Editor is normally located in the Utilities folder in the Applications folder.

New Feature

In Mac OS X 10.6 Snow Leopard, Apple has renamed its script editing utility from Script Editor to AppleScript Editor. It also now resides in the Utilities folder within the Applications folder, not in the no-longer-available AppleScript folder in the Applications folder.

Tip

If you end up doing a lot of scripting, you may want to replace AppleScript Editor with a more capable script development application, such as Script Debugger from Late Night Software ($199; www.latenightsw.com**). Make sure you get a version made for Mac OS X.**

Scriptable applications and environments

The scripts you create with AppleScript Editor can control any *scriptable application*. A prime example of a scriptable application is the Finder. Other scriptable applications included with Mac OS X include Apple System Profiler, ColorSync Scripting, Internet Connect, iCal, iChat, iPhoto, iSync, iTunes, Safari, Mail, Print Center, QuickTime Player, Sherlock, StuffIt Expander, Terminal, TextEdit, and URL Access Scripting. Interestingly enough, even the AppleScript Editor is scriptable. In addition, many Mac OS X applications not made by Apple are scriptable.

Looking at a script window

When you open AppleScript Editor, an empty script window appears. Each script window can contain one script. The top part of the script window is the script editing area, where you type and edit the text of the script just as you type and edit in any text-editing application. The bottom part of the window is the script description area. You use this area to type a description of what the script does. Figure 25.1 shows an empty script window.

FIGURE 25.1

A new script window appears when AppleScript Editor opens.

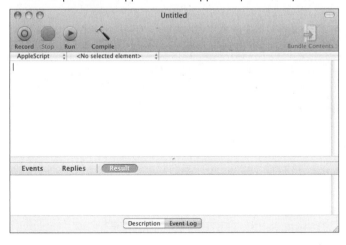

Tip
You can change the default size of a new script window. First, make the script window the size you want and then choose Window ⇨ Save as Default in AppleScript Editor.

The toolbar of a script window has five buttons. You find out more about each of them in later sections, but the following list summarizes their functions:

- **Record.** AppleScript goes into recording mode and creates script statements corresponding to your actions in applications that support script recording. You can also press ⌘+D to start recording. You cannot record scripts for every scriptable application because software developers must do more work to make an application recordable than to make it scriptable. You can find out whether an application is recordable by trying to record some actions in it.

- **Stop.** Takes AppleScript out of recording mode or stops a script that is running, depending on which action is relevant at the time. Pressing ⌘+. (period) on the keyboard is the same as clicking Stop.

- **Run.** Starts running the script that is displayed in the script-editing area. You also can press ⌘+R to run the script. Before running the script, AppleScript Editor scans the script to see if you changed any part of it since you last ran it or checked its syntax (as described next). If the script has changed, AppleScript Editor checks the script's syntax.

- **Compile.** Checks for errors in the script, such as incorrect punctuation or missing parts of commands. If any errors turn up, AppleScript Editor highlights the error and displays a dialog box explaining the problem. AppleScript Editor also formats the text to make keywords stand out and the structure of the script more apparent. AppleScript Editor may even change the text, but the changes do not affect the meaning of the script.

  If the script's syntax is correct, AppleScript Editor tells AppleScript to *compile* the script, which means it converts the text of the script into codes. These codes are what Apple event messages actually contain and what applications understand. You don't usually see these codes in AppleScript Editor because AppleScript translates them into words for the enlightenment of human beings.

- **Bundle Contents.** We talk more about bundles later in the chapter. However, if you are editing a script that is saved as a bundle, this button shows you the contents.

Creating a Simple Script

An easy way to see how a script looks and works is to type a simple script into a new script window. If AppleScript Editor is not already the active application, open it or switch to it. If you need to create a new script window, choose File ➪ New Script or press ⌘+N. In the script-editing area at the bottom of the new script window, type the following statements:

```
tell application "Finder"
activate
set the bounds of the first Finder window to {128, 74, 671, 479}
set the current view of the first Finder window to icon view
set the icon size of the icon view options of the first Finder window
    to 32
select the first item of the first Finder window
end tell
```

Check your script for typographical errors by clicking the Compile button in the script window. If AppleScript Editor reports an error, carefully compare the statement you typed in the script window to the same statement in the book. Pay particular attention to spelling, punctuation, omitted words, and omitted spaces.

When you click Compile, AppleScript Editor formats your script, changing the text formatting as it compiles the script by using different type styles to show different kinds of terms. The statements that you typed probably changed from Courier font to Verdana font after you clicked Compile. AppleScript Editor normally formats text that hasn't been compiled as 10-point Courier. Most other words, including commands from scripting additions and application dictionaries, are normally formatted in plain 10-point Verdana. Verdana 10-point Bold normally indicates native words in the AppleScript language. Figure 25.2 shows how AppleScript Editor formats the script that you typed.

FIGURE 25.2

Check your script for errors and format it for readability by clicking the Compile button.

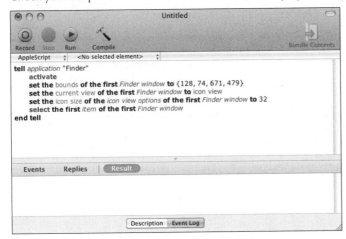

Before running this script, return to the Finder and make sure that a Finder window is displayed. If you really want to see the script in action, set the front Finder window to list view and resize the window so that it is very small.

After setting the stage for the script, switch back to AppleScript Editor and click Run in your script's window. AppleScript executes each script statement in turn. When the script finishes running, the Finder window should be a standard size and set to icon view. The item that comes first alphabetically in the window should be selected.

Switch to AppleScript Editor again and examine the script. You find that the script is fairly understandable. It may not be fluent English, but many of the commands should make sense as you read them.

Analyzing a Script

Having looked through the script that you wrote in the previous example, you may be surprised to learn that AppleScript doesn't know anything about the Finder's operations. Although your recorded script contains commands that set the position, size, and view of a Finder window and selects an item in it, AppleScript doesn't know anything about these or other Finder operations. In fact, AppleScript knows how to perform only the six following commands:

- Copy
- Count
- Error
- Get
- Run
- Set

AppleScript learns about moving and resizing Finder windows from the Finder. More generally, AppleScript learns about commands in a script from the application that the script controls. The application has a dictionary of AppleScript commands that work with the application. The dictionary defines the syntax of each command. AppleScript learns about more commands from scripting addition files on your computer. Each scripting addition file contains a dictionary of supplemental AppleScript commands.

Learning application commands and objects

Look at the sample script you created. The first statement says:

```
tell application "Finder"
```

To AppleScript, this statement means "start working with the application named Finder." When AppleScript sees a `tell application` statement, it looks at the dictionary for the specified application and figures out what commands the application understands. For example, by looking at the Finder's dictionary, AppleScript learns that the Finder understands the `select` command. The dictionary also tells AppleScript which objects the application knows how to work with, such as files and windows. In addition, an application's dictionary tells AppleScript how to compile the words and phrases that you write in scripts into Apple event codes that the application understands.

After learning from the `tell application` statement which application it will send event messages to, AppleScript compiles the remaining statements to determine what Apple event messages to send. One by one, AppleScript translates every statement it encounters in your script into an Apple event message based on the application's dictionary. When the script runs, the Apple event messages are sent to the application named in the `tell` statement. The application receives the messages and takes the appropriate action in response to the Apple events.

AppleScript stops using the application dictionary when it encounters the end tell statement at the end of your script.

A complex script may have several tell application statements that name different scriptable applications. In each case, AppleScript starts using the dictionary of the application named by the tell application statement, compiles subsequent statements by using this dictionary, and stops using this dictionary when it encounters the next end tell statement. Because AppleScript gets all the information about an application's commands and objects from the application itself, you never have to worry about controlling a new application. As long as the application has a dictionary, AppleScript can work with it.

Inspecting a dictionary

Just as AppleScript can get information about an application's commands and objects from its dictionary, so can you. Using AppleScript Editor, you can display the AppleScript dictionary of an application to see which commands the application understands and which objects the commands work with. You can also look at the dictionaries of scripting addition files.

Displaying a dictionary window

In AppleScript Editor, choose File ➪ Open Dictionary or press Shift+⌘+O. A dialog box appears, listing scriptable applications and scripting additions. Select an application or scripting addition file in the list and click Open. AppleScript Editor displays a dictionary window for the application or scripting addition you selected, as shown in Figure 25.3.

FIGURE 25.3

An AppleScript dictionary defines suites of commands and objects for a scriptable application or a scripting addition file.

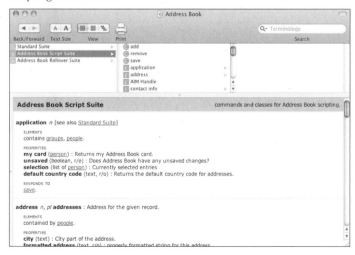

Tip

In the Open Dictionary dialog box, you can select several applications and scripting additions whose dictionaries you want to display (each in a separate window). To select adjacent items in the list, drag across or Shift+click the items. To select nonadjacent items, ⌘+click each item that you want to select.

Looking at a dictionary window

The top of the window shows hierarchically the commands that are available to you. In the leftmost pane is a list of groups of related commands called *suites*. They appear with a box with an *S* in it next to them. When you click a suite, its constituent commands appear in the middle pane. Commands are depicted with a square with the letter *c* inside. Clicking a command displays its constituent elements and properties (depicted with an *e* and a *p*, respectively). Verbs are shown with a blue square, and nouns have a purple square; elements have orange squares, and properties have purple. Below the triple-paned view, you will see the full explanation of the commands. The commands appear in bold, and objects appear in italic. AppleScript Editor groups related commands and objects into suites and displays the names of suites in bold. You don't have to worry about suites when you're scripting.

The description of a command briefly explains what the command does and defines its syntax. In the syntax definition, bold words are command words that you must type exactly as written. Words in plain text represent information that you provide, such as a value or an object for the command to work on. Any parts of a syntax definition enclosed in brackets are optional.

The description of an object very briefly describes the object and may list the following:

- **Plural Form.** States how to refer to multiple objects collectively. For example, you can refer to a specific window or to all windows.

- **Elements.** Enumerates items that can belong to the object. In a script, you would refer to `item of object`. For example, you could refer to a file named `index.html` in the Sites folder as `file "index.html" of folder "Sites"`.

- **Properties.** Lists the attributes of an object. Each property has a name, which is displayed in bold, and a value, which is described in plain text. Scripts can get and set property values, except that properties designated [r/o] (means read-only) can't be changed.

Saving a Script

In AppleScript Editor, you save a script by choosing File ⇨ Save or pressing ⌘+S, or by choosing File ⇨ Save As or pressing Shift+⌘+S. When you choose one of these commands, AppleScript Editor displays the Save dialog box. (The dialog box does not appear when you choose Save for a script that is open and has previously been saved.) In the dialog box, you can choose any of several different file formats for the saved script. The five options are Script, Application, Script Bundle, Application Bundle, and Text.

When you save a new script or a copy of a script, you specify a file format by choosing the format from the Format popup menu in the Save dialog box. AppleScript Editor can save in the following file formats:

- **Script/Script Bundle.** Saves the script as Apple event codes rather than plain text. You can open it with AppleScript Editor and then run or change it. In versions of Mac OS X prior to 10.4 Tiger, you run compiled scripts by using the Script Runner application and applications that have a script menu, such as Apple iWork. In Mac OS X 10.4 Tiger and later, the Mac OS manages the running of the scripts. You can save scripts as Run Only so they cannot be edited, only run.

- **Application/Application Bundle.** Saves the script as an application, complete with an icon. Opening the icon (by double-clicking it, for example) runs the script. When you choose the application format, the following three options appear at the bottom of the Save dialog box:

  - **Run Only.** Script application cannot be edited, only run.

  - **Stay Open.** Causes the application to stay open after its script finishes running. If this option is turned off, the application quits automatically after running its script.

  - **Show Startup Screen.** Displays an identifying window that appears when the application is opened. The Startup screen confirms that the user wants to run the script.

- **Text.** Saves the script as a plain text document. You can open it in AppleScript Editor, in a word-processing application, and in many other applications. Although a more portable file, this format is not as efficient as the others because the script must be compiled in AppleScript Editor before it can be run.

A handy capability is being able to save scripts as Mac OS X bundles. Mac OS X's applications are bundles (another name for packages) that, though they appear as a single item or application, are actually a collection of the files and resources that the application needs to run. (Apple calls this style of application packaging *Cocoa applications*.)

If you Control+click or right-click a Cocoa application, you can see inside of an application's bundle by choosing Show Package Contents from the contextual menu. You'll see all the necessary files and folders that make up an application's contents. The application bundle enables developers to make their applications installable via drag-and-drop instead of using an installer that places files all over your computer. When you save a script as either a Script Bundle or an Application Bundle, it creates a similar package from your script, and you can Control+click or right-click your saved document and see the package contents just like any Cocoa application.

Cross-Ref

See the AppleScript documentation for developers online at http://developer.apple.com/documentation/AppleScript/ if you are interested in more information about bundles and how they can be used. Access to this documentation requires registration with the Apple Developer Connection; you can find information about the ADC and sign up at http://developer.apple.com/index.html.

Creating a More Complex Script

You now know how to use AppleScript Editor to create a simple AppleScript script. This type of script, however, has limited value. A simple script that doesn't take advantage of the full AppleScript language is not very intelligent.

More frequently, you'll use AppleScript to create more complex scripts. This section explains how to create a full-blown script quickly and use the resulting custom utility to augment an application's capabilities.

Making a Finder utility

Your Mac OS X disk is full of special folders, but when someone sends you a file, it's up to you to figure out where the file belongs. For example, you have to sort TIFF and JPEG files into your Pictures folder, QuickTime files into your Movies folder, and MP3 files into your Music folder. You also have to classify and put away fonts, sounds, and so on. The Finder doesn't help you sort out any of this.

You can, however, write a simple script that recognizes certain types of files and uses the Finder to move files to the folders where you want the files to go. The destination folders can be any folders that you have permission to change. These include all the folders in your home folder. If you log in as a user with administrator privileges, the destination folders can also include folders in the main Library folder.

Beginning the script

To begin writing a new script in AppleScript Editor, choose File ⇨ New Script or press ⌘+N, and then type the following statement in the script editing area of the new script window:

```
choose file
```

This command gives the script user a way to specify the file to be moved. The `choose file` command displays a dialog box for choosing a file. This command is part of a scripting addition that is preinstalled in Mac OS X. The name of this scripting addition is Standard Additions.

Tip
You can change how AppleScript Editor formats text by choosing AppleScript Editor ⇨ Preferences or pressing ⌘+, (comma) and then going to the Formatting pane. A dialog box appears listing various components of AppleScript commands and the text format of each component. You can change the format of any component by selecting it in the dialog box and then choosing different formatting from the Font and Style menus.

Seeing the script's results

The script isn't finished, but you can run it now to see the results of the one statement you have entered thus far. Click Run to run the script in its current condition. When AppleScript performs the `choose file` statement, it displays a dialog box for choosing a file. Go ahead and select any file and click Choose. Because there aren't any more script statements, AppleScript stops the script.

AppleScript shows you the result of the last script action in the result window. If this window isn't open, choose View⇨Show Result or press ⌘+3. The result window contains the word *alias* and the path through your folders to the file you selected. This wording does not mean that the file is an alias file. In the context of a script, *alias* means the same thing as *file path*. Figure 25.4 shows an example of the result window.

AppleScript Editor's result pane shows the result of running a script.

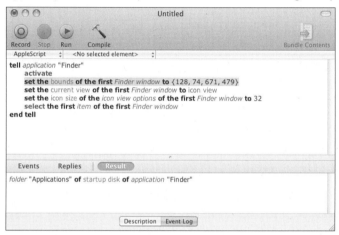

Using variables

The result of the `choose file` statement is called a file specification, or *file spec*. A file spec tells Mac OS X exactly where to find a file or folder. You need the file spec later in the script, so you must put it in a *variable*, which is a container for information. You can place data in a variable and then retrieve it whenever you want to before the script finishes running. The data in a variable is called the variable's *value*. You can change a variable's value by placing new data in it during the course of the script.

On the next line of the script, type the following statement:

```
copy the result to thisFile
```

This statement places the result of the `choose file` statement in a variable named `thisFile`. You can include the `thisFile` variable in any subsequent script statements that need to know the file spec of the chosen file. When AppleScript sees a variable name, it uses the current value of the variable. In this case, the value of variable `thisFile` is the file spec you got from the first statement.

When you run the script, you see that the `copy` command doesn't change the result of the script (as displayed in the result window). Because the result is just being copied to a variable, the result doesn't change.

Capitalizing script statements

You may notice the capital *F* in the `thisFile` variable and wonder whether capitalization is important when entering AppleScript statements. In general, you can capitalize any way that makes statements easier to read. Many AppleScript authors adopt the convention of capitalizing each word in a variable name except the first word, hence `thisFile`. This practice helps you distinguish variables from other terms in statements, which are generally all lowercase.

Getting file information

Ultimately, the script you are creating decides where to move a selected file based on the type of file it is. In Mac OS X, a file's type may be indicated by a filename extension (suffix) at the end of the file's name or by a hidden four-letter code known as the *file type*. Therefore, the script needs to determine the name and the file type of the selected file. You can use another command from the Standard Additions scripting addition to get this information. (Standard Additions is preinstalled in Mac OS X.) Enter the following statements beginning on the third line of the script:

```
copy the info for thisFile to fileInfo
copy the name extension of the fileInfo to nameExtension
copy the file type of the fileInfo to fileType
```

The first of these statements uses the `info for` command to get an information record about the selected file that is now identified by the variable `thisFile`. The first statement also copies the entire information record into a variable named `fileInfo`.

A record in AppleScript is a structured collection of data. Each data item in a record has a name and a value. AppleScript statements can refer to a particular item of a record by name, using a phrase similar to `item of record`. This is the phrasing used in the second two statements listed earlier.

Each of the second two statements gets an item of a record and copies it into a variable. The item names in these statements, `name extension` and `file type`, are taken from the AppleScript dictionary definition of the record. In this script, the record was obtained by the `info for` command in a previous statement.

To test the script so far, run it, choose a file, and look at the result. The result window contains the four-letter file type of the file you chose, displayed as a piece of text. Figure 25.5 shows the whole example script so far.

FIGURE 25.5

The StandardAdditions dictionary description of the `info for` command shows what the command returns.

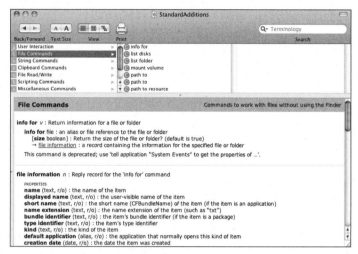

Using parentheses

You may notice that when AppleScript compiles the example script, which happens when you run the script or check its syntax, AppleScript adds parentheses around `info for thisFile` but does not add parentheses in other statements. AppleScript adds parentheses around a command that returns a value, which any `info for` command does. However, AppleScript does not add parentheses around a command at the end of a statement, such as the `choose file` command in the first statement of the example script. Nor does AppleScript add parentheses around elements that refer to a property, such as the `name extension of the fileInfo` in the example script.

Parentheses group elements of a command together. You can type your own parentheses around elements that you want to group in a statement. Parentheses make a complex AppleScript statement easier to read. They may also affect the result of a statement because AppleScript evaluates elements within parentheses before evaluating other elements of a statement.

Working with an application

For the next part of the script, you need to add statements that move the chosen file to the folder where it belongs. The script can use an application — the Finder — to move the file. Add the following statement to have AppleScript start using the Finder:

```
tell application "Finder"
```

After AppleScript encounters this statement, it knows all the commands and objects from the Finder's AppleScript dictionary. This means that subsequent statements use commands and objects that the Finder understands. AppleScript sends these commands and objects to the Finder in Apple event messages. The script doesn't yet include any statements for the Finder, but we add some next. Later we add an end tell statement to have AppleScript stop using the Finder.

Performing script statements conditionally

When creating complex scripts, you may want to give your script the ability to decide what to do based on the factors you specify. AppleScript, like all programming languages, lets you include a series of conditional statements, or *conditionals* for short. Each conditional begins with an if statement, which defines the condition to be evaluated. The if statement is followed by one or more other statements to be performed only if the condition is true. The conditional ends with an end if statement. In AppleScript, a simple conditional looks like this:

```
if the fileType is "MooV" or the nameExtension is "mov" then
move thisFile to folder "Movies" of home
end if
```

In this example, the if statement contains a two-part condition. The first part of the condition determines whether the current value of the fileType variable is MooV, which is the four-letter file type of QuickTime movie files. The second part of the condition determines whether the filename ends with mov, which is the filename extension for a QuickTime movie file. If either part of the condition is true, AppleScript performs the included move statement. If both parts are false, AppleScript skips the included move statement and goes on to the statement that follows the end if statement. Remember that AppleScript sends the move command to the Finder because of the tell application statement earlier in the script.

Note

AppleScript considers the dot, or period, between the filename and the extension to be a separator. The dot is not part of the extension or the filename as far as AppleScript is concerned.

Include as many conditionals in the example script as you want. In each conditional, use the four-character file type and corresponding filename extension for a different type of file, and specify the path of the folder to which you want AppleScript to move files of that type. A quick way to enter several conditionals is to select one conditional (from the if statement through the end if statement), copy it, paste it at the end of the script, and change the relevant pieces of information. You can repeat this for each conditional you want to include.

Finding a Folder Path

If you don't know the full path of a folder, you can use a script to get this information. Open a new window in AppleScript Editor and type the following command in the script editing area:

```
choose folder
```

Run the script and select a folder. The result is a file spec for the folder you selected. You can copy the text from the result window and paste it in any script.

You may notice that the file spec has a colon after each folder name. AppleScript uses colons in file specs to maintain compatibility with Mac OS 9 and earlier. Outside of AppleScript, Mac OS X generally follows the Unix and Internet convention of putting a slash after each folder name.

You can make the previous script a bit more interesting by using the `choose folder` command in the second line in place of a hard-coded folder path:

```
if the fileType is "MooV" or the nameExtension is "mov" then
move thisFile to choose folder
end if
```

This asks the user where to place the file after it is moved.

Finding a File's Type

You may not know the file type of the files that you want to move. For example, you may know that you want to put font files in your Fonts folder, but you may not know that the four-letter file type of a font file is FFIL. To make a script that reports the file type, copy the following three-line script to a new AppleScript Editor window:

```
choose file
copy the result to thisFile
copy the file type of the info for thisFile to fileType
```

Run this three-line script and select a file whose four-character file type you need to learn. If the result window is not visible, choose View⇨Show Result or press ⌘+3. The result of the script is the file type of the selected file. You can copy and paste the result from the result window into a conditional statement in any script window.

If you choose a file that has no file type, one of two things happens: The result window displays an empty value (indicated by quotation marks with nothing between them) or AppleScript reports an error, saying that it can't get the file type.

Breaking long statements

When you type a long statement, AppleScript Editor never breaks it automatically (as a word processor does). Long sentences wrap to the width of your window. Remember that each *line* is a statement and a *return* delimits a line, whereas a *break* only *visually* ends the line and doesn't change the *statement*. You can break a long statement manually, for better readability, by pressing Option+Return. (Do not break a statement in the middle of a quoted text string, however.) AppleScript displays a special symbol (¬) to indicate a manual break. Here's an example:

```
if the fileType is "JPEG" or ¬
the nameExtension is "jpg" or ¬
the nameExtension is "jpeg" then
move thisFile to folder "Pictures" of home
end if
```

In this example, the first statement, which goes from `if` through `then`, takes three lines because it has two manual line breaks.

Ending the use of an application

After the last statement that is directed at the Finder, the script needs a statement that makes AppleScript stop using the application. Type the following statement at the end of the script:

```
end tell
```

This statement doesn't include the name of the application to stop using because AppleScript automatically pairs an `end tell` statement with the most recent `tell` statement. Subsequent statements in the script can't use the commands and objects of that application.

Now is a good time to recheck the script's syntax. If you tried to compile recently, you got an error message about a missing `end tell` statement. Click Compile now, and after AppleScript compiles the script you see AppleScript Editor neatly indent statements to make the structure of the script more apparent. If AppleScript encounters any errors while compiling your script, AppleScript Editor advises you of them one by one.

Trying out your script

After creating a new script, you must run it and test it thoroughly. To test the script that moves files according to their type, follow these steps:

1. **Run your script.**

2. **When the dialog box appears, select a file that is of a type your script should recognize but that is not in the destination folder, and then click Choose.**

3. **Switch to the Finder, and make sure that the file you selected actually moved from the source folder to the destination folder.**

4. **Repeat the test, selecting a different file type that your script should recognize.**

Figure 25.6 shows an example of a script with four conditional statements that move a selected file depending on its file type or filename extension.

FIGURE 25.6

This script uses conditional statements to determine where to put a file.

Creating a Drag-and-Drop Script Application

Although the sample script you created is useful, it would be more useful as an application with an icon on your desktop. Then you could drag files that you wanted to sort into folders and drop them on the application's icon. This would cause the application to run and move the files to their appropriate folders. You wouldn't have to open AppleScript Editor every time you wanted to sort files into folders, and you could sort more than one file at a time. Applications respond to this type of drag-and-drop Apple event, and so can Apple Scripts.

You already know that AppleScript can save a script as an application. With a little extra work, you can make an application with drag-and-drop capability so that you can simply drag files to it to choose them.

Retrieving dropped files

Remember that when you drop a set of icons on an application in a Finder window, the Finder sends that application an Open Documents message that includes a list of the files you dropped on the icon. This message is sent to all applications, even to applications that you create yourself with AppleScript.

You need to tell your script to intercept that event message and retrieve the list of items that were dropped onto the application icon. Place the following statement at the beginning of your script, and delete the `choose file` line we added earlier:

```
on open itemList
```

Now enter the following statement at the end of your script:

```
end open
```

This on open statement enables the script to intercept an Open Documents event message and puts the message's list of files in a variable named `itemList`. The end open statement helps AppleScript know which statements to perform when the open message is received. Any statements between the on open and end open statements are performed when the script receives an Open Documents event message.

Save this script by choosing File ➪ Save As. From the File Format popup menu in the Save As dialog box, choose the Application option. (You may want to save the script on the desktop, at least for experimental purposes.) If you switch to the Finder and look at the icon of the application you just created, you can see that the icon includes an arrow, which indicates that the icon represents a drag-and-drop application. The application has this kind of icon because its script includes an on open statement.

Processing dropped files

The script won't be fully operational until you make a few more changes. As the script stands, it places the list of files in a variable, but it doesn't do anything with that information. If you dropped several files on the application now, the script would still display a dialog box asking you to pick a file and then quit, having accomplished nothing.

First, you need to eliminate the script statements that obtain the file to be processed from a dialog box. Delete what now are the second and third lines of the script (the ones beginning with the words choose and copy) and replace them with the following:

```
repeat with x from 1 to the number of items in the itemList
copy item x of the itemList to thisFile
```

Between the end tell and end open statements, which are the last two lines of the script, enter the following statement:

```
end repeat
```

Figure 25.7 shows the complete sample script modified for drag-and-drop operation.

This script application processes items dropped on its icon.

Save the script so that your changes take effect and then switch back to the Finder. You now have a drag-and-drop application that you can use to move certain types of files to specific folders.

Using a repeat loop

In the modified script, AppleScript repeatedly performs the statements between the repeat and end repeat statements for the number of times specified in the repeat statement. This arrangement is called a *repeat loop*. The first time AppleScript performs the repeat statement, it sets variable x to 1, as specified by from 1. Then AppleScript performs statements sequentially until it encounters the end repeat statement.

In the first statement of the repeat loop, variable x determines which file spec to copy from variable `itemList` to variable `thisFile`. The rest of the statements in the repeat loop are carried over from the previous version of the script.

When AppleScript encounters the `end repeat` statement, it loops back to the `repeat` statement, adds 1 to variable x, and compares the new value of x with the number of items that were dragged to the icon (as specified by the phrase `the number of items in the itemList`). If the two values are not equal, AppleScript performs the statements in the repeat loop again. If the two values are equal, these statements are performed one last time, and AppleScript goes to the statement immediately following `end repeat`. This is the `end open` statement, which ends the script.

Extending the script

Anytime you want the application to handle another type of file, open the script application in AppleScript Editor, add a conditional that covers that type of file, and save the script.

The script in its drag-and-drop form now no longer functions if you double-click it. You can modify the script to restore this functionality by placing a copy of the original script at the end of the `end open` statement.

Tip
You can't open a script application to edit it by double-clicking it because doing so causes the application to run. To open a script application in AppleScript Editor, choose File ⇨ Open or drop the script application on the AppleScript Editor icon in the Finder.

Borrowing Scripts

An easy way to make a script is to modify an existing script that does something close to what you want. You simply duplicate the script file in the Finder, open the duplicate copy, and make changes. You can do this with scripts that have been saved as applications, compiled scripts, or text files. (You can't open a script that has been saved as a run-only script.)

Apple has developed a number of scripts that you can use as starting points or models for your own scripts. You can find some scripts in the Example Scripts folder, which is in the AppleScript folder in the Applications folder. Another place to look is the Scripts folder, which is in the Library folder. The official AppleScript site has some (www.apple.com/applescript/). Check out the Learn and Explore areas of this site. You'll find snippets of code, links to third-party resources, and even some scripts to download directly.

Enabling the Script Menu

After you've built up a collection of scripts that you run frequently, you're not going to want to switch to AppleScript Editor every time you want to run one. This reason is precisely why Mac OS X has included the Script menu (which displays as a stylized *S* icon) since version 10.2 Jaguar, which replaces the Script Runner application in Mac OS X 10.1 Puma and earlier.

The Script menu sits in the toolbar at the top of the Mac OS screen. You can run any of the listed scripts by choosing the script from the Script menu. To activate the Script menu, run the AppleScript Editor application from the `/Applications/Utilities` folder, open the Preferences dialog box by choosing AppleScript Editor ⇨ Preferences or pressing ⌘+, (comma), going to the General pane, selecting the Show Script Menu in Menu bar option, and closing the Preferences dialog box. (You can also change the default script editor, should you find a third-party editor you prefer, in the AppleScript Editor Preference dialog box's General pane.)

New Feature

Mac OS X 10.6 Snow Leopard eliminates the AppleScript Utility found in earlier versions of Mac OS X. Its functions now reside in the AppleScript Editor's Preferences dialog box.

Linking Programs Across the Network

You have seen how AppleScript can automate tasks on your own computer. Ever since Mac OS X 10.1 Puma, AppleScript can send Apple events messages to open applications on other Macs in a network. As a result, you can use AppleScript to control applications on other people's computers. Of course, the reverse is also true: Other people can use AppleScript to control applications on your computer.

Sharing programs by sending and receiving Apple events messages across a network is called *program linking*. For security reasons, program linking is normally disabled. Computers that you want to control with AppleScript must be set to allow remote Apple events. Likewise you must set your computer to allow remote Apple events.

Every version of Mac OS X since 10.1 Puma uses TCP/IP (Transmission Control Protocol/Internet Protocol) to send and receive Apple events messages over a network. Therefore, Mac OS X can send and receive Apple events messages over the Internet as well as over a local network. No version of Mac OS X can use the AppleTalk protocol to send or receive Apple events over a remote network as could Mac OS 9 and earlier. (Chapter 12 explains networking protocols.)

Allowing remote Apple events

If you want a Mac OS X computer to receive Apple events from remote computers, you must set it to allow remote Apple events. First, open the Sharing system preferences and go to the Remote Apple Events pane. Select the check box to the left of the Remote Apple Events label to turn on Apple events. You can restrict the execution of Apple events to specific users by selecting Only These Users and then clicking the + iconic button to add the permitted users, as Figure 25.8 shows.

Caution

The All Users option can compromise your Mac's security by providing an entry point for hackers to control your Mac. If you must use this option, us it sparingly, being sure to turn it off when not needed. Preferably, you use the Only These Users option to restrict access to your Mac to people you trust.

New Feature

Mac OS 9 has been gone for nearly a decade, so the chances of encountering Mac OS 9 users is pretty slim these days. Mac OS X 10.5 Leopard dropped the ability to run Mac OS 9, and now Mac OS X 10.6 Snow Leopard drops support for Mac OS 9 in its remote Apple events. Thus Mac OS 9 users cannot access your Mac's application and system capabilities via Apple events. That's why the Options button is gone from the Sharing system preference's Remote Apple Events pane.

FIGURE 25.8

Set Mac OS X to receive remote Apple events by using the Sharing system preference's Remote Apple Events pane.

Scripting across a network

Using AppleScript to run a program across the network doesn't take much more work than writing a script to use a program on the same computer. For example, the following script sends commands to the Finder on the computer at IP address 192.168.1.203:

```
set remoteMachine to machine "eppc://192.168.203"
tell application "Finder" of remoteMachine
   using terms from application "Finder"
         activate
         open the trash
   end using terms from
end tell
```

The example script begins by setting the value of variable `remoteMachine` to the URL of a remote computer. A URL for remote Apple events begins with `eppc://` and is followed by the remote computer's IP address or DNS (Domain Name Service) name. (The prefix `eppc` stands for *event program-to-program communication*.) Starting with Mac OS X 10.3 Panther, Macs can also be called by their Bonjour name (the name you see in a Finder window's Shared list when connected to another Mac) in scripts, so no URL is required.

The second statement of the example script names the application, in this case Finder, and uses the variable `remoteMachine` to identify the remote computer.

Inside the `tell application...end tell` block is another block that is bracketed by the statements `using terms from` and `end using terms from`. When AppleScript encounters the statement `using terms from`, it compiles subsequent statements by using the named application's scripting dictionary but does not send the resulting Apple events to this application. The Apple events from a `using terms from` block are sent to the application named in the enclosing `tell application` block. In the example script, AppleScript compiles the `activate` and `open the trash` statements by using terms from the Finder's scripting dictionary on the local computer (your computer) but sends the resulting Apple events to the Finder on the remote computer.

When you run a script that sends remote Apple events, AppleScript has to connect to the remote application. Before doing this, AppleScript displays a dialog box in which you must enter a name and password of a user account on the remote computer. If you connect successfully, the script continues. At this point the example script should cause the remote computer's Finder to become the active application and open the Trash in a Finder window.

If you run the script again, you don't have to go through the authentication process. After AppleScript is connected to an application on a particular remote computer, you don't have to go through the authentication dialog box each time you want to send an Apple event.

AppleScript Studio

You have seen that AppleScript is a very powerful scripting language, and you should now have some ideas as to how you can make your own life more automated. Although AppleScript is billed as a scripting language, it is, for all intents and purposes, a programming language as well. Apple knows this, and has built into the developer's tools a means to easily create an application-quality front end to your AppleScripts.

Using AppleScript Studio in concert with AppleScript Editor, you can build full-fledged applications with icons, menus, and all the interface elements associated with a complete application. AppleScript Studio has been incorporated into Apple's Xcode and Interface Builder development tools and is included for free with Mac OS X 10.6 Snow Leopard on the Developer Tools CD.

Automating with Automator

You have seen that using AppleScript is an extremely powerful tool to create your own applications and make your life easier by scripting repetitive tasks simply and cleanly. In Mac OS X 10.4 Tiger, Apple introduced an even easier tool to automate your life: Automator. Automator is kind of a visual analog to the AppleScript language. Instead of building scripts by using natural language pseudo-sentences, you can drag and drop commands into what Apple calls a *workflow* to tell programs what to do.

Automator has a very basic windowed interface, as shown in Figure 25.9. It has three basic sections: a paned section similar to a Finder window where you can choose from a list of applications, a description pane on the right, and the workflow pane on the bottom. The top-left frame contains three panes; one that groups actions by application or name, one that holds your application "library," and one that holds the actions available for each application. To the right of these three panes is a frame that provides descriptions for actively selected actions. The pane on the bottom is your workspace — you drag actions from the left to build your workflow here.

The Library pane contains available actions and workflows that you can drag to the right frame in order to create new workflows to automate your life. In this example, you begin by making a PDF. You first have Automator help you choose your files. Click the Files and Folders library in the Library pane to show the available actions for the Finder. Click and drag the list — Find Finder Items — action to the workspace pane. You can use this action to predefine a specific search in the same way that you would use the find function in the Finder. Type `.png` in the name field.

Note
You can leave the text fields blank, click the Options button in the upper-bottom portion of the action, and select Show this action when the workflow runs. Then when you run your workflow, you will be prompted to specify the parameters for the search. Alternatively, you can use one of the other file-choosing actions in the Finder library to get files, such as Get Selected Items From Finder, which enables you to select whichever files you want manually and then run your workflow.

FIGURE 25.9

The Automator interface has a paned application selector, a description pane, and a workspace on the bottom.

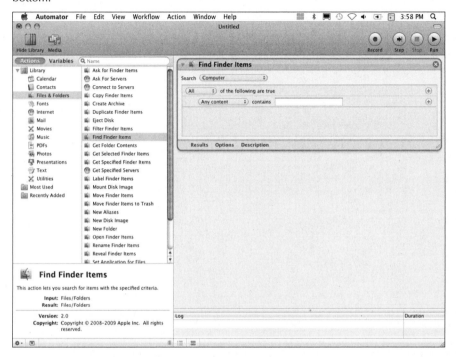

Next, drag the Open Files action to the workspace. You'll see the action pop into place right below the action you already placed: Find Finder Items. Notice that there is a little white triangle at the bottom of the Find Files In Finder action, which is dovetailed with the gray portion of the action just below it, Open Files. This is a graphical representation of the idea that the output of the previous action is passed to the action just below it, which in this case is a string of found files. The workflow you have just created searches your computer for PNG files and when found, opens them in the default application for JPEG files on your system, usually Preview. This is not particularly useful for your purposes, so you'll remove the Open Files action from your workflow.

You can remove an action from your workflow in several ways that should be familiar to you by now. First, you can click the gray X in the upper right of each action; alternatively, you can click and drag an action out of the workspace. You can also select an action and press Delete on your keyboard. Because you probably don't want to create a PDF contact sheet out of PNG files that have the word *John* in them, you should use one of these methods to clear your workspace of actions and begin again.

Begin again by dragging the Ask for Finder Items action from the Finder Library, and then select Desktop in the Start At popup menu and Folders in the Type popup menu. If you want to select multiple folders at a time, make sure that you specify multiple selections can be made by using the Allow Multiple Selections option, as shown in Figure 25.10; otherwise, you will only be able to select one folder in the dialog box during runtime.

FIGURE 25.10

Get ready to make a slide show by telling Automator to choose files during runtime.

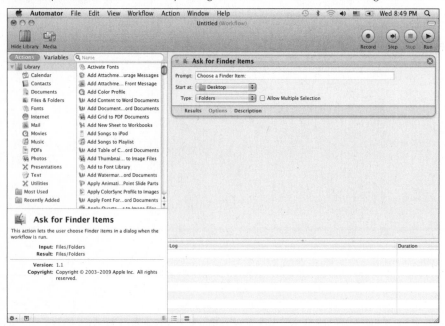

Next, you can make things interesting by using CoreImage to do some image processing. From the Photo actions, drag Apply Quartz Composition Filter to Images. Apple has made it as easy as possible to prevent accidents from happening. Because the Quartz Composition Filter makes changes to the original files, the act of dragging the action over to the workflow triggers Automator to ask you if you'd like to add an action it's been programmed to "suspect" you want; in this case, make a copy of your files before applying the filter action.

Choose to add the copy action, and specify in the resulting action that you would like to choose where to put the duplicated files when the workflow runs. In Figure 25.11, you can see the runtime option is checked for the copy action, but not for the filter. Choose Sepia from the popup menu in the Apply Quartz Composition Filter pane to make an old-style contact sheet.

Still in the Photo actions library, choose New PDF Contact Sheet and drag it into your workflow after the Filter action. Configure the options such as paper size and number of columns.

FIGURE 25.11

You can use the Apply Quartz Composition Filter action to make your pictures look like old-time photos.

You have just created a contact sheet-making workflow that you can use over and over again. To reuse the workflow, however, you need to save the workspace. Similar to AppleScript scripts, there are two forms in which you can save a workspace: as an application or as a workflow document. Like AppleScript applications, Automator applications can't be edited without directly opening them from within Automator, and workflows can't be run outside of Automator.

Another neat way to use Automator workflows is to create a plug-in for other programs out of your workflow. By choosing File ➪ Save As Plug-in, you can add the workflow as a contextual menu item in supported applications such as the Finder.

Recording Actions

Mac OS X Snow Leopard enables you to record your actions to build workflows and create Automator actions. This addition makes Automator even easier to use to automate your life. Be aware that Automator records mouse movements and keystrokes, and will play them back in sequence, so its recording capability is not as elegant a solution as using an application's built-in workflow actions. However, if an application developer has not provided the interface that you need to build a workflow, or you want to do something more complex, this can be an easy way to accomplish your goal.

Note

To use this recording feature, you have to have Assistive Devices enabled in the Universal Access system preference (see Chapter 6). If you do not have Assistive Devices enabled and try to record an action, Automator prompts you to enable it.

To begin recording an action, click the Record button in the main Automator window. Begin the procedure you want to record. When you are done recording the set of keystrokes, return to Automator and click the Stop button. Your recorded keystrokes and mouse movements will be grouped together in a single new workflow action that you can see and edit.

Summary

AppleScript makes applications perform tasks by sending applications Apple event messages. AppleScript is a programming language designed with everyday users in mind, but with enough power for advanced users and programmers.

Use the AppleScript Editor application to create, edit, and run AppleScript scripts. AppleScript Editor can also make scripts into applications. Apple has developed a number of scripts that you can use as starting points or models for your own scripts.

Many AppleScript terms come from the applications the script is controlling. AppleScript terms also come from files called scripting additions. AppleScript Editor can display the AppleScript dictionary of an application to see which commands an application or scripting addition understands and which objects the commands work with.

You can save a script in any of three formats: text, compiled script, or application.

You type AppleScript statements into a new AppleScript Editor window, check the syntax for errors by using the Compile button, and run the script to test it. Your script can use a `copy` statement to set the value of a variable. To start controlling an application, you use a `tell application` statement. A matching `end tell` statement stops controlling the application. With `if` statements, you can have AppleScript perform some operations only when specified conditions are met. Repeat loops execute a group of statements over and over. To make a drag-and-drop script application, you include an `on open` statement and a matching `end open` statement.

You can use the Script menu to run compiled scripts no matter which application is currently active. AppleScript can control applications over a network or the Internet on computers that are set to allow remote Apple events.

Automator is a graphical interface to AppleScript that doesn't give you the same fine control as AppleScript does, but that is much easier for the average person to use. You can save Automator documents as plug-ins to extend the usefulness of other programs that support Automator, or as stand-alone applications you can provide for other people to use.

Making Use of Unix

by Timothy R. Butler

O n the surface, Mac OS X presents a friendly and graphically driven interface that takes many cues from its 1990s-era predecessor, now known as Mac OS Classic. Traditionally, this graphical user interface (GUI) was the only way you would interact with a Mac. This changed with the introduction of Mac OS X in 2000. Underneath its tame-looking exterior, Mac OS X descends from a long line of resilient, capable operating systems, known as Unix, that are very capable of complex server operations far beyond what the average desktop computer will ever do.

Few desktop users aspire to turn their computers into servers, but Unix is useful for much more than that, even in today's GUI-oriented environments. As you see in this chapter, you can use many traditional Unix tools for everyday tasks.

> **IN THIS CHAPTER**
>
> **An introduction to Unix**
>
> **Using the Unix shell**
>
> **Writing scripts and scheduling programs**
>
> **Compiling and installing Unix software**

Introduction to Unix

To understand the value of Unix, it first helps to understand where Unix comes from. The heritage of Unix goes back significantly farther than either the Mac OS Classic operating system that powered most Macs from 1983 until 2001 or the Microsoft Windows operating system that powers most PCs. While relatively unknown until recent times to the average computer user, Unix reaches back to the days before the average person could even own a computer and, because of this rich heritage, offers a consistent and highly capable set of tools from which even the modern user can benefit.

A legend begins

The Unix operating system underlying Mac OS X traces its roots back to the AT&T (then called American Telephone & Telegraph) Bell Laboratories in the late 1960s. Arising out of several interesting but less successful research projects, Unix began as almost a hobby for Bell Labs programmers Ken Thompson and Dennis Richie, but began to show signs as a useful product in 1969.

Over the next decade, Unix was provided to the University of California at Berkley, which created a variant of it known as BSD (Berkeley Software Distribution). This began a distinction that has continued somewhat even to today between what later became known as the System V (AT&T's Unix) and BSD families of Unix. Various commercial developers with licenses to develop Unix created derivatives from one of these streams.

This can often lead to confusion, because there is no single product a person can buy called Unix. Rather, a variety of products, such as Sun Solaris and IBM AIX, are known as Unix.

The rise of GNU/Linux

During the 40 years since its creation, the system has gone from huge mainframes to the tiniest PDAs (personal digital assistants). Without knowing it, you may very well have many Unix or Unix-like devices in your home or office. The system's best-known representative, GNU/Linux, which is technically only Unix-like, runs on many desktops, netbooks (the new breed of inexpensive notebooks), cellphones, and even — quite possibly — your digital video recorder from your cable company.

GNU/Linux emerged primarily out of two projects. In 1991, a university student named Linus Torvalds published a new operating system kernel — the central core of an operating system — known as Linux. About a decade earlier, Richard Stallman had founded the GNU Project to create a complete, free, and open source Unix clone. While the project had fulfilled many of its goals by the early nineties, its kernel project had progressed slowly (even now it remains in an experimental state). Torvalds realized the benefits of using the GNU tools to fill out his fledgling operating system and so the tools were soon combined with his kernel. This created the system known as GNU/Linux, often simply referred to as "Linux."

This combination soon morphed into a phenomenon, capturing much attention in the late 1990s as the most serious threat to Microsoft's dominance of desktop and lightweight server computers. While both Torvalds and the programmers of the Free Software Foundation aimed to create something very much like Unix, Linux was written separately from Unix and has never undergone the costly process to be certified as Unix.

The NeXT step

Unlike GNU/Linux, however, Mac OS X draws not just its inspiration but also its programming heritage from Unix. Mac OS X's particular flavor of Unix arrived at Apple by way of the company's purchase of NeXT Computer in the mid-1990s. That purchase was most famous for bringing Apple's cofounder and current CEO, Steve Jobs, back into the fold. NeXT, which was founded by Jobs after he was ousted from Apple in the mid-1980s, produced a BSD derivative known as

NeXTStep. Apple had been working for years on a replacement for Mac OS Classic but had several failures that never came on to the market. After taking over Apple, Jobs decided to try again, this time using Unix-type technologies as the basis.

As Mac OS X began to progress under Jobs' leadership, it started pulling in updated code from the FreeBSD project and other open source software projects for Unix-like systems. While Mac OS X shared an affinity with FreeBSD — indeed, Jordan Hubbard, one of the FreeBSD Project's founders, was brought on to the Mac OS X development team — it is not accurate to say that Mac OS X is FreeBSD-based. Mac OS X's core system, Darwin, continues to trace its lineage back to NeXT and is, therefore, in some ways actually a predecessor to FreeBSD.

The Mac OS X-Unix relationship today

Until Mac OS X 10.5 Leopard, Apple's operating system was properly referred to as a Unix-like operating system, in a similar vein to FreeBSD and GNU/Linux, because while it had a Unix heritage, it had not undergone the Single Unix Specification certification by the Open Group, which is required for a product to be formally known as Unix. With Mac OS X 10.5 Leopard for Intel systems, Apple became fully compliant with those standards, and Mac OS X is now properly called a Unix operating system.

Because of the popularity of Linux, many users' expectations with relation to Unix functionality are, ironically, colored more by the Unix-like Linux than by any certified Unix. As such, while early versions of Mac OS X favored BSD software, an increasingly large amount of software from the Free Software Foundation and other major Linux-related developers has shown up in Mac OS X in an effort to reduce differences.

The blending of GNU/Linux with BSD, mixed with Mac OS X's own unique heritage and Unix certification, makes Apple's operating system a patchwork of the history of Unix. In many ways, it benefits from the best of that heritage. The many Unix commands and functions brought forward into Mac OS X have been tested over many decades, and while this can make them sometimes seem peculiar and intimidating, with a little knowledge, they quickly become powerful tools that can save you significant amounts of time.

Going Back to the Command Line Interface

Although you benefit from the stability of Unix whenever you're using Mac OS X, to access much of the traditional power that system administrators have enjoyed with Unix over the years, you need to return the command line interface (CLI) that most people associate with computers of yesteryear. For most people who remember a CLI at all, it is likely the MS-DOS command prompt that used to appear when PCs started up and looked like this:

```
C:\>
```

You would enter your command lines after that command prompt, and press Return to tell the computer to execute them. While that command line is rightly viewed as archaic and it disappeared long ago behind the cover of Microsoft Windows, you can still access a descendant of that command line in Windows (choose Start⇨Programs⇨Accessories⇨Command Prompt in Windows Classic mode or choose Start⇨All Programs⇨Accessories⇨Command Prompt in standard Windows mode). Unlike Windows, Apple's Mac OS did not traditionally have a CLI; however, after Apple released Mac OS X with its entirely reworked Unix foundation, Macs gained a CLI.

Unlike the old DOS CLI, you shouldn't view the modern Unix CLI as an outdated tool replaced by the point-and-click GUI that you use most of the time, but rather as an advanced tool that gives you a much faster way to perform many tasks — especially often-repeated tasks.

Much as there are many variations of Unix, as discussed previously, there are also many variations of the Unix command line, which is called a *shell*. Early releases of Mac OS X defaulted to the tcsh shell, such as in FreeBSD, but more recent releases, starting with Mac OS X 10.3 Panther, have used the Bash shell typically used with GNU/Linux. Bash, a pseudo-acronym for Bourne-Again Shell, was created by the GNU Project and designed to offer many of the features of the old Unix Bourne Shell.

Working with the Terminal

The first step to getting started with the Unix CLI on Mac OS X is to launch Apple's Terminal program. You can find the Terminal in the Utilities subfolder of your Mac's Applications folder. The Terminal can perform a variety of different tasks, but its simplest function is accessing the Unix shell. When you launch the Terminal, it appears as shown in Figure 26.1.

FIGURE 26.1

Mac OS X's Terminal application is relatively simplistic looking at startup.

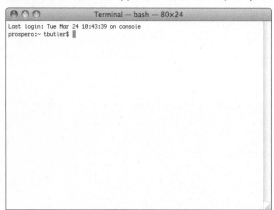

Terminal basics

When you launch the Terminal, you are looking at a working Bash shell prompt. Much like the Safari Web browser, the Terminal enables you to open multiple windows and tabbed panes so that you can perform more than one task at a time. You open new windows and panes via the Shell menu; each window or pane has an independent copy of Bash running in it; so, for example, you can copy a file while another is being used to create a document. The Terminal's Preferences dialog box (choose Terminal⇨Preferences or press ⌘+, [comma]), enables you to perform additional customization with themes and keyboard adjustments, as Chapter 21 explains. Figure 26.2 shows one way to customize the Terminal.

New Feature

In Mac OS X 10.6 Snow Leopard, you can have multiple Terminal sessions running in the same Terminal window, so you can switch among sessions from one location. Choose Window⇨Split Pane or press ⌘+D to open a new pane for a new session in the Terminal window. (You can open as many as you like.) To close a pane, be sure it is the active pane, then choose Windows⇨Close Split Pane or press Shift+⌘+D.

FIGURE 26.2

Mac OS X's Terminal customized with a theme and sporting several panes

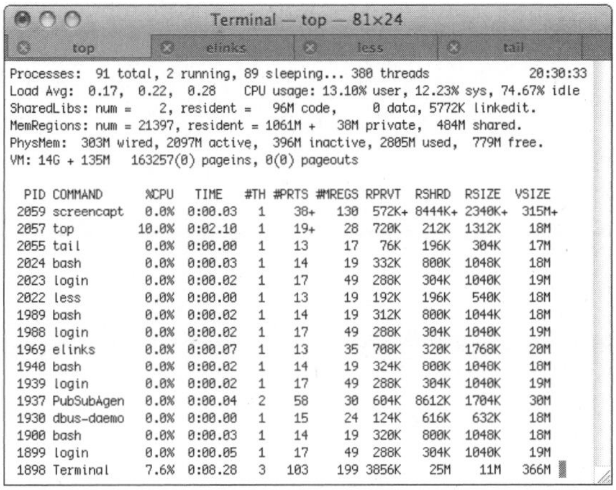

How to Change Shells

If you want to use a shell other than Bash, you can. Open the Preferences dialog box (choose Terminal⇨Preferences or press ⌘+, [comma]) and go to the Startup pane. Select the Command (Complete Path) option in the Shells Open With area and be sure the text field below has the entry /bin/shellname, such as /bin/tcsh for tcsh or /bin/bash for Bash. Quit and relaunch the Terminal for the change to take effect.

If you use tcsh, note that the command prompt differs slightly from the Bash command prompt:

* Bash: prospero:~Documents tbutler$

* tcsh: [prospero:~/Documents] tbutler%

The prompt is the text already present before you begin to type. It looks something like this:

```
prospero:~ tbutler$
```

In this example, `propero` is the name of the Mac given in the Sharing system preference (see Chapter 13), the ~ (tilde) signifies you're in the user's Home directory (`/Users/tbutler` in this example). Finally, `tbutler` indicates which user is logged in. If you go into the Documents folder, the prompt then looks like this:

```
prospero:Documents tbutler$
```

Note that everything stayed the same except the tilde has been replaced with `Documents`, denoting you have moved from the home folder to the Documents subfolder.

Most of the time, you can ignore the prompt itself. When you type a command, what you type immediately follows the prompt on the same line.

Remote access

The Terminal is an ideal way to connect remotely to other Unix systems, including other Macs. Although the Unix shell's remote access functionality was traditionally used by typing various commands, you can tap into much of it by choosing Shell ➪ New Remote Connection. A dialog box opens with the various types of remote access services available. When you click a given service, the server column takes advantage of Apple's Bonjour networking protocol, listing nearby computers to which it can connect. If the desired computer is not listed, you can enter a domain name or IP address for that system in the text field at the bottom of the dialog box. Click Connect to start a session.

For most purposes, using the Secure Shell (SSH) service is best. This provides a shell environment like the one you have seen on the local system, except this shell is running on the remote system and any commands run in it apply to that system.

Tip
You can enable SSH on your Macs to make it simple to remotely access those Macs. To enable SSH on the system you want to be available for remote access, choose ➪ System Preferences, click the Sharing icon to open the Sharing system preference, and select the Remote Login option. Most GNU/Linux systems come with SSH enabled by default. Among other purposes, this sort of remote access can be helpful if the GUI has become unresponsive.

Getting Information In and Out of the Shell

The shell is an extremely powerful tool, but to make good use of it, you need a grasp of some basic concepts behind it. Two key concepts that aid in moving information in and out of the shell are special characters used to control the shell and shell scripting.

Understanding common special characters

There are a variety of useful special characters that the shell recognizes for various purposes. You can use these symbols to do various powerful things with the shell. For example, the asterisk (*) is known as the *wildcard*. Much like its namesake, the wild (or trump) card in a card game, the wildcard can represent anything. To tell the shell to show files by the name of * shows all files; to tell it to show files named *.doc shows all files with the filename extension .doc.

The tilde (~) is also useful when you're dealing with filenames. As in most modern operating systems, Mac OS X gives each user a Home folder. For example, the user Jenny Doe would likely have a Home folder named /Users/jdoe on the Mac's startup disk. This is the folder that the Finder opens up to by default when Jenny logs in, and it contains subfolders such as Documents and Pictures. In Unix, you can refer to the home folder in shorthand by using the tilde. The system interprets this as equivalent to typing the whole path of the folder.

Perhaps two of the handiest more-advanced symbols are the inequality symbols you likely best remember from the frightening days of math classes (< and >, respectively). When used in the form of commands, the item on the side containing the "lesser" value in mathematical equation (for example, the side that appears to be pointed to) "receives" whatever is on the other side. As we explain later in this chapter, this can be used to feed information into programs. For example, whatever is to the left of < receives from whatever is to the right of <, while whatever is to the right of > receives whatever is to the left of >.

Note

Whenever you see a letter preceded by a caret (^), that convention notes a key combination of Control plus the letter indicated; that is, ^c means to press Control+C. You don't actually type the caret itself. (Note that in the Terminal's documentation and Preferences dialog box, the Control key is referred to as Ctrl, for consistency with the standard Windows and Unix PC keyboard convention.)

Much like other programs on a Mac, sometimes programs running in the shell go awry. The two special characters to deal with these sorts of problems are often represented as ^c and ^z (which you enter as Control+C and Control+Z, respectively). These keystrokes send what are known as *signals*, and the two commands are analogous to Quit and Force Quit, respectively. While it is best to terminate a program by using whatever means it offers directly (or enable it to complete its action and end by itself), if for some reason you need to expedite its termination, ^c is a good way to do so. If the program refuses to end by using ^c, you can resort to ^z, which force-quits most programs.

Caution

As with choosing ➪ Force Quit or pressing Option+⌘+Esc for applications running in the Mac's GUI environment, using the ^c and ^z commands can result in data loss if the program has unsaved data.

Another key special character is the dollar sign ($). The dollar sign does not generate money for you, but it does enable you to tap into *variables*. Variables are like boxes that hold information temporarily; referring to a variable's name is equivalent to referring to whatever value is stored in the variable. The Bash shell provides a variety of variables automatically (such as $PATH and $HOME). You can also create variables, as we demonstrate later in this chapter.

One of the most useful special characters in the repertoire is the backslash (\), which is often known as an *escape character*. What the backslash does in most cases is influence how Bash processes the following letter. This is helpful, for example, if you want to use a dollar sign as a dollar sign and not as a symbol denoting a variable. For example, to type the phrase "I have $20.00" in Bash, you would enter

```
I have \$20.00
```

If you enter the phrase normally (as I have $20.00), Bash interprets $2 as a variable and the phrase is interpreted as I have 0.00.

You can use the backslash to invoke other special characters. For example, if you want to create a variable with a carriage return in it, pressing the Return key does not work from a Bash prompt, because Bash interprets the Return key being pressed that as signifying that you are executing the command. Instead, you can type \r to enter an actual carriage return in the text string. These sorts of symbols are especially useful when scripting the shell.

Scripting the shell

Scripting can be a huge time-saver if you use a set of commands over and over on a regular basis. Much of Mac OS X can be scripted (or otherwise automated) by using AppleScript and Automator, as covered in Chapter 25. Scripting in Bash accomplishes a similar goal; Bash scripts are also relatively similar to batch scripts (.bat files) that longtime computer users will remember from Microsoft's MS-DOS.

At its simplest, a Bash shell script is essentially a text document with one Bash command on each line. When run, such a simple shell script acts just as if you had stood there and entered each of those commands individually. For example, you might write such a simple script if you were frequently moving all the Word documents on your desktop to the Documents/Word folder and Excel documents to the Documents/Spreadsheets folder. Rather than having to individually select those files and move them, a shell script enables you to automate the entire process by simply typing in the right commands into a text document created in any text editor, such as TextEdit.

Tip
You can use all the commands covered in the following sections individually or in combination to create Bash shell scripts. We explain how to write shell scripts toward the end of the chapter.

Although not required, shell scripts typically have the file extension .sh, as in myscript.sh.

Notably, the Unix shell can be scripted with a variety of programming languages and not just the built-in commands included in Bash. You can even use commands from other shells. For example, you can write a C Shell (csh) script even if you continue to use the Bash shell. You can also use other scripting languages included with Mac OS X such as Perl, a very powerful scripting language beloved by Unix administrators for its ease of manipulating files. You can even use a Bash shell script to run other scripts by using other scripting languages. As you can see, shell scripting is both very powerful and very flexible.

Learning Basic Unix CommaIn a GUI interface such as the Mac OS X's Quartz, you don't enter the commands as text. Instead, you use the mouse to work with items. But behind the scenes, those mouse-based actions invoke commands. For example, if you want to check e-mail, you can click the Mail icon (the postage stamp icon) on the Mac OS's Dock or navigate to the Applications folder and double-click the Mail application, and Mail launches. Or you could use the Terminal to move to the Applications folder (type `cd /Applications`) and then launch Mail (type `open Mail.app`). The GUI and CLI methods differ, but the result is the same.

When using CLI systems like Bash, note that most Unix commands observe a specific way of typing commands, known as a *command syntax*.

Understanding the Unix command syntax

Unix command syntax typically involves typing a command (frequently a program name) followed by parameters that specify how that command should perform. These parameters are important because many Unix commands, unlike common GUI programs, do not seek further user input after they have been launched (contrast this with Mail, which remains open and has various buttons, such as Get Mail, which you can click to issue further commands after it has started). After typing a command, you must always press Return (often referred to as Enter in Unix help documents and labeled as such on PC keyboards) to issue the command, much as you would click OK to confirm your selections in a dialog box. For example, to view files via the command line, type `ls`.

Note

In this chapter, when covering commands, we assume you know to press the Return key at the end of a command or at the end of each line of a series of commands.

After typing `ls` and pressing Return, you see the files in the current folder. However, if you want to see only Word documents, you can add the simplest form of parameter, one dealing directly with files:

```
ls *.doc
```

This command tells the `ls` command only to show files ending with the `.doc` extension common to most versions of Microsoft Word. If you also want to display the results in a detailed list, rather than multiple columns, you can add another parameter:

```
ls -l *.doc
```

Many commands can have dozens or even hundreds of different parameters and parameter combinations. While some of these are shared from program to program, the combinations may not be intuitive; therefore, you need to read documentation for a specific command to get the best use out of it.

Reading man pages

Man pages (short for *user manual pages*) are a relatively brief source of documentation on how to use a given command. They are particularly helpful in learning the syntax of the command in question. You access these manual pages by using the man command. The syntax for man itself is simply the program's name, man, followed by the name of the program you want to read about. For example, man ls provides the manual page for the ls command.

The typical man page is divided into several sections, as shown in Figure 26.3. At the top is the header, which displays the name of the command and the section of the manual it is in. The header section is followed by a section that provides a short summary of the command, a synopsis of the parameters available for the command, and a description. Following a paragraph or two of explanation about the command is a typically exhaustive, or near exhaustive, list of parameters. An examples section often follows this. Finally, and sometimes most usefully, is a See Also section, which can often point you in the direction of a related, and more appropriate, command for a given job.

FIGURE 26.3

A man page loaded within the Terminal

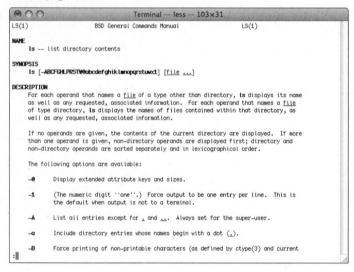

Logging in and logging out as a normal user

When you open the Terminal, you are automatically logged in with your Mac OS X user account. This enables you to view, edit, and delete the same files and run the same sorts of procedures you can do from within Mac OS X's GUI as a normal, non-administrative user. To log out of a shell session, most commonly you simply close the Terminal window (click the Close iconic button for the window or choose Shell ⇨ Close Window) or close the individual tabbed pane, if you are using more than one pane (click the Close iconic button on the pane's tab or choose Shell ⇨ Close Tab).

Note

If you have multiple tabbed panes open, you can close the active one by pressing ⌘+W, and you can close the entire window (and all panes) by pressing Shift+⌘+W. If you have only one pane open, pressing ⌘+W closes the entire window.

Sometimes, however, you may want to work as a different user. For example, if you share a computer among family members, there may be an account named John Smith and another account named Guinevere Smith. If the user named John wants to "become" Guinevere, so as to work with her files or perform some other task for her, it is not necessary for him to log out or use fast user switching and pull up the other account (see Chapter 20). Instead, John can simply use the su command, placing the other user's username as a parameter.

Note

If a user's name includes a space, such as if it is a proper full name (for example, `Guinevere Smith` and not `GuinevereSmith`), the username must be surrounded by quotes (") when the command is given. Also note that it's more common to use an account's short name (see Chapter 20), such as `jsmith` and `gsmith`, when using the Terminal.

So, if John Smith wants to log into Guinevere Smith's account, he simply types su `"Guinevere Smith"` – and presses Return. The shell reappears after he enters Guinevere's password, logged in as Guinevere and not as John. This lets him run commands as if he had logged into the Mac as Guinevere, with permissions over her folders and data. After John has finished whatever work needs to be done logged in as Guinevere, he can log out by using the `exit` command. After entering that command, he returns to the first shell (in this example, John's shell).

Note

In the su `"Guinevere Smith"` – example, note the hyphen after `"Guinevere Smith"`. The hyphen tells su to launch the new shell just as if Guinevere herself had launched it. For most cases, this is the most useful procedure. However, there may be times when you want to act as another user, but want to work with a file in the current folder. To do this, you'd leave the hyphen off the command, such as su `"Guinevere Smith"`. Note that the hyphen-less command only works as expected if the current directory is one that both the current user and the user account you are trying to log into have permission to view.

Running commands and logging in as a superuser

For most purposes, the ability to use su to assert someone else's privileges is fine; however, you occasionally may need system administrator access to perform commands. Traditionally, this access is permitted on Unix systems by logging into what is known as the *root* user, also known as the *superuser*. However, Mac OS X and some other recent Unix variants, such as Ubuntu Linux, have discarded the root user by default. In its place, if your Mac OS X user account has been made an admin account, you can use the `sudo` command to achieve the same powers previously available to the separate superuser account. For example, if you want to view files belonging to another user account, you can type:

```
sudo ls /Users/otheruser
```

This command then prompts you for your account's password, much as Mac OS X's GUI asks for your password before performing administrative tasks such as installing or updating certain software programs.

Cross-Ref

Chapter 20 explains how to create different types of user accounts, as well as set their permissions.

While some users have resorted to enabling the *root* account to get a full root shell, rather than having to constantly use the sudo command to run administrative tasks, a simpler option is available. The Bash shell itself is a program that may be run (you can run multiple bash shells within each other, that is), and so it too may be run by sudo via the command sudo bash. Running Bash this way means that everything you do in that Bash shell has superuser privileges. You can also use sudo su to run a true root user shell, as opposed to merely a shell with root privileges. Note that when using sudo su, unlike sudo bash, Bash will consider /var/root to be the current user's home directory.

Tip

There is a five-minute timeout within sudo, after which it requires you to enter a password again to regain superuser privileges. To get around that need to enter a password every five minutes, use the command sudo bash or sudo su. This should be used with caution; leaving a root shell open allows anyone with access to your system to do virtually anything to it.

Keep in mind that any program run within sudo can delete, change, or view nearly every file on the system. This means you should proceed with the utmost care when running commands in the superuser mode provided by sudo. Unix features very few safeguards, meaning you can delete or modify critical system files in ways that keep your system from booting without receiving any warnings first. You should think twice before running sudo commands — using them cautiously will save you a lot of headaches in the future. Likewise, if you run Bash under sudo, you should never stay logged into that shell when leaving your Mac unattended.

Tip

If you are unsure what a command will do, and think it might have widespread consequences, consider trying it first without sudo and in an unimportant folder. This enables you to see the effects of the command without unnecessary risk.

Managing files and directories

One of the most common tasks that can be performed in the shell is file management, including locating, copying, and moving files. You can accomplish these sorts of tasks very simply from Bash.

Moving about folders

The first step to managing files is to place yourself in the folder containing the files you want to manage. When launching a new Bash shell, you typically starts in your Home folder, as explained earlier. You can get the full path to the open folder by using the pwd command. This gives a response something like this: /Users/tbutler/Documents/Assignments.

You can copy and paste this path into another command in the Terminal, or even paste it into the Go to the Folder sheet in a Finder window (choose Go ⇨ Go to Folder or press Shift+⌘+G) to bring up the same folder.

To change directories, you can use the Change Directory command, **cd**. Typing cd without any further parameters takes you back to the current user's Home folder. Typically, however, you'll want to go to a specific folder, and you can do so by typing a command like this:

    cd /usr/bin

This command moves the user into the folder /usr/bin.

If you want to go into the Documents folder of the current user, we recommend you use the tilde shorthand for the Home folder:

    cd ~/Documents

This is equivalent to typing

    cd /Users/tbutler/Documents

You can also easily move up from a subfolder to its parent folder using cd. To do this, you merely type

    cd ..

Viewing a folder's contents

Being able to move from folder to folder is not terribly helpful if you do not have a way of viewing what is in those folders. To see a listing of a folder's contents, use the ls command. Entering the command without any parameters returns a multicolumn list of all the files in the folder that are not hidden. Adding –a displays all files in the folder, including hidden files. Frequently you may want to see some basic information about the files along with the list — for example, the date modified and the file size, much as is shown in the Finder's detailed list view. To do this, type ls –lh (omitting the h displays the file sizes in bytes rather than the typically more useful megabytes and kilobytes).

You can also use the ls command to view a folder other than the current one by typing the path of that folder after the other parameters. For example,

    ls -lh /usr/bin

This shows the contents of /usr/bin in a detailed list.

Copying and moving files

By now, you have probably noticed that many Unix commands follow the common syntax command /path/of/files. This is true of the commands to copy and move files, as well; however, they add a small twist: A second path is included to specify where the file or files will be copied or moved to. The two commands to move and copy files are mv and cp, respectively. The move command in most cases is very simple. Consider:

    mv ~/Documents/Important\ Word\ Document.doc ~/Desktop/

This command moves the file `Important Word Document.doc` from the user's Documents folder to the user's desktop. (The \ preceding the spaces is an escape character, telling Bash to process the space as a space in the filename, not as a separator of shell commands and variables.)

The mv command is *recursive* by default, meaning that if you move a folder, it automatically takes the folder and all its contents and relocates them. Conversely, cp is *non*recursive by default, and asking cp to copy a folder (as opposed to a file) causes an error. Therefore, if you want to copy entire folders, you must add the -r switch to the command. This switch tells the command to copy recursively. For example:

```
cp -r ~/Documents/Movies/* ~/Movies/
```

This command moves any files located in the first location, including folders, to the second location (the Movies folder in the user's Home folder).

Note

Many Apple file types are not actually normal files at all, but folders with a special extension on the end. Mac OS X applications and iMovie projects are two examples. While the Finder displays these as if they were a single file, Bash and other Unix applications view these "packages" as folders with a collection of files in them. This means that to copy them, you need to use the -r flag, just like when copying other folders.

As in the Finder, the primary difference between moving and copying a file is that copying a file results in copies of the file existing in two places, whereas moving it relocates the file to its new destination.

Getting disk and file system statistics

The Unix shell is an extremely useful and powerful way to find out what is going on in various parts of your system. Using shell commands, you can find out details about mounted volumes, see where disk space is being consumed, and so on.

Discovering information about mounted volumes

You can see currently mounted volumes and find out how full they are by using the df command. Using this command without any parameters shows all the mounted volumes, including external hard disks, any CD or DVD in your Mac's optical drive, USB (Universal Serial Bus) flash drives, and network shares. Like ls, the df command needs the -h parameter to tell it to use human-friendly megabytes and kilobytes for the disk size and usage. Typing df -h produces a result like this:

```
Filesystem      Size    Used   Avail Capacity  Mounted on
/dev/disk0s3    699Gi   343Gi  355Gi   50%     /
devfs           115Ki   115Ki    0Bi  100%     /dev
fdesc           1.0Ki   1.0Ki    0Bi  100%     /dev
map -hosts        0Bi     0Bi    0Bi  100%     /net
map auto_home     0Bi     0Bi    0Bi  100%     /home
/dev/disk1s3    234Gi   210Gi   24Gi   90%     /Volumes/Tim's PowerMac
/dev/disk4s1    975Mi   544Ki  974Mi    1%     /Volumes/CANON EOS 40D
/dev/disk2s1    122Mi    74Mi   48Mi   61%     /Volumes/TIM'S KEY
/dev/disk3s1s2  260Mi   260Mi    0Bi  100%     /Volumes/NT Apparatus 5
```

Each storage device in Unix is assigned a name, which is the name listed under the Filesystem column. The label /dev/disk0s3 indicates that the disk mounted as / is the system's primary hard disk (its startup disk) and that the partition mounted is number 3. You can see that this disk has a capacity of 699GB of which 50 percent is used. If the disk had been partitioned with multiple partitions (for example, a second partition for Boot Camp), the overall size would be reduced proportionately and there would be another disk entitled /dev/disk0s4 listed here.

Tip

It often may prove useful to display only standard local volumes, and you can do so by typing df -lg.

Finding where space is being used

Oftentimes, it is more helpful to know *where* on a disk the space is being used, rather than merely that the space has been used. This is where the du command can come in handy. The disk usage command looks at your entire hard disk or at a specified folder, and shows where your space is going. Run without any parameters, it starts in the current folder and reports how much space is being used in each subfolder. As with other commands, adding the -h parameter turns the sizes into convenient kilobytes and megabytes.

Often, du provides way too much information to be useful when it is run without further syntax. You can quickly remedy this by using the -d (depth) parameter; this parameter is followed by how many subfolders down the du command should display. Typically it is best to go with a depth of 1, which simply shows the subfolders located in the current folder and how big they are. (All their subfolders' contents will be included in the tally of the parent folders, rather than showing each folder individually.)

For example, typing du -d 1 -h in the iPhoto Library produces output like this:

```
16K      ./2002
48K      ./2004
24K      ./2005
 0B      ./Auto Import
4.0K     ./Contents
2.8G     ./Data
8.0K     ./Desktop
4.5G     ./iPod Photo Cache
28G      ./Modified
184G     ./Originals
220G     .
```

Viewing and Editing Files

The Terminal offers many useful utilities for manipulating files efficiently and quickly. Unix terminal commands are especially helpful for working with text files; obviously Photoshop files are not nearly as easy to work with from a text-based environment (though it is possible). With a little practice, you can likely accomplish quite a bit more by using command-line utilities than you can with applications such as TextEdit.

Using standard input, standard output, and pipes

Standard input (STDIN) is a feature you have already been using just by following along with the steps already suggested in this chapter. In its most basic visible form, STDIN is where Unix command line applications look to see what you are typing on the keyboard. Unless you plan to engage in more-advanced programming, knowing much about STDIN really is not a necessity.

Note
STDIN often becomes more useful with specialized applications. For example, if you are using the MySQL database and its corresponding command line application, a fast way to input an entire database worth of data into the system is to take a SQL text file and dump it into the program by using STDIN. Using the command `mysql --d roundtable < gawain.sql` would send all of the SQL commands in the file gawain.sql into the database roundtable.

For most users *standard output* (STDOUT) is far more useful. Using the inequality signs mentioned (< and >) earlier, you can quickly save information to a file. At its simplest form, you can use this to create a text file from lines of text. For example:

```
echo "Hello World" > hello.txt
```

This command creates (or overwrites) a file named hello.txt with the text "Hello World." If you double up the inequality signs (>>), it instead appends "Hello World" to the end of the file.

Practically, this is very useful when you're trying to deal with large amounts of information output by a command. For example, if you use du to list every folder and its usage on your system, you could easily end up with hundreds of pages of output. You can deal with that scenario by sending the output to a text file that can be read later either in the Terminal or in another program such as TextEdit or Microsoft Word. To do this, you use STDOUT to send the du output to a file:

```
du -h / > directoryreport.txt
```

This command outputs the results of du into a file named `directoryreport.txt`. You might want to specify an output folder, in addition to a file name — this too is a simple enough process; to save directoryreport.txt to the Home folder, you could simply type:

du –h / > ~/directoryreport.txSometimes you may want to peruse the information immediately, but a command like du –h run in the main folder of a hard disk is too much to fit on the screen. This is where the shell's pipe character (|) can become very useful. The pipe character, like the inequality signs, enables you to manipulate interactions with a program's output. The simplest example is causing a program like du to pause its output every time it fills up the screen, so you can easily move up and down the results list at your leisure. For example:

```
du -h / | less
```

By adding | less to the end of the command, you can use the arrow keys on the keyboard to move up and down through the results generated by the command. The less command also provides a variety of handy more-advanced commands modeled after the Unix vi text editor. For example, if you want to search the output, when the output has appeared, all you have to do is type a forward slash (/) followed by the text you want to find. For example typing /sangreal searches for sangreal in the output.

Editing text files

One of the most common tasks that you may want to do is edit a text file. You have already seen how you can do rudimentary text manipulation with STDOUT, but what if you want to perform more normal text-editing functions like you might do with TextEdit?

Many initiates to Unix have been scared away by the answers their nearest "Unix guru" offered for this task. Frequently the suggestion is to use the vi text editor, which is, admittedly, a strong choice in that virtually every Unix system has a copy of it installed and ready to go. Unfortunately, vi is also cryptic and can seem counterintuitive to anyone who has not spent a significant amount of time learning it.

Another text-editor option is GNU Emacs. This editor does try to offer some helpful suggestions within the program itself to guide the user, but it too can be daunting to learn. For most projects it is simply overkill: It is one of the rare text editors that can do everything from simple text editing to serving as your Web browser and e-mail client.

A better option for everyday use is Nano, the GNU Project's clone of Pico, an extremely simple text editor. Like vi and Emacs, Nano is available on most Unix systems, including Mac OS X 10.6 Snow Leopard. (Early Mac OS X versions did not have Nano, but you can usually get Pico for them.)

To edit a text file with Nano, simply enter nano filename.txt, such as nano lemorte.txt, at the shell prompt. This command launches Nano and opens the file lemorte.txt. Leaving off a filename launches Nano with a new, empty file. Nano keeps its learning curve low by putting all of the major commands at the bottom of the screen at all times. For example, to save ("WriteOut") the file, simply press Control+O (indicated in Nano as ^O). The status bar near the bottom of the screen prompts you to confirm the filename to save as. To exit, press Control+X. You control the editing cursor by using the arrow keys on the keyboard.

Tip

Nano has a basic clipboard, separate from Mac OS X's Clipboard, for cutting and pasting. To cut text, you repeatedly press Control+K. As long as you keep up a relatively rapid pace, this cuts one line at a time and combines them into the Nano clipboard. To paste, simply press Control+U.

Learning permissions

Understanding *permissions* is critical to taking full advantage of Unix functionality. You may already be somewhat familiar with permissions from the Finder. In the Info window for a disk, folder, or file, there is a Sharing & Permissions section, which enables you to tell Mac OS X who can do what with a given file. By default, there are permissions for your username, your user group (which defaults to "staff"), and everyone.

Cross-Ref

Chapter 2 explains the Info window and its controls over sharing. Chapter 13 explains file sharing in more detail.

Unix offers a similar division of user, group, and world. The group often is a set of related users — say all of those working on a given project. A user may belong to more than one group. Permissions are shown by `ls -oh` as follows:

```
-rw-r--r--@ 1 gawain  roundtable   5.5K Feb  9 20:52 greenknight.csv
```

In this example, the file is owned by the user named gawain and the user's group is roundtable. Likewise, at the beginning of the line you see —rw-r--r--. The rw- indicates that Gawain has read and write permissions to the file (that is, he can view the file and edit or delete it). Conversely, group and world, which are represented by the pair of r-- entries are only given read permissions. This is a fairly standard setup — the user allows other users on the Mac to read the file, but not to write to it (writing includes actions such as deleting!).

While most users are concerned with the ability to read and write files, if you are working with Unix scripting, the execute "bit" is also relevant, as it sets whether the file can be executed as if it were a standard system command. An executable file might look like this via `ls`:

```
-rwxr-xr-x@ 1 guinevere  roundtable   59.2K Dec 20 21:08 galahad.pl
```

You can set these permissions in the shell by using the Change Mode (chmod) command. This command is quite powerful, but at its simplest can be used to change the permissions on just one file. To set the user's permission, you use the u to set the user's permissions, g to set the group's permissions, o to set the world's permissions and a to set all three at once. For example, if you want to make the unreadable file bookofquests.doc readable to all, enter the following command:

```
chmod a+r bookofquests.doc
```

The read permission (r) is "added" to all three permissions settings (a) by way of the plus sign (+). To reduce the permission level of a given file, you can likewise use a minus sign (–):

```
chmod go-r bookofquests.doc
```

This command prevents anyone fitting into the group or world categories from reading the book ofquests.doc file. The equal sign (=), notably, forces a group's permissions to fit what is passed along, rather than merely adding or subtracting permissions.

Commonly, permissions are also represented numerically. For example a=rwx (for example, giving everyone permission to do anything) can be represented numerically as 777. This comes from adding up numbers representing what each user is permitted to do (see Table 26.1). To use chmod in this view, you simply use the numerical combination in place of the letters used previously:

```
chmod 777 bookofquests.doc
```

TABLE 26.1

Permissions Overview

Symbolic (Letter-based) Permissions	Numeric Permissions	Representation in ls	Result
a=rwx	777	-rwxrwxrwx	All users can read, write, and execute the file.
a=rw	666	-rw-rw-rw-	All users can read and write the file.
a=r	444	-r--r--r--	All users can read the file.
a=w	333	--w--w--w-	All users can write the file.
a=e	111	---x--x--x	All users can execute the file.
u=rwx, go=rx	755	-rwxr-xr-x	Owner can read, write, and execute the file; others can read and execute the file.
u=rw, go=r	644	-rw-r--r--	Owner can read and write the file; others can read the file.

Often times, it is useful to apply permissions to more than one file at a time. The recursive (-r) parameter works on chmod much as it does for cp. Using it applies the given permissions to every file matching a pattern in the current folder or any subfolders. For example:

```
chmod -r 644 *.doc
```

This command makes every Word document in the current folder (and any subfolder) available to be read and written by the current user and be read by all users.

Advanced Unix Topics

Much of what is going on in Unix happens under the surface. Taking some time to understand these bits of Unix functionality can help you control the system more efficiently.

Working with environment and shell variables

In Unix, many settings used by the system are held within what are known as *variables*. Variables can be set permanently by editing various configuration files, but are often edited temporarily as needed or are oriented toward read-only use.

The one you'll need to use most frequently is the $PATH variable. $PATH specifies where Bash looks when you enter a command; any program located in a folder listed in $PATH can be loaded simply by typing its filename. (For example, you can launch /usr/bin/nano simply by typing nano, because /usr/bin/ is included in $PATH.)

Tip
When trying to run a program located in the current folder, when the current folder is not in $PATH, **simply prefix the program's name with** ./. **So, if the program is named quest, type** ./quest.

You can modify variables by typing export VARIABLENAME=value. To change $PATH, you can type export PATH=/home/guinevere/bin/. Note that in the case of $PATH, this command could be a bad idea, because it would remove other important locations of commands from the path for the remainder of the session. A better way to deal with path is to include $PATH itself within the value, so that the other paths are carried along:

```
export PATH=$PATH:/home/guinevere/bin/
```

Note
Path uses a colon (:), not a comma (,), to divide multiple entries. Look at the example export PATH=$PATH:/home/guinevere/bin/, **where a colon divides** $PATH **(referring to existing entries) from the new path being added.**

To view a variable, it is helpful to use the echo command. The echo command simply prints what is fed to it; if you enter echo $PATH, it returns something like this:

```
/sw/bin:/sw/sbin:/usr/bin:/bin:/usr/sbin:/sbin:/usr/local/bin:/usr/
    X11/bin:/usr/X11R6/bin
```

A variety of other useful variables exist. The $EDITOR variable is especially helpful, because many programs look to it to see what text editor to use when a file needs to be edited. This becomes relevant, as the next section shows.

Cross-Ref
Variables are covered in more detail in the section on writing shell scripts later in this chapter.

Scheduling tasks

In Mac OS X (and in Unix), many processes are running behind the scenes constantly while others are scheduled to run at startup or at regular intervals. Traditionally, Unix launches programs in a variety of ways. During bootup, the system runs `init`, which launches most of the core system background processes (known as *daemons*) before turning the system over to the user. One of the daemons launched typically is `crond` (Cron Daemon, or *Cron* for short). Cron is one of a Unix system administrator's favorite tools for system maintenance and other useful tasks: You feed it information on when a program ought to run — once a month, or once a year, or every day at 2:48 p.m. — and `crond` makes sure that the program runs on schedule.

Using Cron

To use Cron, you need to edit or create a *crontab* file. To see if you already have one, type the command `crontab -1`. This lists any existing `cron` entries. Whether any exist, you can enter new crontab entries or delete old ones by entering `crontab -e`.

Tip

Before running the command to edit your crontab file, it is a good idea to set the editor environmental variable. This ensures the editor of your choice — Nano is a very good one — is used to edit the configuration, rather than the default vi. To set this, type `export EDITOR=nano`**.**

Cron uses a relatively straightforward format for its scheduled entries: the minute, hour, day of the month, then month and day of the week that the event should run. This is followed by the command Cron should run (using standard shell command syntax). For example, a line might look like this:

```
1 2 * * * rm -r /tmp/junk/*
```

This command runs at 2 a.m. every morning and deletes (`rm`) all the files in the `/tmp/junk` folder. Different combinations can result in commands being executed at specific times, as shown in Table 26.2.

Caution

Running commands such as `rm` in a crontab can be dangerous. It is always good to test the command manually before inserting it into a crontab file. Failing to do so could result in disastrous results.

TABLE 26.2

Breakdown of a Cron Command

Minute	Hour	Day of Month	Month	Day of the Week	Result
*	*	*	*	*	Runs the command every minute.
*/3	*	*	*	*	Runs the command every three minutes.
1	0	*	*	*	Runs the command everyday at 00:01.
1	0	1	1	*	Runs the command on January 1 at 00:01.
*	*	*	*	0	Runs the command every minute of every Sunday.

Note that you can implement a systemwide crontab command — as opposed to one running as the current user — by running `sudo crontab -e`. A program launched by Cron is limited by the permissions of the type of user it is running as, so if a command you type won't function properly without `sudo`, make sure to add it to the systemwide crontab rather than to the user crontab.

Tip

Cron is limited by its expectation that the Mac will be turned on at the times that programs are supposed to run. This was a fine assumption when it was running primarily on servers, which typically operate 24/7, but it can cause trouble if the Mac is often asleep or shut down. One way around this would be to indirectly run the command via a script multiple times per day, with a check within that script to see if it had already executed that day.

Tip

You can edit the crontab file by using GUI utilities in addition to the command line. The free program Cronnix (`http://h775982.serverkompetenz.net:9080/abstracture_public/projects-en/cronnix`) is a good example.

Using Launchd

The operative word noted in the beginning of this section was "traditionally." Apple now suggests that administrators use its relatively new Launchd system, introduced with Mac OS X 10.4 Tiger, as opposed to Cron. Launchd replaces not only Cron, but also Init and several other traditional program-launching features and places them all into one large bundle. Nevertheless, Mac OS X 10.6 Snow Leopard continues to support the use of Cron, and Cron is significantly simpler than creating a time-based Launchd "agent."

In addition to simplifying the overall system by combining various launching programs into one system, Launchd solves one major weakness of Cron: the problem of events scheduled for when the Mac is turned off. In cases where a Launchd agent was supposed to run while the system was turned off, Launchd runs it at the first opportunity it has after the Mac has launched.

If you want to use Launchd, Apple has published a template of a crontab entry-like agent (you can see this in Code 26.1). Code 26.2 shows what that might look like for the process of deleting certain files every two hours.

CODE 26.1

Apple's timed Launchd plist file

```
<?xml version="1.0" encoding="UTF-8"?>
        <!DOCTYPE plist PUBLIC -//Apple Computer//DTD PLIST 1.0//EN
        http://www.apple.com/DTDs/PropertyList-1.0.dtd >
        <plist version="1.0">
          <dict>
             <key>Label</key>
             <string>com.example.happybirthday</string>
             <key>ProgramArguments</key>
             <array>
```

```
                    <string>happybirthday</string>
            </array>
            <key>OnDemand</key>
            <false/>
            <key>StartCalendarInterval</key>
            <dict>
                <key>Hour</key>
                <integer>00</integer>
                <key>Minute</key>
                <integer>00</integer>
                <key>Month</key>
                <integer>7</integer>
                <key>Day</key>
                <integer>11</integer>
                <key>Weekday</key>
                <integer>0</integer>
            </dict>
        </dict>
    </plist>
```

CODE 26.2

A timed Launchd plist file that deletes /tmp/junk/*

```
<?xml version="1.0" encoding="UTF-8"?>
        <!DOCTYPE plist PUBLIC -//Apple Computer//DTD PLIST 1.0//EN
        http://www.apple.com/DTDs/PropertyList-1.0.dtd >
        <plist version="1.0">
          <dict>
            <key>Label</key>
            <string>com.example.deletetmp</string>
            <key>ProgramArguments</key>
            <array>
                <string>rm</string>
                <string>-r</string>
                <string>/tmp/junk/*</string>
            </array>
            <key>OnDemand</key>
            <false/>
            <key>StartCalendarInterval</key>
            <dict>
                <key>Hour</key>
                <integer>2</integer>
                <key>Minute</key>
                <integer>1</integer>
            </dict>
          </dict>
        </plist>
```

In Code 26.2, you can see several differences from a crontab file. First, the command to run the program is split up into separate lines surrounded by `<string>` and `</string>`. Each of these string lines represents one of the segments of the command — a new string line must be started in each place there would be a space if the command were typed in Bash (or included in a crontab file as it was earlier in this section).

Note that, compared to Code 26.1, the time elements specified in Code 26.2 are the hour and minute. Omitting specifications in a Launchd plist file is equivalent to using the wildcard in a crontab file.

After a Launchd plist file has been created, save it in your text editor with the file extension .plist. You should place it in your Home folder under `Library/LaunchAgents` if the activated program should be run as your user, or under `/Library/LaunchAgents` on your startup disk if it should be run with administrator privileges.

Tip

Although adding a scheduled task to Cron via the command line is rather straightforward, working with Launchd is substantially more complex. Using a GUI utility such as Peter Borg's Lingon (`http://tuppis.com/lingon/`) is a big help in taking advantage of the system.

The X Windowing System

In the Mac world, it is natural to think of the operating system's GUI as the entire operating system. Those of you who have used PCs, especially PCs from before Windows 95, will remember that PCs often consisted of Windows (or another graphical interface) placed on top of DOS. In fact, this arrangement is no different today to how the Mac OS X GUI (called Quartz) runs on top of Unix, though it is hidden from the user. But there's another GUI choice when running Unix on the Mac: the X Windowing System.

You can boot Mac OS X into what is known as *single-user mode*, which provides a traditional Unix text-based startup of the operating system. (To use single-user mode, when starting the Mac, press and hold ⌘+S until you see the Unix command prompt.) In addition to being a useful mode for system recovery, this is a helpful demonstration of how Mac OS X is actually several separate components.

Until the Quartz-driven Mac OS X was produced, the X Windowing System (or X for short, pronounced "ex") was by far the dominant graphical environment for Unix and Unix-like operating systems, and it remains the system used by GNU/Linux and many other operating systems. For even longer than Mac OS has been "stuck" in version 10, X has been "stuck" in version 11; in fact, the current release is known as X11R7, denoting it is in the seventh major release of the eleventh version. Because of this long-standing 11, many users call the system X11 for short, which is less confusing than calling it X, especially when on a Mac. X11 is included in Mac OS X by default.

Note

You pronounce the "X" in X Window System as "ex," but you pronounce "X' in Mac OS X as "ten," because the "X" represents the Roman numeral 10. And when you see Mac OS X 10.6 Snow Leopard, you say, "Mac OS 10.6 Snow Leopard."

Similarly to how Mac OS Classic could be run on Mac OS X 10.4 Leopard and earlier, and similar to how Parallels and VMware have modes that enable Windows programs to intermingle with Mac OS X applications, X11 on Mac OS X enables X11-based programs to be mixed with normal Mac OS applications. This is known as a *rootless* X11.

Note

Unlike either Mac OS X's Quartz or the Windows GUI, X11 is minimalist. Basic elements such as window title bars, the Clipboard, icons, and so on are provided by additional layers, often known as window managers and toolkits. By default, Apple provides a window manager known as QuartzWM, which provides X11 applications with standard Mac OS X title bars. If you want to run many X Windowing System apps, however, you will likely need to download a desktop environment from Fink (see the section on installing Fink later in this chapter). Popular desktop environments on Unix include GNOME and KDE. Both Gnome and KDE provide a window manager for many basic applications (like those included with Mac OS X) and the infrastructure for other applications. For example, Ubuntu and Red Hat Enterprise Linux both boot up into GNOME on X11 by default.

To launch X11 on Mac OS X, you can double-click on its application icon in the Application folder's Utilities subfolder. After a few moments, it starts up with a copy of XTerm, the default X11 terminal application. XTerm is relatively similar to the Terminal application used throughout this chapter, however without some features such as tabbed panes. It does have a few nice additions, such as the ability to use the mouse to control some text-mode applications. Figure 26.4 shows X11 with several X applications open.

If you compile or install graphical Unix applications, typically the simplest way to launch them is by typing the appropriate command into XTerm or the Terminal (we recommend using the Terminal). You can also add favorite applications to X11 by choosing Applications ➪ Customize. Optional desktop environments ease the launching of applications, but they also add typically needless complications, such as a second Dock-like panel, their own file managers and desktops, and nonmatching title bars. They have these redundancies because they are designed to be run on platforms such as GNU/Linux, where they are expected to handle these functions. But the Mac OS already provides such capabilities and doesn't need desktop environments to provide them.

Tip

X11 is deceptive in its simplicity. Unlike Quartz, X11 is made up of two components: a client and server (roughly analogous to a Web browser and Web server). In some corporate environments, it may be that there is an X server already on the network. Your system administrator needs to provide you with an account on that server so you can access it.

FIGURE 26.4

X11 loaded with a few basic X applications

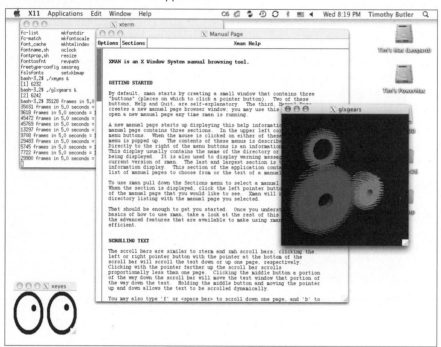

Writing Shell Scripts

Scripting the shell is one of the best ways to harness the power of Unix. As you observed in the introduction to the shell, shell scripts are relatively analogous to Automator actions or AppleScript scripts (see Chapter 25).

Basics of scripting

Shell scripts are essentially simplistic little programs. While you can achieve more advanced command of Unix functions through powerful scripting languages such as Perl, shell scripts are handy for doing repetitive tasks that otherwise would require typing the same commands over and over.

For example, say that you have a program that runs once a week and creates a folder full of data named 1. It might be useful to keep previous weeks' folders for a month, and you could do this manually by using the commands covered previously in this chapter. But, with a shell script, you could automate these commands by using a rudimentary shell script, as you can see in Code 26.3.

CODE 26.3

A simple shell script

```
#!/bin/sh
#Rename folders, upping their numbers by 1.
mv 5 6
mv 4 5
mv 3 4
mv 2 3
mv 1 2
#Delete the oldest folder.
rm 6
```

This simple example script is made up of three elements: shebang, comments, and code.

Shebang

The first line (#!/bin/sh) is known as the *shebang*. This line tells the shell what kind of script it is dealing with. In this particular case, it notes that the *interpreter* for the script, the program that turns the commands into actions, is /bin/sh —, that is, Bash. If the program were coded in Perl, it would instead have a Perl shebang, #!/usr/bin/perl. When the script is run, Bash grabs this line and runs the script.

Caution

If you write scripts intended to run on a variety of systems, and not just on Mac OS X, it may be wise to use the #!/bin/bash shebang line rather than the traditional #!/bin/sh. This is particularly relevant now that Ubuntu Linux, one of the leading GNU/Linux distributions, has begun favoring a shell known as Dash over Bash. Failing to use the #!/bin/bash shebang line results in problems running the script if the script depends on any of the unique characteristics of Bash.

Comments

The second type of line is one that, like the shebang line, begins with # (called a hash or number sign). These lines are known as comments, and the interpreter ignores them. As you can see, these lines are plain English explanations of what the code is doing, meant for people to read to understand the code better. These lines are optional, but they make life easier — especially when you're working with more complex code.

Code

While the example in Code 26.3 is a relatively simple string of Bash shell commands, that's all code really is. While some commands rarely make much sense outside of a script — for example the echo command, which prints out the text you feed it — virtually all of the commands in a Bash shell script are useable at the shell prompt as well.

More advanced scripting

If you imagine taking the various commands that have already been covered in this chapter and stringing them together in a simple script like that in Code 26.3, it is already clear how useful shell scripting can be. However, the limitations also become clear relatively quickly. That's why a few advanced scripting functions are worth noting.

Conditional statements

Perhaps the signature of "programming" is the conditional statement. Conditional statements are often referred to as "if-then-else," which neatly summarizes the basic structure they use.

A simple example checks to see if a certain file exists and then reports back the results. For example, imagine if you want the sample script to only run if a folder named 6 doesn't already exist (to avoid collisions of old files with new ones). Code 26.4 shows what that could look like.

CODE 26.4

A conditional script

```
#!/bin/sh
if [ -a ~/sangreal ]
then
        echo "It has been found!"
else
        echo "It has not been found."
fi
```

In this example, the program checks to see if a file named `sangreal` exists in the current user's Home folder. The lines beginning with `if` and `then` are the parts that set up the condition. The condition itself is specified in between the square brackets after `if`. In this case, the condition uses the `-a` switch, known as a *primary* (see Table 26.3 for some key primaries), to tell Bash that the following text is a file that needs to be checked for existence.

TABLE 26.3

Helpful Primaries for Conditional Scripting

Primary	Result Is true If
`-a` *filename*	*Filename* exists
`-f` *filename*	*Filename* is a regular file that exists
`-d` *filename*	*Filename* is a directory that exists
`-o` *filename*	*Filename* is owned by the current user

After the first echo command line (which is run if the Mac successfully finds sangreal), the optional else statement gives Bash something else to do if the file cannot be found. The fi, the reverse of "if," is Bash's amusing way of noting that the conditional statement has come to an end.

How could this be practically useful? Recall that Code 26.3 was a small script that pushed a series of folders up to rotate backups. The script, however, makes a dangerous assumption: There is no folder named 6 until the script is run. Especially because the script eventually deletes that folder, bad things could happen if it is not the folder the script expects. A modified version of the script protects against this problem, as you see in Code 26.5.

Caution

The time comes for every script writer when a safeguard is left off and some or all valuable data goes into the great bit bucket in the sky. Using conditions and other sensible safeguards is almost always advisable, unless you are positive that the script is operating in a totally controlled environment (a very rare scenario).

CODE 26.5

A safer shell script

```
#!/bin/sh
#Check to see if the folder 6 exists already.
if [ -a 6 ]
then
      quit
fi
#Rename folders, upping their numbers by 1.
mv 5 6
mv 4 5
mv 3 4
mv 2 3
mv 1 2
#Delete the oldest folder.
rm 6
```

As you see in Code 26.5's revised script, a small conditional section has been added at the very beginning of the script. Often in these cases, the simplest way to go is to simply use the quit command to terminate the process if the (dangerous) condition is found to be true. This keeps the script simple and easy to understand. However, you could use a full if-then-else condition, much more like Code 26.4, and place all the following commands within that condition. This is mostly a judgment call of what will be easiest to read later on and what the exact needs of the script are.

Variables

One of the most useful elements when programming, even using a basic scripting language, is the variable. You've already encountered environmental variables that influence the Unix working environment, but variables' value becomes even clearer when you're programming. Variables are placeholder names that point to additional content. In a sense, they are a *synecdoche*; much as "the White House" is often used to refer to the president and his administration, or "the Crown" is used to refer to the queen and her authority, variables typically are shorthand for something larger. Code 26.6 shows a simple use of variables.

CODE 26.6

A simple use of variables

```
#!/bin/bash
CROWN="Her Majesty, the Queen of England"
WHITEHOUSE="the President of the United States of America"
ROUNDTABLE="King Arthur and His Knights@dp
echo "The monarch of England is $CROWN and the leader of the U.S. is
    $WHITEHOUSE; but Camelot was controlled by $ROUNDTABLE."
```

In Code 26.6's example, the first three lines after the shebang define the variables $CROWN, $WHITEHOUSE, and $ROUNDTABLE. The following echo command references each of the three variables. When Bash interprets the script, it replaces each variable with what it represents. Here's what the output would look like:

```
The monarch of England is Her Majesty, the Queen of England and the
    leader of the U.S. is the President of the United States of
    America; but Camelot was controlled by King Arthur and His Knights.
```

Tip

Variables are typically written with a dollar sign ($) before them, but when defining them in a Bash shell script, the dollar sign should be omitted.

Parameter variables

Variables can be used for all sorts of functions. One of the most helpful for creating reusable shell scripts comes in the form of variables that return the parameters fed to the script. Much like other Unix command line applications, shell scripts can take parameters. These appear in a range of variables where $1 equals the first word passed to the program, $2 the second word, and so on. $@ is a special variable that provides the entire set of parameters fed to the script.

This could be useful, for example, if you want to create a small program to take any given file, add the current date to the file name, and then move it into a folder named `processed`. You could accomplish this very simply by using just one line of code other than the shebang line, as you see in Code 26.7.

CODE 26.7

datemove.sh: a simple file mover

```
#!/bin/bash
mv $1 processed/`date "+%Y.%m.%d"`-$1
```

You activate this command simply by typing `datemove.sh filename`. One notable trick comes into play in this script: Note that around the date command there is a grave accent (`` ` ``) rather than a standard apostrophe. This tells Bash to execute the command inside the graves and use the output of that command — this is not unlike how the variable `$1` is transformed into the filename the user enters.

Installing Additional Software

Traditionally, parts of the basic Unix subsystem of Mac OS X were optional installs. If you have experience working with Mac OS X 10.3 Panther or earlier, or if you encounter documentation referring to those versions, you often see references to installing the BSD subsystem. This is now installed by default as part of the Mac OS, as is X11 for Mac OS X. However, you can add a few other packages to greatly expand the functionality of Unix in Mac OS X.

Installing Xcode

Apple's Xcode integrated development environment (IDE) might seem primarily of interest for those planning to do serious software development. And, while this is true, it also includes programs such as the GNU C Compiler (gcc) that are essential for installing many Unix programs that you may want to use. Here's how to install Xcode:

1. **Insert the Mac OS X 10.6 Snow Leopard DVD.** The Xcode IDE is included under the optional installs section of the DVD-ROM. (You can also go to `http://developer.apple.com` to download the latest edition of Xcode.)

2. **Launch the installer.** When the disc's Finder window opens, double-click Optional Installs, then double-click Xcode Tools, and then double-click Xcode.mpkg.

3. **Follow the installer's prompts.** The installer asks you to accept Apple's licensing agreement, then guides you through the installation of Xcode.

After completing the installation of Xcode, your Mac is now ready to install Unix software that is distributed in source code form — either directly or through Fink (see the section on Fink later in this chapter).

Compiling third-party software

Many software programs for Unix are released in source code form (the code the programmer used to create them) so that they can run on the various forms of Unix and Unix-like operating systems in existence. For example, while the final, compiled program your computer produces only runs on Mac OS X, in source form, it can be compiled to run on GNU/Linux variants such as Ubuntu, Sun Solaris, IBM AIX, and many more.

Fortunately, while compiling source code can sound intimidating, in most cases it is actually a relatively simple undertaking. To begin, you want to open up a Terminal window.

Next, you navigate to the folder to which you downloaded the program. Most likely it came in a Gzipped Tarball archive (with either a `.tar.gz` or a `.tgz` extension), which is a tar archive that has been compressed with Gzip. Unlike a Zip file, which compresses files and combines them into a handy package, tar only combines the files into a package; so tar files are commonly "gzipped" after packaging. By default, Safari activates the extractor and decompresses the tarball, but Mac OS X only extracts the files out of the tarball itself if you double-click the file in the Finder.

Depending on what state the files are in, you can issue one of two commands to continue:

- **Decompress and extract the files.** If you have automatic launching of "safe" downloads disabled in Safari (see Chapter 10), you need to perform two tasks on the file. Because these two are commonly combined, tar can handle both for you.

  ```
  tar -xzf filearchive.tar.gz
  ```

  In this example, tar removes the Gzip compression from `filearchive.tar.gz` and then extracts the files from the resulting `filearchive.tar`.

- **Extract the files.** If Safari decompressed the archive for you, you will have a file named simply `filearchive.tar`. This requires a slightly modified tar command:

  ```
  tar -xf filearchive.tar
  ```

Typically, if the archive was called `filearchive.tar.gz`, there will now be a subfolder in your current folder named `filearchive`. You can then go into the folder itself. Typically a Unix source code folder includes a number of standard files, such as README, INSTALL, and configure. In most cases, you need only run the configure program by typing `./configure`. In most cases, you need only run the configure program. This launches a process that searches to make sure your Mac has all the software needed to compile the new code. Typically, you can ignore what this process says unless it offers an error message.

Following the end of the configure program, if it has finished without reporting any problems, type `make`. Depending on the complexity of the program, this may require some time to complete — anywhere from a few minutes to many hours.

Finally, when that process is complete, you need to install the program. You do so by using the `sudo make install` command. Sudo is needed to complete the installation because, like normal software installation, Unix programs typically install in places that require administrator authorization.

Code 26.8 shows what you would need to enter to install most Unix source-based software.

CODE 26.8

A typical software compilation and installation process

```
tar -xzf percival-2.9.3.tar.gz
cd percival-2.9.3
./configure
make
sudo make install
```

The new program is typically installed in `/usr/local/bin/`, which means you can run the new programs simply by typing the program's name, much like the standard Unix commands. For example, if the program file's name is percival, you can now run it simply by typing `percival`.

Using third-party installation tools

It can be time-consuming to find and make various Unix programs piecemeal in an effort to add functionality to the Mac, especially if the program is a complicated one. Many software programs have what are known as *dependencies*. Dependencies are *libraries*, software meant specifically to be used by other programs, or full-fledged programs that the new program must be able access to run.

It would not be an exaggeration to say some programs could end up with many layers of dependencies. We have tried to install software that led to the installation of dependencies for the dependencies of dependencies. This is, needless to say, a headache.

Solving the headache

Various Unix and Unix-like operating systems have taken different approaches to dealing with this potential cranial pain. These approaches generally group hundreds or thousands of programs into *packages*, which contain descriptions and machine-readable lists of dependencies so the web of dependencies can be handled automatically without concerning the user. FreeBSD went with what is known as *Ports*; the Ports system is available for Mac OS X from a project known as *MacPorts*.

The best-known package management tools are two that originated in the Linux world. Red Hat's Linux distribution (originally known as Red Hat Linux, now split between Red Hat Enterprise Linux and Fedora) uses a package management tool known as the RPM Package Manager. This package management tool is perhaps the best known by virtue of the popularity of Red Hat's products and the plethora of other GNU/Linux variants that adopted RPM as they tried to clone and adapt Red Hat Linux. It is still used by Red Hat Enterprise Linux, the related Fedora Core Linux distribution, Mandriva Linux, CentOS, and various other distributions.

Parallel to the development of Red Hat package manager, the developers of Debian created the Debian package system, often known as dpkg. This system is very similar to RPM on the surface, although Debian's system became lauded by those who used it when it was combined with a program called APT (Advanced Packaging Tool). APT became famous for being the first successful tool for easily installing Linux packages over the Internet with automatic dependency resolution. This system is now used by Ubuntu and Xandros in addition to Debian GNU/Linux.

The Fink project began before the very first version of Mac OS X was released; Fink had the goal of providing the same sort of functionality to Mac OS X as tools such as RPM and Debian Package did for Unix. Fink builds on top of dpkg and APT to create a convenient, mostly automated way of installing Unix software on the Mac. Nearly a decade later, Fink maintains a repository of nearly 10,000 software packages.

Installing Fink

Installing Fink is a simple process, extremely similar to the procedure used to install other Mac OS X software.

To install Fink, you need to download the Fink installer from www.finkproject.org/download/. Download the latest version of the Fink binary installer; we also recommend that you grab a copy of FinkCommander from http://finkcommander.sourceforge.net. FinkCommander provides an easy-to-use GUI interface to Fink, making installation of Unix software as simple as pointing-and-clicking. Figure 26.5 shows FinkCommander in action.

Cross-Ref

Chapter 7 has more information regarding installing programs in Mac OS X.

Using Fink to install software

Upon launching FinkCommander, the first thing you should do is get the most up-to-date package descriptions. To do this, choose Binary ⇨ Update Descriptions. You also want to choose Source ⇨ Selfupdate. During both of these processes, you may be prompted about a question that the main Fink command-line program has (which is displayed in the bottom half of the window). Typically answering the dialog box with the default answer is the best choice, unless you know that a different answer is appropriate.

FIGURE 26.5

FinkCommander prompting the user about a question (shown in the lower pane)

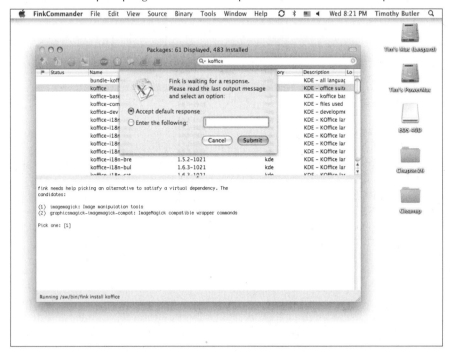

To install a software program, you simply select one from the list and choose between the Install from Binary and Install from Source functions from the toolbar. In almost all cases, it is fine to use the Install from Binary function, and doing so will make life easier and get the software installed faster.

Like iTunes and many other common Mac OS X applications, a search box is on the right side of the toolbar. You can use it to search either the descriptions or names of packages to find the software you want to install. For example, to find the Elinks Web browser, simply type **elinks** and the relevant packages will be immediately visible below.

You also can control Fink easily from the command line. The project's system is made up of two key programs on the command line. The `fink` tool is used behind the scenes when clicking "Install from Source" in FinkCommander. Typing `sudo fink install elinks` compiles and installs Elinks and any required dependencies. To update Fink itself via the command line, type `sudo fink selfupdate`. For installations from binary packages, the entire Debian package system, with its excellent `apt-get` frontend is also available. The command for binary installations is very similar to the previous one: `sudo apt-get install elinks`. Like the `fink` source package database, the `apt-get` database should be updated before performing new installations; you can update it by typing `sudo apt-get update`.

Removing a package installed using either `fink` or `apt-get` is also simple. To remove Elinks, simply type `sudo apt-get remove elinks`

Note

Fink makes a distinction between stable and unstable packages. The default is to use stable packages, packages the project is convinced are stable and perfectly safe to use. However, many programs are relatively outdated in the stable group, so it makes more sense to switch, using the unstable package selection. To switch to the unstable packages in FinkCommander, choose the FinkCommander ⇨ Preferences, and go to the Fink pane. Select the Use Unstable Packages option and click OK. You want to install unstable packages from the source.

Using the Command Line on the Internet

The Internet largely originated from Unix, and its fingerprints are present when you access the Internet on any device. Even Microsoft Windows's Internet network code has a line of descent from BSD. Interestingly, the first Web browser was written for NeXTStep, the predecessor to Mac OS X. While today the Internet is often associated with graphically rich Web 2.0 applications that seem to be totally unrelated to the Unix command line, the CLI is actually quite adept at many Internet-related tasks.

Tip

Many of the following applications are not included with the basic Mac OS X installation. Refer to the preceding section on using Fink to install Lynx, Elinks, NcFTP, or Wget.

Browsing the Web with Lynx and Links

Web browsing wasn't always a graphically rich experience. For many users, the Web was first experienced in a text-based environment, quite frequently with Lynx. More recently a family of browsers known as Links has appeared that offers many of the benefits of Lynx without nearly the number of downsides. Figure 26.6 shows Safari and two Unix browsers: Lynx and Elinks.

Lynx

Lynx is a relatively rudimentary Web browser that can display basic-text Web pages, but little else. To navigate Lynx is like navigating through Nano. By default, you start Lynx by using the simple command `lynx`; however, you can also provide a URL as a parameter to start Lynx on a particular Web site. To access an address box to go to another Web site, press the G key; you can then enter the address and press Return to load it.

Like Nano, you navigate pages by using the arrow keys, which take you from hyperlink to hyperlink (or Web form). Web pages displayed in Lynx don't include any tables, so pages may look substantially different. However, if the Web designer has coded the site thoughtfully, the site will begin with what were originally the contents of the left column of the page, and moving down a page will slowly take you column by column through the site. Pressing the spacebar moves you down one screen at a time.

To click a link or enter text into a text box of a Web form, press the Return key. Lynx offers helpful information, as well as prompts you for more information in the status bar towards the bottom; the bar is colored blue to make it easy to spot. To exit Lynx, press the Q key (for quit) and then press Y (for yes).

As a benefit of Lynx's limitations, Lynx can be useful when you're viewing intrusive pages that have annoying JavaScript, flashing images interspersed with useful (or objectionable) content. Its text-based nature also makes it very speedy on slow dial-up or cellular Internet connections. However, generally speaking, the Web has progressed beyond the point where Lynx is convenient for day-to-day use.

Tip

Lynx's other strength is a rich collection of command-line parameters. For example, Lynx can push the contents of a requested page to STDOUT, ideal for postprocessing by using another command, such as Grep. Typing `lynx --dump http://www.ofb.biz`, for example, outputs that page as plain text with footnotes denoting the URLs of the page's links. Using `-f-source` instead of `--dump` outputs raw HTML source code for the page.

Links

In a naming decision that was not exactly helpful for making it easy to distinguish from Lynx, the major alternative to Lynx is Links. The homonymic-named Links browser offers the same sort of speedy, text-driven browsing of Links, but it also can display tables, run some JavaScript, and otherwise interact with modern Web sites.

The Links variant known as Elinks is available via Fink and, when installed, you can run it by typing `elinks` in the Terminal. Like Lynx, typing `elinks http://www.apple.com` causes Elinks to begin with that page.

You access the address box in Links, like the one in Lynx, by pressing G. Unlike Lynx, you can access most of Links' other functions by using menus accessible by pressing the Esc key. You navigate all the menus and Web pages by using the keyboard in the Terminal. While unsupported in the standard Mac OS X Terminal application, when using Elinks in another terminal program such as XTerm (which launches by default when you start X11), Elinks actually responds to mouse actions much like a normal Web browser.

You can close Elinks either via the File menu or by pressing Q and clicking Yes in the resulting dialog box.

FIGURE 26.6

Safari (background), Lynx (middle), and Elinks (foreground) try to render the same Web page.

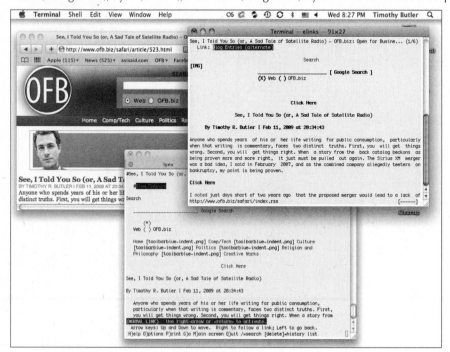

Transferring files with NcFTP

It is often useful to exchange files with a remote server, such as a Web hosting server, using FTP (File Transfer Protocol). While the Finder can browse to FTP sites, it can only view — not edit — the servers it connects to. NcFTP, on the other hand, enables you to upload and download files to the remote FTP server. To launch NcFTP, simply enter the command `ncftp`. This brings you into an NcFTP shell, which is reminiscent of Bash.

To connect to a server, you use the `open` command. For example, if you want to connect to Apple's FTP server, type:

```
open ftp.apple.com
```

This logs in to Apple's FTP server *anonymously*. Many FTP servers allow anonymous login, allowing for FTP browsing as you do with Web sites. If you want to upload files to the FTP server, however, you typically must log in with a username and password. To let NcFTP know that you need to login with a username and password, you use the –u switch. For example, assuming you have an FTP account on Apple's server, logging in would look like this:

```
open –usteve ftp.apple.com
```

After a moment, NcFTP prompts you for a password.

You can perform many of the tasks you perform on an FTP server precisely in the same way you approach those tasks in Bash. Actions such as changing folders with cd, finding out the current path by using pwd, and viewing a folder's contents with ls all work. The caveat is that actions such as viewing and editing files by using editors and other commands are *not* supported. Instead you use put and get to upload and download files, respectively. To download a file, you simply type get filename, where *filename* is the name of the file you want to download. This downloads the file into the folder you were in when NcFTP was launched. Optionally, you can provide a local path or full filename so that NcFTP places the file in a different location. For example:

```
get sangreal.txt ~/completedquests/galahad.txt
```

This downloads sangreal.txt and places it in the current user's Home folder in the completedquests subfolder with the name galahad.txt. The put command works precisely in reverse of get; it takes the first filename specified from the local Mac and uploads it to the FTP server. Unless you specify a second filename, put places the file in the current folder on the server.

The More Secure FTP Alternative

At the beginning of this chapter, we looked at remote access via Secure Shell (SSH). In addition to providing access to a remote system's shell, SSH can perform file transfers much like you can do in NcFTP or another FTP client. SSH file transfers, however, benefit from advanced encryption and are generally easier to perform, as long as you have SSH access to the server you want to upload to.

Unlike FTP, you do not need to start a separate SSH client before performing the copy. Rather, SSH file transfer uses the scp command directly from Bash. The scp command syntax is frequently analogous to that of the cp command, including the need to use the -r switch to do recursive copies, such as for folders. Like cp, scp works by specifying a source folder (or file) and a destination folder (or file). For example,

```
scp -r /home/bors/ steve@apple.com:~/www/bors
```

This command copies the local folder /home/bors to the server apple.com using the username steve. The information after the colon in the destination folder specifies where the files will be uploaded to on the remote server (in this case, it is the www/bors folder located in Steve's Home folder). If you want to reverse the direction and download something from the server, the command would look like this:

```
scp -r steve@apple.com:/home/bors/ /home/guinevere/Documents
```

This command copies the files in /home/bors/ on apple.com's server to /home/guinevere/ Documents/ on the local Mac.

Typically after pressing Return, scp prompts you for the server password before performing the transfer. You can also use more advanced key-based encryption to compliment or eliminate password login.

Retrieving files with Wget

Wget is useful when the files you want to copy into a folder are not local files at all, but are instead located on an HTTP (Web) server or an FTP server. In essence, Wget is like a Web browser, except that instead of displaying what it retrieves, it downloads it to a specified location for later use. Lynx can do the same thing, but Wget makes it simple.

At its most basic, you can merely type wget http://www.apple.com and the front page (index.html) of apple.com is downloaded into the current directory. This can occasionally be handy, but the real payoff is when you are downloading files. For example, if you have the URL of a software program that needs to be compiled, Wget enables you to download it to your working directory and get started on the compilation steps covered earlier without need of using a full-fledged Web browser like Safari first.

Wget is anything but limited, however. It can "crawl" entire Web sites and download the entire contents of that site. For example, if you want Wget to dig down eleven links into a site, ensuring it grabbed all the required images and other files that are on the pages, you type:

```
wget -r -l11 -k -p http://www.apple.com
```

The -r switch causes Wget to go into recursive mode, moving through the site, rather than down-loading a single page. The -l switch limits it to only 11 levels of links, the -k switch tells Wget to change links on the pages it downloads so that one downloaded page links to other downloaded pages rather than the original online copies, and the -p switch tells it to grab all the images and other required files that the pages need to look as they should.

Manipulating Images

When you think of manipulating images on the Mac, typically the first thing that comes to mind is Adobe Photoshop. Photoshop offers a capable, yet elegant, set of tools to handle nearly any image-related task. Adobe's own Photoshop Elements, along with newer products such as Pixelmator, aim to make that sort of flexibility more affordable and accessible. From the realm of Unix-like applications, however, two alternatives appear with the most appealing price of all: free.

Neither GIMP (GNU Image Manipulation Program) nor CinePaint should be taken as second-class applications merely because they do not carry a hefty price tag. Like so much of the Unix software you have seen in this chapter, these products are free because they have been largely developed by dedicated teams of volunteers interested in sharing code to create better software. In many ways, GIMP has become the closest thing to a rival as there is for Photoshop, and CinePaint — with a somewhat off-beat focus on film retouching — has a claim to fame of having been used for a variety of blockbuster films.

It is appropriate to deal with these applications together because they descend from a common heritage. CinePaint, originally known as Film Gimp, was a *fork* of GIMP (that is, an offshoot based the other project's code). The projects have diverged somewhat, and FilmGimp is based on the very old Gimp 1.0.x code base, but much of the interface remains similar enough to avoid a huge learning curve when switching between the applications.

Getting the applications

Both GIMP and CinePaint are available from Fink by using the instructions previously outlined, with their respective packages known as gimp2 and cinepaint. For best results, we recommend that you enable the "unstable" Fink system so the much-newer GIMP 2 can be used rather than the now-archaic GIMP 1.

Tip

While Fink can install GIMP, Aaron Voisine has created a project known as Gimp.app, which packages GIMP much like a traditional Mac OS X application, avoiding the need to manually launch it from the command line. The latest Gimp.app packages are native Quartz applications, meaning that they do not require X11 to run. In most cases, we recommend you use Gimp.app instead of compiling GIMP via Fink. You can find Gimp.app at `http://gimp-app.sourceforge.net`.

Adjusting images with GIMP

To launch GIMP, if you compiled it via Fink, go into the Terminal after opening X11 and enter the command `gimp-2.6`. If you are using Gimp.app, double-click the Gimp.app application icon, just as you would any normal Mac OS X program.

GIMP has a user interface somewhat inspired by Adobe Photoshop, as Figure 26.7 shows. It is made up of several key elements, primary among them is the Toolbox window (the equivalent of Photoshop's Tools panel). Because GIMP does not yet have a specially designed Mac OS X interface, the main menu bar appears in the main document window (which is empty upon launch) rather than on the Mac OS menu bar. The Toolbox provides access to all of the paintbrushes and other tools you may want to use to do image manipulation.

From the Toolbox, you can paint, draw, sample colors, and so on. The lower portion of the Toolbox also contains settings for the current tool. When in text mode, for example, it contains settings to change the font, justification, and so on.

A second floating panel, somewhat like the Inspector in Apple's iWork, contains such useful functions as management of the layers and a visual list of undo actions available. Attached to this panel is another one with management of brushes, textures, and gradients.

Many of the functions necessary for basic image adjustment are under the Colors menu. This menu has tools to adjust color balance, brightness, contrast, and so on. It also had a submenu of "auto" functions to enable the program to try to fix things by itself. For more complex changes to images, GIMP offers a selection of filters under the Filters menu, many of which are analogous to those included in Photoshop.

FIGURE 26.7

GIMP with several images open

GIMP also has some rather interesting automated image-creation functions. Under the File ⇨ Create submenu are functions to create a variety of customizable buttons and logos, handy for Web design and light desktop publishing.

Tip

GIMP saves project files into a format known as XCF by default. While this works fine if you plan to only work with the file in GIMP, it cannot be opened in Photoshop or other major image editors, save for CinePaint (see the next section). Therefore, it is often wise to select another format, such as Photoshop's PSD format, for projects that need to move between programs. Of course, finalized projects destined for the Web should be saved in a format such as PNG or JPEG, but keep a native XCF copy in case future editing is needed.

Retouching film with CinePaint

You accomplish basic tasks in CinePaint in a nearly identical fashion to GIMP. The primary strengths of CinePaint are its more capable, 16-bit image-editing capabilities, which are geared toward professional film retouching, and the Frame Manager.

The Frame Manager is designed so a film editor can take a folder of sequentially numbered film cells (likely scanned in from 35mm film), load them, and quickly move from frame to frame or even play them in order.

To get the Frame Manager loaded (see Figure 26.8), choose File ➪ Open in the Cinepaint Toolbox. The resulting file selection dialog box looks somewhat unfamiliar — folders are located in the left column and files are located in the right column. To move up to a parent folder, you can either use the folder popup menu at the top of the two columns or click the `../ directory` button in the Directories (Folders) column.

Next, find the folder in which the numerically sequenced set of images are located and choose one of the images to open (which one is not a terribly important matter; however, if you plan to retouch all the frames, starting at the beginning may make the most sense).

When that image is loaded, choose File ➪ Frame Manager in that image's window (not in the Toolbox window) and click Create. The Frame Manager window loads with just one image in it. Choose Store ➪ Add in the Frame Manager window; this opens the New Store Option dialog box. From here, you can select how many of the image sequence frames to load — and whether those images should be taken from earlier in the sequence or later in the sequence than your original image. Click OK to load the images.

FIGURE 26.8

CinePaint with Frame Manager open

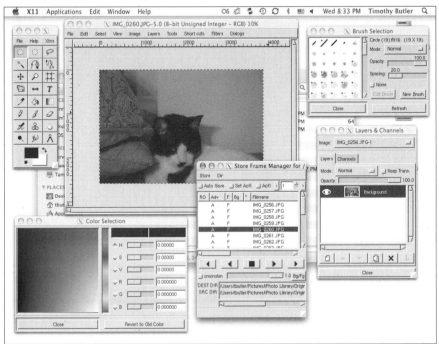

In the Frame Manager window itself, you can now move forward and backward through the images using either the list of images or the movie-player-like controls directly below the list. You can manipulate the loaded image — the one in the image-editing window — just as you would in GIMP, using the Toolbox's paintbrushes, text editor, and so on. When finished, choose Store ➪ Save All to save all of the frames at once.

Summary

Unix operating systems offer a capable and mature way to do virtually any task you could want to do with a computer. In the case of Mac OS X, many Unix functions parallel those available in more traditional Mac form; however, you can accomplish some of the functions — or accomplish them more efficiently — only by tapping directly into the Mac's Unix core. With the addition of Fink, Unix also opens up the door to thousands of mature, powerful applications to perform a wide variety of tasks. Although Unix can seem intimidating at first, the payoff for learning some of its nuances is huge.

Glossary

AAC (Advanced Audio Coding) A standard for creating digital music files, it is the default format for iTunes music and is higher in quality than the more commonly used MP3 format.

absolute pathname A pathname that specifies the exact location of a single directory. An absolute pathname begins at the root directory, a slash (/), and traverses through the Unix file system, ending at the desired directory or file, and naming each directory that is passed through. Each directory that is passed through is named and separated by a slash. /Users/galen/Documents is the absolute pathname of the user Galen's Documents folder. Compare to *relative path*.

active application The application visible in the foreground. If iTunes is the active application, its name is visible in bold in the menu bar, directly to the right of the (Apple) menu.

ActiveSync Microsoft's technology to keep e-mail, contacts, and calendars continuously synchronized between its Exchange servers and computers by using its Outlook and Entourage applications. Mac OS X 10.6 Snow Leopard (as well as the iPhone OS) includes ActiveSync, allowing Apple's Mail, iCal, and Address Book to synchronize automatically to Exchange servers as well.

adapter A device that lets devices with different connector standards connect to each other.

admin See *administrator account*.

administrator account This type of Mac OS X user account gives the user access to system-wide resources, including the abilities to modify system preferences, create and edit other user accounts, and install applications. When Mac OS X is initially set up, the first user created is an administrator.

adopted ownership When a Mac OS X user account is deleted, its contents can be transferred to an existing administrator account. The admin is said to be adopting ownership of the previous user's files.

Advanced Memory Management This Mac OS X capability automatically and dynamically assigns and handles the allocation of both physical RAM and virtual memory to applications and processes as needed.

AirPort Apple's name for its implementation of the IEEE 802.11 family of standards for wireless networking, popularly known as *Wi-Fi*. See *IEEE 802.11a, 802.11b, 802.11g, and 802.11n*.

AirPort Base Station An Apple wireless router that connects 802.11-equipped computers (Macintosh or otherwise) and other devices (such as printers and hard disks) to it, allowing them to connect to each other and to an Internet gateway. The Extreme and Express versions can also wirelessly share attached USB printers, while the Time Capsule model includes a disk for wireless data backup.

alias Also known as a *shortcut*, an alias is a pointer file that can dynamically locate its target file or folder. (You would use it to place a pointer from, say, the desktop to a file buried deep in your Mac's folder hierarchy for easy access.) The pathway is not lost if either the original or the alias is moved to a different location on the same volume. Under the Mac file system, each file has a unique identifier, which can be traced even if the file has moved.

Glossary

anti-aliasing A technique that causes text and graphics to appear smoother when displayed using the relatively low resolution of a computer screen. Shading and blending of otherwise jagged lines are used to fool the eye into seeing a cleaner image.

Apache An open source Web server provided within every copy of Mac OS X and Mac OS X Server. Apache is the most widely used Web server (powering more than two thirds of Web sites) on the Internet. It runs on a variety of platforms, including Unix-based and Windows servers.

API See *application programming interface.*

AppleCare Knowledge Base Located at `www.apple.com/support`, the Knowledge Base is Apple's official Web-based library of articles and information pertaining to the usage and support of its products.

Apple Filing Protocol (AFP) The Mac OS's built-in technology that lets Macs share files with each other over network connections.

 (Apple) menu Located at the top leftmost corner of the screen, this menu contains commands that affect the Mac as a whole, no matter what application you may be running at the time. Example functions include changing the settings of the Dock, updating the Mac OS, and shutting down the Mac.

AppleScript A Mac-only scripting language used for automating tasks and customizing application features, as well as creating stand-alone applets. The language is heavily English based (more so than most scripting languages), making it easy to learn and decipher. AppleScript is included with every copy of Mac OS X. An application that lets you create AppleScripts for its functions is called *scriptable*.

applet A mini-application program that is usually Java- or AppleScript-based. Java applets are often embedded within Web pages (like an Internet search engine), and AppleScripts are often integrated within

a larger application to perform a certain function; within Apple's DVD Player application, for example, you can use the Scripts menu to run an AppleScript that accesses a specific time within a movie.

AppleTalk A networking protocol created by Apple that dates back to the early Macintosh days (the mid-1980s). Mac OS X 10.6 Snow Leopard removes the last vestiges of AppleTalk from the Mac OS, relying instead on more efficient protocols such as TCP/IP and Bonjour.

application A software program such as Adobe Photoshop, the Finder, iTunes, Microsoft Word, Safari, and TextEdit.

application programming interface (API) The method by which an application or operating system makes its functions available for use by other applications and system components. For example, the QuickTime API would be called upon to add movie and sound features to an application.

Applications folder The default location for all applications installed on the Mac. Applications do not have to be placed in this folder, but it is a good idea to keep them here, both so you can easily find them later and in case their software update features require them to be in that folder.

Aqua Apple's name for the look and feel of the graphical user interface that distinguishes Mac OS X from competitors such as Microsoft Windows. The pulsating OK buttons, the photorealistic icons, and the fancy Genie effect that occurs when a window is minimized to the Dock are all examples of Aqua.

archive A single compressed file containing files and folders. These archives typically take less space, making them more efficient for e-mailing and backup storage. The StuffIt and Zip formats are common archive formats for the Mac, with Zip format supported natively in Mac OS X.

argument A piece of information that is passed to a Unix command on the command line. Arguments are usually filenames or directory names. For example, in the command % `chown mark:staff /Users/mark/Documents`, the argument is the Documents folder's file path (`mark:staff/users/mark/`).

ASCII (American Standard Code for Information Interchange) The most basic character set used by almost all modem computers. ASCII uses the codes 0 through 127 to represent uppercase and lowercase letters, punctuation, space, and numbers. An enhanced ASCII version uses the codes 0 through 255 to support a wider variety of characters, but ASCII has largely been supplanted by Unicode and the ISO/IEC 10646 Universal Character Set (UCS) standards. Mac OS X uses both Unicode and UCS, both of which support the original ASCII codes as well.

authentication The process of verifying that someone is, in actuality, who he or she claims to be. Under Mac OS X, when you type a correct password into the login screen, you are being authenticated before being allowed to log in to the system.

Automator Mac OS X utility used to create workflows that let you automate functions in Automator-compatible applications, and then save those workflows for later reuse.

autoscrolling When you drag an item to the edge of a window, Mac OS X automatically scrolls the workspace for you, instead ofrequiring you to manually click the window's scroll arrows or drag the scrollbar first to reveal the off-window workspace.

background program A program that, while running, is usually not visible to the Mac's user. Launch the Activity Monitor utility to see examples of this. The iChat Agent is one such example. This process runs in the background and can sign the user on to the instant messaging service even if the iChat application is not open yet.

Back to My Mac A service within the MobileMe service that provides remote access to your Mac from another Mac via the Internet.

backup A backup is a copy of files and other data meant to help recover from data loss, which may occur due to hardware failure, corruption, viruses, natural disasters, theft, and human error. A backup can be as simple as a collection of files copied to a disk or CD, or a complete replica of your Mac's files and system preferences stored on a hard drive or network file server automatically by using a program such as EMC's Retrospect or Mac OS X's own Time Machine.

binary The number system that computers use, which is base two, unlike the number system humans use, which is base ten. In binary, there are two number choices, a one or a zero. A single binary digit is called a *bit*.

binary file A type of compressed and encoded file, usually containing the `.bin` filename extension. MacBinary files are encoded so that the data contained in them can be stored on other operating systems (like Microsoft Windows) and transferred back and forth without issue. Mac OS X can decode these files; just double-click them.

BinHex A method of encoding and compressing binary files for download and transfer. BinHex files have a `.hqx` filename extension and are a common format in which to receive Macintosh software downloads. Mac OS X can decode these files; just double-click them.

bit Stands for *binary digit*. A bit is the smallest unit of information storage, a one or a zero, a yes or a no, an on or an off, a true or a false.

bit depth The number of bits of information that are required to represent the number of colors available on the screen. For example, a screen that can display thousands of colors is set at a bit depth of 16 bits (2^{16} supports up to 65,536 colors).

Glossary

bitmap font Same as *fixed-size font*.

Bluetooth A short-range wireless networking technology standard supported by most Macs, typically used to connect headphones, headsets, smartphones, and other devices to a Mac.

Blu-ray A recent standard for high-capacity optical discs. It is not natively supported in Mac OS X 10.6 Snow Leopard, though programs such as Roxio's Toast enables Macs to work with Blu-ray drives.

Bonjour An Apple networking technology requiring zero configuration. Connect and turn on the device, and your Mac can see it and use it. Because it is an Apple standard, non-Apple devices (as well as some fairly old Apple devices) may not offer support for the technology. Note that Apple provides Bonjour software for Microsoft's Windows operating system as well; the software is available at `http://support.apple.com/downloads/Bonjour_for_Windows`.

bookmark A saved hyperlink in a Web browser, which lets you click the link to get to its Web page easily in the future. For example, if, when using Safari, you want to save *Macworld*'s Web site (`www.macworld.com`) for future viewing, you can go choose Bookmarks ➪ Add Bookmark to save the location, then just click the bookmark in the future to get to the Web site, instead of retyping `www.macworld.com` each time.

boot The act of powering on a Mac and having the operating system loaded and started. Also called *bootup* and *startup*.

Boot Camp Apple's technology that enables Mac OS X to create a separate disk partition from which you can run Microsoft Windows on a Mac with an Intel-based processor. You can boot between the Mac OS and Windows, but not run both simultaneously under Boot Camp. Using a technology called virtual machines, applications such as EMC VMware's Fusion and Parallels' Desktop let you run both Mac OS X and Windows simultaneously.

bootup See *boot*.

bridge A piece of hardware used to move traffic between two different types of networks or networking hardware. An AirPort Base Station is a bridge when it routes information from a wired Ethernet network to its wireless one.

browser See *Web browser*.

BSD (Berkeley Software Distribution) There are many different versions or "flavors" of Unix, including distributions called Linux, Solaris, and AIX. BSD is an umbrella term for the Unix flavor that has been released by the University of California at Berkeley. Mac OS X is based on this version.

BSD subsystem Together with the Mach kernel, the BSD subsystem makes up Apple's own flavor of Unix, called Darwin. On top of Darwin, Apple placed its proprietary frameworks (such as Carbon, Cocoa, and QuickTime) and its Aqua user interface, resulting in Mac OS X.

bug An error in a piece of software (like a program) or hardware (like a printer) that causes an unwanted behavior, usually resulting in a malfunction. A well-known bug was the Y2K bug, which left many computers (Macs excluded) vulnerable to reverting to the year 1900 instead of the year 2000, due to the two-digit year limitation encoded in most software. Updates, or patches (also known as *bug fixes*), are usually released to repair bugs.

built-in memory Apple's terminology for the RAM (random access memory) that is physically installed in the Mac.

bundle Another term for *package*.

burn When information is recorded onto a CD or DVD, the disc is said to be burned. The term stems from the way optical discs are recorded, which involves using a laser beam to heat a layer of photosensitive dye.

burn-in 1. A condition affecting CRT monitors in which a vestige of an unchanging screen image remains visible after the image changes, and even after the computer has powered off. Today's computer screens are no longer susceptible to burn-in. 2. The process of letting a new or hardware-upgraded Mac run for at least several hours to make sure that the system is functioning correctly.

button A displayed control that — when clicked — causes an action to take place. (Apple's formal name for this control is *push button*.) A label on the button indicates the action that the button performs. The label may be text or an icon. Buttons with text labels are generally rectangular with rounded ends. Buttons with iconic labels may be any shape.

byte One byte is comprised of eight bits. A byte is the smallest unit of storage that the Mac recognizes. Bytes are commonly measured by many thousands (kilobytes, or K), millions (megabytes, or MB), billions (gigabytes, or GB), and trillions (terabytes, or TB) at a time.

Carbon Apple's technology that enables developers to create applications that run in both Mac OS 9 and Mac OS X, appearing to be "native" applications in both OSes. Given that Mac OS 9 was discontinued more than a decade ago, few developers still create Carbon applications.

CardBus A compact form of the PCMCIA add-in card slot standard used for many years by Apple in its laptops. It has been replaced by the ExpressCard standard. See *ExpressCard* and *PCMCIA*.

case-sensitive *Case-sensitive* means that it matters whether or not letters are capitalized. Passwords in Mac OS X are case-sensitive. In some instances, such as in the screen saver password window, the dialog box informs you if the Caps Lock key is pressed, alleviating the frustration of being sure you have the correct password but unknowingly having entered it in all caps.

character A written representation of a letter, digit, or symbol. A single character could be the letter W or an exclamation point. Also called a *glyph*.

check box This type of user-interface option gives you the option of activating or deactivating a setting, offered by an application or within the operating system. A check box has three different states: blank, checked, or dashed. A check indicates a setting is chosen; a blank means a setting has not been chosen; and, in the case where a check box has a disclosure triangle that reveals sub-check boxes, a dash is shown if some sub-check boxes are checked and others are not. Compare this option to *radio buttons*.

Classic The Mac OS 8 and Mac OS 9 operating systems' application environment. The term is used to refer to applications designed to run in these pre-Mac OS X applications. Mac OS X 10.6 does not support Classic applications, unlike earlier versions of Mac OS X.

clean installation A type of Mac OS X installation in which a new, fresh copy of the system is installed, and the original System folder left unaltered and moved into a Previous Systems folder at the root level of the startup disk. An option for preserving the user folders is available.

CLI See *command-line interface*.

click-through The ability to interact directly with an item in an inactive window. For example, you can operate the Close, Minimize, and Zoom buttons in most inactive Aqua windows.

client A program (or a computer running a program) that requests and receives information or services from a server.

clipping file A file created by the Finder to hold material that has been dragged from a document to the Desktop or a Finder window.

Glossary

closed network A Wi-Fi network that requires you to type its name to connect to it. Such a network does not display in the Mac OS's list of available networks, and is meant to essentially be hidden from all but those who know the network exists.

Cocoa Applications that are specifically developed for Mac OS X. Cocoa applications are incompatible with older Macintosh operating systems, such as Mac OS 9. Cocoa applications take advantage of all of Mac OS X's modern OS features, such as advanced memory, preemptive multitasking, multiprocessing, and the Aqua interface.

codec (compressor-decompressor) A tool — software, hardware, or both — that compresses data so that it takes less space to store and decompresses compressed data back to its original form for playback or other use. Codecs are typically used for audio and video files.

collated The process of printing multiple copies of a document so each copy has all its pages in the correct order.

color depth See *bit depth*.

color picker The panel in which you specify a custom color either by clicking within a color wheel or by clicking a color sample or other form of preselected color values.

ColorSync Apple's technology to ensure accurate reproduction of color as graphics move from application to screen to printer.

column view A view of files and folders in a Finder window in which each folder's contents is displayed in its own column, providing a horizontal hierarchy of your disk's contents.

⌘ (Command) The key used to invoke Mac OS and application functions from the keyboard. For example, ⌘+A is used to select all, while ⌘+Q is used to quit an application. It is often combined with other modifier keys such as Option, Shift, and Control.

command-line interface A keyboard-only method of interacting with the operating system. The Mac uses the Terminal application to accept command lines.

comment An AppleScript line or a Unix command line that with a number sign or hash character (#), which in either case means that the line is descriptive and not a command to be performed.

compile To convert the human-readable text of a programming language (such as C or any of its derivatives) into command codes that a Mac can execute. In AppleScript, compiling checks the script for nonconformance with AppleScript grammar, such as the use of a parenthesis.

compression algorithm A method for compressing data so that it fits in less space and can be transferred more quickly. Each compression algorithm generally works best with one type of data, such as photographs, video or motion pictures, and computer-generated animation. Three characteristics of a compression algorithm determine how effectively it compresses: compression ratio, fidelity to the original data, and speed.

compression ratio Indicates the amount of compression and is calculated by the size of the original source data by the size of the compressed data. Larger compression ratios mean greater compression and generally (although not always) a loss of quality in the compressed data.

conditional A programming command that evaluates a condition (stated as part of the conditional) to determine whether another command or set of commands should be performed. (Also referred to as a *conditional statement*.)

connector The part of a cable, usually a plug, that connects into a device's jack.

contextual menu A contextual menu lists commands relevant to an item that you Control+click or right-click.

Control A modifier key on the Mac used both for application and system shortcuts and for opening contextual menus (when the Control key is held and the mouse button is pressed). Applications' menus use the symbol ^ to indicate this key.

cooperative multitasking A scheme of multitasking used by Classic applications whereby multiple applications are open in the Classic environment and voluntarily taking turns using the Classic environment's processing time. While each Classic application is idle, cooperative multitasking allows other Classic applications to use the processor. Compare to Mac OS X's *preemptive multitasking*.

Core Location Core Location is a technology that uses known WiFi hotspots to triangulate your current position. In Mac OS X 10.6 Snow Leopard it is used to automatically determine your present time zone, and adjusts the clock accordingly.

Cover Flow view A view of files and folders in a Finder window in which files and folders are represented as a series of album-coverlike icons that you can "thumb through" by using the → and ← keys. This view is based on the popular Cover Flow view in iTunes for visually finding music by album cover.

CPU (central processing unit) The key component in a computer for processing the instructions that let the operating system, drivers, and applications operate. It is a silicon chip that contains millions of circuits.

CPU core Modern CPUs contain several independent processing engines, called cores, that act as if they were separate CPUs. This multicore CPU approach allows more processing power to be delivered by computers, using less energy, costing less to produce, and taking less space than having multiple, separate CPUs.

crack A means of circumventing a program's security.

crop markers Small triangles that indicate the beginning and end of a selected part of a movie in iMovie HD.

crossover cable A cable whose wires are reversed inside the plug at one end of the cable. Such a cable is required for most pre-2002 Macs to allow direct-connection networking.

custom installation The process by which you can selectively install Mac OS X packages' components.

daisy-chaining The process of connecting one peripheral or network device to another device, linking them so that they can share data. This is often done with Ethernet networking hubs to extend the size of an Ethernet network: One hub is connected to another to allow more connections in total than the first hub can support by itself. The same technique is used with FireWire and SCSI devices to connect one to the next and eventually to a single Mac, which can then access them all.

Darwin A joint project between the open source community and Apple. The primary objective of the Darwin project is to build an industrial-strength Unix-based operating system core that provides greater stability and performance compared to the existing iterations of the Mac OS to date.

Dashboard Mac OS X's window containing active widgets and the controls to activate and deactivate widgets.

dead keys The keys that generate accented characters when typed in combination with the Option key and in proper sequence. For example, typing **Option+E** then typing **O** generates Ó on a U.S. keyboard.

desktop The default screen in the Mac OS after you boot up, showing all connected drives and any folders or files you placed on the desktop. It is used both as the starting point for navigating your Mac's disks, folders, and files, as well as a convenient place to put frequently used files and folders or the aliases to them.

device A piece of hardware attached to a computer, either internally or externally. Some examples include keyboards, scanners, and disks.

device driver Software that controls a device, such as a printer or scanner. The driver contains data required to fully use the device.

DHCP (Dynamic Host Configuration Protocol) A networking service in which a host device, such as a router, dynamically assigns network information (such as TCP/IP addresses) to client computers to grant them access to other network services.

dialog box A movable window that displays options you can set or select; when open, a dialog box usually prevents you from accessing other controls in the application. A dialog box typically has a button for accepting the changes and another button for canceling the changes. Both buttons close the dialog box.

digital signature Like its handwritten counterpart, a digital signature identifies the person who vouches for the accuracy and authenticity of the signed document. A digital signature typically involves a code appended to or included with the file that is verified against an independent database of authenticated codes on the Internet or network.

DIMM A DIMM (dual in-line memory module) is a small circuit board containing memory of the format standard in desktop Macs. A SO-DIMM (Small Outline DIMM) is the laptop version.

directory Another name for a folder.

Directory Services Directory Services provide a consolidated user list that can be shared via multiple network services or servers for authentication. Directory Services do not provide the user list data itself but rather describe how they are set up and enable the communication of the data.

disclosure triangle A user-interface control that regulates how much detail you see in a window. When the window is displaying minimal detail, clicking a disclosure triangle reveals additional detail and may automatically enlarge the window to accommodate it (this is called *expanding the option*). Clicking the same triangle again hides detail and may automatically shrink the window to fit (this is called *collapsing the option*).

disk cache Improves system performance by storing recently used information from disk in a dedicated part of memory. Accessing information in memory is faster than accessing information on disk.

disk image A file that, when mounted by using Disk Utility or a similar utility, appears on the Desktop as if it were a removable disk.

display mirroring See *video mirroring*.

DisplayPort A recent standard for video-display connections that is becoming the standard on newer Macs.

DNS (Domain Name System) A service that resolves domain names to IP addresses, and vice versa.

Dock Mac OS X's quick-access launchpad for applications, as well as for access to the Trash, the Downloads folder, and open files.

domain name The part of a URL that identifies the owner of an Internet location. A domain name has the form companyname.com, organizationname.net, schoolname.edu, militaryunitname.mil, governmentagencyname.gov, and so on.

dongle A hardware adapter or device that typically plugs into a jack and either sticks out from that jack or dangles from a short cord plugged into that jack.

double-click speed The rate at which you have to click the mouse button so that Mac OS X perceives two clicks in a row as a single event.

download The process of receiving software or other files from another computer or server, whether over the Internet or a local network.

dpi (dots per inch) A measure of how fine or coarse the dots are that make up a printed image. More dots per inch means smaller dots, and smaller dots mean finer (less coarse) printing.

drag To move the mouse while holding down the mouse button; this moves, or drags, the selected object.

drag-and-drop editing To copy or move selected text, graphics, or other material by dragging it to another place in the same window, a different window, or the Desktop. Some applications do not support drag-and-drop editing.

drag-and-drop open To drag a document onto a compatible application in the Finder or Dock; when you release the mouse button, the application launches (if it's not already running) and opens the document.

drop box A shared folder located inside a user's Public folder in which other users may place items (when peer-to-peer file sharing is enabled), but only the folder's owner can see them.

drop-down menu See *menu*.

DSL (Digital Subscriber Line) An Internet access service that uses standard telephone wiring. It typically is offered as an add-on to regular phone service, but can also be offered without phone service.

duplex A method of automatically printing on both sides of the page.

DVI (Digital Video Interface) The video-display connection standard used on many Macs. The newer DisplayPort technology is beginning to displace DVI on newer Macs.

dynamic IP address See *DHCP*.

dynamic RAM allocation An operating system technology that allows the Mac OS to respond to an application's request for more or less memory as needed.

Easter egg An undocumented "feature" usually hidden inside an application by a programmer without the publisher's knowledge. An Easter egg might be a hidden message or credits reel. You reveal it by performing secret combinations of keystrokes and mouse clicks.

enclosing folder A file's (or folder's) enclosing folder is the folder in which the file (or folder) exists.

encryption The process of scrambling the data in a file or message so that it cannot be understood by anyone without the correct decryption key.

escape character Escape characters are used in programming languages and command-line interfaces to indicate that the next character is to be used literally, not interpreted as a wildcard or other special character. In Unix, a backslash (\) is used as the escape character, but some languages use other characters.

Ethernet A high-speed standard for connecting computers and other devices in a wired network. Ethernet ports are built into most Macs, in many printers, and even in some disk drives.

event message A means of interprocess communication. Applications can send event messages to one another. When an application receives an event message, it takes an action according to the content of the message. This action can be anything from executing a particular command to taking some data, working with it, and then returning a result to the program that sent the message.

Exchange Microsoft's server software for managing e-mail, contacts, and calendars. This server software is typically used in businesses, and now is supported natively in Mac OS X 10.6 Snow Leopard.

Exposé Apple's window management function, which is designed to afford users easy access to all open applications, windows, or the desktop.

ExpressCard A connection standard for a hardware device that can be inserted into a slot in a laptop. The ExpressCard standard replaces the CardBus standard; CardBus devices cannot be used in an ExpressCard slot, or vice versa, without a special adapter.

extension See *filename extension*.

filename extension The last part of a file's name, typically three or four letters, following a period. The extension helps to designate an item's file type.

file server A computer running a program that makes files centrally available for other computers on a network.

file sharing The technology that lets you share files with people whose computers are connected to yours in a network. The Mac OS X uses Apple Filing Protocol but also supports Windows' SMB protocol for file sharing.

file system A method of organizing data on a volume. Mac OS X uses either HFS+ or the UFS file system for its hard disks, UDF for DVDs, and either HFS or ISO 9660 for CD-ROMs.

file type A four-letter code associated to a file that identifies the general characteristics of a file's contents, such as plain text, formatted text, picture, or sound. This was used in Mac OS 9 and earlier Mac operating systems; Mac OS X uses filename extensions instead for this identification purpose.

FileVault A secure file storage method that encrypts your user folder's contents automatically.

filter A technology that applies special effects to an image, such as a visual effect to a QuickTime movie.

Finder The core system application that allows users to graphically interact with the operating system, such as opening folders and using windows.

firewall A device or software that places a block between your Mac and other computers and devices in your local network or on the Internet. The firewall is meant to keep out unauthorized users and applications, and can also be used to prevent local users from accessing unauthorized services or sharing unauthorized data with outsiders.

FireWire Apple's name for the IEEE 1394 standard of device connections, typically used for external storage drives and video cameras. See *IEEE 1394*.

firmware Low-level programming stored on a device that tells the hardware of a computer (or device) how to operate.

fixed-size font A font format that contains exact pictures of every letter, digit, and symbol for one size of a font. Fixed-size fonts are called bitmap fonts because each picture precisely maps the dots, or bits, to be displayed or printed for one character. Such fonts are rarely used in Mac OS X.

folder-action script An AppleScript script attached to a folder so that it can watch and respond to user interaction with that folder in the Finder.

font A set of characters that have a common and consistent design, such as Helvetica Bold or Apple Gothic.

font family A collection of differently styled variations (such as bold, italic, and plain) of a single font. Many fonts come in the four basic styles: plain, bold, italic, and bold italic. Some font families include many more styles, such as light, medium, black, and condensed.

Fonts folder The Mac OS X has several Fonts folders, each of which can hold fixed-size, PostScript Type 1, OpenType, and TrueType fonts. Fonts stored in /System/Fonts are available for the Mac OS, for all applications, and for all users; only fonts installed by Mac OS X should be kept here. Fonts stored in /System/Library/Fonts are also available for the Mac OS, all applications, and all users. Fonts stored in /System/Users/ username/Library/Fonts are available only for the Mac OS and applications when that specific user account is active.

fps (frames per second) A measurement of how smoothly a motion picture plays. More frames per second means smoother playback. This measurement is used when discussing the frame rate of time-based media.

frame One still image that is part of a series of still images, which, when shown in sequence, produce the illusion of movement.

frame rate The number of frames displayed in one second. The TV frame rate is 30 fps in the United States and other countries that use the NTSC broadcasting standard, and 25 fps in countries that use the PAL or SECAM standard. The standard movie frame rate is 24 fps. See also *fps*.

frameworks Mac OS X frameworks contain dynamically loading code that is shared between applications. Frameworks alleviate the need for applications that utilize identical code to load multiple iterations of the same code simultaneously.

freeware Free software primarily distributed over the Internet and from person to person. Most freeware is still copyrighted by the person who created it. You can use it and give it to other people, but you can't sell it. See also *shareware*.

FTP (File Transfer Protocol) A data communications protocol that the Internet and other TCP/IP networks use to transfer files between computers.

FTP site A collection of files on an FTP server available for downloading.

full motion Video displayed at frame rates of 24 to 30 fps. The human eye perceives fairly smooth motion at frame rates of 12 to 18 fps. See also *fps* and *frame rate*.

gamma The relationship between the intensity of color and its luminance.

gamma correction A method of compensating for the loss of detail that the human eye perceives in dark areas.

Genie effect The visual effect used when minimizing or maximizing an application to or from the Dock, in which it appears to expand or shrink much like a genie going into or out of a bottle. Mac OS X also offers the Scale effect.

Genius A technology used in iTunes that analyzes music for patterns to determine what other music is similar. It is meant to help create playlists of similar music and to provide suggestions of similar music users may want to also purchase when buying a specific song.

gestures A user-interface technique in which you use one or more fingers' motion across a Mac's Multi-Touch trackpad (typically available on MacBooks since 2008) or on an iPhone or iPod Touch to control the device. Example gestures include pinching, expanding, swiping, rotating, tapping, and dragging. See *Multi-Touch trackpad*.

glyph A character in a font, such as a letter, punctuation, space, or symbol.

GPU (graphics processing unit) A processing chip that can reside on a computer's motherboard or on its graphics card, designed to handle the delivery of video, such as in games and movies to the computer screen. Mac OS X 10.6 Snow Leopard's OpenCL technology lets it use the GPU for nongraphical operations when the GPU is not in use, speeding up application performance.

Grand Central Dispatch The technology, new to Mac OS X 10.6 Snow Leopard, that automatically divides up tasks within an application across each CPU core, allowing faster processing than in previous versions of Mac OS X.

group A method of assigning privileges, such as access rights, to multiple users at once so they have identical levels of access and can all have their privileges changed simultaneously by changing just their group's settings.

Glossary

guest A network user who is not identified by a name and password.

guest account The user account that you can set up for a Mac that provides limited access to the Mac's files and applications for guests, such as the babysitter or your kids' friends.

GUI (graphical user interface) A means of interacting with and controlling a computer by manipulating graphical objects shown on the display, such as windows, menus, and icons. Also see *command-line interface*.

H.264 A video standard used by Apple to compress and play video. Also known as MPEG-4 Part 10 and MPEG-4 AVC. Also see *MPEG-4* and *codec*.

hack A programming effort that accomplishes something resourceful or unconventional. The term is also often used as a disparaging term for a quick fix, or for a poorly skilled technician.

hacker 1. A person who likes to tinker with computer technology and especially with computer software code. Some hackers create new software, and enable existing hardware to do things unintended by the original manufacturer, but many hackers make unauthorized changes to existing software. 2. Someone who maliciously breaks into secure systems over the Internet or other network connection.

handler A named set of AppleScript commands that you can execute by naming the handler elsewhere in the same script instead of repeating the entire set of commands several times in different parts of a script. This is also sometimes called a *subroutine*.

helper application A program that handles a particular kind of media or other data encountered on the Internet. Examples include the Adobe Reader and Adobe Flash helper applications that let browsers open PDF files and play Flash files, respectively.

help tag A short description of the object under the mouse pointer in a Mac OS X application. The description appears in a small yellow box near the object. These are also known as *Tool Tips* when used in panels and dialog boxes.

HFS (Hierarchical File System) A file format designed for hard disks and CD-ROMs, it is now used just for CD-ROM drives on the Mac OS. Also see *ISO 9660*.

HFS+ (Hierarchical File System Plus) An extended file format designed for high-capacity hard disks, it is the standard format for disk drives in Mac OS X. In Mac OS X's Disk Utility, the HFS+ formatting is called Mac OS Extended.

Home folder The folder in which users store all of their personal files; each user account has its own Home folder, which is found in /Users. The Mac OS X system also preserves settings for the user in his or her Home folder's Library folder.

Home page The main page of a Web site, the one that appears when a Web browser first opens a Web site if no specific page is indicated (such as www.apple.com).

hot spots 1. For networking, a hot spot is an area in a public place that has Wi-Fi wireless Internet access. 2. In QuickTime VR, hot spots are places in a panorama that you can click to go to another scene in the panorama or to a QuickTime VR object.

hub On an Ethernet network, a device that passes signals from any device connected to one of the hub's RJ-45 ports to all other devices connected to the hub; these are rarely used in modern networks because they do not intelligently manage traffic as switches and routers do. *Hub* can also refer to a device that provides multiple USB or FireWire ports from a single connection.

HTML (Hypertext Markup Language) The language used in creating Web pages to control their appearance and functionality.

hyperlink Text or graphics on a Web page or in a document such as a PDF file or Word file that when clicked opens a new page or resource on the Internet or in a local network. Hyperlinked text is often underlined and displayed in blue, while hyperlinked graphics often have a blue border around them. Whether or not they have such highlighting, the mouse pointer changes from an arrow icon to a hand icon when it passes over the hyperlinked element.

icon A small picture that represents an entity such as a program, document, folder, or disk. Icons are used in folders to represent file types and contents and in application user-interface elements such as buttons.

icon view A view of files and folders in a Finder window in which each folder's contents is displayed as a grid of icons.

iDisk A service within the MobileMe service that provides remote storage accessible via the Internet.

IEEE 802.11a, 802.11b, 802.11g, 802.11n A set of wireless networking standards that includes 802.11b (the oldest), which can deliver data as fast as 11 Mbps; 802.11a and 802.11g (the next oldest), both of which can run as fast as 54 Mbps; and 802.11n (the newest), which can run as fast as 108 Mbps. Apple's AirPort base stations use 802.11b technology, while its AirPort Extreme base stations use 802.11g or 802.11n technology, depending on when they were made. Each Mac model also supports a specific standard, depending on when it was made. Each standard supports all standards previous to it, so older equipment can always run on newer equipment; the sole exception is 802.11a, which uses different radio spectrum than the other standards and thus can work only with 802.11a-compatible equipment.

IEEE 802.1x An authentication standard used in Ethernet and Wi-Fi networks to verify that a user's credentials have not been compromised during a login attempt.

IEEE 1394 A standard for high-capacity device serial-bus connections, typically used for external hard disks and digital cameras. IEEE 1394a, known as FireWire 400, has two versions: the 8-pin version used by many Macs, and the 6-pin version (which lacks the ability to transfer power to the device) that requires an adapter to be connected to a Mac. Beginning in 2008, Macs began shipping with the faster IEEE 1394b technology, known as FireWire 800.

iMac Apple's line of all-in-one Macs.

IMAP (Internet Message Access Protocol) A protocol for allowing access to e-mail servers, it is typically used by corporate e-mail servers such as Microsoft Exchange, IBM Lotus Notes, and Novell GroupWise to provide users access to e-mail when working outside the corporate networks.

inbound port mapping A scheme for directing all requests coining into a local network from the Internet for a particular service, such as a Web server, to a particular computer on the local network.

inherited permissions Privileges that are inherited from a parent folder to child folders and all files within.

initialization A process that creates a blank disk directory. The effect is the same as erasing the disk, even though it's only the directory of files that is deleted, not the files themselves. (Without the directory, Mac OS X and applications can't find those files, so they appear to be deleted as well.)

insertion point A blinking vertical bar in a text window or field that indicates where text is inserted when you start typing.

installation The process of putting a new or updated version of software on your disk.

Internet A global network that provides e-mail, Web pages, news, file storage and retrieval, and other services and information.

Glossary

Internet gateway A device such as a router that enables all the computers on a local network to connect to the Internet, optionally sharing a single public IP address on the Internet.

Internet service provider (ISP) A company that gives you access to the Internet via a phone line, cable line, or other technology.

interpreted The technique used by Unix shells and other scripting languages such as Perl to perform each command as it is encountered instead of converting all commands to machine instructions in advance.

interprocess communication The technology that enables programs to send each other messages requesting action and receive the results of requested actions. Mac OS X has several forms of interprocess communication, one of which is Apple events, which is the basis of AppleScript.

IP address In IPv4, a 32-bit binary number, such as 192.168.0.1, that uniquely identifies a computer or other device on a network. IPv6 is the 128-bit successor.

iPhone Apple's mobile device that combines phone, Web, e-mail, contact management, media playback, gaming, and application launching. A version without the phone and camera capabilities is called the iPod Touch.

iPod Apple's line of music- and video-playing devices.

ISDN (Integrated Services Digital Network) A telephone technology used mainly in businesses that allows for medium-speed network transmissions over long distances.

ISO 9660 The International Standards Organization's formatting standard for CD-ROMs. Mac OS X can read and write the CDs in the ISO 9660 format, but its native CD format is HFS. (Windows PCs use ISO 9660 as their default CD format.) Also see *HFS*.

ISO/IEC 10646 Universal Character Set (UCS) See *UCS*.

iSync Apple's technology to synchronize data across applications and devices, such as between a smartphone and iCal.

jack The receptacle for a cable to plug into.

Java A programming language developed by Sun Microsystems. Java is platform independent, allowing its applications to function within any platform as long as the Java virtual machine software is available and installed. (Mac OS X comes with a Java virtual machine preinstalled.)

JavaScript A scripting language typically used by Web pages to deliver functionality not supported by HTML.

kernel The kernel is the core of Mac OS X. The kernel provides services for all other elements of the operating system. See also *Mach 3.0 Microkernel*.

kernel panic When Mac OS X encounters a critical error it cannot recover from, it suspends all operations and displays a black screen telling you to power down the Mac and restart; this is called a kernel panic. (Windows users are no doubt familiar with the PC's equivalent, the Blue Screen of Death.)

kerning Adjusting the space between specific pairs of letters so that the spacing within the word looks consistent.

keychain The technology that enables you to store passwords and passphrases for network connections, file servers, some types of secure Web sites, and encrypted files. The Keychain Access utility lets you manage the Mac OS X keychain.

label A means of color-coding files, folders, and disks in the Finder. Each of the eight label types has its own color and title.

LAN (local area network) See *local network*.

landscape A page or image orientation that is wider than it is tall.

launch The act of getting an application started.

LDAP (Lightweight Directory Access Protocol) A software protocol that enables the location of individuals, groups, and other resources such as files or devices on a network.

Library folder Contains resources and preferences for Mac OS X. There are several Library folders in Mac OS X: /Library, which is the core library used by Mac OS X and should not be altered; /System/Library, which holds additional features you or applications install meant for use by all user accounts; and /Users/username/Library, which holds additional features you or applications install for just that user account.

ligature A glyph composed of two merged characters. For example, f and i can be merged to form the *fi* ligature.

link See *hyperlink*.

list view A view of files and folders in a Finder window in which each folder's contents is displayed as a list. Folders have a disclosure triangle that, when clicked, expands the list to include that folder's contents.

little arrows The informal name for *stepper controls*.

localhost The current Mac's generic network address (typically the same as the IP address 127.0.0.1), used when in Unix or in network testing utilities to indicate the current Mac no matter what IP or network address it may have been assigned by a router or other device (and thus useful when troubleshooting networking issues).

localization The development of software whose dialog boxes, screens, menus, and other screen elements use the language spoken in the region in which the software is sold.

local network A system of computers that are interconnected for sharing information and services and that are located in close proximity, such as in an office, home, school, or campus. Compare to *WAN*.

log in The process of entering a username and password to begin a session with Mac OS X or another secured resource such as a network connection.

log out A command to quit current user settings and return the Mac OS X system or other secured resource back to the login screen.

loop To repeat a command, movie, song, or an entire playlist.

lossless A type of compression algorithm that regenerates exactly the same data as the uncompressed original.

LPR (Line Print Remote) printer A printer that contains a protocol that allows it to accept print jobs via TCP/IP.

.Mac See *MobileMe*.

MacBinary A scheme for encoding the special information in a pre-Mac OS X file into a file format appropriate for transmission over the Internet.

MacBook Apple's name for its laptop computers. The MacBook Pro is a separate line of more capable MacBooks. The MacBook Air is a very thin, light MacBook model.

Mach 3.0 Microkernel Developed at Carnegie-Mellon University, the Mach 3.0 Microkernel has a closely tied history to BSD (Berkeley Software Distribution) Unix. Mach gives Mac OS X the features of protected memory architecture, preemptive multitasking, and symmetric multi-processing.

Mac Mini Apple's line of small computers that do not come with a built-in monitor.

Glossary

Mac OS Extended See *HFS+*.

Mac Pro Apple's line of large, tower-style Macs, typically used for high-end, performance-heavy tasks.

mail account The configuration settings that provide an e-mail client application, such as Apple's Mail, access to a specific user's e-mail from a server.

mailbox In Apple's Mail, a collection of messages and folders that are typically associated to a specific mail account but can also include content from other mail accounts, such as when setting up a smart mailbox.

malware Software that is intended to do harm. Common types include Trojan horses, viruses, and worms.

man pages Documentation for some of the Mac OS X Unix commands (which are actually Unix programs) and other Unix components.

marquee The rectangular selection area that appears when you hold and click the mouse button, then drag the mouse. Release the mouse button to complete the selection.

maximize The act of expanding a dialog box or application window that has been collapsed to an icon in the Dock or to a title bar within the application window. Compare to *minimize*.

memory protection An operating system technology that makes it impossible for one active application to read and write data from another active application's space in memory. Memory protection helps applications run with fewer crashes.

menu A list of commands that is typically accessible from a drop-down menu, in which a clicked menu label causes the list of available commands to display below it, or from a popup menu, in which a click menu opens a menu that usually displays over the popup menu.

menu bar The row at the top of the Mac OS X screen that begins with the menu, is followed by the current application's menus, and then provides iconic menu items provided by Mac OS X and other applications. The and iconic menu items are always available, while the application's menu items change based on which application is currently available.

Microsoft ActiveSync See *ActiveSync*.

Microsoft Exchange See *Exchange*.

MIDI (Musical Instrument Digital Interface) Developed in 1983 by several of the music industry's electronics manufacturers, MIDI is a data transmission protocol that permits devices to work together in a performance context. MIDI doesn't transfer music; it transfers information about the notes and their characteristics in a format another MIDI device can reconstruct the music from.

minimize The act of collapsing a dialog box or application window to an icon in the Dock or to a title bar within the application window. Compare to *maximize*.

MobileMe An Apple service that provides users with e-mail accounts, Internet-based storage, the ability to share and synchronize calendars and address books data among several devices and users, and the ability to remotely control other Macs with a technology called *Back to my Mac*. The MobileMe service was previously called .Mac.

modem A device that connects a computer to the telephone system. It converts digital information from the sending computer into analog-format sounds for transmission over phone lines and converts sounds from phone lines to digital information for the receiving computer. (The term *modem* is a shortened form of modulator/demodulator.) This term is also used informally for devices that connect computers by using digital technologies — such as cable, DSL, and ISDN "modems" — that perform no digital/analog conversion.

modem script Software consisting of the modem commands necessary to start and stop a remote access connection for a particular type of modem.

modifier key A key on the Mac's keyboard used to access an application shortcut, special character, or other special function; typically in combination with other keystrokes or mouse-button presses. The Mac's modifier keys are ⌘ (Command), Control, Option, and Shift.

motherboard The main circuit board of a computer.

mount To connect to and access the contents of a disk or other volume. Mounting of connected (and powered) internal and external disks (disk, DVD, CD, and so on) is automatic and occurs every time you start up the computer or connect such disks to the Mac.

MOV Apple's QuickTime-based format for organizing, storing, and exchanging time-related data.

movie Any time-related data, such as video, sound, animation, and graphs, that change over time.

MP3 A standard for digital music files that is widely used but provides lower quality than the AAC format used as the standard in iTunes.

MPEG-4 (MP4) A standard for digital video files commonly used on the Mac, Windows, and the Internet.

multicore CPU See *CPU core*.

multimedia A presentation combining text or graphics with video, animation, and/or sound, presented on a computer.

multitasking The capability to have multiple programs open and executing concurrently.

multithreading An operating system technology that allows tasks in an application to share processor resources.

Multi-Touch trackpad Apple's trackpad technology that enables the trackpad to detect the motion and pressure at multiple locations simultaneously, which allows the use of multiple finger movements to perform complex touch gestures that can control the Mac. See *gestures*.

navigate To open disks and folders until you have opened the one that contains the item you need; to go from one Web page to another.

network A collection of interconnected, individually controlled computers, printers, and other devices; together with the hardware, software, and protocols used to connect them. A network lets connected devices exchange messages and other information.

network adapter A device that provides a network port to devices that don't have one built in. One type, called a network interface card (NIC), inserts into a Mac's CardBus, ExpressCard, or PCI slot. Another type, called a network adapter or dongle, connects to a USB jack.

network administrator Someone who sets up and maintains a centralized file server and/or other network services.

networking protocol See *protocol*.

network interface card (NIC) See *network adapter*.

network location A specific arrangement of all the various Network system preference settings that can be put into effect all at once (for example, by choosing it from ⇨ Location).

network name See *SSID*.

network time servers Computers on a network or the Internet that provide the current time of day.

newsgroup A collection of people and messages on the Internet pertaining to that particular subject.

Glossary

NFS (Network File System) The Unix equivalent of personal file sharing. NFS allows users to view and store files on a remote computer.

object A kind of information — such as words, paragraphs, audio, images, and characters — that an application knows how to work with. An application's AppleScript dictionary lists the kinds of objects it can work with under script control.

ODBC (Open Database Connectivity) A standard used by Mac OS X to allow applications to connect to external databases.

OpenCL (Open Computing Language) A technology new to Mac OS X 10.6 Snow Leopard that lets applications use the Mac's GPU, when otherwise idle, to speed processing.

OpenGL (Open Graphics Library) An industry standard for three-dimensional graphics rendering. It provides a standard graphics API by which software and hardware manufacturers can build 3-D applications and hardware across multiple platforms on a common standard.

open source Typically refers to software developed as a public collaboration and made freely available.

OpenType A standard for fonts that provides a very wide range of characters, including contextual variants. The OpenType standard is based on a hybrid of the PostScript Type 1 and TrueType font standards.

operating system Software that controls the basic activities of a computer system. Also known as *system software*.

option In panels, dialog boxes, and other user-interface elements, a selectable control to enable or disable a specific attribute or feature. The most common types of options are check boxes and radio buttons; other forms include sliders and stepper controls.

Option A frequently used modifier key on the Mac, indicated in applications' menus by the symbol ⌥.

original item A file, folder, or disk to which an alias points, and which opens when you open its alias.

orphaned alias An alias that has lost its link with its original item (and, therefore, Mac OS X cannot find it).

outline font A font whose glyphs are outlined by curves and straight lines that can be smoothly enlarged or reduced to any size and then filled with fine dots during printing. Example outline font formats are PostScript Type 1, TrueType, and OpenType.

owner The user who can assign access privileges to a file or folder.

package A folder that the Finder displays as if it were a single application file. The Finder normally hides the files inside a package so users can't change them. A package is also a logical grouping of files that are related, such as all of the items that make up fax software or all of the parts of QuickTime. Sometimes referred to as a *bundle*.

palette See *panel*.

pane An Aqua GUI element comprised of separate screens within a single window. In many dialog boxes and panels, only one pane is visible at a time; you switch among them by using a button, popup menu, or tab. Panes may contain their own set of panes, called *subpanes*.

panel An auxiliary window that contains controls or tools or that displays information for an application; it usually floats above regular windows of the same application. Panels are also called *palettes*. Also see *dialog box* and *sheet*.

parental controls A set of restrictions that can be applied to user accounts, such as to prevent children from accessing X-rated Web pages or spending more than a specified number of hours per day using the Mac.

partition An identifiable logical division of a hard disk. Sometimes referred to as a volume. Also, to divide a hard disk into several smaller volumes, each of which the computer treats as a separate disk.

passphrase Like a password, but generally consisting of more than one word. (The larger a password or passphrase, the more difficult it is to guess or otherwise discover.)

password A combination of letters and/or symbols that must be typed accurately to access information or services on the Internet or a local network.

path A way of writing the location of a file or folder by specifying each folder that must be opened to get at the file. The outermost folder name is written and each folder name is followed by a slash (/). See also *absolute pathname* and *relative path*.

PCMCIA (Personal Computer Memory Card International Association) In the small-factor version known as Cardbus, PCMCIA is a hardware interface typically found in laptops. Small credit-card-sized devices are easily installed and removed from the laptop to expand functionality. Also see *ExpressCard*.

PDF (Portable Document Format) A platform-independent file format developed by Adobe Systems. PDF files are often used in lieu of printed documents, as electronic transmission methods get more and more commonly accepted.

peer-to-peer file sharing A technology for allowing computers to access files and folders located on other computers rather than on a central file server. Less powerful than server-client file sharing, it is cheaper and easier to configure.

peripheral A device typically connected to a computer from the outside, as opposed to installed within it, such as printers, scanners, external disk drives, and digital cameras.

Perl A scripting language typically used by Web pages to deliver functionality not supported by HTML.

permissions See *privileges*.

PHP A scripting language typically used by Web pages to deliver functionality not supported by HTML. It originally stood for Personal Home Page but now has no meaning.

Ping A support tool that can be used to verify and validate the connectivity status of IP-aware network devices.

pipe A means of directing the output of one Unix command to the input of the next Unix command. Expressed in a Unix command line with a vertical bar symbol (|).

pixel Short for *picture element*, a pixel is the smallest dot that a display can show.

pixel depth See *bit depth*.

playhead A marker that tracks movie frames as they are shown, indicating the location of the current frame in relationship to the beginning and end of the movie.

playlist A collection of songs arranged for in a particular sequence.

plug The end of a connector or cable that is inserted into a receptacle such as a jack.

plug-ins Software that works with an application to extend its capabilities. For example, plug-ins for the Firefox browser application are available to integrate FTP services and to access related files used to create the page being viewed.

podcast A set of audio files that is typically used to provide a series of episodes of a radio or other radio-like program. Podcasts are often delivered via iTunes, but can also be delivered as RSS feeds and from Web pages.

pooling A technique that lets the Mac choose from multiple printers or fax machines, to minimize send delays.

POP (point of presence) A telephone number that gains access to the Internet through an Internet service provider.

POP (Post Office Protocol) A standard for accessing e-mail from a server. It is the most common e-mail protocol in use, especially for consumer-grade e-mail accounts such as those provided by MobileMe, Gmail, and Yahoo Mail. It is less adept at supporting multiple devices' access to the same e-mail account as the IMAP and Exchange protocols are.

popup menu See *menu*.

port 1. As referred to within the Network system preference, a port is some form of physical connection to a data network. 2. A synonym for a jack.

portrait A page or image orientation that is taller than it is wide.

PostScript Adobe's language for converting the mathematical equations used to represent text and shapes into the pixels and dots used, respectively, to display items on a monitor and to print items on a printer.

PostScript printers Printers that interpret Adobe-developed PostScript language to create printed pages. Commonly used in environments where precise and accurate printing is a must.

PostScript Type 1 font An outline font that conforms to the specifications of the PostScript page description language. PostScript fonts can be smoothly scaled to any size, rotated, and laid out along a curved path. Compare to *TrueType* and *OpenType*.

PPD (PostScript Printer Description) A file that contains the optional features of a PostScript printer, such as its resolution and paper tray configuration.

PPP (Point-to-Point Protocol) An industry standard for the communication between computing devices over dial-up connections.

PPPoE (Point-to-Point Protocol over Ethernet) An implementation of PPP over Ethernet, used by ISPs that want to regulate access or meter usage of its subscribers, like DSL (Digital Subscriber Line) connections.

PRAM (parameter RAM) A small amount of battery-powered memory that stores system settings, such as time and date.

preemptive multitasking A technique that prioritizes processor tasks by order of importance. Preemptive multitasking allows the Mac to handle multiple tasks simultaneously. This method of managing processor tasks more efficiently allows the Mac to remain responsive, even during the most processor-intensive tasks.

primary script The language script system used by system dialog boxes and menus. If you are working on a computer that is set up for English, Roman is your primary script; your secondary script can be any other installed language script, such as Japanese.

printer driver Software that prepares pages for and communicates with a particular type of printer.

print job A file of page descriptions that is sent to a particular type of printer. Also called a *print request* or *spool file*.

print request See *print job*.

print server A device or software that manages one or more shared printers on a network.

private IP address An IP address for use on a local network. Compare to *public IP address*.

privileges Privileges provide the control mechanism for regulating user access to files, folders, and applications within Mac OS X.

process Programs or threads (tasks) within a program that are currently running on the computer.

processor See *CPU* and *GPU*.

program A set of coded instructions direct a computer in performing a specific task. Also called an *application*.

program linking The process of sharing programs by sending and receiving event messages across a network.

protected memory This technique isolates applications in their individual memory workspaces. In the event of an application crash, the program can be terminated without having a negative effect on other running applications or requiring a restart of the computer.

protocol A set of rules for the exchange of data between computer systems.

proxy icon A little icon next to the title of a Finder window. It represents the folder whose contents currently appear in the window. You can drag the proxy icon to any folder, volume, or the Trash.

proxy server A device that acts as an intermediary between a user's workstation and the Internet. When a request is made for Internet content, the request is passed along to the proxy server. The proxy server acts on behalf of the client and forwards the request on to the Internet. It then relays the retrieved response to the user.

public IP address An IP address for use on the Internet. Compare to *private IP address*.

push button Apple's formal name for a button.

Quartz A powerful two-dimensional graphics rendering system. Quartz has built-in support for PDF, on-the-fly rendering, compositing, and anti-aliasing. It supports multiple font formats, including TrueType, Postscript Type 1, and OpenType. Quartz supports Apple's ColorSync color-management technology, allowing for consistent and accurate color in the print/graphics environment.

Quick Look Mac OS X's technology that lets you preview many types of files' contents from the Finder, rather than having to open them in an application to see their contents.

QuickTime Apple's proprietary, cross-platform multimedia authoring and distribution engine. QuickTime is both a file format and a suite of applications. Mac OS X 10.6 Snow Leopard uses a performance-optimized version called QuickTime X.

radio buttons A type of user-interface control in which you can select only one setting from a group. They work like the station presets on a car radio. Also see *option*.

RAID (redundant array of independent disks) A set of standards for using multiple hard disks as if they were one disk. One type of RAID configurations creates an automatic backup of the primary disk, while others store data across multiple disks to reduce the impact of a hardware failure on any one disk.

RAM (random access memory) 1. The high-speed, quickly rewritable memory space available for use by a computer to load applications, data, and other active information. 2. A common label for the memory chips used to provide random access memory capabilities. On a Mac, the specific RAM chips are called *DIMMs* or *SO-DIMMs*, depending on the type of Mac you have.

RAM disk Memory set aside to be used as if it were a very fast hard disk.

raster image An image made of lines of discrete dots for the display screen or the printer. Compare to *vector image*.

record A structured collection of data in AppleScript (and in other programming languages), in which each data item has a name and a value.

regular expression A shorthand method of expressing a string of characters or various permutations of a string of characters. Used in Unix command lines.

relative path A path that does not begin with a slash character and is therefore assumed to start in the current directory.

remote installation The process of installing the Mac OS or an application onto a Mac from another Mac over a network. This is required for the MacBook Air, which has no DVD drive, but it is also useful for businesses that want to centrally manage software installation on all users' Macs from one master system.

Rendezvous The original name for Apple's Bonjour technology.

repeat loop An arrangement of AppleScript commands that begins with a Repeat command and ends with an End Repeat command. AppleScript executes the commands between the Repeat and End Repeat commands for the number of times specified in the Repeat command.

resolution 1. The horizontal and vertical pixel capacity of a display or printer, measured in pixels. 2. The number of pixels per inch for a display, scanner, or printer; a higher number means there is more data per square inch, resulting in a more accurate rendering. 3. The perceived smoothness of a displayed or printed image.

resolve an alias What Mac OS X does to find the original item represented by an alias.

resources Information such as text, menus, icons, pictures, and patterns used by Mac OS X, an application, and other software. Also refers to a computer's processing power, memory, and disk space.

right-click Pressing the right-hand mouse button on a multibutton mouse or on an Apple Mighty Mouse that can detect which side of its single button you are pressing. In Mac OS X, right-clicking opens a contextual menu for whatever object is right-clicked, if one is available. With one-button mice that cannot detect right-clicks, you can Control+click the object instead to open its contextual menu.

rip To convert tracks from audio CDs, typically into MP3 or AAC format, into files stored on a computer or other device.

RIP (raster image processor) Software that translates PostScript code into an image made of rows of dots.

ROM (read-only memory) Non-editable information, typically located within a hardware device, usually used to provide specifications as to the device's behavior. Compare to *RAM*.

root 1. The name of the user account that has control over all folders and files on a computer, including the contents of the normally off-limits /System folder. 2. The top-level directory of a file system.

root level The main level of a disk, which is what you see when you open the disk icon.

Rosetta Apple's technology that enables Intel CPU-based Macs to run applications designed for the PowerPC CPU that Apple had previously used. In Mac OS X 10.6 Snow Leopard, Rosetta is no longer installed by default when you do a clean installation of Mac OS X.

router A network device that manages the delivery of information among computers and between computers and the Internet and other network devices. Unlike a hub or bridge, a router sends information only to the intended recipient, instead of broadcasting information to all devices and letting them figure out if it was intended for them. That makes routers much more efficient for managing network traffic than bridges or hubs are. Also see *Internet gateway*.

Samba A open source version of Microsoft's SMB protocol for file sharing. Mac OS X uses Samba to permit file sharing with Windows PCs.

Scale effect The visual effect used when minimizing or maximizing an application to or from the Dock, in which it appears to expand or shrink in a rapid series of steps. Mac OS X also offers the *Genie effect*.

screen saver Software that was originally designed to protect against monitor burn-in by showing a constantly changing image on the display while the computer is idle. Although modern monitors do not suffer from burn-in, screen savers remain popular as a way to personalize the computer or to indicate that the user has been away for some time.

script 1. A set of commands that a computer program can execute directly, often as an adjunct to an existing application, without having to be compiled into a separate software application. Example scripting languages include AppleScript, JavaScript, Perl, and PHP. 2. A collection of AppleScript commands that perform a specific task. 3. Short for language script system, which is software that defines a method of writing (vertical or horizontal, left to right or right to left). A language script also provides rules for text sorting, word breaking, and the formatting of dates, times, and numbers.

scriptable application An application that can be controlled by AppleScript commands.

script applet AppleScript scripts saved as applets (small applications).

scripting additions Plug-ins that add commands to the AppleScript language.

script recording A process in which AppleScript watches as you work with an application and automatically writes a corresponding script.

scroll track The area in the scrollbar that you move the scroll thumb through to navigate the window.

scrolling list This user-interface technique displays a list of values in a box with an adjacent scroll bar. Clicking a listed item selects it. You may be able to select multiple items by pressing Shift or ⌘ while clicking each desired one.

scrub To move quickly forward or backward through a movie by dragging the playhead.

search path An ordered search for resources within a Mac OS X system.

Secure FTP (SFTP) A variant of the FTP protocol that encrypts the transmission to keep the information secure during transit. See *FTP*.

selection rectangle A dotted-line box that you drag around items to select them all.

service Available from the Services submenu in the application menu, a service is a function, typically for simple needs, that can be used in most applications. Services provided with Mac OS X include a translator between traditional and simplified Chinese, a screen-capture utility, and a tool to read aloud selected text. Applications may install their own services.

server Software or a device that provides information or services to clients on demand.

settings sheet See *sheet*.

Glossary

shared folder The place where local user accounts can share files among themselves locally on the system.

shareware Software distributed over the Internet and from person to person on a trial basis. You pay for it if you decide to keep using it. See also *freeware*.

sheet A user-interface element containing additional options that applies to and is attached to another window (usually to a dialog box), ensuring you won't lose track of which window the options apply to. Also called a *settings sheet*.

shell Part of the Unix operating system that interprets command lines.

Shift A frequently used modifier key on the Mac, indicated in applications' menus by the symbol ⇧. Its main use is to produce uppercase versions of letters.

Sidebar The Sidebar is located at the left side of all Finder windows and contains shortcuts to mounted volumes and commonly used folders.

single-user mode Entered during the system startup by pressing and holding ⌘+S during the boot process after the startup chime. Single-user mode goes straight to the command line, eliminating the GUI until a reboot occurs. This mode is typically used for troubleshooting.

sleep A mode available in the Mac OS that does not power down the Mac but does suspend most operations to preserve power while keeping the Mac ready to be reactivated quickly. It's used as an alternative to shutting down and restarting, both of which are more time consuming. Note that a sleeping laptop does use power, so eventually a laptop not connected to a power cord will deplete its battery when in sleep mode.

slider A displayed control consisting of a track that displays a range of values or magnitudes and the

slider itself, also known as the *thumb*, which indicates the current setting. You can change the setting by dragging the slider's thumb.

slot An opening in which you can insert a compatible device or disk. For example, laptops often have an ExpressCard slot in which to insert hardware devices, and most Macs have a slot in which you can insert a CD or DVD.

smart folder A folder whose contents are determined by setting up a series of rules in the Finder; these rules let you manage folders' contents automatically. The smart folder contains aliases to the original files and folders, so the original files and folders are also available in their normal locations.

smart mailbox A mailbox created by setting up a series of rules in Apple's Mail; these rules let you manage e-mail automatically. The smart mailbox contains aliases to the original e-mails, so the original e-mails are also available in their normal mailboxes.

smart playlist A playlist created by setting up a series of rules in iTunes; these rules let you manage music and other media files automatically, as well as transfer an ever-updating playlist to your iPod or iPhone, such as music you've not heard recently. The smart playlist contains aliases to the original files, so the original files are also available in their normal playlists and albums.

SMB (Server Message Block) The Windows protocol used to enable peer-to-peer file sharing. Mac OS X uses the open source version called Samba to provide file sharing between Macs and Windows PCs.

smoothing See *anti-aliasing*.

SMTP (Simple Mail Transfer Protocol) A protocol typically used to send e-mail through a server to the recipient.

SO-DIMM See *DIMM*.

software One or more programs that consist of coded instructions that direct a computer in performing tasks. Also called *applications*, though *software* is a broader term that includes utilities, widgets, scripts, and all other forms of coded instructions.

soundtrack The audible part of a movie.

splat Unix jargon for the number-sign symbol (#).

spool file See *print job*.

spooling A printer-driver operation in which the driver saves page descriptions in a file (called a *spool file*) for later printing.

Spotlight Mac OS X's technology for indexing and searching all contents available to the Finder. In Finder windows, the Spotlight technology lets you search by filename, file attributes, and file contents, using user-configurable queries.

SSH (Secure Shell) A protocol for securely accessing a remote computer.

SSID (Service Set Identifier) The name that a wireless access point or router broadcasts to identify itself to Wi-Fi devices so they know it's available for making a connection to. Mac OS X calls this a *network name*.

SSL (Secure Socket Layer) A technology that protects data over a network or Internet connection by encrypting the data. Some Web pages use SSL to protect sensitive data in forms such as credit card numbers, and some e-mail servers use SSL to protect passwords and e-mail messages.

Stack A user-interface element in Mac OS X's Dock that presents the contents of the Downloads, Documents, and other folders as a stack of documents when you hover the mouse over it.

standard input The source of Unix commands, which is the keyboard by default.

standard output The destination for the result of Unix commands, which is the Terminal window by default.

startup See *boot*.

startup disk A disk that contains the software needed for the computer to begin operation.

static IP address An IP address that doesn't change when you begin an Internet session or when your computer starts up.

stationery pad A template document that contains preset formatting and contents. Also called a *template*.

status bar A strip in the top part of a Finder window that shows how much free space is available on the volume that contains the currently displayed folder.

stepper controls Iconic buttons that contain triangle-shaped arrows; these controls let you raise or lower a value incrementally. Clicking a stepper control or pressing the corresponding arrow key on the keyboard changes the value one increment at a time. Clicking and holding a stepper control or pressing and holding its corresponding arrow key on the keyboard continuously changes the value until it reaches the end of its range. These are informally called *little arrows*.

streaming media Movies, audio, and other time-oriented media files designed to be played over the Internet while they are downloading, as opposed to needing to be completely downloaded before they can be played.

stuffed file A file (or group of files) that has been compressed in the StuffIt file format from Smith Micro. See also *Zip file*.

submenu A secondary menu that pops out from the side of another menu. A submenu appears when you click a menu item that has a right-facing triangle icon at its right side. Submenus are sometimes referred to as *hierarchical menus*.

Glossary

subnet mask A 32-bit binary number used to identify a segment of a network.

subpane See *pane*.

suite In AppleScript, a group of related commands and other items.

SuperDrive Apple's name for a recordable DVD drive. Different Mac models have different capabilities in their SuperDrives, such as support for dual-layer recording, based on the technology available when the specific Mac model was designed.

superuser See *root*.

switch 1. A central device on an Ethernet network that passes signals from any device connected to it to any other device connected to it. See also *hub*, *Internet gateway*, and *router*. 2. Options you can specify as part of a Unix command.

symbolic link A representative file that contains exact information as to where a file or folder resides.

symmetric multiprocessing The technology that allows the operating system to take advantage of two processors by assigning applications to a specific processor or by splitting an application's tasks among multiple processors simultaneously.

system administrator A person who has the knowledge and authority to make changes to settings that affect the fundamental operation of a computer's operating system.

system file Contains sounds, keyboard layouts, and language script systems, as well as the basic Mac OS 9 software for the Classic environment.

System folder The folder that contains the essential components of the Mac OS.

system preference A set of controls used to control the configuration and capabilities of a specific aspect of the Mac OS or the Mac hardware. Choose System Preferences to access the System Preferences application in which you set the individual system preferences.

system software Software that controls the basic activities of a computer system. Also known as the operating system.

tabbed pane The name for a pane that you access by clicking a tab-like label to expose its available controls. See also *pane*.

tasks Functions that an application, script, or utility executes for a specific purpose, such as sending a file to the printer or opening a window.

TCP/IP (Transmission Control Protocol/Internet Protocol) The basic communication protocol of the Internet.

Telnet An application that allows remote users to interact with Mac OS X's command line over TCP/IP, assuming they are authorized to do so.

template The common name for what Mac OS X calls a *stationery pad*.

Terminal An application that allows local users to interact with Mac OS X's command line.

text behavior The set of rules used in a particular language for alphabetizing, capitalizing, and distinguishing words.

thread 1. A string of messages about the same subject in a newsgroup. 2. A single task being executed within an application; the term is typically used to indicate a task that can operate at the same time as other tasks.

3G Indicates third-generation cellular communications technology, which is capable of providing Web and e-mail access over a cellular network. There are many standards that qualify as 3G, including CDMA2000 1XRTT and EVDO, EDGE, and HSDPA, and each carrier chooses which ones it supports. iPhones support the EDGE and HSDPA flavors of 3G; 3G cards for MacBooks support whatever 3G technology the cellular carrier they are tied to uses.

thumb The movable part of a slider control that indicates the current setting.

Time Capsule An Apple hardware device that acts as a Wi-Fi router and as a backup drive that multiple Macs can back up data to wirelessly.

Time Machine Apple's utility, included in Mac OS X, that automates the backup of the Mac's applications and data and permits easy restoration of backed-up data in case of accidental deletion, file corruption, or other error.

title bar The top row in a Finder window or document window that indicates the name of the folder or document, respectively.

toolbar The top area of a Finder window, directly below the title bar, that provides access to various options through the use of iconic buttons, as well as to the Spotlight search field.

Tool Tips See *help tag*.

track One channel of a movie, containing video, sound, closed-captioned text, MIDI data, time codes, or other time-related data.

tracking The overall spacing among letters in an entire document or text selection. Text with loose tracking has extra space between the characters in words. Text with tight tracking has characters squeezed close together.

tracking speed The rate at which the pointer moves as you drag the mouse.

trackpad handwriting A technology new to Mac OS X 10.6 Snow Leopard that enables you to enter Chinese characters by drawing them with your finger on a Multi-Touch trackpad.

Trash The Mac OS's folder for deleted items. It is accessible from the Dock, and you can drag items out of the Trash to undelete them. After the Trash is emptied, the items are no longer recoverable without special software.

translator A program that translates your documents from one file format to another file format, such as a PICT graphic to a GIF graphic.

Trojan horse Destructive software that masquerades as something useful, such as a utility program or game. Compare to *virus* and *worm*; see also *malware*.

trough See *scroll track*.

TrueType The outline font technology built into Mac OS X (and Microsoft Windows). TrueType fonts can be smoothly scaled to any size on-screen or to any type of printer. See also *PostScript Type 1 font* and *OpenType*.

Type 1 font See *PostScript Type 1 font*.

UCS Formally the ISO/IEC 10646 Universal Character Set standard, this joint standard from the International Standards Organization and the International Electrotechnical Commission defines how characters for any language are encoded and interpreted by operating systems and applications. Mac OS X uses this standard as well as the similar Unicode standard to provide access to fonts' characters.

UDF (Universal Disk Format) The standard for formatting regular DVDs. Recordable CDs can also be formatted by using this standard. See also *Blu-ray*.

UFS (Unix File System) An alternative to the HFS+ file system format for Mac OS X.

Unicode A standard for encoding characters in any language used by Mac OS X to access and render more than 100,000 characters from languages throughout the world. Unicode is similar to the UCS standard also supported by Mac OS X.

Universal Access Apple's term for assistive technologies meant to help the hearing, visually, and physically impaired use the Mac.

universal binary A format for Mac applications that lets them run on both PowerPC-based and Intel-based Macs natively.

Unix A complex and powerful operating system whose TCP/IP networking protocol is the basis of the Internet. The name *Unix* is actually a pun: It was the single-user derivative of a multiuser, time-shared mainframe operating system at Bell Labs called Multics (the Multiplexed Information and Computing System). It was created so researchers could play space-war games on less-expensive computers instead of the mainframes they managed.

unmount To remove a disk's icon from the Desktop and make the disk's contents unavailable.

upload The process of sending files from one computer to another computer.

URL (Uniform Resource Locator) An Internet address. This can be the address of a Web page, a file on an FTP site, or anything else that you can access on the Internet.

Usenet A worldwide Internet bulletin board system that enables people to post messages and join discussions about subjects that interest them.

user 1. Someone who uses a computer. 2. Someone who can log in to your computer with a unique name and a password.

user account The set of permissions that can be set up for each individual who uses a specific Mac. Each account can be configured differently, providing access to different folders and applications. Each user has a Home folder in which his or her applications and data are stored separately from that of other users.

user group An organization that provides information and assistance to people who use computers. For the names and phone numbers of user groups near you, check Apple's Web page (www.apple.com/usergroups/find.html).

username A name that can be used to log in to a Mac OS X system, application, or network service.

user preferences Unique settings where users configure the behavior and appearance of applications and system software.

Utilities folder A folder within the Applications folder that contains the utilities that Apple includes with Mac OS X. You can store other companies' utilities here as well.

variable A container for information in a script. You can place data in a variable and then use it elsewhere in the script.

vector image A form of computer artwork comprised of lines and shapes, each defined by mathematical formulas. Unlike raster images, vector art can be resized to any dimension with no loss of quality, because it is not comprised of a finite amount of dots, but rather geometric lines and shapes. See also *PostScript*.

verbose mode Useful for troubleshooting, this bootup mode displays all system activity in text format during the boot process. Press and hold ⌘+V during bootup to get verbose mode.

video mirroring The duplication of one screen image on two displays connected to a computer.

virtual machine A disk file that appears to be a functional computer when opened, complete with operating system, applications, and files. A virtual machine is used to run Java programs on Macs, as well as to run Windows alongside the Mac OS by using the EMC VMware Fusion and Partallels Desktop applications.

virtual memory Additional memory made available by Mac OS X treating part of a hard disk as if it were built-in memory.

virus Software designed to spread itself by illicitly attaching copies of itself to legitimate software. Some viruses perform malicious actions, such as erasing your hard disk. Even seemingly innocuous viruses can interfere with the normal functioning of your Mac. Compare to *Trojan horse* and *worm*; see also *malware*.

VNC (virtual network computing) A protocol used to allow one computer to remotely access and manage another over a network or the Internet. Mac OS X uses VNC in its Back to My Mac and screen-sharing utilities.

VoiceOver Apple's technology that reads text and user-interface elements to the visually impaired, to help them use the Mac.

volume A disk or a part of a disk that the computer treats as a separate storage device. Each volume can have an icon on the Desktop. See also *partition*.

WAN (wide-area network) Typically, a network composed of two or more LANs, a WAN is a network that is typically spread out over a large area.

Web browser A program that displays and interacts with Web pages on the Internet.

Web page A basic unit that the Web uses to display information (including text, pictures, animation, audio, and video clips). A Web page can also contain hyperlinks to the same page or to other Web pages (on the same or a different Web server).

Web server A computer or a program running on a computer that provides and delivers Web pages and associated files to a Web browser.

Web spot An Apple technology that automatically identifies sections of a Web page, such as individual stories, to help the visually impaired navigate the page using the VoiceOver utility.

white point A setting that determines whether colors look warm (reddish) or cool (bluish). Measured in degrees Kelvin, with warm white points having lower temperatures than cool white points.

white space Any combination of blank spaces, tab characters, or line returns; in other words, characters that are blank.

widgets Lightweight utilities that run in Mac OS X's Dashboard. Some come with Mac OS X and with various applications, but the Safari browser can also create widgets from snippets of Web pages.

Wi-Fi The computer industry's marketing name for the IEEE 802.11 family of wireless networking standards.

wildcard A character that represents a range of characters in a regular expression. For example, an asterisk (*) stands for any individual character.

workflow A series of steps that can be recorded and repeated by Mac OS X's Automator utility.

worm that replicates like a virus but without attaching itself to other software. It may be benign or malicious. Compare to *Trojan horse* and *virus*; see also *malware*.

WPA (Wi-Fi Protected Access) A security standard meant to secure access to and transmissions over Wi-Fi networks.

write-protect The process of locking a disk so that it cannot be erased, have its name changed, have files copied to it or duplicated from it, or have files or folders it contains moved to the Desktop or Trash.

X11 X11 provides a GUI environment for BSD Unix applications.

Xgrid A technology that enables your Mac to share its processing capabilities with other Macs, in what is known as *grid computing*.

Glossary

XNU At the heart of the Darwin operating system lies a XNU (X is not Unix) kernel developed by NeXT, and later Apple.

Zip file A file (or group of files) that has been compressed by using Mac OS X's Archive command. Mac OS X opens Zip files when you double-click them. Windows and Unix systems create Zip files as well, using the WinZip and gzip applications, respectively.

Index

Symbols and Numerics

Index

Index

Index

Index

Index

Index

Index

Index

Index

Index

Index

Index